Children

OF THE

Arbat

Anatoli Rybakov

Translated by Harold Shukman

Hutchinson
London Melbourne Auckland Johannesburg

By the same author

Heavy Sands

This edition first published in Great Britain in 1988
by Hutchinson, an imprint of Century Hutchinson Ltd,
Brookmount House, 62–65 Chandos Place, London WC2N 4NW

Century Hutchinson Australia Pty Ltd,
89–91 Albion Street, Surry Hills,
New South Wales 2012, Australia

Century Hutchinson New Zealand Limited,
PO Box 40–086, Glenfield, Auckland 10, New Zealand

Century Hutchinson South Africa (Pty) Ltd,
PO Box 337, Berglvei, 2012 South Africa

British Library Cataloguing in Publication Data

Rybakov Anatoli Naumovich
Children of the Arbat.
I. Title II. Peti Arbata. *English*
891.73'44 [F]

ISBN 0–091737–42–7

Printed and bound in Great Britain by
Mackays of Chatham PLC, Chatham, Kent

Part 1

etween Nikolsky and Denezhny streets (today they are called Plotnikov and Vesnin) stood the biggest apartment block in the Arbat — three eight-story buildings, one close behind the other, the front one glazed with a facade of white tiles. Signs attached to the walls announced "Fine Embroidery," "Stammering Cured," "Venereal and Urinogenital Diseases." Low, arched, iron-clad passageways linked two deep, dark courtyards.

Sasha Pankratov came out onto the street and turned left toward Smolensk Square. Girls were already strolling up and down arm-in-arm, whiling away the time in front of the Arbat Art Cinema, Arbat and Dorogomilov girls, and from Plyushchikha Street. Carelessly turned-up coat collars, lipsticked mouths, long curling eyelashes, a colored neck-scarf. Autumn chic of the Arbat. The movie was over and the audience was pushing its way out onto the street through the narrow doors, where a gang of boisterous teenagers was jostling, long-standing claimants to the territory.

The Arbat had finished for the day. Early Soviet Gaz and Amo automobiles rolled along the asphalted center of the road and tried to avoid the potholes. The area between the tramlines was still cobbled. Trams were coming out of the depot towing two, even three cars in a vain attempt to satisfy the transport needs of the great city. The first line of the Metro was being laid underground, and a steel derrick poked up into the air above the shaft being sunk in Smolensk Square.

Katya was waiting for Sasha at Devichy Field Boulevard at the Rubber Works Club. High cheek-boned and gray-eyed, she had the look of a girl from the steppes. She was wearing a sweater made of thick country wool, and she smelled of wine.

"I had some red wine with the girls. Did you celebrate the holiday, too?"

"What holiday?" he asked.

"You mean you don't know?"

"No."

"It's . . . the Protection of the Virgin."

"Ah."

"That's it, 'Ah'?"

"Where are we going?"

"Where? To my friend."

"Should we bring something?"

"There'll be snacks there. Let's buy some vodka."

They walked along Great Savinsky Street past the old workers' barracks, where they could hear drunken voices and tuneless singing, and the sound of an accordion and a phonograph. Then down the long, narrow passage between the wooden factory fences, and finally down to the embankment. To the left were the big windows of the Sverdlov and Lever factories, to the right the Moscow River, in front, the high walls of the Novodevichy Monastery and the metal transoms of the circle-line railroad bridge, behind them the marshes and water meadows of Kochki and Luzhniki.

"Where are you taking me?" Sasha asked.

" 'Where, where?' Just come. Nothing's out of the way for a beggar."

He put his arm around her shoulders and she tried to throw it off. "Be patient," she protested.

He squeezed her more tightly. "Calm down," she urged.

The four-story, unplastered cement building stood somewhat apart. They walked down the long, ill-lit corridor past numerous doors. As they reached the last one, Katya said, "Marusya's living with a friend. Don't ask any questions."

A man was asleep on the divan, his face to the wall. A boy and girl, aged around ten or eleven, were sitting at the window and turned to greet Katya. Marusya, a small woman, was busy at the kitchen table, next to the sink. She had a pleasant, kind face and was a lot older than Katya.

"We got tired of waiting; we thought you weren't coming," she said, wiping her hands and taking off her apron. "We thought you must have gone off somewhere else. Get up, Ivan Petrovich, the guests are here."

Thin and sullen, the man rose, smoothing back his skimpy hair and rubbing his hand over his face to wipe away the sleep. His collar was creased and his tie was undone.

"The pies have dried out." Marusya took the dishcloth off a plate of pies. "This has a soybean filling, this one's with potatoes, and that one's got cabbage. Toma, bring the plates."

The little girl put plates on the table.

Katya took off her jacket and began laying the table with knives and forks from the sideboard. She knew where everything was. She'd been here before.

"The room needs tidying," Katya observed. It was an order.

Marusya cleared clothes off the chairs. "We had a nap after dinner," she said, justifying herself, "and the kids have been cutting up paper. Pick up the paper, Vitya."

The boy crawled about the floor, picking up bits of paper.

Ivan Petrovich washed at the sink and straightened his tie.

Marusya cut the children a piece from each of the pies and set them down by the window. "Eat!"

Ivan Petrovich poured out the vodka.

"Here's to the holiday!"

"See you under the table!" Katya responded, looking around at everyone except Sasha.

It was the first time she had brought him to meet her friends. Here she drank vodka. With him it was always red wine.

"You've got yourself a nice dark-eyed one!" Marusya nodded toward Sasha with a grin.

"Dark-eyed and curly haired," Katya laughed.

Ivan Petrovich reached for the bottle. "Curly when you're young, bald when you're old." He talked as if he wanted to get acquainted, and Sasha no longer thought him sullen. Marusya gazed at them both with a look of gentle understanding.

Sasha enjoyed Marusya's solicitude. He liked the house on the outskirts, and the sound of the songs and the accordion coming from the next apartment.

"You're not eating?" Marusya asked.

"Thank you, I am eating. It's delicious."

"They're not what I would have given you, if I could have got anything to make them with. You can't get proper yeast, and what you can get ... Ivan Petrovich brought it."

Ivan Petrovich said something serious on the subject of yeast.

The children asked for more pie.

Marusya cut them each another piece. "You think I made them just for you! You've had your feast, now go and get washed!"

She gathered up their bed linen and carried it out of the room to the neighbor's.

The children went to sleep next door. Then Ivan Petrovich got ready to leave and Marusya went to see him out, saying to Katya as she left, "There are clean sheets in the cupboard."

"What does she need him for?" Sasha asked, when Marusya had shut the door.

"Her husband won't support her. It's hopeless to chase him. She still has a life to live."

"But with the children here?"

"Would they be better off starving?"

"He's an old man."

"She's no youngster."

"Why doesn't he marry her?"

She gave him a look of distrust. "And why don't you marry me?"

"Do you want to get married?"

"Yes. Okay! Let's go to bed."

Another surprise. Usually, he had to win her as if they were meeting for the first time. But now, she made the bed herself and then undressed. All she said was, "Put out the light."

Afterward, she ran her fingers through his hair. "You're strong. I bet the girls all love you. But you're not careful." She leaned over him and looked into his eyes. "Aren't you afraid I'll produce a little dark-eyed Sasha?"

It had to happen sooner or later. Well, she would have an abortion. Neither of them wanted a child.

"Are you pregnant?"

She buried her head in his shoulder and pressed against him, as if to find shelter from the miseries and misfortunes of her life.

What did he know about her? Where did she live? With an aunt? In a hostel? Did she rent the corner of a room? An abortion! What would she tell them at home, what would she tell them at work? All of a sudden she's missing her periods? Where would she be able to go with the baby?

"If you are, have the baby and we'll get married."

Without raising her head, she asked, "But what shall we call it?"

"We'll think of something. There's plenty of time."

She laughed and moved away from him.

"You won't get married, and anyway I don't want to marry you. How old are you? Twenty-two? I'm older than you. You're educated, but look at me — only six years of school. I'm getting married, but not to you."

"Who to, I'd like to know?"

"You'd like to know? He's a boy from my village."

"Where is he now?"

"Who, where ... He's in the Urals. He's coming for me."

"What is he?"

"What? A mechanic."

"Have you known him long?"

"I've told you, we're from the same village."

"Why didn't he marry you before now?"

"He wanted to sow his wild oats first, that's why."

"And now he has?"

"He's thirty and he's had a few girls, I can tell you."

"Do you love him?"

"Yes. I do."

"So why do you go with me?"

"Why, why, why. I also want to live. What is this, the third degree? So many questions!"

"When is he coming?"

"Tomorrow."

"So we won't be seeing each other again?"

"Do you want me to invite you to the wedding? He's strong, you know. One swipe and that'd be the end of you."

"We'll see."

"Ho, ho."

"But you're pregnant."

"Who said so?"

"You did."

"I didn't say anything. That was your idea."

There was a quiet tapping at the door. Katya got up to open the door to Marusya and then got back into bed.

"Did you see him off?"

"Yes." Marusya switched on the light. "Would you like tea?" Sasha reached for his trousers.

"You can stay as you are," Marusya said.

"He's bashful." Katya grinned. "He's ashamed to be seen with me, but he wants to get married."

"It doesn't take long to get married, or to get divorced," Marusya said.

Sasha poured what was left of the vodka into a glass and ate a piece of pie.

He felt all in all he should be grateful to Katya that things had ended as well as they had. What she had said about the mechanic was probably true, but that wasn't the point. The point was, she'd been teasing him and like a fool he had been taken in.

He got up.

"Where are you off to?" she asked.

"Home."

"What are you talking about?" Marusya protested. "Sleep here. You can leave in the morning. I'll sleep at my neighbor's. Nobody will disturb you."

"I have to go."

Katya looked at him sullenly.

"Can you find your way home?"

"I won't get lost."

She pulled him toward her. "Stay."

"I'm going. Be happy."

Still, she was a good girl! It would be a pity if she didn't telephone him and they didn't see each other again. He didn't know where she lived, she wouldn't give him her address: "My aunt would be angry." She hadn't even told him which factory she worked at. "Be under the lamppost at the entrance."

At first, she would call him from a phone booth. They would go to the movies or the park; later, they started going into the depths of Neskuchny Park. The wicker benches appeared white in the moonlight. Katya pulled back. "What are you doing? . . . Leave me alone! . . . You think you can touch me any way you like?" Then she pressed against him, a girl from the steppes, her lips dry and chapped, and ran her rough hands through his hair.

"You know, I thought you were a Gypsy when I first saw you. We had Gypsies next to our village, and they were dark, just like you. Except that you've got smooth skin."

She came to see him in the summer, when his mother was away at her sister's dacha. Her eyes were angry and she was embarrassed by the women sitting at the entrance.

"All eyes! I'll never come here again in my life."

When she telephoned, she usually said nothing, then she would hang up and call again.

"Is that you, Katya?"

"Yes, it's me."

"Why didn't you answer when you called before?"

"That wasn't me."

"Are we going to meet?"

"Where do you want to meet?"

"Next to the park?"

"You've already made up your mind. Come to Devichy."

"At six, seven?"

"I'll arrive there at six," she said.

Sasha recalled all this now, as he waited for her to phone, and the next day he wanted to get home from the institute as soon as he could, just in case she did. But he had to stay late to get the student newspapers ready for the October holiday. And then he was summoned to a meeting of the Party committee.

2

There were no empty seats near the door and Sasha had to edge his way between the crammed rows of chairs, pushing through the closely packed audience and attracting an irritated look from Baulin, the Party committee secretary. Baulin was red-haired and brawny, with a round, simple, open face, and his broad chest bulged under a blue satin peasant shirt that was fastened at the neck with two white buttons. He waited until Sasha had found a seat and then turned to Krivoruchko.

"So, Krivoruchko, you have sabotaged the construction of the hostels. Nobody's interested in your alibis. You say the funds were diverted to crash programs? You're not responsible for building a steel plant like the Magnitka — it's only a hostel for the institute. Why didn't you warn us that the timetable was unrealistic? ... Ah, the timetable *was* realistic. So why wasn't it kept to? ... You've been in the Party for twenty years? Your past services have earned our deepest respect, but we still have to punish you for your mistakes."

Sasha was astounded by Baulin's tone of voice. Krivoruchko was the deputy director of the institute and the students were afraid of him. People often talked about his brilliant war record, and he wore his military tunic, breeches, and boots as a constant reminder of it. He was stooped and had a long, miserable nose with bags under his eyes. He never stopped to chat, and even when greeted, he would reply with no more than a nod of the head.

Krivoruchko was leaning on the back of a chair, and Sasha could see his fingers were trembling. It was pitiful to see weakness in a man who was usually so formidable. But the building materials had in fact not been delivered, although now nobody cared.

Janson, the dean of Sasha's faculty and a Latvian who was not easily ruffled, turned for support to the director of the institute, Glinskaya, and asked in a conciliatory tone, "Maybe they'll give us another completion date?"

"What date?" Baulin asked with sinister benevolence.

Glinskaya was silent. Her aggrieved look showed how she felt about having such a worthless deputy forced on her.

Lozgachev, a postgraduate student, got up. Tall, smooth, and impressive, he raised his arms in a theatrical gesture.

"They surely didn't send the shovels to Magnitka as well? Did the students dig the frozen ground with their hands? The Komsomol* organizer is right here — let him tell us how the students managed without shovels."

Baulin watched Sasha with interest as he got up.

"We didn't have to work without shovels. The storeroom was closed on one occasion, but the manager came back and issued the shovels."

"Did you have to wait long?" Krivoruchko asked, without raising his head.

"Maybe ten minutes."

Having been let down by Sasha as a witness, Lozgachev shook his head reproachfully, as if the blunder was not his but Sasha's.

"So you managed?" Baulin grinned.

"We tried," Sasha replied.

"How long did you work and how long were you idle?"

"We had no materials."

"Why not?"

"Everyone knows."

"Don't play lawyer with me, Pankratov," Baulin warned, his words strung out for effect. "It's out of place."

Averting their eyes from Krivoruchko, the committee members voted to expel him from the Party. Only Janson abstained.

Krivoruchko left the room, even more stooped.

* *Translator's note:* The League of Communist Youth.

"A complaint has been received from senior lecturer Azizyan," Baulin announced, looking at Sasha as if to say, *And now it's your turn, Pankratov.*

Azizyan had given Sasha's group a short course on the fundamentals of socialist accounting principles. He had not dealt with the subject at all, he had taught them nothing about accounting or even about its basic principles. Instead, he had lectured about people who distorted those principles, and Sasha had complained that the group should be learning something about bookkeeping as such. Cunning and unctuous, a dark, balding little man, Azizyan had laughed. *Then* he had laughed; now he was accusing Sasha of attacking the Marxist basis of the science of accounting.

"Is that how it was?" Baulin's cold, pale blue eyes were on Sasha.

"I did not say that theory was unnecessary. I simply said we weren't getting instruction in bookkeeping."

"The Party's concern with theory doesn't interest you?"

"Of course it does, but so does concrete knowledge."

"Is there a difference between the Party's concern with theory and concrete knowledge?"

Lozgachev was on his feet again.

"Comrades! When people openly preach that a science is politically neutral ... And, also, Pankratov tried to foist his own personal opinion about Krivoruchko onto the Party committee, acting as a spokesman for the student masses. Tell us Pankratov, honestly, just who do you represent here?"

Janson gloomily drummed his fingers on his tightly packed briefcase. It wasn't right to argue with a lecturer, but still — to say that science was "politically neutral"...

In a voice weary from the burden of high office, and implying that this was a trivial matter, involving only a paltry student, Glinskaya addressed Baulin. "Perhaps this should be handed over to the Komsomol...."

Lozgachev looked at Baulin; it was clear that Glinskaya's idea did not appeal to him.

"The Party committee should not evade —"

His casual use of that one word settled the issue.

Baulin scowled. "Nobody's going to evade anything. But there is a procedure. Let the Komsomol discuss the question. We shall see how politically mature they are."

Sasha saw the brown leather coat as he came in — Uncle Mark! His uncle greeted him. "Been having a good time?"

Sasha kissed his uncle's smooth-shaven cheek. Mark gave off the scent of good pipe tobacco and fragrant eau de cologne — "the cozy smell of a bachelor," in his mother's words. Portly, jolly, balding, and avuncular, he looked older than his thirty-five years. The sharp eyes behind the yellow-tinted spectacles revealed the iron will of a man who was known throughout the whole country as one of its industrial chiefs, almost as much a legend as his gigantic construction in the east, the new metallurgical base of the Soviet Union. Out of range of enemy aircraft, it would be the strategic rear of the proletarian power.

"I almost decided not to wait for you, I thought you might be out for the night. . . ."

"Sasha comes home every night," his mother said.

There was a bottle of port on the table, choice pink sausage, sprats, and some cakes — the kind of delicacies that Mark always brought when he visited. There was also the traditional pie that his mother always baked for Mark. He must have let her know he was coming to Moscow.

"Are you here for long?" Sasha asked.

"I got here today and I leave tomorrow."

"Stalin summoned him," his mother said.

She was proud of her brother and proud of her son. She had nothing much else to be proud of — abandoned by her husband, a woman on her own, small, plump, though her white face was still pretty and her gray hair was thick and wavy.

Mark pointed to a parcel on the divan. "Undo it."

Sofya Alexandrovna tried to untie the knot.

"Give it here!" Sasha said, cutting the string with a knife.

Mark had brought his sister a length of cloth for a coat and a downy shawl and for Sasha a suit of dark blue wool. The slightly creased jacket fitted him perfectly.

"Like a glove," Sofya Alexandrovna observed with approval. "Thank you, Mark, he has absolutely nothing to go out in."

Sasha looked at himself in the mirror with satisfaction. Mark's gifts were always just what one needed. When he was a child, his uncle had taken him to the shoemaker to have a pair of tall, soft leather boots made for him. Nobody, neither in the apartment building nor at school, had boots like those. He had been very proud of those boots and could still recall their smell and the sharp scent of hides and tar in the shoemaker's tiny shop.

Several times that evening Mark was called to the phone. In a low, firm voice he gave instructions about the allocation of resources, budgets, special trains, and he warned that he would be spending the night in the Arbat and that his car should be there at eight the next morning.

He came back into the room and cast a sidelong look at the bottle.

"Hmm!"

" 'Drink, comrade, wherever you can, to drown life's sorrows.' " Sasha sang Mark's favorite song. When he was still a child he used to hear Mark singing it.

" 'Softer, softer, all our worries will go tonight.' " Mark picked it up. "Is that it?"

"That's it!" And Sasha piped up again.

> Maybe this time tomorrow
> The Cheka* will get here,
> And maybe this time tomorrow
> We'll execute Kolchak . . .

He got his voice and his ear from his mother. She had once been asked to sing on the radio, but his father wouldn't have it.

> Maybe this time tomorrow
> Our comrades will arrive,
> But maybe this time tomorrow
> They'll take us to be shot.

---

* Translator's note: Cheka, from the initials for the Extraordinary Commission for Combatting Terrorism, founded in December 1917, was the security police organization of the Soviet State.

"It's a good song," Mark said.

"And you can't sing it properly," Sofya Alexandrovna said. "Like a choir of blind men."

"A duet of blind men," Mark said, laughing.

A bed was made up for Mark on the divan and Sasha slept on a canvas camp bed.

Mark took off his jacket and shirt, and, in his undershirt, which was trimmed around the neck and the sleeves in pale blue, went to the bathroom.

Lying with one arm under his head, Sasha waited for him.

When he had gone downstairs after the Party meeting, Janson had run past and given him a pat on the back as he did so. It was the only good, encouraging gesture shown to Sasha, and it emphasized the sense of emptiness he now felt. Everyone else suddenly seemed to be in a great hurry, either to get home or to the canteen. He walked to the tram stop along the dirty road of the straggling suburb and was passed by a large black car. Sitting in front was Glinskaya, who was turning around to say something to the other passengers. The way they were talking and laughing and driving right past him, without the slightest awareness of him, again aroused the feeling of emptiness and of sudden, unjustified rejection.

Sasha had known Glinskaya since his schooldays. He had noticed her at meetings of the parents' committee, and he had been in the same class as her son, Jan, a gloomy, taciturn youth who was interested only in mountaineering. She was married to a Comintern official, and her Polish accent gave her categorical pronouncements a note of falseness. Even so, he had not expected her to keep quiet at the committee meeting. After all, she was just as responsible as Krivoruchko for the construction of the hostels. Yet she had remained silent.

Mark returned, washed and fresh, took a bottle of eau de cologne out of his toilet kit, and patted some on his face. Then he lay down on the divan, twisted around to make himself more comfortable, took off his spectacles, and sought myopically for somewhere to put them.

"Shall I turn out the light?" Sasha asked.

"Yes."

They lay in silence for a while, and then Sasha asked, "Why has Stalin summoned you?"

"It wasn't Stalin. I've been called here to pick up his new instructions."

"They say he's not very tall."

"He's about the same height as you and I."

"And yet he looks tall on the rostrum."

"Yes, he does."

"When it was his fiftieth birthday," Sasha said, "I didn't like the way he replied to the speeches praising him — things like 'the Party created me in its own image' and so on."

"His point was that the praise belonged to the Party and not to him personally."

"Is it true that Lenin wrote that Stalin was rude and disloyal?"

"How do you know about that?"

"It doesn't matter. The point is I've heard it. But did he really say it?"

"They are exclusively personal characteristics. The important thing is the political line."

"But can you separate them?" Sasha objected, and at that moment Baulin and Lozgachev came into his mind.

"Do you have any doubts?"

"I didn't think so, somehow. I mean, I'm for Stalin, but I just wish there was a bit less glorification. It grates on me."

"Something not understood is not the same as something wrong," Mark replied. "You must believe in the Party and its wisdom. Things are going to get tough."

Sasha laughed. "Yes, I learned what that's like today."

He told Mark what had happened at the Party committee session.

"Bookkeeping? But was that a question of principle for which —" Mark was incredulous.

"Well, you can wait your whole life for a question of principle to turn up."

"It's tactless to argue in the lecture room," Mark said.

"They're not accusing me of being tactless, but of being nonpolitical. And they're demanding that I admit it."

"If you were wrong, admit it."

"Oh, no, that's not what they want. Anyway, what is there to admit? The whole thing's fake, phony."

"Is Glinskaya still the director?"

"She is."

"And she was there, at the committee meeting?"

"She was."

3

Mark Alexandrovich told his driver to go on ahead, while he walked.

It was a brilliantly clear autumn morning, with a steady, bracing chill in the air. Office workers were hurrying to their jobs, a noisy line of women waited at the bakery, a silent column of men waited at the tobacco stand.

He had always singled Sofya out from among his sisters. He loved her and pitied her. She was weak and not adaptable, and now, having been left by her husband, she was especially helpless. He loved Sasha, too. Why were they getting at the boy? After all, he had said the right thing, spoken honestly, and yet they were now trying to destroy his spirit, demanding repentance for an act he hadn't committed. But he, too, had urged Sasha to repent.

Mark crossed Arbat Square and walked along Vozdvizhenka Street, which seemed suddenly quiet and empty after the lively Arbat. There was only one large crowd, and it was waiting for the Voentorg store to open. A smaller group huddled at Kalinin's doorway. Mark Alexandrovich got into his waiting car and traveled along Mokhovaya Street, Okhotny Row, across Theater and Lubyanskaya squares and onto Nogin Square, where, in the former Business Court, in a vast five-story building with long corridors and myriad rooms, the People's Commissariat of Heavy Industry was housed.

Thousands of people came to this building from every corner of the country. It was here that everything was decided, coordinated, elaborated, planned, ratified. As was his custom, Commissar

Ryazanov began his tour of the commissariat not with the management, but in the clerical departments and sections. And because, although chief of the greatest construction project in the world and Ordzhonikidze's favorite, he went first to them, the rank-and-file workers were delighted. He took notice of them, he recognized their strength, the strength of the organization. And so they eagerly responded to his problems and dealt with them as befitted the interests of the factory that was the pride and joy of the Five-Year Plan; in other words, they dealt with them the way Mark Alexandrovich wanted.

Having made his tour of the departments, Mark Alexandrovich went up to the third floor, passed through several corridors, ascended one staircase, descended another, and arrived in a quiet, unfrequented wing of the building. The offices of the people's commissar and his assistants were located here. The secretaries at their desks in the carpeted anteroom knew Mark Alexandrovich, and he went through unannounced to Budyagin's office.

A member of the Central Committee and a friend of Stalin's from their days in Siberian exile, Budyagin had been recalled a few months earlier as ambassador to the most powerful European state and was now deputy people's commissar. It was rumored that his recall had not been accidental, and that he was somewhat out of favor. His lean face, however, with its black mustache and gray eyes under thick brows, gave nothing away. Worker-intellectuals, like Budyagin, who had traded their army commander's cloak for a diplomat's morning coat, or their local Cheka chairman's leather coat for the manager's two-piece suit, had always embodied for Mark Alexandrovich the formidable, implacable spirit of the Revolution, the all-shattering power of the dictatorship.

They discussed the fourth blast furnace. It was now supposed to start up by the time of the Seventeenth Party Congress, in five months, not in eight, which had been called for in the original plan. Both Mark Alexandrovich and Budyagin knew that economic wisdom was being sacrificed to political necessity, but that was what Stalin wanted.

After they had been over the whole question, Mark Alexandrovich said, "You know my nephew, Sasha Pankratov. He was in the same class as your daughter at school."

"Yes, I know him." Again, Budyagin's face was inscrutable.

"It's nonsense, really. . . ." He told Budyagin what had happened.

"Sasha's an honest young man," Budyagin said.

"The political neutrality of bookkeeping! Can you imagine! The director of the institute is Glinskaya. I don't know her, but you do. Please talk to her, if it's not too difficult. It's a shame for the boy, they're persecuting him. I could go to Chernyak, but I don't feel like taking it to district level."

"Chernyak isn't the district secretary any longer."

"What?"

"He isn't."

"What are we coming to?"

Budyagin shrugged his shoulders.

"The congress is in January," Budyagin said, and without pausing, went on, "Sasha's a good boy. He comes here from time to time. He hasn't said anything to me."

"He wouldn't, and anyway this just happened yesterday."

"Is Glinskaya capable of doing something?" Budyagin sounded dubious.

"I don't know," Mark Alexandrovich replied. "But I will not let him be torn to pieces. We mustn't allow our children to be crippled; they're just beginning their lives."

"It isn't only your nephew it's happening to now," Budyagin said.

Mark Alexandrovich went down to the barbershop for a haircut and, something he never did, a shave. He wished he hadn't, for the barber sprayed him with a powerful eau de cologne.

The alien, persistent perfume annoyed him as he entered the restaurant reserved for members of the directorate.

The barmaid turned to him. "Comrade Ryazanov, they asked for you to call on Comrade Semushkin."

He went upstairs. Anatoli Semushkin, Ordzhonikidze's secretary, greeted him coldly and expressed his irritation that Mark Alexandrovich never seemed to be available when he was needed. Semushkin addressed everyone in the familiar form, he acknowledged nobody but his boss — Sergo — and he was feared scarcely less than Sergo himself. He had been his adjutant during the Civil War, then from 1921 he served as his secretary, in the Transcaucasus and the Central Control Commission, and now in the Commissariat of Heavy Industry.

With an especially significant look on his face, and the same expression of annoyance, he dialed a number. "Comrade Ryazanov is here." He handed the receiver to Mark Alexandrovich.

He was expected at the Kremlin at four o'clock.

He suspected that this was the reason for summoning him to Moscow. He had already bought his return ticket, thinking the meeting was off. And now, in forty minutes, he would be with Stalin.

On another phone Semushkin called the Bobrinsk Chemical Works, where they replied that Ordzhonikidze was out on the site. Semushkin hung on, delaying Mark Alexandrovich but calculating that it was better to be late for Stalin than turn up there without Ordzhonikidze's instructions.

That wasn't the way Mark Alexandrovich saw it. Semushkin only moved and functioned in higher circles, but Mark Alexandrovich couldn't allow the other man's bureaucratic zeal to stand in his own way.

He remained calm and unruffled. The only thing troubling him was the awful barber's scent. It was ridiculous to show up at the Kremlin smelling like this, and to see Stalin, no less. He went back to the barbershop and washed his face and hair, while the barber stood by with a towel. This wasn't the good-natured Comrade Ryazanov who had been joking with him about balding men half an hour earlier. The commanding face, especially without the spectacles, now looked ruthless.

He poked his Party card through the hatch at the Troitsky Gate. The hatch slammed shut, then opened again, showing a soldier's silhouette behind the glass. It was only when he leaned forward that Ryazanov could see him.

"Do you have any weapons?"

"No."

"What's in the briefcase?"

Ryazanov lifted it up and opened it.

The sentry gave him back his Party card with a permit tucked inside.

Two soldiers with rifles stood at the door of the special entrance. They asked for his permit and checked his papers. After examining the photograph on his Party card, the sentry cast a formal but attentive glance over his face.

Ryazanov left his topcoat in a small cloakroom and went up to the third floor. Outside the office, a man in civilian clothes checked his papers once more.

Inside sat Poskrebyshev behind a desk. It was the first time Mark Alexandrovich had seen him and he thought his face coarse and unattractive.

Ryazanov announced himself.

Poskrebyshev led him into a small anteroom, indicated the sofa, and went through to the inner office, firmly closing the door behind him. He came back.

"Comrade Stalin will see you now."

The left wall of Stalin's elongated office was hung with an enormous map of the Soviet Union. Bookcases lined the wall on the right. A large globe stood in one corner, and in the other a writing desk and chair. The middle of the room was occupied by a long green baize–covered table and chairs.

Stalin stopped pacing the room when the door opened. He was wearing a handsome dark khaki jacket with matching breeches tucked into his boots. He was less than average height, solidly built, somewhat pockmarked, and his eyes were slightly Mongol. Above a low brow his thick hair was streaked with gray. He took a few light steps toward Mark Alexandrovich and shook his hand. It was a simple, formal action, yet the importance of the gesture was clearly conveyed. He then pulled out two chairs at the table. They sat down. Mark Alexandrovich could see that his eyes were light brown and lively, and even seemed rather jolly.

Ryazanov began his report with a description of the project.

Stalin immediately interrupted him. "Comrade Ryazanov, don't waste time. The Central Committee, and its secretary, know perfectly well where the site is and what it's for."

He spoke with a strong Georgian accent, and, as Mark Alexandrovich discovered, was well informed about progress at the site.

"The Komsomols are running away?"

"Yes."

"So, we mobilize them and they run away. How many have gone?"

"Eighty-two."

Stalin gave him a penetrating, searching look.

"Show me your report."

From his briefcase Mark Alexandrovich took out tables indicating the deployment of the labor force and pointed to a graph.

"Don't be so hard on yourself, Comrade Ryazanov! If as few as eighty-two workers ran away from a factory in Moscow, the manager would regard himself as a hero."

He smiled, causing a deeply etched network of wrinkles to appear around his eyes.

When Ryazanov complained about the factory that supplied his equipment, Stalin asked for the manager's name.

"The man's a fool. He makes a mess of everything." Suddenly his eyes looked yellow and wary, like a tiger's, and Mark Alexandrovich saw in them a flash of anger toward a man he knew to be an efficient manager but who found himself in a difficult situation.

Ryazanov changed the subject to a more delicate one, the building of the second open-hearth furnace.

"Can you build it in a year?" Stalin asked.

"No, Comrade Stalin."

"Why not?"

"I don't gamble with engineering."

Immediately he was afraid of what he'd said. Stalin looked at him intently. Again his eyes looked yellow and wary, and one of his eyebrows was raised almost vertically.

"So, the Central Committee gambles with engineering?" He spoke slowly, stretching out his words.

"Forgive me, that wasn't what I meant. What I want to say is . . ." He then proceeded to give a detailed, precise, and convincing explanation of why the second open-hearth furnace could not be completed within a year.

Stalin was listening carefully. Clutching his pipe to his chest, his left hand appeared cramped and stiff.

"You've spoken plainly. We don't need Communists who

promise anything you like. What we need are those who tell the truth." He said this without smiling and with great emphasis. His words seemed to be addressed to the whole country.

Ryazanov was about to go on, but Stalin touched his elbow.

"I listened to you, now it's your turn to hear what I have to say."

Stalin spoke about the metal industry, the east, the second Five-Year Plan, the defense of the country. In a quiet, thick voice, slowly and precisely, as if dictating to a secretary, he spoke about things that everyone knew, but which now, said by *him,* acquired new and special importance.

He made no mention of the fourth blast furnace, as if he wanted to save Mark Alexandrovich from harming his own position by raising objections that Stalin would not have accepted.

"When are you leaving?" Stalin got up.

"Today."

"If you can, put it off a couple of days. I think my comrades in the Politburo would be interested to hear what you have to say."

The awkwardness and anxiety that Mark Alexandrovich had felt during the meeting with Stalin receded, and what remained was a sense of the greatness with which he was involved. The vast project he was in charge of demanded an iron will. If it were not for the iron will of Stalin above him, he would be unable to exercise his own. And his was tough, too. What choice was there? Great historical revolutions weren't achieved by being soft.

The staff in the commissariat knew about his talk with Stalin and were already drafting a decree for the Politburo. All the required personnel, from the Central Directorate to typists and even the manageress of the buffet, stayed at their jobs all evening and all night. Members of the board whose official stamps were needed for the draft decree would arrive at the commissariat by dawn, and the documents would be delivered to the Central Committee by special messenger in the morning.

Nobody asked Ryazanov what Stalin had said. The tale would only be garbled in the retelling. Stalin himself dictated what he thought necessary. The dates and sites that Mark Alexandrovich had indicated were what Stalin wanted.

The main thrust was that the completion date for the second

open-hearth furnace had been postponed for a year, and this augured a new and more realistic approach to the composition of the second Five-Year Plan. After all, metal was the basis of everything.

Budyagin also occupied himself with the draft decree, then left, returned at eight in the morning, and stamped it without a word.

Their friendship gave Budyagin the right to inquire about "the conversation," but he didn't. Mark Alexandrovich sensed some opposition to Stalin in Budyagin, but banished the thought that it might be political. It was most likely something personal, as often happens between former friends. Maybe he was offended at being recalled from abroad and given a job that, however senior, was lower in rank, and that might be a step farther down the ladder.

Ordzhonikidze arrived. Mark Alexandrovich always felt relaxed with him. He might explode in appalling anger, but he never bore a grudge and was good-natured. It was to him that Mark Alexandrovich owed his present high position. Sergo had spotted him when he was manager of a small factory in the south and had promoted him to become the top metallurgist in the country. Sergo had a gift for finding people and then giving them the protection they needed to do their work.

He was sitting at an enormous desk, a tired man with a fleshy, aquiline nose and puffy face, graying hair, and a thick, uneven, drooping mustache; the top button of his tunic was undone and the collar of his lilac-colored shirt hugged his thick neck.

The windows of the office gave onto a narrow side street that led to an ancient little church, the kind that had abounded in this old quarter of Moscow between the Yauza, Solyanka, and Moscow rivers. This one must have been very special to have survived and not been wiped off the face of the earth.

"Well done!"

The praise was aimed as much at the draft decree as the fact that Ryazanov had not lost his head in front of Stalin and had pleased him. It also applied to himself for having picked the right man, the sort of man who could be relied on in complicated and critical situations.

"Tell me all about it!"

As Ryazanov recounted the conversation, Ordzhonikidze listened tensely, trying to capture the very essence of Stalin's every word.

The farther the meeting with Stalin receded, the more significant it seemed to Mark Alexandrovich. Such meetings occur only once in a lifetime. Above all, he had a radiant sense of the great man's understanding and the genius that cast its light over the times.

" 'I don't gamble,' you said that?"

"That's what I said."

"So, the Central Committee gambles?" Ordzhonikidze repeated the question and laughed.

"Yes, that's exactly what he said."

There was great meaning in Ordzhonikidze's bulging brown eyes as he looked at Ryazanov.

"Be at the Central Committee by ten. You'll have five minutes to present your report — don't count on more than that. Don't give them any pep talks about Soviet power, just stick to the facts that support your position. Answer questions, ignore critical comments. And don't get nervous, you'll have me behind you."

In the waiting room outside the auditorium where he was to give his report was a table laden with a large permanently boiling samovar, a supply of sliced lemon, sandwiches, and mineral water, but no barman or waiter. Along the walls and at the windows were desks where one could arrange one's papers.

Provincial Party secretaries, people's commissars and their deputies and heads of directorates, a number of military, and a large group from the Caucasus were all waiting to be called.

A middle-aged female secretary would call out, "Comrade So-and-so, to the session, please."

If she had to call several people together, she would say, "The comrades from such-and-such province" or "the comrades from this or that commissariat."

She called on Mark Alexandrovich by his name.

He went through the secretaries' room and on entering the auditorium saw rows of people sitting in armchairs. Standing behind the chairman's table was Molotov. To his right was a rostrum, to his left and slightly to the rear sat the person giving the report, the stenographers sitting still farther to the left.

"Comrade speaker, please come here." Molotov indicated the rostrum.

A notice on the inside edge of the rostrum read: "Readers have five minutes." On the wall opposite the rostrum was a black clock with gilded hands, like those on the Kremlin.

Stalin was sitting in the third row. The rest of the row to his left was empty, so that he could get up and leave easily. Mark Alexandrovich had heard about his habit of pacing up and down his study. Now, however, he remained in his seat, just as he had two days earlier.

Mark Alexandrovich ran quickly through the draft decree. He spoke in terse, mostly technical terms, but in a clear and simple way that was convincing to people used to political verbiage. He underlined the early start-up of the fourth blast furnace and did not linger over the delay of the second open-hearth furnace, which was actually the more important. The main thing here at this moment was to highlight precisely what needed emphasis.

"Any questions?" Molotov asked.

Someone pointed out that the draft decree called for the supply of wood and that approval had not yet been given by the Wood Industry Commissariat.

Mark Alexandrovich was about to reply when a sudden silence fell. He heard the voice of Stalin.

"Let Comrade Ryazanov go back to his plant and start making metal. It would be wrong to detain him for the sake of a few papers."

He spoke not only very quietly, but had also turned away, so that one had to strain to hear what he was saying.

"I think we ought to be able to get the necessary approvals without Comrade Ryazanov. The decree has been considered; there are no outstanding questions. In helping Comrade Ryazanov, we will be carrying out the Party's orders."

He stopped as suddenly as he had started.

Nobody asked any more questions.

4

*C*omfortable before the Revolution, the first apartment block on the Arbat had now become the most over-crowded. The apartments had been subdivided and crammed with tenants, though one or two people had somehow managed to protect themselves and gain a small victory over the new order. Such a one was the tailor Sharok.

He had started as a boy in the workshop, become a cutter, then a master tailor, and finally had married the boss's only daughter. Such was Sharok's career. Then the Revolution had cut off his expectations. The workshop he expected to inherit was nationalized. He went to work in a clothing factory, supplementing his income by working at home. Exercising the caution of a man determined never to confront a finance inspector, he accepted clients only on reliable recommendation.

Aging handsomely, the portly tailor still had the dignified and deferential manner of the owner of a lady's dress shop.

Six evenings a week he was at his tailor's table with a tape measure around his neck, marking fine lines with chalk, cutting cloth, sewing, and pressing seams with his heavy iron. He was earning money. Sundays he indulged his passion for pari-mutuel betting at the racetrack. Sharok might have reconciled himself with life, were he not in constant fear of the house management committee, his neighbors, and, quite simply, of the unexpected. One such surprise was the eight-year camp sentence imposed on his elder son, Vladimir, for robbing a jewelry store.

He had never trusted the fidgety little freak. The boy had his mother's simian looks. But Sharok took consolation from the fact that Vladimir had completed a chef's course at the Prague restaurant and had brought home a pay envelope.

Of course, restaurants were not what they used to be — not the restaurants nowadays! But it was a well-chosen profession for the physically weak boy who was no good at schoolwork. Since he enjoyed himself betting at the races, Sharok thought nothing of the fact that Vladimir gambled at cards. But robbery! That meant prison by any country's laws, not only Soviet.

Sharok's younger son, Yuri, was a reserved, fastidious youth. Cunning and cautious, he had grown up on the back streets of the Arbat close to the Smolensk Market and Protochny Street, the breeding ground of Moscow's crooks and down-and-outs. He knew what his brother was doing, but said nothing at home. The laws of the street meant more to him than those of the society they lived in.

From childhood, he grew up in the belief that somehow the Revolution was thwarting him. He did not know precisely how, only that it did. He had no idea how life might be under a different system, only that it would be better. Of that he had not the slightest doubt. He referred sarcastically to the Komsomols at school as "the comrades," the way the new bosses were referred to every day at home. Those arrogant activists imagined the world belonged to them. When Sasha Pankratov, the secretary of the school Komsomol cell, got up on the platform and started speaking, gesturing vigorously, Yuri felt defenseless.

He detested politics and regarded the career of engineer as the only one worth considering, as it might give him some independence. But his brother's arrest led him to change his plans.

The old man had been looking for a defense lawyer, and after consulting his clients he had at last found one who agreed to take the case for a fee of five hundred rubles. It was a colossal amount and Sharok was afraid to hand it over without a witness, so he took Yuri along with him.

The lawyer didn't waste time counting the money, but carelessly threw it into a drawer, and with that the visit was at an end. Yuri, however, had taken a good look around and saw the pictures in their gold frames, the gold bindings on books in glass cases. He had never seen such a luxurious set-up.

When they were out on the street again, the old man sighed enviously, "The way some people live!"

The lawyer impressed Yuri even more, however, in court. The little man with a flabby face and sleek beard could twist the awesome proletarian court around his little finger. That, at any rate, was how it looked to the young Sharok. The lawyer showered the court with laws and statutes, paragraphs and points, he resorted to tricks and stratagems, called new witnesses, appointed supplementary experts, and wrangled sarcastically with the judge and the prosecutor. The gloomy judge and the remorseless prosecutor had the law in their hands, but it seemed to frighten them, and this discovery determined the plans Yuri Sharok now made for his own future. Engineering was forgotten. The path to a career as a lawyer lay via a higher education, and the path to higher education lay via the Komsomol and the factory.

Thus it was that in his ninth year at school, Yuri Sharok joined the Komsomol. As the son of a worker, a preferred status at a school attended by the children of the Arbat intelligentsia, he kept himself aloof. The girls thought him enigmatic. It was the clever, serious, active ones who liked him. They thought they were educating him politically, shaping and developing him. Being honest and trusting, they found him attractive, handsome, simple, and reserved.

Later, working in the factory, he acquired the confidence he had always lacked. Now he was a worker! The blue overalls, which were always clean, suited his good physique. He cultivated a degree of rudeness, which he passed off as working-class directness and contempt for intellectuals. Once a shy, silent schoolboy, now he would often speak at meetings, sensibly assuming an ability to speak in public to be an asset for a future advocate.

Once he was at the institute, however, he spoke much less, nor did he distinguish himself there in any other way. He presented himself as a future efficient and dependable public servant. Not that he tried to distinguish himself. The newspapers were full of attacks on wreckers and saboteurs and deviationists. *Show them up! Punish them mercilessly! The scoundrels! Human carrion! Destroy them! Finish them off! Root them out! Exterminate them! Wipe them off the face of the earth!* These short, implacable words and phrases, like shots from a pistol, reawoke his fear. He understood everything perfectly and weighed his future in a calculating manner. When he finished at the institute, he would be sent to a province or district, either to a people's court or the prosecution service. He didn't give the slightest hint that he wanted to be a private defense lawyer. "Don't try to wriggle out of your duty, Sharok!" they would say. Surely he wouldn't have to relinquish the goal he had worked so hard and so stubbornly to attain?

Sharok made Yuri a suit. It was in the latest "Charleston" style, wide-cut trousers and a short, fitted jacket with high square shoulders. With his blue eyes and pale skin, Yuri looked very good in it. They had bought the cloth at Torgsin, the imported goods store on Tverskaya Street.

"The neighbors are nosy," the old man said. "Their tongues would hang out. 'The Sharoks have got gold hidden away and more money than they know what to do with.'"

He had regretted having to sell the gold bracelet and gold studs, but the old man was well aware that, to land a good position in Moscow, one had to be well dressed. The days of the leather coat and peasant shirt were gone, thank God. For all his selfish indifference toward his family, Sharok did have something akin to fatherly feeling for his younger son, in whom he saw himself as a young man. There was also the matter of the second room in the apartment, which worried him. The house management committee had their eye on it even now, and if Yuri were to leave, they would grab it.

"Contacts, contacts, you must make contacts," he urged Yuri.

But Yuri didn't make friends, either in the factory or at the institute. Friends were not permitted in the Sharok household. Their relatives were poor and Sharok saw them only as an additional burden, so they were neither visited nor invited. The father spent his free time at the races, the mother spent hers in church. At Easter the children got a slice of Easter cake, at Shrovetide they got pancakes, and that was the extent of their festivities. Although Sharok claimed he didn't believe in God, he couldn't forgive Him for his ruin. Still less could he forgive the Soviet system. On May Day and the Seventh of November, he worked just as he did on other days.

Yuri's links with his schoolmates turned out to be the firmest. Three of them lived in his apartment block. Sasha Pankratov, the Komsomol secretary, Maxim — Max — Kostin, the son of the woman who worked the elevator, and Nina Ivanova, one of the soft-hearted Komsomols who had wanted to improve Yuri. Together with Lena Budyagina, whose father was the famous diplomat, they formed a tight group of activists.

They used to meet at Lena's, in the block of apartments known as the Fifth House of Soviets. Budyagin then lived abroad and the children had the run of the apartment. Yuri would show up, vaguely feeling that these might turn out to be useful friends. One day, this vague sensation turned into a concrete hope. The one man who might help him, Budyagin, had been recalled from abroad and put in charge of heavy industry.

From Vozdvizhenka, Yuri turned into Granovsky Street. This was where *they* lived, in the Fifth House of Soviets, a building of gray granite. *Their* children were playing in the small garden fenced around with spiked railings. Yuri waited in the lobby with an impenetrable look on his face while the ancient doorman phoned the Budyagins. He then went up to the third floor and rang the bell.

The door was opened by Lena, smiling her usual shy smile. She wore her black hair in a heavy bun and, being tall, kept her head slightly bowed. Her bright red mouth and pouting lips were slightly too large for her beautiful, long, milky-white face. Nina said Lena had a Levantine profile. Yuri had no idea what that meant. All he knew was that Lena Budyagina was the most beautiful girl in the school.

He pulled her toward him with the rough familiarity of an old friend and she did not pull away.

"Have the others come?"

"Not yet."

"Is Ivan Grigoryevich at home?"

She led him along a hallway smelling of freshly waxed floor to her father's study.

"Papa, Yuri wants to see you."

She gave Yuri a happy and devoted smile and let him slip past her into the room.

The narrow room was darkened by a neighboring wall that

projected half across the window. Books, magazines and journals, newspapers, and Russian and foreign pamphlets lay strewn over a table, piled on bookshelves, heaped on chairs, and scattered across the floor. Above a battered couch hung a map of the world with steamship routes marked in dotted lines. Yuri noticed a three-digit number before Budyagin closed the file he had been reading and pushed it to one side. It contained secret documents circulated only to members of the Central Committee and Central Control Commission. Yuri also noticed a Parker pen, Troika cigarettes, rubber boots, and a jacket of the particular cut that the celebrated tailor Entin made only for diplomats of the highest rank.

"Yes?" Quietly businesslike, Budyagin's tone was that of a man who was accustomed to being asked for favors.

"I'm just finishing in Soviet law at the institute, Ivan Grigoryevich," Yuri said, "and my brother's in jail. . . ."

The ring of the doorbell and the sound of the door being opened came from the hallway.

"They'll never let me join the court or the public prosecutor service," Sharok went on. "That leaves economic legal work. I'd like to work in a factory. Before the institute I worked in a factory in Frunze. I understand people and I know about production."

Budyagin cast a detached glance over Sharok. He was confident of his right to supervise others. What could Yuri and his ilk mean to him? He was used to commanding the masses, to deciding the fate of the masses.

"Go and see Egert. I'll tell him."

"Thank you, Ivan Grigoryevich."

"What did your brother do?"

"It was a criminal offense. He's young, he got into bad company. . . ."

"We got rid of the old system of justice and the new one is only half-literate. We need educated people."

"I understand, Ivan Grigoryevich," Sharok eagerly agreed. "But it doesn't depend on me. Work for the court or the prosecutor's office, and my brother's a convict."

"Egert, go and see Egert," Budyagin repeated. "I'll phone him. So, you'd like to be a legal counsel?"

The deliberately ironic way he said "legal counsel" wounded Yuri.

But he had attained his goal. Only the result mattered. That's the way it's done! Some find it hard; for others everything's easy. It used to be that you had to have money. Now you had to have power.

He was finished with the institute and its canteen that always smelled of sour cabbage, finished with the hated "voluntary" Saturday work, the boring meetings, the endless homework, and finished with being afraid of saying the wrong thing. He hadn't even worn his new suit to the institute, not wanting to stand out among the students who for years had been trying to get an order for a pair of cheap woolen pants out of the trade union.

Of course, they would hold meetings, utter their phrases. He could imagine their hostile faces, their spiteful looks, and the sullen impenetrability of their leaders. "You're trying to get out of doing your duty, you're deserting, Sharok...." He would just smile, calm and derisive. What was all this about? Why the complaints? He was just going back to the factory he'd come from, going to rejoin the collective he'd grown up in. There used to be seven hundred workers there, now there were five thousand. It was the firstborn of the Five-Year Plan! It was an honor for a young specialist to work there. Had he asked for the post himself? No, why should he? He'd never lost touch with the factory, and when they had asked him if he wanted to come back after he'd finished at the institute, he'd said yes. What else should he have said? He was proud of the concern being shown for his future. And him a simple Soviet man.

That would shut them up! They'd change their tune. They'd be slapping him on the back, "Okay, Sharok, that's fine, you do what you have to do!"

He felt his power and his triumph over the people at the institute, and also over these people at the Fifth House of Soviets. These imperious intellectuals, they had always merely tolerated him. But let Sasha Pankratov try asking Budyagin for the same thing, and Budyagin would refuse, he'd tell him to work where the Party sent him. Yet Sharok could be thrown a crust. They don't respect Sharok, so they could throw him a crust. And these kids, his schoolfriends, all sitting together in the vast school refectory, they had never respected him, either. And now they'd despise him for running to Budyagin for help.

Let them think what they liked. After all, he might have gone to Budyagin for advice. Like an old comrade. Yes, exactly, just like going to an old comrade! Of course, being polite, they just might not ask at all why he'd gone.

"Hi!" Sharok said.

"Greetings!" Max Kostin answered for the rest.

In his well-pressed tunic and highly polished boots, his red hair carefully combed, broad-shouldered, fresh-faced, and smiling, Max was radiant, as a young student should be when he has been given the day off.

Next to him on the sofa sat Nina Ivanova, her heels treading down the backs of her crumpled shoes.

Should have bought them a size bigger, you silly fool, Sharok thought to himself. Nina hadn't a clue about clothes. She wore the same old jacket wherever she went. She had no idea how to do her hair, either, combing it back instead of covering up her high horsey forehead.

He clapped Vadim Marasevich on the shoulder. Yuri behaved affably toward this harmless windbag, the son of a famous Moscow doctor. Vadim was lolling in an armchair discussing H. G. Wells. He was fat, his lips were thick, and he had short, tufted eyebrows, like a rat's, above his small, dull eyes.

Little Vladlen Budyagin was doing his homework, sitting with his legs, in long brown stockings, folded under him. Lena distractedly followed the movements of his pen as it formed sloping letters. She smiled at Yuri and nodded to him to sit.

This was the entire group except for Sasha Pankratov.

"Wells predicts wars, epidemics, the disintegration of the United States," Vadim said, "and then the scientists and aviators will take power."

Nina objected. "The history of mankind isn't science-fiction. It's classes that take power."

"Undoubtedly," Vadim agreed condescendingly. "But it's the line of thought that's so interesting. Scientists and aviators, the levers of future power, the technocrats who will conquer space."

"My friends, if Germany rearms, everyone will rearm," Max said.

"Hitler won't last long," Nina protested. "The Social Democrats got eight million votes and the Communists got five million."

"Yet they couldn't protect Thälmann." Yuri entered the conversation, thinking that if five million people couldn't protect one man, they weren't worth much.

Nobody present even thought to look for a hidden meaning in his words. Their beliefs were too strong to doubt the faith of a fellow comrade. They could argue and debate and even quarrel, but they were unshakable in their belief that it was Marxism, the ideology of their class, world revolution, the final aim of their struggle, and the Soviet state, the indestructible bastion of the international proletariat, that together gave their lives meaning.

"They have forgotten how to act conspiratorially," Max said.

"Dimitrov will shake that regime," Vadim Marasevich said. "Like shaking a pear off a tree. It'll be a magical sight, the trial of the century!"

He aired his views on the forthcoming trial of Dimitrov, and on the possibility of war, or rather on the symptoms of its outbreak, which only he could discern.

But Vadim Marasevich's theories were well known here, and they wouldn't let him prattle on. A new slaughter? Mankind had hardly forgotten the last war, which had cost ten million lives. An attack on the Soviet Union? The world's working classes wouldn't allow it. And Russia was not the country she once was. They were already turning out cast-iron at Magnitogorsk and Kuznetsk, the tractor factories of Stalingrad, Chelyabinsk, and Kharkov, and the automobile plants in Gorky and Moscow were under way, and the first Soviet rolling-mills had been built.

Their hearts swelled with pride. This was their country, the shock brigade of the world proletariat, the embodiment of the advancing world revolution, an island of hope in a world torn by crises, unemployment, moral decline, spiritual poverty. True, they had ration cards and denied themselves everything, but they were building a new world. The well-stocked windows of the Torgsin store were an obscene spectacle as long as the people went hungry, but the gold the store earned helped build factories. It was a pledge of future abundance.

They always spoke this way. Everything here was as it always was. The polished floors, the long table under the low lampshade, the marmalade on the table, the tranquillity of a high state official's orderly home. Pouring the tea, Lena's mother asked, "Maxim, lemon for you?" And, as always, coming from this Armenian woman, the Russian name sounded strange and artificial to Sharok.

And yet, what had they achieved, after all? With all the possibilities open to them, Nina was a schoolteacher, Lena did English translations in a technical library, Max was finishing infantry school and would sweat it out in the army. They were openhearted, and that was their fatal weakness.

Such were the thoughts of Yuri Sharok. But he then asked, "What's happened to Sasha?"

"He's not coming," Max replied.

Sharok detected in Max's brief reply the irritating restraint of the Komsomol leader who always knew something others weren't to know.

"Has anything happened?"

Lena replied that Sasha was having some problems and her father had telephoned Glinskaya.

So, the unbending Sasha! Well, what do you know? It put Yuri in a good mood. When he had applied to join the Komsomol, Sasha had made a little "no confidence" speech and abstained in the voting. At the factory, Sharok had been made a trainee milling-machine operator, while Sasha had unloaded trucks and had spent a whole year stuck with stevedores — the country, of course, needed stevedores, too. Sasha had wanted to study history, but got into engineering instead, and the country, of course, needed engineers. Coming from the same background, it wasn't surprising that Budyagin liked him. But what had happened? Budyagin would never have intervened if it had been only a minor matter.

Yuri said, "One of the kids at the institute made the following crack: 'What is a wife? A thumb tack on a chair.'"

"He read it in Mendel Marants," Vadim Marasevich said.

"He said it at a meeting about International Women's Day. He was expelled from the institute, the Komsomol, the trade union."

"The joke was out of place," Nina Ivanova said.

"If they expel everyone, who'll be left?" Max frowned.

$$\text{5}$$

Lena Budyagina was born abroad in a family of political émigrés, and when she had first come to Russia after the Revolution with her father, who was by then a diplomat, even her knowledge of her native language was uncertain. But she had not wanted to appear different from her friends, and the special nature and exclusiveness of her situation was a burden to her. She was acutely sensitive to everything she saw as genuinely national and Russian.

She was immediately attracted by Yuri Sharok, a simple working-class boy, independent, touchy, and enigmatic, and she joined with Nina Ivanova in trying to educate him, though she knew well enough that her interest was not entirely educational. Yuri knew it, too. But at that time, love affairs were regarded in school as unworthy of real Komsomols. As children of the Revolution, they genuinely believed that any personal distraction was a betrayal of society.

After they had left school, and without making any effort to get closer to her, Yuri had consciously maintained the relationship at the exact level of intimacy it had reached in school. Sometimes he would telephone and suggest a movie or café, other times he would drop by when the whole group was there. The embrace in the hallway had been a step across the artificial threshold Yuri had previously set. He had acted unexpectedly and crudely, but with the sort of decisiveness that would conquer such a nature as hers.

For a few days, she waited for him to telephone, and then, unable to wait any longer, she casually called him, the way they used to phone each other. She spoke in an even, quiet voice, trying to make sure her word endings were correct and that the stress on each word fell in the right place, and she spoke slowly and calmly, so that even on the phone her shy smile was detectable.

Yuri had been waiting for her call.

"I was just going to phone you. I've got two tickets for the dance at the Business Club on the sixth. Want to come?"

"Yes, of course I do," she replied.

He came for her on the evening of the sixth of November. In her long blue-green evening dress, a string of pearls glimmering in her black hair, and wearing an exotic perfume, she was strikingly beautiful — a woman from another world. Only her shy smile was familiar, and seemed to be asking if he liked what he saw and whether he realized that she had dressed for him.

She opened the door to the dining room.

"Be in bed by ten o'clock, Vladik."

"Okay." Vladlen was building something on the windowsill.

"Where are your folks?" Yuri helped her on with her coat.

"Papa's in Kramatorsk and Mama's in Ryazan."

"For the holiday?"

"Papa always makes the rounds of the factories during the holidays, and Mama's a lecturer."

She gathered up the long dress beneath her coat and laughed. "Long dresses are rather awkward."

They were in luck. A car was just coming out of the driveway and as it happened Lena recognized the driver, who gave them a lift. A middle-aged man, he worked as a chauffeur for senior officials and had the self-important manner that went with the job. He was attentive to Lena but took no notice of Yuri, who did not let it bother him but instead concentrated on the fact that Lena was alone and that he would be taking her home after the dance. Her nearness on the soft seat in the back of the car aroused him, but it was the thought that tonight was the night anything might happen that excited and alarmed him even more.

He had known other women, but not like this. The neighbor's cleaning woman, a pickup in the courtyard, girls in the village he visited with his father. With them things were much simpler: they knew how to look after themselves. Now he was the one who was responsible for whatever happened, and it was dangerous to toy with a Budyagin. Anyone else in Yuri's position would eventually ask her to marry him, but he was afraid it would be too big a jump. Anyway, could he be sure that Lena would make him the sort of wife he needed? He couldn't imagine her strange, hostile family next to his own. He should wait. He hadn't given up hope of becoming a lawyer and achieving independence. If he married Lena, he would be hitching himself to her wagon.

They pulled up outside the Business Club, and Yuri had no idea how to open the car door, turning first one handle and then another to no avail. Lena leaned across, opened the door, gave him a smile and said, "The handles in this car are very uncooperative!"

Her attempt to smooth over his clumsiness only irritated him further, underlining the fact that he had never been in such a car before. But he controlled himself. Giving the chauffeur a cold look, he followed Lena into the club. He would do as he liked and live as he liked, and at this moment he liked Lena. Sitting next to her, he felt the looks they were getting. He was used to women looking at him, but their glances now were different, special. They were curious about the man who had the attention of the most striking woman there that evening.

Ruslanova sang and Khenkin read stories by Zoshchenko, and then the dancing started. Lena was an obedient dancer, maybe not as light on her feet as the girls he met at the dance halls, but she laughed at her own awkwardness and pressed trustingly closer to him.

When Lena went to the powder room, Yuri leaned against a column and looked around at the assembled crowd. Here were the leaders of industry, top executives, scientists, the cream of Moscow's technical intelligentsia who worked in commissariats and trembled before their bosses, but earned good salaries and bonuses, bought their goods in restricted stores, and got sent on profitable missions. Yuri knew all too well that the lucky ones who got into the best institutions after graduating moved up fast, and what a sweat it was for those who were sent to work in industry.

What would he achieve in a factory? He'd be running from one people's court to another, doing petty cases of firings and absenteeism, lawsuits about trivial shortages or the poor quality of protective gloves. To work in the legal department of a commissariat or a directorate or even an enterprise group, that would be something else. Big cases, handled in the high courts, the Supreme Court of the Soviet Union and the Republics. That would be useful for a future career as a lawyer. But all that was for later. First, he had to avoid being allocated to the regional courts by the institute along with the rest, and then everything would be much simpler.

It was eleven o'clock. Yuri wanted to get Lena home before the doorman locked the entrance.

"Tired?" he asked.

"Let's stay a bit longer." She smiled.

It was one o'clock before they left. After the stuffiness of the club, the light rain outside was pleasantly refreshing. There was not a soul about and, apart from the rain-streaked streetlamps, the only sign of life was the light inside the security police building on Lubyanskaya Square.

They arrived at Lena's.

"Come upstairs for a while."

Yuri was surprised by her straightforward, trusting tone of voice. He followed her in silence.

The old doorman opened up for them. He didn't ask what a guest was doing going up to the Budyagins' at this hour — he was well trained and showed no surprise at anything.

She switched on the light in the entrance hall and peered into the dining room.

"He's asleep."

She was evidently relieved that the child was sleeping, not because she didn't want him to see that Yuri was there.

"Go and sit in Papa's room while I change."

She switched on the overhead light in the study and left Yuri alone.

He browsed through a pile of books. There was a volume of Lenin with slips of paper serving as bookmarks, there were books on metallurgy, and Alexei Tolstoy's *Peter the First*. He couldn't find any official papers or secret files or banned books such as only *they* could get hold of, and there was no sign of the revolver *they* all had (it would have to be a Browning, Yuri was sure, as that was the easiest to slip into the back pocket). He had a powerful desire to see something forbidden, inaccessible; he longed to be able to touch the secret of their power.

She would be back any minute, so he had to hurry. He pulled at the middle drawer of the table and, finding it locked, tugged at the rest with the same result. He just managed to lean back in the chair as she entered, dressed as he was used to seeing her, in a white blouse and dark blue skirt.

"Shall I make some coffee?"

They made chance physical contact as they moved together around the small room. She smiled at him. And when she leaned forward to pour the coffee, he saw her breasts. He had never been alone with her at night, he had never drunk such coffee, such liqueur.

"More?"

"I've had enough."

He moved over to the sofa.

"Let's sit here."

She joined him, still carrying her cup of coffee. He took the cup from her hand and set it down on the table. She smiled in surprise and gazed at him. He looked straight into her anxious eyes and, with crude familiarity, pulled her close to him.

6

On November 7, Sasha waited for the institute's column at the corner of Tverskaya and Bolshaya Gruzinskaya streets.

The procession was making slow progress. Above the marchers, banners, pennants, and portraits uniformly fluttered their celebration of Stalin. Middle-aged men blew their trumpets with grim determination, discordant singing came from the ranks, and people were dancing in the middle of the street. Loudspeakers carried the sounds of Red Square, voices of radio commentators, greetings from the Mausoleum, the triumphant roar of the demonstrators as they marched across the square.

The institute's column arrived a couple of hours later and came to a halt. The ranks broke up and the marchers mingled. Sasha pushed through the crowd to join his own group. At once, he was aware that everyone was looking at him the way people do with someone who's in trouble and doesn't yet know it. This had nothing to do with the committee. This was something different.

Nobody said anything and he didn't ask. Only his friend Runochkin apparently wanted to say something but couldn't let go of the banner he was holding.

"Get in line, get in line!" the marshals ordered.

The ranks had all been prearranged, and Sasha was at the end of the column among students from other courses. He could see his faculty's flag and the banner that Runochkin and another student were carrying on two poles. Whipped by the wind, the banner unfurled, streamed to the rear, then twisted and finally straightened out. The column moved off.

It stopped again before reaching Triumphal Square. The ranks mingled once more. Sasha went over and was met by Runochkin.

"Our wall newspaper's been taken down."

Runochkin was small and crooked, and one of his eyes was crossed, so he would stand somewhat sideways and twist his head as he spoke. Why had they taken down the wall newspaper? It had never happened before.

"Who did it?"

"Baulin. Because of the rhymes. He claims they debase the shock-work campaign."

Runochkin was the editor of the newspaper, but it had been Sasha's idea to write the rhymes about the pace-setting student workers, and he had even composed one himself, poking fun at Kovalyov, the group's leader. *"Since it now is the fashion/To work with a passion,"* his limerick ended, *"Kovalyov thinks he's haute couture."* The other three were written by Rosa Poluzhan. Boris Nesterov she teased for his insatiable appetite (*"When he reaches heaven's gate/He'll trade his wings for a full plate."*); Peter Puzanov for his constant napping; and Prikhodko because he liked to do a bit of hunting during work trips, so he made more trips than anyone else. The rhymes were hardly works of genius, they weren't even funny, but they were innocent.

"Debase the shock-work campaign! What's so debasing?"

Runochkin tilted his head. "It was the rhymes. 'Why *only* about shock-workers?' I explained that we had only included photographs of shock-workers, so the rhymes went together with them. They wanted to know why there was no editorial, as well."

It had also been Sasha's idea not to include an editorial. Why repeat what every other paper would be writing about? The paper must be bright and cheerful, a holiday number that people would actually read and that wouldn't just hang miserably in the corridor. The others had agreed with him then. Only the cautious Rosa Poluzhan had given him a meaningful look and said, "It would be better if you wrote an editorial and signed it."

"Are you afraid of Azizyan?" he had asked her.

Good God, how things had turned out. There was still the other business with Azizyan dragging on, and now this had to happen. Okay, we'll just have to defend ourselves!

The columns halted again at Strastnaya Square. From here on there would be no more stops. The marshals checked carefully to see that no outsiders had slipped in among the ranks. They got the columns into line and drew the ranks closer together, so that they could be made to run the last lap of the march onto Red Square without stopping.

Baulin and Lozgachev came up to the group. Lozgachev was wearing a red armband, as leader of the institute column.

Baulin looked at Sasha severely. "Don't you think you have to turn out for the demonstration, Pankratov?"

This was unfair. It was usual for those who lived in town to join the procession as it passed along. And, anyway, Baulin could have no idea which of the thousand students had showed up at the institute and which had joined the column later. Yet he had known Sasha's movements, which meant he had kept an eye open specially for him and now he had come over precisely to make his remark and put Sasha's "misdemeanor" on public record. The injustice was all the more humiliating because Baulin knew that Sasha wouldn't dare to contradict him in front of everyone. Or would he?

"I *am* at the demonstration. You can see me, apparently. I am not a hallucination." Sasha spoke with the deliberate politeness the intellectual youth of the Arbat used when faced with a brawl.

"Mind you don't go too far." Baulin said no more and moved on without waiting for Sasha to reply.

Flowing in two streams around the Historical Museum, the columns poured into Red Square, moving closer together as they increased their pace, and practically ran across the square, where they were separated from each other by compact ranks of Red Army soldiers.

Sasha's column passed close to the Mausoleum. Among the people standing on the tribunes were military attachés in their operetta uniforms, but nobody took any notice of them. All eyes were focused on the Mausoleum; everyone was excited by a single thought: Was Stalin there and would they be able to see him?

They could see him. The face with the black mustache, looking as if it had just been taken from the countless pictures and sculptures. He stood motionless, his cap pulled well down. The roar grew. "Stalin! Stalin!" Like the rest, Sasha marched with his eyes fixed on him, shouting "Stalin! Stalin!" The marchers tried to look back after they had passed the Mausoleum, but the soldiers hurried them on. "Move it! Move it!"

At St. Basil's Cathedral, the columns broke up and the disorderly crowds moved down to the river, onto the bridge and the packed embankment. Drums, trumpets, banners, placards, and pennants were all loaded onto trucks. Tired and hungry, everyone was rushing to get home, hurrying to Kamenny Bridge, the Prechistensky Gates, the tramcars.

At that moment the roar on the square reached a crescendo and echoed down to the embankment like a roll of thunder. Stalin had raised his arm in salute to the marchers.

An urgent meeting of the Party committee and Party activists of the institute was convened after the holiday in a small assembly hall.

At the podium, Lozgachev was sifting papers.

He spoke. "Two anti-Party actions have taken place in the institute. The first was Pankratov's assault on the application of Marxism to accounting, and the second was the publication of a wall newspaper, also by Pankratov. His accomplices turned out to be Komsomol members Runochkin, Poluzhan, Kovalyov, and Pozdnyakova. They met no rebuff from the Communist or Komsomol members of the group. This is proof that political diligence has become blunted."

He went on. "The holiday issue of the newspaper carried no editorial on the sixteenth anniversary of October, the name of Comrade Stalin was not mentioned once, portraits of shockworkers were accompanied by malicious, slanderous so-called verses. Here is a bit of one of them, composed as it happens by Pankratov himself. Just listen to this: 'Since it now is the fashion to work with a passion' — what does 'it now is the fashion' mean?"

Lozgachev swept the audience with a severe look.

"Do we really regard work as a *fashion?* It is the work our people are doing that is creating the foundations of socialism; we regard work as an honor. For Pankratov, however, it's just another 'fashion.' Only a malicious critic could have written in this way, someone who is prepared to slander our people. And it was at the last meeting of the Party committee that some people tried to whitewash Pankratov by reassuring us that his attack during Azizyan's lecture and his defense of Krivoruchko were mere coincidence."

"Who were these 'some people'?" Baulin knew as well as everyone else whom Lozgachev meant.

"I have Janson in mind — the dean of the faculty. I don't think he should walk away from his responsibility."

"He won't walk away," Baulin promised.

"The easygoing, carefree atmosphere, created in the faculty by Comrade Janson, permitted Pankratov to carry out his political sabotage."

"Disgraceful!" The cry came from Karev, a pleasant-looking fourth-year student whom everyone in the institute knew to be a demagogue and a scrounger.

"The Party committee of the institute responded decisively to Pankratov's assault and removed the newspaper. This shows that all in all our Party organization is in a healthy condition. Our firm and merciless decision confirms that this is so."

Lozgachev gathered up his papers and left the podium.

"Is the editor here?" Baulin inquired.

Everyone started shifting around to locate Runochkin. The small cross-eyed man climbed up to the podium.

Baulin adopted his customary tone of malicious geniality. "Tell us, Runochkin, how you arrived at this situation."

"We didn't think it was worth repeating the editorials that were going to appear in the main paper."

"What has the main paper got to do with it?" Baulin frowned. "It hadn't come out when you issued yours."

"Yes, but it did come out later."

"And did you know what its editorial would be about?"

"Of course we knew."

There was laughter in the hall.

"Don't act the fool! Who decided it shouldn't be written? Pankratov?" Baulin was angry.

"I don't remember."

"You don't remember. Weren't you surprised?"

Runochkin shrugged.

"And weren't you surprised by Pankratov's suggestion to include the verses?"

"We'd done it before."

"Do you understand your error?"

"Put the way Comrade Lozgachev put it, yes, I understand my error."

"And how would you put it?"

Runochkin was silent.

"Made an idiot of himself!" It was Karev again.

Baulin looked at his papers. "Is Pozdnyakova here?"

Smiling, Nadya Pozdnyakova went to the podium. She was a good-looking girl.

"What can I say? Sasha Pankratov decided not to write an editorial — he's the Komsomol organizer, so we had to do as he said."

"So, if he told you to jump from the fifth floor, you'd do it?"

"I don't know . . . ," she replied in confusion. "And I thought —"

"You didn't think," Baulin interrupted. "And do you like to see training for shock-work being mocked in this way?"

"No."

"Why didn't you object?"

"They wouldn't have taken any notice of me."

"But you could have come to the Party committee."

"I . . ." She put her handkerchief to her eyes. "I . . ."

"All right, sit down." Baulin looked at his papers again. "Poluzhan!"

There were shouts from the audience. "We don't need to hear any more of them. Let Pankratov answer for himself!"

"Pankratov will get his turn. Poluzhan, tell us what happened," Baulin said.

"I regard the whole affair as a big mistake," Rosa Poluzhan began.

"Mistakes can be of all sorts," Baulin reminded her.

"I regard this one as a political mistake."

"You should have said so straightaway; we shouldn't have to drag it out of you."

"I regard it as a gross political error," Rosa went on. "I would only ask you to take into account the fact that I had suggested that we include an editorial."

"You think that exonerates you?" Baulin retorted. "You washed your hands of it, made sure you were covered, made things safe for yourself. But the fact that such a vulgarity was hanging on the wall didn't bother you? You wrote some of the verses yourself, didn't you?"

"Yes."

"Which ones?"

"On Nesterov, Puzanov, and Prikhodko."

"Oh, yes — the glutton, the sleepyhead, and the cheat! And you think that's the way to glorify shock-work?" Baulin asked mockingly.

"That was my mistake," Rosa whispered.

"Sit down! Kovalyov!"

White-faced, Kovalyov took his place on the podium.

"I must confess in all honesty that on my way here I hadn't realized the full political essence of this affair. It seemed more like a joke, stupid and inappropriate, but just a joke. I now see that we were all tools in Pankratov's hands. True, I did try to insist on including an editorial. But I said nothing when the verses were being discussed. One was written about me, and I thought that if I protested the others would think I was trying to evade being criticized."

"You were embarrassed?" Baulin smirked.

"Yes."

"Kovalyov came to the committee and told us honestly what had happened," Lozgachev intervened.

"It would have been better still if he'd come before the paper was put up," Baulin retorted.

Siversky, the topography lecturer, got up. Sasha had never imagined that he was a Party member. A silent man with military bearing, in high boots, dark blue cavalry tunic, and long white Caucasian shirt, he looked more like a tsarist army officer.

"Kovalyov, you say you were too embarrassed to protest against the verses about yourself."

"Yes, that's right."

"Then why didn't you object to the verses about the others?"

"That's a provocative question!" It was Karev again.

"You're confusing the issue," another voice called out.

Baulin raised his hand to silence the audience.

"You can hear what the meeting thinks of your question, Comrade Siversky."

"I wanted to tell that young man, Kovalyov, that this is not the way to start out in life," Siversky said calmly and sat down.

"You'll have your chance to speak during the debate," Baulin replied. "For the moment, let us hear what the chief organizer has to say. Pankratov, please!"

Sasha was in the back row among students from other departments, listening and thinking over what he ought to say. They expected him to admit his mistakes. They wanted to hear him repent and they wanted to hear what he would say to justify himself.

Did he regret what had happened? He did. He didn't have to argue with Azizyan; he could have published the paper the way they always had. If he'd acted differently this whole business, which had suddenly erupted into his life and into his comrades' lives so unpleasantly, would never have happened.

He must stand his ground and defend the others. He must make them hear him out. Baulin, Lozgachev, and Karev weren't the only ones here. There were also Janson and Siversky, and his comrades, too. They sympathized with him.

The hall fell silent. Those who had gone out for a smoke now came back. Some people left their seats to get a better view.

"Heavy charges have been laid against me," Sasha began. "Comrade Lozgachev used such terms as political sabotage, anti-Party assault, malevolence —"

"And quite right, too." The cry was probably from Karev, but Sasha had decided not to take any notice of hecklers.

Baulin tapped his pencil on the table.

Sasha went on. "Lecturer Azizyan was unable to combine the theoretical and the practical aspects of the subject in his lectures and was therefore depriving us of familiarization with important parts of the course."

Azizyan leaped up, but Baulin stopped him with a gesture.

"As for the newspaper, as Komsomol organizer I take full responsibility for that issue."

There were cries of "That's noble of you!" "Show-off!"

"I was the one who said we didn't need an editorial and I also suggested putting in the verses, and I wrote one of them myself. The others might have thought there was a directive."

"A directive? Who would have given *you* a directive?" Baulin glared at Sasha.

For a moment Sasha did not understand the question, but when it finally sank in, he replied, "You have the right to ask me any question you like, except those calculated to insult me. I'm not expelled yet."

"You will be, don't worry!" It was Karev again.

"Also, we didn't print an editorial because we didn't want to repeat what our main paper and the faculty bulletin would be saying. They have more experienced journalists . . ."

"Judging by the verses, you're a poet, too," Baulin declared sarcastically.

"Scribbler!"

"I have already agreed that it was a mistake to omit the editorial. Now, about the verses. They contain nothing reprehensible. The mistake was to print them underneath portraits of the shock-workers. It distorted their meaning."

"Why put them in?"

"Just to give people a laugh for the holiday."

"Things have certainly turned out cheerful, no arguing about that!" Baulin remarked.

Everyone laughed.

"But I categorically reject the accusation of political sabotage," Sasha went on.

"Tell me, Pankratov, did you ask anyone for help?"

"No."

Baulin looked across at Glinskaya and then again at Sasha.

"Not Deputy Commissar Budyagin?"

"No."

"Then why did he intercede for you with the director of the institute?"

Sasha hadn't wanted to mention Mark, but now he had no choice.

"I told my uncle, Ryazanov, about it and evidently he spoke to Budyagin."

"Evidently," Baulin mocked. "But surely Ryazanov is in the east?"

"He came to Moscow."

"Ryazanov is by chance in Moscow, you by chance tell him the story, he by chance mentions it to Budyagin, and Budyagin by chance telephones Glinskaya. Aren't there just a few 'chances' too many here, Pankratov? Wouldn't it be much more honest just to say straight out: 'Yes, I tried to find ways out'?"

"I have explained the circumstances as they were."

"He's wriggling!" "He's not telling the truth!" "He's dishonest!" Karev had been joined by some of the other shouters of the institute.

"Have you anything more to say?"

"I told you everything."

"Sit down."

Sasha left the podium.

"Who wishes to speak?" Baulin asked.

"Janson! Janson! Let Janson speak!"

Janson stepped to the podium with an angry face.

"Comrades, the question we are discussing here today is a very important one."

"We don't need you to tell us that!" came from the hall.

"But the objective results must be distinguished from the subjective motivation —"

"They're one and the same! Don't start philosophizing!"

"No, they're not one and the same. But let me make my point —"

"No, we won't let you. You've said enough!"

Siversky got up to speak again. "Comrade Baulin, bring these rowdies to order. It's impossible to achieve anything under these circumstances."

Baulin gave the impression of not having heard the request.

Janson stubbornly persisted. "Pankratov took up an apolitical position and hence a philistine one —"

"Not enough, not enough!" Karev shouted.

Janson winced. "Wait a moment, comrades, hear me out —"

"There's nothing to hear!"

"In order to call these acts anti-Party, or to call them political sabotage, we first have to show premeditation. Only if there is evidence of intent —"

"You're evading the issue!"

"What about yourself, tell us about your own role!"

"So, the question is, did Pankratov mean to cause damage to the Party? I believe he had no such intention."

"Compromiser! Appeaser!"

"Papering over the cracks!"

"Comrade Janson, you are being asked to tell us about your own part in what happened," Baulin pointed out.

"I had no part in it at all. I had no hand in preparing the paper, nor the right to allow or not allow its publication. Lecturer Azizyan didn't complain to me, but to you."

"But why didn't you remove it from the wall?" Baulin asked.

"You must have seen it before I did."

"But why didn't you see it? It was nearer to your office, wasn't it?"

Janson shrugged his shoulders. "If you think that's of any importance —"

"Enough!" "He's had his say!"

Janson stood for a moment longer, shrugged again, and then went back to his seat.

With his jacket hanging over the back of his chair, Baulin spoke from his seat at the chairman's table. He wasn't smiling or grinning anymore, and he spoke in chopped categorical phrases.

"Pankratov was counting on his impunity. He was counting on protection in high places. He was sure that, faced with such names, the Party organization would not act. But the Party organization regards Party business, and the purity of the Party line, above any name or any authority."

He paused to allow applause, but as only two or three claps were forthcoming, he made it appear he didn't want any applause and continued.

"One is ashamed to look at the Komsomols Runochkin, Pozd-nyakova, Poluzhan, and Kovalyov. These are people who are only a step away from becoming engineers, Soviet specialists. Such are the toothless, politically helpless people trained by Comrade Janson!

That's why they so easily became toys in the hands of the class enemy. And that's what we are accusing Janson of. Janson, you created the right soil for Pankratov. Even here you tried to shield him. And that makes one suspicious."

⚘ 7 ⚘

Yuri told Lena to keep quiet about their affair. He loved her, she loved him, and that was all he wanted of her. He avoided her family, her home, and her friends. Afraid of injuring his self-esteem, she went along with his wishes.

His father had never let him bring girls home before, but a commissar's daughter was serious business! Yuri had never gone with such a girl before. Sharok and his wife were reserved with Lena. So a girl was visiting Yuri, fine, it was the young people's own affair. If they suit each other, they'll marry, if they don't, they'll part. They were only in step with the times. But if they did get married, she'd have to show respect to her in-laws, even if she was the daughter of a commissar. And she should be grateful to the girls who'd gone to bed with him before and hadn't been crazy about getting married afterward.

Lena, however, took their reserve as a sign of their dignity. In her eyes, Yuri's parents were also special and something out of the ordinary. His father was a handsome and imposing master crafts-man and his mother was a devout old lady. Theirs was a patriarchal way of life, a completely different world, a world of the people, simple and genuine.

Sometimes they discussed the letters Vladimir sent from the White Sea Canal, letters from a convicted criminal, which began with "Dearest Papa, Dearest Mama," "My own dear brother Yuri." There were poems, tearful prison poems about the young man's ruined life, and his dream of "flying, light as a bird." Yuri would wince, visibly embarrassed in front of Lena, but she was moved by his father's gloomy attentiveness and his mother's sad and worried look, and by the resilience with which Yuri bore this complication in his life.

Everything about them pleased her: their simple food, the way the father would wipe the chalk from his fingers, pick threads off his jacket, sit down at the table in the measured way of a working man for whom a meal in the bosom of his family was the reward for his hard toil. She liked the way Yuri's mother would always serve his father, as the breadwinner, the first helping, then the second to Yuri, also a working man, and the third to Lena as the guest, and finally help herself to what was left — as the mother who worked in the kitchen, she would always be satisfied. This was a real family, bound together and totally unlike her own, where each member lived his or her own life and they didn't see each other for weeks on end.

She and Yuri sometimes went to the Metropole to hear Skomorovsky or to the Grand Hotel to hear Tsfasman. She always insisted on paying her own way — after all, she worked and earned a salary and not to pay her share would be uncomradely. Yuri accepted her argument about comradeliness and tolerantly agreed. He was flattered that such a beautiful girl would waste herself on him, just as he was flattered by the attentiveness of the waiters. There were beautiful women and well-dressed men at the neighboring tables, the lights would be turned low, multicolored projectors would illuminate the fountain in the middle of the hall, and they would dance to the Metropole dance band. He would smile at Lena and squeeze her hand, delighted by the attention they attracted.

She would leave him late at night, but occasionally, if he let her, she would stay until almost dawn. The gates would be locked and she would have to ring the bell. The sleepy doorman would stumble out and eye her suspiciously every time, and she would slip him a ruble and run outside into the street, her high heels clicking loudly on the dark streets of the Arbat. At home, they noticed her coming in late and guessed what was going on, but they asked her nothing. Her father didn't like Yuri; he spoke about him derisively, even with contempt. Well, that was his business. She had ties to her family, but if need be, she would leave home, and without hesitation.

* * *

At the beginning of December, Yuri was summoned to the Commissariat of Justice. In the personnel department, in a large room with many unoccupied desks, he was received by a flat-chested, middle-aged woman named Malkova, with reddish hair and small, mobile features. She gestured to him to take a seat on the opposite side of her desk.

"Comrade Sharok, you're about to finish at the institute and we'll have to start thinking about a job for you, so I thought it was time I got to know you a bit better. Tell me about yourself."

To avoid being recruited into the security or prosecution services, Yuri knew he should present himself in an unfavorable light. But the habit of self-protection had over the years built up an automatic response in him, demanding that he make himself look irreproachable, absolutely spotless, and that he conceal anything that might compromise him. He spoke about himself in his customary way: he was the son of a clothing-factory worker, had himself been a lathe-worker, was a member of the Komsomol, and had a blemish-free record. There was one complication, however: his brother had been convicted of robbery. Mentioning this could only give his story an added note of sincerity, he thought.

Malkova smoked as she listened intently, then she stubbed out her cigarette in an ashtray and asked, "How was it that you, a Komsomol, didn't keep an eye on your brother?"

"I was only sixteen when he was put inside."

"Sixteen-year-olds commanded regiments in the Revolution."

She spoke as if she herself had commanded a regiment at sixteen. Maybe she had. She held herself like a soldier, lean as she was, in her leather jacket, with a cigarette between her teeth. No, perhaps not. After all, not everyone could have commanded a regiment; there wouldn't have been enough to go around! But this red-haired spider's opinion would decide whether they'd send him to work in a factory or somewhere in the back of the beyond. There was talk in the institute about the whole graduating class being sent to western and eastern Siberia.

Yuri smiled.

"My brother's a lot older than me; I couldn't have had any influence on him."

Malkova searched among the papers on her desk and found what she was looking for.

"The Chemical and Pharmaceutical Board wants you for their legal department. How did that come about?"

"I worked in the Frunze Chemical Works before the institute," he explained eagerly. "They need a lawyer. I've kept up my contact with them and so they asked for me."

Malkova frowned. "Everyone wants to stay in Moscow. But who's going to fill the jobs in the rest of the country? What about the courts and the prosecution service?"

Slowly, weighing each word, Yuri said, "To work in the courts and the prosecution service, one must be trusted absolutely. With a convict for a brother, what trust would I have?"

"To work in the courts and the prosecution service you have to be a true Soviet person, first and foremost," Malkova said in an instructive tone of voice. "The business of your brother won't prevent that."

"But you yourself asked me why I hadn't kept an eye on him. Apart from that, I think industry needs competent lawyers."

Malkova got up. "I'll take your request up with the head of the directorate. Then, it's up to the assignment commission. They decide everything."

Yuri also got up. "I'll work wherever they want to send me."

"You're telling me you will!" She smirked. "You've been getting a grant — now you have to earn it."

"I would obviously like to stay in Moscow," he said with conviction. "My father and mother are here and they're both elderly and not well, and in effect I'm the only son they've got left. But that" — he pointed to the file lying on the desk — "that wasn't my idea, it was the factory's. They don't need just any lawyer, they're looking for someone who knows their industry, the chemical industry."

"Everyone who wants to stay in Moscow has very weighty arguments," she said, "and they can all produce valid reasons, just like this one."

She fell silent and then added suddenly, "On the other hand, the Party organization of the institute is recommending you for a different job, and as it happens it's in Moscow, too."

"I don't know anything about that. But what is it exactly?"

Her reply was evasive. "Well, there are some vacancies. The prosecutor's office, for example. But you would prefer the factory?"

"Yes, I prefer the factory. I worked there, I grew up there, they were the ones who sent me to study. I owe the factory a lot."

The pride in his voice softened her.

"We will take note of your wishes and also of the request from the Chemical Board. In any event, the commission will make the decision."

This hag held his fate in her hands! She'd probably just got out of some dump in the sticks herself, but she was ready to send him, a native Muscovite, to some godforsaken hole miles from anywhere. His father was right, the peasants had invaded Moscow and there was nowhere for the city folk to go. The old man was now starting to push him. "They're recommending you for a job in the prosecution service in Moscow." But he wasn't being straightforward, or maybe he was. He was probably thinking about the apartment.

Even if they were recommending him, it didn't mean he would get the job. They might ask him why his brother was a criminal. There shouldn't be criminals in a real working-class, proletarian family. It means the family's not what it seems. Surely there were others, people who could be trusted, their own people.

With time, the childish and romantic image of the glamorous and independent defense lawyer had faded. The institute practice course, where he had sat in, and observed the courts and the prosecution service, had shown him the other side of the coin. He had seen famous lawyers not only making brilliant speeches, but also in a fluster, squabbling with other lawyers, shamelessly chasing after fees, ingratiating themselves with secretaries and clerks in the court, trying to drum legal advice into the head of some uncomprehending old woman during a consultation that paid five rubles. He knew the price of the luxurious offices they installed in their homes and which were turned back into dining rooms and bedrooms after the last client had gone. Even so, this had been the only thing he wanted to do.

But it was odd. The thought that he might be turned down for an official job stung him. Once more, they would be showing their disregard of him. They kept the good jobs for their own people, but him — reliable, obedient, a potential executive — they would give donkeywork. At the very best, they would throw him a crust and let him go to the factory as a "legal adviser," as Budyagin had put it contemptuously.

He told nobody about his interview at the commissariat, but he could not conceal his anxiety from Lena. They were sitting in the theater — at long last, they'd managed to get seats for O'Neill's *The Emperor Jones*.

"What's bothering you?"

She looked at him searchingly, lovingly.

He smiled and gestured to her not to disturb the people sitting near them.

At home, as she lay in his arms, she asked him again. He said it was nothing in particular, just that there was some difficulty about the factory's offer.

"I could talk to my father, if you want."

"He's already done what he could."

She didn't insist, knowing that her father wouldn't do more than he already had.

"Sasha Pankratov came to see us yesterday. I feel sorry for him."

"Why's that?"

"Don't you know? He's been expelled from the Komsomol and the institute."

Yuri propped himself up on his elbow.

"That's the first I've heard about it."

"Don't you ever see him?"

"I haven't run into him for ages." This wasn't true. He'd seen Sasha only recently, but Sasha had said nothing to him. Yuri couldn't tell Lena this. "Was it because of the business with the accounting lecturer?"

"Yes, and the newspaper business."

"What happened with the newspaper?"

"He wrote some verses."

"Is he a poet?"

"He wrote some verses or put someone else's in, I don't know. He was in a rush and wasn't making much sense and then he left. I feel so sorry for him."

*   *   *

So, Sasha Pankratov had been expelled, and him a true believer, such an activist, rock-hard, unbending! And now he's been chucked out. Even Budyagin hadn't helped. And with the famous Ryazanov for an uncle! It's terrifying. If it can happen to Sasha . . .

If the same thing were to happen to him, who would help? His father, the tailor? His brother, the convict? He didn't have Sasha's resources, not that they had done Sasha much good. He shouldn't have turned down the prosecution service: he would have been safe there, nobody could have got at him, and he would have been able to get at anyone he liked and they wouldn't be able to get away.

He ran into Sasha the next day as he got home.

"Greetings!"

"Hello."

"I heard you had problems at the institute."

"Who told you?"

"I saw Lena."

"It's been fixed." Sasha was frowning.

"Really? That's good." Sharok didn't try to hide his grin. "I'm happy for you. It didn't take you long to get back on your feet."

"I managed it. See you around."

"I t's been fixed." Sasha said the same thing to everyone. He didn't want any rumors to reach his mother.

Glinskaya's decision had been posted the day after the bureau meeting. As the "organizer of anti-Party attacks," Sasha was to be expelled from the institute, Runochkin, Poluzhan, and Pozdnyakova were to be admonished, and Kovalyov reprimanded.

The machine was in motion, documents were collected, reports compiled. Before he was even asked, Lozgachev, who replaced Janson as dean, had drawn up Sasha's record. Smooth and pink-cheeked, he seemed to be saying, "Personally, I have nothing against you, it's just the way things worked out, but I'll be truly pleased if you are reinstated."

Sasha said good-bye to everyone, but refused to shake hands with Kovalyov.

"I don't associate with vermin."

Runochkin agreed that Kovalyov was vermin, and thought the rest of them were, too. Little Runochkin wasn't afraid of anyone.

The class bell rang and the corridor emptied. No one had any more time for Sasha. He had collected his papers and only needed to get them stamped and then leave.

Krivoruchko was still the deputy head of the provisions section. As he stamped the papers, he said under his breath, "The December applications have already been sent to the ration-card office."

"Thanks," Sasha replied. The applications were usually sent in later, but Krivoruchko was making sure Sasha got his rations. He didn't have to do it.

Now Sasha's mother wouldn't suspect anything was wrong before the end of December, and by that time he'd be reinstated, anyway.

He went from one institution to another, waited interminably for interviews, gave tedious explanations in the face of mistrustful looks, and heard insincere promises to "look into the matter." But nobody wanted to do anything. Why should they? Getting him reinstated would mean taking the responsibility on themselves.

His case was being handled at the district Party committee by a nice-looking young woman called Zaitseva. All Sasha knew about her was that she played basketball well, even though she was short. She listened to what he had to say, asked him a few questions, none of them very significant, in his view, concerning Krivoruchko, and then she advised him to get a character reference from the factory where he used to work. She told him that his case would be dealt with at a session of the district Party bureau and Komsomol.

Traveling to the factory brought back memories of getting up early, the freshness of the morning streets, the stream of people pouring through the factory gates, the cold emptiness of the workshop. He had wanted to work in a factory, even though he had not been particularly attracted by engineering. The very word *proletarian* appealed to him, made him feel part of the great revolutionary class. It was a poetic and unforgettable beginning of life for him.

On the very first day, they had put him to work loading trucks. He could have refused, like Yuri Sharok, who had got himself a place on the engineering side, as a trainee milling-machine operator. But they put Sasha on the loading platform and forgot about him, and he didn't remind them of his existence — someone had to load the trucks. Life then had seemed endless — everything was ahead, in the future, still to come. On the open platform of the goods depot, in rain or snow, in heat or freezing cold, he unloaded and loaded trucks in his denim jacket and thick gloves. He was doing something the country needed. And he despised Yuri, neat and clean, comfortably settled in the warm, light workshop.

The whole gang used to pile into the canteen as one. The other workers would scramble out of their way to avoid the dye, whitewash, alabaster or coal dust on their jackets. They were noisy and foulmouthed. Sasha recalled Morozov, who had once been a divisional commander, a quiet man who'd left the Party over the New Economic Policy and become a drunk. He remembered Averkyev, the foreman, another drunk whose wife had left him, and a few more names and faces came back to him.

They hadn't cared about a bigger pay envelope; as long as they got enough for a bottle they were happy. They avoided piecework and wrangled with the foreman. They bargained for lighter work. They also preferred having a set time for a job or, better still, a set job, a precisely defined piece of work that they could finish and go home. Then they worked fast, really exerted themselves, but only so as to get off earlier. Sasha didn't regard them as genuine workers, yet something touching and human about them appealed to him — they were people whose lives had gone wrong. They would finagle all they could when the work was being doled out, but they never cheated each other, never tried to shove more work onto one of the team. And though Sasha took no part in their boozing and didn't exchange dirty jokes or compete in their invention of obscene limericks, they liked him well enough.

Usually this mixed and motley crew would be given miscellaneous unloading jobs, but sometimes they were put on the main loading dock to handle finished goods, which were drums of dye. Once, the trucks failed to arrive for a while and the drums of dye were piling up in high stacks in the goods depot. Then suddenly the trucks began pouring in, one lot after another, and every loading team was sent to help, including Sasha's

A drum of dye weighed around a hundred and fifty pounds. They were rolled up wooden ramps into the trucks and stacked one row on top of another. The ramps were steep and you had to take them at a run to make it to the top. Once inside the truck you had to stand the drums tight up against each other to make sure the proper number were loaded. The work went on for eight hours at a stretch, without a break, rolling the drums up the steep ramps and stacking them upright. And you had to move, because running right behind you was your mate, and he wouldn't be able to slow down on the steep ramp. And if you fumbled with your drum for a second too long, you held up the entire chain and broke the rhythm. At first, Sasha couldn't stack the drums precisely. So, they showed him how, by taking a drum with hands at its base, lifting it with a swing, turning it on its edge, and stacking it. Once he'd been shown, he didn't hold anyone up again.

Generally, two main teams worked on the dye, one lot Tatars who'd come from Ulyanovsk province for the money, and the other lot Russians, professional stevedores who were also there just for the money. Loading the drums paid well.

One day, Malov, the chief foreman, told Averkyev to send one of his men to the first team, which was a worker short.

Averkyev turned to the Tatar Gainullin and told him to go.

"I'm not going," Gainullin replied.

"Lifshits!"

Lifshits, a strapping Odessa Jew with a low brow, tried to joke his way out. "I can't work with them, they eat pork."

Malov gave up. "I'm not standing here any longer. Work it out among yourselves, but send a man over."

He was a decisive man, a demobilized platoon commander who looked like a fighter; he was a former stevedore himself and he could keep even Averkyev's bunch in line.

"You decide," was Averkyev's response.

Malov's gaze fell on Sasha.

"Pankratov, get over to the first team!"

Malov wasn't especially fond of Sasha. Having completed high school, Sasha was the most educated man there. Maybe Malov didn't like the idea of educated stevedores. Malov now watched Sasha half-questioningly, half-mockingly, expecting him to refuse.

But Sasha said, "Sure, I'll go."

"Can't keep you out of anything." Averkyev was not pleased.

The Tatars didn't roll the drums. At the double, they carried them on their backs across planked runways, up the steep ramps into the trucks, and swung them right into place. It was quicker to work this way, but it was a totally different, unendurable kind of work. You had to run with a hundred-and-fifty-pound drum on your back along shaky wooden planks, up steep ramps, and then drop it so it didn't crush your foot or land on the wrong spot, and you did it all day long. It felt the whole time as if the drum was about to slide off your back and pull you down with it; but you couldn't stop for a second, you could hear the heavy breathing and smell the sweat of the man behind you, and if you stopped he would fall on top of you. You pulled with all your might, taking the ramp at a run, you ran into the wagon, dropped your drum, and started running back, desperate not to fall behind these more experienced, tough stevedores who made no allowances, especially for you, an outsider.

The noon whistle! Sasha collapsed by a stack of drums. Red circles floated before his eyes and a dull roar echoed in his head.

As he lay there, drifting in and out of sleep, he thought only of the moment he would have to get up, get back in line behind the brawny Tatar he'd been behind in the morning, and start again, across the rickety planks with a drum on his back. He knew he wasn't going to make it through the full shift; he knew he would collapse and fall sprawling on the runways.

He could have gone to the office and complained that he hadn't been sent to hump hundred-and-fifty-pound drums of dye on his back. He'd been sent to do a stint of production work. What the hell did they think they were doing! He'd volunteered for the workshop and they were sticking him with the stevedores.

He could have done it, but he knew that, as soon as the whistle went, he'd get up and stand in line behind the brawny Tatar, bend his back and carry the next drum into the truck.

The other workers were starting to come out of the canteen, which meant the break would be over soon. He made an effort of will and stretched himself, sat up, moved his arms, his legs, and his head. Everything ached and felt alien.

They were shouting to him. He raised his head and saw his gang boss Averkyev and the loader Morozov. They'd obviously had a few at lunch. Averkyev's puffy face was all red and Morozov's pale blue eyes looked even bluer and more bemused than usual.

"Here, eat!" Averkyev tossed him a hunk of bread and a bit of boiled beef.

"Thanks."

"You have to take the drum on your whole back, right down the spine, got it?" Averkyev explained to him. "Like this: okay, put it on me."

He bent his back and stretched his hands out behind him.

Morozov and Sasha put a drum on his back. It lay evenly along the length of his back.

"And try this!"

Averkyev bent farther forward and as the drum slid up onto his shoulders he carried it over his head and set it down in front of him.

"Don't carry it on your shoulders, put it on your back. You try."

Sasha stood up and bent over. Averkyev and Morozov laid a drum on his back.

"Don't drop your shoulders!" Averkyev shouted.

Sasha straightened his shoulders; the drum touched his back right along the spine and felt balanced.

"That's how you do it, get it straight and take it away."

Sasha felt steadier after that; he didn't wobble running up the ramps and the drums didn't slide off his back. But their weight was just as crushing and his legs were failing. As he ran back to pick up another drum, his back wouldn't straighten. He had no idea how he lasted the second half of the shift, and he couldn't remember how he managed to get home, but when he did, he collapsed on his bed and slept until morning.

When he got to work the next day, Malov told him to do another couple of shifts in the first team and then he would move him.

In fact, he humped the drums for two weeks, by which time he had the hang of it. The Tatars got used to him and he got used to them, and he even wrote an appeal for them to their local soviet about some tax problem.

Nor did he go back to his old gang. Instead, he was sent to the transport section as a truck-loader.

"You'll learn to be a driver," Malov told him. Sasha couldn't decide whether Malov was trying to make him happy or just getting rid of him.

Sasha worked in the transport section and learned to drive a truck but, returning to the works now, it was his days as a stevedore that came back to him. Those first months had been the most memorable time of his life at the factory.

He wondered if any of the old gang would still be around. It hadn't been all that long ago, only four years.

The wooden loading docks were gone, and a large stone structure had been built on a different site. The old gates had also given way to wide-set stone pillars. A new office building now faced the main yard, and new buildings could be seen above the high stone wall. The yard itself had been paved and there were now shops, stalls, and sheds around it. The factory was a going concern; it had grown and developed. This was what gave the country its reality, and it's what he ought to be doing, no matter what.

The secretary of the Party organization turned out to be Malov, not an altogether pleasant surprise.

He still had the look of an old fighter, but now he was balding, not as ruddy as he used to be when he was foreman in the goods depot. He was thinner, and he looked tired and sallow. He was behind a large desk, half-sitting on his chair, signing worksheets on the windowsill. He recognized Sasha at once. He acted as if four years hadn't passed and Sasha were still working there.

"Well, Pankratov? What's up?"

Sasha told him his story.

"Okay," Malov said. "I'll go to the committee and tell them."

So, even Malov was backing away. He didn't want to give Sasha a reference.

"Zaitseva told me I should bring a written reference."

"She wants it in writing? She'll have it in writing. Remind me what section you were in, what you worked on."

He jotted down what Sasha had done, then looked up and said, "So, put your foot in it at last?"

"Why 'at last'?"

"It was bound to happen. Well, go take a stroll for an hour while I write up your reference."

"I'd like to see some of the gang. . . ."

The new buildings had been erected along the boundary of the site and the old main part of the works had remained the same. He went through the first three workshops — the machine shop, boiler shop, and main stores — and came to transport. The manager's black Ford was standing over the pit and Sergei Vasilyevich, the chauffeur, was at his bench. As always he was wearing his black leather outfit, his peaked cap, felt boots, and rubber overshoes. He was a solid man, pompous and independent; he'd been a chauffeur before the Revolution, and he was loyal to the manager. He, too, recognized Sasha at once.

"Come back to work?"

"I'm here on business."

Sasha was amazed how much he had forgotten of the place, and how only now, coming back and seeing the workshops and passageways and hearing the sounds of the factory, he remembered. Everything had been so simple and straightforward back then — just work, the pay, and his Komsomol duties. He never heard of anyone here having a political case made against him. Here people were too busy with production and with building a plant. Maybe times had changed. Maybe things weren't the same here, either. It'd be interesting to see what Malov had written about him.

The reference read:

This is to certify that Pankratov, A.P., worked at this plant from 1928 to 1930, first as a stevedore and later as a driver. He was diligent in his work and carried out the tasks assigned to him. He took part in social work as secretary of the Komsomol cell of the transport section. He committed no breach of conduct.

"I'll say more when I'm at the committee," Malov promised.

When he got home, he saw a blue envelope through the slit in the mailbox. It was from his father, he recognized from the handwriting. His father's letters gave him no pleasure.

His father was asking him to send some technical handbooks. "They're on the bottom shelf of the bookcase. You presumably know where the bottom shelf is. I wouldn't dare to burden you with this request, except that I have no one else to ask. I could come to Moscow for them, but I don't think my presence would please anyone."

He could hear his father's voice; it was his usual way of speaking. If his mother asked, "Are you going to have dinner?" he would reply, "I don't have to." "Are you going to the meeting?" "No, I'm going dancing." As he was a bit hard of hearing, he often missed what they said, and would imagine they were talking about him. He swore if he didn't get his apple in the morning, or his glass of yogurt at night. Sasha's mother would be struck dumb with fear the moment she heard his footsteps in the corridor. He came home from work with his grievances ready — dissatisfaction with his home, his wife, and his son — and primed to start an argument that he would trigger with a remark or a rebuke.

Only when she became jealous was his mother unafraid. Then, Sasha's soul would be drained by the screams and slammed doors, the rabbitlike look on his mother's face as she cried and raved hysterically and flung her accusations.

It was six years since his father had left, yet she was still afraid of him, even at a distance. When she saw the letter now, the old, familiar, and depressing look of fear and alarm reappeared.

"From your father?"

"He wants me to send him some handbooks."

The frightened look did not leave her face as she took the letter, nor did her expression change as she read it.

More than anything else, Sasha was worried about how she would react when she heard of his troubles, and he did his best to see she found out nothing. He left the house every morning as if he were still going to the institute. He earned his wages for December by unloading trucks at Kiev Station. When he ran out of places to go, he went to Nina Ivanova's.

She'd given him a key to her apartment, and he spent the mornings there alone, reading or studying. One day, Nina's younger sister, Varya, came home from school in her dark coat and dainty shoes. She took off her scarf, and her long dark hair fell to her shoulders. She sat on the bed, crossed her legs, pouted her lips slightly to blow a wisp of hair off her forehead, and looked at Sasha the way pretty teenaged schoolgirls do to embarrass the boys.

The room was divided by a table covered with a tattered oilcloth. In Nina's half, books and papers were strewn over her desk and broken-down house slippers were stuffed under her bed, while Varya's half had a bright cushion cover, a phonograph on the windowsill, and a lampstand made of a bronze athlete holding up a muscular arm.

"Why have they thrown you out of the institute?"

"They'll reinstate me."

"I'd throw *them* out. We've got rats just like them at school, who'd ruin you as soon as look at you. Just yesterday, we had a test and Lyarkin says, 'Ivanova's got crib-notes on her knees.' I stretched my legs out and said, 'Show me.' "

She stretched her legs out as she had in class.

"Kuzya, the mathematics teacher, went as red as a beet and said, 'Stop that, Ivanova!' Why me? It was Lyarkin's fault. Last year he behaved like an animal, pulling girls' bookbags out of their hands, but now he's on the classroom committee! He's a cheat himself, but he snitches on others. I can't stand people like him."

"How do you crib?"

"It's simple." She tapped her knees, which were covered in cotton stockings. "I write with an indelible pencil and I'm all set!"

"Couldn't you pass without cheating?"

"Oh, yes, but I don't want to."

She looked at him challengingly as she sat there with her legs apart, like a small insect. Sasha found the situation funny, but tried to look serious, knowing what a worry Varya was to her older sister.

The girls had grown up without a father and then their mother had died. Sasha remembered a committee meeting where they had discussed helping Nina to bring up her sister. An allowance had somehow been scraped together and she was given a paid job as a youth leader. Then they'd left high school and gone their separate ways, and it only came back to Sasha when he saw Varya with other teenagers hanging around in the yard.

"Are you a Komsomol?"

"What for?"

"It's better than just hanging around."

"I like it."

"You don't spend the night at home."

"Ha, ha! One night I slept at a girlfriend's dacha because she was too scared to go to the station on her own. Nina won't go out alone at night, either. She's a much bigger coward than me, a hundred times bigger. She ought to marry her Max — she can't do anything and Max doesn't need to, they could eat in the canteen."

"Aren't you a bit young to give advice?"

"She shouldn't poke her nose into my business, she makes a fuss but she doesn't understand a thing."

"What do you want to be?"

Instead of replying, she sang in her high childish voice:

> *Like a flower of the fragrant prairie,*
> *Your laughter is sweeter than the pipe,*
> *Your eyes are bluer than the sky above,*
> *Daring cowboy of the native steppe.*

The bell rang in the hallway.

"Nina's home," she announced without getting up. "She's forgotten her keys again."

"How do you know it's her?"

"I can tell everyone who lives here by their ring."

Nina came in and saw Varya posing immodestly on the bed, with her legs spread. She started in on her.

"Boys on the brain, painted fingernails, lipstick the color of carrots, she knows it all. She spends hours trying to curl her eyelashes with a kitchen knife."

"Kitchen knife?" Sasha said in amazement.

"And she's always on the telephone, you should hear her — crepe georgette, velvet, red voile this, blue silk that . . . For five years, I've worn the same blouse, I've washed it every day but I can't tell you what it's made of. But she'll spend three days running round the shops looking for special buttons for a dress. She won't wear galoshes, hates felt boots, stole a pair of my shoes and ruined them at a dance, and then just threw them into the bathroom. Today it's shoes, tomorrow she'll be taking money and, if I haven't got any, she'll go and steal from someone else."

"Don't frighten her!" Sasha said. "Don't frighten her and don't frighten yourself!"

But Varya wasn't a bit frightened. She pretended to yawn and rolled her eyes in utter boredom; she'd heard it all a hundred times before.

"What surprises me is her hardness. She laughs at Max. What business is it of hers? It's despicable and tactless."

"Max does have a sad look." Sasha said diplomatically.

Nina's eyes darkened.

"I treasure Maxim, he's a lovely, fine boy. But what can I do? I still have to get this one on her own feet."

"Don't blame me, if you please," Varya pouted.

"They were told to make a wall newspaper," Nina went on. "So, she goes into the neighboring classroom and copies theirs — word for word, and she was even too lazy to change the names. What is she going to do next? What is she capable of?"

Varya slipped her feet into her shoes and got up.

> *Like a flower of the fragrant prairie,*
> *Your laughter is sweeter than the pipe....*

Sasha went to the district Party committee feeling confident. This was one place where they weren't afraid to make decisions, and the session was going to be chaired by First Secretary Stolper himself.

As he waited in the corridor for them to call him in, he could hear voices and fragments of speeches, and Stolper's high sharp voice continually interrupting. Terrified staff scuttled in and out to grab files from cabinets, with Stolper shouting irritatedly after them. It pleased Sasha to hear Stolper getting on these officials, just as he would get on Baulin and all the others who had stuck the label of enemy on him.

The door opened.

"Pankratov!"

The room was full, with people sitting along the walls and around a long green baize–covered table. Stolper, a thin man with tired, malevolent eyes, looked at Sasha sullenly and nodded to Zaitseva.

"Make your report! And keep it brief!"

Like a diligent schoolgirl, Zaitseva read out the facts of the case. Someone laughed when she came to the verses, and they did indeed sound silly.

She then declared that these facts should be taken in the context of the main issue.

For the first time Sasha learned that Krivoruchko had once been a member of some opposition group or other, but he couldn't make out which. Zaitseva mentioned the Eleventh Party Congress, 1922, the "workers' opposition," a collective letter to the Central Committee, which Krivoruchko had signed, though she didn't spell out the contents of the letter. She then announced that Krivoruchko had at one time been expelled from the Party for "failing to break off his contacts," though which contacts she didn't make clear. She did add, however, that the Party had reinstated him with a reprimand. He was later again reprimanded for obstructing the railway with "socially alien and class-hostile elements." Which railway and what connection Krivoruchko had with it she did not say. And now he had been expelled again, this time for disruption of a building program.

Although the list of expulsions and reprimands was all there in Krivoruchko's personal file, Zaitseva acted as if she had unmasked him herself, exposed him to the light of day, and as if she was personally shaken at having discovered someone so steeped in crimes.

Zaitseva's testimony made it plain to Sasha that the case against Krivoruchko was much more complicated than it had first appeared at the committee. He had a past hanging over him, but Sasha couldn't imagine what that had to do with him.

He soon saw the connection.

Stolper picked up Sasha's file and leafed through it. Everyone was silent; only the rustle of pages could be heard as Stolper flipped them irritably.

"What's going on at your place, Baulin?"

Baulin stood up. "We expelled Krivoruchko from the Party," he snapped.

"He didn't build the hostel," Stolper rebutted. "That was his *job*" — he banged his hand down on the file — "or had you forgotten that? You remembered *that* only when they put out their anti-Party pamphlet."

"We had no evidence of a connection between Pankratov and Krivoruchko."

"He had no evidence!" Stolper curled his lip. "Pankratov attacks Marxism in class and *after that* he's allowed to publish the holiday issue of the paper, which he duly turns into an anti-Party pamphlet. Pankratov defends Krivoruchko, and the dean — what's his name —?"

"Janson." Zaitseva was anxious to show how thoroughly she had studied the case.

"Janson defends Pankratov. We're talking about a *network* here! Where's your political judgment? Explain to me, why precisely was it *Pankratov* who defended Krivoruchko?"

"Pankratov has been expelled for it," Baulin retorted.

"No, it wasn't for that!" Stolper yelled. "He was expelled only after he'd come out in the open. Why weren't you on your guard when he defended Krivoruchko? The committee proposed a resolution but you, Comrade Baulin, you wouldn't have it. Comrade Lozgachev proposed it, but you put off dealing with the affair and gave Pankratov his chance to publish his anti-Party newspaper. Right there under your nose, Krivoruchko was corrupting the students. Or perhaps you imagine that Pankratov published the paper *all by himself*, that he attacked Marxism on his own? Who's behind him? *That*, you don't want to know! Why is that? Are you afraid?"

"We're not afraid of anyone," Baulin replied, with Stolper obviously in mind.

Stolper saw this and, staring hard at Baulin, abruptly but quietly said, "We'll have to look into things at the institute."

"Please do," Baulin responded.

"What do you mean, 'Please do'?" Stolper exploded. "We're not asking your permission, Comrade Baulin. Why hasn't Janson turned up for the hearing?"

"He's ill."

"Ill. And what about the director of the institute?"

Baulin shrugged his shoulders. "She didn't come."

"Some organization!" Stolper sneered. "No wonder they can twist you around their little fingers. Yes, and Comrade Malov was also kind enough to issue a good character reference. Malov, you knew why Pankratov wanted it?"

Malov stood up, a tall, broad, stooping figure, looking like a prizefighter in a two-piece suit. He had been sitting against the wall almost next to Sasha, without Sasha's realizing it.

"Yes, I knew."

"He told you why he'd been expelled?"

"Yes, he did."

"Did he tell you the same as you have heard here today?"

"Exactly the same."

"Yet you gave him a reference?"

"That's right."

"How are we to understand that, Comrade Malov?"

"I wrote about him as he was four years ago."

"Perhaps he was deceiving the Party then?"

"He wasn't deceiving the Party then. He was carrying drums of dye on his back."

"What kind of dye?"

"Like that." Malov pointed at the table. "The kind they used to dye your green baize."

"What do you mean, '*your* green baize'?"

"Well, it's on *your* table, isn't it?"

"What's that got to do with anything?"

"He was a boy, a Komsomol, he was working and helping to build the factory. What else should I write? That's how it was."

"That's how it started, but it has ended up rather differently." Stolper became conciliatory. "If Pankratov had gone only to you for help, that'd be one thing, but when someone starts running around to see people's commissars and using his family connections, that's something else. You failed to take that into account, Comrade Malov."

"Maybe," Malov objected, "but I only saw him at work, and I can't believe he's an enemy of the Party."

"It's not just people like him who've become Party enemies. Let's hear what Pankratov has to say."

Sasha got up. Obviously, he was not going to be reinstated. Everything that had been said here was absurd, but the farther the case went, the more the accusations grew and there was no way he could break out of the vicious circle. He'd never be able to convince them of anything. The stupid verses, the incident with Azizyan, and Krivoruchko, all these were explainable facts, but an implacable force was at work here. Still, he had to defend himself.

"As far as Krivoruchko is concerned, I told the committee meeting about the problem with the shovels."

"What shovels?" Stolper broke in.

"Shovels, to work on the building, the storekeeper wasn't there —"

"Stop talking rubbish!" Stolper interrupted him savagely. "Answer the question — why did you defend Krivoruchko?"

"I didn't defend him. All I said was that in fact there were no building materials."

"So, it wasn't just shovels, but materials in general," Stolper said sarcastically. "Then, that's what you should have said. All right, carry on." He sounded tired, as if it was pointless asking Sasha anything, since he could always talk himself out of it.

"I was not an acquaintance of Krivoruchko's; I had never spoken to him in my life."

Stolper shook his head and pursed his lips, but said nothing.

"As far as the accounting lecturer is concerned, his course was just hackwork."

"Marxism is hackwork?" Stolper stared at Sasha.

"No, but —"

"That's it, Pankratov, we've heard enough!" Stolper got up and pulled on his tunic. It looked wrong on him, the way an army uniform always looks wrong on a small-chested, narrow-shouldered civilian. "We've heard what you have to say. You show no desire to repent; you've tried to deceive the Party here. You can go!"

9

hey saw in the New Year at Nina Ivanova's. The meal was crowned with a roast goose that Nina had managed to get hold of and that Varya had cooked. The party would go on till morning, as nobody would be able to get home during the night. They would go straight to their jobs from Nina's, the first of January being an ordinary working day.

Sitting in the only armchair, with her legs crossed and smoking a cigarette, was Vadim Marasevich's sister, Vika. She had been a plump, lazy child, forever asking "What shall I do?" when everyone else was busy, and she had grown up into a tall, blonde, arrogant woman. She was the kind of girl you'd meet on a Saturday night at the Metropole or the tea-dances on Sunday afternoon at the National. She'd broken up with her boyfriend just before New Year's and that, as she made clear with her look of utter boredom, was the only reason she was here.

Yuri Sharok started flirting with her, as if to cheer her up, but actually to conceal his relationship with Lena. It had a strange effect, since everyone had known about them for a long time — except Vadim Marasevich. Vadim was still a virgin and he couldn't accept the idea of relations that he himself hadn't experienced and that he believed must cause a profound change in a person. And he hadn't noticed any such change in Lena.

Vadim was holding forth on everything under the sun, jumping from the Reichstag fire to the new production of *Dead Souls* at the Moscow Arts, from Roosevelt's New Deal to the death of Lunacharsky in Menton. He made it sound as if he were the only one who knew everything about events that were, in fact, well known to everyone.

Yuri Sharok had had a drink with his father before coming to the party and he was lively and relaxed. If his flirting with Vika was going to get everyone mad, let it! He'd flirt with her all the more!

Varya had stayed home, ostensibly for the sake of the goose, not wanting to trust the cooking to Nina, but in fact she preferred older company to that of her schoolmates. Max had promised to bring along a friend who could dance the rumba. At the moment, this young student with the strange name of Serafim was earnestly winding up the phonograph.

A sad-looking Max was standing next to Serafim. He had just proposed to Nina and she had turned him down flat, giving him no hope. He loved and admired Sasha and was also upset by his problems.

Sasha had decided that whatever his situation, he wouldn't avoid his friends and their celebration; he must live his life as he had before.

Nina was seated at the head of the white linen–covered table, with Max, Sasha, Varya, and Serafim on her right, and Vadim, Lena, Yuri, and Vika on her left. Everything was perfectly arranged, shining and sparkling, and the delicious smell whetted the appetite and aroused a mood of pleasure. The night outside was freezing, the room was warm and cozy, the girls were wearing lisle stockings and high-heeled shoes. The planet was spinning on its relentless orbit, the stars in the universe were in permanent motion, they had vodka and port and white wine and roast goose, there was mustard sauce for the herring and store-bought ham, and they were seeing in 1934, just as they had seen in 1933, and would see in 1935 and '36 and '37 and many more years to come. They were young, with no thought of death or old age; they had been born for life and youth and joy.

"Let's bid a fond farewell to the old year," said Vadim. "It was, after all, one year of our lives. Nobody has strewn our path with roses, as they say in Odessa, and anyway a path covered with roses wouldn't be real life. The path of real life is strewn with thorns. . . ."

The sound of the clock rang out midnight and they all stood up and raised their glasses.

"A happy New Year to everyone!" Vadim declaimed.

Their glasses clinked, plates were passed around, and Max did an expert job of carving the goose.

"A master!" Sasha exclaimed.

"So long as there's a goose." Yuri laughed and held out his plate.

"Give me a leg, Maxim." Vika finally deigned to say something.

"I'll have the other!" Vadim was fond of his food.

"The Maraseviches will take everything!"

"Stop the Maraseviches!"

Vadim tapped his knife on his plate. "A toast to Max, the pride of the Red Army!"

"Max!"

"Hey, I'm not getting my fair share!"

"Comrades, someone's snatched my fork!"

Again Vadim tapped his knife.

"Let's drink to Serafim, our only guest and also the pride of the Red Army."

"Your health, young man!"

"Being young isn't a vice, it's just a pain in the neck!"

"Serafim, where's your brother George?"

Serafim's face had turned pink as he stood up and bowed; he was shy in this noisy company.

Always a great talker, Vadim proposed a toast to Lena, "our beauty," and then to Vika, "also not so bad," and he wouldn't give up the center of the stage.

"Let's drink to our school!" This was Max's idea.

"Here's to sentimentality!" Yuri sneered.

Max looked at him, astonished. "Should we just forget it, cast off those years like an old boot?"

"I'm for Max's toast," Vadim intervened. "We mustn't deny our old household gods, our alma mater and hearth and home."

"To the school, our united labor school!" Yuri raised his glass with obvious irony. Driveling babies — the hell with them! If they want to toast the school, he'd toast the school; he couldn't care less what he toasted.

"Don't do us any favors, Yuri," Nina snapped. She was annoyed with him for flirting with Vika. She couldn't stand Vika anyway —

nobody had invited her — and she was indignant at the way Sharok was humiliating Lena.

Vadim tried to negotiate the troubled waters. "Here's to Yuri Sharok, the future chief prosecutor!"

"You'll get us out when they put us in jail," Max added good-naturedly.

"And now," Vadim said, wiping his lips with a napkin, "to our hostess, to our Nina, the heart and soul of the party!"

"Nina! Nina! Nina!"

Sasha turned to Varya. "Now we should drink to both our hostesses."

Slim and elegant, the youngest one there, Varya had remained silent, afraid of saying the wrong thing. Serafim had made a shy effort to talk to her. Sasha was amused at their embarrassment and now tried to draw Serafim into his conversation with Varya. She replied eagerly and turned to Sasha, who gazed closely into her oriental eyes and sweet face.

They pushed back the chairs and table and started dancing to records. *"Those black eyes have me enthralled, I can never forget them."* Yuri danced with Vika, Vadim with Lena, and Varya with Serafim. Then Nina and Max joined in.

"Come on, I want to dance, too," Sasha said when the record was being changed.

He danced with Varya, feeling her lithe body, her light step, her joy. He realized that everything that annoyed Nina — the makeup, the perfume, hanging around the apartment yard, the boys — was sheer nonsense, nothing more than the eagerness of a young woman entering into life, into the beautiful world, the young, bright world from which he was being torn, body and soul.

The fight erupted suddenly. Yuri and Vika had gone out into the hallway and Nina was incensed.

"I *did* ask people not to make any noise. I *do* have neighbors." Her face was red with anger as she spoke. "But no, *they* have to go out into the hallway to talk, as if there wasn't enough room in here."

"Don't, it's all right," Lena protested, smiling. Yuri's behavior was bad enough, without Nina's drawing attention to it.

"Don't get worked up," was Max's good-natured advice.

"I can't believe anyone would be so brazen." Nina was still flushed and highly agitated. "They can go into the hallway, but *I* have to live with these people."

"Stop it!" Sasha didn't like the way Yuri and Vika were carrying on, but he was determined not to let it spoil the party.

Vadim tried to turn the whole thing into a joke.

"My sister can't even find the bathroom by herself."

They were all familiar with the usually rational Nina's occasional outbursts of fury and knew that they passed as quickly as they came. But it was the hour when even at New Year's parties everyone was tired enough to be rankled by the slightest offense.

Yuri sat down next to Lena, laying his arm along the back of her chair, and said coldly, "Typical old-maid hysterics." He had spoken quietly and deliberately, with his hand on Lena's shoulder as if to demonstrate that the matter only concerned the two of them. His remark was anything but an outburst.

"Shut up, Sharok!" Sasha snapped. Now he had an excuse to settle scores with him. When Yuri's mother told Sasha's mother that Sasha had been expelled from the institute, she had made no effort to conceal her malicious delight. Sasha had sensed Yuri's ill-will behind it.

"Everyone's had too much to drink. . . ." Vadim made an effort at reconciliation.

"I've known what you are for a long time," Sasha went on. "Would you like me to entertain the others with my discovery?"

Yuri went pale. "What do you know? What, come on tell us!"

"This isn't the time or place, and anyway, the others wouldn't be interested."

"Not the time or place. What makes you think *you're* going to choose the time and place? Who are *you* to dictate? You're pretty arrogant for someone who's just had his ass kicked — officially!"

"Shut up!" Max snapped.

"That was below the belt," Vadim muttered.

"That's my business," Sasha replied calmly. "It has nothing to do with you or your relatives. You want to know what I think of you? You're small-minded, vain, conceited, and that's the end of it as far as I'm concerned."

"And you're an emperor without any clothes, a general without an army. And that's the end of it as far as *I'm* concerned." Yuri got up. "Come on, Lena."

"Lena!" Sasha called to her.

"What?" She smiled, vainly hoping to cool things down.

"Couldn't you find yourself a bigger piece of shit than that?"

Lena flushed red and ran out of the apartment. Yuri paused in the doorway and looked at Sasha before following her out.

"You shouldn't have said that," Max remarked mildly.

"I can't stand rats."

But he became gloomier; he'd been unable to prevent himself from spoiling the celebration.

10

He would rather his mother had cried. Instead she froze, was struck dumb, did not ask him to explain what had happened and didn't want to know the details. A catastrophe had hit and that was all that mattered.

He was tormented by the glazed look in her eyes. She sat reading without seeing the words, turning pages automatically, day and night thinking only of one thing: that there was no man to stand behind Sasha because she hadn't been capable of keeping her family together, and their unhappy life had affected the boy since childhood.

His father had announced that he couldn't get away for another six weeks. She knew him well enough to guess that he was counting on everything blowing over by the time he came. "Surely Mark can do something?" Sasha's father had asked. It was the usual taunt he aimed at her family. She wrote to Mark, who replied that he would soon be attending a congress and hoped to sort things out then. She was not reassured. Sasha was still alone and defenseless.

She started going out for long periods. Sasha would watch her walk across the courtyard, a small, dumpy, gray-haired, lonely woman. He would warm up his own meal, although sometimes there was no dinner to warm up. Where did she disappear to? He rang her sisters, but she wasn't there. Maybe she was making the rounds of different offices, pleading on his behalf, trying to find influential friends? But she didn't have such friends.

"Where've you been? Where did you go?" he'd ask.

Either she'd keep silent or claim she'd been walking in the Arbat or sitting in the square.

Sasha also wandered in the Arbat, along the streets he'd known since childhood, past the old mansions with their columns, plaster moldings, bright green roofs, and white stuccoed facades. In Krivoarbat Street, where the old schoolyard had been, the architect Melnikov had built himself a strange, round house. The chintz-curtained windows of the school basement still gleamed as they had when engineering workers had lived there.

He remembered when, as a youth leader, he'd taken a group of Young Pioneers to camp at Rublevo, and how they'd sung on the way: *"We're off to camp at Rublevo, the camp's got everything we need!"* He'd ruled them with iron discipline, and they'd been somewhat afraid of him. The only one he hadn't been able to control was Kostya Shabrin, the son of the school carpenter, a mischievous, disobedient boy. After one of his regular capers, Sasha had decided to send him back home.

The school cook had said to him, "Don't do it, Sasha, his father will kill him."

What did she mean, "kill him"? Nobody had the right to kill anyone. Sasha was sorry for Kostya, the other children had pleaded for him, but to go back on his decision would have undermined his own authority.

When they returned from camp and classes had resumed, Kostya's father said nothing to Sasha, but once, when they passed each other in the corridor, he stopped and gave Sasha a long hard stare, and Sasha had never been able to forget it.

He had behaved so harshly, and so stupidly, that time. The interests of the group had demanded discipline and he had sacrificed poor little Kostya for the sake of it. He had thought the punishment would be good for the kid, but had he asked himself what it would be like for Kostya to face his father?

From Plotnikov Street he turned into Mogiltsevsky and then Mertvy. It was here, opposite the Dutch embassy, in the house where the district Komsomol committee used to be, that he had been admitted to the Komsomol eight years earlier. He had worn a leather jacket and despised anyone who dressed more elegantly. He valued nothing but books, which he gave to a library after he'd read them, and he had even tried to form a commune at school. His imagination and fantasy had carried him God knows where.

But why did this thing have to happen to him? Shouldn't he rely on the opinion of the majority? But Baulin, Lozgachev, Stolper, they weren't the majority.

Maybe he should write to Stalin. Stalin knew that the country needed specialists, not the semieducated. Stalin despised gossips, and Azizyan was a gossip. Stalin didn't like careerists, and Lozgachev was a careerist; he hated bullies, and Baulin was a bully. With his sense of humor, Stalin would see the innocent rhymes for what they really were. But it would be arrogant to approach Stalin on a personal matter.

He spotted his mother once, as he was coming home. She was standing at the gates, looking for someone.

As they got to the entrance of their building, she said, "You go in, I'll walk a little longer."

"You'll freeze."

"I'll walk a little longer," she repeated. Her face had its stubborn, rabbitlike expression, the one that had foreshadowed another scene and a row with his father.

Another time he caught sight of her on the Arbat. She was walking slowly past the gates of their block. She stopped in front of the watchmaker's and pretended to be looking at the watches in the window, then she walked back, looked across to the other side of the street, walked to the pharmacy, stopped, turned back. She was looking for someone, searching someone out, the way she had searched out his father when she thought he was carrying on with their neighbor, Militsa Petrovna. But his father wasn't here anymore, there weren't any supposed mistresses, no more jealousy, and yet she was obviously in the grip of some new obsession, gazing at a single spot with her fixed, tense, stubborn stare. Then she crossed the street, her head bent very low, as usual, not looking to either side, afraid of seeing the cars that were coming toward her. Drivers would jam on their brakes, stick their heads out their windows, and swear at her. Without looking around or turning her head, she would gain the sanctuary of the sidewalk.

"Who were you looking for?" Sasha asked her when she got home.

She fidgeted, afraid he wasn't going to believe her.

"What are you trying to hide from me?"

Her eyes were wide with fear when she looked up at him.

"They're following you."

He was amazed.

"Who's following me?"

"One wears a hat with the earflaps pulled down, another one is small and has a squirrel coat, and the third one wears felt boots — he's tall and nasty-looking. There are three of them and they take turns following you."

"Well, of course they would, wouldn't they. What sense would there be in them all following me at once?" He was laughing at her.

"I know their faces," she went on. "I can even recognize them from the back and by their voices. I was standing in the bakery and the one with felt boots was standing right behind me. I didn't turn around, but I knew he was there, all right. I bought my bread, I went out and he went out, too, but he didn't buy any bread, he just stood behind me and pointed me out to one of the others. That's how they work. They guessed that I found them out and when I looked around they disappeared, ducked into Nikolsky, and then came out on Denezhny. But I went straight to Denezhny and ran into him, and he turned away, but I knew it was him."

"Who are they following, you or me?" He was laughing again.

"They're watching our house. Who comes here, who leaves, when you go out, who you go with, who you talk to. I was in the butcher's and I tore off a fish coupon and he was standing right behind me and he said, 'You need a number four coupon.' I looked around, but he'd turned his back, but I knew his squirrel coat."

" 'You need a number four coupon,' he said that?" Sasha couldn't stop laughing.

She nodded her head in time with her words.

"And the militiaman on duty at Smolensk Street is in with them, too. Once I was following the tall one and he pointed someone out to the militiaman with a look, and the militiaman went over to the man and asked to see his papers, and then the tall one turned around and saw me and gave me a black look and I didn't see him for two days, and the little one said he'd got in trouble with his boss."

"Who did he say that to?"

"Me. He told me while he was standing behind me, he said it so as nobody else would hear. I don't look around anymore, I don't want to get him into trouble; after all, he's not supposed to talk to me. I know his voice very well."

Sasha looked at her in horror. Something terrible had entered their life. He had fallen into a whirlpool and was being sucked down to the bottom. At this moment, all he could think about was that the whirlpool mustn't drag his mother down as well. His mother was the dearest thing in the world to him.

"Once I felt he was standing behind me," she went on. "I didn't turn round, but I asked him, 'Are you going to take Sasha in?' He didn't say anything, didn't answer me. I couldn't help myself, I turned round, and he put his fingers to his lips, backed away, and disappeared in the crowd."

"It's all in your imagination," Sasha said. "Nobody's watching me, or you. What do they want us for, what are we, state criminals? It's ridiculous! If they wanted to pick me up, they'd have done it ages ago, they wouldn't waste their time following me around. Anyway, everything's going to be all right, I'll be reinstated soon. They're all tied up with the congress just now, they haven't got time for me, but after the congress, they'll deal with it. Put it out of your head. You're making yourself miserable over nothing."

She stared at her fixed spot with hunched shoulders and said nothing, just shook her head, as if she had a nervous tic. Whatever he said, however much he tried to persuade her, she repeated the same thing: it happened just as she'd said. That's how it was today, the same as yesterday, and it would be the same tomorrow. She'd go out and see one of them, and if the little one was on duty, he'd say something again. Maybe he'd answer her question: Were they going to take Sasha in, or not?

But the little man in the squirrel coat only gave her a look of sympathy and turned away. He still wouldn't answer her question. So now she waited for the thin one. Every sound alerted her, and silence seemed ominous. For hours she stood at the door, listening for footsteps on the stairs, or sat perched on the windowsill to see who was in the yard. Once, she spotted a militiaman, which made her rush mindlessly around the room in stark fear. He didn't come to their apartment, but went to the neighbor's, obviously to check up on Sasha. There was nothing bad they could say about Sasha, but people can easily dream up something if they think it will distract attention from themselves.

Everyone knew about Sasha's situation, the whole house and all the tenants, and no doubt every one of them had been questioned or visited. She sat on a bench in the yard under a shelter and sized up the way people walked by, the way they looked at her, the way they greeted her.

They telephoned from the housing office and asked her to tell Sasha to come in. She had always been afraid of them, but she went herself. They wanted more precise information about the reference from Sasha's place of work. That was their excuse! She had known the manager of the housing office for twenty years. Viktor Ivanovich Nosov had played in the yard as little Vitka, and she had known his mother when she was alive; he knew her well and he knew Sasha, too. Now, he hardly glanced at her, and he didn't even ask her why Sasha, a student, was working as a stevedore, which of course meant he already knew. And he said good-bye coldly. The woman in charge of identity cards didn't bother to say good-bye at all — she pretended to be too busy.

Someone once rang up and asked to speak to Sergei Sergeyevich. She said there was no Sergei Sergeyevich living there. Five minutes later, a different voice asked for Sergei Sergeyevich. Then they called again, but said nothing, and all she could hear through the receiver was the sound of breathing. Several times there were calls for their neighbor Galya, who had rarely had a telephone call before. Galya spoke evasively, ambiguously. She would hang up and hurry back to her room with her eyes averted.

Her old rival, Militsa Petrovna, who had once roused her jealousy, promised to help. They had become friends. In her youth, Militsa had had influential admirers, but there was nobody now. Sofya was fed up with all of them. She often sat on the bench with Margarita Artemovna, a calm, wise, reliable old Armenian woman, who suggested that Sasha should go and stay with her relatives in Nakhichevan for a while.

Sofya Alexandrovna seized on the idea. She was afraid to suggest it to Sasha herself and asked their next-door neighbor, Mikhail Yurevich, to do it for her. Advice like this was best coming from a man.

An intellectual bachelor who affected a pince-nez and collected books and etchings, Mikhail Yurevich lived alone, in a room piled high with albums and files, his ancient furniture permanently impregnated with dust from his folios and the smell of paint, glue, and India ink. He enjoyed talking to Sasha and usually showed him his recent acquisitions.

His latest was Dante's *Inferno* with illustrations by Doré, a vortex of human beings swept around in the underworld, men, women, and children, heads, arms, legs, and the eternal fires of desire, suffering, and passion consuming mankind.

Apart from the Dante, Mikhail Yurevich had also got hold of an Academy edition of Machiavelli's *The Prince*.

"I know the book," Sasha said. "His ideas on power are naïve, far from a scientific understanding of its true nature."

"Possibly," Mikhail Yurevich conceded. "But it's useful to study the history of the good and the evil in any period.... You must forgive me for interfering, Sasha, but your mother has told me about your troubles and I want you to promise you won't get angry with her for speaking to me about it. God helps those who help themselves, you know. Why don't you go and stay with your father or your uncle?"

"Go away?" Sasha asked, amazed. "I can't see why I should. The case can't be straightened out with me away. Mama's got herself into a state about it. Actually, nothing happened. It's a typical story, and there are plenty of them around, unfortunately. You think they want to arrest me? Out of the question. And even supposing they did, it wouldn't be any harder for them to get me at my father's or my uncle's. Maybe you think I ought to go underground?" He laughed at the thought of himself, Sasha Pankratov, hiding from his own people.

"I'm sure your mother's fears are exaggerated," Mikhail Yurevich agreed, "but it's a feature of any political case, that with each appeal you draw more people into the circle, and more official bodies, and the case grows like a snowball."

Sasha looked at Mikhail Yurevich with surprise. For a man who had nothing to do with politics, he obviously knew what he was talking about.

"I believe in the Party," he said. "And I have no intention of running away from it."

It was morning when Sasha arrived in Staraya Square, where great holes yawned and heaps of ancient snow-covered bricks lay where Kitaigorod Wall had once been.

He entered the Central Control Commission, which was housed in a pleasant, large, gray building. He found the number of Solts's office on a board in the lobby and went up to the second floor.

A line of people sat waiting silently along the walls of a long corridor. A young man in a dark blue suit, white shirt, and tie came out of Solts's office. Sasha decided he must be a visitor, and since nobody in the line moved, he opened the door and went in.

There were two desks in the large room, a small one by the door for a secretary and an enormous one at the far end, behind which sat Solts. He was a heavy man and with his disheveled gray hair, short neck, fleshy nose, and harelip, he resembled the famous chess-master Emanuel Lasker. Beside him, laying papers before him for signature, stood a round figure with the featureless face of a bureaucrat.

Since Solts appeared to be busy, Sasha sat down by the door. Solts looked up and saw him there, but said nothing. He had poor eyesight and couldn't tell exactly who had come in, but as nobody was allowed to enter without permission, and since Sasha had indeed come in and sat down, he assumed his secretary must have let him in and that he must have a reason for being there.

The assistant went on handing him papers. They were court sentences relating to cases of convicted Party members. Sasha realized this from the assistant's brief comments, giving the name of the convicted, his Party record, the relevant article of the criminal code, and the length of sentence. The articles he recited meant nothing to Sasha.

Silently, his lower lip hanging, his face worn out, scowling and miserable, as if he was thinking of something even more unpleasant than these sentences, Solts signed the papers that would ensure the expulsion of the convicted from the Party.

It dawned on Sasha that he must have got in by accident, out of turn, and that he had no right to be there, but he couldn't get up and leave. If he did, there was no way of knowing when he'd get an appointment, if at all. He had just realized that the people in the corridor were waiting for an interview with Solts, and they'd probably been there for months.

Suddenly Solts exploded: his gray head shook, his fingers drummed impatiently on the desk.

"Eight years for forty yards of wire!"

"Article twenty-six, clause B."

"Article, article ... Eight years in prison for forty yards of wire!"

The assistant bent down to get a closer look at the papers and glanced quickly through them. Calm returned to his face. The file was in proper order. And no matter how loud Solts screamed, he didn't have the authority to alter a court sentence.

Solts also knew he hadn't the right to change the sentence: the convicted man would be expelled from the Party and it was his job to confirm the expulsion; it was senseless to take out his irritation on his assistant.

His gaze fell once more on Sasha. This unknown man sitting at the door also irritated him. Who was he, what was he doing there?

At that moment, Solts's secretary returned. He was the young man in the dark blue suit Sasha had taken for a visitor. Having worked for Solts for many years, the secretary saw at once that Solts was infuriated by one of the sentences, that he was irritated by the presence in his office of an intruder, and also that this boy had managed to get in because of his own blunder in stepping out to get some cigarettes from the cafeteria.

Solts pointed a long finger at Sasha. "What does he want?"

Sasha looked at the secretary and read in his rapid glance, *Say what you've got to say quickly!*

Sasha got up.

"I've been expelled from my institute . . ."

"What institute's that?" Solts shouted. "What do I want to know about some institute for? What do you want here?"

"The Transport Institute," Sasha said.

"The comrade is from the Transport Institute," the secretary reported briskly. "He's a student, and he's been expelled from his institute."

He added under his breath, "Go over to him."

Sasha approached Solts's desk. "I've been expelled over a wall newspaper and a dispute about the course in accounting."

"What newspaper, what accounting? What is it you want from me?"

"It has been classified as political sabotage."

Solts looked hard at Sasha, apparently unable to understand what he was talking about, what was going on in general, why he had come into his office, taken a seat, eavesdropped on court sentences, and was now going on about a wall newspaper and an accounting course. . . .

The assistant gave an almost imperceptible, indulgent snicker, as if to say, from the heights of his official self-confidence, *This is the sort of thing that happens when people ignore the established order and proper procedure.* It was precisely because Solts did not see the need for such procedure that people could get in to see him without going through the proper channels.

The self-satisfied snicker was not lost on Solts. Eyeing Sasha under beetling brows, he said with unexpected calm, "Summon them all."

Sasha remained where he was.

"What are you standing there for?" Solts shouted. "Get out!"

Sasha backed away. The secretary signaled him to come over.

"Who has to be summoned?" he asked in an undertone, laying a list in front of him stamped "Central Commission All-Union Communist Party (Bolsheviks): Party membership."

It was only then that Sasha realized that Solts wanted to summon everyone connected with his case. For the first time, his heart thumped and a lump rose in his throat.

The secretary was waiting for him to reply.

"Baulin, the Party committee secretary at the institute," Sasha began.

"Forget their jobs, just their names!" The secretary noted them all down on a summons list.

"Glinskaya, Janson, Runochkin . . . the students, too?"

"Don't waste time, just tell me the names!"

"Poluzhan, Kovalyov, Pozdnyakova." As he spoke, Sasha could hear Solts's assistant behind him muttering names and articles.

"Is that all?" the secretary asked.

"Yes."

"When for?"

"Could it be tomorrow?"

"Do you think you can tell them all?"

"Yes."

"You'd better get moving!"

Sasha turned at the door and saw that Solts was glowering at him, his head lowered.

"You are requested to attend the Party Membership Bureau on 10 January at 3 P.M. for an interview with Comrade Solts." Then the list of names. The only one missing was Sasha's. Solts's secretary hadn't asked him for it. It was absurd, but it didn't matter. He'd won, anyway. He didn't doubt it for a moment. Solts didn't need the opinion of other departments, or their documents and decisions. "Summon them all!" But what if he hadn't gone into the office by mistake, and if the secretary hadn't felt he had to do something to cover up his blunder? Nothing would have happened. And then the assistant's supercilious smile, which had annoyed Solts. Now things were happening, it was turning out all right!

Something was bothering him, nevertheless. Those silent people sitting on benches along the walls, dumb, patient, waiting for the fate of their nearest and dearest to be decided. The dictatorship of the proletariat must defend itself, that was obvious. And yet the air in those corridors was thick with human misery. Then there was the unknown man who'd got eight years for stealing forty yards of wire. Maybe he had played a part in Sasha's case; maybe the sympathy he'd been shown had been intended for the other man.

But he was young and he wanted to live, so he tried to think about himself and about the fact that his miseries were coming to an end, and not about the people sitting silently on the benches along the oppressive corridors of the bureaucracy.

Glinskaya was on the phone when Sasha walked into her office without waiting for her secretary. She looked at him in surprise, then fear, and covered the mouthpiece with her hand.

"What do you want?"

Sasha put the summons in front of her.

She read it and muttered in confusion, "Why me? This is for Baulin."

She looked pitiful.

"Please sign it."

"But why? Go and see the Party committee," she mumbled.

"I have been instructed to give this to you. Please sign."

She finally put down the phone and picked up the list.

"You've been to Solts?" Suddenly she was using the familiar form with him.

"Yes."

She looked at the list. The membership committee of the Central Control Commission had become involved. . . . It couldn't have happened without Ryazanov, or Budyagin, which was only to be expected. And on the eve of the congress. She imagined how Solts or Yaroslavsky, or even Rudzutak himself, might mention the Pankratov case in his speech as an example of a heartless attitude to a future young specialist. Sasha had been expelled from the institute in his last year — she'd signed the order herself. Yes, she had submitted to the Party committee's decision and signed it. But she had warned Baulin. They'd received a letter forbidding the failure of final-year students, but Baulin had taken no notice, so now let him get out of the mess himself.

She smiled at Sasha.

"This is all junior school stuff, rhymes and whatnot."

He pushed the list toward her.

"Just sign, please."

"I'll be there."

"Please be kind enough to sign here."

Frowning, she signed alongside her name.

When Baulin read the summons, he grinned sarcastically. "So, you managed to get to the top? Sure you won't fall from there, too?"

He signed with an offended look, as if Sasha had delivered a personal insult.

Janson peered at Sasha through the thick lenses of his spectacles and there was a flicker of hope in his eyes. He said nothing, only asking which floor he should go to.

The list was passed around Sasha's group from hand to hand. "This'll worry them," Runochkin said. "Kovalyov, are you going to repent now?"

"Sasha, you're wonderful," Pozdnyakova said.

Rosa Poluzhan was more cautious, and asked quietly, "Does it mean victory?"

Solts had plainly forgotten all about Sasha. He watched mystified as eight people walked into his office. He must have called a meeting, but there was nothing in his diary about it.

Glinskaya held out her hand to him. They knew each other; he recognized her and rose in a clumsy gesture of gallantry. He turned out to be extremely short.

"The Transport Institute case," his secretary announced.

It meant nothing to Solts, he knew nothing about cases at the Transport Institute, and being so nearsighted he didn't recognize Sasha. From force of habit, he nevertheless gestured them all to sit down.

Glinskaya unrolled the wall newspaper before him. It had been kept rolled up and she had to use a paperweight and a huge pencil jar to keep it flat. Solts watched her uncomprehendingly.

"Here are the rhymes," she said.

He leaned forward over the paper, wondering what the rhymes were about. At that moment he spotted Sasha and looked at him hard. He then remembered the young man from the day before who had come in and sat down in his office. Frowning, he read another verse.

"The issue was dedicated to the sixteenth anniversary of the October Revolution," Baulin said.

Solts squinted nearsightedly around the group trying to locate the source of the voice. In front of him sat Nadya Pozdnyakova, the good-looking blonde, Sasha, twisted little Runochkin, terrified Rosa, and a perplexed Kovalyov.

"The October Revolution didn't abolish rhymes," he replied sternly.

"They were inserted beneath portraits of shock-workers," Baulin insisted.

Solts now understood whom and what he was arguing with. "It used to be forbidden to write rhymes about people in high places, but rhymes were still written."

"But to suggest that labor is only a 'fashion,' can that be right?" Baulin stood his ground.

"Labor, labor!" Solts snapped back. "Bourgeois constitutions also begin with words about labor. The question is what kind of labor and what it's in the name of. How does this jingle attack labor?"

"Look ..."

"I am looking, and I can see that you're going to ruin these young lives." With a sweep of the hand, he indicated the students ranged in front of him. "I can see that you'd like to torment and torture them. It was them Lenin had in mind when he said, 'You will live under Communism.' What kind of Communism are you offering them? You've thrown him out of the institute, but where's he supposed to go, what's he to do? Be a stevedore?"

"He's working as a stevedore already," Janson remarked.

"We've taught him and trained him, he's supposed to be a specialist, and you throw him out onto the street. And what for? Because of some rhymes? The young have their own rules, and their first rule is to laugh."

With the same clumsy attempt at gallantry, he turned again to Glinskaya.

"We used to laugh when we were their age. Now it's their turn, and thank God for it! If the young people are laughing, it means things are all right, it means they are with us. And you want to kick them in the teeth! They wrote the rhymes about each other.... Who would you rather they wrote them about? Me? They don't know me. So, who are they supposed to laugh at?"

"His expulsion was confirmed by the district committee," Baulin protested.

"Confirmed!" Solts yelled, purple in the face. "You managed to get that done quickly enough!"

Glinskaya, who felt on much firmer ground here than at the institute, asked in a tone of compromise, "What shall we do, then?"

Solts replied decisively with a frown, "Reinstate him!"

❧ 12 ❧

When they were outside, Runochkin scanned the others. "We have to celebrate."

"I'm in favor," Nadya agreed excitedly.

"I have to be somewhere else," Rosa declined.

"I've got to go, too," Kovalyov announced somberly.

"Give our regards to Lozgachev," Runochkin shouted after him. They only had a few rubles among them.

"We'll go to my place and get some more," Sasha said.

At home he embraced and kissed his mother.

"Say hello to my friends! I've been reinstated! Hooray!"

Sofya Alexandrovna burst into tears.

"Cheer up!" he said.

She wiped her eyes and smiled, but she was still consumed with fear.

"Nina called."

"We're going to pick her up."

Nina was not in when they got there. Varya was on the phone in the corridor.

Sasha put his hand on the phone and cut her off. "Get ready!"

"Where are we going?" She took in the good-looking Nadya with a glance.

"We're going to have a drink and a bite to eat."

It was getting dark quickly and the streetlights were going on. Sasha loved the busy, last-minute activity on the Arbat in the early winter evenings. Everything was as it should be and in its proper place. He was walking in the Arbat as he always had, and *that business* was now a thing of the past.

They ran into Vadim on the corner of Afanasyevsky Street. He was wearing a deerskin coat and a Yakut hat with long fur earflaps that reached down to his belt.

"The conqueror of the Arctic! Come with us!"

"Celebrating a victory?" He guessed at once.

"You got it."

"Let's go to the Kanatik, it's a great place," Vadim suggested, eyeing Nadya.

"Nina's meeting us here."

They negotiated a steep stairway down into the Arbat Cellar, which was little more than a low basement, partitioned by thick square pillars, and found a free table in the far corner. The place smelled of cooking, starched tablecloths, and spilled beer — tavern smells. It was dimly lit by ungainly lamps, hanging awkwardly from the low arches. On the stage towered a double bass, still in its cover, and a saxophone lay on a chair. The musicians had arrived.

Sasha held out the menu across the table. "What'll we have?"

"It's expensive," Nadya breathed. "One portion of cattle fodder."

"We didn't come here to eat salad," Sasha protested.

"The only thing worth coming here for is the coffee and Cacao-choix liqueur." Vadim spoke like an old hand.

A coffeepot stood over the blue flame of a spirit stove on the next table, and two nattily dressed men were drinking coffee and liqueur from dainty cups.

"We're hungry," Sasha said. "Varya, what do you want to eat?"

"Beef Stroganov."

They ordered a bottle of vodka for the boys, a bottle of port wine for the girls, and beef Stroganov for everyone.

"We should have ordered different dishes," Vadim remarked.

"And now Nina's arrived." Varya, who was facing the entrance, said it as if to herself.

"All tucked away in the corner?" Nina was in a lively mood. "Congratulations, Sasha!" She kissed him. "I realized as soon as I read your note, but then I never doubted." She glanced at Varya. "You here, too?"

"Yes, I'm here, too."

"It's a pity Max doesn't know," Nina said as she sat down between Vadim and Runochkin.

The band started up. *"Oh, little lemons, my little lemons, growing on Sonya's balcony . . ."* The waiters were scurrying up and down the crowded, narrow spaces between the tables.

"To Solts, a real human being!" Runochkin said.

"But he was terribly nervous," Nadya added.

Between mouthfuls of his beef Stroganov, Vadim said, "Sasha's been through the fires of purgatory. But mind you, without suffering . . ."

"I hate whiners," Sasha interrupted him.

Vadim was trying to impress Nadya. "To paraphrase Proudhon, 'After the oppressors, I most hate the oppressed.' But circumstances vary. This, for instance . . ."

He indicated the next table. The two men had been joined by a girl with a beautiful, but haggard, face.

"A social evil," Nina said.

"Or possibly a pathological phenomenon," Vadim objected.

"It's neither pathology nor sociology, it's just plain, old-fashioned prostitution," Sasha said. "I'm not interested in why she makes her living that way, and I have no desire to speculate about her psychological state. Look at Nina and Varya and Nadya — they're the girls for me; I'm ready to love, respect, and honor them. Man is a moral being, that's what distinguishes him from the animals. And his vital function is not confined to suffering."

Varya softly sang along with the band. *"We loved you, tender and honest were you. . . . We all wanted you. . . ."*

"Why do people like these depressing songs so much?" Vadim answered his own question. "So-and-so's dying, the poor lad's been abandoned and forgotten, and nobody even knows where his grave lies. Man *suffers*, that's the whole point."

"Don't try tearing at our heartstrings," Sasha interrupted.

Vadim pouted. "Well, so much for tolerance!"

"Don't be offended, but to you it's just an abstraction. I've been through it. Anyway, let's see how much we've got left, maybe we can afford another bottle?"

They ordered another bottle for the boys and ice cream for the girls.

"But don't rush," Vadim warned. "Let's make it last the evening."

"You've got school tomorrow, Varya," Nina reminded her sister.
"I want to listen to the music."

"Leave her alone," Sasha said. "Let her stay."

He wanted to make Varya happy. He was happy himself. It wasn't just that he had *shown them all,* he had also fought for something more important: he had defended his friends' faith. Never before had he felt so tormented by others' defenselessness. In his place, Runochkin would have shrugged his shoulders and walked away. Nadya Pozdnyakova would have had a cry and walked away, too. And as for Vadim, if he'd had to face what Sasha had just been through, he would have collapsed at the start.

Only Varya hadn't thought Sasha's saga especially important. She'd be only too delighted if they'd expel her from school. Here she was, sitting in a restaurant, a dingy tavern she found beautiful, with young people in modern suits, jazz musicians on the stage, the trumpet player blowing out his cheeks, the drummer absently juggling his sticks, the girl at the next table.

Two drunks were now pestering the girl, trying to drag her to their table. They were taunting the two characters sitting with her, who didn't look very willing to defend her. She was swearing and crying drunken tears; the waiter was getting ready to throw her out.

"A dogfight," said Sasha, his eyes narrowing.

"Stay out of it," Vadim warned, but he moved his chair away, knowing it was no good trying to stop Sasha.

Sasha stood up, his head thrust forward, his shoulders hunched. He knew how to fight. Smiling grimly, he went over to the next table.

"Why don't you just leave her alone?"

Two fat ugly mugs in lilac-colored shirts, one wearing felt boots, the other wide-cut trousers, a couple of bullying sons-of-bitches.

The one in felt boots pushed Sasha out of the way dismissively; the other one tried to get between them. "Back off, the two of you!"

But Sasha knew that technique: the first one to hit him would be the one trying to make peace. Sasha landed a short, sharp blow that doubled him up, gasping for air. Sasha turned to the second man, but he stepped backward, turning over a table with a crash. The girl screamed, and her two pals jumped out of their chairs. The trumpet player watched the scene out of the corner of his eye and blew out his cheeks, the pianist swiveled around but his fingers went on tinkling the keys, the drummer went on juggling his sticks. . . . *"How do you do, Mr. Brown. How do you, do you, do you do!"* The band played on, they were happy, everything's fine, ladies and gentlemen, dance the fox-trot and the tango, drink your coffee and Cacao-choix, pay no attention, it was nothing, a minor incident, a little misunderstanding, it's all over. The felt boots and wide trousers retreated to their own table. The two fops paid their bill and left with the girl; the waiter was already changing their tablecloth. Everything's just fine, ladies and gentlemen!

"They'll be waiting for us outside," Vadim said.

"Vadim's scared." Nina laughed.

"Forget it," said Sasha.

He was usually calm when he got into fights, but now that it was over, he was trembling and had to make an effort to control himself.

"Varya, let's dance."

The band was playing a slow waltz, "Ramona." He moved around the tiny floor with Varya and felt everyone's eyes on him. To hell with them, let them think what they liked. The two thugs were also watching him. To hell with them, too!

Here he was, waltzing with a pretty girl. She smiled at him, admiring him for the way he'd acted. Her hero, he'd stood up for a girl who only five minutes before he'd been condemning. Varya sensed something of herself in this: Were they alike, the two of them, he only pretending to be politically conscious?

She was looking at him, smiling at him, and pressing herself against him. The band was sobbing, the trumpet howling, the drummer's sticks were poised in the air, the pianist was slouched over the keys. *"Ramona . . ."*

"You're a good dancer," Sasha said.

"Let's go skating the day after tomorrow," Varya said.

"Why the day after tomorrow?"

"It's Saturday, they have music. You can skate, can't you?"

"I used to, once upon a time."

"What about it, then?"

"I don't even know where my skates are."

13

"In view of student Pankratov's admission of his errors, he is to be reinstated in the institute with a strict reprimand."

There were no celebrations. His expulsion had excited everyone; his reinstatement left them all cold.

Only Krivoruchko said, as he signed Sasha's new student card, "I'm happy for you."

For someone who used to be so terrifying, he now looked like a lonely man waiting out his last days in his office.

"How're things with you?" Sasha asked.

Krivoruchko indicated a stack of files in the corner. "I'm being replaced."

He took a stamp out of his enormous desk, which the students called his deck. They often had to see him, as he handled their stipends, their lodgings, ration cards, requisitions.

"As a matter of fact, I know your uncle. We used to be in the same Party organization. It was a long time ago, back in 'twenty-three. How is he?"

"He's well."

"Please give him my regards when you next see him."

Sasha felt ashamed — he'd escaped, whereas Krivoruchko hadn't.

"Maybe you ought to see Comrade Solts?"

"Solts can't do anything in my case. It depends on someone else ..."

He added, almost to himself, not looking at Sasha, "And this is a chef who likes to make peppery dishes."

And he frowned.

Sasha knew which chef he had in mind.

He then went to see Lozgachev, who smiled as if he were delighted at Sasha's success.

"Have you seen Krivoruchko?"

He knew Sasha had, but still he asked.

"He has taken care of my card and permit," Sasha replied.

Baulin walked in and overheard Sasha's reply, and dryly asked Lozgachev, "Krivoruchko's still got the stamp?"

"The new man starts on Monday."

"She could at least have taken the stamp."

Lozgachev shrugged, as if to say Glinskaya thought herself too grand to wield a rubber stamp.

Just as before, they busied themselves with their affairs, their squabbles, as if nothing had happened; they felt neither guilt nor any pangs of conscience. In fact, now that they had reinstated him, Sasha would have to behave differently.

They were talking about Glinskaya sarcastically in front of him, making no effort to conceal their hostility to her — surely such frankness implied that they trusted him?

In effect they were saying: "Pankratov, you've got to start acting smart. You're flawed now, you've got a record, you won't get off the hook so easily next time. Solts is a long way away, but we're right here — stick with us and you'll be all right. You're still young and inexperienced, green, you slipped up, all right, we can understand that. Now you know what sort of person Krivoruchko really is, help us defeat him. There is only mutual trust where there are common enemies. 'Tell me who your friends are' — that's outdated. 'Tell me who your *enemies* are, and I'll tell you who you are,' that's the question today."

"Did Krivoruchko complain to you?" Lozgachev asked.

It wasn't worth getting involved with them. But he wasn't the one who'd been beaten — they'd had to tuck their tails between their legs, and they shouldn't be allowed to forget it.

"Why should he complain to me? I'm not the Party membership committee."

Lozgachev smiled encouragingly.

"We're all comrades in misfortune."

" 'Comrades'?" Sasha mocked. "He still hasn't been reinstated."

Baulin's sullen look was a signal to Sasha not to go too far.

Instead, it only spurred him on. What was Baulin warning him about? Were they going to expel him again? Let them try! They'd just burned their fingers, and now they're pretending they won. "It wasn't Solts who forgave you," they were saying, "it was the Party. And as we are the Party, it's *we* who have forgiven you." But, no, you are *not* the Party!

"You think Krivoruchko will be reinstated?" Lozgachev asked derisively.

"They reinstated me."

"You're different, you committed an error, but Krivoruchko's an old hand. . . ."

"He was expelled once before for political errors and was reinstated then, but this was only about the hostels. . . ."

"This is new," said Baulin, sinking into an armchair and looking at Sasha intently. "You never used to talk like this."

"Nobody ever asked me before. Now I'm being asked."

"You disowned Krivoruchko before," Baulin went on. " 'I don't know, I don't know him, we haven't exchanged more than a couple of words.' "

"It's still true. I *don't* know, I *don't* know him, we *haven't* exchanged more than a couple of words."

"Really?" Baulin sounded sinister.

"You're wrong, Pankratov," Lozgachev pronounced. "The Party must purge its ranks —"

Sasha broke in, "Of careerists, above all."

"Whom do you have in mind?" Lozgachev frowned.

"Just careerists in general, nobody in particular."

"No, you're wrong." Lozgachev shook his head. "The Party is purging its ranks of ideologically unstable, politically hostile elements, and you say it has first got to get rid of the careerists. Obviously, it must do that, but why compare the two?"

Sasha was irritated by Lozgachev's smooth, hypocritical voice, by his cold face, by the blindly narrow-minded formulas he'd learned to mouth by heart.

"Perhaps we ought not to stick labels on people, Comrade Lozgachev. You've just had some experience with that. I say that one careerist can do the Party more harm than all the errors of an old Bolshevik like Krivoruchko. Krivoruchko committed his errors in support of the Party, whereas a careerist is only concerned about his own skin and his own cushy position."

Silence.

Then Baulin pronounced slowly, "Not bad, Pankratov, not bad."

"I do my best," Sasha replied.

Of course, they would reinterpret and twist his words, Sasha thought, as he left Lozgachev's office.

These were people he could be frank with! He wasn't afraid of them. But it was all too stupid!

Sasha was in his usual seat in the lecture hall, his name hadn't even been removed from the register, but he still couldn't believe that it was all over. The whole business with Solts now seemed unreal. It was this institute that was real, Baulin, Lozgachev, broken Krivoruchko.

He was going home in an overcrowded tram. Outside, the early winter evening was turning dark quickly. Opposite him sat a clumsy-looking peasant with a scruffy red beard, the ends of his floppy-eared fur cap hanging down over his sheepskin coat. His enormous felt boots were planted on one bag, while another was on the seat next to him, clumsy great peasant bags, getting in everyone's way in the crowded car. He kept looking around nervously, and asking where he should get off, though the conductress had promised to tell him in plenty of time. Yet somehow, deep down behind the peasant's look of supplication, Sasha sensed something hard and stern. At home this man would no doubt be quite different. On the cover of his bridges and road-building notebook, Sasha jotted down the idea that people change with their environment, meaning to write it down properly in the diary he had started, given up, and had now made a firm decision to keep up.

❧ 14 ❧

Katya telephoned out of the blue one night as Sasha was going to bed.

She was playing her old games. First complete silence, then a second call.

"Is it you, Katya?"

"Didn't you recognize me?" Her voice seemed to come from afar, as if she was calling from a pay phone outside town.

"How could I recognize you if you didn't make any noise?"

"Noise ... People around here don't shout. How are you?"

"I'm okay. I think of you."

" 'Think of you' ... Haven't you got enough girlfriends?"

"They've all gone off and left me. How're you?"

"So-so.... Marusya misses you. You remember Marusya? She fell in love with you and she says I must bring my black-eyed friend home."

"Fine, when shall we go?"

"Go ... What do you mean, I'm a married woman!"

"You married the mechanic?"

"Mechanic ... Tinker, tailor, soldier, sailor."

"Are you drunk, or something?"

"No thanks to you!"

"When are we going to meet?"

"*Where* are we going to meet? It's thirty below outside, your thing'll drop off...."

"But Marusya's expecting us."

"Expecting us ... Her husband's come back. Okay, be at Devichka."

"But where'll we go?"

"To Kudykin Hill."

"So, it's tomorrow at Devichka. At six or seven?"

"I'll be there by six."

Katya was back in his life. All his old desire for her was revived, not that it had really died. They'd been together in September or October and now it was already January, four months. Of course, she hadn't got married and Marusya's husband hadn't come back, and they'd go to Marusya's tomorrow, that's why she'd mentioned her. She couldn't talk straight, always in circles. A strange, enigmatic girl.

He thought of her as he lay in bed, and the more he thought, the more he desired her. Tomorrow he would kiss her warm lips and hold her, and the thought kept him awake.

He was abruptly woken by the shrill ringing of the doorbell in the corridor. It was two in the morning and he had barely dropped off. The bell rang again, insistently and firmly. He went out into the corridor dressed only in his underwear and took off the chain.

"Who is it?"

"House management."

Sasha recognized Vasili Petrovich's voice and unlocked the door.

The janitor was standing in the doorway. Behind him was a stranger, a young man in an overcoat and soft hat, and two Red Army men in greatcoats with crimson tabs. Pushing first Vasili Petrovich and then Sasha out of the way, the young man entered the apartment; one of the Red Army men remained at the door and the other one followed Vasili Petrovich through to the kitchen and took up his post at the back door.

"Pankratov?"

"Yes."

"Alexander Pavlovich Pankratov?"

"Yes."

Watching Sasha guardedly, he handed him a warrant for the search and arrest of Citizen Pankratov, Alexander Pavlovich, a resident of the Arbat. . . .

They went into Sasha's room.

"Your papers!"

Sasha took his identity book and student card out of his jacket, which was hanging over the chair. The young man studied them closely and laid them on the table.

"Weapons?"

"I don't have any weapons."

The young man nodded toward Sasha's mother's room.

"Who's in there?"

"It's my mother's room."

"Wake her up."

Sasha pulled on his trousers, tucked in his shirt, and put on socks and shoes. The young man, in his coat and hat, waited for him to dress.

Sasha opened his mother's door carefully, trying not to wake her up suddenly and alarm her.

She was sitting hunched in bed, clutching her white nightdress to her breast, her gray hair falling over her forehead and into her eyes, and looking at the young man with her fixed sideways stare as he followed Sasha into the room.

"Mama, don't worry. . . . They're here to search me. It's a misunderstanding. It'll be all right. Just stay calm."

With her distrustful, sideways stare, she was looking past Sasha at the unknown man standing at the door.

"There, there," Sasha muttered. "I've told you, it's a misunderstanding. Lie down. Please."

As they left the room, he was about to close the door, when the young man stopped him; the door had to remain open.

The young man was only carrying out his orders; it was pointless to argue with him. Sasha felt he must remain confident and cheerful, for it was the only way to keep his mother calm.

"What are you looking for? Perhaps I could find it for you."

The young man took off his coat and hat and hung them in the corner. He was wearing a dark blue suit and a dark shirt and tie. He was the kind of perfectly ordinary young man, beginning to fill out, that one would meet in any government office.

Sasha's notebooks, summaries, and textbooks from the institute were lying on the desk. The young man picked them up one at a time and leafed through them, scanning the pages and stacking them neatly in a pile.

His attention was drawn to the note Sasha had made on the cover of his bridges and road-building notebook that day in the tram. "Peasant in tram, confused, pitiful, but at home important, authoritative, despotic." The notebook was lying alongside his identity book and student card.

The drawers of his desk contained papers, photographs, letters. The young man was not interested in the contents of the letters, but in who had sent them. When he couldn't decipher a signature, he asked Sasha, who answered curtly. The young man laid the letters to the right; he had no need of them. Sasha's documents, his diploma, the reference from work, and other such things were left where they were, but his Komsomol and trade union cards were put on the left.

"Why are you taking my Komsomol card?"

"I'm not taking anything for the moment."

Childhood and school photographs were of no interest to him either, but those with adults in them attracted his attention. "Who is this? And this?"

Sasha's mother got up. He heard the creak of her bedsprings, her shuffling slippers, and the noise of the wardrobe door. When she came in, she was wearing her dress, hastily thrown on over her nightgown. Smiling pitifully, she went over to Sasha and stroked his hair with a trembling hand.

"Go and sit in your room, ma'am," the young man said. He spoke in a tone of official finality, one that had always terrified her, as if she had done something that could harm her son. Her head started nodding in small, frightened movements.

"Perhaps we should all lie down on the floor?" Sasha asked sarcastically.

The young man, who was going through the books on the shelf, glanced around in surprise but said nothing.

"Go and sit in your room," Sasha said to his mother.

Her head shook more rapidly and, with a look at the young man's broad back, she went back to her room.

Do they know about Solts? They can't, otherwise they wouldn't have dared to come here like this. A cog in the machine had obviously got stuck. What a pain! This misunderstanding was going to make life complicated.

The young man ordered him to open the cupboard, empty his jacket pockets. His notebook with all his addresses and phone numbers now lay on the table.

The young man looked around the room to see if he had missed anything, spotted a suitcase under the bed, and told Sasha to open it. It was empty.

He was doing his duty, a thorough, conscientious public servant. If Sasha had his job, if the Party were to post him to the GPU security force and he were given the job of carrying out a search and arresting someone, he would do it exactly the same way, even if the man he was arresting was innocent. Mistakes are inevitable in this sort of work. One has to rise above personal reactions. He would prove his innocence as he had at the Control Commission. Meanwhile, let the man do his job.

"Come into the next room," the young man said.

His mother was leaning on the top of her chest of drawers with her head in her hands and looking sideways at the door.

"Mama, the comrades want to look over your room. You sit down."

But she remained standing and barely moved when the young man approached her.

There were photographs of Sasha, Mark, and of her sisters on the chest of drawers.

"Who's this?"

"My brother, Mark Alexandrovich Ryazanov."

Let them know that her brother was the famous Ryazanov and that Sasha was his nephew. She had been thinking all the time that as soon as she told them this they'd stop the search and not arrest Sasha. The whole country knew Mark, Stalin knew him.

And she added with a pathetic smile, "And this is Sashenka, when he was a little boy."

The young man frowned and picked up the photograph of Mark, undid the frame's catch, removed the matte, and examined the back of the picture. Nothing was written there. He put it all back on the chest of drawers, the photograph, the stand, the glass, the matte. Sofya Alexandrovna sank into an armchair, covered her face with her hands, and gave a moan.

The young man poked around in the chest of drawers. The scent of fresh laundry rose from the linen as he turned it over, the way it did when Sasha's mother made his bed.

"I thought I was the one who was being searched," Sasha said.

"You live as a family," the young man replied.

They went back to Sasha's room. Sofya Alexandrovna followed them; the search was over and they hadn't told her to stay in her own room. The thought that they were going to take Sasha away stirred her from her torpor, prompted her into a flurry of feverish activity, rushing about not knowing what she was doing, fussing around Sasha, anxiously watching the young man. He wrote out his report at the table. *On such-and-such date, at such-and-such place, by order number so-and-so . . . The following items were removed: identity book number so-and-so, trade union card number so-and-so, Komsomol card, student card, notebook.* He held the bridges and road-building notebook in his hand and then put it to one side. He had decided not to take it.

"Where can I wash my hands?"

Sofya Alexandrovna sprang into action. "Let me show you. Please."

Busily she opened drawers and produced a clean towel and while the young man was washing his hands she stood at the door of the bathroom holding the towel, which she handed to him with a pathetic and pleading smile: maybe this man will make things easier for her boy *there*.

The young man dried his hands and went out into the corridor to use the telephone. What he said was incomprehensible, only one word meant anything — Arbat.

He hung up the receiver and leaned against the doorjam with the unconcerned look of a man who has done his job. The Red Army man at the door was at ease and the other one came out of the kitchen, leaving both the front and back doors unguarded. The janitor had gone. Although nobody had told the neighbors the search was over, Mikhail Yurevich and Galya appeared in the corridor.

Sasha's mother was collecting his things, her hands trembling.

"Put in warm socks," the young man told her.

"He should probably also take something to eat," Mikhail Yurevich added politely.

"Money," the young man said.

"Dammit!" Sasha said. "I'm out of cigarettes."

"I'll go and get some of mine." Galya came back with a pack.

"Have you got any money, Sasha?" Mikhail Yurevich asked.

Sasha dug in his pockets. "Ten rubles."

"It'll do," said the young man.

"The store there's cheap," one of the Red Army men explained. It was all so calm, as if Sasha were setting off on a trip to some unknown town and they were advising him on what he ought to take.

The young man was smoking in the doorway, one of the Red Army men was chatting with Galya, the other one was squatting on his heels and was also smoking. Mikhail Yurevich gave Sasha a smile of encouragement, and Sasha also smiled, aware that his smile was weak, but it was the best he could manage.

"Sashenka, look what I've put in for you." She lifted the corner of the bundle with trembling hands. "Look, there's soap, tooth powder, a brush, a towel, a razor ..."

"No razor," the young man said.

"Sorry," she said, taking out the razor. "Here are your socks, a change of underwear, handkerchiefs ..."

Her voice began to shake.

"Here's your comb, your nice scarf ... nice scarf ..."

Her words became a sob. She was exhausted, she was dying, sorting out these things, things belonging to the boy they were tearing away from her, the boy they were taking to prison. She collapsed into the armchair, and her sobbing shook her plump little body.

"Now, now, take it easy, everything's going to be all right." Galya stroked her shoulder. "They took away the Almazovs' boy, kept him for a while and then sent him home. No need to cry now, if that's how it turns out for your son."

But Sofya Alexandrovna shook and mumbled, "It's the end, it's the end. . . ."

The young man looked at his watch. "Ready?"

He threw away his cigarette butt, straightened up, and frowned. The sentries also straightened up, returning to their responsibilities. They weren't giving advice anymore, they had their weapons ready for escort duty. The young man gestured to Mikhail Yurevich and Galya to stand aside so the arrested man could be led away.

Sasha put on his coat and fur hat and picked up his bundle.

One of the Red Army men fumbled with the French lock and finally managed to open the front door.

Sofya Alexandrovna had been waiting for this moment, dreading it. She ran out into the corridor, saw Sasha in his coat and hat, grabbed him and clung to him, shaking and choking with tears.

Mikhail Yurevich gently took her by the shoulders.

"Sofya Alexandrovna, really, you shouldn't, you shouldn't."

Sasha kissed the top of her head, on her untidy gray hair. Mikhail Yurevich and Galya held her back as she wailed and writhed to break free.

Sasha left the apartment.

A car was waiting for them nearby. The young man and one of the soldiers sat on either side of Sasha in the back, while the other escort sat in front alongside the driver. They drove without speaking through the night streets of Moscow. Sasha couldn't make out which way they were going to the prison. Huge iron gates opened to allow the car into a long, narrow, enclosed courtyard. First the escorts got out, then Sasha, then the young man in charge. The car left immediately. They took him into a vast, low-arched, empty space, an enormous basement totally without furnishing, neither benches nor tables, smelling of bleach, with dilapidated walls and a worn cement floor. Sasha realized this was the assembly point — from here prisoners were sent to the cells, or grouped for dispatch to other prisons, or exile; it was the entrance and exit of the prison, its first and last stage. It was empty at the moment.

The young man and the escorts were no longer watching Sasha's every movement, for there was no chance of his running away now; one didn't run away from this place. They had carried out their mission successfully, they had delivered the arrested man, they were no longer responsible for him.

"Wait here," the young man ordered, and left.

The escorts left as well, to go to the guardhouse. Through its open door came the smell of damp army greatcoats and cabbage soup.

Sasha put down his bundle and stood by the wall. Nobody was guarding him or watching him during this pause in the operation as the arrest stage was completed and the concluding stage had yet to begin.

In those moments, left on his own, Sasha became acutely aware of his position. Were he to take even one step, they would stop him and order him to stay where he was; he would have to obey and that would humiliate him still further. He must give them no excuse. That way he could retain his dignity, the dignity of a Soviet man who had been put in this situation by mistake.

A small military figure with two square tabs on his collar appeared and, without stopping, ordered Sasha to follow him.

Sasha picked up his bundle and did so, feeling nothing but curiosity.

There was a small office desk beyond the first arch. The man sat down and pulled out a blank form. Name? First name? Father's name? Year of birth? Any distinguishing marks? Tattoos? Scars? Traces of injury? Burns? Birthmarks? He noted the color of Sasha's hair and eyes. He proffered a sort of ink pad and Sasha marked the form with his fingerprints. His belongings were noted down: coat, fur hat, boots, sweater, trousers, jacket, shirt. He then told Sasha to sign.

"Money."

He counted the money, wrote on the form, and got Sasha to sign again. He put the money in a drawer.

"You'll be brought a receipt." He indicated a door. "Go through there."

A drowsy fat man in civilian clothes was waiting for Sasha in the tiny room.

"Take your clothes off."

Sasha took off his coat and hat.

"The boots."

Sasha took off his boots and stood there in his socks.

"Take out the laces."

The fat man put the laces on the table and pointed to the corner.

"Stand over there."

There was a plank in the corner marked off for measuring height. The fat man moved the slide down onto Sasha's head and called out to someone on the other side of the wall, "Five foot six."

He then ran his hands over Sasha's coat and hat, opened up the linings with a knife and groped around, then he put them back on the iron bench. He indicated Sasha's suit.

"Take it off."

Sasha took off his jacket.

"Take off everything!"

Sasha remained in his underpants and undershirt.

The fat man felt through the trousers and jacket, opened up the linings, unrolled the cuffs on the trousers, pulled out the belt and put it next to the laces, throwing the trousers and jacket on the bench.

"Open your mouth."

He brought his somnolent face close to Sasha's, looked inside his mouth, pulling up his lips to see if there was anything concealed behind or between his teeth. Then he indicated the underpants and undershirt.

"Off!"

He searched for tattoos, scars, traces of burns or injuries, and found none.

"Turn around. Spread your legs. Wider. Bend over."

Sasha felt the cold touch of the man's fingers on his buttocks. The fat man inspected his rectum.

"Get dressed."

Then, under escort, holding up his beltless trousers with his hand, his laceless boots flopping, Sasha went through a series of short corridors, up and down iron staircases, the escort clanging his keys on the iron handrails and grating them in locks. All around were blank cells and blank metal doors.

They came to a halt. The sentry who was waiting for them opened a cell. Sasha went in. The door clanged shut.

s Stalin had demanded, the fourth blast furnace was started up earlier than planned, at seven o'clock in the evening of the thirtieth of December in thirty-five degrees below zero. Mark Alexandrovich Ryazanov would leave for Moscow only when he was sure there would be no repeat of the catastrophe they'd had with the first one, when they'd started it up at a similar temperature. For that reason, he didn't travel with the local delegation, but left on his own on the ninth of January.

His official railway car had already been hitched to the locomotive and the snow plow had gone on ahead. There were high snowdrifts and the few signal lights, rocking in the fierce wind, were faint. The station and the town were at the outer limit of the electrical grid, which extended only to the factory, where it was needed to make metal.

Around the Dutch stove in the little station house his staff had gathered with their last-minute problems that he would now settle. They followed him into the train in their wet boots and galoshes, their caps and collars covered with snow, and they brushed themselves off, stamped their feet, and started smoking, much to the annoyance of the conductor, who had polished everything till it shone and stoked up the stove, as he always did when *he* was traveling.

Mark Alexandrovich took off his sheepskin coat and hat, but still felt too warm. The lights shone brightly, if unsteadily. He looked quickly through his papers, making sure he had everything he needed for Moscow. The date given by the Central Committee for completing the factory was 1937. And the national pig-iron target for the Five-Year Plan had been reduced from twenty-two million to eighteen million tons. Realism had prevailed. Now was the time to demand at the top of one's voice everything one had previously only whispered about — housing, mechanization, social and consumer amenities.

The stationmaster looked in. "I'm giving the signal to depart, Mark Alexandrovich."

The conductor, in his black uniform topcoat and black fur hat, came through the car carrying a lantern and muttering sullenly, "Time to leave, citizens, time to leave."

The others left the car, letting in an icy blast. The conductor kicked away the snow that had built up on the step and closed the door.

A whistle blew, the engine hooted in reply, and the train lurched and gradually picked up the rhythm of the rails, rocking from side to side.

Mark Alexandrovich took off his boots, got his house slippers from his bag, and contentedly walked up and down in them, stretching his legs. He went to the window and drew aside the curtain.

Chugging through the snow-covered steppe, the little train skirted the town perched on a hill and illuminated by the flickering flames of the furnaces. Four years earlier they had come to a bare site, and now there was a population of two hundred thousand, a gigantic world-class factory that was already supplying the country with a million tons of pig iron, hundreds of thousands of tons of steel, three million tons of iron ore.

He wasn't given to reminisce — for many years he hadn't had time to; he'd had barely enough time to think about what had to be done at the moment. With the congress in front of him, he now thought of Lominadze, who'd already left with the local delegation.

Lominadze, once a member of the Central Committee, had been removed from all his important posts for theoretical errors and sent as secretary of the town committee. This really meant he was secretary of the factory Party committee, since the town was in practice the factory. He was the same age as Mark Alexandrovich, though he'd been in the Party two years longer, since 1917. He was regarded as an impressive politician, intelligent, tactful, imaginative, and creative. But if one of the aims of the congress was the defeat of former oppositionists, Lominadze would be a target, and that could mean the factory could become a target, too. Metal was important, but politics was more important.

All things considered, Mark Alexandrovich was inclined to think the congress would pass peacefully; even its title — the Congress of Victors — suggested it. The three preceding congresses had been conducted in an atmosphere of conflict, but the time had now come to demonstrate the unity and solidarity of the Party around the new leadership. Still, one had to be ready for any eventuality.

In the days when he hadn't had his own separate railway car and had gone back and forth to Moscow in the heated freight car, or even on the roof of the car, wearing his army greatcoat and carrying his backpack, he never used to worry about a thing. Now he controlled the lives of hundreds of thousands of people, he was invested with full power, firmly believed in the correctness of the Party line, didn't belong to any opposition group and never had. He was liked by Sergo, he was valued by Stalin. Yet now he had to assess everything anew, and worry in case there might be complications simply because a year ago Lominadze had been sent as Party secretary — Lominadze who had committed errors that had nothing whatever to do with Mark Alexandrovich or his team.

And, in addition, there was this incomprehensible arrest of Sasha.

His nephew's plight had filled him with anguish and despair. But he didn't know all the circumstances, he kept telling himself. The nonsense with the accounting lecturer was no reason for an arrest, especially as Solts had already reinstated Sasha. The causes must be connected with what Sasha had said that night, about Stalin's arrogance and Lenin's letter. . . . Had he read Lenin's letter? When, where, who'd given it to him? Stalin's arrogance . . . Had he said this to anyone else? To whom? Had he been expressing his own ideas, or had someone put them into his head? If so, who?

He had the right to know all the facts — it was, after all, his own nephew who was involved — and he had the right to expect a thorough and objective investigation.

*   *   *

He was met in Sverdlovsk by Kirzhak, the factory's representative at the provincial soviet. The Moscow–Vladivostok express, which he was to catch, was late, and, avoiding the main building, the stationmaster took him straight from the train to a room set aside for government officials and similar important persons.

A waitress brought tea and sandwiches. Kirzhak, a nervously fussy little man, reported on the present state of affairs: the suppliers were not reliable, there was insufficient transport, funds were unrealistic, the paperwork created bottlenecks, the local organizations were of little help. Mark Alexandrovich was used to the aggrieved tone that Kirzhak used to compensate for his lack of power.

The business with Kirzhak over, he went out onto the platform. Every corridor and gangway in the station was cluttered with bundles, bags, and trunks. People were sitting and lying on benches and the floor, crowding in lines at the ticket offices and the hot-water boiler; there seemed to be a great many women and children. This was peasant Russia, the Russia of sheepskin and birch-bark shoes and rope, unfit and stunned at having to pull up its roots and resettle. This was the village in sad confusion, in miserable poverty and decay, turned upside down, torn from the land, and cast into the unknown.

It was nothing new to Mark Alexandrovich — he'd seen it on every road in the country. Masses of people with their bags and baggage, their wives and children, were arriving continually at the factory. And the factory dormitories reeked of the same acrid stench of sheepskin and sweat and garlic. Such were the implacable laws of history and industrialization. It was the end of the old village life, the primitive, worn-out, myopic, ragged, ignorant village life, the end of private ownership. A new kind of history was being made. All the old ways were collapsing in pain and loss.

The transcontinental car was half empty, and Mark Alexandrovich got down to work straightaway, going out into the corridor only when it was already getting dark, around three o'clock.

The carpeted floor muffled the rhythmic click of the wheels. All the other compartment doors were closed, except one, from which he heard a man and woman speaking French.

The woman came out into the corridor and smiled in embarrassment when she saw Mark Alexandrovich. She was in her dressing gown and bedroom slippers, with her hair undone, on her way to the bathroom, and here looking at her was this strange Russian who must have boarded while they were sleeping. She was a big woman of about thirty-five, and she wore large horn-rimmed spectacles. She smiled at him again on her way back from the bathroom and closed the door of the compartment behind her.

The door opened again and the man emerged, equally large and portly, and Mark Alexandrovich at once recognized him as a famous Belgian Social Democrat who was prominent in the Second International. He remembered reading a month earlier a brief mention in the press of his trip through the Soviet Union and China to Japan, where he was to give a series of lectures. He'd thought then that the report was an indication of new contacts, which were entirely sensible in the present climate of international relations.

As usual with traveling companions who know they have a long journey ahead of them, they soon fell into conversation. Mark Alexandrovich's English was good, and he could manage in French well enough. Hearing her native language being spoken, the Belgian's wife came out to join them, dressed now in a gray wool skirt and sweater that only emphasized her magnificent bosom. Her smile this time expressed pleasant surprise at finding at last another traveler who could speak French.

They chatted about the Russian winter, the great distances, and the difficulties of communication and travel. In Tokyo and Osaka it was warm, in Nagasaki it was hot, but here it was cold. The Russians were evidently invigorated by the frost. The Belgian regretted that though they were traveling through Siberia and the Urals, they hadn't seen the famous Kuzbass or the famous Magnitostroy. All you could see out of the train window was the famous Russian snow. He would like to have seen the "Russian experiment," he said, excusing himself for the banality of the expression with a smile.

He reached into their compartment for the latest precongress issue of *Pravda,* which had a map showing the main sites of the second Five-Year Plan. These were marked by symbols of blast furnaces, cars, tractors, combine harvesters, locomotives, railway cars, car tires, hydroelectric power stations. Mark Alexandrovich explained that rolls of textile represented textile mills; lumps of sugar, sugar mills; small circles, ball-bearing factories. The Belgian smiled his approval, but pointed out that such an ambitious plan could only be fulfilled at the cost of other sectors of the economy, above all agriculture.

Mark Alexandrovich knew these Menshevik, moderate socialist arguments. Russia was going through its second revolution, but this well-groomed, respectable gentleman, this polished parliamentarian, didn't understand what was happening, just as he hadn't understood what had happened in the first revolution.

He said nothing, however; he didn't want a political discussion. He'd been abroad and was used to talking to foreigners, but he always avoided political argument, having decided long ago that nobody could ever convince anyone of anything. Not that he wanted the man to think he was afraid of a discussion —'in that sense Mark Alexandrovich was somewhat vain and was not accustomed to losing an argument.

And so instead he shared his impressions of America, where he'd spent two years working in a steel foundry. He recounted an amusing scene he'd witnessed in New York. A frail old lady, dressed from top to toe in old-fashioned black with something resembling a bird's nest on her head, came out of church. She was supported by a young girl, probably her granddaughter or maybe even her great-granddaughter. Carefully the girl steered her down the church steps and led her to the waiting Packard at the curb, helped her gently in, kissed her tenderly, and shut the door. And the old lady who had scarcely been able to get to the car under her own steam, once behind the wheel, switched on the engine and roared away.

He told the story without comment, just told it good-humoredly while puffing on his pipe, but he inserted it in the conversation at a moment when his companion could not mistake its meaning: America was an out-dated social order equipped with the latest technology.

The Belgian appreciated his subtlety, the diplomatic way he had indicated the level of conversation he was used to. Mark Alexandrovich loved to show off his intelligence in front of foreigners, his wit and the breadth and open-mindedness of his views; he thought it was the way a man who had power and prestige in his own country should behave.

The Belgian's wife did not see the point of the story, but she thought it funny nevertheless, and laughed long and hard.

From the station Mark Alexandrovich went to the Third House of Soviets on Sadovaya and Karetny. All the delegates had arrived, and the hall set aside for the organizing commission was empty, though there were clerks on duty who registered him, issued him his credentials, gave him his hotel voucher and food coupons and a notebook bearing the title *Delegate of the Seventeenth Communist Party Congress*. He had entered the familiar atmosphere of the Party congress, with its strict order and procedures, to which he found it agreeable to subject himself. He felt himself elevated to something more important, something higher than the life he had been living the day before, and it felt as if his everyday burdens had been lifted from his shoulders, a feeling akin to that of an old soldier rejoining his unit.

At the hotel they put him in a room with two others, and all he would have was a bed and a stool, which was fine because he needed nothing more. He knew he would see many old comrades among the delegates, some of whom he'd already met in the lobby. They stood gazing at each other with pleasure and excitement, and the feeling of stability and reliability, a sense of the rightness of their mission, was strengthened in Mark Alexandrovich. The Party and the Party members were mature, tempered by experience, aware of how their work should be done. The fact that they supported Stalin was no more than a sign of their strength.

These were honest people, selfless people, people whose sense of justice would never allow lawlessness. What had happened to Sasha was an absurdity. Maybe Sasha had already been let out?

He telephoned his sister and from the first sound of her voice he knew nothing had changed.

"Are you coming?" she asked.

He didn't want to go to the Arbat just then. It was late, he had no car, friends were waiting for him in the next room. But if he didn't go now, he didn't know when he'd be able to get away.

"If you're not going to sleep right away, I'll be around in an hour or so."

"Who can sleep?"

The visit to his sister upset him. She spoke to him now in a pitiful, servile way, scurrying about looking for documents, which she smoothed with trembling fingers, and then watched him with mixed feelings of hope and fear. At this moment he was not her brother but one of the powerful of this world, someone who might or might not help her son, someone who could or maybe could not save him.

Suffering had sharpened her senses: she realized that he didn't like this business, that he wanted to weigh all the circumstances, whereas the only thing that mattered to her was that Sasha was in prison.

An oppressive sense of numb hopelessness descended on him and he felt a pain in the back of his neck. He loved Sofya, he loved Sasha, but he couldn't make empty promises. He had experience, he was a Communist.

"I'll deal with this tomorrow. If Sasha is not guilty, they'll release him."

She stared at him in disbelief and alarm.

"Sasha guilty? Can you even think it?"

He was firm. She must be ready for anything. Otherwise if it fell, the blow would be all the harder to take.

"He has been accused of something. . . . I won't leave Moscow until I find out exactly what it is."

Mark Alexandrovich called on Budyagin. Because of him Budyagin was in a difficult position: he'd petitioned for someone who was now under arrest.

Budyagin was in a sour mood; he did not mention the congress once and seemed busy with ordinary, everyday work. Perhaps he was offended at not being elected to the congress? But he was a delegate with consultative status, which was quite normal for many Central Committee and Control Commission members. It was no mark of demotion, it was an old practice. Perhaps the congress was troublesome for him, maybe it meant more work, more problems?

Still . . . Budyagin exuded an air of gloom, of intensity, of unfriendliness.

"You know about my nephew?" Mark Alexandrovich asked.

"Yes."

"I never expected this to happen when I came to see you about him."

"Of course not." Budyagin spoke calmly, making it plain he held no grudge against Mark Alexandrovich.

"He's my nephew and I have the right to expect some information."

Budyagin said nothing. He sat at his desk with his chin propped on his palms and looked at Mark Alexandrovich.

"I'm going to try to talk to Yagoda or Berezin at the congress," Mark Alexandrovich said, ending the conversation that Budyagin apparently had no desire to continue.

But Budyagin said, "They know he's your nephew."

Mark Alexandrovich stared at him.

"What are you getting at?"

"They knew you'd intervene. They counted on it." Budyagin looked intently at Mark Alexandrovich and added, "Sasha was no accident."

He spoke in the same measured way he had when they were last together and he had mentioned that Chernyak was no longer the district Party secretary. Then he had been giving information, now he was opening a conversation.

Was something about to happen at the congress? But what? A group, a faction, was there lobbying going on, were votes being collected? Was there another split in the leadership? Whom do they want to put in *his* place? The old guard were already compromised. New people? But whom? It was doomed to failure, the Party wouldn't support them, Stalin was the embodiment of the Party line, the Party policy.

The conversation with Budyagin and its possible consequences were far too serious for there to remain the least hint of misunderstanding or ambiguity in his position.

"I don't think one should put too much meaning into Sasha's arrest. Pure coincidence is not a sound basis for remote conclusions," Mark Alexandrovich said firmly.

He gave Budyagin an open, straightforward, uncompromising look. Such a pity. A good Communist, a worker with great natural talent, a major figure. But he'd lived abroad for many years, he'd become cut off from the country, he didn't know what made the people tick anymore, or the Party, or himself, Mark Alexandrovich, for that matter. People such as Budyagin were being left behind, falling by the wayside; they'd lost their way in unfamiliar times, amid the sacrifices these times demanded.

"The Party is not blind, Ivan Grigoryevich. You know that as well as I do."

He looked at Budyagin. Their youth together, the Civil War and everything he held dear and would never forget, had forged a bond between them. But, at the moment, the most important thing in his life was his town on the hill, lit up by the flames of the blast furnaces and the open hearth. That was where the Revolution was now, and it would continue, even if Budyagin deserted it, as others had.

Nothing Budyagin thought mattered. Everything he'd said or might say was petty and unimportant, and Mark Alexandrovich paid little attention to his reply. Ivan Grigoryevich's voice even sounded muffled and distant and Mark almost missed the words he uttered, and it would not be until much, much later that the bitterness in them would finally sink in.

"We're putting Komsomols in prison," Budyagin said.

The lobbies and vestibules of the Great Kremlin Palace, the wide, upward-sweeping marble staircase, and the foyer outside the meeting hall were crowded with delegates. They were standing talking in groups, or wandering about calling to each other, or were huddled around the tables where congress papers were being handed out.

Mark Alexandrovich picked up his papers and exchanged waves and greetings with colleagues from the Donbass, where he used to work. Then bells rang and everyone moved into the hall.

The hall had been refurbished. A large visitors' gallery had been installed, and everything was new and fresh and smelling of wood and paint. As the papers reported the next day: "The hall now has a more severe appearance, but it is also majestically simple. The tastelessly opulent gilt has been removed, the columns, crests, and regalia have gone, the rubbish of several epochs has been scraped off the walls. The hall is now spacious and bright."

The delegation's seats were in the fourth and fifth rows centered on the podium. Standing, facing them, were Kaganovich, Ordzhonikidze, Voroshilov, Kossior, Postyshev, Mikoyan, Maxim Gorky. Kalinin was sitting on the steps, writing rapidly in a notebook, glancing up at the hall through his peasant's metal-framed spectacles.

The applause that greeted Molotov, when he took his place at the presidium, exploded with a different magnitude when Stalin appeared at his side. The noise grew and was amplified by the clatter of chairs and desks being pushed back, and by the stamping of feet as everyone rose. "Long live Comrade Stalin!" came the shout. Everyone shouted, "Hurrah! Long live the great general staff of Bolshevism! Hurrah! Long live the great leader of the world proletariat! Hurrah! Hurrah! Hurrah!"

The ovation to Stalin was repeated every time Molotov pronounced his name, and again, when Khrushchev proposed the names of the new presidium, and finally, loudest and longest of all, when the chairman announced, "Comrade Stalin has the floor."

Mark Alexandrovich stood up like the rest of them and clapped and cheered. Stalin, wearing a slightly lighter colored tunic than the others on the platform, took the podium, sorted out his papers, and waited patiently for the ovation to die down. His demeanor indicated he regarded the clapping and cheering as meant not for himself, but for what he personified, the great victories achieved by the people and the Party, and he himself even applauded this idea of Stalin. It was something he noted in his speech, when he commented ironically, "Of course, we have also sent greetings to Comrade Stalin, did you think we wouldn't?" This created an intimacy and understanding between himself and the people who were applauding him so ecstatically.

"If, at the Fifteenth Congress, we still had to prove the correctness of the Party line and to carry on a struggle against certain anti-Leninist groups, at this congress we don't have to prove anything, and there's nobody to overcome. Everyone can see, the Party line is victorious."

Mark Alexandrovich felt that these words vindicated his prediction: the congress was going to be peaceful, and there would be no complications because of Lominadze. Stalin himself wanted solidarity. The battle was over, and all the extreme measures associated with it should now disappear. And with them would go all those monotonous toasts.

His thoughts were confirmed when Stalin declined to make a closing speech: "Comrades! The congress debates have demonstrated the total unanimity of our Party leadership on all questions of policy, I think we may say. The main report, as you know, raised no objections. This shows an exceptional ideological and organizational solidarity in the ranks of the Party. One wonders, therefore, whether there is really any need for a closing speech. I think not. Allow me therefore to refrain from making one."

Lominadze spoke immediately after Stalin, and then several other former oppositionists — Rykov, Bukharin, Tomsky, Zinoviev, Kamenev, Pyatakov, Preobrazhensky, Radek. There was no repentance this time, as there had been at the Sixteenth Congress. Now, they gave systematic analyses of their mistakes and joined their voices to that of the Party. Nobody interrupted them or demanded that they bend more. Their speeches were not considered inadequate. Only once, during Rykov's speech, did someone call out impatiently, "Order!"

Pyatakov was approved as a Central Committee member, and Rykov, Bukharin, Tomsky, and Sokolnikov were approved as candidates.

And the list of candidates for the new Central Committee was virtually the same as the old one, with the normal changes as some people came forward into the leadership while others left.

Mark Alexandrovich saw his own name on the list — he'd been proposed as a nonvoting member of the Central Committee. He valued this recognition of his contribution to the second Five-Year Plan. The list contained the names of managers of other large sites and great enterprises. They were signs of the times, symbols of the country's industrialization.

Budyagin was not on the list.

And Sasha had been a frequent visitor at the Budyagins'. Ivan Grigoryevich had probably had wide-ranging conversations with him. Maybe it was he who had shown Sasha Lenin's letter. Maybe he'd involved him in more than mere conversation.

Mark Alexandrovich knew neither Yagoda nor Berezin, but in any case an approach to Yagoda, the chairman of security police, was out of proportion to the importance of Sasha's case. An approach to Berezin was more appropriate, as he dealt with just such cases. But someone always managed to detain him during the recesses, or else he simply couldn't find him in the crowds.

A convenient moment came on January 31 during the demonstration in honor of the congress.

It was the most grandiose of such occasions Mark Alexandrovich had ever witnessed, and he'd seen quite a few. For over two hours, at night in the freezing January weather, more than a million people passed through Red Square, which was illuminated by searchlights, giving the demonstration an especially imposing atmosphere.

"Stalin." It was the only word that appeared on the billboards and banners, that was shouted out and declaimed, and that hung in the frosty air. All eyes were turned to the Mausoleum, where he stood, wearing his army greatcoat and cap with its earflaps down. Everyone else on the Mausoleum was wearing a warm hat, but the earflaps were turned down only on Stalin's. He was cold, and this only made him all the more human and simple for the million people who saw him. They were moving about, but he had to stand on the Mausoleum motionless for several hours just to greet them.

Mark Alexandrovich stood with the other delegates in the stands by the Kremlin wall. He was used to worse frosts than this, but even his feet were frozen. He was wearing only shoes and should have put on his felt boots. He walked through the stands and stood a little way off from Berezin. As the procession began, he went up to him.

Berezin's bronzed Eskimo face had the stolid, enigmatic look of a man one approached only on matters of life and death. Berezin nodded respectfully — a congress delegate was a congress delegate — and when Mark Alexandrovich introduced himself he even gave him a good-natured greeting.

Mark Alexandrovich outlined Sasha's case briefly, mentioning the wall newspaper and Solts, and said that he vouched for his nephew, even though he admitted that out of youth and hot-headedness the boy might have said something he shouldn't have, when he was accused unjustly. If Sasha had been arrested for something else, he would like to be told what it was, as his nephew's case could not but concern him.

Berezin listened attentively, glancing occasionally at the procession passing through the square, and when his face was lit up by the searchlights it looked tired, puffy, and sagging. He listened without speaking, only asking for Sasha's name to be repeated, and, in reply to Mark Alexandrovich's request for information, smiled and said, "He's hidden in the deepest mists," which sounded as if he didn't know about the case, and that even if he did, this wasn't the time or place to discuss it. And even if it were the right place, he wouldn't be able to tell Mark Alexandrovich anything, such was the nature of his work.

"Ill look into it and do what I can. The investigation will be carried out thoroughly and fairly."

The reply seemed to Mark Alexandrovich a serious one, sincere and benevolent. He left Berezin feeling somewhat reassured.

He had also wanted to have a word with Solts, but Solts was ill and hadn't appeared at the congress. It didn't seem appropriate to visit the sick man at home, and in any case after his chat with Berezin it didn't seem necessary.

⚔ 16 ⚔

While the Muscovites were trooping across the searchlight illuminated Red Square and greeting Stalin as he stood on the Mausoleum, it was suppertime in the Butyrki prison.

Felt boots shuffled quietly along the corridors, locks rasped and clanked, spoons scraped in bowls, there was the sound of boiling water being poured into mugs.

The round flap over the spy-hole slid open and a point of light was visible momentarily, disappearing as the head of the guard got in the way. He inspected the cell, then slid a bolt and opened the hatch.

"Supper!"

Sasha held out his bowl, and the prisoner who was serving dumped a ladleful of buckwheat in, spooning it out of a large can that another prisoner was holding for him with both hands. He then poured boiling water from a kettle into Sasha's mug. The guard watched to make sure Sasha didn't try to pass anything to the other two, and that they didn't look at Sasha.

This corridor was for politicals. Like Sasha, the others approached their hatches, held out their bowls and mugs, got their buckwheat and hot water.

Who were these people? In three weeks, apart from the men who brought him his food, Sasha had caught a glimpse of only two other prisoners. One was the barber, a feeble old man with a low brow, a pointed beard, and the pitiless eyes of a murderer. He shaved with a blunt razor, so Sasha decided to grow a beard instead. The other one was a young criminal with a doughy womanish face. He cleaned the corridor and stood with his face to the wall when they brought Sasha past, as he was forbidden to look at another prisoner or to show his own face. Yet Sasha had felt his eyes on him, his sideways, curious, even cheerful look.

When Sasha was taken out for exercise or to the washroom, all the other cells seemed empty. But on the first night, after supper, there was an urgent tapping on the wall to his right — rapid, light taps, then short pauses and a scraping noise, as if something was being moved across the surface of the wall. Then silence. His neighbor was waiting for him to reply, but not knowing how to tap messages, he did nothing.

Next evening, after supper, the tapping came again.

To let his neighbor know he'd been heard, Sasha tapped a few times with his knuckles, and he was now doing this every evening. He could not make out what his neighbor was trying to convey, though he could detect a certain pattern in the tapping: a series of taps, a short pause, then another series, and finally the scraping noise. He was excited by this cautious communication that seemed to convey something of the prisoner's stubborn hope.

There was nobody tapping on his left wall, nor did anyone reply to his taps in that direction.

Sasha finished up his buckwheat, licked his spoon, and then used it to stir a little sugar into what was left of the tea in his mug. He drank the cold brew, sat for a while longer, then got up and began pacing the cell: six steps from wall to door, and — in defiance of the laws of geometry — six steps from corner to corner, the difference between the diagonal and the sides in this case being imperceptible. In one corner of his cell was the slop pail, in another was his bunk, a small table stood in the third, and the fourth was bare. A dim bulb burned in the ceiling behind a metal grill, and high up, close to the ceiling in a deep, steeply sloping recess, behind thick iron bars, was a tiny, dirty pane of glass.

His laceless boots dragged and clattered along the concrete floor. He kept his unbelted trousers from falling down by putting one of his shirt buttons into the top buttonhole in his fly. The trousers would twist and make it hard for him to walk. Yet there wasn't the same feeling of humiliation as when one's trousers fall down.

He wasn't summoned, interrogated, or accused of anything. He knew charges had to be brought within a certain period, but what that period was he had no idea and no way of finding out.

Sometimes he thought they'd forgotten about him and that he'd be incarcerated forever. He tried to keep his fear at bay by not thinking about it. He must just wait. Eventually he'd be called and interrogated, everything would be cleared up, and he'd be released.

He imagined himself going home. He'd ring the doorbell. "Who's there?" No, that would be too unexpected. He'd telephone first and say, "Sasha's coming home soon." Then he'd just show up. "Mama, it's me!"

He found the thought of her suffering unbearable. Maybe she didn't even know where he was and was running from one prison to another, waiting in endless lines, small and frightened.

Time heals everything, they say, but he knew she'd never get over the shock of his imprisonment. It made him want to bang on the walls of his cell, to hammer and shake the iron door, to shout and scream and fight.

The lock rasped and the door was opened.

"Slopping out!"

Sasha threw his towel around his neck, picked up his slop pail, and went down the corridor ahead of the guard.

The stench of chlorine was even stronger in the washroom than it was in the cell. He emptied his pail and swilled it out with chlorine solution. It stank, even though he hardly ever used it. Then he went back to his cell; the iron door clanged behind him and wouldn't be opened again until the next morning.

The stars in the dim glass of his window hadn't yet faded when he heard movement in the corridor again and his cell door rattled as bolts elsewhere were drawn. "Slopping out!"

Another prison day was beginning. The spy-hole slid open. "Breakfast!"

Hanging from the neck of the server was a large plywood tray with hunks of black bread, lumps of sugar, tea and salt, packs of Boxing cigarettes, cut in half, matches, and strips of phosphorus torn from matchboxes. To each prisoner they doled out eight cigarettes a day, but a pack contained twenty-five. Whoever was third down the line got nine, and he also got the remains of the pack itself, or rather a piece of the half-pack — but a piece of paper, however you looked at it. It was Sasha's luck today to get the piece of paper, and maybe he'd get the chance to scribble a note on it. The trouble was, he couldn't think where to hide it, and stuck it behind the radiator.

The bread they doled out was heavy and badly baked, with the crust peeling off. But in the mornings it still smelled like the real thing, fresh, sourdough bread. It reminded him of the time his mother had had bread baked with flour his father had been given at work as his half-yearly ration instead of bread. The bread they'd got back from the bakery had weighed more than the flour, a mysterious surplus that had puzzled him for a long time. He had helped his mother bring it home on a sled, and the sensations of that cold winter, the crunching of the iron runners on the crisp snow, the warm smell of the mounds of freshly baked bread, and his mother's joy — they would dry the bread and live on it through the winter — all came back to him now, as he sat drinking his tea and dunking his bread. These memories of childhood made his heart ache; they were too human for prison and the dark cell he'd been locked up in for reasons he couldn't fathom.

The lock rasped, the door opened. It was the escort in his sheepskin, carrying a rifle.

"Exercise!"

He had to leave the cell, turn left, go to the end of the corridor, and wait while the escort opened the door into the little yard. Then, by the same route, with the same opening and closing of doors, go back to the cell. The whole operation, including the exercise, took twenty minutes.

The little square yard was enclosed on two sides by the walls of the prison building itself, there was a tall stone wall along the third side, and the fourth was bounded by a round brick tower. He walked in a circle along a path trodden in the snow. There were paths trodden down diagonally across the yard as well, where prisoners who didn't want to follow the circle had preferred to go from corner to corner.

The sentry stood guard in a prison doorway, leaning on the doorpost with his rifle in his hand, sometimes smoking, sometimes watching Sasha with half-closed eyes.

The snow crunched underfoot. The blue sky and pale blue frosty stars, the distant hum of the busy streets, and the smell of smoke and burning coal had a powerful effect on Sasha. The bulbs burning in the other cell windows were proof that he was not alone. After the stench of the cell, he felt drunk from the fresh air. Life goes on, even in prison. A man is still alive as long as he breathes and hopes, and at the age of twenty-two, life is all hope.

The escort straightened up, tapped his rifle, and opened the inner door.

"This way!"

Sasha completed the circle and left the yard. They went up staircases, keys rasped again, the cell door closed behind him again, again there were the bare walls, the bunk, the table, the slop pail, the spy-hole in the door. But the sensation of the bracing frosty air and the distant sound of the street stayed with him for a long time, and he stood staring up at the tiny patch of winter sky in his window, the blue, untroubled sky that had only minutes earlier been right above him.

His one other joy was the shower.

He was taken to it at night, once a week. The door would open and the escort would wake him up with the question: "Is it long since you washed?"

"Yes, a long time."

"Get going!"

He'd leap out of his bunk and dress rapidly, grab a towel, and leave the cell. In the changing room, the escort would give him a tiny bar of gray soap and he would enter the cubicle. The water flowed sometimes hot, sometimes cold, and there was no means of controlling it. Sasha would stand under the shower and sing with the sheer joy of it. He thought the sound of the running water would drown his voice and that the escort, sitting outside in the changing room on the windowsill, wouldn't hear him. The little Red Army man had a cheerful and obliging look, and he didn't rush Sasha. He sat patiently. After all, he had to wait for someone, and if it wasn't Sasha it would be someone else. Sasha would take his time soaping himself until the soap became a tiny, soft scrap, and he would go on standing under the shower, turning to let the water run onto his back, his belly, his legs, and singing all the time.

Returning to the changing room, he would rub himself down while the escort watched him with curiosity, perhaps wondering why this nice-looking, apparently educated young man was being held here, or perhaps he was admiring Sasha's muscular physique.

One night the escort woke him with his usual question: "Is it long since you washed?"

Sasha had showered the previous night; the escort must be mixing things up.

"Yes, a long time."

"Get going!"

As he was coming out of the cubicle, toweling himself, he said, "It'd be nice more often. . . ."

The little escort said nothing, but he came by the next night, and Sasha began to take a shower every night. Sometimes he didn't feel like getting up and wanted to sleep, but he knew that if he refused, the escort might not come the next night.

Why was he being indulged like this? Maybe others had refused, and the escort was bored with nothing to do at night, or maybe he just didn't like to think of the hot water going to waste? Maybe he was well disposed toward Sasha because Sasha seemed to appreciate him, appreciated the shower he was in charge of?

Sasha was woken by the scraping of the lock. An escort, one he hadn't seen before, strode into the cell with a great bunch of keys hanging from his belt. The corridor guard stood at attention in the doorway.

"Name?"

"Pankratov."

"Get dressed."

Sasha got off his bunk. Where was he going? Was he being freed? Why at night? What time was it, anyway?

He was about to put on his coat.

"You won't need that."

The escort nodded to the right and followed him down the corridor. The keys clanked on his belt.

They walked a long way through innumerable short corridors,

up and down staircases enclosed in metal cages, and each time before unlocking a door the escort knocked on it with a key, and only when he had received a similar signal from the other side in response would he unlock the door.

Sasha went ahead of the escort and tried to work out which part of the prison they were in. They had gone up and down from floor to floor and he reckoned they were now on the first floor.

The doors here — and there were many — were no longer iron, but were ordinary wood ones, without ventilation hatches or spy-holes. The escort knocked on one of them.

"Come in!"

A light dazzled Sasha as he entered. A man seated at a table was directing a lamp at his face, and Sasha stood, blinded by the narrow beam, not knowing what to do or where to go.

The lamp was deflected downward, illuminating the table and the man.

"Sit down!"

Sasha sat down. The investigator turned out to be a puny, fair-haired young man in large horn-rimmed spectacles, with three bars on the collar of his tunic. He was a type Sasha knew well, and liked. A rural Komsomol organizer, perhaps a village librarian or schoolteacher, if one could imagine him out of uniform. He began filling out a form that lay in front of him on the table. Name? First name? Father's name? Date of birth? Place of birth? Address?

"Sign."

Sasha signed. The investigator's name appeared on the form — Dyakov.

Dyakov laid the pen next to the inkwell and raised his eyes to look at Sasha.

"Why are you here?"

Sasha hadn't expected the question.

"I thought you were going to tell me that."

Dyakov pushed back in his chair in an impatient, irritated gesture.

"Save your wit! And don't forget where you are! *I* ask the questions here and *you* give the answers. Now, I asked you, why were you arrested?"

He said it as if someone else had arrested Sasha and it was his job to find out why. And since Sasha obviously knew why he'd been arrested, he shouldn't be obstinate and waste time — the sooner they got on with it, the better. The room was in total gloom, except for the pool of light thrown onto the table by the desk lamp. Dyakov's face vanished when he leaned back in his chair, and his voice came out of the darkness.

"I suppose it's because of the affair at the institute," Sasha said.

"What affair?" Dyakov sounded tired and uninterested, as if he already knew all about it and had known for a long time that it had nothing to do with Sasha's being arrested. People under interrogation always start off with such little tricks and you had to listen to them, however monotonous, pointless, and boring.

Was this a ploy? Or did the investigator really know nothing about it?

Sasha felt unprepared. He was gripped by a stifling, sickening feeling, such as he'd felt as a child when he had climbed up the fire escape to the roof and the top rungs had pulled away from the wall. The end of the ladder had swayed and he had had to wait for the right moment for it to get close enough to the roof so that he could jump the gap. Looking down from the eighth floor, he'd seen the kids below in the depths of the courtyard craning their necks up at him, watching and waiting. He'd been struck with terror and felt he wouldn't be able to jump that far, that he wouldn't take his feet off the ladder in time and would go crashing down to the asphalt below.

Sitting in front of the investigator now, he felt the same sensation of playing a deadly, fatal game, the same sinking feeling of doom. His case was a trivial nonsense, but decked out with all the trappings of a political crime, with the arrest, prison, and interrogation, it had become terrifying. The man sitting opposite him was his comrade, another Communist, but to him Sasha was an enemy.

Yet Sasha knew he must say what he had prepared himself to say. In the same words he had rehearsed over and over to himself in the cell, he now went over the whole story of his conflict with Azizyan, the wall newspaper, Solts.

"But you just said the Central Control Commission reinstated you."

"Yes, they did reinstate me."

"So, that's not why you were arrested. You must have been arrested for something else. What was it?"

"There is nothing else."

"Think about it, Pankratov. You don't imagine you were arrested because of some argument with a teacher of accounting or an unsuccessful issue of a student newspaper. Do you think we're here to pop off sparrows with an air gun? A strange idea you've got of the Cheka!"

"What are the charges against me?"

"You want to be charged formally? You think it'll be better for you?"

"I want to know why I was arrested."

"But we want you to tell us that yourself. We're meeting you halfway, we're giving you a chance to present yourself to the Party as honest and frank."

"You tell me what you suspect me of doing, and I'll give you an answer."

"With whom have you had counterrevolutionary conversations?"

"Me? I've never had a counterrevolutionary conversation with anyone. I couldn't."

"Then who has had any with you?"

"Nobody has had any with me."

"Do you stand by that?"

"Yes, I do."

Dyakov frowned and turned over some of the papers on the table.

"Well, that's a great pity. We were hoping for something better from you. You obviously don't intend to be honest and sincere. It won't make your situation any easier."

"Apart from the affair at the institute, I am not aware of having done anything."

"So, you were arrested for nothing, for no reason? We put innocent people in prison, do we? You even carry on counterrevolutionary propaganda in here! But we're not the tsarist police, we're not the old Third Section, and we're not just a punitive organization. We are an armed detachment of the Party. And you, Pankratov, you're a double-dealer, that's what you are!"

"How dare you call me that!"

Dyakov smashed his fist down on the table. "I'm going to show you what I dare to do and what I don't! Where do you think you are — in a rest home? We have other places for people like you. Double-dealer! You've never had kulaks shooting at you with sawed-off shotguns. You've spent your whole life on the back of the working class, and even now you're living off the state, being educated and getting your stipend from the state, and still you are deceiving the state!"

He sat silent and frowning for a while, then said, in a dissatisfied tone of voice, as if he were carrying out an unnecessary and pointless duty, "Oh, well, let's get the rubbish you've spouted down on paper. Sit down!"

He began to write, occasionally putting short questions to Sasha about when and with whom he had put out the newspaper, when the difference with the accounting lecturer had occurred and what it had been about, when and where he had been expelled, and what charges had been brought on that occasion.

When he'd finished, he pushed the paper toward Sasha.

"Read it and sign."

He leaned back in his chair and Sasha felt his steady gaze on him. Dyakov was watching, using this moment to take a good look at him.

Everything had been written down correctly, yet it sounded one-sided, somehow. They had published a holiday edition of the wall newspaper, they'd inserted some rhymes that had vulgarized shock-work, so-and-so had been involved, he'd been expelled by the Party cell and the district committee.... Naturally, it had been written this way according to formula, just to get the interrogation down on paper, and the reason for his arrest would appear elsewhere.

Nevertheless, he said, "It doesn't say here that I was reinstated by the Central Control Commission."

Dyakov frowned and took back the paper.

"What did they say in the order about reinstatement?"

"They didn't get it quite right —"

Dyakov interrupted him.

"I didn't ask you how they *ought* to have written the order, just *what* they'd written."

"'In view of student Pankratov's admission of his errors ...'"

Dyakov picked up his pen and wrote at the bottom of his report, "I was later reinstated at the institute, having admitted my errors."

He pushed the paper over to Sasha once more.

Sasha signed. Dyakov took the paper and pushed it to one side. "I advise you to think seriously, Pankratov. We don't want to lose you for the cause. That's the only reason we are taking trouble over you. We're being merciful with you, you must understand that. And you ought to appreciate it. Dig into your memory, dig deep!"

He got up and opened the door, nodding to the escort.

"Take him away!"

Sasha went back to his cell and the bolt slid shut behind him. The winter stars were glimmering in the dim window. Was it night or morning?

He heard tapping on the wall. His neighbor obviously wanted to know where he'd been. He gave his usual three taps in reply and lay down on his bunk without undressing.

What did Dyakov want from him? What was he supposed to confess? "With whom have you had counterrevolutionary conversations?" What conversations? He couldn't figure it out. He'd been sure they'd arrested him because of what happened at the institute. The fact that this wasn't so stunned him; everything now was confused, upside down. He had been hoping for understanding, for trust. What he got was the opposite. If the institute wasn't the reason for his arrest, that meant there was another one, and that the prosecutor had found it convincing. But who could have accused him of counterrevolution? He had no differences with the Party. Sure, he didn't like the way toadies and time-servers sang Stalin's praises, but he'd never spoken to anyone about this, and in any case it wasn't about Stalin himself. He had mentioned this only to Mark, but Mark wouldn't have told anyone else about their conversation.

Maybe Mark had been arrested? During the search the man in charge had seized on his photograph, turning it over and inspecting it from all angles. Was Dyakov trying to extract evidence against Mark? Was he counting on Sasha to provide it?

What about Budyagin? Maybe he was a friend of Eismont or Smirnov — and the Smirnovs also lived in Fifth House. Budyagin had been summoned back from abroad just after the disastrous Smirnov-Eismont affair. And they knew that Budyagin had phoned Glinskaya, that Sasha frequented the Budyagins' home. So they were trying to get information against Budyagin.

Bullshit! He was twisting everything inside out. They wouldn't have arrested him just for being someone's nephew, or because he knew someone who knew someone who had got in trouble. But they were holding him here for something. This investigator wasn't fooling around.

Day after day, Sasha went over the last few months of his life. Had he blurted out something in the heat of the moment? He hadn't even talked to anyone about what had happened at the institute. Only the others in his group knew — Nina, Lena, Vadim, Max, Yuri . . .

Yuri Sharok! That fight they'd had at New Year's . . . But even Yuri wasn't capable of something this low. What about the others in the group?

Kovalyov? No, the institute wasn't involved in this. So, what was it?

During the day a prison official, with two bars on his collar, appeared in the cell.

Sasha stood up mechanically, as he was used to doing at home. It was a gesture he wouldn't forgive himself for later.

"Name?"

"Pankratov."

"What is your complaint?"

"I'm not getting any mail."

"Tell your investigator."

"What about newspapers or books?"

"Ask the investigator."

And with that he left. The sentry locked the cell door.

One learns the ways of prison only by being there. The individual prisoner gradually acquires all those unwritten rules that previous generations of prisoners have worked out.

The prison official's visit made clear to Sasha that he had been moved into a new category: the investigation of his case had begun. The official wasn't interested in his requests. He made Sasha understand that not only his fate but also his conditions here depended on the investigator.

From that day Sasha's life, while remaining outwardly the same, in fact changed sharply.

Before, he'd looked forward to the interrogation with impatience and expectancy, but now he did so with secret terror. He was terrified that the investigator would suddenly spring something unknown and unexpected on him, something he hadn't prepared for and might not be able to explain, and that he might only widen farther the chasm of distrust and suspicion that lay between them.

17

Old Sharok and his wife didn't like the Pankratovs. They didn't like the father, the engineer, or the "overeducated" mother, and they certainly didn't like the uncle who was "one of *them,*" one of the *bosses.* While Sasha's mother was apt to sit in the yard talking with the "intellectuals," Mrs. Sharok would more likely be found with the elevator women or the janitors. They decided that Sasha's arrest was a case of the "comrades" scrapping among themselves: "Well, let's hope they tear each other's throats out."

But Yuri Sharok could not remain unaffected by Sasha's arrest. They were, after all, in the same group.

And yet, what made Yuri a member of the group? There was no real friendship between them, they only tolerated him — Nina the hysteric, Maxim the blockhead, Vadim the bigmouth. They'd be crying over Sasha now, but not him.

Lena. She was a nice girl, and good-looking, but what did he have in common with her? She wouldn't make much of a wife. Did she even know how to make a cup of coffee? When she tried to please him, she only irritated him with her clumsiness. Besides, they were the same age. His own father at sixty was still a handsome man. But at forty, Lena would be fat, with a mustache, just like her Armenian mother.

Stalin wasn't pleased with Budyagin, Lena had told Yuri that herself. He knew all too well what "Stalin isn't pleased" meant and what it would lead to. The luxury apartment in the House of Soviets was just a facade. Budyagin had given him a lecture on Soviet justice, but how much of it did he understand himself? He was naïve when it came to the Party, he was out of touch. There was a force that was bringing stronger men than Budyagin under control. How would he look to his father if Budyagin went under? "So much for your commissar's daughter!"

That's it! Yuri had had enough! There were plenty of pretty girls in Moscow. There was Vika Marasevich, Vadim's sister, she was there for the asking. Or Varya Ivanova, she was delicious.

He hadn't telephoned Lena for a week. Let her call. She'd never do it again after the way he was going to talk to her.

But when she did call and he heard her deep and disturbing voice saying, "Yuri, what's happened to you?" he became confused and mumbled that he'd been busy — working for his diploma, running around about his job, getting home at midnight, and that the only pay phone at the institute was out of order.

She cupped the mouthpiece with her hand.

"I miss you."

"I'll phone you as soon as I'm free. Later this week, maybe."

He didn't phone her that week, or the next. He had no intention of calling her. He wasn't going to give her any explanations!

But she called him herself.

"Yuri, I have to see you."

"I told you I'd call you as soon as I'm free."

"I must see you."

"Okay, nine o'clock on the Arbat outside the Art Theater." They walked around Arbat Square and along Nikita Boulevard. There was a harsh frost. Lena was wearing a fur coat, red gloves, and a round fur hat over a wool scarf that covered her ears. Her high boots hugged her full, straight calves, a sight that always excited him. And she was wearing that familiar perfume. Was this going to be their last time together? It was hardly the weather for a stroll.

"It's too awful about Sasha!" she said.

He shrugged his shoulders. "So, they arrested him. . . ."

"Aren't you sorry for him?"

"It's not a question of being sorry. He despises everyone. I don't trust him, no, I don't trust him."

"Not trust Sasha?"

"When I was trying to get into the Komsomol, Sasha said, 'I

don't trust Sharok.' Nobody minded what he said then, but when I say I don't trust him now, it annoys you."

She was flustered and his anger upset her.

"The others think well of you, believe me."

"They're a condescending lot, just like you."

She stared at him in surprise. He was trying to start a quarrel. He hadn't phoned her for two weeks, and now she was afraid to tell him why she had wanted to see him.

They walked in silence as far as the Nikita Gates.

"Shall we turn around?"

"Let's go as far as Pushkin's monument. Tell me how things are with you."

He shrugged again, he had nothing to tell, he was bored.

"What about the job?"

"Nothing's happening."

Pushkin loomed in the square, snow-covered.

"Let's sit. I'm tired," she said.

Scowling, he swept the snow off the bench for her. He remained standing, and he would go on standing like that, looking at the Passion Monastery. . . . He didn't so much hear as feel that she had drawn a deep breath.

"Yuri, I'm pregnant."

"Are you sure?"

"Yes."

"Maybe you're just late?"

"It's more than two weeks. . . ." She sounded uncertain.

The two weeks he hadn't seen her. How could it have happened? He'd been so careful. Surely she had some foreign pills or tablets for this sort of thing?

"Have you tried anything?"

"I wanted to talk to you first."

"I'm not a doctor." Sullenly, as if Lena had got herself pregnant just to annoy him, he added, "This is not the way I want to become part of your family."

She was startled. "What do you mean by that?"

"We have to wait." He took her hand and felt the patch of warm flesh between her hand and her glove. If only she agrees, if only she doesn't become stubborn. "Look, there's the institute and the job. Nothing's settled yet, it's all vague. . . . And there's Sasha. We're all involved with him, no matter what. Everything's become mixed up and complicated, we don't want to make things worse. It's not a good moment. I know it's a rotten operation, but it only takes a few minutes. Let's be patient, let's wait, we'll have children one day. And there's my parents. They're old-fashioned . . . first one son a convict, and now an illegitimate baby. I know it's small-minded, but I can't stand people gossiping, it outrages me, you must understand that."

"I do understand," Lena murmured sadly.

"Let's go before you freeze to death."

He got up and held out his hand to her, unable to resist the temptation to glance quickly down at her figure, though he knew that nothing would show yet. Even so, he thought she had filled out a bit and was taking her time getting up from the bench. He was seized with terror at the thought of what might have happened. He could have become a father without even realizing it. And that would have been for life.

She smiled shyly. "It's still too early to notice anything."

It was a night they would never forget. She agreed to have an abortion for his sake; he was more precious to her than anything else in the world. Her compliance mellowed him, made him proud. He in turn was tender with her and tried to win her over, to tie her to him, to make her completely submissive. Everything in life repeats itself and will go on repeating itself a million times over, she wasn't the first and wouldn't be the last, it was a normal female thing. His mother had had several abortions. Pregnant village girls were known to jump off the top of a gate and come to no harm. They survived. One mustn't complicate one's life. In the summer they'd go to Sochi. It was supposed to be a first-class resort, and at last he'd get a chance to see the sea — after all, what had he seen besides Moscow? Lena had been lucky, she'd seen the world, but what about him?

He stifled her deepest feelings; his arguments seemed to her full of simple, sound common sense. Of course she mustn't burden him with children right now, or with worries that would only push him away from her, instead of binding him to her. She would never stand in his way, he must never be able to blame her for anything. As for her being pregnant, who else should she tell but him? He mustn't even think about it, he mustn't worry.

What had happened brought them closer together. He'd never been so affectionate and sincere, or so vulnerable. For the first time, she saw him worried and scared, and she was overcome with feelings for him. She fell even more in love with him.

He dozed in the morning, his hand over her breast, and she was careful not to wake him. Normally, he didn't stop her from going, and sometimes, with indifference, would send her away during the night. Now he didn't want her to go. But at last, with his cheek pressed against hers, he accompanied her to the door, not on tiptoe, as usual, but openly, talking loudly and smiling, unconcerned by the squeaking of the door or the noise of the lock.

And the doorman didn't even seem to look at them suspiciously but took his ruble, not as if he was expecting it, but with a "Thank you kindly." Her high heels clicked along the Arbat as she walked home quietly and with assurance along *his* street, *her* street.

It was only when she reached Arbat Square that it dawned on her that she had walked downstairs right past Sasha's apartment. Why did she think of this just now? Had being in love put everything else out of her head? And there was Sofya Alexandrovna, probably lying awake at night, staring at the ceiling and wondering how Sasha was.

Even a brief stay in the hospital couldn't be easily concealed. The Budyagins would get the truth out of her in no time — there's not much you can hide from a mother; mothers know about such things. Lena wasn't any good at making excuses, and it would be beneath her dignity to try. But suppose they heard it from someone else? They might try to persuade her to have the child: "We'll manage even without your Sharok."

What was going on inside her head?

He called her at work and spoke tenderly, but his voice betrayed his fatigue: he was busy, he had worries, she shouldn't add to his burdens with her troubles.

The simple, straightforward girls of the Arbat had never given him problems like this: they knew how to look after themselves. Whether they did it with mustard or potassium permanganate or quinine, it wasn't any business of his. But this spoiled little daddy's girl didn't know anything, she couldn't do anything for herself, dammit, she was just a novelty from abroad! He had to get her out of his hair now, or he never would. If only she'd have a miscarriage. People were falling down on the icy sidewalks all the time, especially nearsighted, clumsy ones like her. . . .

Frank discussion was not a common occurrence in the Sharok household, but Yuri decided he had to talk with his mother. She knew all kinds of secret old wives' remedies the peasants used, or at any rate she knew people she could turn to for help. He watched her exchanging secrets and whispering with the other old women in the yard and he guessed from the expression on her face that they were talking about his affair.

Now her face was blotched, and she was fixing him with a stare. So, the whore's got herself pregnant. What was she thinking of, the slut! It just shows, the educated ones are worse than ordinary girls. The bitch was trying to hook a husband. She should have thought about what she was doing, she's not a kid, she's of age.

Only that day she had been boasting that her Yuri was going to marry a commissar's daughter and live in the Kremlin, and now she was oozing malice. It was all because of *them,* because of the *comrades,* the bosses and managers. They wouldn't let Yuri's parents so much as cross their threshold, and they wouldn't even let Yuri in, either. They'd tell Lena she could take her brat and live with her husband — after all, he had his own room. He had a room, but they had three rooms. And there was an old woman at the husband's, they'd say, there's a ready-made nanny for you. Well, they got the wrong one there, all right, I can tell you, I'm not nannying any of their brood. She's not even Russian! Just look at her nose! A kike, if I ever saw one! And now she wants money for an abortion. A race of vipers!

"Shut up!" Yuri yelled. "Just tell me what to do!"

She pursed her lips and asked in a businesslike way, "What month is she?"

"It's been hardly any time," he lied, afraid that if he said how long it had been she would refuse to help.

"She should make a mustard bath and soak her feet. And the hotter the better, as hot as she can take, hotter, even. I don't suppose *they've* got something as common as a bucket."

"They'll find one."

He didn't say he knew Lena wouldn't be able to do it at her own home. It would have to be here, at his place.

He couldn't find any mustard on the Arbat, but managed to buy some on Usachev Street and tucked it away in his briefcase. His mother wouldn't dare look in there, since she'd be afraid of damaging the complicated lock. He looked into the kitchen to check on the bucket and found there were two.

That evening he and Lena went to the Revolution Theater to see *The Man with the Briefcase* by Faiko. Yuri liked Granatov. He felt an affinity with the fatal course of events in Granatov's life.

During the intermission, he surveyed the crowd in the foyer and inhaled the scent and powder. For him, going to the theater was like taking a holiday. He could never understand Sasha Pankratov or Nina, who would go to the theater in between their other activities, almost without stopping, or Vadim Marasevich, who would take a play apart as if he were dissecting a frog.

He said, "I've got some good news for you. There's this man in the department, Kolya Sizov, his father's a famous doctor. Have you heard of him?"

"Sizov? No, I don't think so."

"He's professor of gynecology at the medical school."

She winced when she realized what he was talking about. But surely it wasn't going to happen so soon?

He went on mercilessly. "There's a safe method. A mustard bath for the feet, you know, just like people do for a cold."

She relaxed slightly. "Will it help?"

"So they say, yes."

His assertiveness alarmed her.

"Maybe I should go to a doctor."

He persisted. "It's not an abortion, you won't have any pain, you'll just have to stand the hot water. What have we got to lose? You haven't changed your mind, have you?"

"No, I haven't changed my mind," she said softly, "but how can I do it at home? They'll see ..."

Then, as if he'd just thought of it, he said, "We'll do it at my place. My father always does it for a cold, so there'll be mustard there."

18

"Hot?" Yuri asked.

"It's all right.... It's even rather pleasant."

Lena was sitting on the bed with her feet in a bucket full of a brown solution, twisting her face away from the mustard fumes, which stung her eyes.

Her large feet would hardly go into the bucket. She had pulled up her slip and uncovered her round white knees, which she kept pressed close together. Leaning forward, with her hands over her stomach, her fallen shoulder straps baring her plump shoulders, and her breasts covered by pale blue lace, she swished her feet in the water and tried to smile.

Yuri added some more boiling water, holding the spout of the kettle next to the side of the bucket, so as not to pour it onto her legs.

She hunched her shoulders and swished her feet around more vigorously.

"It's hot...."

"Try to take it, it'll cool down quickly."

Holding the kettle with one hand, he tested the water in the bucket with the other. It didn't seem hot enough, so he added more.

"Ow!" Her face was contorted, she was moaning with her eyes tightly shut, and she was breathing heavily.

"Take it easy, take it easy, it'll soon be over, just give it another minute, Lena...."

Her fingers clutched at her slip and then let go as she leaned back until her head touched the wall.

"Any minute now, any minute, Lena, hang on...."

There were beads of sweat on her upper lip and forehead.

He felt the water and poured some more.

She moaned and pulled her feet out of the bucket, and he saw that her calves were crimson red and swollen. The room was saturated by the stench of mustard.

"Yuri, I can't take any more," she pleaded. "Let me take my feet out, just for a minute, only a minute. . . ."

"It'll all be over in a little while, just a little while longer, try to hang on. . . ."

"My feet have gone numb, I can't feel them, they don't belong to me. . . ." She lay contorted on the bed, her teeth clenched and bared. "I can't breathe. . . ."

He leaned over her prostrate body, undid her shoulder straps and brassiere, and stroked her knees.

"There, there, take it easy."

And carefully he poured more hot water into the bucket. She moaned softly, barely moving her feet now, her large, white, lifeless, naked body scarcely covered by the crumpled blue slip.

He went into the kitchen and fetched a second kettle from the stove. The handle rattled noisily, threatening to wake up the family. Damn bucket had been patched and repatched. They were too stingy to throw out their old junk!

He sensed that someone had come in and he looked over his shoulder in alarm to see his mother standing at the kitchen door.

They looked at each other in silence, which she broke, saying, "Don't boil her feet."

He said nothing, but picked up the bucket and returned to his room, closing the door firmly behind him. He heard his mother switch off the light in the kitchen.

Lena's head was on the pillow, her legs were dangling, her calves were blazing crimson.

"Lena, are you sleeping?"

Her eyelids were trembling and she was breathing very quietly, hardly perceptibly. Large drops of sweat shone on her forehead, eyebrows, upper lip, and chin. He wiped her face carefully with a towel.

"Lena!"

"I feel sick," she whispered without opening her eyes.

He lifted her head and put a mug to her lips. Her teeth chattered lightly on the rim as she made an effort to swallow. She took a long drink of water and fell back exhausted on the pillow.

Covering her with a blanket, he poured more hot water into the bucket, but missed and poured some on her legs.

"Ow ..." she moaned, throwing off the blanket, her face twisted with pain.

"That's all now, that's the last."

She was trembling as if she had a chill, her shoulders hunched and her clenched hands shaking.

He covered her with the blanket again.

"That's it."

She began to sob, softly and hopelessly.

"It's all right, I'm not going to do any more."

He looked at the clock. It was a quarter to two. It had taken forty minutes. He'd wait another five.

She'd stopped weeping and was lying with her head buried in the pillow as if she were dead. He bent over her and felt her forehead. It was cold. He listened. She was breathing.

Carefully he lifted her feet out of the bucket. They looked as if they really were boiled. She'd be all right. . . . The room still reeked of the sharp smell of mustard. He laid her legs on the bed and covered them with the blanket, then he took the bucket out to the kitchen, emptied it, washed the mustard off the sink, wiped everything clean, put the bucket in its place, and went back to his room.

She was asleep. He went to the window and drew the blind. The staircase lights in the neighboring building gleamed dimly, the bulbs burning forlornly in their wire cages. It had to work. What a spoiled brat! Anyone else wouldn't have so much as squeaked. It's not as if you can die from a little hot water. She can put some cream on her feet.

He undressed, put out the light, and got into bed next to her, carefully moving her legs away and pulling an edge of the blanket over himself. He felt the heat radiating from her feverish body. She was sprawling, motionless, almost dead, she seemed like another woman. She exuded a sharp, exciting scent. . . .

He took her as she lay there, sprawling, lifeless, unresponsive, and therefore all the more irresistible. The act was exciting in a way he had never experienced — it was something animal, bestial. He was trying to evoke a shock that would destroy the living being inside her, that would tear out the tiny embryo that had all but destroyed his life. And when she moaned, he thought at last the other life that had been forming inside her was finally killed.

The next morning she couldn't put her stockings on.
"My feet hurt so."
Then she couldn't get into her boots.
He found her some large felt boots with openwork uppers.
"That's better," she said, walking cautiously and awkwardly across the room. She at once looked much shorter and stockier, like a peasant woman with a pale puffy face and dark rings under her suffering eyes.
She sat down suddenly on the bed. "My head's spinning."
He decided he'd better accompany her home; she might fall down in the street. He ought to give her a cup of hot tea, but he could hear his mother already busy in the kitchen, and he wasn't going in there with her.
They met no one as they went out through the yard. They crossed to the other side of the Arbat, as there were people from the apartment house lining up at the bakery. Lena walked slowly, holding on to him — she had found a moment to hold his hand. This was going to be their final walk together, so she had better make it last. As long as she didn't fall, as long as she could hang on until they reached her home. She didn't work today, so she could sleep it off.
She walked across her own yard alone, glancing around the lobby and smiling at Yuri.
He wanted to call her during the day to find out how things were, but he didn't, knowing that would give away his concern and emphasize the danger of what they had done. He'd phone her the next day at work. If she was there it would mean she was all right, and if it had worked she'd tell him.
She was at work. Softly, but clearly, with her hand cupping the mouthpiece, she said, "Everything's all right."
He heard the pleasure in her voice at telling him something she knew would make him happy.

"Congratulations! Well done! A big kiss! I'll call you again later." He hung up.

He wasn't going to call her anymore. That was it, he'd got rid of her!

When he got home from the institute that evening, his mother said, "Nina Ivanova telephoned."

"What does she want?"

"For you to call her."

She would only whine about Sasha and go on and on. To hell with them!

Nina called him again.

"You know about Lena ... ?"

His heart stopped.

"What?"

"She's had a hemorrhage."

"My God! We were talking on the phone only today. She was at work." He added: "Of course, it's been a while since we saw each other."

"They had to take her to the hospital from work."

"Which one is she in?"

She gave him the name of a hospital in the Marinaya district.

After a moment's hesitation, he said firmly, "What happened to her?"

"I don't know."

"Who told you she's in the hospital?"

"Her mother. Lena's in a very bad way."

"Thanks for letting me know. I'll go and see her."

He went back into his room, closing the door after him, and sat down at his desk. Jesus! What a mess. He knew the law — he was a lawyer, after all. An illegal abortionist, that's what he was! "Any such act ... leading to the death of the woman so aborted ..." What an idiot he'd been! What had induced him to do it here, in his own home? She could have managed it at her place, no one would have seen anything, she had her own room. He had been a fool! A fool!

She wouldn't give him away, if she survived. And if she died, he'd deny everything. There was no evidence. Yes, he'd known she was pregnant and that she hadn't wanted the baby, and that she was doing something about it. But he'd assumed she had some kind of foreign drug, and he had no idea what she had actually done to herself. She'd looked unwell the other evening and he'd taken her home, then he'd called her at work a few days later, which was a perfectly natural thing to do, given their friendship.

Anyway, how could a mustard bath be equated with an abortion? Why should the lawmakers use that particular word — "abortion"? Is it a word that lends itself to a wide interpretation? "Artificial termination of a pregnancy" was a phrase that could be read almost any way you liked. But the lawmakers hadn't said that, they'd made it perfectly clear: abortion in the medical sense of the word, that is, surgical intervention.

He must refine his story, add some more details. Where, when, the day, the hour and minute, the place — convincing details. If Lena were to die, Budyagin would get him. Though he might want to avoid a scandal. The daughter of a senior official getting rid of her baby in the most primitive way, like a peasant. And if one really got down to the bottom of it, the Budyagins were most to blame: after all, they had been against the marriage, and because of them Lena hadn't wanted to have the baby, so, looking at it objectively, they were the ones who had pushed her into doing what she did. They hadn't wanted any publicity. That's how it really was, that's the way to see the affair, if one looked right into it, right into the essence of it. What had they prepared her for? What had they taught her? To translate from English? Not much of a preparation for life. He'd always hated that family, and now he was in their hands, floundering in his tiny room, while they were in their impregnable fortress in the Fifth House of Soviets, mobilizing doctors to save Lena. No doubt they would save her. And then later, they would deal with him.

His mother was sullen and said nothing. She'd guessed, but was afraid to say anything in case the conversation turned into accusations. But what about the girl? She's used to the best, but she did what everyone else does. Imagine, a young lady like her! And him, what about him, he just rushed blindly into it, and managed to scald her feet, he did. He hadn't a clue.

Yuri went to the hospital, but he didn't go in. He walked past at a distance, in case he ran into the Budyagins or someone saw him. The fewer people who saw him the better.

He returned to the Arbat and called the hospital from a booth, not from home. He inquired about the condition of Elena Ivanovna Budyagina. "Her condition is serious, her temperature is 103.6."

He rang every day and only at the end of the week did they say, "Her condition is stable, her temperature is down to 100.7." Three days later her condition was satisfactory and her temperature was back to normal. At the end of the second week her mother took her home.

That evening Yuri's mother asked him, "How's your princess?" He grinned. "In the pink."

He didn't phone her, as he couldn't imagine that she would talk to him. He hadn't visited her once in the hospital, he hadn't written, and he had no excuses. To hell with it! He'd been right not to go. He needed to know only one more thing, and that was whether she'd told anyone. But he still couldn't bring himself to pick up the phone. Nor did she call him. Nina did.

"Yuri, the gang is meeting today to visit Lena. Will you come?"

"I'm tied up today."

"Come later."

"I won't be free till late."

Had she called on her own initiative, or had Lena put her up to it? He must make sure.

He phoned Lena. He heard her soft, deep, caressing voice.

"I was so worried about you," she said.

"I was the one who was worried, about you."

"I was thinking all the time: How would you get through this? Why didn't you visit me?"

"I called every day to ask how you were," he said.

"Really?" This delighted her. "The others are coming to see me today. Won't you come, too?"

"I don't think so, not with such a mob."

"Yes, I don't blame you. But when?"

"I'll call you."

✢ 19 ✢

ina got home from school at five and found Varya and her friend Zoe sitting on the stairs by the door.

"The door slammed shut and I'd forgotten my key."

Forgotten her key. The little liar. She was forbidden to bring Zoe into the apartment, so they sat on the stairs instead: "The stairs don't belong to you, you can't stop us from sitting there."

"You've got thirty seconds for reflection, and two minutes for completion." Varya was talking like a schoolteacher to Zoe, who fled down the stairs.

"Did you visit Sofya Alexandrovna?"

"Yes."

"Did you buy everything?"

"Yes."

"What about the cards?"

"They're ordered."

"How much money's left?"

Varya held out the change.

"I've kept fifty kopeks for skating."

"What about your homework?"

"I'll do it."

They each had their chores to perform. Nina worked all day, rushed home for a meal, and then out again to teach at evening school, as they couldn't manage without the extra salary, while Varya went skating, or to the theater or the movies, or met her boyfriends and girlfriends, so it wasn't as if the household chores took up much of her time.

"You can warm up the kasha for your supper. I'll leave it in the pan, the butter's in the sideboard," Varya said.

"Don't come home after eleven," Nina warned, buttoning her coat.

As soon as the door slammed after her, Varya was on the phone to Zoe.

"Come on over, Nina's taken off."

She cleared the table, prepared the supper, washed the dishes, and put everything away in its proper place. She liked things to be in order. Nina never put things away properly.

The phone rang. Still holding the dishtowel, Varya picked it up.

"Is that you, Natasha?"

It was her "telephone boyfriend," a boy she'd got to know only on the telephone — she'd never seen him and he hadn't seen her. He was called Volodya, but she refused to tell him her name.

"It might be Natasha," she had said.

And he had started calling her Natasha, but he asked her every time, "Natasha, come on, what's your real name?"

She liked the sound of his voice, and she was frank with him: because she'd never meet him, she could tell him everything. He said he was not as open with anyone as he was with her.

"Natasha should be a blonde."

"I am a blonde, as it happens."

"What about your eyes?"

"Orange, on a blue background."

"Does anyone have eyes like that? Where did you go last night?"

"I had a great time. We went to a dance at the polytechnic where they played all kinds of instruments that were perfect for doing the rumba to."

"I'm jealous. I had to do homework."

"Study, my friend, study, do your best, learning is a sweet fruit, learning is a sure path that will lead you out of the gloom into the light."

"When are we going to meet?"

"Never."

"But we might fall in love."

"No, we wouldn't, we think too much alike."

"What are you going to do today?"

"I'm going skating."

"Which rink?"

"The one near the factory."

"Which factory?"

"The soap-and-nail factory."

"Let me come with you, I'm a good skater."

"But I'm not, so you'd be bored. Anyway, I have to say good-bye, my friends have come for me."

Pale and pimply, a flower of the dung heap, Nina called her, Zoe was dressed for skating, with a white hat and long pants under her skirt. Her mother worked in the box office at the Carnival Cinema and let the girls in without paying.

"Why are you wearing the white?" Varya asked, eyeing Zoe's hat. "I thought we'd agreed."

"The elastic went on the red one. It snapped as I was putting it on. You wear your red one, it suits you so well!"

"You want me to wear a *red* hat with a *white* sweater? You take the red, and I'll wear your white one."

"Why do we always have to do what *you* want?"

"It's not what I want, it's what we agreed."

Zoe shrugged, offended. "Oh, well, if you must . . ."

"Don't do me any favors! I'm not going skating, anyway." She threw off her shoes and sat on the bed with her legs tucked under her.

"That's silly," Zoe mumbled. "All right, I'll wear your red hat."

"I'm not going skating."

They sat for a while not saying anything. Zoe was miserable and sorry they'd quarreled over such a trivial thing.

"Let's go," she pleaded.

"I can't go out at all, not as long as *he's in there.*"

"But you were getting ready."

"Yes, I was getting ready, but now I've changed my mind."

With Sasha's arrest, Varya saw herself as different from all the other girls. She was waiting for a friend who had suddenly disappeared and would reappear just as unexpectedly and who would deal with her severely if she were disloyal. Everyone knew she'd danced with Sasha at the Arbat Cellar, they'd been seen there together, and people had seen the fight. Now Varya had become friends with Sasha's mother, and took packages to him in prison.

Despite the cold, Varya would join the lines waiting outside the prison early in the mornings. When Sofya Alexandrovna arrived, they would stand in line together, inching toward the guard's little window. Sofya Alexandrovna didn't know how to argue. She was afraid of making the man behind the little window angry. It embarrassed her to hold up the line of tired people who had been standing along the high, long, cold prison wall since five in the morning. Varya wasn't afraid of anyone and nothing embarrassed her. They searched all the prisons for Sasha. They would be given a form at each little window asking for the name and father's name and address of the arrested. Sofya Alexandrovna would fill out the forms, and they would go back in the line, then hand the form in and then have to wait another two or three hours only to be told, "He's not here."

"Well, where is he?" Varya would snap.

"It's not known."

"But who is supposed to know? You're the ones who arrested him, you ought to know."

Varya listened to all the advice that was proffered in the all-knowing Arbat courtyards. One Novinsky Boulevard girl, whose boyfriend was in the Taganka prison, showed her how to hide a note in clean underwear, and instructed her to send more sugar and apples, as they could be used to make wine. Sofya Alexandrovna shook her head as she listened.

"No, Varya, Sasha doesn't need wine. . . ."

From an attractive, middle-aged woman Sofya Alexandrovna had aged overnight. At first, she thought she had only to appear before those who had arrested Sasha and their hearts would melt — after all, they had mothers, too. But then she saw so many other mothers, and nobody's heart melted at the sight of them. They stood in long lines, each afraid that what little sympathy that might exist behind the closed office doors would be given to the one who had just entered.

She saw armed sentries, impenetrable stone walls, and behind them her Sasha was locked up, her boy was being deprived of what every living being had the right to, the freedom to breathe the earth's air. What did they have in store for him? She didn't sleep at night — what was he sleeping on? She couldn't eat — what was he eating, bent over his prison bowl? He was precious to her, he was her life, her blood. The scent of his hair as a child still lingered on his pillows, his shoes smelled of the dry earth he'd run barefoot on as a boy, and his desk of the inky smell of his school exercise-books.

She walked the streets, hoping to see the men who'd followed Sasha before his arrest. They must know what kind of trouble he was in, and how to help him. If she saw the small one in the squirrel coat, she would ask him about Sasha. She would say she had nothing against him, he'd just been doing his job. But now that they'd done what they had, they could surely be merciful — after all, what difference could it make to them?

She walked up and down the Arbat, first on one side then the other; she went into shops and pretended to join a line. But she saw neither the small man in the squirrel coat, nor the one in the hat, nor the tall, unpleasant one.

Stiff with cold and crushed by the knowledge that she was powerless, she would return home to the empty, dark room, alone and suffering, and she would pray to a God she had long abandoned, and she would pray for the spirit of goodness and mercy, omnipresent and all-pervading, to soften the hearts of those who were going to decide Sasha's fate.

In the mornings the noise of the postman would get her out of bed. She was waiting for a reply from the prosecutor, or a letter from some secret but powerful well-wisher, and she was waiting for a letter from Sasha himself, sent through someone who'd been in prison with him, now let out, or maybe who'd already been sent into exile — letters did arrive that way. She'd been told of such instances. She gazed at Stalin's portraits in the newspapers: he dressed modestly, he had good-natured wrinkles around his eyes, and he had the wise, calm face of a man with a clear conscience. His fiftieth birthday had been celebrated not long ago, so now he must be fifty-four, no fifty-three, the same age as Pavel Nikolaevich, her husband. Stalin's elder son must be the same age as Sasha, and there was another son, and a daughter — he knew what it was like to have children, and he knew what family grief meant: after all, he'd lost his wife quite recently. If only Sasha's case could be laid in front of him. She put all her hopes on Mark. Mark would tell Stalin about Sasha. Stalin would call for his file, maybe even have Sasha brought to him. And he'd like Sasha. Everyone liked Sasha.

Pavel Nikolaevich came. He was upset, of course, but he didn't think it was such a catastrophe. They weren't going to shoot Sasha, or sentence him to life imprisonment, there was no life imprisonment. He was young, he had his whole life ahead of him. Obviously something had to be done, but only people in authority could do anything in a case like this. He had no access to such people. Mark had access.

Why couldn't she understand that, or even try to? He'd come here with the firm intention of being patient, even good-humored. But as soon as he entered the hateful apartment and saw this old woman who had once been his wife and heard that whining in her voice and saw that stubborn look that came into her face when she was struggling not to show her fear, all the old irritation and impatience and anger came back. It was all her fault; she and her brother had raised Sasha.

They were sitting opposite one another, she gray, her lips trembling and her head shaking, he smooth shaven, well groomed, his large gray eyes showing his irritation. They were at the table they had sat at for so many years. It was still covered with the same oilcloth, under the same tacky lampshade. She was nervously wiping the cloth with the palm of her hand, needlessly smoothing it out, and the movement irritated him.

"You want me to go around to all the different authorities? It won't make any difference, I've tried to explain, you can only appeal against a *decision*. And they haven't made a decision yet, because the investigation is still going on."

Maybe she was using this as a way of getting him back?

"What do you want me to do? You want me to leave my job at the factory? They wouldn't let me. And I've no intention of coming back to Moscow. Just remember that.... What?"

He thought he'd heard her say something, but so quietly that he wasn't meant to hear it.

But she hadn't, she was only moving her trembling lips silently.

"No, nothing ... I'm listening to you."

"Yes, I know you're listening. You're listening and thinking what a rotten father I am for not helping my own son. You've always thought I was a rotten father, and you've made him think so too."

His abuse and his accusations had always tormented her. Now the old feelings returned and she was horrified that she could not overcome that fear, especially now when they had to save their son, *their* son.

She could hear his hostility to Sasha and the effort he was making to shield himself from Sasha's suffering. How dare he air his hard feelings, *his* grievances at this moment? And how could she be afraid of him now, when Sasha's life was at stake? She mustn't be afraid of anyone, she had no right. She was his *mother!*

"If you'd been here when they took him away ..."

She spoke bitterly. She knew she would have to speak louder; she would virtually have to shout to make him hear.

"Oh, yes, of course, *I'm* to blame, it was *my* fault. ... You're the martyr, you're the sufferer, and I'm the swine who just likes to have a good time boozing and chasing skirts. ..."

My God, he was just the same, not even this disaster had made any difference, the way he went red in the face and pouted his lips and mimicked her. She had waited for him to come, hoping he might be able to help, being a father and a man! What should he be thinking about, except Sasha? He had no right to think about anything else. And she was going to force him to think about Sasha.

She went to the desk and took out her appeal to the prosecutor.

"Here." She handed it to him.

His face showed displeasure and distaste. The stupid woman was still trying to make him do something about this hopeless business. Why should anyone bother with her appeal, why should anyone even take the trouble to read it?

But he would have to read it. Everyone would condemn him if he refused her now, just at this moment. He wanted the world to see him as a decent person, a decent father. He wasn't going to give her the chance to say, "He wouldn't even read the appeal."

But what on earth had she written! "This is a mother writing to you ... give me back my son." Naïve, sentimental, unconvincing. "I appeal to our fair and merciful government. ..." Just words, only words. "I know that my son is not guilty of anything. . . ." Who's going to believe *that*? "If he has committed an error, it was entirely unintended, he's no more than a child. . . ." Twenty-two years old, some child! Anyway, what error? Why confirm his guilt indirectly?

She was sitting on the sofa with her head cocked, listening to his remarks, hardening herself to his sarcasm, remarks meant to underline her stupidity. All right, she didn't know how to write an appeal — let him improve on it, as long as it helped Sasha.

She laid a sheet of paper in front of him and pushed the inkwell nearer.

"You write it the way it ought to be."

He glanced at her in anger and confusion, realizing how foolish he'd been. If the appeal was pointless, what difference did it make how it was written? Now he had to write something, but what could he possibly write? He didn't even know the charges they'd brought against Sasha.

"Look," he said, "send it in as it is. You could maybe take out the bits about errors and 'give me back my son,' but the rest . . . Yes, send it in as it is."

"Fine," she said, picking up the letter. "I'll send it."

She hadn't expected anything else from him. She wouldn't send it in any case without first showing it to Mark.

"When are you going back?"

He exploded again. "You know I have to be back at work tomorrow!"

"Please leave some money," she said firmly. "I'm buying things for Sasha at the good shops."

He almost swore at her. He was only an ordinary engineer on ordinary wages, but it wasn't the money. It was her tone, that awful demanding whine, that he couldn't stand. All she ever needed him for was money.

He took out a hundred and fifty rubles.

"That's all I can spare."

℁ 20 ℁

gain it was at night that Sasha was awakened by the metallic scraping of the hatch. Yesterday's guard conducted him again along the numberless short corridors, the great bunch of keys jingling from his belt, and again he tapped with a key either on the door handles or on the metal cages enclosing the staircases to signal that he was escorting a prisoner. This time Sasha figured they were on the first floor. He could hear voices coming from an open door at the end of the corridor, and even the sound of laughter. This area had a different smell, not a prison smell.

Dyakov didn't point the light at him this time; obviously he only used that ploy for becoming acquainted. Nor was he in uniform, but had on a brown jacket over a blue pullover. He nodded to Sasha to sit and went on writing with his head bent low. He wrote and read over what he'd written without paying any attention to Sasha. All that stood between the two of them was a massive inkstand and an equally massive paperweight. It occurred to Sasha that it would be an easy matter to pick up the paperweight and smash it down on Dyakov's head. Among all the prisoners who sat on this chair there must be one who would want to do it, and someday would do it. Everything else here had been thought out, every step, every movement, but they hadn't taken this into account. Maybe there was some secret mechanism that would be set in motion if you touched the paperweight. Of course, nobody could escape from this place, but a person might commit such an act in a fit of desperation. And yet Dyakov wasn't afraid of its happening. On the other hand, maybe *genuine* prisoners were interrogated somewhere else in the prison.

Dyakov gathered up his papers and left the room, leaving the door open. He was wearing felt boots with his brown trousers tucked into them. Seeing how warmly dressed Dyakov was, Sasha suddenly felt the chill of the cement floor through his thin shoes.

Everything was different, not at all like the last time. Dyakov appeared to be busy with some important and urgent case. It was as if they'd brought Sasha here not realizing that Dyakov was going to be otherwise occupied. The civilian clothes and felt boots gave Dyakov a simple and unofficial appearance. He'd gone out and left Sasha alone with all sorts of papers lying right there on the table, and he wasn't afraid that Sasha might look at them, just as he wasn't afraid that Sasha might hit him on the head with the paperweight.

The sound of slamming doors and voices came from the corridor. Dyakov was talking to someone. He reentered the room, moving somewhat clumsily in his felt boots, closed the door, sat down at the table, fumbled in one of the drawers, and brought out a slim file containing the notes of the last interrogation, then searched for something else, fishing and digging around, and then, without looking at Sasha, said:

"So, Pankratov, what are you going to tell me about today?"

He said it casually and steadily, and there was even a note of humor, as if he couldn't remember what they'd talked about last time.

"Well . . ." Sasha began.

"Ah!" Dyakov had at last found the document he had been looking for and left the room with it.

He came back and, still standing, slipped the papers back into the drawer, then sat down and opened Sasha's file.

"So, Pankratov. Have you thought about my advice to you?"

"Yes, I have, but I still don't know what it's all about."

"That's not good." Dyakov shook his head. His voice carried a note of reproach and regret, perhaps even sympathy, as if to say, *You're not making things easy for yourself, my friend, not one bit.*

He pondered for a moment and then nodded at the file. "Are you going to try to drag this business out?"

"I don't know what counterrevolutionary conversations you meant last time."

Dyakov frowned. "You're not being sincere, Pankratov. You want to divert us from the *main* thing and concentrate on the business at your institute. And you're not even being honest in that. There's much that you've kept back. And that also tells us a lot about you."

"What have I kept back?" Sasha asked, amazed.

At that moment a middle-aged man with the face of an Eskimo entered the room. He was dressed in a dark blue suit that fitted his solid physique well.

Dyakov stood up. The man nodded for him to sit and sat down alongside him.

"Carry on."

He fixed his gaze on Sasha. Sasha realized this must be Dyakov's superior officer, but in that look Sasha sensed something more than normal official interest in someone undergoing a routine interrogation. He had a sudden flicker of hope that this man was going to change his fate.

"So, Pankratov," Dyakov said, "where were we?"

"You were saying that I was hiding something. What am I hiding?"

"One has only to glance at the minutes of the Party meeting. You sought the protection of some people in high office. . . ."

Dyakov watched Sasha expectantly, searchingly.

So, that was it. It had to do with Mark, or Budyagin, or both of them. He took the hint. Dyakov hadn't said *"comrades* in high office," but *"people* in high office," and he'd said it intentionally. And he had named no names. Well, he was going to have to name them, because Sasha was not going to do it for him.

"Whom did you have in mind?"

"Pankratov!" Dyakov twisted his mouth into a disapproving, censorious grimace. "You should be ashamed of yourself, Pankratov, playing cat and mouse with us. We know more than you think. You want to make *us* talk, but we want *you* to do the talking, and it's for your own good. Ryazanov and Budyagin made representations on your behalf, you admitted as much at the Party meeting, yet here you are, spinning us a yarn."

Again it was just plain "Ryazanov and Budyagin," not "comrades."

"I didn't ask for anyone's protection," Sasha protested. "I told my uncle Ryazanov about my case, but I didn't ask him to get involved. He went to Budyagin without my knowledge and asked him to telephone Glinskaya, the director of the institute."

"All right," Dyakov agreed, "but why didn't you tell me about this last time? Why is it you didn't mention precisely those names? You named a pile of other people." He took from Sasha's file a thin sheet that Sasha had not seen before. "Baulin, Lozgachev, Azizyan, Kovalyov, but no Ryazanov and Budyagin. Why's that?"

Sasha's mind raced. One word could prove fatal for both Mark and Budyagin. They were what all this was about, it was obvious now. But what were they being accused of?

"I didn't think it mattered. It was purely a family tie. I can't see why you think it's so important." He said this firmly, making it clear that he neither wished nor intended to discuss it further. Dyakov had indicated the path he wanted Sasha to follow, but he wasn't going to.

Dyakov looked at him, as it seemed to Sasha, with attentiveness and curiosity, and a degree of caution.

"Did your uncle also arrange for Solts to deal with the case?"

"No one arranged that. I went to Solts on my own."

Dyakov smirked. "People wait months for an interview but you ... you, he received right then and there and settled the case, just like that. Who's going to believe *that*?"

"But that's exactly what happened," Sasha said. "I went into his office, he noticed me, asked me what I wanted —"

"Just pure luck?"

"Absolutely.... Surely I had the right to apply to the Central Control Commission? Surely my own uncle had the right to petition for me? Is that what I'm guilty of? Are you keeping me here for that? For nothing, for no reason!"

A grimace passed across Dyakov's face. He said nothing, but glanced at his superior as if to let him see what he had to cope with here; perhaps he also expected him to say something.

But the man with the face of an Eskimo said nothing. He heaved himself up from his chair and left the room.

Scowling and using a different tone of voice, Dyakov declared: "What you are guilty of is insincerity and dishonesty before the Party. You've concealed a lot of other things, as well. You named all your accusers, but not once have you mentioned the names of those who defended you. And quite a few people are involved in your case. Krivoruchko, for instance . . ."

Sasha sensed danger. Everything could come apart at any moment. Obviously as far as Mark and Budyagin were concerned, he couldn't say anything that would compromise them, nor would he. But what about Krivoruchko? "This is a chef who likes to make peppery dishes." Krivoruchko had said that about Stalin. And if he, Sasha, said nothing about it now, he would be taking the path of insincerity and lies.

"I have been in his office twice. The first time he stamped my expulsion papers, the second time he took care of my reinstatement."

Dyakov burst out laughing.

"First we expel you, then we reinstate you, then we throw you in prison. . . . Didn't he say anything to you?"

"He seemed to me distraught, depressed — after all, he had been expelled from the Party."

"And you were expelled, too. Surely, he must have said *something* to you?"

Dyakov kept his gaze fixed firmly on Sasha. Did he know something or was he just guessing, just feeling his way, perhaps aware that Sasha was now confused?

"Surely he must have expressed some opinion on the fact that you'd been expelled and were now being reinstated?" he persisted. "He surely asked you about your case? Especially as you had come to his defense at the Party committee meeting."

"All I did was tell him what had happened," Sasha protested.

"Precisely. And all *he* did was to wield his rubber stamp?"

He mustn't give way! Dyakov was just feeling him out, trying to trap him, diverting him from the main issue of Mark and Budyagin, confusing him. . . .

"Any personal conversation was not possible. He's the deputy director, and I'm just an ordinary student."

Dyakov looked at him piercingly. "But we have information that he carried on anti-Party conversations with other students. Yet, with you, an *aggrieved* student, and on top of that one who had *defended* him, he didn't say anything. Very strange!"

Krivoruchko knew Mark and had asked Sasha to give him his regards. He mustn't mention that.

"Well, that's the way it was."

Dyakov was still watching him intently and suddenly, a malicious grin spreading over his face, he pulled a blank interrogation form toward himself.

"All right, Pankratov, we're very patient people here: we can wait till you decide to be honest — until you remember what you're supposed to."

Dyakov's report on this occasion began with the words *Further to the evidence earlier recorded by me . . .* and contained Sasha's admission that he had been in Krivoruchko's office and spoken in his defense at the Party meeting, and that Janson and Siversky had spoken in Sasha's defense. There was no mention of Mark or Budyagin in the report.

Everything had been noted down correctly, but again Sasha had a vague sense of danger. He couldn't fathom why. The only amendment he asked Dyakov for was that he had gone to see Krivoruchko on business.

"You're a student, so obviously you went on business."

Damn him! Sasha signed the statement.

"I'm not getting any packages from my mother, and I'm worried. Also, I'd like a newspaper and books from the library."

Dyakov shook his head.

"Not permitted while the investigation is still going on. If you decide to be more frank and open, everything could change. You'd get your parcels and books and a newspaper. And keep in mind, Pankratov, our next meeting will be our last — I can't drag this out any longer." He pointed a finger up at the ceiling. "I also have to produce results. And I would like to conclude this case favorably for you. Keep that in mind."

Either Mark or Budyagin, or both of them together. Both honest Communists, dedicated to the Party. He didn't know Budyagin that well, but he knew Mark very well indeed: he would swear by him;

he wouldn't allow himself even to imagine anything. If Mark was arrested, it would have to be some kind of misunderstanding. Like his own arrest, or even worse, because there was at least the business at the institute. In Mark's case, what could there be? A leading engineer, a fine administrator, a selfless, genuine Communist, his whole life had been his work and nothing but his work. Could they have arrested him? Maybe he was here, right in this corridor, maybe even in the next cell. Mark in a cell like this, myopic and with a weak heart?

He knew Mark never would have done anything wrong; he was convinced of his honesty. If they thought he was trying to protect Mark, let them. He was willing to share Mark's fate. If that's the way things turned out, so be it, there was nothing to do but see it through and wait for the time when they would both prove their innocence.

Now that he saw things clearly, he had no need to go on dreaming up explanations. He was an honest Party member, he was hiding nothing, holding back nothing, he could say nothing bad about Mark, nor would he. That's all there was to it.

The only thing that worried him was Krivoruchko. It was the only point where he felt himself vulnerable. One way or the other, he had concealed something. Perhaps it was an insignificant triviality, but he had concealed it. He wanted to have a clear conscience, and Krivoruchko got in the way of this sense of honesty and clarity.

During the day a new guard appeared with a notepad and pencil in his hand.

"Write down what you want from the library."

He'd been allowed to use the library!

He had no idea how many books he could ask for or for what length of time. But he was not going to reveal his ignorance. The prison staff took less advantage of the experienced prisoners.

Tolstoy's *War and Peace,* Gogol's *Dead Souls,* Balzac's *Illusions perdues,* Stendhal's *La Chartreuse de Parme,* the latest issues of the important literary journals ... He wrote without thinking — there was no time to think with the guard waiting; the prisoner was supposed to have decided in advance what he wanted. He wrote whatever came into his head; it was important to get hold of books, the thicker the better, so they would last till the next time, whenever that might be.

There was one item he ordered deliberately, and that was the *Soviet Criminal Trial Code*. He wouldn't get it, but he added it nevertheless to express his protest against his present situation.

Why had Dyakov allowed him to have books? Was he trying to win him over? It was in his interest to make Sasha's life so miserable that he would be forced to start confessing. Maybe he was afraid of breaking the rules about prisoners having books? Was it pity? There was no room for pity when someone was accused of counterrevolution.

Perhaps Dyakov had nothing to do with it; perhaps it was like getting his daily shower. What if it was discovered and he didn't get his books?

The next day the new guard turned up with a package that had been wrapped in a clean white cloth scorched yellow from ironing. Sasha recognized it at once as the damp-cloth he used at home for pressing his trousers. So, he was going to get packages as well as books.

"Name?"

"Pankratov."

"Sign."

The guard handed him a list of the parcel's contents and a stub of pencil. The list was written in his mother's broad, almost indecipherable hand, except the word *chocolate* had been added in an unfamiliar, precise, stylish hand. Half the list had been crossed out with an indelible pencil.

Sasha sorted through the bags and packages his mother had wrapped so carefully, and which had been roughly opened by alien hands. A long white loaf, cheese, cold meat, sausage — these things had been cut into pieces during the inspection. There was butter wrapped in grease-proof paper, sugar, a change of underwear, socks, handkerchiefs.

So, his mother was alive, she was getting by, and she knew where he was.

"Can I send back laundry?"

"Wrap it up."

He wrapped his dirty underwear in the cloth. The iron-scorched scrap of white linen brought the smell of home to him, his home.

"Write on the back that you received it."

On the back of the list he wrote, *Received everything. Don't send anything except white bread, meat, and underwear. All's well, I'm fine, a big kiss. Sasha.*

"The pencil!" the guard demanded.

❧ 21 ❧

Sofya Alexandrovna touched the scrap of paper, felt it between her fingertips, read and reread a thousand times what he'd written. It became a symbol of her son's suffering and his bitter fate, but it also told her that he was alive. She showed it to everyone — Mikhail Yurevich, her neighbor Galya, Militsa Petrovna, her sisters, Varya Ivanova, Max Kostin... *Received everything.... All's well, I'm fine, a big kiss....* Only he could have written it, only her good, brave boy.

Everything now acquired a new meaning. The crumpled note, the laundry with its prison smell, the meat and bread that he asked for — until now, there hadn't been enough of such tangible details for her to imagine him alive. The evenings and nights were now no longer so lonely; she felt she was with him, knew his every minute, sensed his every movement. If her heart ached, it meant he wasn't feeling well; if she couldn't sleep, he was lying on his bunk with open eyes; if she felt a surge of mortal fear, it was because they were taking him to be interrogated and he was racked with pain, writhing and suffering. She remembered punishing him as a child because he didn't want her to go to the theater, and he'd cried not from pain but because she had humiliated him, small as he was. Now it was life itself that was beating him.

Mark was seeing senior and influential people about Sasha. She trusted Mark, he didn't deceive her or try to reassure her, he did everything he possibly could. Yet even more than she trusted him, she trusted the women she stood in line with at the prisons. In the lines everything was clear, simple, just. These poor women learned ways to protect their dear ones, they warmed them with the warmth they'd given up standing for hours in the cold, eased their hunger with the little they could eke out of their own meager rations, and through the dense stone prison walls they sent them their love and hope.

Sofya Alexandrovna could now think of the lines outside the prison without fear. She no longer felt isolated standing there, and although it did not diminish her sufferings, it helped to remove the sting of their individuality. She had to do what the others did. The world that had earlier been so terrifying to her demanded action, and action stifles fear.

She had learned from the women how to locate Sasha, how to make up a parcel and what to put in it, to which offices she should apply and to whom she should write. And their advice always turned out to be right. She managed to get an interview at the Directorate of Public Prosecution. The answer she got — "When the investigation has been completed, you'll be told the outcome" — was also exactly what they had predicted, but it was important, because it meant the prosecutor was looking into Sasha's case. That could make a difference.

They also knew what to do if Sasha was sentenced, they knew every inch of the path that would lie before him: it was another of life's paths and people still went on with their lives, even that way. This reassured her more than hopes and promises. Where they sent Sasha would depend on whether it occurred to him to demand a medical examination, because with his weak chest he might get the Volga region, instead of Siberia. If they telephoned and told her to pack his warm clothes, it meant Siberia or the north, and if they didn't, it would be Central Asia.

And she was ready when the housing office manager, Viktor Ivanovich Nosov, came to seal Sasha's room — the women had warned her. He was obliged to do it, even though it probably made him uncomfortable. She was only afraid that his discomfort might make him abusive, so she prepared a little speech: "Viktor Ivanovich," she would say, "if you will speak to me calmly, I'll understand you better."

In any event, Viktor Ivanovich was not rude.

"It's the system, Sofya Alexandrovna. When Sasha returns, we'll unseal the room. Like this, you won't be bothered. You know what people are like, nosing about, and you can't get rid of them. I'll get the janitor to come and help move a few things, and you can leave what you don't need there, since the room is yours."

He told her that she needn't take everything out of Sasha's room, and she realized that as long as things were left there, nobody could move in without permission. She turned down his offer of the janitor's help, however, as she'd have had to pay him and she had no money.

The room she decided to give up was not the main one, where Sasha had slept and studied, but her own small bedroom. Everything she needed had to be moved out, and Sasha's desk, his divan, and clothes stand moved in.

She was busy doing this when Varya turned up. She took off her hat and coat and quickly got down to work, carrying piles of linen, dresses, rugs, pillows, blankets, and she did it without dropping or misplacing a single thing. She knew exactly what to put where, and made sure that everything was properly arranged.

The girl's help gave Sofya Alexandrovna pleasure, as did Varya herself. She had at first thought it was wrong to let this young girl into her life, with its unhappiness, but Varya's sympathy was so unswerving, her desire to help so firm, that she couldn't imagine how she could send her away.

The girl's presence made their work seem like normal everyday household chores, the routine moving of furniture, and to keep up this pretense, Sofya Alexandrovna said nothing to her. But she felt her nerve failing. Her husband had left her, they'd taken her son away from her, now the room. . . . She ought to have given the room to him long ago. He was a grown man and it was awkward for him to have to live in the main room, but she hadn't given it up, hadn't wanted to deprive herself of the extra convenience. How petty and selfish she'd been! And he, so kind and so unselfish, had never tried to persuade her to do it.

They couldn't dismantle the big iron bedstead, a foot was broken on the wardrobe, and they couldn't budge the chest of drawers, even without the drawers.

Mikhail Yurevich came home from work, then Galya turned up, and together they moved the chest and the wardrobe, took the bed apart, and moved Sasha's divan, desk, and bookcase into the small room. Sofya Alexandrovna laid out his writing materials and some of his books, and hung the curtain.

Varya didn't leave until everything had been moved, even though Serafim, the young student Max had brought to the New Year's party, was waiting for her at home.

He'd phoned her the very next day, bold as brass, and asked her to meet him on Arbat Square. She decided to go along, but just as a joke, and not alone, with Zoe and another girl. Her friends stood on the other side of the street as this good-looking soldier approached Varya, and then they watched them stroll along the Arbat. The girls walked along the other side making silly gestures at Varya that she didn't understand, and she made signs back at them that they didn't understand. Serafim asked her to go dancing at the Red Army Club, but she had already agreed to go to the movies that night. However, she knew how hard it was to get into the Red Army Club, so she promised to go the following Saturday. He knew all the latest dances and they went every week, to the envy of her friends.

She even got used to his funny name — anyway, one of the famous Znamensky brothers — the long-distance runner — was also called Serafim. Of course, he wasn't like the boys from the neighborhood, real Muscovite boys of the Arbat. He was provincial and shy. But he was serious in his courting, which flattered her, as it made her feel grown up, and Nina couldn't say anything against him, because Serafim was a friend of her own Max, and Max couldn't possibly have friends who were bad.

Nina greeted her with a scowl. Serafim had been waiting an hour, sitting on the bed with a book in his hands and irritating Nina by rustling the pages while she was trying to mark her pupils' exercise-books. Her look said: *You made the date, you should have been here. It's not up to me to entertain your boyfriends.*

Varya didn't explain why she was late; it would keep till later. She asked Serafim to go out into the corridor and wait while she changed.

The mirror hung on the door of the wardrobe and Varya opened it so she could stand sideways to the light. She stripped and began changing. Even this annoyed Nina, who thought the dress she had been wearing was good enough. Look at her putting on her stockings! She stretched her leg out, holding it in a pose and admiring it in the mirror. Where did she pick up this habit of parading around the room half-naked? And at sixteen!

"Forgotten someone's waiting for you?"

"No," Varya answered curtly, and in the same tone asked, "Can I borrow your good shoes?"

Nina didn't feel like lending her her one pair of good shoes, but she wanted Varya to get the hell out.

"Take them."

Varya found the shoes and inspected them thoroughly. When she'd put them on she stood up to look at herself in the mirror again, then she sat down and admired her outstretched leg.

When she was finally ready, she opened the front door. "Come in, Serafim."

She already had her coat on, her scarf tied around her head, and had taken a last look at herself in the mirror, when she turned to her sister and said, "I was at Sofya Alexandrovna's. I helped her move things. Sasha's room's been sealed up."

Varya's parting shot was instinctive, but it found its mark. Nina could find out what was happening at Sasha's home only from Varya.

Of course, neither Nina nor anyone else could do anything to help him. What could they possibly do? And not knowing the facts or what he had been accused of?

Yet she felt guilty because she was free and he was in prison. He was the best of their bunch! And all of them had kept very low profiles. She hoped it was just a misunderstanding that would be cleared up. But they'd sealed his room and that meant he wasn't going to be released. So what now? Did that mean that Sasha was an enemy of the Soviet government? Did it mean they should turn their backs on him?

They had all left Sasha to his bad luck and walked away. She had expressed her sympathy to Sofya Alexandrovna, but what good was that?

They must do something: they must write a letter. They should collect everyone's signature — after all Sasha had been the secretary of their Komsomol cell, and they could write that they stood behind him. Max would sign, and Vadim and Lena, and the others, too. And the head of their school and the teachers who knew Sasha. She and Sasha used to be pupils at the school where she was now a teacher, so she felt sure she'd be able to get the signatures. Yuri of course wouldn't sign, damn him.

She phoned Lena and Vadim and they agreed to meet the next day at Lena's. Then she went downstairs and told Max's mother to have him stop by when he came home on leave next day.

The meeting of the friends turned out not to be a happy one.

Lena, shrouded in a shawl, sat and said nothing, except to agree that a letter must be written and that she would sign anything.

Even Max looked miserable. He knew a letter from them would be useless, and he knew what the consequences of sending it would be, but he didn't want to refuse, didn't want Nina to think him a coward.

Only Vadim spoke up.

"What would the letter achieve? Would it help Sasha? It would only make things worse; we'd only complicate the issue. We'd be summoned and asked what we know about Pankratov. 'In school he was a good Komsomol.' 'But it's six years since you were at school together. What sort of person is he now? Do you know what happened at the institute? Did he tell you? *What* did he tell you?' And then they'd get hold of Sasha and ask him what he'd told us. I don't doubt Sasha's innocence, but I want to show you how it would turn out."

"Are we supposed to leave Sasha to his own luck?" Nina asked.

"Why his own luck? His case is being looked into. Why do we think it won't be straightened out? All right, *we* know Sasha, but they've undoubtedly collected character references on him. They didn't arrest him just because he's Sasha Pankratov, but because there's some sort of case. We just don't know what it is."

"We've got to help him," Nina said.

"Think about it," Vadim objected. "Sasha won't even know of the existence of our letter. On the contrary, they'd start asking him about each one of us, and that could only make his position worse."

"Are you afraid they'd ask him about you?"

"I'm not afraid of anything!" Vadim reddened.

They all knew he was right. Nina knew it, too. But there was a more important truth than simply knowing. And there was another realization, at once bitter and shaming: they were afraid of complicating their own lives. Suppressing that fear was more difficult than sending the letter.

"Let's ask my father," Lena suggested.

"Definitely!" Nina exclaimed, secretly hoping that Ivan Grigoryevich would intervene and help Sasha.

The idea also suited Vadim: Ivan Grigoryevich would talk them out of sending such a reckless letter. Vadim had made up his mind not to sign it, in any case.

It was Max, with his plain common sense, who realized that it was unfair to put Ivan Grigoryevich in such an ambiguous position.

"We should decide for ourselves."

"We can at least get some advice," Nina insisted.

Lena's mother and father came into the room for tea.

"Papa," Lena asked, "what should we do about Sasha?"

"What *can* be done?"

"We want to write a letter to the authorities."

Budyagin frowned. "What good would a letter from you do?"

"But we must do something," Nina said.

"They'll manage without your help," he answered angrily.

🌷 22 🌷

ot once, since his return from abroad, had Budyagin been called in by Stalin. And this despite his having much to report that he had had to omit from his dispatches, and which demanded immediate attention, given the growing tension in international relations. He asked for a meeting and was told, "Wait, you'll be summoned." He'd waited more than a year. This was not accidental, just as his omission from the new Central Committee was not accidental. Maybe Stalin wanted him to repent. But he had nothing to repent. As ambassador to one of the most powerful Western countries, he had carried out the policy dictated by the Central Committee, although he had had the right to express his view to that body.

Budyagin was not afraid of Stalin, but dealing with him was always complicated. In exile, Stalin had once refused to talk to a comrade who'd teased him for sleeping in his socks. Small of stature and puny, he had appeared especially vulnerable in Siberia. He was always cold, so he slept in his socks. Stalin owned a multicolored, quilted silk blanket, and that, too, became the butt of jokes, which Stalin took as proof of his own inability to adapt and as a sign of weakness. Eventually they stopped laughing at him. They realized it was impossible to quarrel with Stalin, as he was incapable of reconciliation. His strong Georgian accent and cumbersome turn of phrase did not make him a good orator; in debates, he was vulnerable, and the others were reluctant to offend by contradicting him.

Arguments and differences flourished, but never prevented the exiles from getting along together. Only Stalin could never compromise — an ideological opponent became a personal enemy. He thought it only natural that a comrade would lend him his felt boots, even though the comrade might need them himself. But he would petulantly refuse the offer of boots from someone he'd argued with the night before. Capricious, complaining, and prone to painful misunderstandings, he was often unbearable.

The other exiles would hunt or fish, but Stalin never went anywhere, spending the evenings working by the light of a kerosene lamp. People felt sorry for the solitary, stiff-necked Georgian, in his peasant hut at the edge of the village — he always found a spot for himself on the edge of the village — in the depths of the Siberian taiga, among the Russian peasants with whom he found it hard to get on. And he never did get on with them. His comrades forgave him much, the way the strong forgive the weak, or the way adults will forgive a difficult — at times impossible — child.

Budyagin had been the only one who managed somehow to get along with Stalin. A working-class lad from Motovilikha, as soon as he spotted the Georgian, he felt sorry for this southerner banished to icebound Siberia, to ferocious conditions that few Russians could endure. Budyagin performed small services and did whatever he could for Stalin, and Stalin accepted this as normal. In this respect it was easier for Budyagin than for the others — he was a capable blacksmith and metalworker, he could handle an ax, even manage a plow, and he knew how to use a gun and loved fishing, especially at night in the autumn, with a pitch-flare at the bow of the boat.

In silence Budyagin listened to his intellectual comrades argue and debate and philosophize. He read a lot and even learned English. Most people learned German or French. Stalin was the only one who didn't learn any language. The exiles gave Budyagin books to read, which they then analyzed and explained to him. Stalin also explained things to him. Stalin's dogmatic plain speaking, his seminarian's liking for interpretation, his implacable certainty that what he knew was the very frontier of knowledge, carried a conviction that made a bigger impression on Budyagin than the bookish rhetoric of the others. But Budyagin developed quickly, and as he met other people along the way who were stronger, more educated, and more brilliant than Stalin, he was less impressed. Those eight months of exile together, however, remained not only in his memory but in his heart — his first attachment to the cause that was to become his life's work.

Budyagin also saw Stalin occasionally during the Civil War, just as Stalin was beginning to play an important role. Stalin's willpower and energy were of service to the Revolution at a time when his rudeness, disloyalty, and grasping for dictatorial power were tolerated, a time when the Revolution required extreme measures. But when the time came for construction, these character flaws would be dangerous. Stalin's desire for power had become all-embracing and uncontrolled. Lenin had warned of this in his letter to the Party.

For Stalin, devotion to an idea was a measure of devotion to himself. What Ryazanov had thought of as the end of a process — that the Party leadership was now united — Budyagin knew was only the beginning. He had expected changes to be made at the congress, but they hadn't occurred. But Budyagin knew that, having confirmed his exceptional status at the congress, Stalin would now proceed to confirm his uniqueness and Stalin's measures would be all the worse when they came.

Whatever the Revolution did, Budyagin accepted the responsibility. Every action carried out in the name of the Revolution, he considered as his own, its mistakes were his mistakes, all its injustices he regarded as his own. He possessed the superior courage of the revolutionary, and he took responsibility for the fate of those who had been thrown into the furnace of social upheavals. Guilty and innocent alike, people had fallen, but he believed it was blazing a path for future generations; the real Revolution was not great because of *what* it destroyed, but because of *whom* it created.

Budyagin fully understood that Stalin appreciated Ryazanov, and when the nephew of a Central Committee member was arrested, it was known by everyone. The arrested nephew would be Ryazanov's Achilles' heel, forcing him to loyal service to a man who was indifferent to the facts of the case. Interference by Budyagin in Sasha's case would then only complicate Ryazanov's relations with Stalin.

Yet he felt he must intervene.

The thought of those young people in the next room discussing how they might help Sasha made him tremble. He'd seen them, upright and selfless, carrying on the cause of the Revolution. Yet here he was, an old Bolshevik who had prepared, carried out, and consolidated the Revolution, and he had nothing to say to them. He couldn't tell them that Sasha's arrest had been just, because he knew it was not so. Nor could he tell them Sasha's arrest was unjust, because he would have to explain to them how such a thing could happen.

Knowing that it was useless to intervene, Budyagin phoned Berezin. He knew Berezin as an honest and courageous Chekist. He told Berezin that he would vouch for Sasha Pankratov and he asked him to look into his case.

Berezin knew that Sasha Pankratov was guilty of nothing. He was familiar with the case, having been present at Sasha's interrogation, and thought him an honest young man. The thick black beard had failed to conceal the handsome young face and the expression of honor, courage, and decency. Berezin had admired Sasha's short, dignified responses and the quick smile of youth that is afraid of nothing and that still has the whole of life before it.

Berezin in fact knew a great deal more than either Budyagin or Ryazanov, and he could make assumptions they could not.

Lominadze, who had once been a leading figure in the Comintern, had expressed opinions of the Chinese revolution that differed from Stalin's, and had discussed the problem with Shatskin and Syrtsov. This event had led Stalin to label them "right-leftist freaks," and to remove Lominadze from his post and send him to the Urals as secretary of a town Party committee.

A file on him had been opened. It contained the evidence of a certain Cher, a former Comintern employee, to the effect that Lominadze was secretly preparing the creation of a new International. Cher was a man of uncertain nationality, loyal to a number of different countries. He was an adventurer and a scoundrel who alleged that a number of people were connected with Lominadze, among them Glinsky, a former activist in the left-wing of the Polish Socialist Party, who had given Lenin substantial assistance while he was an émigré.

Glinsky's wife was the director of the Transport Institute. Allegedly an underground opposition had been discovered in the institute, led by Glinskaya's deputy, Krivoruchko, who had been a member of the Workers' Opposition. Yagoda — head of the secret police — had seized on this at once. A link between Glinsky's wife and an underground opposition gave substance to Cher's allegations: any indirect links would add dimension and credibility to a case, any fact would add weight, any name was of significance if it was found in the file, and if it was skillfully attached to the basic version.

Berezin knew perfectly well that there was no such underground at the institute, nor any connection between Sasha Pankratov and Krivoruchko, just as Krivoruchko was in no way connected with Glinsky, nor was Glinsky connected with Lominadze, who in turn was not planning a new International. Lominadze's case, however, was being prepared according to Stalin's instructions and was under the personal supervision of Yagoda himself, and, as Berezin realized, it was a case that was going to reach farther and higher, though how far Berezin could only guess. If Yagoda knew about Sasha's case, Berezin foresaw the worst. The links formed a terrifying and ominous chain. To request the release of Pankratov could be seen as the attempted removal of one of the links, a trivial one, maybe, but a link just the same. Yagoda would never permit it. Nor would Vyshinsky. Solts had reinstated Pankratov; Vyshinsky had sanctioned his arrest. The only hope for Pankratov was to keep the boy in the background, not to draw attention to him. Everything should stay as it was for the time being. Dyakov could go on with his case, which was limited to the affair at the institute, and which was all he knew about. The only thing Berezin did was to authorize Sasha to receive parcels and to be given books from the prison library.

Dyakov had received Berezin's orders respectfully. He always listened to Berezin with respect, though he guessed that Berezin's days in the central apparatus were numbered. True, the parcels and books were an indulgence, but this was sometimes done in the interests of the investigation, and therefore not something to find fault with.

"It will be done," Dyakov had replied.

Berezin truly professed the spirit of the Revolution and regarded his work in the Cheka as his revolutionary duty. As chairman of a provincial Cheka during the Civil War, he had applied the Red terror, though he had released a number of luckless liberals or terrified bourgeois, if he was sure they were not a danger to the Revolution. Dyakov was different: nobody ever got out of his small but tenacious grip, and to fall into his hands was in itself enough to establish one's guilt.

What mattered to Dyakov was not whether someone was actually guilty. He was concerned with the *general* version of their guilt. This *general* version had to be skillfully applied to the *particular* individual and hence create the *concrete* version. Having created the concrete version, he would control it, through both the investigation itself and the person being investigated. If the subject repudiated the version, this would merely serve to add further evidence of his hostility to the state, which, to Dyakov's mind, he, Dyakov, was here to represent.

Dyakov's version, which he sincerely believed to be balanced, logical, and incontrovertible, came down to the following: the institute was run by Krivoruchko, a former oppositionist, long since defeated and therefore bearing a grudge and, to Dyakov's way of thinking, embittered forever. Such a man could not remain inactive: the enemy did not slumber, the enemy subverted wherever and whenever the opportunity arose, especially among politically immature young people. Now, just such a group of young people had put out an anti-Party newspaper. Was there a connection between these two circumstances? It was impossible for there *not* to be! The leader of the young people, the student Pankratov, had defended Krivoruchko. In *no way* was this mere coincidence! Was it mere coincidence that Krivoruchko's case occurred at the same time as Pankratov's? Impossible! Behind Pankratov stood the inspirer, the former oppositionist, Krivoruchko, and there was your counterrevolutionary organization.

That Pankratov would *fall apart,* thus proving this version, Dyakov had not the slightest doubt.

For Dyakov there were two kinds of people who were investigated: those who trusted in the process and hence in the Soviet system, and those who did not. He further subdivided them into the trivial, who argued with every word written down in the record, and the nontrivial, who did not. Pankratov believed in the security organization and he wasn't trivial. He'd been shaken by the arrest, he was hoping for release, he was looking for trust, he was inexperienced, straightforward, he would defend his comrades, take everything on his own shoulders, even more than necessary. He was an easy case.

Krivoruchko was arrested the same night as Sasha. He said he'd heard about the Pankratov case, but didn't remember Pankratov himself: there were thousands of students at the institute.

In fact, Krivoruchko had not forgotten Pankratov at the committee meeting, and he remembered him coming to have his papers stamped. He denied knowing Pankratov not because he thought it might harm himself — nothing could either harm or help him. His denial was the reflex of anyone who had at any time belonged to an opposition group. He had not even figured out the *version:* he didn't yet know that Pankratov was in prison. He denied knowing Pankratov because he knew that any mention of any name by him could only harm its bearer.

❧ 23 ❧

Sasha was given four books, none of them on the list he had submitted, though the librarian had evidently tried to come close. Instead of Balzac's *Illusions perdues* he got *César Birotto,* instead of *War and Peace* they'd given him Tolstoy's *Childhood, Adolescence and Youth,* plus the magazine *Nature and People* for 1906 and a 1925 issue of *Red Soil.* They'd all been read over and over and were dog-eared and bore the oval stamp "Butyrki City Prison Library." The Balzac was an 1899 edition, the Tolstoy 1913. Many pages were missing, and the list of missing pages at the back of each book was incorrect.

Still, for Sasha there was a week's respite ahead of him. He looked through the magazines first, then read the books, then the magazines again. He found a poem of Esenin's he hadn't come across before: "Blue mist. Snowy expanse." He'd already read Balzac's *César Birotto,* but before, the story of the luckless parfumier had seemed melodramatic, whereas now he was touched by it. "Unhappiness is a step toward the rise of genius, a purifying font for the Christian, a treasure for the deft, an abyss for the weak." He was not a genius or a Christian, nor was he deft or weak. Yet he felt something in these words that was important for him.

He indulged himself for a week with books, clean underwear, and the delicacies his mother had sent. He dropped a few pieces of meat in the soup, and when it was warmed up he added it to the kasha and made himself an edible dinner. Mornings and evenings he made sandwiches with rolls, butter, and salami or cheese, and his cell was filled with the smell of a school lunch-break. Well fed and washed, he would lie on his bunk and read. Lying down was forbidden during the day, but he took no notice of the corridor guards' rules and they left him in peace, only becoming insistent when a superior officer was approaching. He had a week of satisfied, lazy life with books, salami, and chocolate. He seemed to be getting used to it, settling down, adapting.... "We will all become calm, we will all be there, whether you are cared for in this life or not." It was not convincing, but it was comforting.

His world of books and magazines was utterly divorced from his present life, and indeed from his past. The suffering and bitterness in *Childhood, Adolescence and Youth* were not like those of his own childhood and youth.

He'd said to his father, "I won't let you hurt Mama."

His father had looked at him with his gray, bulging eyes and sunk his head in his hands and said, "You're a good son," and then seemed to cry.

A father is a father. Maybe he had a cold hand, but he recalled its touch from his childhood. It made him want to console him and to ask his forgiveness.

His father took his hands from his face. His eyes were angry and dry. "Who gave you the right to interfere!"

"She's my mother."

For days, his father would get up and move about silently, he'd shave and spend a long time washing and dressing, then he'd look at himself in the mirror, sit down at the table without a word, eat in silence, stuff his papers into his briefcase, mutter something, and without a good-bye go off to work. When he returned, he would look angrily around the room, eat his supper without saying a word, clear away his plates with a clatter, not reply to his wife's timid questions. And only late in the evening, when they had gone to their room, would Sasha hear his father's muffled voice, and then his mother would be silent and Sasha was afraid that the silence would cause her heart to burst.

Later his father said to him, "We have to have a chat."

They went out of the house and walked along the Arbat. Snowflakes flurried in the light of the streetlamps. His father was wearing his high fur hat, made of the same fur as the collar of his topcoat, and he walked along, tall and handsome, smooth shaven, arrogant, a man who would brook no opposition.

He hadn't wanted their son involved in their relationship, but *she* had poisoned the boy against him from childhood. *She* was to blame for their discord, *she* was to blame for his failures, she didn't share his ambitions or his interests, she cared more for her sisters and brother. Envy, that was all she was capable of.

Sasha had been seized by a feeling of hopeless depression. What could he possibly reply to his father, there on the street? His father was hard of hearing; one had to shout to be heard.

All he had said was, "If people can't live together, they ought to separate."

A month later his father went to work at the synthetic rubber factory in Efremov, and everything fell onto Sasha's shoulders, at the age of sixteen.

Dyakov didn't call for him and Sasha didn't care. He'd waited for the first interrogation with hope, the second with fear, and now he felt neither. The only thing that worried him was the thought of Krivoruchko. They might arrest Krivoruchko and he might confess that he'd said to Sasha, "This is a chef who likes to make peppery dishes." They'd be able to trap Sasha in a lie, in which case they wouldn't believe him about the main issue, which had to do with Mark.

But why had Krivoruchko said it at all? Look at the absurd position his gossip had put him in! How would Sasha have acted if the question had come up at a committee meeting? He wouldn't have concealed those words there: "Comrade Krivoruchko must explain what he meant, he must make himself clear!" Why should he behave any differently here? Why must he protect Krivoruchko *here*?

He would tell everything the way it happened and remove the burden from himself. His conscience would be clear and they could do what they liked with him. "Siberia is awful, Siberia is far away, but people live there, too." What was that from?

But he was here, living in prison, lying on his bunk, reading, indulging himself with salami and chocolate, singing away under a hot shower every night, thinking, remembering. He'd grown a beard, he could already stroke it, and he'd like to have seen how he looked, but there was no mirror.

*　　*　　*

The guard appeared again with pencil and paper and collected the books. Sasha wrote out his new order. This time he asked for ten books. Just on the off-chance they might be available, he repeated his request for *War and Peace* and *Illusions perdues* and the January, February, and March issues of the serious magazines. He added Stendhal, Babel, Gibbon's *Decline and Fall of the Roman Empire,* which he'd begun reading not long before his arrest, Gogol, whom he loved, Dostoevsky, whom he did not but whom he felt he must master. Again he put down the *Criminal Trial Code* so that they would at least know that he had asked for it. Dyakov would obviously check the list, and he should be aware that Sasha wanted to know his rights.

Two days without books returned him to his previous state. Blank walls, oppressive silence, secret shufflings, the all-seeing eye in the door, the urinal, and, now that he'd eaten up what his mother had sent, the heavy food and indigestion.

He thought about Katya, her hot hands and her lips dry from the wind. Unable to sleep, he got up and paced. But the guards banned moving about at night.

"Prisoner, lie down!"

He lay down but he couldn't fall asleep, and when he did drop off, he had the agonizing dreams of a boy, exhausting visions he'd had as a teenager.

When he was seventeen, he'd gone with his mother to Lipetsk. While they were there, the landlady's daughter-in-law, Elizaveta Petrovna, came to visit from Samara, where her husband was working on the railway. She was a skinny blonde who wore a thin wrap that barely covered her naked body. She gave Sasha a narrow, sideways glance, smiled at him ambiguously, and put on a show of mock modesty, a typical little hick from Samara. But she excited and confused Sasha with her ambiguous smile, her cheap perfume, and her body, which he glimpsed through the half-open wrap. During the day she would lie in the garden with the wrap open, exposing her shapely white legs to the sun. Sasha didn't look in her direction, but he was aware of her lying under the apple tree, the splash of color of her wrap, the lovely bare legs, the rounded knees, and he sensed her glance and her smile.

"Sash-sha ..." she said one day, drawing out the *sh-sh*.

He went over and sat down next to her.

"Sash-sha," she repeated, turning toward him and letting her wrap fall open, revealing her thin white shoulder and small breast.

"Sash-sha, where do you go all day? With girls? Tell me about your girlfriend!"

He was gazing at her legs pressed tightly together and her small white breast, and he was struck dumb. He felt debilitated by the baking sun, by the buzzing wasps and the scent of apples, he couldn't stand up, he didn't dare move, and he was ashamed that she could see and understand everything, as she smiled her mysterious smile and silently mocked him.

"Nothing but books, books — you'll read yourself silly." She snatched the volume of Anatole France out of his hand. "I won't give it back!"

She hid the book behind her.

He reached for it, their hands met and clasped, he was overcome by the heat of her body, she cast a quick glance at the gate, threw back her head, and gave a deep sigh. A distant, secret expression appeared on her face. She put her warm hands behind his neck and drew him closer, their lips touched, and she lay back.

Then she looked into his eyes and laughed.

"Now look what you've done. They'll have to be washed.... And you didn't like it, did you? Don't worry, darling, it's not always good the first time. It is your first time, isn't it? Tell the truth."

He felt ashamed and avoided her for the rest of the day, but the next day at lunch she said, "Sasha, be a man and take me for a ride in the boat."

"Yes, go on, Sasha," said his mother, who was worried that he was bored by Lipetsk.

They took the boat to the other side of the Voronezh, as the river was called, and there, in a clearing in the woods, as she had so obviously intended, she gave herself to him again.

She came to him that night where he slept in the dining room on the divan. Every night she came to him, and every day she took him to the other side of the Voronezh.

"Talk about cradle-snatching," whispered the mother-in-law. "The little trollop!"

Sasha's mother took no notice.

Elizaveta's husband arrived and looked at Sasha suspiciously — obviously his mother had said something. Elizaveta played the tender young wife and made Sasha out to be a hopelessly love-struck boy. Drawing out her words and laughing, she said to her husband, "And this is my admirer."

Sasha hated her play-acting, and he couldn't stand the whispering and laughing that went on in her room at night. As he had to start work at the factory soon, he left his mother in Lipetsk and went home to Moscow.

He avoided women for a long time after that.

Then, the factory organized a voluntary Saturday work project. They had to clear some ground, unload firewood, and shovel snow. A tall, sleek, good-looking girl called Polya, a machine operator from one of the workshops, was working alongside him, joking and flirting, and at the end of the day she said quietly: "Come to my place and warm yourself up." She added, "I'm alone today."

But he didn't go. She'd made it too obvious.

Now, he wished he had gone.

His blood was seething, and he couldn't take his mind off it; he knew what being alone sometimes led to and he was afraid of it.

He exercised in the morning and evening, he didn't lie down during the day, but paced from corner to corner, fixing a daily quota at ten thousand paces, took his shower cold, lay down as late as he could, and got up early.

Two days later they brought his books and once more he could bury himself in reading. But he read either sitting up or leaning against the wall, not lying down. He'd been given the first two volumes of Gibbon, Dostoevsky's *Brothers Karamazov,* and Gogol's *Taras Bulba* instead of his *Dead Souls.*

One day a cellmate materialized: a thin, exhausted young man in a tattered, light overcoat, worn-out shoes, and a cap. After he was brought in, a bed, mattress, and blanket followed.

His name was Savely Kuskov, he was a third-year student at the

Moscow Teachers' Training Institute, and he had been in the Butyrki for five months. There had been four of them in a cell the size of Sasha's, and today they had been dispersed; no doubt a new intake was expected.

The impression he made on Sasha was of someone who, if not entirely crazy, was at least touched. He would lie for hours without moving or saying a word, then suddenly leap up and start pacing, stumbling over the bed and singing quietly and monotonously: *"Cornflowers everywhere, the field was full of cornflowers."*

He didn't go out for walks in the yard or go with Sasha for a shower, and he didn't exercise. He had no relatives or close friends in Moscow, and though he received no packages, he didn't eat the prison meals when they came, but waited until the food, which was never hot anyway, was thoroughly cold. Then he would give his bowl a perfunctory rinse and watch with indifference while Sasha washed his own bowl out thoroughly. Sasha received a second package from his mother and laid out everything on the table, but Savely would hardly touch anything.

He picked up Gibbon briefly and then put it down. As for Gogol and Dostoevsky, he'd already read them. He wasn't interested in Sasha's case and spoke about his own with indifference. He was from the district of Sebezh, a village on the frontier, and just before he had been about to go home for his vacation his mother had written to say there was a shortage of small currency and they couldn't buy or sell anything or get change. So, he'd started collecting silver money, and when he was searched they found he had twenty-eight rubles and forty kopeks. He was accused of planning to escape abroad, and to make things worse, he was in the foreign languages department. He had confessed at the preliminary hearing, the investigation had been terminated, and he was now awaiting sentence.

"Why did you confess?"

"How could I prove anything?" Savely asked phlegmatically. *"They* have to prove it, not you."

"And they would, too: 'You saved up silver.' "

It was ludicrous and absurd. Still, if anyone had been told that he, Sasha, had been arrested over a student newspaper or because of his uncle, they wouldn't have believed it either.

Savely only came to life when he recounted the legends of those who'd escaped. They had sawed through the bars over their windows, climbed out onto the roof, from there to the next roof, then jumped onto the wall and down the wall into the street. Just recently two currency speculators had jumped from the fourth floor to the street.

Sasha had been in prison long enough to know it was impossible to escape. But he didn't argue. Savely's general ignorance and lack of education amazed him. But when he tried out the few words of German he remembered from school, he found that Savely spoke it well, fluently and without hesitation, which dispelled any doubt that he might not be a student at the Teachers' Training Institute at all.

Savely became equally animated when he spoke about the prison hospital. It had clinics and consulting rooms for everything, including electrotherapy and dentistry. Whatever was wrong with you, a boil, a carbuncle, lumbago, straightaway they put you on a daily dose of sunlamp treatment, or they might even put you into the ward, where you got white rolls and milk. Hearing him talk about white rolls and milk with such ecstasy made even less sense, since he ate almost nothing.

He said one thing that Sasha found of value. If the doctor came to your cell and asked if you had any health problems, it meant you were being sentenced to exile and they were deciding where to send you. If you wanted to go to the south, either Central Asia or Kazakhstan, you should say you had tuberculosis, rheumatism, sciatica, or slipped disc, and if you wanted to go north, you should say you had a bad heart. And if the doctor didn't come, it meant the camps, and that could be anywhere.

Sasha also learned the name of their block and those of the other blocks and how they were arranged. The tower inside the yard was called the Pugachev Tower. It was the smallest yard; there were bigger ones, and the best of the lot was the one with workshops, where the criminals worked, because through them you could get a note to the outside.

They took Savely away on the third day. He left in the same state of indifference as he had arrived. Two days had been spent in the company of someone he hadn't known, and now he was departing from someone he still didn't know.

But as Sasha watched him go, not turning around or saying good-bye, and he looked at his narrow, hunched, submissive shoulders in the doorway, he had a sense of the endless prison *road*. He'd meet many others along that road. Savely was only the first.

❦ 24 ❦

"**C**omrade Budyagin, please hold the line."

Then came the familiar voice. "Hello, Ivan!"

Budyagin wasn't used to calling Stalin by his surname and he hadn't the nerve to call him by his first name.

He replied, "Hello!"

"You came home, but you haven't been in to see me. You've become proud, or maybe you forgot the way."

"When would you like me to come? I'm ready any time."

"If you're ready, come over. We live next door to each other."

The last time Budyagin had been at Stalin's was two years earlier, just a month before the death of Nadya, Stalin's wife. Coming home in those days had meant dealing with Litvinov, who ran foreign affairs and was then trusted by Stalin.

Stalin's conception of foreign affairs boiled down to the belief that the Soviet Union's enemies were England, France, and Japan. England saw the U.S.S.R. as a threat to its colonial empire, Japan saw it as a threat to its sovereignty in Korea, and France saw it as a threat to its influence in Europe. At the same time, England and Japan were rivals of the United States on the world market. Defeated Germany stood in opposition to her conqueror France.

In this way, all complex problems had been rendered simple. England, France, and Japan stood on one side; the U.S.S.R., the U.S.A., and Germany stood on the other. Stalin believed that he had a great talent for reducing the complex to the simple.

Budyagin regarded Stalin's ideas, which he had formed during the period of the Weimar Republic, as outdated, and his desire to simplify everything as catastrophic. Hitler's rise to power had changed the disposition of forces, and the German problem was now fundamental.

Litvinov evidently shared Budyagin's view, but didn't say so. Perhaps he was hoping that time would alter Stalin's position? *"Laissez passer,"* he'd said to Budyagin. He was a diplomat, he knew that were he to point out Stalin's mistakes, Stalin would replace him with someone who would toe his line without complaint.

Stalin didn't know Europe, didn't like Europe, and despised the émigré Party intellectuals — they were conceited know-it-alls of the same stripe as the Western labor leaders who wore evening dress and morning coats. While Stalin had been living the life of an underground activist, sent into exile, escaping, and going into hiding, they had been living abroad in perfect safety, doing a bit of reading, a bit of writing, and becoming famous. During the Fifth Party Congress in London, he'd had a chance to take a good look at them at close quarters.

Until then, Stalin had been abroad only to Party meetings in Tammerfors and Stockholm. But they had been nothing compared to the London congress, where more than three hundred delegates had gathered, among them Bolsheviks, Mensheviks, Bundists, and Polish and Latvian Social Democrats. For the first and only time in his life, Stalin saw the capital of a world power, a city such as he had never seen, the capitalist Babylon, the stronghold of bourgeois democracy.

Among all those confident people who had grown up with their incomprehensible and alien traditions, Stalin, who didn't know the language, felt humiliatingly insignificant. It was cold in London that May and he'd lost his scarf, so he went with Litvinov to buy a new one. He didn't want too coarse a wool that would scratch his neck, and it was hard to find one that satisfied him. They ended up buying him the softest and most expensive, but he still complained and turned around to swear at passersby he thought were staring at him.

Litvinov had had to leave him for a while in the docks area, and when he returned he found Stalin was being beaten up by some longshoremen. Maybe they'd asked him something and, not knowing the language, he hadn't replied. Litvinov, who was fearless and who spoke English like a native-born Londoner, had driven them off. This incident remained unnoticed at the time, as nobody at the congress was interested in Stalin. Later Litvinov had told Budyagin about the scarf, but he'd never talked about the incident on the docks. Stalin would never have forgiven him. Puny and frail as a child, he was pathologically sensitive about anything that cast doubt on his physical strength and courage. It was a psychological condition that later gave rise to his suspiciousness.

While they were still in exile, he'd said to Budyagin, "You have to reply to rudeness with greater rudeness. People take it as a sign of strength."

It was in the course of one of the long winter nights that Stalin himself had talked about the incident with the longshoremen; they had mistaken him for an Indian and were going to beat him up, but they got one in the eye and ran away. He loved that expression, "one in the eye."

"And that's the famous English working class for you," he said. "Colonialists, just like their bosses."

Budyagin had been waiting for over a year to see Stalin, and regarded it as his duty to express his point of view. He knew it would be hard to get Stalin to change his mind: he was a man who gave up his likes easily, but his dislikes never. But he also knew that Stalin was afraid of a war.

Budyagin would soon realize that his efforts were doomed to failure. Time had not changed Stalin's position — he was as convinced as ever of his infallibility, and Budyagin knew exactly what would ensue if he were to contradict him.

Budyagin walked to the Kremlin, not along the Vozdvizhenka, as he normally had, but by way of Herzen Street, then across Manezh Square and along the railing of Alexander Park to the Troitsky Gate. He prolonged the walk a few minutes longer, for he wanted to give careful thought to the conversation that was about to take place, and perhaps he also wanted to delay the meeting that he felt sure was going to play a fateful role in his life.

He had always kept away from the internal Party squabbles and the dogmatic rigidity of the Party intellectuals. Nor had he joined in the universal chorus of glorification. Stalin had more than enough of that.

He hadn't joined the Revolution to better his life. His family had been quite comfortable: his father, brothers, and he himself were all qualified forgers at the Motovilikha plant. It had been a state-owned enterprise, one of the biggest in the country; and its fifty-ton press was said to be the most powerful in the world. Motovilikha was on the left bank of the Kama, on the mainline of the railroad, an industrial, commercial suburb of Perm, and a busy, prosperous, and relatively sober town.

As a bright young worker, he had been spotted by Nikolai Slavyanov, the inventor of the arc-welding process, and had been recruited to work on the first arc-welding projects.

Working with advanced technology and its brilliant exponents stimulated his mind. He became involved with the many Social Democrats who were to be found both among the educated workers at the factory and the political exiles in the town.

No doubt he too would have become a rank-and-file Social Democrat. He registered for courses in general education in Tomsk, where they issued school diplomas that entitled one to enter the Institute of Technology.

He was already a professional revolutionary by the time of the first Russian Revolution. In December 1905 he took part in the general political strike, and then in the armed clashes with the troops. He was arrested and exiled to Narym.

Everything had been clear as long as the struggle was against the autocracy. The Revolution had been clear: the final aim was to be victory of their idea. Extremes were unavoidable: the people's frenzy had burst upon their age-old oppressors, the Red terror had been justified, the Revolution had to defend itself.

The Civil War had come to an end and everything took its proper place. The NEP was not merely a new economic policy, it was a new policy altogether. Revolutionary Russia had become a legal state. A new order of life had arisen, which promised to produce the new man of whom the young Budyagin had once dreamed.

But the policy that Lenin had meant to apply "seriously and for a long time" did not last long. Stalin terminated the NEP, he destroyed and deported millions of peasants to Siberia, eliminated those who thought differently, created a regime of fear, lawlessness, and arbitrariness, claiming that in doing so he was carrying out Lenin's wishes. He loved swearing by the name of Lenin, loved referring to him, although he had told Budyagin in Siberia that Lenin didn't know Russia well enough, which was why he had launched the slogan of nationalization of the land — something that wouldn't appeal to the peasants, as Stalin had asserted at the time. And then, at Tsaritsyn, during the Civil War, he had told Budyagin that Lenin didn't understand military affairs very well, either. But Stalin had always understood the significance of Lenin's role in the Party and had never opposed it. When it turned out that Lenin was right, and that he'd always been right, Stalin proclaimed himself his confederate, carrying out Lenin's policies without hesitation. Even now at every step he made obeisance to Lenin, presented himself virtually as the initiator and inspirer of Lenin's decisions. But instead of the socialist democracy that Lenin was trying to install, Stalin created a totally different regime.

Stalin was alone, sitting at the dining table. There was a bottle of Ateni wine, two bottles of mineral water, some glasses, a bowl of fruit, and an open book. Even when he was at home, he still dressed in his semimilitary style, with his breeches tucked into crimson-tooled, light morocco boots.

Stalin turned his head. His drooping jowls and heavy chin covered the white edge of his collar, and his tunic swelled over his stomach. There was the familiar low forehead, the pockmarks, and the soft, well-shaped hand. Budyagin sensed that this would be his last visit.

Without extending his hand, Stalin got up slowly and continued to look straight at Budyagin. Although he was short, he did not look up, nor even straight ahead, but rather as if he were looking through his heavy, lowered eyelids. Stalin did not like tall people.

Budyagin was waiting for Stalin to tell him to sit down and end the awkward moment.

Stalin nodded toward the window.

"Are they cursing me out there?"

He didn't mean the foreign country Budyagin had left a year before, or the one he was now in, he meant the whole world, all of mankind, in fact everything that lay beyond the window: the lonely Georgian exile in his Siberian hut had stirred in the bosom of this implacable Asiatic god. Except that beyond the window lay not the silent taiga, but a vast country that was obedient to his will.

And he could ask this after the triumph he had just won at the congress. He didn't trust anyone, just as in the old days, and he needed to convince himself that this distrust and suspicion were justified, and to check yet again what sort of people Budyagin and those like him were. He had already adopted a hostile attitude toward Budyagin: he didn't smile or ask about his family, or evince the slightest trace of their former relationship.

"There are bound to be some who do," Budyagin replied.

Stalin moved his hand in a minimal gesture, and Budyagin sat down.

Grasping his pipe in his fist, Stalin moved around the room with his familiar light, springy step.

"What do you think of Ryazanov?"

The question was unexpected. Stalin had received Ryazanov and heard him address the Politburo, and he had promoted him into the Central Committee. Perhaps the arrest of his nephew was giving Stalin cause for doubt.

"He's a practical, knowledgeable man," Budyagin replied.

"I hear he's started building something that's not in the plan."

A message had come into the commissariat to the effect that Ryazanov, on his own authority, was building a movie theater and a sports center, and was even laying the foundations for a health resort, which they were calling the "Urals Matsesta."

"Pyatakov sent a commission there," Budyagin answered with restraint.

Stalin looked him straight in the eye. Budyagin knew this meant Stalin didn't trust him, didn't like his reply. But why? He had spoken the truth. On the other hand, he was all too familiar with Stalin's way of sowing confusion by showing distrust where it was unjustified, and giving the impression of trust where there were grounds for doubt.

Stalin looked away slowly and smirked.

"Sergo proposed Ryazanov for the Central Committee. He wants to pack it with economic planners."

He fell silent and waited for Budyagin's reaction.

It was typical of the man to play one off against the other: Sergo had proposed Ryazanov for the Central Committee, but not Budyagin.

Raising his voice, Stalin went on. "With all due respect to Sergo, we're not going to turn the Central Committee of the Party into the Supreme Council for the National Economy. The Central Committee is like our supreme court. The economic planners and the politicians and the military people and cultural leaders all have to be there. All our Party's resources have to be represented in it, especially its young resources."

He stopped opposite Budyagin.

"We have to move aside and make way for men of the people. The people want to see their own sons running the state, not a lot of newcomers, not a new nobility. The Russian people never liked the nobility. The history of the Russian people is the history of its struggle against the nobility. The Russian people loved Ivan the Terrible and Peter the Great, in other words tsars who destroyed the nobility. Every peasant movement, from Bolotnikov to Pugachev, was a movement in favor of a good tsar and against the nobles."

He was off on one of his typical excursions into history, which was the only thing he had much relatively sound knowledge of, especially the history of the Church and the religious heresies. But it was also possible that he was saying that people like Budyagin were the new nobles. And the people didn't want them around anymore.

Stalin went on. "Why was it that the peasants in the central provinces supported the Revolution, but not those in the border-lands, in Siberia, for instance? Because in the central provinces there were landlords and nobles, whereas in Siberia there weren't any. And as soon as Kolchak — a noble — fought us, the peasants came over to the Revolution."

He looked at Budyagin with darkened eyes. Then he moved away to the window and stood with his back to Budyagin.

"But not all young people can be counted among the new forces. I happened to be going through the Arbat and I noticed young idlers in Western raincoats, standing on the street corners, laughing. I ask myself: What is more important to them, their Soviet motherland or their Western raincoats?"

He was talking about the youth, which meant he knew about the intervention for Sasha.

"It is possible to wear a Western raincoat *and* love the Soviet motherland," said Budyagin.

"You think so?" Stalin turned and looked at him. "That's not what *I* think. *My* children don't wear Western raincoats; *my* children are happy with Soviet ones. *My* children couldn't get hold of Western raincoats. I ask myself, where *do* these people get hold of them?"

Perhaps he had Lena in mind? Maybe one of the wives had gossiped spitefully that "Budyagin's daughter wore Western clothes." Trivial facts were important to Stalin: he always paid attention to them, using them to show how well informed he was, proud of his ability to form generalizations and to draw conclusions from trivialities.

"I'm wearing a foreign suit myself," said Budyagin, making it plain that, having lived abroad for nearly ten years, he and his family had naturally bought their clothes there.

Stalin took the hint and with mock respect spread his hands.

"Yes, but *you* act for us on an international level. How could you . . ."

He came slowly toward Budyagin and suddenly reached out to touch his head. "You look so young, still handsome, black hair . . ."

The thought occurred to Budyagin that Stalin would as easily cut off the head he had just touched with his soft hand.

Stalin lowered his hand, almost as if he had read Budyagin's thoughts, and a grin moved his mustache.

"You always liked to argue, Ivan, always the desperate, incorrigible debater."

He moved again to the window and stood with his back to Budyagin.

"We love our young people, they are our future. But they must be properly raised. You have to cultivate the young the way a gardener cultivates a tree. You mustn't flatter or humor them, nor should we forgive them their mistakes. . . ."

Yes, he was definitely talking about Sasha. He was showing how well informed he was. But he was revealing only a small part of what he knew. When the time came, he would display it all.

"One mustn't seek cheap popularity with the young," he went on. "The people don't like leaders who court cheap popularity. Lenin didn't do it — he didn't wander around the streets. The people don't like phrase-mongering leaders. Trotsky was a real windbag, and look where it got him."

This dart was in fact aimed at Kirov. Kirov liked to mingle with the people in the streets of Leningrad, and he was the best orator in the Party.

But what was this all about? Was he preparing a new assault? No, he wasn't ready to rid himself of Kirov and Ordzhonikidze just yet. He would remove them and leave those two pawns, Molotov and Kaganovich, in the Politburo. But not just yet. The time wasn't right, the Party wouldn't swallow it.

For the moment he would start with Budyagin, feeling him out as someone who had been close to Kirov and Ordzhonikidze since the defense of Astrakhan and the military operations in the north Caucasus. That was the reason he'd called him in. He wasn't interested in international problems. If he had been, he'd have summoned him a year earlier.

As always, Stalin's frankness when talking about close comrades was startling, as was his conviction that what he said would not be passed on. If Budyagin were so much as to hint to Kirov or Ordzhonikidze what he had just heard, he'd be branded an intriguer. After all, Stalin hadn't actually criticized anyone, he'd merely remarked on Ordzhonikidze's efforts to get more planners into the Central Committee and expressed a legitimate concern about the casual and open way Kirov wandered around the streets of Leningrad.

"By the way," he went on, without turning around, "what sort of person is Kodatsky? Wasn't he with you at Astrakhan?"

"Yes, he was, he ran the fishing industry of the province. But you *must* know him, he's chairman of the Leningrad Soviet."

Stalin pretended not to have noticed the implied sarcasm in Budyagin's reply.

"Well, Kodatsky is a Zinovievite," he said calmly.

Budyagin was genuinely amazed.

"Kodatsky? But he came out *against* Zinoviev."

"Yes, he *apparently* came out against Zinoviev," Stalin agreed. "But when the Leningrad workers demanded the expulsion of Trotsky and Zinoviev from the Party, Comrade Kodatsky wasn't very enthusiastic. He wavered. And on an issue like that! And then it was Comrade Kirov himself who proposed that Kodatsky be relieved of his post as secretary of the Moscow-Narva District Committee. And he was relieved. But he was kept in the Economic Council, and now he's been made chairman of the Leningrad Soviet. So, in place of Grigory Zinoviev as chairman of the Leningrad Soviet, we have a new chairman who is also a Zinovievite. What are the workers of Leningrad supposed to make of that?"

"As far as I know, Kodatsky never took part in the opposition," Budyagin said. "If he wavered in matters of *organization* ... but nobody can claim to be totally free of such wavering, especially eight years ago."

"Nobody is asking for Comrade Kodatsky's blood," Stalin replied calmly, turning to Budyagin. "Even so, in an organization like the one in Leningrad, one has to be all the more alert over the selection of personnel. As a matter of fact, the Party left it to Comrade Kirov to select his assistants. We won't interfere."

This last sentence carried a warning that the conversation about Kodatsky was of a personal character, and was not official.

As a matter of course, more for the sake of form, Stalin then asked Budyagin the question he had been expecting.

"What about Hitler?"

"Hitler means war," he replied.

Stalin said nothing, then asked, "Has he got anything to fight with?"

"Germany's industrial potential is very great. It wouldn't be hard for them to rearm."

"But will they let him rearm?"

"He won't ask anyone's permission."

"Will he be able to stay in power?"

"Yes, it looks like it."

Stalin said nothing, but ran his finger around the inside of his collar.

"You think the Germans will fight?"

"If they have to, they will."

Slowly and with conviction, Stalin proclaimed, "England and France bound Germany hand and foot at Versailles, the reparations stripped her bare, they took her colonies, the Sudetenland, Danzig, the Polish Corridor, and they sliced off East Prussia. So, what do the Germans propose to fight with?"

"England and France will try to make a deal with Germany at our expense," Budyagin commented.

Stalin turned to him. It was plain that he felt no need to conceal his own point of view; on the contrary, he felt he must express it right here in front of Budyagin, in his own home. He maintained his outwardly calm appearance.

"England and France will never allow a strong Germany to exist in the heart of Europe. Whereas we, on the contrary, want to see a strong Germany, as a counterweight to England and France."

"Germany is the real threat to us," Budyagin responded with conviction.

Stalin frowned.

"To exaggerate the German threat is to overlook the main danger. Obviously, the English imperialists would like that. But it is not in our interest."

"I stand by my opinion," said Budyagin.

"That's why you're no longer where you were," Stalin replied, with a threatening stare.

Budyagin stared back.

Stalin said nothing, then, turning away as if to speak to someone else, he said: "The Party doesn't need the parading of *shades* of opinion. What the Party needs is hard work. Anyone who doesn't understand that is of no use to the Party."

"The Party will decide if I'm of any use to it," Budyagin said.

Stalin sat down at the table, turned away and picked up a book.

"I'm busy. Excuse me."

25

The door closed behind Budyagin. Stalin put aside his book, got up, and paced around the room clutching his pipe. He stopped at the window and gazed out at the familiar sight of the yellow and white Arsenal building and the bronze cannons lined up along its facade.

The diplomat from Motovilikha! It wasn't an unarmed Germany that posed a threat, it was Japanese troops in Manchuria, in our rear in the Far East. Budyagin knew that perfectly well, however limited his outlook. He hadn't come to talk about Hitler.

He'd come to make it known that there were people in the Party who had their own point of view, and that they were defending their right to their point of view, and that at the proper time they would advance it against *his* point of view. Budyagin hadn't come on his own initiative, he was too unimportant. He'd come on *instructions* from the same people who had allegedly helped *him*, Stalin, to rout his enemies, the same people *he* was supposed to rely on, and was relying on, because he had to, otherwise they'd get rid of him the way they'd got rid of the others. They thought he was indebted to them for everything.

They were profoundly misguided. The true leader emerges *by himself*, he owes his power to himself alone. Otherwise he is not a leader, but a puppet. They hadn't chosen him, he had chosen them. They hadn't pushed him to the front, he had pulled them along behind him. It wasn't they who had helped him to consolidate himself, it was *he* who had raised *them* to the pinnacles of state power. They had become what they were solely because they had taken their places alongside him.

To whom had Lenin been indebted? Some émigrés in London and Geneva? And Peter the Great? To Menshikov and Lefort? The fact that his power had been inherited didn't change the essence of the point. To reach the pinnacle of power, the monarch had to destroy the entourage that had become accustomed to seeing him as a puppet. That's how it had been with Peter, and the same was true of Ivan the Terrible.

Stalin hadn't become leader because he had managed to wipe out his opponents. He had wiped out his opponents because he *was* leader. It was *he* who had been destined to run the country. His enemies hadn't understood that and therefore they were defeated. They still didn't understand it, and so they had to be destroyed. The failed pretender is always a potential enemy.

History's choice had fallen on him because he was the only one who understood the secret of supreme power in *this* country, the only one who knew how to rule *this* nation, the only one who knew its every virtue and shortcoming. Especially its shortcomings.

The Russians were a nation of the collective. The commune had been their way of life since time immemorial; equality was at the root of their national character. This provided the right conditions for the sort of society the people were building now in Russia. Tactically, Lenin's NEP had been the right maneuver, but the idea that it should be applied "seriously and for a long time" had been mistaken. The move had been a temporary deal with the *peasants* in order to get more food. "Seriously and for a long time" implied a policy based on the wealthy land-owning *farmer,* the kulaks. Farmers implied the path of inequality, and that was contrary to the psychological makeup of the people.

Stalin went to the bookshelf and took down a volume of Lenin and reread the passage where Lenin had said: "To get every member of the population to take part in the cooperative venture by way of the NEP would take an entire historical epoch. Without universal literacy and adequate know-how, and without teaching the population how to use books, without the material basis and some measure of assurance against, say, crop failure or famine and so on, without all this we will not attain our goal." He closed the book and put it back.

This was the reasoning of an émigré who did not know Russia

or the Russian village or the peasant. What had happened to the famous electric plow that Lenin had gazed on with such naïve hope in 1922? Where was it now? It wasn't that Lenin didn't understand technology, just that he didn't understand the Russian village and the Russian peasant. In order to make the peasant literate and cultured and in order to safeguard the village from famine and so on, we needed not decades but centuries.

That approach, the approach that tried to inculcate the psychology of the farmer, was alien to the peasant. The farmer didn't need the dictatorship of the proletariat. The farmer, the private farmer and the individualist, has to be stifled at birth in the Russian peasant. As for cooperatives, by all means, but the kind in which the peasant will be a simple worker. That's what *he* had accomplished: the second Russian revolution, and it was no less important than the first one.

In the October Revolution we had the peasants on our side, and in the collectivization we had them against us. Yes, of course we need books and science and protection against crop failure, but we need all that, not as *preliminaries* of collectivization, but on the *basis* of it. Lenin had said: first culture, then collectivization. Stalin's way was: first collectivization, *then* culture.

What Lenin had called bureaucratic perversion was in fact the only possible way to run the country. It had its dangers: the bureaucracy tries to stand between the people and the leadership, it tries to supplant the leadership. That has to be stamped out without mercy. The apparatus must be the unquestioning executor of the supreme will, it has to be kept in a state of fear, which it will in turn pass on to the people.

Did *he* have such an apparatus? No, he did not! The present apparatus had been formed in the struggle for power and was not yet an instrument of the leader; it regarded itself as a partner in the victory. Budyagin's visit had been a reminder of this.

The apparatus of the true leader is the one he creates for himself *after* he has come to power. Such an apparatus must not be eternal or permanent, otherwise ties become cemented and the apparatus acquires a monolithic quality and strength of its own. One must keep shuffling it, renewing and replacing it.

The creation of such an apparatus is more complicated than just getting rid of rivals. The apparatus consists of hundreds of thousands of people who have been concentrated into a single organism, linked and welded together from top to bottom. The present members of the Politburo were no longer those who had returned with Lenin from abroad. The Politburo members now had their own connections within the apparatus, their own links, which stretched from the top to the bottom. You only had to touch one link for the whole chain to rattle.

Did *he* trust his own entourage?

In politics you trust nobody.

Molotov, Kaganovich, and Voroshilov were the most reliable of the lot — they had no ambitions for independent leadership. They were good executives. Molotov was dull-witted and Kaganovich was more lively, but all of them had shown themselves to be capable of carrying out orders, and of committing themselves to those orders. Yet without *him* they were nothing. Voroshilov was potentially capable of desertion, but he would cling to *him,* because he was afraid of the military intellectuals, especially Tukhachevsky. Voroshilov was counting on the cavalrymen in the army, Budenny, Timoshenko, Shchadenko, Gorodovikov, but they were not much support; the age of the saber had gone.

Kalinin and Andreyev. The oldest and the youngest members of the Politburo. One was fifty-nine, the other thirty-nine. Both of them had come up through the ranks, Kalinin from peasant stock, Andreyev from the working class. They'd support the majority.

Finally, there were those who couldn't be counted on — Kirov, Ordzhonikidze, Kossior, Kuibyshev, and Rudzutak.

Lenin had privately recommended that Rudzutak replace *him* as general secretary *then,* at the time of his famous letter. It was possible Lenin hadn't discussed the question with Rudzutak himself, hadn't actually asked for his agreement. The letter was known only to Lenin's wife, Krupskaya, Lenin's sister Marya, and Stalin's wife Nadya, who was then working in the secretariat. It was she who told him about it. But later, others also heard about it from Nadya, and he never forgave her for it. Rudzutak was being very careful. He had no major connections in the organization. Right up to the February Revolution of 1917 he had spent nearly ten years in hard labor. Even so, he was the man Lenin had thought of putting in *his* place. That must never be forgotten. Rudzutak would never forget it.

Kuibyshev came from gentry background; he'd been through the old Cadet School. He was fond of the good life. He'd gone into private life: he was sickly and wanted to be left alone. A good Party worker, but it was easy to find plenty of other good Party workers.

Kossior came here and walked with him along the corridor and constantly shifted to the right and left. Why? He was not a sincere person. He couldn't be trusted.

Sergo Ordzhonikidze. A difficult case. He was the only one who was close to *him,* going back thirty years to their time together in Tiflis. And that was the point: Sergo had known him far too long, he'd seen him in too many situations and regarded himself as an accomplice. But a real leader doesn't have accomplices, he has *comrades in arms.* Pupils, not friends, became disciples. Sergo was a romantic and openhearted: he believed too much in what he said and did, dangerous characteristics in a politician. When the opposition had capitulated, Sergo had proposed reinstating all of them in the Party. Didn't he understand that anyone who had come out against *him* had to be destroyed? The people had to be made to realize that anyone against *him* was against the Soviet regime. Why hadn't Sergo wanted to destroy the enemies of the Soviet regime when those enemies had appeared not outside the Party but within it? That had been no error, it was a *policy:* it was intended to preserve a counterweight to *him* inside the Party, it was directed at a future situation in which Sergo would act as judge; he was creating reserves that he could unleash against *him,* should the need arise.

Lominadze was the proof of it. Sergo knew about Lominadze's letter to Shatskin, which had been intercepted in 1930. And how had he reacted? He'd shrugged it off: "He's just a boy." But what had this "boy" written about *him* in his letter? Childishness has no place in politics, politics is not child's play. Lominadze and Shatskin had been grooming themselves as *successors,* and they were in a hurry. They regarded *him* as an ignoramous, an uneducated semi-Marxist. But what was Lominadze? If he'd been born three years earlier he'd have been at home among the Georgian Menshe-viks, the likes of Zhordania, Chkheidze, and Tsereteli, and they also thought *he* was an ignoramus. Those Georgian intellectuals had all the worst national characteristics of the Georgians: they saw themselves as a European island in an Asiatic sea. Now Lominadze was in the Urals, but Sergo was still protecting him. Was this by chance? No, it was not by chance. Lominadze was one of the links in his chain.

Was Sergo's policy his own? No, it was not. It was a common policy that he was pursuing with Kirov. They were inseparable companions and friends! When Kirov came to Moscow, he invariably stayed at Sergo's. What lay behind such *tender* friendship? What bound them together? What friendship can there be between political leaders? Why should two members of the Politburo set themselves apart from the rest by friendship? They were both about forty-eight years old, they'd both been in the northern Caucasus and Georgia, both had been members of the Politburo since 1930, but none of that was a basis for such unanimity.

Friends are never equals. In friendship, as in politics, one leads and the other is led, one exerts influence and the other is influenced. The leader in this instance was Kirov. Like many half-educated people, he was vain, like many a run-of-the-mill small-town journalist, he was a rabble-rouser, and like most rabble-rousers he had the gift of the gab, which meant he had fans who thought he was the best speaker in the Party, if not the "tribune of the Revolution."

When Stalin originally sent Kirov to Leningrad, it was to show the Leningraders that their city was not the second capital, but that it was just a provincial town in the northwestern corner of the country. There couldn't be two capitals: a second capital will always be a rival to the first. The Leningraders had become accustomed to having highly placed people there, but then they'd got the unknown Kirov from far-off Azerbaijan, and at that time he wasn't even a member of the Politburo. The Leningrad workers — the *Peterites* as they liked to be called — were fond of flaunting their revolutionary history, and now they had a man who before the Revolution had been a rank-and-file contributor to a pathetic little magazine called *The Terek*. He'd been sent to Leningrad as an outsider, an agent whose job it was to root out the seditious opposition.

The idea was that the Leningraders wouldn't stand for it, the situation would worsen and the conditions would be created in which the final liquidation of this permanently dissident center would be possible.

But in the eight years that he'd been there, Kirov had become his own man, he was the "favorite," he had gained the support of the Party organization and actually reinforced Leningrad's importance as the country's second city, encouraged their deep-rooted separatism and the ridiculous conviction Leningraders had that their city was special, exclusive, the only European city in Russia.

In his hunger for popularity, Kirov had opted for the simple style. He lived on Kamennostrovsky Boulevard in a large house, inhabited by all kinds of people, he walked to work, wandered on his own around the streets of the city, took his children for rides in his car and played hide-and-seek with them in the yard....

A comrade in arms should model himself on his leader. The leader's life-style sets the tone of the epoch that he personifies; he sets the style of the state that he governs. By flaunting his openness and accessibility, Kirov was challenging *him,* as if to emphasize that Stalin lived in the Kremlin, with guards, didn't wander the streets or play hide-and-seek with his children, thus underlining the idea that Stalin was afraid of the people, whereas Kirov was not.

At the Seventeenth Congress, Kirov had said: "The only thing that is old in Leningrad are the revolutionary traditions of the Petersburg workers. Everything else is new."

That was not true. Civil servants from before the Revolution were still there, as were the gentry, the bourgeois intelligentsia, Latvians, Estonians, Finns, and Germans, agents working for bourgeois intelligence services, petit bourgeois workers who thought of themselves as the makers of the October Revolution, and tens of thousands of people who had supported Zinoviev in his attack on the Party. The *entire* Leningrad Party organization had supported Zinoviev. *All* the Communists and Komsomols had voted for the opposition. What had become of them? They were all alive and kicking and they now comprised the majority of the Leningrad Party organization. The cronies had remained in place, and there were many of them. Why did Kirov refuse to root them out? He relied on Chudov, Komarov, and a few others who had come out against Zinoviev. But why? Because Zinoviev had offended them, that's why. A talentless bunch! Zinoviev knew that, which was why he kept them down. *He* would keep them down, too; otherwise they would stir up trouble against *him*. Yet Comrade Kirov surrounds himself with such people.

How could he say, then, that the only old thing left in Leningrad was the "revolutionary tradition"? It was nothing more or less than an open defense of the Leningrad oppositionists, both the known ones and the secret ones, those who had been unmasked and those who had remained concealed; he was flattering the Leningrad petit bourgeois workers in order to win their sympathy and to show that he was defending them from Stalin, but all of it was an attempt to retain Leningrad for himself as a stronghold. Just like Sergo, he was preparing a counterweight to *him*. The same tactics and the same policy.

They thought they could deceive Stalin, did they! They won't get away with it! However much they heap praise on him and swear by his name, they won't pull the wool over *his* eyes!

He'd spent a week with Kirov the previous year. Voroshilov had been with them, too. They went to look at the White Sea Canal and the ports at Soroka, Murmansk, and Leningrad. *He* sensed that Kirov had some reservations about the canal. And yet the northern seaway would serve as their outlet to the Pacific Ocean, their route to the Japanese rear. Kirov had a different view of this strategic question: he had his sights on the West, not the East, and he'd acquired this from the Leningraders, who regarded themselves as Europeans. He took the same position as Budyagin, and therefore Budyagin had come not with just a *general* warning, but with a quite specific one.

Kirov was good at appearing enthusiastic, but he didn't even make a show of doing so about the White Sea Canal; he felt no need. He just kept his mouth shut. He tried to take a back seat, but then came a temptation he couldn't resist. When the Murmansk port manager showed them a new crane, Kirov tried to *explain* how it worked, imagining that he was demonstrating his superiority. And how! After all, he hadn't been educated in a seminary, he'd been to a technical school and was a certified mechanic. The only problem was that for some reason Comrade Kirov hadn't worked as a mechanic for the last twenty years. Newspaper work was evidently cleaner. Nothing remained of his *secondary* technical education, and he never should have displayed his outdated, superficial knowledge. Nobody wants to hear a politician talking about technology, trying to teach everyone else about it, when he himself hasn't studied it, has only got a superficial knowledge of it, and can't even really understand it himself. *Whom* did he think he was trying to teach?

That night, *that* night, Nadya had screamed at him, "They think they can influence you to be a better person. How naïve they are! They don't know you! Nobody can influence you, you're beyond it!"

She was talking about Kirov and Bukharin, her closest friends. They'd taken her over! *They* had! Through her they had tried to influence him, and had planted distrust in her toward him. They were prepared to use a politically naïve woman; they'd deprive him of his personal sanctuary, deprive him of his home, his wife, and family, they'd attacked him from behind, they'd stabbed him in the back. He'd never forget they'd done that to him. They would pay for it in full. As if she had been so good! She had found herself some jolly companions and clever fellows, handsome friends! Even her death had been like a challenge to him. Nadya had also been from that damned city — she'd grown up there, a Petersburger through and through. Everything about her was hostile to him, and *they* had just added to it. You couldn't trust anyone, not even your wife. They wanted to isolate him. So what! Even alone he was more than a match for them, all of them.

Influence. Sergo also wanted to influence him. Influence *him!* The conceited idiots!

Kirov was a worthless, semi-intellectual upstart, and a rabble-rouser. He got an ovation at the Seventeenth Congress. He got another one at the celebration for the congress on Red Square. A member of the Politburo should appear before the Muscovites as a representative of the *whole* Party, not just the Leningrad organization. But he didn't decline the invitation, he spoke.

He couldn't be trusted.

Kirov has to be transferred to Moscow where an eye can be kept on him and where he'll be out in the open. The entire second capital business had been going on long enough.

Look who they'd sent: Vanya Budyagin! They couldn't find anyone more intelligent. *He'd* caught him with his very first question, about Ryazanov: "Pyatakov sent a commission there." He hadn't given a straight answer. After all, Ryazanov had put the Moscow commission under house arrest and then sent them back to Moscow. Budyagin didn't mention that. Why should they hide something like this from *him?* They want to hide their own differences, they want to present their organization as united and monolithic. Ryazanov's town Party secretary was Lominadze, and they were trying to conceal his role. As if they could keep anything from *him.* He knew their every step and every intention.

The arrest and dismissal of the commission was an isolated incident and Ryazanov would answer for it. But the incident was also evidence of serious things going wrong in Ordzhonikidze's organization. It was a slap in the face to Ordzhonikidze, even though Pyatakov had organized the commission.

They were trying to keep it from *him* because they hoped to localize the conflict. They were mistaken. *He* would deal with it himself.

Stalin left the window, picked up the telephone, and told Poskrebyshev to summon Ryazanov to Moscow urgently.

⚘ 26 ⚘

Ryazanov was expecting the call, and when it came he left the same day.

He thought he knew what would happen: he'd be taken off the job and expelled from the Party. He had always known it, and he had been ready to answer for his actions.

Apart from the housing complex, he had indeed begun to build a movie theater, a clubhouse, a Young Pioneers camp, a nursery school, and a medical center alongside the sulfur hot-spring they called the Urals Matsesta, after the one in Sochi. It was hopeless trying to get a supply of permanent, highly qualified staff for the plant if they weren't provided with the normal services.

Ryazanov knew as well as anyone that the country needed metal. He was producing it. But he also knew that there was more to it than just turning out metal. The country needed industry: it was not going to be an Asiatic Russia with a few factories, the way it could be done in the Congo; it was going to be a European, industrial, socialist Russia. You couldn't achieve it with peasants getting their training haphazardly on the job; you needed a well-educated work force supplied with the amenities of modern civilization. The standard of living was an integral part of the standard of production. It was possible to build factories in blizzards and snowstorms, and on the blood and bones of people, but a modern industry couldn't be built that way.

It wasn't as if he'd done that much — just one movie theater, a clubhouse, a nursery school, and a medical center — but everyone knew it was only the beginning. The people had given up their evenings and worked on their days off with the same energy and enthusiasm with which they had built the blast furnaces.

But Moscow had received a report that Ryazanov had started non-plan construction to the detriment of the plant and that he was forcing people to work without pay.

Pyatakov had sent a commission. It was headed by an economic planner who was a has-been, a man with no imagination, who knew only that Ryazanov was supposed to do one thing and who had no room in his mind for anything else: and that one thing was pig iron. Imagine, wooden barracks! On the front during the Civil War, the men had slept under the snow!

The chief expert in the commission was an economist of the Bukharin school. At the end of the 1920s, he had expressed the opinion that the prospects for the Urals were not good and that it made more sense to build in Siberia, where there was more coal and oil and above all the water resources necessary for electrification.

Right from the start it was obvious that the commission would not support Ryazanov in his building program, and that it would cast doubt on the future development of the plant. To let people like this loose on the plant would demoralize everyone.

He gave orders for the distinguished commission to be accommodated in the Country House, a residence for government visitors, with a special kitchen and special services, and located in a picturesque spot some twelve miles from the plant. The distinguished members of the commission were delighted, except for one problem: no cars had been put at their disposal and they had no way of getting to the plant. They were given three good meals a day, but they couldn't get through to either Ryazanov or Moscow by phone. On the first day, with their stomachs full, they made jokes about the fact that Ryazanov hadn't even been able to supply them with transportation. On the second day, they started cursing him, and by the third day they realized they'd been led up the garden path. On the fourth day, they were deposited on demand at the railroad station, their documents were stamped, first-class tickets were issued, and they went back to Moscow.

Ryazanov had carried out the whole operation without Lominadze's knowledge. Stalin didn't like Lominadze and it would only make things worse if he were involved.

Ryazanov's relations with Lominadze had become difficult after the Seventeenth Congress. Lominadze had been removed from the Central Committee and Ryazanov had been put on it so he now occupied a higher political position than Lominadze. Ryazanov was an engineer, but Lominadze, for all his intelligence and ability, had no understanding of engineering. The plant manager was not a new recruit to the Party and most of the foremen in the workshops were Communists. They weren't like the tsarist "military specialists" used by the Red Army in the Civil War — they didn't need political commissars breathing down their necks.

By all means, brilliant speeches and historical parallels were fine, but not now! Ryazanov had spent two years in the United States and had traveled throughout Europe. He knew how much ground still had to be covered, how much work was needed to catch up. All the rest was hot air. Communism had to be built, not discussed.

Using Lominadze's former influence would make perfectly good sense, but Ryazanov's word now carried more weight, whether at the center or in the regional offices or here at the plant. True, Lominadze was a favorite of Ordzhonikidze and had a direct line to him, but whatever the plant needed, Ryazanov could get himself from Ordzhonikidze. In any case, one didn't go to a people's commissar for every little thing — that was what the industrial organization was for, and it only acknowledged Ryazanov. The plant and Ryazanov were one; it was his life and death.

Ryazanov had carefully considered how to handle the commission and he knew the risk he was taking. But in the event of success, the reward would be enormous and his position would be secure for a long time to come. He counted on Ordzhonikidze's support: Pyatakov had sent the commission without his knowledge. Sergo would also know that Ryazanov would never get Lominadze mixed up in the affair. And Ryazanov also counted on Voroshilov's support. A month earlier, Voroshilov had dropped in on his way back from the Far East and had been very pleased with everything he saw; he'd slapped Mark on the shoulder and said, "I've got a Bolshevik nose, I can smell metal!"

Ryazanov was also hoping that Stalin would understand him, since he understood Stalin. In his place, Stalin would have done the same thing, and that had been Ryazanov's guiding principle. Ryazanov was Stalin's man, he was *his* plant, *his* Urals. Stalin could not fail to take account of that.

The affair was discussed in the Kremlin by Stalin, Voroshilov, Ordzhonikidze, and Yezhov, who was a quiet, polite man with violet eyes, the new head of the Central Committee organizational bureau.

Ryazanov gave his explanation. He hadn't arrested anyone — the members of the commission had been free to come and go as they liked. He had simply delayed their visit to the factory until he had spoken to Comrade Ordzhonikidze. He wanted to ask Comrade Ordzhonikidze to order the commission back to Moscow, as he regarded their presence at the factory as harmful. He'd rung Moscow and been told that Sergo was in the south and would be back in a few days. The commission could wait a few days, there wasn't a fire anywhere. As for building the social amenities, it was being done within the limits of the agreed funding and the workers were giving their labor voluntarily. All this could have been checked out by sending an auditor, rather than such a prestigious commission.

They listened to him in silence and without interrupting him. Stalin walked around the room, pipe in hand. Ordzhonikidze was frowning. Yezhov was sitting quietly at a corner of the table with a large notepad in his hand. Voroshilov gave Ryazanov an encouraging smile, and when Ryazanov called the commission prestigious he laughed out loud.

He spoke first.

"I visited the factory recently and it's beginning to take off: it's supplying metal, the teamwork is solid, the management has authority. Why send a professor there who had originally objected to the plant's establishment? Ryazanov did the right thing; I can't see any reason to criticize him. He waited for Comrade Sergo, and the commission should have waited, too, but they didn't. All right, but this is Ryazanov's business. And he's right about something else: we're too fond of sending vast commissions where a simple inspector would do. I believe we should support Comrade Ryazanov."

They were all waiting to hear what Ordzhonikidze would say. His tone was cool.

"The facts are as stated. Let us agree, that's how it was. But, Comrade Ryazanov, you deprived the members of the commission not only of transportation, but also of communication. You wanted to talk to me, that's your right. But they wanted to talk to Moscow, and that was their right."

"You've been misinformed, Grigory Konstantinovich," Ryazanov protested. "Our regular telephone line is erratic, as we all know, and to get through on it to Moscow is practically impossible, whereas we have two direct lines to you, Grigory Konstantinovich, the one I have and the one Comrade Lominadze has. The commission didn't approach Comrade Lominadze, and he is not involved in this matter at all, and I did not think it appropriate to put my line at their disposal, as they would only have contacted Comrade Pyatakov and he would naturally have confirmed their authority. And so I was waiting for you, because, quite frankly, I did not believe you would confirm their authority."

When he mentioned the direct lines that he and Lominadze had to Ordzhonikidze, Ryazanov saw Stalin stiffen.

Stalin immediately began to speak, enunciating his words slowly, with his heavy Georgian accent. He was plainly agitated.

"We don't want people in the Urals who don't recognize the importance of the place. Let those who don't recognize the importance of the Urals stay in Moscow at their desks. Sending this particular commission was a gross error. That should be pointed out to Comrade Pyatakov."

He paused. Yezhov was making rapid notes.

"Building accommodation and social amenities on a reasonable scale is also essential, especially where production demands are being met successfully. The working class must be able to see the tangible results of socialism. And not only in their pay envelopes — capitalists also pay wages. The working class must be able to see the results of socialism in cultural and social institutions, like medical facilities and nursery schools for their children, for the workers' children. Industrial complexes that fulfill the plan have that right. That's what caring for people is all about. Is it practical? It is. Is it plain to see? It is. Is it convincing? It is."

He filled his pipe.

"What part has the town *Party* committee played in this conflict? I see no evidence of its role. What is it doing in general? Why didn't the plant manager talk to the Party committee about the commission? Why was it not taken into account?"

Ryazanov began to reply but Stalin stopped him with a gesture and went on.

"Doesn't it have any authority? Why doesn't it have any authority? If Comrade Lominadze doesn't concern himself with the factory, one has to ask what does he concern himself with? He's an active man, he can't be sitting and doing nothing. Is he too busy with world problems? Why isn't he carrying out his immediate duties? Wherever the Party fails to carry out its immediate duties, the economic managers are compelled to take measures that, in *other* circumstances, could compromise them. Why does the town committee secretary have a direct line to the people's commissar? What he needs is a direct line to the regional Party secretary."

"The direct line's not important," Ordzhonikidze said with a frown.

"Yes, a triviality," Stalin agreed, and suddenly smiled benevolently. "But it's a distraction from work, you see. Other town committee secretaries don't have a direct line to you, but they get by, all the same. So why should we put our dear Comrade Lominadze in this special situation? It's not a very helpful way to treat a young Party leader like Comrade Lominadze. It gives him a false sense of his own identity. We are doing him a disservice in this."

Ryazanov had been right about Stalin. And Stalin had been right about him. They had become close and this lifted Mark's spirits. All the people and committees and documents that had divided them literally disappeared, floated off, lost their meaning. Now Stalin alone guided him. He turned to him in his thoughts for advice, he measured and assessed his own actions by reference to his idea of Stalin.

He was filled with pride and an awareness of his own power and importance. Authoritative by nature, he now no longer tried to conceal it. Not that he changed his way of doing things. When in Moscow, rather than going straight to the people's commissar he still visited the departments and sections and spoke to the ordinary staff. As before, he still tackled his problems with zeal and still resolved them in the interests of the factory, which in fact meant doing pretty much what he wanted. And nobody noticed that there was something new about him: his authoritativeness was more emphasized. Before, when he talked to his assistant, he would sit down; now he remained standing and the assistant would get to his feet. Conversation was still friendly and considerate, but it was made on the move. It seemed natural: it wasn't just the famous manager of a famous factory who was talking, nor even just the favorite of Stalin and Ordzhonikidze, but possibly a future people's commissar.

Ryazanov's relationship with Ordzhonikidze, however, became somewhat strained. At the meeting in the Kremlin, Ordzhonikidze had not disagreed with Stalin and Voroshilov, even though he felt that Ryazanov should have behaved more diplomatically and avoided a skirmish from which he, Sergo, might not have emerged too well.

Ryazanov could see that Sergo was displeased and annoyed with him, though he consoled himself with the thought that Sergo was not vindictive, that he couldn't conceal his anger. In any case, he, Ryazanov, had been fundamentally right and he wasn't responsible for Sergo's differences with Stalin over Lominadze.

He didn't go to see Ordzhonikidze, but waited to be summoned, and meanwhile busied himself with various jobs in the organization, Gosplan and the State Bank. Any trip to Moscow, even on the most urgent government business, always meant that a mass of details that one could handle only in Moscow could be dealt with.

He also had to call on Budyagin, even though Budyagin's days at the commissariat were numbered. Ryazanov pitied him more than he pitied Lominadze. Budyagin was not a theoretician or a speaker, he was a Party worker, and though he was not an engineer, he understood what was going on, he could grasp things quickly. But he had fallen behind, the times had overtaken him, and the times were Stalin. Budyagin didn't like Stalin, he resisted him, and that meant he was resisting the country and the Party.

Ryazanov was talking to Budyagin in a cool, businesslike way, as he would with his boss, a deputy commissar, when it suddenly struck him that Sergo's deputies were Pyatakov and Budyagin and that Sergo's entourage consisted of a number of people whose loyalty to Stalin was dubious. Had Sergo picked them himself or had they been picked for him? If so, for what purpose?

Budyagin was also restrained in talking to Ryazanov and did not even mention the commission. But when he'd signed his papers and completed their business, he asked, "How is your nephew?"

Mark had not been expecting this question. He had planned on seeing his sister later on, but as it turned out, he had to leave the city that evening.

"He's still inside. . . ."

Budyagin said no more and Mark left the office. But there was an unpleasant aftertaste. Budyagin knew that Sasha had been arrested. He was saying something else: Why hadn't Ryazanov used the opportunity of his meeting with Stalin to inquire about Sasha? The question was offensive.

Did he have the right to take up Stalin's time for a mere boy who was probably being held for some good reason? He had obviously done some silly things. If Mark's visit to Berezin hadn't resulted in freeing Sasha, that meant they had something on the boy.

Under these circumstances, how could he approach Stalin? Stalin had put him on the Central Committee, even though his nephew was under arrest. Stalin was keeping a distance between him and his nephew, keeping the case at arm's length. What if he now raised the question with Stalin himself? It would be tactless, and Stalin could see it no other way! And then their inner affinity and mutual understanding would be destroyed forever. That's how it was. Budyagin, he hoped, didn't imagine that he was simply too scared to talk about it to Stalin.

"Budyagin's a primitive man, and he's finished politically," he thought to himself with annoyance.

🙠 **27** 🙡

Savely had taught Sasha how to communicate by tapping. The alphabet was divided into six rows with five letters in each row. The first tap indicated the row and the next indicated the position of a letter in the row. Short pauses between taps meant a row was coming next, slightly longer pauses meant letters were coming, and still longer pauses were used to separate words; scratching meant "I've finished" or "stop" or "repeat." Pauses and intervals were quite short, and experienced prisoners could manage with fractions of a second. The pauses created the greatest difficulty: if you missed one, the tapping merged, you got the wrong letter, and the following ones lost their meaning.

Sasha wrote out the alphabet on a cigarette packet with a burnt match and began communicating with his neighbor. Lying on his bunk with the blanket over him to prevent the guards from hearing, he tapped slowly and with long pauses.

His neighbor understood him, but he had trouble understanding his neighbor: Sasha mixed letters up, asked for repeats, and got it wrong again, even though his neighbor tapped clearly, precisely, and with long pauses, and tapped short words. He asked Sasha his name and gave his own as Chernyavsky, a Party member. He asked if Sasha was getting newspapers and reported that he wasn't getting any, either.

But he had information, which probably came from his other neighbor. There had been a Party congress; nothing much had happened at it. He gave Sasha the news every evening. If a guard came to either of their cells, they had to stop and then start from the beginning again. Two evenings were taken up reporting that the ice-breaker *Chelyuskin* had been crushed by the ice in the Arctic Ocean and sunk, and the next two evenings he reported that an anti-Fascist general strike had been called in France.

Sasha could not but feel gratitude to this man who, at the risk of being thrown into a punishment cell, was communicating with him, just to brighten up his solitude. The whole country was seething with activity and construction, and he was sitting here in a solitary cell looking anxiously at the door in case, God forbid, the guard should discover that he, Sasha Pankratov, was interested in events that had been reported that day in the Soviet press.

His feeling of resignation evaporated, and with it his willingness to accept his fate. No! He would *not* accept such a fate, he didn't want to reconcile himself, he didn't want to. That was not the path he intended to take. His path lay with the Party, with the people, with the state.

What should he do? To whom should he write? To the prosecutor? The prosecutor had sanctioned his arrest. To Stalin? His letter would get no farther than Dyakov. And what would he say? That Mark wasn't involved in the case? But he didn't even know what the case was about or whether his arrest was connected with Mark anyway.

It was then that Sasha began to form a plan. It was not much of a plan, but it was worth trying.

That evening, he contacted his neighbor and asked whether anything had appeared lately in the press about Mark's plant, and he got the answer: "I'll find out and let you know."

Next day came the report, "They've started the blast furnace and been awarded a medal."

Sasha asked, "Ryazanov?"

His neighbor replied, "The Order of Lenin."

Mark was free and still running the project. The case had nothing to do with him! How could he have thought it had? It all had to do with the institute, but the other way around — not because of the wall newspaper, but because of Krivoruchko. That's what they had been pressing him on at the district committee. It was his last conversation with Baulin and Lozgachev that had done it. He'd realized it then — he'd sensed that he'd made a mistake — and now he was having to live with its consequences.

And Dyakov was constantly asking him about Krivoruchko: "Who has had counterrevolutionary conversations with you?" That was the root of everything that had happened to him! Maybe Krivoruchko had also been arrested and had admitted to having talked to Sasha about Stalin, even if only because he was afraid Sasha had already mentioned it. That would mean that Krivoruchko had been honest and admitted it, whereas Sasha had been dishonest and had tried to shield him . . . "Who has had counterrevolutionary conversations with you?"

Dyakov was right: he was devious, he had passed up his chance, he deserved what he got. He hadn't been questioned for three weeks, maybe he wouldn't be questioned anymore; after all, why question him when he denied everything, even established facts? Maybe the case was closed, maybe they were deciding it now, maybe they'd already decided.

He paced his cell, listening for steps in the corridor, expecting them to come and read out his sentence, and realizing that everything had been lost through his own guilt. Even if a decision hadn't yet been made and Dyakov was to question him once more, it was too late to confess: he had deceived them, he had concealed everything before. If only he'd told the whole truth at the first interrogation, his confession would have seemed voluntary, sincere, and honest. Now it would be a confession they'd forced out of him; it would be insincere and dishonest.

He stopped wanting to get up in the mornings and he no longer waited for the evening visit to the washroom; he started using the slop pail, just like Savely. He didn't feel like having a shower at night, and after his second refusal the escort stopped coming for him. He only wanted to eat. He waited impatiently for the servers to come and dish out his portion; he started daydreaming about the food his mother would send and he regretted instructing her to send him only white bread and meat. A nice big hunk of sausage would go down well right now. He had the right to that, at least. His life was finished, however you looked at it. The smear of counterrevolutionary was something you never got rid of.

Chernyavsky was tapping. Sasha didn't reply. Who was Chernyavsky and why should he communicate with him? What did he have in common with the others here? He had thought that Mark and Budyagin were here, honest Communists, innocent of any crime. But Mark and Budyagin weren't here. The people in here were not honest Communists, but criminals. Savely was in here for a reason, so was Chernyavsky, and so was he, Sasha — he was here because he had felt sorry for Krivoruchko, and he was now paying for that moment of weakness. He didn't have a clear, unequivocal position, which was why the incidents with Azizyan and the newspaper were no accidents, in the first place, just as his doubts about Stalin — the great Stalin! — were no accident. He was small-minded and overconfident, he wanted to think everything out his own way, but there were things you couldn't fathom on your own, things other, more powerful minds had thought through.

A thin ray of April sunshine came through the dim glass behind the iron grill. It was the first real spring day, and Sasha wanted to experience the joy of it. He climbed up on the table and opened the vent that was kept closed except when he went out for exercise. Immediately the cell bolt rasped and the guard appeared in the doorway.

"Shut it! Come away from the window! Do you want a taste of the punishment cell?"

Sasha shut the vent and jumped down from the table.

"I felt like a breath of fresh air."

Still, he'd caught the distant sounds of the bustling street: the tram bell, automobile horns, and children's voices. He imagined the asphalt on the sidewalks drying out. The girls would soon be wearing their light dresses with open necks and showing bare arms and long legs. Was he really going to have all that taken away from him? Now, while he was still young and healthy? No! He longed to be out there on the spring street; he wanted to live, like everyone else.

During the spring the year before he had taken a course at the auto depot. The garage always reeked of gasoline, there was a permanent fog of exhaust fumes, and most of the glass in the roof had been broken and patched over with sheet metal. It was an old garage, one of the oldest in Moscow, built way back for Moscow

Food Products, and there were even some old Model T Fords still there, one-ton vans for bread deliveries.

Sasha liked the depot manager, Antonov, a young man, with light brown hair and glasses. He liked his quick wit and common sense, his thirst for knowledge, and the fact that he was at the depot day and night, twenty-four hours. This worker, who'd been promoted to a responsible job, personified what the Revolution had brought: people raised from the lowest levels of society and put into creative work, they were the real strength of the working class, they were the people! He ought to be with the people, too. His place was with Antonov, the ex-driver, and with Malov, the ex-stevedore; they didn't try to be clever or discuss everything, they just got on with the job. They thought this was a beautiful way of life, and he hadn't appreciated its value. But he would return to it, *whatever it took!*

They brought him his books. He looked through them with indifference, with none of his earlier delight.

There were the third and fourth volumes of Gibbon, an old magazine without its cover, and a dog-eared little book in a cardboard binding called *Impressions of a Journey through the U.S.S.R.* by some left radical French senator named de Monzie, a petit bourgeois politician who'd toured the Soviet Union in the mid-1920s and written this lively, if rather superficial, little book about it. Sasha hadn't asked for it. Why had the librarian sent it?

De Monzie wrote about the Soviet Union in general sympathetically, though with some criticisms, especially about the criminal and judicial procedure. As evidence he cited Article 58. It was obviously because of that article that the librarian had sent the book. It was in place of the *Criminal Trial Code* that Sasha had asked for and that couldn't be sent.

Sasha learned nothing of any great importance for himself about this article. Article 58 was not the point, however.

The point was that some unknown prison librarian had responded to his cry, echoed his prayer, and had shown Sasha an example of humanity, fearlessness, and trust.

What had made him do it? Had he violated his duty? Probably he had, but he had fulfilled another, higher duty, his human duty. The laws made by men should not conflict with the laws of the conscience. Those who condemned the innocent and left the defenseless without any defense and denied the rights of those who had no rights — they were the ones who violated their duty.

He didn't jump off his bunk or start pacing his cell. What had happened was as pure, bright, and clear as everything real and human in him, and he felt no tremblings of excitement or shock. He had found what he had to find. And he only felt ashamed that he had lost his courage.

Sasha went to his next interrogation without any hope, knowing what to expect and feeling no fear. Saying that Stalin liked to cook peppery dishes didn't make a man into an enemy. But what difference did it make: Dyakov ignored the meaning of what was said; he interpreted statements, and Sasha wanted no part of the process. Certainly, he wanted to get out of Butyrki, but he wanted to get out with a clean record, both before the Party and before his own conscience.

Dyakov was formal.

"We shall conclude the affair at the institute," he said in a businesslike way. "Your admissions have been noted. Now it's up to you yourself to evaluate them politically."

"I admit that publishing the newspaper was an error," Sasha replied.

"A subjective error," Dyakov interjected. "But errors have objective causes and objective consequences. Isn't that so?"

The *interpretation* begins. For Dyakov, a man was nothing more than a unit for completing the record, and the record was required for carrying out the sentence.

"So, Pankratov, what are the objective reasons and objective consequences of your errors?"

Sasha looked right into Dyakov's little-boy face. If he ever ran into him on the Arbat . . .

Dyakov launched into a lecture. "Lets think about it. If there had been a healthy political environment at the institute, it would not have been possible for your newspaper to come out. But the political environment was not healthy. Krivoruchko was running an underground anti-Party organization. It has been discovered, its members have been unmasked and arrested. They are here, with us, and they have confessed to everything."

The clerks and bookkeepers in the personnel section at the factory used to jumble facts and figures in the same crude way. What could Dyakov do to him? He had carried one-hundred-and-fifty-pound drums on his back, and tree-felling wouldn't kill him. He could go back to work for Averkyev or Morozov. There were people like that everywhere, they were the real people. It was people like Dyakov who were the real enemies of the Party.

"You're naïve, Pankratov, you don't know these people. Krivoruchko delayed the completion of the hostels in order to cause student discontent, to create political confusion among the student masses. In this atmosphere of political disorientation it was possible to issue a newspaper of the sort you put out. Whether you wanted or not, objectively you became a tool in the hands of Krivoruchko and his gang, and they used you for their counterrevolutionary ends. That's why you have ended up here, especially as you were not willing to make a political assessment of your errors. But, Pankratov, it is still not to late to do so. *Believe us!*"

Believe us . . . Oh, yes, he'd believed enough! He'd believed just such words — how many times had he heard them, how many times had he uttered them himself? They weren't human words, they were ritualistic incantations. Lozgachev had practiced this ritualism with Azizyan, Baulin had done so, too, and Stolper, and now Dyakov was doing his ritual bit. But it was the lives of innocent, suffering people that were lying on their ritual altar.

Dyakov looked at Sasha. "Do you understand, Pankratov?"

"Yes, I understand."

"That's good. Let's write it down."

"As long as it's convincing," Sasha said in an unctuous tone that would never take in anyone on the Arbat. But this weakling didn't understand anything: he was so sure of his ability to frighten people, his right to decide their fate, he was so puffed up like a turkey, that he didn't know that here, inside these walls, there were others wearing the same uniform he wore, who would see through the lie and the ritualism, and who knew that it would all come to an end sooner or later and in the meantime they were risking their lives to help people.

"But of course," Dyakov replied gravely.

Glancing at the copy of Sasha's previous deposition, he wrote on a new form, read it over to himself and then aloud to Sasha.

" 'Having thought over my behavior and my actions and wishing to give them a pure-hearted and sincere evaluation, and as a supplement to my previous statements, I hereby declare the following: I acknowledge that publishing an anti-Party issue of the newspaper on the occasion of the sixteenth anniversary of the October Revolution, and involving students Runochkin, Kovalyov, Poluzhan, and Pozdnyakova in this newspaper, was a political error. I also acknowledge that my defense of Krivoruchko was a political error. These errors were the result of the political circumstances created in the institute by the deputy director Krivoruchko. I acknowledge that the issue of an anti-Party edition of the newspaper for the sixteenth anniversary of the October Revolution was part of the anti-Party course being followed in the institute by Krivoruchko.' "

He slid the form over to Sasha.

"Here, Pankratov, you can check for yourself that it is just as I read it. And then you can sign it."

"I will never sign this," said Sasha, looking Dyakov straight in the eye.

❧ 28 ❧

ife in the Arbat went on as before. The April sun shone through the windows and warmed up the streets and the sidewalks. Blackened heaps of snow still lay along the boulevards. The warm smell of the reviving soil came through the cracks in the asphalt. Schoolchildren played football in the side streets without hats and coats. Scaffolding appeared, and masons and painters emerged to repair and decorate the houses and to build extensions.

The lights still shone in the movie theaters in the evenings — the Arbat Art, the Carnival, the Prague.

Arbat and Dorogomilov girls were out in the streets again, and the girls from Plyushchikha, with their coat collars now turned down, their colorful headscarves untied, and wearing light shoes and fine flesh-colored stockings. The same huddle of teenagers hung around the entrance of Sasha's house. Varya went past them without stopping, waving a hand in salute, as she hurried to the military school's graduation celebrations being held at the Red Army Central House.

Varya had never been to such a grand occasion before. Presiding on the stage were nationally famous army commanders. She recognized Budyonny, and of those whose names Serafim whispered in her ear she remembered Tukhachevsky, one of the best-looking men she had ever seen in her life. Normally she did not like meetings and speeches and reports. But she was taken with the festive atmosphere of this occasion: the splendor of the hall, the romance of the feat of arms about which the legendary army commanders addressed the graduating classes, the atmosphere of masculine, martial unity, when the boundaries of seniority became blurred and the graduates saw themselves in the famous army officers and the army officers saw themselves as young again in the new graduates.

The officers' wives seemed special, sharing the burdens, frustrations, and dangers of their husbands' profession. Even the girls who had been invited behaved ceremoniously, as if they were already used to this way of life. Varya studied them closely. Some of them were very beautifully dressed. The Red Army Song and Dance Ensemble had never appealed to her particularly before, but now she enjoyed the soldiers' singing and dancing and their typical Russian dash and exuberance.

A military band in the foyer played fox-trots, rumbas, and tangos as well as any dance band. Compared to the smartly turned out cadets, who looked so adept, so uncomplicated, and so radiant, young civilians in their two-piece suits and wide flapping trousers, loud ties, and unpolished shoes appeared absurd and ridiculous.

Nina also behaved differently. She didn't nag. She was pleasant and good-humored, if rather sad, no doubt sorry that Max was going away and that she had refused his offer of marriage.

Serafim was also going off to the Far East, but Varya wasn't sad, because that evening she had agreed to marry him. She would finish school first and then go out to join him. In the meantime, he would write to her and she would write back, and everyone in school and on the block would know that in a year's time she'd be going out to the Far East to her *husband*. She would stand out from among her friends. None of *them* had anyone waiting in the Far East. She'd go alone to the theater and movies and the skating rink, but she wouldn't go dancing at all. And if she did go, she'd only dance with Zoe. On the other hand, she might dance with a man, but she wouldn't let him get to know her. Thank you, but . . . No, I'm sorry . . . I can't . . . Alone, solitary and unapproachable, and about to leave for the Far East, she would attract a lot of attention.

As far as Sasha was concerned, Varya hadn't stopped going to see his mother, which meant she hadn't forgotten him. So, with Serafim waiting for her in the Far East, and Sofya Alexandrovna and Sasha needing her here in Moscow, she would seem even more interesting and original in her own eyes.

Varya was very happy. She and Serafim looked good dancing together, and even the senior officers and their wives watched them. She tried to linger as long as possible near where the handsome Tukhachevsky was standing.

Max danced with Nina. His round, snub-nosed face radiated benevolence. When his friends asked Nina to dance, Max smiled good-naturedly and waited for her in a corner. Tall, broad shouldered, and powerfully built, he was unusually strong physically, and like most strong people, he was careful about using his strength. He was afraid of stepping on someone's toes or breaking something.

His father had been a steamfitter, a heavy drinker who had died of alcoholism, leaving his mother, an elevator operator, with four children. Maxim was the eldest. A childhood of poverty had made him thrifty, which his school friends had taken for stinginess and had teased him about. He kept his comb in a leatherette case, his paper money in a wallet, and his loose change in a purse. His pencil had a metal cover over the end to protect the lead point. He had a notebook with addresses and phone numbers, which he hung on to for years. He loved things that lasted. He liked his food simple but filling, but he had never got used to spending much money on it, and when he had to, he could go without.

Being so careful and thrifty, he was given all the practical jobs at school. He used to take the minutes at meetings, collect membership dues, file the district committee's instructions in loose-leaf binders, write up reports. Max did everything, from fetching and carrying, making the rounds, seeing that everyone was notified, writing announcements, posting notices, finding red bunting for holidays, buying the tickets for group outings to the theater, taking names for circles and seminars, to doing the roll call and counting votes. It was not that he was not thought capable of better things, but just that it turned out that way. Everyone got used to it.

A year, and in some cases two years, older than his fellows, he could see through their trivial quarrels and would change the subject, make a joke, laugh, and remove the barb with his good humor. He had the quick, agile mind of a peasant and knew how to avoid trouble. And he could be cunning when necessary, though he never compromised his convictions or his loyalty to his friends.

Over the years, something simple, soldierly, firm, and unbending had developed in him and had become an integral part of his character.

Max entered the military school after he had done his compulsory labor service. The army gave him financial security and enabled him to help his sick, exhausted mother and the family. As a young, strong, well-educated officer, he found the army way of doing things appealing. His place was there among the troops, on the frontier where the tension was mounting. Still, he was sad to be leaving Moscow. . . .

It was sad to leave his friends behind, Nina, Sasha, Lena, Vadim. They personified the life to which he and thousands like him had risen out of their dark, dank basements.

Sometimes, when he was a boy, he would clean the stairs for his mother. Nina would help him, not because he needed help but just to show others that no job, however menial, was beneath them. It was the act of a Komsomol, an act of comradely solidarity, and from it Max learned more about the meaning of the new morality than he did from any book. Then, there was that awful affair when they were in ninth grade. . . . Max's father had stolen and drunk the money that Max had collected to help build an airplane called "Moscow Komsomol." It had amounted to about thirty rubles, a considerable sum in those days. Max had wanted to kill himself. Where on earth could he get hold of thirty rubles? How would he explain it to his friends? Nina realized he was in a state and managed to pry the story out of him, and then she immediately went and told Sasha Pankratov.

"Come on!" Sasha had said to him. "You don't put much value on your life!"

And he gave him the money, fifteen rubles that he had got from his mother and fifteen from his Uncle Mark.

He would not have friends like that now. Sasha had saved him, but what had he done for Sasha . . . ?

He had liked Nina even when as children they had played hide-and-seek in the backyard, and then later he had liked her at school. She was a mature sort of girl, strong and decisive. He also liked her ineptness, her sharp temper, her stubbornness, and her helplessness. He did not believe her pose that she supposedly did not love him. She didn't know that herself. He had brought Serafim to the house on purpose, hoping that Varya would marry him, as he was a good boy, not stupid and very handsome. Then Nina's continual excuse — that she couldn't do anything until Varya was on her feet — would be out of the way.

That, however, was not the way Nina saw it. She had no doubts about how impressive the army officers were, but they were after all political thinkers, strategists, public figures. Max wasn't going to be one of them. His career would be spent drilling Red Army men on the parade ground. Look at him, standing there, waiting for her, all broad shoulders and ruddy cheeks, his light brown hair carefully slicked down, his boots gleaming and his buttons shining, a creaking new leather belt, and steel studs on his boots, which clicked on the parquet as they danced. He would end up an old campaigner.... Pity! He could have reached for more. The war will come and everyone will have to fight, but in the meantime one must live and work.

She had said all this to Max when he entered the army school, but he hadn't listened. Fine, he was entitled to decide his own fate. Nina had made a firm decision that she was not going to marry Max and leave Moscow.

Hamlet was playing at the Vakhtangov with fat little Goryunov in the title role. Yuri Sharok loved the Vakhtangov. He called Vadim Marasevich and asked him to get them tickets, adding that he would call in that evening at the Marasevich apartment on Starokonyushenny Street.

Professor Marasevich was a famous Moscow doctor who once a month attended the Central Clinic for Scientists on Gagarin Street, where an appointment with him had to be booked six months in advance. A clinic on Pirogov Street was named for him, as was a department at the Institute of Medicine.

Distantly descended from a Ukrainian Cossack chieftain, Professor Marasevich, like his father before him, who had also been a doctor and professor, was a Muscovite born and bred, with old, well-established connections among the Moscow intelligentsia.

He entertained only close friends at home and his apartment on Starokonyushenny was frequented by such celebrities as the pianist

Igumnov, the stage director Stanislavsky, the composer Prokofiev, the singer Nezhdanova, Geltser the ballerina, Kachalov the actor, Sumbatov-Yuzhin the actor-playwright, the director Meyerhold, and even by Commissar Lunacharsky himself. No famous Western artist on tour or currently popular performer could fail to be invited to the elegant if somewhat disorganized apartment.

Guests would be received by the beautiful daughter, out would come the cut glass and the starched linen tablecloths. Young actors often dropped by after the performance and would fall eagerly on the veal and pale pink salmon.

They would enliven the party with their improvisations, or their miniature dramatizations, with Vadim providing impromptu reviews of their performances, and not without some wit of his own, as his father noticed. Vadim had finished at the university with a degree in art history. He had already given some lectures and conducted art tours, and now he was trying his hand as a theater critic.

Professor Marasevich, who drank only Georgian Borzhomi mineral water, would tell an amusing anecdote or two from his own or his father's medical practice and before midnight would get up and wish everyone good-night, with the remark that in his job it was important to keep to a regular routine.

Vika was also trying to get into the theater or films, but so far with not much to show for it, apart from her affairs with a number of well-known actors, some promising directors, and one or two up-and-coming journalists. Her affairs always began on an elevated level, with flowers, letters, restaurants, and taxis, and ended in petty quarrels, recriminations, and fights on the phone.

Only her affair with Yuri Sharok began and ended simply.

They ran into each other on the Arbat and strolled along together in the spring sunshine.

Yuri said: "Come and see how I live."

She knew exactly what he had in mind, and the ritual invitation had its usual automatic effect on her. She was also prompted by a secret rivalry with Lena Budyagina. She did not know that Lena and Yuri were no longer seeing each other.

Finding out how Yuri "lived" occurred without words or explanation, as if they had been lovers for years. By comparison with present and past admirers, Yuri satisfied her requirements, but his room and the pathetic apartment and the smell of the pressing iron reminded her of what his father was. . . .

She worried that when the time came to dump him — which she usually did as casually as she might drop in on someone — Yuri might be difficult.

But he turned out to be quite *decent,* and the son of a *tailor,* no less!

However, he was tactful for his own reasons: she left him indifferent. He thought her cold and stupid. Also, he compared her with Lena and found her wanting. How casually she would jump into a strange bed! The fury of the petit bourgeois who sees his own wife in every licentious female simmered in him.

He stopped by to see Vadim about *Hamlet.*

Vadim was late, so Yuri waited for him with Vika in her room. She was lying on her bed, half-dressed, looking at foreign magazines. He sat next to her and they flipped through the pages together. There were pictures of men's fashions as well as women's, and they were chatting as if there were nothing between them.

Vika could not but appreciate his discretion and gentlemanly behavior, and she decided he deserved a reward. As Yuri reached for another magazine, their hands touched and she said quietly, looking into his eyes: "Do you want to . . . ?"

He nodded his acceptance.

She said, "Wait, I'll shut the door."

The reward had been bestowed just as Vadim came home. Yuri was sitting in an armchair and Vika was fixing her hair in front of the mirror. She said that any moment now a famous actor from Vakhtangov's theater would be arriving. He was a real matinee idol; Yuri had last seen him in *The Intervention.*

"You can keep him company," Vadim said. "Yuri, you come and have something to eat with me."

They went into the dining room, which was as big as the entire Sharok apartment.

Vadim ate greedily. He was thick-lipped, with little eyes, and he had a shattering voice, very masculine and rumbling, and the subtle intellectual intonation he used when he spoke made a strange contrast to his appearance.

Spreading butter thickly on his bread — which he was eating with soup — he began.

"He confuses jurisdiction with jurisprudence, rarity with parity, precedent with proceeding. And yet, he *is* the *new man,* call him what you like — shock-worker, new entrant. He is in tune with his theme, the *main* theme, and with his hero, the hero of the *future.* But are we really going to trade our future for a quarter pound of butter?" He pushed away the butter dish. "After all, those who grieve, grieve precisely for that quarter pound of butter...."

Yuri listened to Vadim's musings on the heroes of the future without irritation. They did, after all, add something to his own knowledge of a world that was completely foreign to him. Not long before, Vadim had said exactly the opposite, deriding bad taste and extolling artistic skill. Vadim was remarkably good at tacking with the wind, and he had always been drawn to stronger personalities. In school it had been Sasha Pankratov, then someone else at the university, and now it was a well-known critic who was writing articles about poetry that aimed at sounding moronic. Yuri never pointed out Vadim's inconsistencies to him, however.

He liked the Marasevich household, with its actors and its constant stream of the amusing, the carefree, and the famous. There was something effortless and jauntily cynical in the conversations of these people who had had fame lavished on them. And somehow their fame itself seemed effortless and simple, a matter of chance or deftness or impertinence. And despite their seeming indifference, they behaved like privileged individuals.

He liked Professor Marasevich, too. He was a gentleman with a carefully tended face, a handsome little beard, and soft hands, and he also carried himself with that privileged air.

Yuri began to see Vadim almost every day. Vadim took him to the theater. Yuri also went to the theater on his own, if either Vadim or someone else he had met at Vadim's telephoned for a complimentary ticket.

It was an extraordinary and rather wonderful time. Yuri Sharok would remember the spring of 1934 for a long time to come. His nomination for the Prosecution Service had not yet been processed, but Malkova had promised that it would be decided soon. For the last few months Yuri had lived a free and easy life, one without worries and one in which he lived in as full and interesting a manner as he could. Only the thought of Lena occasionally troubled him. When he entered a theater, he would scan the auditorium, hoping and fearing that he would see her.

Lena had not been to the theater since her illness. She hardly ever went out of the house. She did not telephone anyone, and she had not seen any of her friends since the day they had met to discuss helping Sasha.

Then one day, unexpectedly, Gera Tretyak stopped by. She was also the daughter of an ambassador, and they had been friends since childhood. They used to see each other when their families both happened to be in London or Paris or Berlin at the same time, but in Moscow they had practically lost touch with each other.

Gera was a pretty little brunette with a sharp wit, who could make even the most trivial things sound absorbing. Lena smiled as she listened to her chatter away. She recalled the time they had traveled to South Wales together and stayed in a cheap little hotel in Cardiff. Some Scottish football players were also staying there, and two of them had suggested they run off to some town where girls of fourteen were allowed to get married. Lena and Gera were then just fifteen. Then there was their trip to the palace at Fontainebleau and the woman guide who, when they were looking at Napoleon's bed, had pointed out that he was only five feet tall. Gera was surprised and said surely she meant five foot three. The guide was angry and said that her husband was five feet tall, and everyone knew that he was exactly the same height as the emperor Napoleon. For some reason this seemed even funnier than it had at the time, and they were convulsed by laughter. Lena was delighted that Gera had spent the evening with her. She hugged and kissed her as she was leaving and said sadly: "Don't forget me."

⚜ 29 ⚜

It was about eight in the evening — the same evening that Varya, Nina, and Max were dancing at the Red Army Central House, and Yuri was having supper with Vadim Marasevich, and Gera Tretyak was paying her visit to Lena Budyagina — that Sofya Alexandrovna was telephoned and told to report at ten o'clock the next morning to the commandant of the Butyrki prison, where she could see her son, Alexander Pavlovich Pankratov. She was to bring warm clothes, money, and provisions. The voice at the other end of the line was level and calm. It was the voice of a man who was used to saying the same thing day in, day out, concisely and clearly. When he had delivered his message, he promptly hung up without waiting for any questions.

Sofya Alexandrovna was afraid he might have left something out, that he had forgotten something important, something essential for her doing everything properly. She was afraid of forgetting something herself, and of mixing things up, so she tried desperately to recall everything he had said: tomorrow, ten o'clock, Butyrki, meeting with son, warm clothes, provisions, and, yes, there was something else, but what was it? Dear God, she had forgotten something. . . . Oh, yes, money, money for the journey. To make sure, she wrote it all down on a piece of paper: ten o'clock, meeting, clothes, food, money. Money and food meant exile, warm clothes meant the north or Siberia.

With only one night in which to do everything, she had no time for an emotional reaction. Although she had been prepared for this, she could not forgive herself for not getting everything together earlier, but she had thought it would be bad luck to prepare ahead of time for such a journey.

Sasha had his winter coat, his cap with earflaps, a sweater, and a warm scarf. But he had no felt boots. Though wherever they sent him at this time of the year, April, he would not need any. He would need them for the winter, but she would be able to send him some by then. What he needed now was leather *boots*. There would be mud and slush out there, and his shoes wouldn't last a day in that. He must have boots; they'd save his life. But he didn't have any, and the stores were all shut. In any case you could only get a pair of boots with coupons, and she didn't have any. You could buy a pair at a second-hand stall, if you were prepared to spend a fortune and take the chance that they weren't made of cardboard instead of leather. But the second-hand stalls were also shut.

Then she remembered that there was a strong pair of rough boots about Sasha's size out at her sister Vera's dacha. She'd buy Vera new ones, whatever they cost. But she must get that pair to Sasha now.

She called Vera, but she and her husband were out at the dacha and would not be back till the day after tomorrow. Just her luck!

Her younger sister, Polina, did not have a phone. But there was one in the neighboring apartment, and Sofya Alexandrovna even remembered the number from the times she used to phone Polina when Polina was still friendly with her neighbor. But it had been several years since the neighbors had stopped talking to her and Polina had asked her sister not to call her there anymore. But call her she did, despite the thought that the neighbors might not take the call, and might be rude to her, as well.

A full-blooded, strident male voice answered.

"I'm very sorry to disturb you," Sofya Alexandrovna said, "but it's urgent. . . . I wonder if you could please ask Polina Alexandrovna to come to the phone?"

"Polina Alexandrovna?"

"Your neighbor in number twenty-six. Please excuse me, it's her sister calling."

"Well, I don't know . . ."

But instead of hanging up, he handed the receiver over to a woman.

"Who do you want to speak to?"

"I'm terribly sorry," Sofya Alexandrovna said. "This is your neighbor Polina Alexandrovna's sister. I'm sorry to be a nuisance, but it's an emergency, it's to do ... Could you be so kind as to call my sister to the phone?"

"All right," the woman replied unpleasantly.

It was some time before Polina finally came to the phone in an agitated and breathless state, having guessed that it was bad news about Sasha.

"They're exiling him tomorrow. You must go out to Vera's dacha and fetch the boots."

"Oh, my God," Polina wailed, "Igorek's got a temperature and Kolya won't be back till after eleven. What on earth can we do? I'll come the minute Kolya gets in, but it'll be too late to go out to the dacha."

"Come anyway. You can help me get his things together," said Sofya Alexandrovna. "I'll think of some other way to get the boots."

"What shall I bring?"

"Nothing, I've got everything."

She'd have to go to Vera's dacha herself, though she was not sure she could find the way at night. It was in a new settlement with paths instead of streets. Nobody knew the names of the paths, the houses were not numbered in any particular order, and there wouldn't be any weekenders around to ask. She must go, all the same. But if she went there, who would go to the late-night store?

She phoned Varya, but neither Varya nor Nina was at home. Should she ask Militsa Petrovna? No, she couldn't go — she had to be careful of her heart and couldn't even lift a can of milk. And there were a lot of things to be bought, like bread and biscuits, sugar and condensed milk, and lemons — he needed the vitamins — and smoked sausage, cheese, bacon ...

She wrote it all down and knocked on Mikhail Yurevich's door. He was in his dressing gown, leaning over his table, working on something.

It was a terrible imposition, she was sorry, but there was no one else to do it. Here was the list and the money. If they didn't have smoked sausage, semi-smoked would do, it wouldn't go bad in this weather, and some sort of fish, nothing too salty, would also be good.

Mikhail Yurevich frowned at her through his pince-nez.

"You can't go out of town at night," he said. "How will you get back?"

"By the night train. It leaves at one something. . . ."

"The trams won't be running," he said.

"I'll manage somehow. . . ."

"You go to the store, and I'll go to your sister's."

"But, Mikhail Yurevich, it's a long way, thirty miles, and then it's twenty minutes from the station. The settlement has no street lights, there are no proper roads or sidewalks, there's mud everywhere. You can't go, you simply can't, it's too much to ask."

"Write down the address and see if you can draw me a map of the place while I get dressed," he said.

She sketched the route and explained it as well as she could. Right next to the station there was a stall that had been boarded up for the winter. The important thing was to turn right at the stall, that way you came to the right path. That was the problem, finding the right path. Then the third street on the left, which was actually called Third Green Street — except that there was no street sign, because the kids had torn it down in the summer. The dacha was number 65, the number was painted on the gate. It was easy to recognize from the picket fence along the front. First there was a solid fence, then farther on another solid fence and the picket in between was Vera's. But he must remember to turn right at the stall to reach the correct path.

Mikhail Yurevich stood there before her in his boots and high fur hat, knitting his brows and looking very grave in his old-fashioned pince-nez, and helpless at the same time. To think of him tramping through the dirty, deserted settlement! He would be searching all night, and tomorrow he had to go to work.

She glanced at the clock and saw to her horror it was already nine-thirty. The late-night store closed at ten.

Both cars of the tram were full, but she pushed her way onto the steps of the second car. She didn't care if they fined her. They wouldn't get her off the tram. But nobody fined her; she passed her money along for the ticket and rode on the steps all the way. She was thinking of everything she still had to do after she'd been to the store. There was the suitcase. She didn't know where the keys were for it, or even if the lock had been repaired. The suitcase hadn't been used for ages. It had to have a working lock, because Sasha might be traveling with a group of criminals who would steal everything.

The thought of Sasha going into exile with a party of criminals, who might rob him, harm him, beat him, brought back to her the full measure of the unhappiness that had been heaped on her son: he was a marked man, persecuted, an outcast without rights.

Moscow seemed improbable, unreal in its immensity. The streets, the squares, the lights, the store windows, and the automobiles and tramcars, everything on the move, going somewhere. Yet it was unreal, unnatural, hazy, as in a bad dream with death masks, waxwork figures, dummies, all bathed in the milky light of the tramcar.

She got off at Okhotny Row. It was a quarter to ten. From the tramcar stop she could see movement in the entrance to the store. It was still open! Breathing heavily, she walked fast, but when she reached the store the crowd was being turned away. They were shouting, complaining that they were only a minute or two late. Some of them tried to push their way in and were stopped. An assistant was manning the door.

Sofya Alexandrovna also tried to push her way in and failed. She was jostled in the small, agitated crowd.

Then the crush thinned out, fewer people were coming out and the lights inside started going off. Gradually everyone left.

Only Sofya Alexandrovna remained. Every time the door opened she begged the assistant to let her in.

The assistant, a rude woman with a fat, red, frost-bitten face, snapped: "Push off, ma, you're in the way!"

"Please let me in, I beg you."

A boisterous group of teenagers piled out of the store and one of them piped up: "Let the old girl in to get her pint!" They then dashed off toward Okhotny Row, laughing.

"I beg you, it's not too late," she pleaded when the door again opened.

The assistant paid no attention. She was used to persistent

customers. Every night there were moaners who went on pestering her right up until the lock was actually put on the door. When Sofya Alexandrovna tried to hold the door open, she gave her usual shout: "No pushing! Keep away from the door!"

The cleaning women were already sweeping the floor, scattering fresh sawdust, and the assistants were clearing the shelves and hurrying to get away.

Sofya Alexandrovna stayed put.

The fat assistant let the last customer out and left her post. Sofya Alexandrovna pushed open the door and entered.

"Where do you think you're going?" The fat assistant came running over to her.

"I'm not leaving," Sofya Alexandrovna replied quietly.

"I'll call the police," the woman warned her.

"It's for my son, he's in prison."

Sofya Alexandrovna looked into the coarse face, the face of a street vendor who sold hot pies and ice cream in the winter.

"He's going into exile tomorrow. I have to get a parcel together for him," she said.

The woman sighed.

"The stories people make up, they'll say anything. We want to get home, too, you know."

Sofya Alexandrovna said nothing.

The other assistants were already putting on their coats and getting their bags.

The fat assistant roared the length of the store, "Mikheeva, serve this lady!"

Polina arrived and then, very much later, Vera and Mikhail Yurevich with the boots, which it turned out were one size too big, but would do.

"They're not good leather dress boots, just everyday working boots," Vera said. "But with woolen socks they'll be perfect, nice and warm and comfortable."

As well as the boots, Vera had brought a knapsack with broad shoulder straps that could be adjusted for length.

"The knapsack for his food, the suitcase for his things."

Vera was the most energetic and businesslike of the sisters, with the typical practical nature of someone who raised a family in the Moscow suburbs. Her husband went hunting and fishing, her children went skiing and on holiday trips. They lived at the dacha and kept an orchard and vegetable garden. "You're much too soft," she used to say angrily to Sofya, while trying to get her to leave her husband. She would defend her sister and quarrel with Pavel Nikolaevich, and she wouldn't tolerate his remarks. But she had finally stopped visiting the Pankratovs altogether.

Efficiently and without fuss, Vera did the packing herself. She said they should put in a knife, fork, and spoon, and a mug. Sofya had completely overlooked them, as well as a razor. She was used to making up prison packages, but this was for a journey, and she could put in whatever she liked.

"Don't give him too much money now," Vera insisted. "It might get stolen. Better to send it later, to the place itself. Tell him when you meet him that as soon as he gets there he's to send you a cable and you'll send money for him to pick up. Don't worry, he'll be all right, he's young."

It was more Vera's energy and efficiency than what she said that was so reassuring. That was what life was all about, and it was also helping to prepare Sasha for life.

✖ 30 ✖

nina did not notice that Sofya Alexandrovna's lights were still on. Varya, who missed nothing, did, but she didn't think it was significant, because Sofya Alexandrovna sometimes lay in bed all night with the light on, as she had told Varya herself. In any case, Varya's thoughts were elsewhere: tomorrow evening, she and Nina would go to the station to see Max and Serafim off.

The dancing at the Red Army Central House had gone on till two in the morning. Most people had left to catch the last trams, and Nina had wanted to leave then, too, but Varya and Serafim had persuaded her to stay. Max had smiled good-naturedly. Nina was in the minority, so they stayed.

They walked home through the dark cold Moscow streets, Varya without galoshes and wearing only a thin muslin dress. Serafim put his army greatcoat around her and his cap on her head. She stopped under a streetlamp to look at herself in her mirror and thought the cap, though it fell forward over her forehead, suited her very well. She looked like a very pretty young soldier. She walked behind with Serafim, his arm around her shoulder, and when Max and Nina turned a corner they would stop and kiss. Serafim kissed so hard her lips hurt. Varya had never kissed anyone *properly,* and she didn't find it very pleasant now, just painful. But she knew what that meant. It meant that Serafim was *passionate.*

Nina knew why they had hung back, but pretended not to notice. And she didn't start lecturing Varya when they got home, but only told her to get to bed quickly and to put out the light, as she had to get up early for work.

Next morning, she left a note on the table addressed to Varya's teacher: "Please allow Varya Ivanova to leave early today for domestic reasons." The domestic reasons were saying good-bye to Max and Serafim.

Varya, however, had no intention of going to school at all. She had to look her best at the station. There'd be a lot of people there to see the young officers off, including the well-dressed, pretty girls she'd seen at the dance. And she was not going to be outdone. She would look grown up and serious. She was, after all, accompanying her future husband. She wouldn't wear black, but something severe and striking. She attended the second shift at school, and there was her hair to be done and her makeup to be put on, and even if she left school early, she wouldn't have enough time to do everything.

Quickly she got Nina's lunch ready, grabbed her schoolbooks, and dashed off to Zoe's.

Zoe wasn't going to school either, but was staying home to help Varya get ready, to do her hair and her eyelashes. She lent Varya her fashionable new boots with the steel buckles and, most important, she lent her her mother's sealskin coat, which Zoe had been allowed to go out in occasionally. When Varya put it on, Zoe said she looked incredibly grown up and that she would stand out in the sealskin coat, the fashionable boots, and the fluffy white headscarf that also happened to belong to Zoe's mother.

At five Varya was finally ready and rang Nina.

"I'll see you at the tram stop."

"Where are you calling from?"

"School."

They both arrived at the tram stop at the same time.

Nina didn't recognize her.

"Why the fancy outfit?"

"The cloakroom was locked, so I borrowed Zoe's coat and scarf."

"What about Zoe?"

"She'll wear mine."

"Where are your books?"

"I left them in my desk — you don't think I'm going to lug them with me to the station!"

The school cloakroom could have been locked, but Nina knew she was lying, just the same: Zoe's coat would have been locked in the cloakroom, too, if this really was Zoe's coat. But Nina wasn't going to interrogate her and argue with her and prove her a liar. Varya wasn't a child anymore. She'd be getting married soon, and thank God Serafim was such a decent boy. Let her live her own life, and let her see Serafim off the way she wants.

The station was crowded and the platform was packed to capacity. Nina and Varya stood at the gate in despair, but Max and Serafim were already running through the crowd to meet them, waving their arms. They elbowed their way alongside the train, taking care not to get separated among the milling pack of people who were hurrying to find their friends and relatives. There were husbands and wives with bundles and going-away presents, and girls carrying flowers and hugging and kissing these marvelous young men, these new Red Army officers, bare-headed in their tunics and cross-straps, having already put their caps and greatcoats on the train. . . . Young, enthusiastic, and zestful, there was also a serious aura about them. They represented the awesome military might of the Soviet state. Nina knew that these ardent, pink-cheeked young men would be the first to go into battle, the first to take on themselves whatever challenges appeared. She thought that her proper place probably was beside Max, who was so strong and calm and good-natured. She'd miss him for those qualities when he was gone.

As for Varya, she was basking in Serafim's loving look, as well as the looks that other cadets were casting at her. She was the most striking, most beautiful girl there, and she was unexpectedly tall, almost as tall as Nina. And nobody else was wearing such a chic sealskin coat, or such a scarf. She was flushed with all the excitement, the bustle of the station, the hoots and whistles of the trains heralding long, unknown, and alluring journeys to come. Max said she looked like a movie star. Serafim whispered that he loved her more than life itself, and even Nina smiled when she looked at her and thought with pleasure what a pretty sister she had.

Varya, very properly for a grown-up woman and fiancée, was totally absorbed in her own little circle consisting of Nina, Max, and Serafim, and in nobody else. It mustn't be thought she had a roving eye. If she was looking around now and then, she was doing no more than giving a casual glance at the station, the trains, and the people hurrying to catch them.

She looked across to the next platform. And she saw Sasha.

With a knapsack on his back and carrying a suitcase, he was flanked by two Red Army men, with a swarthy little officer in a long cloak walking quickly in front and busily pushing people out of the way.

Sasha sensed that someone was looking at him, and as he glanced around Varya saw that his face was deathly white and that he had a curly black beard, like a Gypsy's. His eyes skipped over the departing cadets, over Max, Nina, and Varya, but he recognized no one and he turned away and kept walking toward the train that was waiting farther off at another platform. People carrying suitcases and bundles and bags were scurrying all around them, and they were lost in the crowd.

Varya stared at the spot where Sasha had vanished from her view. She didn't hear the train whistle blow. She didn't notice that the others were saying good-bye, or that Nina was kissing Max on the forehead, or that Serafim was leaning toward her and looking into her eyes.

"Wake up, Varya!" Nina said.

"I just saw Sasha."

"What are you talking about?" Nina screamed, realizing instantly that Varya was telling the truth.

"He was under guard. He's got a beard," Varya muttered, her eyes still fixed on the other platform, as if she might catch a glimpse of him there among the throng of people with their bags and bundles. "He's got a beard, a *beard,* just like an old man." She burst into tears. "Just like an old man . . ."

"Stop it, you can't be right," Nina said, her voice trembling.

Max was struggling to keep calm. "You're mistaken, Varya. They wouldn't send him off that way."

"It was him. . . ." Her voice was shaking. "I recognized him. . . . He turned around and looked. He was as white as a sheet. He looked just like an old man."

In confusion and dismay, Serafim reached out to her. "Good-bye, Varya."

"He was as white as a corpse!" Varya wailed. "And dragging a suitcase, he had to drag a suitcase...."

Serafim, his face red with embarrassment, leaned over and kissed her cheek, which was wet with tears and streaked black from the mascara that ran down her face.

The train was moving slowly. Cadets were hanging out the windows and crowded on the coaches' steps, shouting and waving good-bye to their loved ones, who were walking alongside, waving back and shouting good wishes for the journey. Max and Serafim also waved.

Varya stood in the middle of the platform crying, wiping her eyes with her handkerchief and smearing her makeup all over her face, choking and swallowing her tears. Nina was shaken and worried and tried to calm her down.

"Don't, we can't do anything about it now. Let's go to Sofya Alexandrovna and find out what's happened."

An old woman who was passing stopped, looked at Varya, and shook her head in sympathy.

"The young girls are weeping for their soldier-boys."

Part II

The he old road to the Angara, opened by the first settlers in the taiga, began in Taishet. The new one started from Kansk, where there was the regional NKVD center and a prison and where the rail part of the journey ended and the marching phase began.

Kansk was a quiet little town with boardwalks and no gardens, a typical town in the steppes. Now at last there was blue sky overhead and the heavy scent of life. No more cell, no more Dyakov, no more prison yard with the armed sentry watching. It was hard to believe that it had all really happened. Here he was like everyone else, walking freely along the street, carrying his suitcase, while Boris Soloveichik walked at his side and complained that he hadn't managed to fix things so that he could stay in Kansk.

"Why do they want to send a specialist with my qualifications to some little village? What good is that to the state?"

The post office, a small house with a porch, also served as the ticket office for the district. The young clerks in their housedresses, their fingers covered with glue and ink, knew Soloveichik, the sympathetic, sociable Muscovite who collected his letters there.

"FEELING FINE STOP WRITE KANSK DISTRICT BOGUCHANY VILLAGE GENERAL DELIVERY STOP LOVE SASHA." This was his first cable to his mother.

The girl counted up the words, told him how much, wrote out a receipt, and took his money. The girls were cheerful and very pretty.

Soloveichik's landlady, a thin young woman with a tranquil face, was laying the table. What had prompted her to take up with

Boris? He'd soon leave and forget her. Had she pitied him as an exile? Boris, for all his ways as a ladies' man from the capital, looked pathetic next to her.

Sasha dug a can of sprats out of his knapsack, the last of the food his mother had provided. Boris opened a bottle of vodka. He had his own glasses and napkins, trying even here to live like a civilized human being. It seemed almost a normal life, until they thought of who and what they were, and then it was crazy and weird and awful. Well, maybe not so awful.

Sasha's head began to spin after the first glass.

"It's normal after prison," Boris remarked. "You'll get used to it. We'll drink pure spirits on the Angara, it's cheaper to transport than vodka, since it's nearly four hundred miles by horse. We'll do all right for ourselves. Boguchany's a big village — I'll find my sort of work there, and so will you. You'll be working as a mechanic inside five minutes. They've got tractors and sowers and winnowers — all kinds of machinery."

"But I don't know anything about tractors or sowers or winnowers."

"You'll like all the activity up there; you'll soon learn about tractors. In the old days, young intellectuals used to go abroad, but you and me, we're going to the polar bears. How much nicer to be a nightingale in Moscow than a sparrow on the Solovetsky Islands.* What can we do about it? Wail and cry? I was all set to become the chairman of Gosplan, or anyway the deputy chairman, since I'm a non-Party man. I carried everyone on my back, a universal workhorse I was, never in anyone's way, always at everyone's beck and call. But then my advancement was stopped by a small reading error and one punctuation mark. Remember this: nobody in exile ever tells the truth — if someone's here because there was a real case against him, he makes out he's here for nothing, and if someone's here for no reason, he acts as if they really had something on him.

"But you can believe what I tell you. This is what happened. We had a slogan hanging up in the institute: 'During a period of

---

* *Translator's note:* Soloveichik is punning on his name — *solovei* is Russian for nightingale and is also the name of a penal settlement, and *vorobei* is both a sparrow and a prisoner or old lag.

reconstruction technology decides everything. Stalin.' Do you know it? I read it out one day in the presence of a lovely girl and she accused me of not being able to read properly. Listen carefully. She thought I'd read: 'During a period of technological reconstruction, Stalin decides everything.' She was an educated girl and my ignorance irritated her, so she duly imparted her irritation to the proper quarters. Well, I always had rather poor pronunciation, so I thought I'd get off with a good tongue lashing. Instead I got Article Fifty-eight, counterrevolutionary agitation and propaganda. Better yet, the security organization thought three years would be enough time for me to learn to read properly.

"I haven't done too badly here, though: economist for the Fur Procurement Trust. Make no mistake, since I got here the quantity of furs has gone up. But security has decided that Kansk is too cushy for learning to read, so they're sending me off to the Angara with the first group that comes along, and that happens to be yours. So now I'm dreaming of a job as accountant for the Boguchany branch of the Fur Procurement Trust. What you and I are going to make, Sasha, would be peanuts in Moscow, but for us it'll mean survival."

Perhaps Boris was right, but Sasha had chosen a different path for himself. He was going where they sent him; he'd live the way they meant him to. To try to get something for himself from them would be to recognize the right of the Dyakovs to keep him here, which he was not about to do.

"Where did you live in Moscow?" Boris asked.

"In the Arbat."

"Not bad. I lived on Petrovka, in the house near the skating rink, you know?"

"Yes."

"As you can imagine, much of my youth was spent in Hermitage Gardens. Many a pleasant evening I passed there. But as my grandfather the *tsaddik* used to say — you know what a *tsaddik* is? A *tsaddik* is sort of in between a sage and a saint. Anyway, as my grandfather the *tsaddik* would say on such occasions, '*Genug!*' You don't know what *genug* means either? *Genug* means 'enough,' 'that's it,' 'that's all.' And that's what *I* say: *genug* of reminiscing, *genug* of tears!"

*   *   *

In the morning the landlady went to work before they were up, leaving their breakfast in the oven under a metal cover.

"There you see the enormous advantage of the simple woman," Boris said. "Why do you think I divorced my wife? Only because she wouldn't get up early to make my breakfast. So, she lost a husband. Mind you, she'd have lost me anyway. Now, off we go to the mighty Fur Procurement Trust to see about my discharge. Not much chance of severance pay, I'm afraid, but I'm going to try and wangle a letter out of them to someone in Boguchany. Aren't you going to shave?"

"No."

"Listen, Sasha, shave it off. What do you want a beard for? When we go out, you'll see how pretty the girls are here."

Sasha had already seen some of them — very beautiful, stately Siberian girls with light brown hair, strong bodies, and strong legs. He had imagined his life in Siberia as that of a hermit. He'd learn French, English, politics, and economics — he wasn't going to waste the next three years. Now he began to have doubts. Maybe he should broaden the curriculum a bit?

"And they don't wear any makeup, it's all *au naturel*," Boris added. "The trek leaves in three days' time, so we should enjoy ourselves. But with a beard like that, my friend, you might just as well stay at home."

"I don't feel like being shaved in this place."

"Listen to the voice of experience. You're only on the first day of your exile, I'm already in my third month. If you put off trying to live your life until they let you out, you're a dead man. There's only one way to keep going, and that's to live as though nothing had happened. That way we have a chance of getting out in one piece."

The room was low, the wallpaper faded, the yellow-stained paper on the ceiling bulged in places, and a child was crying next door. But the room smelled of eau de cologne and powder. There were two ordinary barber's chairs; the barbers wore white coats — and boots — and their expressions were the same as those of Moscow barbers, grimly obliging.

Sasha saw his white face reflected in the dim, cracked mirror. His curly black beard had grown evenly and looked as if it had just been carefully trimmed.

"All of it? A clean shave?"

The barber snipped the air with his scissors reflectively and then decisively swooped down on Sasha's beard. Clumps of curls fell onto the unwashed sheet the barber had draped over Sasha.

The clippers clicked and hot lather warmed his cheeks, reminding him of the barbershop in the Arbat, its smells, the bright lights, and the holiday bustle.

"Is that you, or do my eyes deceive me?" Soloveichik spread his arms wide. "Our new lady-killer!"

Walking along the street again, Sasha looked at the girls and they looked back at him.

"If only they'd let us stay here, think what we could do to improve the local breed," Boris said. "The place is full of exiles, what difference would two more make?"

"Who will they leave here?"

"Left, who have they *left* here! The sick, those with large families, the very old. . . . Look, there's one coming now, but don't stare at him, he's a Menshevik, one of the leaders."

Coming toward them was an old man with a stick. He was wearing a coat and soft hat, and his long gray hair fell over his collar. Soloveichik greeted him with a bow. The old man bowed in return, though somewhat uncertainly, the way people do when they're not sure whom they are greeting. Then he recognized Boris, lifted his hat, and smiled.

"He's been through it both ways," Boris said, proud of the respect the old man had shown him. "He was exiled as a revolutionary in nineteen five and then as an *anti*revolutionary in nineteen twenty. How old do you think he is?"

"Sixty?"

"Try seventy-two! He was one of the first. You'll find all sorts here: Mensheviks, Socialist Revolutionaries, Anarchists, Trotsky-ites, national deviationists. These are people who used to be important."

Sasha had never realized that there were still any Mensheviks or Socialist Revolutionaries left in the Soviet Union. Trotskyites he could remember. But the others? Didn't they realize that . . . ? They were still hoping for something to happen. . . . Still carrying on their . . . Or, maybe they weren't carrying on anything.

They ate in the Fur Procurement Trust canteen, a low basement room with square pillars and bare tables. The kitchen was behind a large rectangular serving hatch. Three big saucepans were steaming on the stove and the cook, a good-looking woman, stood by with a ladle in her hand.

"This canteen is supposed to be reserved for employees, but they don't check up on outsiders. You have to have an identity card for the cashier. They have their own fattening station, with pigs, rabbits, and chickens. About half the exile community feeds here. If anyone tells you I fixed it for him to eat here, you can believe it."

The cook spotted Boris, put down her ladle, wiped her hands on her apron, and came out of the kitchen.

"Borscht today, Boris Savelyevich, and beef Stroganov with mashed potatoes, and if you can wait a minute I'll fry the potatoes for you." She leaned toward him. "Also, there's some real butter."

"Fry the potatoes," he replied grandly.

"Are you leaving?"

"I fear so." He frowned. "Did they bring the fur scraps?"

"Yes, they did, four bags, and they promised more tomorrow. But they got the prices wrong again, the goulash should be eight kopeks more than they allowed. And we haven't agreed on a price to repair the stove, and it's smoking badly, which hurts my eyes."

She seemed to be implying that as long as Boris had been there everything had gone right, but that as soon as he left everything would go wrong. And from the look on his face, he wasn't a bit surprised — it was only to be expected — though he was pleased to know that even if he was nobody in this place, he still commanded some respect. He deserved it.

"Here I am yakking away and you want your dinner," she remembered with a start.

"When I got here, there were five people working in the canteen," Boris said. "Now there are two — one helper and her. She's the cook, cashier, waitress, and manageress. As a matter of fact, organizing the canteen was only one small job I did here. I could tell you what I achieved here in two months, but who cares? Nobody is indispensable — one day it's me, the next day it's you. Though if you really think about it, that doesn't make sense. If there's no Pushkin in a library, I can replace him with Tolstoy, but it would be Tolstoy and not Pushkin. They can put someone else in to do my job, but it wouldn't be another Pushkin, if you see what I mean."

A shy little man came into the canteen. Stooped and disheveled, unshaven, the peak of his cap broken, a long, frayed jacket over a filthy shirt, buttons missing, clumsily patched trousers bagged at the knees, and shoes worn down at the heels.

"Ah, Igor!" Boris called. "Come over here, come on!"

Igor approached, smiling shyly. Sasha saw that he had blue eyes and a thin, white neck.

"Take your cap off, you're in a restaurant," Boris said.

Igor crumpled his cap in his hands and his light brown hair, which hadn't been washed or cut for a long time, stuck out in all directions.

"How're things?" Boris asked.

"Mustn't grumble." Igor smiled and revealed his few remaining teeth.

"Mustn't grumble. That means you're going to grumble about something. Got fired again?"

"No, not at all. They didn't need me for the surveying fieldwork, so they let me go."

There was something about his pleasant intellectual voice that Sasha couldn't quite identify. It was familiar.

"Igor worked in the surveyor's office," Boris explained. "A nice clean job, surveying buildings, drawing up plans, and piecework on top of it, so a guy can do all right. But here you have before you a lazy gentleman who hands in his drawings with butter stains on them. Have you really got butter, Igor? Then you should spread it on your bread, not your drawings. As for them letting you go because they didn't need you in the field, that's a lie. Half the staff is staying in Kansk and you could, too, if you were any good."

Igor grinned guiltily and twisted his cap.

"Okay!" Boris stopped lecturing him. "Do you want to eat? Of course you do! Have you got any money? Of course you haven't!"

"I'm getting paid for eight drawings any day now."

"I've been hearing about those eight drawings for the last two months."

Boris called out. "Marya Dmitryevna, you can feed Igor! I'm paying!"

The cook sullenly pushed a bowl of borscht and a hunk of bread through the hatch. Igor stuffed his cap into his pocket, tucked the bread under his arm, and went off to a distant table, holding the bowl of borscht awkwardly in both hands.

"Who is he?" Sasha asked.

"One of the more notable personalities here, a colorful type. A poet. The son of a White émigré. In Paris he became a hardened Komsomol, came to the U.S.S.R., and, hey presto! here he is in Kansk!"

"What for?"

"You do ask naïve questions. Why, to nip sedition in the bud, of course. If I tell the wrong kind of joke, then it follows that I am inclined toward a certain way of thinking and in the right circumstances I would be capable of anti-Soviet actions. You issued an unacceptable newspaper, tomorrow you publish an underground magazine, the day after tomorrow it would be leaflets. It's even humane: they gave you three years for the newspaper, but they'd have to shoot you for the leaflets, so actually they saved your life. Igor grew up in Paris, the son of an émigré, in other words someone who suffered from the Revolution, so nothing good can come of him. Therefore, he has to be isolated for his own good."

Igor was sitting in the corner, wolfing his food.

Watching him, Boris went on. "An ordinary person cleans up after himself, and that way he can be a human being wherever he goes. The aristocrat is used to having someone else clean up his mess for him, and if there isn't anyone, he becomes an animal. Monsieur over there doesn't wish to work, so he eats the leftovers in canteens, he's thrown out of his apartment, he's a bum! He's taken money from everyone here and never paid a penny back. And, as you know, millionaires are not very plentiful among the exiles. The exiles spoiled him themselves, made a regular song and dance about him. A poet, you don't say! From Paris, you don't say! Paris! France! *The Three Musketeers!* Dumas *père!* Dumas *fils!* I'm the only

CHILDREN OF THE ARBAT ✶ 269

one he's afraid of. The ones who fussed over him don't pay for him to eat now, but I do. He has to stomach my style, even though he despises me as a pleb and a lout. And now that I'm off to the Angara, he'll probably die of starvation! But the most interesting thing is something else: he's waiting for his Dulcinea. If she turns up, you're in for a spectacle you've never seen before and never will again. And here she comes."

Into the canteen strode a woman of astounding beauty. About thirty, she was majestic, a goddess with a sharply outlined, large stubborn mouth. She swept the room with a cool gaze, nodded casually to Boris, who bowed his head with restrained dignity. Then she saw Igor, bent over his bowl in the corner.

"That a slouch like him should have a woman like that!" Boris murmured, grief-stricken.

"Who is she?"

"She came from Leningrad looking for her exiled husband and fell in love with that scarecrow. Every day they sit here; he reads her his poems and she gazes at him as if he was the picture of Dorian Gray."

The woman said something to Igor and he giggled, scraping the crumbs off the table and throwing them into his mouth. The shabby, nervous little man had no charm about him whatever. The woman rose and went over to the service window where the cook, still sullen, slid a bowl of borscht across to her. Igor made a move as if to get up and help, but he remained where he was. When the woman went back for some bread and a spoon, he again moved as if to follow her, but did not.

Now she ate and he talked, his face looking simultaneously young and worn out. She listened and occasionally nodded.

Then she went back for a second helping, half of which she poured into Igor's bowl.

"What a pig!" Boris was exasperated. "He can eat from morning till night, and he'll take from any woman. Even in the worst conditions, a human being remains a human being. Just look at what this Parisian man-about-town has come down to. And don't think he's simpleminded. Not a bit! He's a know-it-all and a cynic, he sneers at the people he fleeces. He's a parasite! He spares himself, but sparing oneself means not sparing others, that's what my grandfather the *tsaddik* used to say. He came to the U.S.S.R.! Thought he was doing the Soviet Union a great honor, but then he discovered that in the Soviet Union you have to work. He didn't want to work, so society threw him out, squeezed him out of itself."

Sasha commented with a smile, "It would have been better to squeeze him back to Paris."

Meanwhile the woman had finished eating, pushed her bowl away, put both elbows on the table, and, leaning her chin on her hands, was gazing at Igor.

Igor, however, had turned gloomy. He sank back in his chair, dropped his head, and was muttering. . . .

He was reading poetry in a low voice, so that only the occasional word reached Sasha: crusaders, walls of Jerusalem, yellow sands, boiling sun, women waiting for knights who would never return. . . .

"How do you like that, eh?" Boris asked under his breath. "Knights in shining armor and enchanting ladies. Eh? In Kansk, in the fur agency canteen!"

It was absurd. At the same time, Sasha was fascinated by the situation, by Igor's distant gaze and the profound look in the eyes of the beautiful woman.

Sasha suppressed a momentary shudder. It arose from the intolerance that had been bred into him.

He said to Boris, "We should be more tolerant."

2

The meeting to discuss the general plan for the reconstruction of Moscow was almost over when Stalin arrived. He knew what Kaganovich would say in his opening speech and he'd read Bulganin's report. All opinions and proposals for the reconstruction had been reported to him and discussed twice in the Politburo, and he had determined his point of view, which had in turn been integrated into the general plan for the reconstruction of Moscow. The general plan and his point of view were in fact one and the same thing.

When he appeared on the platform everyone rose and joined the customary eruption of stormy applause. Stalin raised his hand in greeting and sat down at once, signaling everyone else to sit.

Someone at the rostrum was winding up his speech. While appearing to listen attentively, Stalin was doing sketches of the ancient ruined churches in Ateni, a small village a few miles from Gori, where his father, the cobbler Dzhugashvili, had customers, to whom he would take newly finished shoes and spend a day or two doing a little shoe repairing.

He would often take little Josef with him. They would leave Gori early in the morning and follow the vineyards along the banks of the Tana until they reached Ateni, in which there were nine or ten ruins of ancient churches. Among them was the church of the Zion Monastery, which was crowned with a cupola and was built, according to tradition, in the seventh century. Figures of the period could still be seen carved in the facade, and there were more of them on a fresco inside the church.

The most important monuments were architectural ones. They

would last a long time; they stood on open ground and could therefore be seen easily. Lenin had understood the importance of sculpture when he had ordered the creation of monumental propaganda. But Lenin had understood it too narrowly, only as a means of instilling images of the new historical authorities in the minds of the masses. The true purpose of monumental propaganda, however, was to perpetuate the epoch. How many of the fifty or so monuments built in Lenin's time were still standing? One? Maybe two?

The monument to Stalin's epoch would be Moscow itself, the city that *he* was going to create anew, for only cities were perpetual. The modest architecture of the twenties had been a mistake. Contrasting revolutionary asceticism with the ostentatious opulence of the New Economic Policy had allowed the modernist architects to ignore the classical heritage in their work. But it was the classical heritage above all that had to be incorporated.

Peter the Great had understood this and had built Petersburg precisely along classical lines, and that was why, from the architectural point of view, Leningrad (as Petersburg was now called) was a real city. But it was a city of the past, earthbound. Moscow would appear to future generations as a city that reached upward. Skyscrapers built on classical lines, that was the style of the future. The first skyscraper would be the Palace of Soviets. Kirov had proposed it in 1922, but who would remember that? Stalin was going to build the Palace of Soviets, which he would make the architectural focus of the new Moscow; he would lay new highways, install the Metro, put up new, modern apartment houses and administrative buildings, erect new bridges and embankments, hotels, schools, libraries, theaters, clubs, gardens, parks. It would all become a majestic monument to *his* epoch.

These thoughts brought back the memory of the ruined churches in Ateni. As a child, the rumbling emptiness and ancient mystery of those half-destroyed churches had struck his imagination. And now, as he sat sideways at the long table on the platform, he sketched their straight outlines on a sheet of paper. He did not know how to draw, but he could manage rectangular objects even without a ruler. He had a firm hand.

"Comrade Stalin has the floor," Kaganovich announced.

Again they all stood up, again the ovation and the roar of applause.

Stalin walked to the rostrum, cut off the applause with an abrupt gesture, and began speaking quietly.

"Enough has been said about the need for the reconstruction of Moscow. I don't have to repeat it. Moscow as it is now, built of wood, with its narrow lanes and side streets and back alleys and dead ends, is an incoherent sprawl, with its squalid houses and gloomy workers' barracks, and its antediluvial means of transport. Such a city can in no way satisfy the needs of its workers."

He paused and took stock of the tense silence. Nobody moved or made a sound.

Speaking still more quietly, Stalin went on.

"Since the Soviets came to power, we have made great strides to raise the standard of living for the workers of Moscow. We have moved workers who used to huddle in cellars into normal apartments, reducing the living space occupied by members of the former exploiting classes. We have put up numerous schools for the workers' children, as well as workers' clubs and palaces of culture. Our achievements in this area have been considerable, and they arouse a justified sense of pride in the hearts of Soviet people. But it is the future we have to think of. To lead means to see ahead. The plan we create must last for decades. The plan for the reconstruction of Moscow is such a plan."

He left the rostrum and walked up and down at the front of the stage. Then he went back to the rostrum and continued.

"In carrying out this plan, we will be fighting on two fronts: first, against the idea that Moscow should remain a 'big village,' and second, against excesses in urban development. We must not blindly copy Western models. Moscow is a socialist city, the capital of a socialist state, and that should determine its appearance. It isn't a city where the rich live in palaces and the workers live in slums, but, on the contrary, it is a city where the workers are provided with the best and the most advanced amenities.

"It follows that the first aim of the plan is to make the city convenient to live in. We must build comfortable new apartment blocks, preferably in park zones. We must construct comfortable and attractive buildings along the embankments of the Moscow and

Yauza rivers, which would give us an extra thirty miles of improved roads. We must build houses along the city's main streets, clearing away the old stuff and widening the main roads to fifty or seventy-five yards. This would solve the city's transport problems and would again be in the interests of the workers."

He paused once more. He knew that what he was saying was already well known, but he also knew that his audience took his words as revelation because it was *he* who was uttering them.

"Let me now come to the second aim," he continued. "The capital of the first socialist state in the world must be a beautiful city. Already at the dawn of our statehood, a plan for monumental propaganda was devised under the leadership of the great Lenin. The great Lenin wanted our epoch to leave monuments that would last for centuries, and it is up to us to cherish Lenin's wish faithfully and to develop it further. However, we were still poor in those years and we had to make do with modest architectural solutions. Regrettably, that opened up a wide path for formalist art, and the masses do not understand formalist art. It is strange to us. Now we are rich and powerful and we should above all make use of our classical heritage. Of course, we mustn't copy it blindly, as the planners of Petersburg did. We must pour socialist content into the classical mold."

Again he took a long pause and then went on.

"And finally, comrades, the last point: In what directions should Moscow be developed?

"The first proposal is to leave Moscow just as it is, as a museum, so to speak, a memorial, and to build the new Moscow on a new site. With all due respect, we cannot accept this idea. Moscow is the historic center of Russia. It was Muscovy that unified and created the state of Russia. We cannot renounce Moscow, we dare not and we will not.

"The second proposal is to leave the present center of the city untouched, roughly the area inside the Sadovoya ring, and to encircle it with eight satellite districts, creating eight residential conglomerations that would in fact constitute the new Moscow. It's not hard to see that this is just a variant of the first proposal.

"What are these proposals based on? First and foremost, on a lack of confidence that we are capable of reconstructing Moscow. Of course, it would be much easier to build a new city. But we are Bolsheviks, and it is within our powers to accomplish even the most difficult option: to rebuild, to reconstruct our Moscow *and* leave the city in its present place, leave it as the center of our country, the center of the world revolution. Therefore, we will develop Moscow along a radial-ring pattern, which is how it developed historically. Its architectural focus will be the Palace of Soviets, crowned by a grandiose figure of Vladimir Ilyich Lenin. The city's main highways will radiate out from the Palace of Soviets, each of them wide and lined with tall buildings. Moscow will thrust upward, skyward. A skyward-thrusting Moscow incorporating classical ideas, but shaped by socialist thinking — that will be Moscow's future image."

Stalin returned from the meeting to his study at a quarter to ten.

"Shumyatsky has brought the film, Josef Vissarionovich," Poskrebyshev announced.

"Good," Stalin said, "Shumyatsky can go home. Tell Klement Yefremovich to come and watch."

Stalin usually watched films with one of the Politburo members. On this occasion, he put on his spectacles and sat in the back row to one side, to be out of the way of the projector and not have it rattling in his ears.

On very rare occasions, and only if there were guests, he would sit in the middle of the second row without his glasses. He never appeared publicly in his glasses, and was never shown wearing them.

Today he'd ordered Charlie Chaplin's *City Lights*. It was the third time he'd seen it. He loved Chaplin, who reminded him of his father, the only person he ever held dear. Sometimes he thought he saw something of himself in Chaplin's hero, both of them so alone in the world. But he would quickly dismiss the thought as inappropriate, not in tune with reality. Chaplin reminded him of his father, and only of his father. Poor Charlie walked away down the road, looking back and smiling helplessly. It brought a tear to Stalin's eye and he wiped it away with his handkerchief. . . .

Voroshilov leaned toward him. "What's the matter, Koba?"

"This film's about me," Stalin replied without emotion.

But it was not about him, it was about his father, the hapless bootmaker. When he went off to collect his earnings, usually to Telavi or some other place, he would turn around in the road and, just like Chaplin, smile helplessly and wave sadly to Josef.

They were then living in the house of another cobbler, Kulumbegashvili. There were two rooms in the house: one was inhabited by the Kulumbegashvilis, and the Dzugashvilis huddled together in the other. The tiny house was permeated by the smells of bootmaking, as Kulumbegashvili also worked there. Stalin's father was often away, traveling to Kakhetia and wandering in the area. He didn't get on with his wife. Stalin's mother was a powerful woman, a pure Georgian of the Kartveli people, while his father's family were southern Ossetians who inhabited the Gori district. His ancestors had become Georgianized and his grandfather had replaced the Ossetian -ev ending of the name, Dzhugaev, with the Georgian ending, -shvili.

His mother did the cleaning and laundry at the house of a rich widower called Ignatashvili. At school, they said the old man was Josef's real father and that it was he who was responsible for Josef's getting into the seminary. If Josef was really the son of Dzhugashvili, he'd be learning bootmaking from his father, who'd be living at home and not wandering around Georgia.

They were all lying! You could never believe anyone! The young Josef knew perfectly well that his father was the nice, quiet bootmaker, although his mother was always cursing him because they were so poor and because he'd ruined their lives. Josef could not love his mother because of the way she berated his father.

No doubt his mother had wanted the best for him. She wanted him to become a priest, she wanted to give him to God. And she took him with her to the Ignatashvilis to see that he was well fed. He didn't like going there. They were rich and he was poor, they would bring him a bowl of soup and some lamb and sweet corn, which he would eat in the yard, while they were having their meal inside the house, drinking wine and making conversation. When they went to the Ignatashvilis, his mother would try to dress him up. Why? Some people used clothes to show their wealth, others to hide their poverty. But he was not ashamed of his poverty. He was a beggar, he went about like a beggar and he always would. So what if his trousers were in tatters? He hadn't any others. His boots were worn out, and they were his only pair. Later, at the seminary in Tiflis, he was proud of his ragged appearance — it was the only way for a real man to look! Even now, he dressed like a simple soldier. . . .

He did not want to submit to his mother. He loved his father, but he did not submit to him either, for the simple reason that his father had no will of his own. His mother had a will, and it was said he had inherited his character from her. But she put all her willpower and character into getting a crust of bread. His father, on the other hand, was a real man, not a beast of burden. His father wasn't going to break his back for a kopek. He loved to sing and laugh and sit around a table with his friends. At times like that he looked like a real man, sympathetic, charming, cheerful. But when he was with his wife, he changed: he became a small and beaten, silent, weak man!

Then a letter arrived informing them that his father had been killed in a drunken brawl in Telavi. More lies. His father never got into fights, he was a quiet, peace-loving man. Who would have killed him and why? His father had simply died. The boys in school had something else to tease him about, saying that his father hadn't been man enough to stand up for himself. But Josef knew it hadn't been like that, that it was all lies, so he didn't even bother to reply but grinned and kept to himself. He despised the lot of them, all of his schoolmates. He despised the rich ones who boasted of their wealth, and he despised the poor ones who were ashamed of their poverty.

His father was buried in Telavi, though nobody knew where, not even Josef. He had loved his father and his father had loved him and had treated him well, never punishing or reprimanding him. He used to stroke his head tenderly and sing him songs. It was from his father that he had inherited his musicality. He was always in the top row of the choir at school, where the short boys stood, and the choirmaster used to say that he had the best voice and that he had good pitch. That was from his father. He also looked like his father, who had been short and ruddy, whereas his mother was tall and dark. His father loved jokes, whereas his sullen mother never even understood them.

Now the local citizens wanted to change the name of Gori to Stalin. That wasn't necessary! They should rather rename the town of Tskhinavli, the capital of southern Ossetia; then it would serve as a monument to his father and all of his Ossetian tribe. His mother would know that he was honoring the memory of his father, the bootmaker Vissarion Dzhugashvili. She would understand, being no fool. Of course, he would look like an exemplary son to the Soviet people, and his image would be more human, more close and more dear. For him, his childhood meant above all his father.

He recalled again the times he'd gone with his father to Ateni, when the peasants were making their wine, stamping the grapes with their bare feet and pouring the good Ateni wine into enormous basins.

In the evenings, his father would sit with his friends and drink the local wine and they would sing songs in those Georgian harmonies that tug at the heartstrings. They sang well and they drank well, like true Georgians, becoming mellower and merrier with the drink, unlike the Russian peasants who, when drunk, throw their weight around and get into knife fights. Still, they were the Russian people, a people great in number and great in territory, a people you could make history with. Annexation by Russia had saved the Georgians as a nation, and Georgian socialism had become a part of Russian socialism.

The Russians are a coarse nation, they're not like the Georgians. Because of his withered arm, nobody had ever picked on him at school or in the seminary. That was merely ingrained Georgian good manners. In Baku, Batumi, and Siberia, however, the Russians took no account of his physical disability and behaved like pitiless louts. He had stood up to them by being even more coarse himself. Lenin had rebuked him for his rudeness, but it was the only way to command — the coarseness of the administration curbed the coarseness of the people. The intelligentsia had handled the people with kid gloves, and the people had then thrown them out like so much garbage. Even when he was young, he had realized that democracy in Russia would turn out to be only a license to unleash crude force. The people's coarse instincts could be restrained only by a powerful regime, by a dictatorship. The Mensheviks hadn't understood this, but they didn't know the people; it was the Bolsheviks, who did know the people, who had understood it. That was why most Russian Social Democrats had sided with the Bolsheviks and not with the Mensheviks. Bolshevism was a Russian phenomenon, Menshevism was not. Of all the famous Georgians, he was the only one who had understood the Russian people and joined the Bolsheviks. The others, Noah Zhordania, Tsereteli, Chkheidze, and the like, hadn't understood the Russian people and had sided with the Mensheviks. True, he had been opposed to the nationalization of the land. It was impossible to say who had been right *at the time,* he or Lenin. History gives no simple answer to the question of who was right and who was wrong in the past — the victor is right. But he wasn't going to oppose Lenin. His destiny had been with the Bolsheviks and with Russia, which was the only place where he could become known as a political figure. He had steeped himself in the national question and he knew that among nations, as among people, the powerful dominate; as among politicians, there were those who drove and those who were driven. In the Soviet Union, with its hundreds of different nationalities, only one could lead, and that was the Russian nation, which constituted more than half the total population. It was important to declare merciless war on Russian chauvinism, as it provoked local nationalism in response. But it should not be forgotten for one minute that the chief unifying force was the Russian people. For the Russian people he must be a Russian, the way the Corsican Napoleon was a Frenchman for the French.

Stalin was pleased with the meeting. He had not only emerged as the initiator and organizer of Moscow's reconstruction, but he had also preserved the city whose name was dear to every Russian, he had preserved Moscow as every Russian knew and imagined it. *He* and only *he* had satisfied the deep Russian reverence and love for Moscow, not those highbrow Russian intellectuals whose job it was to preserve Russia's culture. And therefore Moscow was now *his* city and the future Moscow would be a monument to *him*. Kirov — a Russian — was floundering in Leningrad, shouting about its reconstruction, but what was there to reconstruct? Leningrad was fully formed, it was a solid stone mass with which Kirov would be able to do nothing. He may only have been a small man, but he had big ambitions.

As always, after demonstrating his originality, a sharp sense of loneliness came over him. They stood and applauded him, but they didn't love him; they were afraid of him, so they stood and applauded him. Should he fail, they would trample on him with the greatest satisfaction and a sense of triumph and joy. They would take out their own feelings of inadequacy and spite on him. They were unable and unwilling to accept his superiority, his originality, and his uniqueness. For them, he was a half-educated seminarian, a lowbrow plebeian. Even his so-called comrades in arms were afraid of his growing grip on power. They talked about collective leadership, the role of the Central Committee, and they were keeping in reserve Pokrovsky's ideas, which denied the role of the individual in history, thinking to belittle *his* role in the history of the Party and the history of Russia.

They would not succeed. He would not only create a new history of Russia, he would also develop a new approach to the evaluation of historical events. It was the only way to ensure that present and future generations made the correct judgment about the epoch, *his* epoch.

Julius Caesar and Napoleon did not become emperors out of vanity, but from historical necessity. Only Caesar, possessing individual power, could defeat the barbarians, and only Napoleon, being an emperor, could subjugate Europe. The supreme power had to be majestic in a *tsarlike* way; the people would submit only to such authority. Only such authority was capable of inspiring fear and trembling in the people. Russian historians depicted Ivan the Terrible as a villain. In actual fact, he had been a great statesman who annexed Kazan, Astrakhan, and Siberia. He was the first in the history of Russia, and maybe not only of Russia, to introduce a monopoly in foreign trade, the first of the Russian tsars to adopt the principle of statehood as fundamental, according to which everything was subordinate to the interests of the state. The nobles were opposed to the creation of a powerful, centralized state, and therefore Ivan's mistake was not that he punished them, but that he didn't punish them enough, he did not destroy the four main noble clans right down to their roots. The kings of ancient times were more farsighted in this respect, they killed their enemies down to the third and fourth generations, wiped out the whole lot once and for all.

The historians were also wrong about the role of the *oprichnina,* Ivan's elite. It was important to distinguish between the concept of the *oprichnina* and its members, the *oprichniks.* The *oprichnina* was Ivan's guard, a progressive armed force designed to fight against the nobles. The *oprichniks* were executives, and there were bound to be executioners among them. Humane parliamentarians and highly educated legislators make the laws on capital punishment, but executioners carry them out.

Peter the First was a great ruler and he created the new Russia. So what did Pokrovsky write about him? These are his words: "Peter, nicknamed 'the Great' by flattering historians, shut his wife away in a monastery, so that he could marry Catherine who had been chambermaid to a pastor in Estonia. He tortured his son with his own hands and then had him secretly put to death in the dungeons of the Peter-Paul Fortress. . . . He died from the effects of syphilis, having first infected his second wife. . . ." And that's all Pokrovsky could see in Peter!

And this rubbish came from the "head of a school of history"! Somehow he'd overlooked the fact that Peter had transformed Russia! That was where the dogmatic interpretation of Marxism could lead, that, and the denial of the role of the individual in history! And this primitive sociologist was the man Lenin had advanced to the front rank of historians, praising his *Condensed Outline of Russian History,* a pathetic piece of work that presented all Russia's historical figures as men of no talent, as nonentities. How could Lenin have praised this? Lenin, who understood so well the role of the individual in history!

Pokrovsky wanted to present himself as the custodian of Leninism, the sole interpreter of Lenin's views. Well, I'm sorry, the only interpreter of the views of Vladimir Ilyich Lenin was his successor, only he who continued Lenin's cause, only he who led the country after him. His successor was Stalin, who was now leading the country. That meant only Stalin could be the interpreter of Lenin's heritage, including the field of history, since it was *he* who was *making* that history. Yet in ten years, Comrade Pokrovsky hadn't said a single word about Comrade Stalin's contribution to the social sciences. Did he not realize that to run a state meant to develop the theory of the state? He realized, all right, but he didn't want to acknowledge Comrade Stalin either as a scholar or as a theoretician.

Pokrovsky's anti-Marxist school of "history" had to be smashed. Lenin's authority must be used to serve the Party's needs today, and what might be necessary tomorrow. And Lenin's authority must pass to his successor. Stalin was the Lenin of today. When Stalin died, his successor would be called the Stalin of his day.

In practical terms, the October Revolution was carried out by the military-revolutionary committee of the Petrograd Soviet. Trotsky was at the head of it. That was all very important then, during the seizure of power, but it was of no significance now that the events were in the distant past and when the Party was facing new tasks. What was needed now was a powerful regime. Trotsky was hostile to the regime and therefore could not be regarded as the hero of October — he would not be dealt that historical trump card.

That was the only way to create an indestructible succession of power, eternally stable and unshakable. Historical science must affirm that Stalin was Lenin's true heir, that there could be no other, and that those who claimed to be were nothing but pathetic pretenders, political adventurers, and intriguers. Historical science must always assert that Stalin had stood shoulder to shoulder with Lenin. Not Zinoviev, who had only been Lenin's secretary in emigration, nor Kamenev, who'd done nothing more than check Lenin's papers, but Stalin, who had done the practical work of building the Party inside Russia. That was why it was called the Party of Lenin and Stalin. The minor tactical differences they had had should be forgotten, they should be expunged from history forever. History should show only that which made Stalin the Lenin of today.

The main task was to build a mighty socialist state. For that, mighty power was needed. Stalin was at the head of that power, which meant that he had stood at its source with Lenin. Together with Lenin he had led the October Revolution. John Reed had presented the history of October differently. That wasn't the John Reed we needed.

Would this be a distortion of history? No, it would not. It was the Party that had carried out the seizure of power in October, not the émigrés who'd returned from Paris, Zurich, and London. At the Parisian sidewalk cafés they had become skilled in discussion and debate and had learned to address meetings, whereas revolutionaries inside Russia had had to learn to keep silent or talk in whispers. But it had been just such ordinary, modest Party workers who at the decisive moment had raised the masses to struggle and revolution and then later to defend the Revolution. *He* was the representative of *those* Party members and therefore *their* role in the history of October was *his* role. That was the essence of the masses' role, and where the true role of the individual in history was to be found.

Trotsky had been a single unit in the Revolution, representing nobody but himself. However important the things he did, he did them as a fellow traveler; it was his own affair and had nothing to do with the real history of the people. But what Trotsky did against the Party and against Lenin certainly did have a direct relation to history, for the history of the Party is the history of the Party's struggle with its enemies, and above all with Trotsky. During the Civil War Trotsky was the commissar of foreign affairs and chairman of the war council. But it wasn't he who won the Civil War, traveling up and down the various fronts and making speeches. Nor had the military experts won the Civil War — they'd only got in the way. It had been won by the tens of thousands of Communists, the Party cadres who created the armies and the divisions, the regiments and the units. *He* represented those cadres, and therefore their role in the Civil War was *his* role, and *his* role was the Party's role.

These and these alone were the principles on which history and the history of the Party must be based.

So-called collective leadership was a myth. There had never been "collective leadership" in the history of mankind. The Roman Senate? How had it ended? With Caesar. The French Triumvirate? With Napoleon. Yes, the history of mankind was the history of class struggle, but the leader emerged as the expression of class, and therefore the history of mankind was the history of its leaders and its rulers. Idealism did not come into it. The spirit of an epoch was determined by the man who made the epoch itself. The epoch of Peter the Great was one of the most brilliant in the history of Russia, and it reflected Peter's brilliant personality. Alexander III's reign was the dullest; it was entirely in keeping with his own mediocrity.

3

Boris went out in the morning to arrange for a driver for their journey, and Sasha sat down to write some letters.

"Dear Mama ..."

Some official had read out the orders of a special meeting to him in the same room where he had been interrogated. Article 58, Clause 10, three years of administrative exile to eastern Siberia, to include the preliminary detention already served.

"Sign!"

Sasha had read the paper. Maybe it would say why he had been given three years? Not a word about it. It wasn't even a real sentence, just an extract from a longer list, and he was maybe fifth, or twenty-fifth or three hundred and twenty-fifth on the list.

He had signed.

The sentence had been announced in the morning, the meeting with his mother had been during the day, and he'd been sent off the same evening.

The evening before, a guard had appeared and given him a piece of paper and a pencil.

"Who do you want to see before you go?"

He wrote down his mother and father. Varya? He could write *Varya Ivanova, fiancée*. They would have to let him see his fiancée. Why Varya? Did he love her, did she love him? Yet it was her he wanted to see. *"Like a flower of the fragrant prairie, your laughter is sweeter than the pipe ..."* He had missed that tender voice.

But he didn't write Varya's name. Did she want to see him, was she waiting for him, did she need him?

The guard had taken Sasha to a tiny room and left, locking the door behind him. Sasha sat at the table and thought of how shocked his mother would be when she saw him with a beard, and how awful it would be for her to walk along the prison corridors.

The key turned and Sasha saw the guard's face appear and behind it that of his mother, her gray hair. The guard stood with his back to Sasha, preventing his mother from going to him, and pointed to a chair on the other side of the table. She scurried to sit down, her head lowered, not looking at Sasha. Once she had sat down she raised her eyes and didn't take them off him. Her lips trembled and her head began to shake very slightly.

Sasha looked at her and smiled, though his heart was beating hard. How she had aged, now unhappy she looked, how much suffering there was in her eyes. She had come in an old lightweight coat she called her "gabardine," and it reminded Sasha that it was already springtime and that he hadn't seen her since January.

The lower half of the window had been blanked out with whitewash, but the spring sunshine streamed through the upper half into the far corner where the guard sat impassively.

"I wanted to shave, but I didn't have time, and the barber's not here today," Sasha said breezily.

She sat looking at him in silence.

"The barber's an amateur — he pulls the hair, so no one likes going to him. Maybe the beard suits me, maybe I ought to leave it?"

She said nothing, nodding her head gently and gazing at him.

"How's everyone, are they all right?"

She understood that he meant, Were his friends all right?

"Yes, they're all fine."

But the thought that they were well and that Sasha was the only one who was having a hard time, that it had to be just him, was too hard for her to bear and she burst into tears, burying her face in her hands.

"No, don't, there's something I want to say to you," he said.

She took out her handkerchief and wiped her eyes.

"I'm going to appeal. The whole case is nonsense; it's connected with the institute."

The guard interrupted him.

"No talking about the case!"

His mother showed no alarm, the way she used to, if someone in authority ever spoke harshly to her. The stubborn look that Sasha knew so well appeared on her face, she strained every nerve as she listened to him, and she heard him out. This was something new that he noticed in her.

"I'm going to Novosibirsk, everything will be all right." He had said Novosibirsk, because he couldn't bring himself to say Siberia. "As soon as I get there I'll send you a telegram and then I'll write. I'll get myself work, don't send me any money."

"I've put in a hundred and fifty rubles."

"Why so much?"

"And food, as well, and boots."

"Boots, that's good, but there's no need for food."

"And warm socks and a scarf." She raised her eyes. "How long have they given you?"

"Hardly anything, three years unrestricted exile. I'll be back in six months. Did Papa come?"

"He came in January, but I couldn't reach him now — they only phoned me last night. How is your health?"

"Perfect! I haven't been ill once, the food's very good here, a real health resort!"

He tried to cheer her up by being cheerful himself, but she could see his suffering, and she was suffering, too. She tried to cheer him up by smiling painfully at his jokes, trying to let him see that he was not alone, that people were concerned about him.

"Vera was so upset that you didn't put her name down. She came with me, but they wouldn't let her in, nor Polina, either."

He had somehow forgotten about his aunts.

Confusing what she had rehearsed with words that came rushing into her head now, she said: "Look after yourself. All this will pass. Don't worry about me, I'm starting a job."

"What job?"

"In a laundry, sorting the laundry as it comes in, on Zubov Boulevard, near us."

"Sorting dirty linen?"

"I've already agreed. Not right now, but after I've come out to see you."

"Come out to see me?"

"I'm coming out to see you."

"Fine, and we'll write to each other," he said to pacify her. "Did anyone from the institute come to see you?"

"The little one, the one with the squint . . ."

Runochkin! That meant they were all all right.

"What did he say?"

"He talked about the deputy director. . . ."

Krivoruchko! That meant he was here. Dyakov hadn't lied.

"The whole case has to do with him," Sasha muttered.

The guard got up.

"The visit is over!"

"The case is all about him," Sasha repeated. "Tell Mark."

She nodded to indicate she understood: Sasha had been arrested because of the deputy director, and she had to tell Mark this. She would tell him, though she knew it would do no good. Nothing did any good. But at least let it be no worse than it was. Three years, they would pass, they would come to an end.

"And also tell him that I haven't given any testimony."

The guard opened the door.

"Please leave, citizeness!"

Sasha got up and embraced his mother. She buried her face in his shoulder.

"There, there," he said, stroking her soft gray hair. "Everything's all right, and you're crying."

"Please leave, citizeness!"

They were forbidden to embrace, to approach each other and kiss, but they did, just the same.

"Come on, come on, you must leave." The guard had shoved her toward the door with a nudge of his shoulder. "You've been told already, now leave!"

Now he was writing to her that everything was fine, he was fit and happy and there was no need to send him anything. She should write to him care of General Delivery, Boguchany Village, Kansk District.

Boris came back angry. Nobody wanted to take them; everyone was afraid of the bad road and was asking enormous sums. The commandant's office wouldn't wait any longer and said they had to get themselves there any way they could. The travel allowance was worthless, barely enough to get them halfway.

They had dinner again at the fur agency canteen. Sitting hunched up at a bare table in the corner was Igor.

"The count is at his post," Boris remarked. "Waiting for me and his Dulcinea. Her to read his poems to, me for a free meal. Well, he's in for a long wait. I'm out of a job myself, now."

The cook didn't come out to greet Soloveichik this time; she was moving saucepans around noisily on the stove and clattering the metal plates.

"Since morning he's been here, Boris Savelyevich, cadging food off the employees. It's impossible — this isn't a church door for him to beg alms."

"I'll talk to him," Boris replied.

Boris had no official standing, yet she ladled an extra portion of sour cream into his soup, as she had the day before.

"You have to understand her position," Boris said. "Beggars aren't allowed in the canteen, and it's her responsibility."

"He's hungry," Sasha replied.

"Look, Sasha," Boris objected vehemently, "I arranged it so the exiles could come in here. Now that I'm going, it doesn't affect me, of course, but for those who are staying here, it's a matter of life and death. It'll end up with them being kicked out. I warned them all not to get here before two o'clock, after the employees have eaten, and not to make any noise, not to be a nuisance, but to be quiet, peaceable, and tidy. Not like that! He turns up first thing in the morning, hangs around the whole day, eating bits and pieces, whatever he can find, reading his poems — and there are poems and poems, as you know, just as there are poetry-lovers and poetry-lovers.... You know what I mean?"

"People meet in cafés in Paris and hang around in them all day, and Igor got used to it," Sasha said.

"I got used to a warm lavatory," Boris snapped, "and a bathroom and a telephone and going out to restaurants. As you see, I've broken the habit."

"Let's give him a last dinner. I'll pay," Sasha said. "Call him over."

Boris shrugged his shoulders and with a frown beckoned to Igor.

Igor, who had been waiting for Boris's signal, came to life, got up awkwardly from the table, and came over, smiling expectantly.

"Well, have you been paid for your drawings?" Boris asked.

"They've promised any day now."

"Where's your lady?"

"Valeria Andreyevna has gone back to Leningrad."

"For good?"

"For good."

" 'Strangely we met, and strangely we part,' " Boris muttered. "Well, sit down."

Igor sat down hastily, putting his crumpled cap on the table, then, remembering himself just in time, moved it to his knees.

Boris nodded toward Sasha.

"Tomorrow we —"

Igor stood up and bowed to Sasha. Sasha smiled at him.

"As I was saying," Boris continued, "tomorrow they're sending us to the Angara. I've got them to agree that you and the others can still come in here as before. But it's high time you understood that this is not a café in Montmartre."

"I understand," Igor whispered, bending low over the table.

"This place is a closed institutional canteen. As soon as you've eaten, you leave. If you've no money, don't show yourself. Those are the rules here, and you are breaking them. They can turn you away, and that would be a minor misfortune, but because of you they'll turn the others away, too, your fellow exiles. Do you understand?"

"Yes, I understand. But I'm not an exile," Igor added hastily.

"Then, pray, what are you, if I may inquire?" Boris asked mockingly.

"I wasn't sentenced, they just called me in and said, 'Go to Kansk, that's where you're going to live.' "

"You carry a note?"

"Yes."

"And a passport?"

"I've never had a Soviet passport."

"Have you got the right to leave?"

"No."

"So, you're the same as us. Come on!"

Boris and Igor went to the serving hatch and returned, Igor carrying a bowl of borscht and Boris a hunk of bread and a spoon.

"Eat!" Boris ordered. "And don't rush — nobody's going to take it away from you."

Igor bent low over the bowl and ate silently.

"You're an artist, you ought to do portraits," Boris said.

Igor put down his spoon and wiped his lips with his fingers. "Nobody wants them; they say photographs give a better likeness and are cheaper."

"Why don't you try doing pretty little landscapes?" Boris persisted. "It's the sort of thing they might like here; you could do some in the club for the holidays. You have to start using your brains a bit and stop thinking of yourself as an aristocrat."

"I don't," Igor whispered.

"Yes you do. And you consider me a pleb."

Igor shook his head. "Not a pleb."

"What, then?"

Igor lowered his head, his spoon poised in the air. "I regard you as a money-grubber.'"

Sasha couldn't suppress a smile, but Boris went white. "That's nothing new for me. Boor, pleb, money-grubber, it's all the same. In Russia, that is. I don't know how it is in Paris. But since it is the plebeians — sorry, money-grubbers — who pay for the nobility to eat, I'm leaving you seven rubles." Boris took his money out and counted seven rubles. "It's enough for ten meals. I'm leaving it with the kitchen; otherwise you'll gobble it all up in one day. And then, when you've got through the ten dinners, either you'll find another 'money-grubber,' which we can rule out, or you'll work, which is doubtful, or you'll die of hunger, which is the most likely."

He went to the hatch and spoke to the cook, leaving her the money. She did not look pleased as she threw it into the plate that served as the till.

Sasha stood up.

Igor also got up. His cap fell to the floor and he bent down and picked it up.

Sasha held out his hand to him.

"Good-bye, Igor. I hope you manage to get things straightened out for yourself in the end."

"I'll try," Igor replied sadly.

"So long." Boris gave him a casual nod.

Their driver turned up next morning in worn-out moccasins and a greasy hat with three flaps. His wrinkled face was covered by a thick reddish stubble. He looked anxious and was worried that he hadn't charged enough.

Sasha and Boris loaded their things onto the cart and the landlady put in a bag of food. She stood for a long time on the porch, watching them go.

As they walked behind the cart, Boris said sadly, "Say what you like, she did a lot for me."

Their companions for the journey were already waiting at the commandant's office. Volodya Kvachadze, a tall, handsome Georgian in a new, black, quilted jacket that he'd got a month before the end of his camp sentence of five years. Ivashkin, a middle-aged printer from Minsk. Kartsev, a former Komsomol official from Moscow, brought to Kansk from a political "isolator," the special prison in Verkhneuralsk, after a ten-day hunger strike.

Boris knocked on the hatch outside the commandant's office and announced that the cart had arrived, and so had Soloveichik and Pankratov.

"Wait!"

The hatch slammed shut.

Volodya Kvachadze, frowning arrogantly, said nothing. Kartsev, who was sitting on a bench with his eyes closed, looking weak, exhausted, and utterly apathetic, also said nothing.

"We haven't gone anywhere yet, and already the driver is fleecing us for a hundred rubles," Boris said. "We've only been given fifty rubles as our travel allowance, so we've got another fifty to pay."

"No way!" Volodya snapped. "Let *them* pay the other half."

"They give what is allocated," Boris explained. "We could manage all right on it in the summer, of course."

"So I'll go in the summer — I'm not in any hurry," Volodya

replied. "Anyway, this is a pointless discussion because I haven't *got* any money."

"I haven't, either," Kartsev said quietly, without raising an eyelid.

"Nor have I," Ivashkin added guiltily.

The hatch opened.

"Ivashkin! Sign!"

Ivashkin looked at the others in confusion.

Volodya pushed him away and bent down to the hatch.

"You're giving us ten rubles each and the cart costs a hundred."

"We gave you what is allocated."

Boris bent toward the hatch. "Not everyone's got the money, so what do we do now?"

"It's up to you to figure it out, that's what," came the reply.

"It's up to *you* to figure it out," Volodya shouted. *"You!"* He banged on the hatch with his fist.

"Cut that out!"

"Get your boss!"

Ivashkin touched Volodya's sleeve. "Let's not start any trouble, boys."

Volodya threw him a look of scorn.

A well-fed man with two bars on the collar of his tunic appeared.

"Who's complaining?"

"We can't pay — and we're not expected to pay for the transport," Volodya said over his shoulder.

"Walk, then."

"What about our things? Are *you* going to carry them for us?"

"Who do you think you're talking to!"

"I couldn't care less. . . . I asked you, are you going to carry our bags?"

"The allocation for travel expenses is set by the people's commissar for internal affairs," the commandant announced, restraining himself.

"Let *him* try and get there on the allowance, this people's commissar of yours!"

"Are you trying to get yourself sent back to the camp?"

Volodya squatted on his heels by the wall. "I don't care!"

"We can make you go!"

"Be my guest."

"Guards!" the commandant yelled, red in the face.

Two guards came out, dragged Volodya to his feet, and tied his hands behind his back.

"Now that you've tied him up, you can't get any money out of him," Sasha said.

"You want some of it, too?" shouted the commandant.

"You'll get no money out of me either," Sasha continued calmly.

The commandant turned away and ordered the cart to be brought into the yard.

Volodya was led into the office.

Ivashkin cleared his throat. "We're done for, mates!"

Kartsev didn't open an eye.

The hatch opened.

"Soloveichik!"

Boris went over.

"Give your travel allowances to the driver immediately. The man in charge at Boguchany will pay him the rest. Give him this packet of documents: they're the papers for all of you. Now get going!"

They pulled out into the street. The cart rolled through the gate followed by two mounted guards carrying rifles. Volodya lay tied up in the back of the cart, his black eyes squinting angrily.

The party moved off.

4

The boys were standing along the brick wall, the teachers were sitting on benches, and the girls, dressed up for the occasion and in a holiday mood, were sitting on the ground. The tenth grade was leaving; they had finished school and were saying good-bye forever. Only Varya wasn't there.

Not to turn up on this of all days! Nina was choked with embarrassment. Not to say good-bye to her class, the friends she'd spent the last ten years of her life with, not even to have a photograph to keep as a souvenir, never mind the position she had put her sister in in front of the whole teaching staff!

Only a few days earlier, the mathematics teacher had come up to Nina in the staff room and praised Varya as a "gifted young lady." "Young lady" had jarred unpleasantly. Her sister had indeed acquired a number of quite markedly uncontemporary traits. She wore her hair straight back, not in a simple bun on the back of her neck, but over her ears, like women in old portraits. And she had taken to turning her head in such a way as to appear to be looking at everything sideways.

Nina considered the expression "young lady" socially alien and therefore offensive and began to think that the conversation with the mathematics teacher was a bad omen, although he looked friendly. The physics and chemistry teachers had also spoken well of Varya, and the mathematics teacher had nodded in agreement when they said that Varya need have no fear of the competitive exams — nobody had any doubts about her passing and about her going on to higher education.

Nina escaped with some general remarks: Varya could paint well and her technical drawing was excellent and when someone had a lot of abilities, it was hard for them to decide what to do.... She couldn't tell them that her sister didn't care what she thought, didn't listen to her advice, lived as she wished and did what she wanted.

Varya smoked. When Nina had asked her how she got hold of such expensive cigarettes — Hercegovina Flor, ten in a slim package — she calmly replied, "I bought them." And as to why she came home so late at night and where she had been, she would answer as curtly, "With friends." She wouldn't say where she got the money for cigarettes or with which friends she stayed up all night. When Nina asked her who gave her foreign phonograph records, she pulled an insolent face and said, "I work for Japanese intelligence. Didn't you know?"

She said it as a challenge, trying to provoke a quarrel. But Nina held her irritation in check, and smiled as if at the joke. "I thought they only used people who had a higher education as spies. Take a look around you, Varya, look at the times we're living in. Everyone has the opportunity to develop their abilities, surely that's the most important thing? Why should you miss your chance, everyone's studying...."

"I'm not interested, can't you understand?"

"Then what are you interested in?" Nina screamed. "Hanging around the streets all day?"

She couldn't think why she had said this, for she knew perfectly well that it had nothing to do with the streets and the people there, and she cursed herself for her outburst.

What did Varya want? To become a draftswoman? A machine operator? To go out to Siberia to join Sasha? She might come up with anything, anything at all.

At the station, when Varya had seen Sasha under escort, she had become hysterical, wailing and refusing to listen to anybody. People in the tram had looked at them: a young girl in a woman's sealskin coat, obviously not her own, crying and covering her face with her handkerchief.

At home, Nina had persuaded her not to go to see Sofya

Alexandrovna, and Varya, who had become feverish, was suddenly obedient and went to bed. Nina had covered her with a blanket, thinking she'd calm down and sleep it off. Varya slept the whole evening and through the night, and she didn't hear Zoe come for her wretched sealskin or Nina getting ready for school in the morning. Nina was worried and came home early, only to find that Varya had gone out.

When Varya came home late, she said she'd been to see Sofya Alexandrovna. Then she went to bed with a warm blanket, as she had the previous evening, and again spent the next day with Sofya Alexandrovna.

A little while later, Nina also went to see Sofya Alexandrovna, who greeted her coolly, not with her usual cordiality, as if it were Nina's fault that Sasha had been sent into exile, while everyone else was walking around free. That was how she was meant to feel. Varya was sitting on the sofa, reading, and barely glanced up when Nina arrived. Conversation was difficult. Sofya Alexandrovna answered Nina in monosyllables, and the sound of Varya turning pages filled the long silences. She, too, no doubt thought that Nina had betrayed Sasha by doing nothing for him.

Let them think what they like. So, Nina wouldn't go to see Sofya Alexandrovna again. She certainly didn't intend to explain herself to Varya. She had no need to justify herself; she had done nothing wrong.

Yet it left an unpleasant taste in her mouth, a feeling that she had been rejected. She was an intruder at Sofya Alexandrovna's, whereas Varya was at home, and that was why she was being so stubborn and doing as she liked.

What ideas had Sofya Alexandrovna put into her head? After all, now that Sasha was *on the other side,* she must be *on the other side,* too. It was crazy, but that's the way it must be. Nina recalled what Sasha had been like in school, but a touching school friendship was no basis for political trust. Childhood was childhood, and real life was real life. What was left of their group? Sasha was in exile. Max was in the Far East — no doubt he'd get married and settle down with a family. Sharok was in the prosecution service. That was also crazy — Yuri Sharok deciding people's fates, a prosecutor, a job which in her eyes was the personification of gallant dedication to the Revolution. And Sasha Pankratov was in exile as a counterrevolutionary!

Even so, there was a firm, if implacable, logic in history. If you judged Communists only by their personal qualities, the Party would become a shapeless mass of eloquent intellectuals.

So, who was left? Vadim Marasevich? He was always friendly, as usual, when they met on the Arbat. He was getting his reviews into the newspapers and magazines and doing well, like the rest of his family, and they had recognized the Soviet regime only in the seventeenth year of its existence.

Varya, wearing a short, faded shift, was standing on the windowsill in her bare feet, cleaning the windows. Drops of dirty water ran over her hands and down the glass to collect in small puddles between the windowframes.

"Why didn't you come for the photograph?"

"I forgot. And when I remembered, it was already too late."

"At least you can remember the other things you have to do, thank God."

Varya threw the rag into the pail and jumped down.

"So I didn't get photographed." She searched through drawers and took out some photographs. "Here I am in sixth grade, and here I am in seventh. And, as a matter of fact, here's the tenth grade, taken last autumn. Nobody's changed much in six months. You can be sure of that."

Nina ignored the photographs and coldly announced: "I'll be leaving in two days to attend a seminar. Decide what you're going to do. I'm only going to help you if you're willing to prepare for the university. Otherwise you're on your own."

"Don't worry about me," Varya replied. "I'm going to get a job."

The shock Varya had felt at seeing Sasha at the station had still not passed. She had been horrified that he was under guard, horrified at how pale he was and how aged he had looked with his beard, surrounded by people running past him along the platform concerned only with getting a good seat on the train — happy, pink-cheeked young officers who didn't even notice that a man was being led away under guard while they set off for the Far East, sure that everything was right with the world.

She had been even more shattered by the *obedient* way Sasha had carried his suitcase, walking *voluntarily* into exile.

Why hadn't he resisted, why hadn't they had to tie him up? If he had resisted and fought, shouted and protested, if they'd had to take him bound hand and foot, two guards wouldn't have been enough, they'd have needed a whole platoon, and not just an ordinary railway coach but one with iron bars. People wouldn't have been so mindless, as they ran along the platform. And all those Maxes and Serafims in their bright new uniforms, perhaps they wouldn't have been so narrow-minded and obedient in their self-satisfied way.

Sasha had been tamed, too.

When she had delivered packages for him to the Butyrki, it had seemed to her that the high, thick, impenetrable walls had been built just for him, so afraid of him were those men with their guns. But, no, it wasn't *they* who were afraid: he didn't scare them, they scared *him*. That was why he walked so meekly between the two young guards whom he could have knocked down with one hand. He couldn't anymore.

But Varya continued to pity Sofya Alexandrovna. She went to see her every day and brought her news to try to cheer her up. When Sofya Alexandrovna started work at the laundry, she went to the shops for her to get her rations.

Sofya Alexandrovna praised Sasha, called him honest, manly, and fearless. Varya did not argue, but she no longer considered him manly. If he could let himself be treated *that* way, then he was just like everyone else. And he always had been just like everyone else, he had always done as he'd been told. Now he'd been told to go into exile, so he'd gone; he'd walked obediently along the platform with his suitcase in his hand.

Sofya Alexandrovna decided to give up Sasha's room, and Varya helped her get the place ready for the new lodger. Sasha's ice skates were lying in the cupboard, blades screwed onto old boots, with long laces that had been knotted and reknotted where they'd broken. Sofya Alexandrovna picked up the skates and started crying. They brought back his childhood.

They reminded Varya of the chill air of the rink, the pool of dim light on the ice, the band on the bandstand, the bustle in the changing room. Her own laces were tied in the same clumsy knots as these, making it difficult to get the laces through the eyelets, so it took a long time to get ready.

Varya also remembered the time they had gone to the Arbat Cellar, when she'd asked Sasha to go skating with her. It had seemed then that everything was wonderful, that Sasha had conquered everyone. They'd had a good time, dancing the tango and the rumba, and the band had played "Mister Brown" and "Black Eyes" and "Oh, Little Lemons" . . . And Sasha had stood up and defended a girl he'd never seen before and had shown how brave he was.

At that moment in the Arbat Cellar he'd been her hero.

Now he was no hero. She knew there weren't any heroes.

There was just a vast apartment house without sunshine or fresh air, with the smell of old cabbage and rotten potatoes wafting from its basements. There were overcrowded communal apartments with their endless squabbles and disputes. Stairs reeking of cats. Lines for bread, sugar, margarine. Coupons that went unused because there were no goods. Intellectual men in patched trousers, intellectual women in worn-out jackets.

And right next door, on the corner of the Arbat and Smolensk Street, was the Torgsin store, where you could get anything, as long as you could pay for it in gold or foreign currency. And right next door on Plotnikov Street was the special, restricted store where they also had everything for those with power and money. And here on the Arbat was the Arbat Cellar where you could get whatever you wanted if you could afford it. It wasn't fair, it wasn't right!

In her sixth year at school Varya had joined a drama group, run by a former actress named Elena Pavlovna. The activists had criticized her for putting on Ostrovsky and Griboyedov instead of plays by Soviet playwrights, and she had lost her job, even though she had a sick daughter to look after. Varya had been appalled that an elderly person could be deprived of her crust of bread. Three years had passed and the drama group floundered along without a leader, because it was impossible to find anyone to take the job for the pittance it paid. Everything was ruined. And nobody would take the responsibility. Varya started skipping meetings — everything was always decided beforehand, anyway, and it was demeaning to have to raise your hand to vote when it really didn't matter. Yet Nina defended them. Nina was an idiot, with a ready-made answer for every question. The questions could all be different, but the answers were always the same.

Varya had found refuge among the boys and girls in the street, dropouts like herself. They weren't supposed to smoke, so the boys smoked; using makeup was frowned upon, so the girls used lipstick and powder, let their hair grow long, and wore fishnet stockings and bright scarves.

But now all this had become uninteresting. The shock she had experienced at the station prompted her to look for a different kind of independence, especially as there was now a new crowd in the street.

One day Varya bumped into Vika Marasevich on the Arbat. She was with a very unpleasant, snappily dressed man of about forty.

Vika had never taken any notice of Varya, but now she stopped to talk and even hugged her. She was wearing an amazing perfume.

"Varya, meet my friend, Vitaly — Vitaly, this is my schoolfriend, Varya."

Vika's slight inaccuracy did not escape Varya — there had been a good five years between them at school.

"See what beautiful girls we have on the Arbat?" Vika went on. "Well, Vitaly, what do you say?"

Vitaly raised his eyebrows like an idiot, spread his arms, and was lost for words.

"You've completely dropped out of sight, Varya, you don't phone or come around anymore."

Varya had never phoned Vika and she'd never been to her home.

"How's Nina?"

"She's fine, working."

"Nina's her sister," Vika explained to her companion. "Varya dear, call me or I'll call you, and we'll get together." She took a small notebook out of her bag, flicked through it, and found their phone number.

"It hasn't changed?"

"No."

"Well, keep in touch."

Two days later, Vika rang and invited Varya over.

When Varya arrived, Vika had evidently just got up: she was wearing her dressing gown, stockings, and silk underwear, and her dress was lying on an armchair where she had thrown it the night before — these rags meant nothing to her, she didn't bother about them. With a small key, she opened a wooden box standing amid a collection of flasks and jars, which contained earrings, beads, and brooches. She showed them to Varya, not to flaunt her possessions, but just to show her what was in fashion, what they were wearing abroad. Leafing through foreign magazines, she showed Varya shivering beauties wrapped in furs and wearing flesh-colored stockings and delicate shoes.

Then they sat at a small table alongside an ottoman and drank coffee and Benedictine from minute glasses, and smoked long gold-tipped cigarettes.

This was another world! Out there, people were standing in lines, waiting to trade their coupons; here they were drinking coffee, smoking cigarettes, and admiring foreign fashions.

"Does Nina know you're here?"

"No."

"Didn't you tell her we ran into each other?"

"I don't have to tell her everything."

"Quite right, too," Vika said approvingly. "I've got a lot of respect for your sister, but she's got a masculine attitude toward things, she's indifferent to what a woman needs — she despises me, I know, because she's a bluestocking, but I don't mind. I admire her ambition. She's socially minded and that's good, that's wonderful. But we're not all made the same way."

"Nina wants everyone to be like her," Varya said.

Vika wound up the phonograph. "Who do you like? Melekhov? 'Girls, tell your friends . . .' No, you can hear too much of him. . . ."

She played Vertinsky, then Leshchenko.

"Vitaly's got some wonderful records. We must go and hear them sometime."

Varya burst out laughing.

"Go to *his* place?"

"What have you got against him?"

"He's proof perfect that man is descended from the apes. Why go and see *him?*"

"You're underrating him, Varya. He's a very influential person."

"Let him influence someone else."

"Are you going to enter drama school?"

"This year I'm through with school. I'm going to start work."

"Doing what?"

"I'll get a job somewhere as a draftswoman."

"Varya! Vitaly can fix you up in a jiffy. He knows absolutely everyone in Moscow. I'll call him right away."

She pulled the phone on its long cord across the ottoman and dialed.

"It's Vika."

Jazz was coming out of the earpiece.

"Turn off the barrel organ," she commanded. "Varya's here, my schoolfriend, from the Arbat. . . . Sure," — she nodded at Varya — "he says hello. . . ."

"*Merci!*"

"Listen, she's looking for a job as a draftswoman. . . . In school . . . the school specialized in it. She does excellent drawing. . . . What? And who have you got there? No, I'm not interested. . . . And where will you find him?" (The conversation was apparently about some man Vika was agreeing to meet.) "No! The day after tomorrow, Saturday. Erik will surely be able to come then, and we'll go to the Metropole. I'll ask her. . . . Varya, are you free the day after tomorrow?"

"Yes."

"She's free. And Erik has to come, too. . . . Because I say so! Otherwise Varya and I won't come. He has to be there, don't forget."

She hung up.

"There'll be another man, his name is Erik. He works on equipment for Magnitostroy."

She looked at Varya.

"Come the day after tomorrow at six, we'll leave from here. We'll get you a job and enjoy ourselves at the same time."

She smiled and stroked Varya's hair.

"I must take you to Pavel Mikhailovich, he'll style your hair for you." Pavel Mikhailovich was a famous hairdresser. His salon, next to the Prague restaurant, was called Paul's. He was known as "Mr. Paul" to his clients, and Vika was showing how well she knew him by using his real name.

ow should she dress tomorrow, what could she wear to go to the Metropole? Next to Vika she was just a girl in a worn-out blouse. All her things were out of date and ugly. What stockings did she have, or shoes? She searched through the wardrobe, dressed and undressed. Only her old blue dress looked reasonable. She would have to ask Zoe for her high-heeled shoes, there was nothing else to do.

Vika was wearing a beaded dress, the hem just below the knee in front, below the calf at the back, and higher on one side than the other. It hugged her bust and waist. Tall and blonde, with smooth skin and large, gray eyes, she was a striking girl.

Unhurriedly, though the date was for seven and it was already nearly eight, she took off the dress and sat down in her pink underwear to change her hairstyle.

The telephone rang and a complicated conversation took place with Vitaly. He hadn't been able to find Erik anywhere and he was suggesting they go to his place. Vika explained that they were fine where they were.

"It would be even nicer with you here, but I'm afraid you have to wait for Erik's call," she said to him.

She was still at her dressing table, clothed only in her underwear.

"Has Lena Budyagina been around to see you lately?" she asked Varya.

"Not since the New Year's party."

"Does she still see Yuri?"

"No. Yuri's an informer, I can't stand him!"

Vika spun around on the revolving stool and looked at Varya

angrily — that was not the way people spoke in her house. Vika, her brother, their father, and everyone in their circle accepted reality, the inevitable conditions of life. The nature of their acceptance was simple: restraint, no ambiguity, no jokes or accusations — they knew only too well what they might lead to.

"Varya, listen carefully to what I'm going to say! I'm going to be introducing you to people. The positions they hold carry a lot of responsibility. You are going to have to weigh every word you say around them."

"But what did I say?"

Vika did not even want to repeat the word *informer;* it wasn't going to be she who had uttered it. "Your vocabulary smacks of the street."

Varya exploded. "So? I grew up on the street!"

"You've misunderstood me. I'm not talking about vulgarity — that doesn't bother me. But it's best to avoid certain topics and certain words. Yuri does his job, and it's not for you and me to try to understand it."

Varya was silent. What was there to understand? Except maybe the lines waiting at the prisons. But Vika was right: she was now moving into a new, unknown world and she would have to behave differently.

"I just don't like Sharok, I think he's repulsive."

Vika embraced her.

"Clever girl! 'Life is short' may be a cliché, but it's got more than a grain of truth in it. All the rest is no business of ours. Right?"

The apartment had been quiet when Varya had arrived. At nine, the place came to life, with voices and footsteps in the corridor and doors slamming. Vika paid no attention to any of it. Everyone lived his own life here, everybody minded his own business, not even Vadim bothered to look in. Varya compared this with life in her communal apartment, where she lived under Nina's tedious, heavy-handed control.

Vitaly phoned at ten and told them to be at the entrance in no more than fifteen minutes.

Vika adjusted her hair languidly, applied more lipstick, and slipped into the beaded dress.

*   *   *

Erik turned out to be a tall, slim young man with shiny black hair brushed smoothly back. Both from the suit he wore and the way it fit him, he was obviously a foreigner. He got out of the car and opened the door for Vika and Varya with the gallantry of a prince inviting shepherdesses to enter his carriage. Then he got in and drove without uttering a word for the entire journey. When they arrived at the Metropole, he helped the girls out of the car.

The line outside the restaurant parted, and a doorman in a braided uniform opened the door for them, the headwaiter in his black suit appeared, a free table in the crowded room was found, and a waiter materialized. Vitaly had spoken with the doorman, the cloakroom attendant, the headwaiter, and the waiter, but Varya noticed that it was Erik they were trying to please, and that was true most of all of Vitaly himself. Vitaly, who was at home here, looked over the menu and advised what they should order, while the waiter hovered attentively.

Vika was transformed. Nothing — the line outside the restaurant, the doorman, the cloakroom attendant, the lack of a table, the headwaiter's attentiveness, and the waiter's willingness to oblige — had concerned her. She turned the short walk to their table into a triumphal procession, so that the glances that focused on her should bear witness to her beauty and reinforce the impression she wanted to make on Erik. She looked straight ahead as she walked, acknowledging no acquaintances who might diminish her impact by showing familiarity. Today *she* would decide to whom she was going to speak and whom she would ignore.

Having sat down she cast a casual and unexpressive gaze around the restaurant and nodded toward a miniature blonde girl who was with a stocky Japanese man in dark glasses.

"Do you recognize Noemi?"

She was treating Varya like an old friend, as she had on the Arbat. Varya had no idea who Noemi was, she only knew that Vika had arranged with Noemi an hour before to meet at the Metropole.

Vika then pointed out a lovely Chinese woman. "Look, Sybilla's here, too."

As the waiter set the table, Vitaly explained to Varya and Erik that Sybilla Chen was the daughter of the Chinese foreign minister. A famous dancer, she was opening her tour the next day in

Moscow; she would be going on to Leningrad and then Europe and the United States. He pointed out several other artists. Most people would be arriving in half an hour, when the theaters let out. The show here would start at eleven. It would be Utyosov's band without Utyosov — he never sang in restaurants.

There were plenty of girls in the restaurant with foreigners. Varya knew they were given fashionable clothes, rides in automobiles, and that they also got married and went to live abroad. She wasn't interested in foreigners but in this restaurant, with its fountain and music and famous people all around her. Wasn't it this she was trying to escape to from her dingy communal apartment?

The starched tablecloths and napkins, the glitter of the chandeliers, the silver and the crystal — the Metropole, the Savoy, the National, the Grand Hotel. Before, these had been nothing but names to her, a Muscovite born and bred, but now her hour had come. A girl from the Arbat, she was quick on the uptake, observant, and she didn't miss a thing, especially the way the men eyed her and the women looked past her. They ignored her because she was badly dressed. Never mind, they'd take notice when she came back dressed more elegantly than the lot of them. She didn't dwell on how she was going to get hold of new clothes. She wouldn't sell herself to foreigners; she was no prostitute. And anyway, not everyone here was like that. Take the table over there: one bottle among the lot of them, they hadn't got money, they'd come to dance. She'd find her *own* kind of company.

They were discussing wines. Vitaly recommended the Château d'Yquem, but Vika wanted Barsac, a wine Varya had never heard of. Erik preferred a glass of vodka, and caviar. His polite smile never left his face. He spoke very good Russian, albeit with a slight accent, and now and again he had to make an effort to recall a word. His father was Swedish, the owner of a famous telephone company that was installing special communications equipment in Soviet factories, and Erik, who was an engineer, was representing his father's firm. His mother had been born in the Baltic region of the Russian empire and had taught Erik Russian, and even his father knew Russian. It was his company that had installed the first telephones in Russia before the Revolution. Smiling, Varya commented that a Swede was supposed to have blond hair and blue eyes. Erik solemnly explained that his maternal grandmother had been a Georgian princess who married a Baltic baron, a general in the Russian army. The name he mentioned was one of those that Varya knew from the history quizzes she loved to take. At school they had learned about the ancestors of the old noble families — but Erik could trace his lineage not just back through the centuries, but to other countries as well. It was fantastic, almost like history itself, the way the old clans had broken up and scattered their fragments around the world.

"Don't look now," Vika murmured, leaning forward, "but behind us, to the right, second table along, you'll see a couple, an Italian and a girl ..."

One after the other, as though not looking at anything in particular, they all turned around and looked at the Italian and the girl who was with him. She had an outlandish face, with enormous eyes and deathly white skin.

"Nina Sheremetyeva," Vika revealed.

"Of *the* Sheremetyevs?" Erik raised his eyebrows.

Taking note of Erik's interest in the countess, Vika replied, "Yes, but from one of the impoverished branches, not the main one."

Vitaly added, "She was living with a newspaper photographer, then an actor, then the actor went back to his wife, and now it'll be interesting to see how the affair with the Italian ends."

It was Vika who had started the gossiping, but now she felt it was time to exercise some discretion. "A pretty woman is always the subject of idle talk, as everyone knows."

The lights were dimmed, spotlights illuminated the fountain, and the band began to play. A young man was looking at Varya. He was short, with the face of an angel, a regularly shaped, slightly elongated oval face, with a high forehead, carefully arranged chestnut hair, a short straight nose, and good-natured, smiling eyes. His suit, his shirt, and tie were impeccable, perfect, even too perfect, not a wrinkle, not a speck of dust on him, he was like something from a picture postcard. Varya decided he must be an actor. Only an actor could be so handsome and so elegant. He danced simply, without elaborate intricate steps, but that was the latest style. Vitaly's dancing, in contrast, was old-fashioned, and Varya was embarrassed to be seen with such a middle-aged partner. The angel smiled at her, not in a loutish way but like a friend, as if to say, *Okay, so here we are dancing in the Metropole, I can see your boyfriend is not a foreigner, he's conceited, impressed with himself because he frequents restaurants like this.*

The music stopped and everyone returned to their tables. The angel passed close to Varya and smiled at her again. He escorted his partner back to her table, thanked her, and went to his own table, which was on the same side of the dance floor as Varya's, only a little closer to the fountain. It wasn't clear how many and just who was sitting at his table, as young people would join him for a while; some would stay, others would leave and new ones arrive. The angel and the only girl at the table, a pretty, freckled, plump girl, the kind it's a pleasure to look at, danced every dance, the plump girl with someone from their table, the angel with whatever girl he asked. When the orchestra struck up a rumba, he appeared at Varya's side, bowed to everyone, turned to Vitaly, and asked for the pleasure of this dance with his lady. Varya thought this was the usual custom at a restaurant — she was perfectly capable of deciding with whom she was going to dance. She got up and led the angel onto the floor.

He danced the rumba the same way he danced the fox-trot — step, slide, step, slide. Varya could dance beautifully even with the worst partners, but with *him* . . .

"I know you," he said, smiling. He had the whitest teeth, though one of them was crooked.

Varya made a little grimace: oh, yes, I'm sure you do. He was playing the guessing game to get to know her, asking her leading questions to get the information he wanted. How primitive!

"Your friend's name is Vika."

She replied with the same grimace: why shouldn't he know Vika's name? Probably everyone here knew who she was.

"You live in the Arbat," he went on, baring the crooked tooth in a smile that was somehow made the more charming for it. He also had a nice voice.

"If you know that Vika lives in the Arbat, it wouldn't be hard to guess that I do, too."

"And you've got another friend called Zoe."

He smiled in triumph — he'd won the game they were both playing.

Varya moved back a little and looked at him. Where had he seen her with Zoe?

"How do you know?"

His enigmatic smile indicated that he knew a lot more than he was going to say; now it was her turn to reveal something.

"My name is Lyova, what's yours?"

"Varya."

"Will you have the next dance with me?"

"I'd be delighted."

She got back to the table at the same time as Vika and Erik. Vitaly hadn't been dancing.

"Varya, let's go for a little walk," Vika said.

The powder room was like a beauty salon, with women touching up their lipstick, putting on powder, repairing their hair. One woman was sewing a button back on her sash. An attendant had needle and thread and handed out towels, for which she was given tips.

"What are you doing?" Vika asked. "You came here with us, but you're dancing with anyone who asks you. Don't you understand?"

"But Vitaly said it was all right."

"He didn't mind your being *asked*, but it was up to you to decline. You've put me in a difficult position — I don't know what Erik will think. Now every man will come over to our table because they know there's a girl who doesn't refuse anyone."

"Suppose I don't want to dance with Vitaly?"

"Then you should come with people you *do* want to dance with. But as you have come with us, dance with Vitaly and Erik, the people we know, after all. Not with anyone who happens to turn up!"

"As a matter of fact, he isn't just anyone. He knows you."

"He knows my name, and I know his, Lyova! Everyone here knows him." She twisted her mouth derisively. "He's a draftsman at a design studio."

That was how he knew Zoe — she also worked at a design studio. He must have seen her when she went to visit Zoe at work.

He remembered her, and she had thought he was an actor. Well, it was even better if he was a draftsman, as that was what she was going to be.

"He's just another dancing partner who hangs around the restaurants," Vika went on. "He's pals with some billiard player who always picks up the bill. If you like him, come with him next time and dance with him and his friends, but tonight please don't make me look like a fool, if you don't mind."

They went back and Vitaly and Erik got up and helped them to their seats.

Lyova was at his table, not with his back to her, but facing her, and when the music started he raised an eyebrow questioningly, but she gave him a barely noticeable shake of the head and he moved to another table. Vika went onto the floor to dance with Erik. Varya told Vitaly she didn't feel like dancing.

The evening had been spoiled, Vitaly grumbled at Vika: he'd done his bit by bringing Erik, and look what he'd got for his trouble. He muttered vaguely about egoists who used others. Vika pretended she didn't know what he was hinting at, and, as for Varya, she didn't give a damn about Vitaly.

They left the restaurant at about three in the morning. Vitaly suggested they go to his place to listen to records. Vika announced that she was tired and that it was late.

"What about you?" she asked Varya.

"I should have been home ages ago."

Erik said he'd drive anyone wherever they wanted to go. Vitaly didn't get into the car, because he lived nearby on Gorky Street and could easily walk. Thank you very much for a pleasant evening!

Vika mockingly waved good-bye to him.

She was altogether pleased with Varya. Varya could be relied on, she wasn't cheap or empty-headed, she was a good, decent girl and her naïveté would be reflected onto Vika. She was just the companion Vika needed. They even looked like a classic pair, one blonde, the other dark, both the same height, both beautiful. Varya just needed to be taught how to dress and do her hair and to learn good manners.

They arranged to meet Erik the next day at the National for tea. Vika would bring Varya and another friend, a well-known architect who had recently won first prize in a competition. Erik was delighted, for he had heard of the architect.

Was Vika thinking of marrying a foreigner and leaving the country with him, like the other girls at the Metropole? She hadn't yet decided. She had grown up hostile to all *this*. As a child, she hadn't been able to stomach the boor who had been installed behind a partition in *their* apartment, the loutish way he had organized things in the corridor and in the kitchen. He was a grubby worker who came home from his night shift first thing in the morning and turned the bathroom into a dirty pond, and who had regarded her father — who owned the apartment — as a surviving counterrevolutionary. And meanwhile her father, a professor with a world reputation, had been forced to accept fees in the form of flour, jam, and fruit-drops that had got stuck together. Even these paltry payments had had to be concealed so they wouldn't be branded as bourgeois. Her childhood had been unforgettable. . . .

Everything had changed since then. They had got back the whole of the apartment, her father was earning fabulous fees, they had the highest standard of living, famous people came to the apartment, she had everything: clothes, cosmetics. Life in Moscow, as one of the most beautiful girls there, wasn't so bad.

But what future was there for her? A professor? A famous artist? A powerful boss? Divorce, alimony . . . Most young people started out with nothing, with four hundred rubles, but she wasn't about to bring a parasite into the house. True, a new elite had emerged — pilots, aircraft designers — and the government gave them nice apartments, good rations, excellent salaries, part of it even paid in vouchers for the hard-currency, foreign goods shops. Vodopyanov, Kamanin, Doronin, Lyapidevsky, Levanevsky, Molokov, Slepnev — the most famous names in Moscow, but where were they all, these famous pilots? They were probably married. Where were the mysterious aircraft designers?

She didn't know what to do with her life. In any case, it wouldn't be a Japanese, or even an American, for they were both from too far away, nor a Herman the German, because things were getting uneasy there. An English lord or a rich Frenchman or even a frivolous Italian . . . Paris, Rome . . . The Swedish heir of a safety-match king would do, or the son of a Dutch oil magnate . . .

They were Swedes or Dutchmen only on paper; they lived in London and Paris. If she became Erik's wife, the girls would die of envy — for them, even a Turkish kebab-vendor was a prince.

Anyway, one could go to restaurants only with foreigners: they were fussed over, everything was done to please them, they could get anything with their hard currency, with them you were treated like a human being. She would go to the National tomorrow during the day. She hadn't decided if she would go up to Erik's room; she might use the excuse that Varya was with her. In protecting Varya, she would be displaying her own virtue.

And so Vika and Varya were sitting at a table in the restaurant of the National with Erik and a well-known architect named Igor Vladimirovich, a lean man in his mid-thirties, with a nervous manner but a quiet voice. Varya had heard about him on the radio. Vika simply called him Igor.

Waitresses were serving tea. The restaurant monogram was on the saucers and sugar bowls and cookie plates. There were pastries and wine. It was all very decorous, sedate, and serene.

Varya spotted a number of people who'd been at the Metropole the night before. There was Noemi and her Japanese, Nina Sheremetyeva and her Italian, and the plump girl with freckles, but without Lyova. The women were wearing short dresses or suits. Noemi was in a bright cardinal-red suit with a suede sash and silver braid and epaullets.

They chatted about music and the ballet. Erik talked about Stravinsky and Diaghilev and Pavlova, and mentioned Russian musicians and artists who were living abroad.

Varya loved music and frequently went to the conservatory with her friends, but when Igor Vladimirovich asked her what kind of music she liked best, she replied, "Loud."

Igor Vladimirovich and Erik burst out laughing, and then so did Vika.

The orchestra, consisting of a violin, cello, piano, trumpet, and drums, began to play, and the four of them got up to dance on a tiny patch of floor.

Igor Vladimirovich danced very well, not as professionally as Lyova, but people watched as they danced. They recognized him.

The plump girl smiled at Varya, making it clear that she had been noticed by her friends.

"You dance beautifully," Igor Vladimirovich said. "You're very easy to dance with."

"So are you."

He was behaving as a middle-aged, educated man should with a young girl, but Varya sensed that he liked her.

As Vika danced with Erik, he invited her to come up to his room afterward. It would have been overly coy to have refused; after all, this was the fourth time they'd gone out together. She could hardly expect him to wait much longer.

Some part in her decision was played by Noemi's red suit. What a suit it was! All Vika had that was halfway decent was the beaded evening gown. The fashions brought from abroad by the wives of Soviet diplomats were copied by tailors in Moscow, but what could *they* make?

She must come to a decision. Today. Not tonight, but right now, following her impulse. Their conversation had been a good beginning, but apart from the entertainment, she longed for an intelligent man in her life. And there was nothing that prevented her from visiting him in his room during the day.

But what about Varya? It would be awkward to ask her up to Erik's room and then send her away; it would be too obvious. Even worse to take her home and then come back alone. She suggested they change partners, and while she was dancing with Igor she asked him to see that Varya got home.

"I have to go to the tailor's. Varya's a wonderful girl, but when it's a question of dressmaking, it's best to keep one's best friends out of the way."

As they came out of the National, Igor Vladimirovich suggested they go for a walk in the Alexander Park. "If you've got time, that is."

A bench had been placed across the entrance to the park, even though it was still early.

"We shall overcome this obstacle."

He pushed one end of the bench out of the way and they walked along the rain-soaked paths by the metal railing, past the tall lime trees and trimmed shrubs. It was a warm evening and still light, and the sunset reflected off the Kremlin battlements.

"Old Neglinka Street used to run through here, once upon a time," Igor Vladimirovich said. "Then the ponds were put in, and the gardens. They were designed by Bové, a truly great architect."

"He certainly was," Varya said mockingly.

Remembering her sarcastic remark about music, he said nothing.

"He built the Manège," she offered, "the Maly Theater, and he rebuilt the Bolshoi after it burned down, the facade of GUM. . . . And what else? The Triumphal Arch, the First City Hospital, Prince Gagarin's mansion on Novinsky Boulevard . . ."

"How do you know all that?"

"The school I went to taught us all about architectural drawing."

He said, "You have very unusual eyes — they slant upwards almost to your temples."

"I've got Tatar blood in me."

"No," he protested, "it's not the same as the Mongol slant; they're more the sort of eyes you see in Persian miniatures."

"And there aren't any Tatar miniatures," Varya said.

They both laughed.

Then he said, "I'm sorry you like loud music, because I prefer it quiet."

"I like *good* music," she replied.

The figure of the park attendant loomed in the distance.

"Are we about to be thrown out?" Varya asked.

"We'll explain ourselves," he said bravely.

"We'd better get out."

Jumping over the puddles, they ran to the exit. A whistle blew behind them, but they had already moved the bench aside and skipped out of the park.

"Saved!" Igor Vladimirovich declared.

Hopping on one foot, Varya was leaning against the railing with one shoe off.

"Did you get wet?" He bent down.

"Worse. My stocking's got a run."

He was standing next to her not knowing what to do, concerned by her distress. She in fact was quite upset, as these were her only good pair of stockings.

He picked up her shoe and wiped it inside and out with his handkerchief. She stood leaning against the railing.

"What's your size?"

"Thirty-five." She put the shoe on. "It's fine, we can go."

They walked to the tram stop.

"May I phone you?" he asked, as Varya was getting on the tram.

"If you like."

6

The full meeting of the Central Committee opened on June 9, and on the thirtieth came news from Germany that Röhm, the head of the Nazi storm troopers, and most of the other storm trooper leaders had been murdered. This operation, known in history as "the night of the long knives," was carried out under the personal direction of Hitler. On July 1, *Pravda* and other Soviet newspapers carried articles by, among others, Zinoviev and Radek, which interpreted the event as a convulsion of the Fascist regime foreshadowing its inevitable collapse.

Stalin did not object to this view. Any weakness in another regime would only underline the power of his own, even though he knew that a split did not weaken a political movement but merely widened its social base, attracting different kinds of supporters and consolidating the central thrust in its fight against dissidents. The most obvious example of this was the case of Christianity.

Splits in the Party had never worried Lenin *before* the seizure of power, but once the Party was the organ of government, he tried to avoid them. That was what had motivated his so-called Testament that had strengthened the claims of Trotsky, Zinoviev, and Bukharin to the leadership. Lenin saw state power as a factor that bound together those who had something to gain from maintaining and consolidating it. In fact, power divided, since all these groups were trying to seize it. Power was a consolidating force only when it was in the hands of someone from whom no one else would either dream or be capable of seizing it.

To achieve this, the people must be made to believe that the regime was indestructible, and those who were capable of infringing on this belief had to be eliminated.

Lenin had brought his own party to the Revolution; he had created it and nobody ever attempted to usurp his leadership. The situation now was different. Stalin was asserting his authority at a time when many aspired to power, convinced that they had a better claim to Lenin's heritage than Stalin had. Even those he had defeated had not lost hope. Such a one was Zinoviev. Didn't he realize that the murder of Röhm, far from weakening, had strengthened Hitler's position? He was not a novice in politics. And that rogue Radek understood, too. Yet they were trying to convince the Party rank and file that a split weakened authority, and that the physical annihilation of opponents was a feature of Fascism, whereas Bolshevism, by contrast, always sought to unite its ranks and its forces. Were *they* a force? They ought to have left politics long ago. But they hadn't. They still write, they make speeches, they remind the people of their existence, they want to be seen, they want to be in evidence. They were merely treading water, biding their time, trying to alarm *him* with the thought of war with Germany! Even more, they were trying to provoke the war themselves. What else did the journal *Bolshevik* intend in publishing Engels's article on tsarist foreign policy? Why that, all of a sudden, forty years after it was first written? To commemorate the twentieth anniversary of the Great War, if you can believe it! It was a primitive ploy of Zinoviev's as a member of *Bolshevik*'s editorial board, which the chief editor, that blockhead Knorin, had fallen for.

Engels asserts in his article that when Russia was at the pinnacle of her military might she was governed by talented foreign adventurers, most of them Germans: Catherine the Great, Nesselrode, Lieven, Giers, Benckendorff, Dubelt, and so on. Why focus on that just at this moment? Why give the Nazi propaganda machine such a trump card by extolling the role of the Germans? Why draw attention to the role of non-Russians in the Russian government altogether? Could it be a hint at *his* Georgian origins? Zinoviev and Knorin weren't Russian, either. But who was paying any attention to *them,* what good were they to anybody? Nobody would think of drawing a parallel. People paid attention to Comrade Stalin, and this was what they were counting on. In fact, the whole issue of the non-Russian element was a play for Kirov, it was a prize for him to pick up, he was the one they were banking on now, just as they had once banked on Comrade Stalin as a means of getting rid of Trotsky.

This time, however, they were preparing to go farther, much farther. For it wasn't merely the non-Russian element they had picked up in Engels's article. Engels had called Russia a bastion of European reaction, he had accused Russia of expansionism, and he depicted a future war against Russia virtually as a war of liberation. He had written: "A victory for Germany would consequently be a victory for the Revolution. . . . If Russia starts the war, then forward against the Russians and their allies, whoever they may be!" Not a word about the conflict between England and Germany, and yet that had been the chief cause of the Great War. Apparently Engels hadn't been able to predict everything.

The point of publishing the article was that *they* wanted Hitler to know that there were political forces in the U.S.S.R. that expected war, that were putting their hopes on war to overthrow the present leadership, and that were therefore ready to trade with Hitler, ready to concede something to him. The purpose of the article was to provide Hitler with the promise of the victory in foreign policy that he needed to justify his own revanchism — the idea of national revenge that constituted his chief strength, the force with which he was welding together the German nation.

The Soviet people, however, had no need of war, the Soviet Union was not prepared for war, the reconstruction of the country's industry was still under way. It was only *they* who needed a war — and only *they* — for they had no other means to overthrow him, they could see no other way to seize power. Rhetorically Zinoviev and Radek appeared to be implacable enemies of Hitler, but by publishing Engels's article at this moment, they were serving Hitler, feeding his arrogance, tossing him paltry ideas for an accommodation with the West, cooking up a deal behind Stalin's back and at Stalin's expense.

Stalin picked up his pen, dipped it in the inkwell, and, in his small, precise hand, wrote a letter to the members of the Politburo about Engels's article. Only about its essence, however. He did not expound his views linking Zinoviev, Radek, and Kirov, nor did he even mention their names. His letter ended thus:

> In view of what we have said, is it worth our while to print Engels's essay in our militant organ *Bolshevik* as a lead article, or at least as a profoundly instructive article? For it is clear that to publish it in *Bolshevik* at all would be implicitly to endorse it as such. In my opinion, it is not worth our while.
>
> J. Stalin.

Then he crossed the room and opened the door to the antechamber that also served as Poskrebyshev's office. Stalin rarely used his bell to summon Poskrebyshev. Normally he would just open his door and call him in, or through him whomever he wanted to see. Poskrebyshev was always in his place, and if he had to leave it briefly, his desk would be taken over by Dvinsky.

Poskrebyshev was there. Stalin went over to the bulletin board hanging on the wall. Every day, information was entered on it — about the sowing in the spring, the harvest in the summer, and the procurements in the autumn. As usual, he studied the board closely and, as usual, made no comment. As he was returning to his study, he told Poskrebyshev to come in.

Poskrebyshev followed Stalin and closed the door behind him carefully (Stalin did not like doors being left open, nor did he like them to be slammed), and stopped a few paces from the desk in order not to stand right next to Stalin (Stalin didn't like that, either), but close enough to hear Stalin's quiet voice and not to have to ask him to repeat anything (Stalin did not like having to repeat things).

"Take this letter," said Stalin.

Poskrebyshev approached and took the proffered letter.

"Acquaint the members of the Politburo with its contents, and send with it a draft decree releasing Comrade Knorin from his position as chief editor of *Bolshevik*. Comrade Stetsky is to be appointed in his place. Zinoviev is to come off the editorial board of *Bolshevik* and Comrade Tal is to take his place."

Almost always and instinctively, Poskrebyshev knew what Comrade Stalin wanted. On this occasion he wanted (a) that there should be no copies made of his letter and that after being read to the members of the Politburo it should be put into his personal safe; (b) that the letter should explain the reasons for the changes at *Bolshevik;* and (c) that there should be no official explanation of these changes.

"Very good!" Poskrebyshev replied.

He did not leave, however. He knew precisely from Stalin's face when it was time to leave and when it was not.

Stalin took a dark red morocco folder from his desk and handed it to Poskrebyshev.

"Take the mail."

Now Poskrebyshev knew it was time to leave; he backed away, then turned and left the room, again firmly but quietly closing the door after him.

He sat down at his desk and began to go through the mail that Stalin had handed him.

Comrade Stalin saw only the most important mail addressed to him. The ability to discriminate between the important and the unimportant, the necessary and the unnecessary, was another of Poskrebyshev's talents. He was of course physically not capable of reading every letter sent to Stalin — for that there was a special staff in the secretariat who sorted the mail and who passed to Poskrebyshev what they thought important. And it was from that presorted mail that he in turn selected what he regarded as worthy of report. The staff in the secretariat also understood their job: they knew what was required, that any letter concerning members of the Central Committee, especially members of the Politburo, must be reported. Every morning Poskrebyshev placed the mail on Comrade Stalin's desk in the same red morocco folder, and he collected it when Stalin gave it back to him, as he had today.

As usual, Poskrebyshev divided the mail into two piles, one of letters that had been touched by Comrade Stalin's pen, the other of those that had not. The first pile he passed immediately to the secretariat for registration and for action according to Comrade Stalin's instructions. The second pile of letters — those on which no instructions had been penned — were not registered but were placed in the safe until Comrade Stalin asked to see them.

There was, however, one further category of letters, those that Comrade Stalin did not return straightaway, and sometimes not at all, but which he kept and on occasion even destroyed. These were letters of exceptional significance.

When he placed the mail on Comrade Stalin's desk in the mornings, Poskrebyshev always counted the letters and made a note of their number, and when they were handed back to him, he counted them again, and thus knew how many Stalin had retained. He also knew which they were. Possessing the bureaucrat's tenacious memory, he had a pretty good idea of what was in the letters that Stalin kept.

On this occasion, everything had been returned, with the exception of a sealed packet containing Yagoda's report. But, then, Stalin always kept Yagoda's reports.

7

mark Alexandrovich arrived in Moscow on the morning of the twenty-ninth of June, just as the Central Committee meeting was opening, and he left the evening of the first of July. He was in a hurry. The rolling-mill was about to be started up, and when that happened his factory would operate a complete metallurgical cycle. The central goal of his life, the creation of the world's biggest metallurgical plant, would be accomplished.

He attended all the sessions of the Central Committee meeting. The questions that were debated — deliveries of grain and meat, improving and developing livestock — were all part of the Party's economic policy and, as an economic manager, he was obliged to keep abreast of all its aspects. He did not bother to visit the commissariat: the main task of launching the rolling-mill would not be settled in Moscow, but at the factory itself.

The only other thing he had to do was not connected with the meeting — to see Sofya. Sasha had been sentenced and exiled and nothing could be done now to help him. His efforts before the sentence hadn't helped, and now he had even less chance, as sentences by the special board were not open to appeal. The fact that he, a nonvoting member of the Central Committee, had petitioned on Sasha's behalf would undoubtedly have been reported at the highest level, yet Sasha had been sentenced, which meant he must have been mixed up in something. But it wasn't a complete catastrophe — he was young, the three years would soon pass, he still had his whole life in front of him.

Nevertheless, thinking about Sasha depressed him. His own life had not been without difficulties, but never anything like this; his life had always been honest and clear, no deviations or factionalism, either by him or by his close friends. He had grown up in an apolitical family and he was the only one who had become a member of the Party. His sisters were non-Party, and so were their husbands. He had thought of Sasha as a Party member, but look what had happened! His own nephew sentenced under Article 58 for counterrevolutionary agitation and propaganda. Mark Alexandrovich felt guilty toward the Party: he hadn't noticed anything; he'd been unaware, negligent. The stain was on him. Had it happened right after the Revolution, it would have been understandable; the Revolution had, after all, divided many families. Even if it had happened in the 1920s, one could have understood; the twenties, after all, were a time when the leadership was continually shifting, when factions formed, when there were oppositions, and when a section of Soviet youth, especially student youth, was seduced by Trotsky's phrasemongering. But now, in 1934, when deviation and opposition were a thing of the past, when the new Party leadership was already consolidated and the Party line had been stabilized, and when in both Party and country there was unprecedented unity and solidarity, what had happened with Sasha was ridiculous and disgraceful. It cast a stain on him, as well.

What had gone wrong? Sasha had everything: Moscow, a home, the institute, a bright future. He couldn't possibly have been arrested because of the fight with the accounting lecturer and the business of the wall newspaper — he wouldn't have been sentenced for that. There must have been something else, something he had concealed. He could have been influenced by someone. But then he wasn't exactly a child — he was twenty-two, a grown man — he should have *thought!* And not only about himself, but about his mother and about his *uncle,* who had become like a father to him; Sasha should have thought how it would reflect on him, on his reputation in the Party and the country. But he hadn't! He hadn't taken this into consideration! He had tried to be too clever. "There ought to be a bit more modesty" — he had dared to say that about Stalin, and him no more than a mere boy. He had dared to judge the way Stalin was supposed to behave! There were eleven thousand Komsomols, boys and girls, working at Mark Alexandrovich's factory, and they were really *working!* Up to sixteen hours a day they had worked, when the second furnace was being erected. It had been winter, with cruel cold and icy wind, and they had worked without days off. He had returned from Moscow — Ordzhonikidze had summoned him for a few days — only to be told that the sand and cement had frozen in the freight cars. The concrete had to be poured warm. So these boys and girls, who had come from the village only yesterday, put their minds to it. They brought up the locomotives and ran pipes that carried steam and hot water around the clock. That was how they worked, and they had earned the right to name the second furnace "Komsomol"! They had stayed on the site, preparing their food right there on camp fires. They'd had to harness the horses in the mud, their wheelbarrows slipped off the ramps, their main tool was the shovel, their main transport was the workhorse. The ditches they dug were endless, there were mountains of earth and clouds of dust that rose to the sky. There was the noise and thunder of machinery, and yet out of this chaos emerged the greatest factory in the world. Those young people, those youthful enthusiasts, hadn't spared themselves; they hadn't discussed difficulties. They didn't live in a nicely furnished apartment on the Arbat, but in tents and dugouts, wooden huts, whole families sleeping in one bunk, or on one mattress stuffed with straw. They had everything — fleas, lice, cockroaches, typhus.... There weren't enough teachers, the children had their schooling in the same wooden huts where they slept, movies were shown outdoors, the shops were set up in sheds — and such shops, with empty shelves. These workers — shock-workers we called them — were paid with vouchers for a pair of trousers or a new skirt or a pair of boots, or even just a package of fruit-drops. And they were proud. They knew they were building socialist industry, overcoming the country's age-old backwardness, strengthening its defense capability, its economic independence. They knew that they were building a new, socialist society.

That was what these young people understood. They would never reproach Comrade Stalin for anything. Stalin was the symbol of their lives and their unprecedented achievement. These boys and girls were making history — *they* were, not like his nephew, who had slid all the way down to prison and exile in Siberia.

* * *

He approached Sofya's building, the house on the Arbat that he knew so well, with its facade of white glazed tiles. There were bright pennants fluttering in the breeze above the Arbat Art Cinema. The close-packed buildings formed a deep courtyard where Sasha used to play and from which he would come running with his little hands outstretched to meet him with cries of "Uncle Mark's here, hurrah!"

Well, the skies are rarely cloudless and life's misfortunes are always with us, and now they had fallen on Sofya, the softest and most defenseless of his sisters. Her husband had left her and now her son was in exile. He felt sorry for her, but he had been powerless when her husband had left, and he was powerless to help her now. He could only give her his love, his sympathy, and material support. She must be strong and brave. Misfortunes are never permanent, they always go away.

He recalled the last time he had visited. She had been so pitiful and trembling, and had spoken in such a servile way, fussing over some papers or other, smoothing them out with nervous fingers. Even before he got to the apartment, he felt the muscles in the back of his neck begin to tense. Again he would see that look of hers, full of hope, but also fearful that her hopes were in vain. There was nothing that could be done for Sasha, and it was time she understood this and reconciled herself. Sasha would be home again in three years.

Sofya Alexandrovna had just got in from work and was warming up her supper. She greeted him calmly, without her usual excitement at his visits. Before, she would have prepared for his arrival, baked a pie, dressed herself up a bit; now he arrived to find a single working woman who hadn't time for baking and welcome-home parties. She greeted him and invited him to share her supper, though she wasn't sure he would want pearl barley soup and corned beef and potatoes fried in margarine. She looked with indifference at the parcel he had brought with him, and the packages he took out of his briefcase. Going out to work was doing her good, he thought; it had changed her. Before, she had been no more than a wife and mother, a housewife. The life at work, being part of a collective and sharing the concerns that lay outside the home, distracted her from her personal suffering, broadened her world, and given her some stability and strength.

He was glad for his sister and for himself. The visit was not going to be as hard as he had feared.

In his heart, however, he also knew that in acquiring this strength, of which he very much approved, Sofya had lost something that was very precious to him, something from the distant past, something very dear: her softness and benevolence. The attractive coziness of her home, which he had become accustomed to, had vanished. The tidiness and neatness, the pleasing little knickknacks, had gone. Now there were only the bare essentials; it was not a place to spend time in. Here one lived in haste. She ate the potatoes straight from the frying pan, which stood on a metal trivet. The tablecloth was turned over at one corner. He saw, however, that she had not let herself go — on the contrary, she appeared straighter, slimmed down, more mobile, more active. Apparently the house had simply lost its meaning for her. Her son was not there.

She told him about the laundry. Linen sorting was not difficult, though naturally there were some awkward customers, but what could one do? — everyone nowadays was nervous and tense. There were problems in the laundry itself: they damaged or lost things. Then the difficulties began. There would be explanations, inquiries, forms to be filled out, with people waiting in line who would start complaining. It was the manager's responsibility to straighten out problems, so that she could do her job, but the manager would never come out and deal with things, he was never where he was supposed to be, he vanished for days at a time, mysteriously. She could still see the funny side of things; she hadn't lost her sense of humor.

But she never said a word about Sasha. She chatted with her brother out of politeness, so as not to remain silent, but she didn't look at him, she avoided his glance, and he sensed that her conversation was by rote, she was uttering ready-made phrases. In her hesitation and inability to look at him, Mark saw the old Sofya.

Suddenly she broke off from what she was saying.

"Oh, yes, Mark, I must tell you, I'm renting the small room. So if you want to stay the night, you'll have to sleep in here, in my room."

"I'm staying at a hotel," he replied.

He already knew his sister had been able to hang on to the room. She and her husband were not formally divorced, and after Sasha's arrest, Pavel Nikolaevich had managed to reserve his living space, claiming he was a specialist who had had to go out of town on his job for a while. But now Mark heard that she was renting the room, and the news did not fill him with joy. She shouldn't take more than the official rent for the room, as it would legally amount to speculation with living space. Nobody took much notice of such things at present because there was a housing crisis, people had nowhere to live, but nevertheless he did not want his sister, the sister of Ryazanov, to live off the rent of a room. He had never refused to help her; he could provide whatever she'd get for the room, and far more than that.

"Do you have to?"

She did not understand. "Have to what?"

"Rent the room."

"Yes, I need the money."

"How much do you get?"

"Fifty rubles."

"Who are the lodgers?"

"There's only one. She's a middle-aged woman."

"How did you find her?"

"The neighbors recommended her. . . . What's the matter?" Finally she looked at him. "Do you think I'm not doing the right thing?"

"You don't know her . . . the neighbors recommended her . . . why do you want to do this? To have problems with the housing office in getting a permit, all the whys and wherefores . . . I repeat, why do you want to do this? I'll give you not fifty but one hundred and fifty rubles a month. I've brought five hundred rubles for you now. You know I don't need money."

She was thinking in silence, then she said calmly: "I won't take your money. I don't need it myself, I earn my living. As for Sasha, he has a father and mother who'll take care of him."

He knew he would not succeed in convincing her, and he did not want to argue. He'd offered her money, but if she preferred to rent the room, it was her own affair, even though she had seen he hadn't been pleased. As for what she had just said, that was no rehearsed statement, but let her say it; the time for insinuation was past.

"How is Sasha?" he asked.

She was slow to reply.

"Sasha — the last letter was sent from Kansk. He was supposed to go to the village of Boguchany, but nothing has come from there yet. I don't know how he got there, on foot or what. I've looked at the map ... Boguchany's on the Angara River, there's no road there, so he must have gone on foot. . . ." She smiled suddenly. "I don't know how people are taken into exile nowadays. It used to be in Stolypin wagons, but now I don't know. . . ."

"Sofya," Mark said reprovingly, "I know it's very hard for you, but I want you to have a clear understanding of the way things are. First of all, there's no hard labor anymore. Second, Sasha has not been sent to a camp, but into exile. I have been to see the highest authorities. They intervened, but it was impossible to do anything. The law is the law. They have something on Sasha, probably nothing very serious, but something all the same. We are living in strict times, and there's nothing to be done. He's been exiled for three years. He'll live in a village, like millions of other people who are living in villages. He'll find himself work out there. He's young, and the three years will fly by. But you must reconcile yourself to the inevitable: you have to wait patiently and calmly and not let yourself go."

She smiled suddenly, and then again. He knew that smile well.

"So, it wasn't such a heavy sentence, only three years," she said.

"Did I say they ought to have given him more? Sofya, be reasonable! What I'm saying is that, given the times we're living in, three years of exile is a trifle. They are *shooting* people, you know. . . ."

She was still smiling and looked as if she might burst out laughing.

"So, you see. . . . They didn't shoot him. For the little verses in the wall newspaper they didn't shoot him, for the little verses in the newspaper he only got three years' exile in Siberia — thanks very much! But what's three years, just a trifle! After all, Josef Vissarionovich Stalin only got three years' exile, and *he'd* been organizing armed uprisings and strikes and demonstrations, he'd published underground newspapers, traveled abroad illegally, but still, only three years, and he escaped from exile, and they *resettled* him for the same three years. But if Sasha should run away, he'd get ten years in a camp, at the very least." She had stopped smiling and was now looking at her brother straight and hard. "Yes! If the tsar had sentenced you Communists according to *your* laws, he'd still be on the throne for another thousand years. . . ."

He smashed his fist down on the table. "What rubbish! You're a fool! Where did you pick that nonsense up? Stop it right now! How dare you speak that way! In front of me! Yes, we do have a dictatorship, and a dictatorship means violence, but it's the violence of the majority over the minority. Under the tsar the minority oppressed the majority, which was why the tsar didn't dare use the extreme measures that we use in the name of the people and for the people. The Revolution must defend itself, otherwise it is not worth anything. Your misery is great, but it doesn't give you the right to become a philistine. You're not thinking what you're saying. If you say that kind of thing to anyone else, you'll end up in the camps yourself. Take note of that, Sofya, if only for Sasha's sake. He shouldn't lose his mother at a time like this."

She sat and listened in silence, feeling for crumbs with the tips of her fingers and pressing them into the table. Then calmly she said: "Listen, Mark. . . . First of all, while you're in my home never bang the table with your fist. I don't like it. Aside from my feelings, I have neighbors and it's embarrassing: my husband used to bang on the table, and now you're doing it. It must never happen again. Bang on your own table in your office, in front of your subordinates. Please don't forget this. As for the camps, don't threaten me — I'm not afraid of anything now, I've had enough of being afraid, and that's it. They can't put everyone inside, there aren't enough prisons. . . . 'A tiny minority.' How easy it is to say it! 'Millions of people are living in villages.' But have you see how they live? Don't you remember, when you were young you used to sing 'Find me the village where the Russian peasant doesn't groan'? You sang it well, with heart, you were good, you pitied the peasant. Why don't you pity him anymore? Who were you singing about in those days? 'For the people, in the name of the people.' Isn't Sasha the people? Such an honest, openhearted boy, and so believing, and they send him to

Siberia. They couldn't shoot him, so they send him to Siberia instead. What's left of your songs? Prisons, exile, camps. Now you pray to your Stalin. . . ."

Mark Alexandrovich stood up and pushed back his chair.

"My dear sister —"

"Don't make a fuss, don't get excited," she continued calmly. "Listen to what I have to say, Mark. You offered me money, but you can't buy yourself off. You've raised your sword against the innocent, against the defenseless, and you yourself will perish by the sword!" She lowered her gray head and, looking at her brother from under her brows, she pointed a finger. "And when your time comes, you'll remember Sasha, you'll think of him, but it'll be too late. You did not defend an innocent man. And there'll be nobody to defend you."

8

The group had been walking for four days, going deeper and deeper into the taiga, the great endless forest. The cart trundled along in front, while bringing up the rear, mounted on a horse with a hunting rifle slung across his back, was the village agent, a sleepy lad.

The village agent was a job the peasants took in turn, and the escorts were changed at each village. Siberian peasants had always done this job, among their other tasks. The young man's father, his grandfather, and his great-grandfather before him had all had to escort exiles, and his great-great-grandfather had been brought here as an exile himself.

The escorting was no more than a formality, for the party was received in one village and passed on for the next stage without any paperwork. The real security guard was the taiga itself. There was nowhere to hide and the peasants could smell a stranger twenty miles off. Security lay in the fact that an illegal existence was impossible when everyone was constantly being checked.

The rare attempts at escape occurred only from the settlements themselves when an exile so longed for freedom that he ran without thought of what lay in store for him. People escaped in the spring when the sights and smells — the same at all latitudes — filled the heart with an irresistible longing for home, and in the early autumn when the thought of the long, dark Siberian winter to come was unbearable. People even tried in the winter, a month before the end of their sentence, when, already at home in their thoughts, they had no more strength to wait and were terrified that when they went to collect their release papers, they would be given another term instead. These winter escapees — these snowdrops — would be found when the snow melted in the springtime.

But people did not run away during the trek itself. Just out of prison, or camp, out of the stuffy railway car, they could walk at large, freely, and it was impossible to get their bundles from the back of the cart unseen. Also, the entire group was traveling on just one document, so if one man escaped, all the rest would be involved. They'd all be accused of aiding and abetting. If you wanted to escape, the decent thing was to escape from your own settlement.

The snow was already melting on the low ground and the sun's rays shone through the trees high above, but the path was murky and dank. All around there were fallen trees and branches, trees rotted down to their roots and covered with a shaggy, gray moss. There were crumbling logs, and not a bush or a flower to be seen, only yellow traces here and there of last year's dried-up grass, and everywhere scorch marks, as though a forest fire had blazed out of control. It was a forest without end, depressingly monotonous, nothing but larch, with the occasional fir or cedar or spruce, and even more rarely a silver birch or aspen. The only sign of life was high up in the treetops, where the breeze blew and the twitter of birds could be heard, where squirrels leaped from branch to branch, rustling the cones. And nothing ahead of you but forest, ridges, and exposed roots.

Villages were numerous at first while they were still in the vicinity of Kansk, but they were hurried through each one of them. People didn't want them in their village overnight. The exiles would arrive at their lodging late in the evening and leave first thing in the morning. The landlord would curse as he rattled the bolts on his door, a woken infant would start crying, the wife would grumble as she threw rags down on the floor, or she might not give them anything to sleep on. They could lie on the bare boards for all she cared. Sleeping on the floor was cold, and Kartsev, who was ill, coughed explosively. Ivashkin sighed heavily as he thought of his wife and children.

Once they were in the taiga, villages became few and far

between, and it took a whole day to get from one to the next. They arrived in their first taiga settlement while it was still light and they had a good sleep at last.

The escorts had untied Volodya once they were out of Kansk: "Now you can walk." He had rubbed his numbed body and then walked with an easy stride. He didn't tire or complain, but looked implacably angry. He had the skills of a veteran camp inmate: any triviality could cost you your life, you had to be on your guard, ready to make an instant decision, never to give an inch in anything, to be afraid of nobody — on the contrary, to make everyone else wary of you. He was condescending toward Boris and Sasha and Ivashkin, seeing them as "accidental victims of Stalin's regime"; he despised Kartsev as a "capitulator" and wouldn't speak to him or take any notice of him. Sasha was surprised at his ability to ignore a man with whom he was traveling, sleeping in the same room and sharing the same hardships.

Volodya Kvachadze walked in front; Kartsev, sick and breathing with difficulty, trudged behind, stopping frequently. Then the whole party would stop. Volodya would stand without turning around, annoyed at the delay. He considered Kartsev's physical weakness as a sign of spiritual weakness, which was how he also viewed Kartsev's recantation. And anyone who walked alongside Kartsev or helped him at a difficult crossing Volodya regarded with suspicion, like a scout from the enemy camp.

Sasha liked Volodya's courage, the resistance he showed to authority, the dignified way he bore himself. But he also saw that Volodya would never accept a point of view different from his own, and it was a failing Sasha recognized in himself. On the very first day, he said: "Volodya, just so there won't be any misunderstandings, I want you to know that I accept the Party line. Let's keep our views to ourselves. No need to have pointless arguments."

"I haven't the slightest desire to debate with Stalinist yes-men," Volodya had replied haughtily. "But since you put me here, don't try to gag me as well."

Sasha smiled. "It wasn't me who sent you here. I've been sent here too, you know."

"They don't recognize their own, do they? You could just as

easily have been the one twisting arms behind us like they did at Kansk, like they did mine."

"I can just imagine how you'd treat us if you had the power," Sasha said.

"You'd have conformed just like the rest," Kvachadze said with contempt.

"No need to fight, boys," Boris interrupted. "That's always the trouble with politicals: they have to quarrel. The criminals stick together, and they get left alone."

"The criminals are scum," Volodya said. "Degenerates and murderers. They'd betray their own comrade for a bowl of camp soup. They're the system's main support, they help our 'administrators.' Kill your wife and you get eight years, and then they knock off four for good behavior. But take a pair of shoe soles out of the factory and they'll give you ten years."

The taiga became steadily more dense: thickly overgrown ridges and plateaus, dips and mounds, the chatter of birds in the treetops, the gloom and dankness of the path. Once in a birch grove they saw a huge, long-nosed elk, which vanished with a crackle of twigs.

They were warmed by the sun from the early morning. Its rays never penetrated down to the path, but it nevertheless made the way more cheerful and easier.

They rested at midday by a winter hut, a tiny wooden structure with smoke-blackened walls, no windows or stove, a floor of beaten earth, scorched by the camp fires lit there in the winter, with only a small opening in the roof for the smoke to escape. A bundle of dried twigs lay in one corner. It had been left there as fuel by the last person who had used the hut. The next visitor might arrive in a blizzard and be unable to find dry wood to start a fire and would freeze to death there on the beaten floor. A really decent man would not only leave dry twigs, but also a box of matches concealed in a dry place.

They lit their fire, brought water from a stream, and made millet porridge and tea.

Boris had got the millet the day before at a village general store. The storekeeper knew him and had opened up his shop at night.

He had also given them a package of tobacco and a bottle of moonshine vodka, which they had drunk that same night.

The realization that he was known even here — in a village buried in the taiga — and that the others would be sunk without him, restored Boris to his customary state of initiative, and strengthened his conviction that even in Boguchany he would manage well.

Boris paid for everyone's lodging and supper, as none of them had any money, except Sasha. But Sasha had no guarantee that he would find work, whereas Boris had a job already waiting for him in Boguchany. He had the look of a commissar, in his service jacket with its turn-down collar, breeches tucked into expensive boots, his rainproof cloak and khaki cap. And he had cultivated the soft, authoritative voice of a superior, one with whom it would be difficult to argue. He would get his way in any case, so better do what he says straightaway.

Boris was in command now, sending one of them for water, another one for brushwood. It was still possible to collect dry wood in the forest, so they decided not to touch the supply they'd found piled in the hut. He spared only Kartsev, who sat on a stump and held his pale suffering face to the sun with his eyes closed.

The storekeeper had also arranged for a good, helpful, capable lad to go with them as an escort, though it was not his turn. He made spoons out of birch bark when they stopped to eat. Fair-haired and light footed, he had walked like the rest of them, leading his horse on a rope. Sasha had been beside him as they left the village and they stayed together through the day. The boy even gave Sasha his rifle to shoot grouse, but Sasha missed.

"It'll be hard on you if you miss a bear." The boy laughed.

"Have you hunted bear?"

"Three times. We go for them when they're in their dens. As soon as the dogs have smelled them, we cut logs and seal up the den, and when the bear starts to fight his way out, we shoot him. Some people go for him with a spear, or a dagger. The bear, he's cunning, he'll fly at a man, but he creeps up on horses and cattle."

He smiled when Sasha told him there were animals that were stronger than bears, like lions and tigers and elephants. He didn't believe him.

He also smiled when he told Sasha how the year before, in the clearing they were then passing through, they had killed three exiled criminals.

"They'd been sent into exile for some reason or other and they were playing cards in the village. Our boys saw they had money on them. When they reached this place, our boys started shooting and the criminals ran off into the forest, vanished they did, snowed in, with a bad freeze. Our boys thought they'd be eaten by wild animals, there's plenty around here. Then the regional boss for the fur agency came out here and his dogs sniffed out their corpses. They started asking questions and our boys were sent off to Novosibirsk. And while they were there, in prison, they were killed by a gang."

"Did they find much money on the dead men?"

"Ten rubles."

This story came up again when they were sitting around the camp fire chatting. Boris had heard it before, from exiles in Kansk, and Kvachadze had heard it, too, in the camp. The two boys had been murdered the night they arrived at the prison. The news of their coming had gone on ahead of them. They had been put in a big cell, where the inmates were all friends, so it had been impossible to find out who had done it.

"And a damn good thing, too," Volodya remarked. "At the most, they would have got five years, and they'd have been let out after a year — they only killed exiles, don't forget. Now, the locals know there's a prison telegraph that works better than the government's. The state doesn't protect us, so we have to protect ourselves. There's no other way."

"Volodya," Sasha said, "you yourself said criminals weren't human! How can you approve them taking the law into their own hands?"

"Hard labor's a law unto itself, and you'd find that out soon enough if you had to do it," Volodya said, brushing the objection aside. "The argument of an intellectual!"

"What have you got against intellectuals? They have their uses," Sasha said.

Volodya raised a finger. "In some cases."

"Anyway, you're one yourself."

"What makes you think I'm proud of it?"

"The first intellectual was the man who discovered fire," Sasha said. "Naturally, his contemporaries killed him. One of them burned a finger, one scorched his foot, so another one killed him just for the hell of it, for getting above himself! Even in the Stone Age, they didn't like people getting above themselves."

"First prize to Sasha for logic," Boris announced. "Do you agree, Volodya, first prize to Sasha?"

"Give it to him, if you've got one."

They were all in a good mood. The sun was setting behind the trees, but they could still feel its warmth as they walked without coats and hats, which they'd thrown into the back of the cart. The helpful young man who accompanied them and let them fire his rifle was not a real guard; this was nothing like going into exile. For the first time they weren't eating at someone else's table, but there in the forest at their own camp fire. The crackle of pine twigs and the scent of resin, the smell of burned porridge, and pine needles in the tea — it took them back to their childhoods. It hadn't been so long ago that they'd sat around the camp fire at their Young Pioneers' camp.

Kartsev turned his sickly face to the sun, twisting his head toward the hazy beams that pierced the trees.

Ivashkin agreed with both Sasha and Volodya; he loved *clever* conversation. He thought of his own profession as an intellectual one, and as special. But if you were in a rush and made a typographical error, they sent you to Siberia, even if you hadn't done the typesetting yourself. In one of Comrade Stalin's speeches, instead of "reveal" they had mistakenly printed "conceal." Six of them had been put inside. Ivashkin had left a wife and three daughters at home.

The escort listened to their conversation and smiled. He ate very little porridge, not wanting to deprive the others of their full share.

The driver of the cart was a gloomy man, who refused the porridge and the tea. He chewed something in the cart and dozed as his horse rested and had its fill of grass. Then he harnessed it up. The men, now relaxed at the fireside, got up reluctantly and the party moved on.

They had gone about three miles when suddenly the wind whistled through the tops of the trees, it became dark, a heavy wind started blowing, and snow began to fall.

The driver urged his horse on and the escort picked up the pace, for they wanted to reach the Chuna River while it was still light. Then the snow stopped as suddenly as it had begun, leaving white snow caps on the bushes and making the path even worse than it had been. The group pushed the cart and maintained the faster pace.

Kartsev couldn't go on. He leaned against a tree and stood there coughing and gasping for breath.

"Get into the cart," Sasha said.

But the driver wouldn't have it. "I wasn't hired to carry people, the horse can't make it, the road's not good enough."

"You've no conscience," Ivashkin said.

Sasha grabbed the horse by the reins.

"Whoa! Kartsev, get in!"

"Don't you touch him, boy!" the driver yelled. "I'll turn around and go right back. They'll show you what trouble is!"

"We're not going to argue, chum," Boris said, in his authoritative voice as he helped Kartsev into the cart.

They had to remove two suitcases, the lightest ones, which the peasant boy tied onto his saddle. Only Volodya said nothing, but just waited indifferently until it was all over. He wasn't going to speak up for a "capitulator," even if the man was giving up the ghost.

They crossed the Chuna in a flat-bottomed boat that couldn't get right next to the bank, so they had to wade, carrying their things and dragging the cart. They got soaked through.

They came to a large, impoverished village, consisting of dilapidated, blackened hovels and broken-down cattle sheds. Some kind of celebration was going on. There were lights on in the huts, though it was early, and they heard the sound of drunken shouts and singing. Peasants were staggering along the street, taiga dwellers, forest folk, people of all shapes and sizes and colors, not like the stately Siberians of the steppes, with their light brown hair. There were boys and girls sitting on logs who called out to the escort that they were celebrating their patron saint's day. The escort at once hurried to find the chairman of the community. He wanted to be relieved of his charges as soon as possible.

While they were waiting for the chairman to arrive, they were approached by the local exiles. One was a portly man, with a full head of hair, unhurried movements, and an attentive look, the typical sort of state official Sasha had seen so often at the Fifth House of Soviets. With him was a thin, red-haired woman with a severe, tormented face. Sasha's group was the first to arrive since the road had become passable and they were anxious to see if any of their *own* people had turned up.

"Good day, comrades!"

The woman's gaze rested on Kvachadze and she evidently sensed a fellow spirit in the glance he returned. Volodya pronounced his name, which they knew, and theirs were familiar to him. They embraced and kissed, but no such welcome was exchanged with the rest of the party. The man smiled as if in greeting, but he offered nobody his hand: after all, he might be shaking hands with someone he ought not to, or his handshake might be rejected. The woman didn't even smile.

They led Volodya away. Tall and lithe in his black padded jacket, his pack on his back, he walked between them, answering their questions, of which there were apparently many, as they had had no mail for two months.

"Adieu!" Boris called after them, offended. Volodya had broken a solidarity that was higher than any political affinity.

A boy with a fat face ran up to them, drunk, bustling, rubbing his eyes and chewing as he came.

"Which of you's the exiles? So it's you lot? Look how filthy you are! Did the Russians do that to you? Come on!"

The dilapidated hut he brought them to at the edge of the village had a broken-down stove, and they needed to warm themselves up, dry out their clothes, lay Kartsev down somewhere warm. While they were inspecting this long-abandoned habitation, the fat-faced boy vanished without trace. The driver also left, after throwing their things on the ground.

"We have to put some pressure on the local authority," Boris said. "Come on, Ivashkin!"

"Come where? The whole village is having a party."

"I'll do the talking," Boris reassured him. "You just come along to bring back the grub."

They left. Sasha got clean underwear out of his suitcase, woolen socks and a shirt, and held them out to Kartsev.

"Here, change into these."

Sasha was amazed at how thin Kartsev was. His skin was stretched over his ribs, his knees were bony, there was no flesh on his legs, and his long arms hung limp and lifeless, his shoulder blades sticking out like the stumps of severed wings.

"You became emaciated from your hunger strike," Sasha observed.

"They force-fed me through a tube." Awkwardly Kartsev tucked the shirt into the underpants. "Then they transferred me to the hospital block, fed me on milk. I slit my wrists, lost a lot of blood."

His eyes shone feverishly, and his face was blotched red. He obviously had a temperature, but they had no thermometer, not that it would have made any difference, because they would still have to be back on the road next morning. When at last he had changed, he wrapped himself in Sasha's flannel blanket, sat on the bench, leaned back against the wall, and closed his eyes.

"Why did you cut your wrists?" Sasha asked.

Kartsev did not reply; maybe he was dozing and hadn't heard.

Sasha inspected the stove. Someone had torn off the doors. He thought of lighting it, but perhaps Boris would find them a better place to stay.

Boris and Ivashkin returned with a loaf of bread and a birch-bark bowl of buttermilk, which was all they'd managed to get. Nor had they been able to find another place to stay. Everyone was drunk and it was impossible to get any sense out of them; nobody would give them a night's lodging.

Ivashkin found a piece of wood outside and split it up into kindling, but it wouldn't burn and they were only wasting their matches.

They ate the buttermilk and bread in darkness.

"A cold supper is better than no supper," Boris pronounced.

Kartsev would eat nothing, but asked for something to drink. There was no water.

"I'm going to Volodya's friends; perhaps they can take him in for the night," Sasha said.

Boris shook his head dubiously. "They won't. Still, there's no harm in trying. I'll come with you."

"Why?"

"The whole village is dead drunk, and those boys on the log looked aggressive."

A full moon in a clear sky made it lighter outside the hut than inside. The young people were still there, sitting on the log. One of the boys, evidently the local wit and troublemaker, said something funny and waved his arms, and the others exploded in laughter. Seeing Sasha and Boris, he called out: "Hey, you, 'the forgotten and abandoned ones,' come over here!"

"Don't take any notice," Boris muttered under his breath.

"Why?" Sasha went over to the log. "What do you want?"

"What are you hanging around for? Looking for girls? Looking for a punch in the mouth?"

The peasant lad who'd escorted them was also sitting on the log, and was smiling silently. But it was obvious that if they started beating up Sasha and Boris, he'd go on smiling just the same.

Sasha turned to Boris.

"Not a bad idea. They've got some good-looking girls here."

"They're good-looking, but they're not for you!" the boy shouted.

"Are they all for you, then?" Sasha grinned. "Do you think *you* can really manage them all?"

The others laughed.

"Oh, yeah? I'll, I'll —"

"Oh, yeah?" Sasha imitated him. "And fuck you, too."

The stevedores he'd worked with at the chemical factory would have been proud of Sasha.

And he walked on.

"You shouldn't get into fights, boys. There are more serious things to think about," Boris added before turning away to follow Sasha.

As they walked, he said to Sasha, "If they don't murder you here, you'll live a long life. You can be quite impressive."

*　　*　　*

The door to the hut was not closed. Volodya, the man, and the woman were sitting at the table. A kerosene lamp was burning.

"It's Pankratov and Soloveichik," Volodya said. "I told you about them."

He had evidently spoken well of them, because the man was smiling. "Please sit down, comrades, and have tea with us."

"Thank you."

Sasha did not sit, but turned to Volodya. "What are we going to do with Kartsev?"

"What do you expect me to do?"

"Would you give up your place here for him?"

The man answered for Volodya: "To a certain extent, it's up to me to decide who spends the night in my house."

"Perhaps you know someone who might give us room for the night?" Boris asked.

"Nobody here will take strangers in, especially if they're sick."

The woman took no notice of them and went on speaking to Volodya. "So, tell me, when did you last see Ilyin?"

When they were back on the street, Sasha said angrily, "So much for my talent to impress!"

"My dear boy, those were political passions at work, and they're the most furious."

9

By the end of the day, Poskrebyshev had returned to Stalin his letter to the members of the Politburo about the Engels article. They had all agreed that the article should not be published. They had also voted unanimously, when canvassed, on the resolution calling for changes on the editorial board of *Bolshevik*.

Stalin had not been in any doubt that both proposals would be accepted: his tactic over Stetsky had been the correct one. Stetsky was a Bukharin man and they were keeping Bukharin in reserve; they weren't yet ready to sacrifice him, just as they had not been ready to sacrifice Smirnov, Talmachev, and Eismont the previous year, or Ryutin the year before.

Nevertheless, all opponents, past, present, and future, had to be liquidated and would be liquidated. The sole socialist country in the world could survive only if it were unshakably stable, and this would also be seen as a sign of its stability by the outside world. The state must be strong in case of war; the state must be mighty if it wants peace. It must be feared.

In order to turn a peasant society into an industrialized country, countless material and human sacrifices were necessary. The people must accept this. But it would not be achieved by enthusiasm alone. The people would have to be forced to accept the sacrifices, and for this a powerful authority was needed, an authority that inspired fear. This fear should be sustained by any means available, and the theory of undying class war provided for all such possibilities. If a few million people had to perish in the process, history would forgive Comrade Stalin. If he were to leave the state undefended, however, he would be condemning it to extinction, and history would never forgive him. The great aim demanded great energy, and great energy could be drawn from a backward people only by great harshness. All the great rulers had been harsh. It was not by chance that Kamenev, now head of the Academy publishing house, had only recently brought out an edition of Machiavelli. He had published it just for Stalin. He wanted to show *him* that the methods he was using had been known as long ago as the fifteenth and sixteenth centuries. But Kamenev was mistaken. Machiavelli's ideas were out of date. In any case, there was no evidence that they'd been of any value even in the fifteenth century! They were pointed but superficial, schematic, undialectic, lacking in logic. "Authority based on the love of the people for a dictator is a weak authority, for it depends on the people. Authority based on the people's fear of the dictator is a strong authority, for it depends only on the dictator himself." This proposition was true only in part: authority based *only* on the people's love is indeed a weak authority. But authority based *only* on the people's fear is also unstable. Stable authority was based on *both* the people's fear of the dictator *and* their love for him. The great ruler is the one who can inspire love through fear. Such love can come when all the harshness of his rule is attributed by the people and history not to him personally, but to his executives.

Sending Trotsky into exile out of the country had been a humane act, and therefore it had been a mistaken one: Trotsky was at large and still active. He would not send Zinoviev and Kamenev into exile abroad: they were going to serve as the first foundation stones of the bastion of fear he must build in order to defend the nation and the country. And they would be followed by their allies. Bukharin was one of their allies. He had secretly run to Kamenev and had said he would prefer to see Zinoviev and Kamenev in place of Stalin in the Politburo. He had found allies of his own, and he would share their fate.

There was no room in politics for pity. If he felt sorry about anyone, it was Kamenev. Sorry in the sense that Kamenev was with that shit Zinoviev and not with him. Kamenev was a "comfortable" man, a nice, compl'ant man, a Tiflis man, moreover. He'd completed high school in Tiflis and lived there for many years. In his gentleness and consideration for others and his affability, he had in him something of both the Jewish and the Georgian intellectual. He was a touch cynical, but in a good-natured way. He was educated and he knew how to take his bearings in the political environment, he was good at formulating arguments cogently and concisely, which was after all what Lenin had valued him for, and with justification. Not a vain man, he had no ambitions for leadership. He was the traditionally *second* man. That's what he had been under Lenin, and that was what he could have been under Stalin. But Kamenev hadn't wanted it! He had preferred that windbag Grishka Zinoviev to Stalin! Once upon a time they had worked well together, they had understood each other perfectly. It was in fact Kamenev who had put Stalin forward as a candidate for the post of general secretary of the Party. But he had done that only in order to use him against Trotsky. Together with Zinoviev, he had decided to use the Party apparatus as a stick to beat Trotsky with, but they had allowed others to do their dirty work for them. However, they had misunderstood the main point, namely that the Party apparatus was not a stick, but a lever of power. And when they put this lever in Stalin's hands, they gave him full power. *His* genius lay in the fact that he was the only one who had realized this. Actually, Lenin had also realized it, but not at once, not for almost a year later, when it was already too late! Yet even then, when Lenin had demanded that the Party remove Stalin from the post of general secretary, Kamenev had not comprehended what was happening, and it was Kamenev who had proposed that the congress take no notice of Lenin's letter. He had seen the light only after Lenin's death, when it was not only Trotsky who lost out in the succession to Lenin, but also Kamenev and Zinoviev. At that moment he ought to have made the right political choice and followed the rest of the Party in support of Stalin. Instead, he had opted for that ignoramus Grishka! Why? Was it that he believed in the great Grishka's talents? Not a bit of it! He miscalculated because he had never understood Stalin. He had not understood that Comrade Stalin's so-called primitiveness and his alleged mediocrity were in fact the simplicity of the leader who not only read lectures in the Communist Academy, but, above all, was speaking to and leading the masses, who were following him.

The Jews had never understood the idea of a *leader*. They had never learned to submit. This was their position throughout history; it was their national tragedy. All the other nations had submitted to Rome and preserved themselves as nations. The Jews were the only nation that would not submit. In all other religions God manifests Himself as a man, whether it was Christ, Muhammad, or Buddha. Only the Jews had no deified leader, only the Jewish religion would not permit the personification of God as man. For them there was no such thing as absolute authority, and for that reason they had not been able to maintain their statehood, for the supreme authority in a state must be personified in the supreme leader. The Jews had argued away their whole history. For them, democracy meant the possibility of arguing. They had to put their own opinion against that of the majority.

There were of course individual Jews who were prepared to recognize a leader and to serve him, Kaganovich, for instance. It was in fact Kaganovich, when he was lecturing at the Institute of Red Professors in 1929, who had actually called Stalin "the Leader." But Kamenev had preferred someone else's superficial learning and rhetoric. He had miscalculated. Learning and rhetoric were not enough for a leader. Where were all those prerevolutionary "leaders" now, all those intellectuals and "men of letters"? Where were Lunacharsky and Pokrovsky, Rozhkov, Goldenberg and Bogdanov and Krasin? And Nogin, Lomov, and Rykov? They weren't around anymore, there was nothing left of them. Trotsky had had certain qualities of leadership. But the Party cadres hadn't been able to stomach his intellectual arrogance, which he demonstrated at every opportunity. People didn't like to be thought fools. People recognized mental superiority only when it was combined with the superiority of authority. Mental superiority was acceptable to them only in a *ruler*, because it meant they were submitting to a *wise* ruler. They did not feel demeaned; on the contrary, they felt uplifted. Their unqualified submission was justified in their eyes. They consoled themselves with the thought that they were submitting to a mind, and not to a force.

Until a leader had attained autocratic power, he must be able to convince people and to create in their minds the belief that they were his willing allies, as though he were merely expressing and formulating their own thoughts. Trotsky had not understood this, just as he had not understood the meaning of the organization. Thinking of himself as a leader, he had imagined that he could draw the masses along with him solely by his rhetoric and his intelligence. Wrong! It took more than brilliant speeches to conquer the masses. One needed a tool, and that tool was the Party organization. "Give us an organization of revolutionaries," Lenin had written, "and we will overturn Russia!" Trotsky had never understood this key Leninist notion. And that was what Lenin had meant when he wrote in his "Testament" about Trotsky's "non-Bolshevism."

Nevertheless, it was in the "Testament" that Lenin had given preference to the "non-Bolshevik" Trotsky over him, Stalin. He had called them both the most prominent leaders of the Central Committee, yet he had given the edge to Trotsky. Why had he done this? Perhaps Lenin had taken the idea of collective leadership seriously? No, he hadn't! Lenin knew the meaning of "Leader." "Soviet socialist centralism in no way contradicts individual leadership and dictatorship . . . a dictator who can sometimes do more on his own and who is often more necessary, can sometimes embody the will of the class. . . ." And again: "To agree to place the dictatorship of the masses *in general* in opposition to the dictatorship of the leaders is ridiculous, absurd, and stupid." Lenin had understood this, but he had thought he would rule Russia with European methods, and he had seen Stalin as an Asiatic.

Lenin had known the importance of organization, but he had wanted to strengthen the state bureaucracy, which he would lean on as the head of government; he had not wanted to strengthen the *Party* organization, on which Stalin relied. For that reason he had proposed removing Stalin from his post as general secretary of the Party. Along with the New Economic Policy, Lenin had evidently had some wider changes in mind for the long term, for if the farmers were going to set the direction, then they would demand their rights. Lenin had seen Trotsky, Zinoviev, Kamenev, Bukharin, even Pyatakov, as more suitable for these maneuvers, and he had regarded *him,* Comrade Stalin, as unsuitable. He had seen in Stalin the chief "apparatchik," and he was afraid of strengthening the apparatus, the organization. And he had been right. The apparatus had the capacity to stagnate. It was formed by ties that had been cemented over many long years, and instead of being a lever of power, it became a brake, a mummy. The chancery in the vast, backward, peasant, and multinational country had been needed to hold on to the gains of the Revolution, but the chancery concealed within it a threat to the Revolution itself: the power of the chancery becomes all-embracing, powerful, and uncontrollable. Lenin was rightly afraid of this happening and therefore he asserted that "we have taken over the worst of tsarist Russia, its bureaucratism and sluggishness, from which we are literally suffocating." That was true. But that did not mean one had to destroy the apparatus and create a political balance. A political balance would mean the end of the dictatorship of the proletariat. The organization had to be preserved and strengthened, but its independence had to be strangled at birth, its personnel constantly replaced, so that mutual ties could never be cemented. An organization that was constantly being changed could have no independent political strength, but it could remain a powerful tool in the hands of a leader, the hands of an omnipotent ruler. This organization as an instrument of power must inspire terror in the people, but it must itself tremble with terror before the leader.

Did he have such an organization? No, he did not. He had long wanted to change the composition of the Party Central Committee, but had not been able to do so, even at the Seventeenth Congress, *his* triumphant congress. But there had not been any reason for rejecting candidates, so he had had to leave the Central Committee members in place. *Their* collective guarantee, *their* solidarity, and *their* surviving mutual relations had worked for them, and he had been unable to overcome them. But enough was enough! This organization had served its purpose and had no further use in its present form; he needed a new one, one that did not argue, one for which there was only one law — namely, *his* will. The present organization had had it, it was so much spent steam, so much garbage. But it was precisely the old personnel who were the most cemented together, the most interconnected. They wouldn't just walk away from their jobs — they would have to be *got rid of.* But they would then be forever aggrieved, forever hidden, potential mortal enemies, ready at any moment to join with anyone who came out against *him*. They would have to be liquidated. Among them there would be people who had performed good service in the past, but history would forgive Comrade Stalin. Their past services had now become a danger to the Party cause, because they imagined themselves the controllers of the state's destiny. So they had to be replaced. To replace meant to liquidate.

Stalin paced his study again and stopped at the window. Yes, Lenin had led the October Revolution, and Lenin had carried it out, that had been his historical service. But having carried out the Revolution and defended the new regime in the furnace of civil war, Lenin had then taken the path suggested to him by the experience of orthodox Marxism, and the New Economic Policy had been the first step along that path. Lenin had completed the bourgeois revolution by extreme revolutionary means, sweeping the path clear for it by destroying the remnants of the old feudal-landlord system. But Lenin had died. History is a great director. She had removed Lenin from the scene in good time and provided a new leader who would lead Russia along a genuinely socialist path. More than one revolution was needed to achieve this. Stalin had already carried out one revolution, no smaller in magnitude than the October Revolution itself, when he liquidated individual agriculture, liquidated the kulaks, those peasants whose private landownership was a vestige of tsarist times, liquidated the very possibility of developing the village by means of the individual farmer. Millions of people had died, but history would forgive him. He had carried out yet a second revolution by putting Russia on the path of industrial development, by turning her into a modern, industrial state that was powerful in the military sense. It had been costly, many lives had been sacrificed, but again history would forgive him. History, however, would not forgive him if he left Russia weak and powerless before her enemies. Now it was time to create a new, special organization of authority. And it was time to destroy the old one. He must start to liquidate the old organization by getting rid of those who had opposed *him*. Zinoviev and Kamenev were the most vulnerable: they had struggled against the Party and they had confessed to so many sins that they would be able to confess to a few more. They would confess to anything. And nobody would dare to defend them, not even Kirov.

Kirov had been in Leningrad for nine years. What had he done in that time to turn the Leningrad Party organization into a real stronghold of the Central Committee, rather than a mere showcase? He had decided to appease the eternally discontented city, instead of smashing it. To smash it would have meant replacing the old organization with a new one, getting rid of the old personnel and putting new people in their place. Appeasement meant leaving the old organization and the old personnel untouched, and merely winning them over to one's side. That was the path Comrade Kirov had chosen. Why had he done that? Had he not understood his task? He had understood it well enough. But it was precisely his own task that he had understood, not the Party's, and he had turned Leningrad into his own stronghold, not the Party's. He had not won the Leningraders over to the Party's side, they had won him over to their side, and made him into their new leader.

Stalin returned to his desk and read through Yagoda's report again. No, Yagoda's protégé, Zaporozhets, wasn't the man to change the situation in Leningrad. He was a nonentity!

Stalin opened the door to the outer office and told Poskrebyshev to summon the people's commissar for internal affairs, Comrade Yagoda, tomorrow.

10

They reached the Angara at midday. The brown, yellow, and red strata of the high limestone cliffs overhanging the mighty river revealed the earth's oldest structure.

An hour later they were in Boguchany. This was where they were to live.

There were bathhouses on the bank, nets stretched over drying frames, boats tied to mooring posts. Along both sides of the wide street there were dark gray log huts with porches, and windows with carved frames, painted blue or violet, looking out onto the street. Their planked roofs were overgrown with green moss and they were separated by high solid fences.

The driver turned into a big yard, with a cattle shed, barns, and an open cattle pen. There were, however, no cattle, only chickens pecking at a dung heap. The driver opened a door into a spacious hut and they were struck with a sour odor. They could make out a homemade table and some benches along the walls. They were in the dwelling of an impoverished widow.

Their hosts were a hunched old woman who sat on a bench, a walking stick beside her, nervously watching every move of her guests, her daughter, a woman of about forty with a sunken chest and swollen belly tied round with a filthy apron, so silent she might have been dumb, and her son, a small, ugly boy of about fourteen.

They dumped their things and went off to find the district NKVD officer. He turned out to be one Baranov, a fat man with a self-satisfied official-looking face, who looked as if he had slept the winter through and would have gone on sleeping if it weren't for his state duties. He opened the package of documents, puffed himself up, and read out the places of settlement appointed for each member of the group. Ivashkin was to stay in Boguchany, Volodya Kvachadze was to go farther down the Angara, while the rest of them would go farther up the river, Kartsev to the village of Chadobets, and Sasha and Boris to the village of Kezhma, in another district and under the jurisdiction of the administrator there.

"But you see," Boris explained, "I've been appointed to the local branch of the Fur Procurement Trust. There's an order from Comrade Khokhlov to Comrade Kosolapov about it."

Khokhlov was the head of the fur agency's office for the territory, and Kosolapov was the Boguchany representative. But Boris did not show Khokhlov's letter to Baranov, because he was afraid it might be confiscated.

"Khokhlov shouldn't meddle in official business." Baranov frowned. "When the next mail boat arrives, you leave for Kezhma."

Volodya went off in search of his own kind.

Ivashkin, who was possessed by the idea that his profession was exceptional, got busy right away; a printing shop had been started up in Boguchany but there were no typesetters. They were in short supply everywhere.

"How do you know about the printing shop?" Sasha asked him.

"I heard something in Kansk," Ivashkin replied evasively and hurried away to find lodgings.

He'd kept quiet about this all the way, afraid that someone else would steal a march on him. It made an unpleasant impression.

Boris looked crushed. Kezhma was a remote village two hundred miles off and he didn't know if there'd be a job for him there. He'd been a fool not to have armed himself with a letter for Kezhma, too.

"I'm going to go and see Kosolapov just the same," he said. "He might be able to do something. Baranov — the sheep — is well named!"

Sasha and Kartsev went back to the hut. Kartsev was utterly exhausted and could barely make it; he collapsed on a bench when they got there and asked for something to drink. He was shivering. Sasha covered him with a blanket and asked the old woman: "Do you have any boiled water?"

"Boiling water? In the kettle, there."

She was sitting in her corner, like an owl.

"You got ill on the road. Never mind. You'll soon get over it, you're young. Want to eat?" she asked.

"When my friends get back."

The first to return was Volodya. He picked up his bag, said he'd be staying at a friend's place three houses past the school, and left.

Then Boris returned. Kosolapov could do nothing, it was all in Baranov's hands. That his life should depend on such a blockhead! The hell with it!

"You know, Sasha, I'm even happy about it. I've got used to you. We set out on the journey together, we might as well finish it together."

He was already planning their lives in Kezhma, setting them both up in jobs, remembering some facts and figures about the Kezhma district that he would use to win over the local Fur Procurement Trust agent.

Ivashkin returned and announced that he'd found himself a place with cheap food, that the local wages were good, with a bonus thrown in because it was the north. He'd be able to send something home, or even bring his family out here. He didn't stay to eat, as he'd already paid for his evening meal.

"I've got to run, friends, the man's waiting for me."

"Look at the way people say good-bye," Boris observed.

"He didn't cry on your shoulder." Sasha grinned.

"You noticed, too? Good boy! You're learning fast."

They ate cabbage out of the same bowl and then set off for the post office, where they left instructions for their mail to be forwarded to them in Kezhma. Sasha wrote to his mother that he felt fine, that the Angara was a mighty river, that he didn't need anything, and that she should write to him in Kezhma.

They went back to the hut. Huskies with curly tails lay on the street and barely raised their heads when a woman carrying a yoke passed by, or even when a crowd of children came flying out through a gate.

"I have yet to see one even slightly possible sign of local talent," Boris said. "Even the girl at the post office, and she was the elite. . . . Mind you, the whole area is overrun with syphilis. You have to watch yourself. And they've got trachoma, so never dry yourself with one of their towels, for God's sake! But, to get back to the main point, did you notice the girl who hovers around outside our place? Did you see those cheekbones? Not bad, not bad."

Sasha had seen her when she was chatting to the old woman's son.

"And she took a look at you," Boris added.

"She's only a kid."

"What are you talking about? She must be sixteen. Quite old enough. Later on they get married and turn into workhorses. You'd better get used to it."

"It's corruption of minors," Sasha said, laughing. "Article Fifty-eight's enough for me to be going on with."

Sitting on the earthen windbreak outside the hut was the very girl herself. She was small and shapely, with good legs, a finely chiseled face, with a steep forehead and full lips. There was a remote hint of the Tungus, Tatar grin in her slightly prominent teeth. She wore a tightly buttoned-up blouse and a long peasant skirt that covered her bare legs down to her ankles. Her strong feet were caked with dirt. She was chewing on a piece of resin and laughing at Sasha with her small, brown eyes.

"What are you laughing at?" he asked.

She giggled and covered her mouth with her hand, jumped up, and ran away, slamming the gate after her. But Sasha could see her looking at him through a crack.

"A wild thing, but a delight, a little Venus," Boris said.

For supper they were given stewed turnips and oatmeal porridge. Again everyone, including the old woman and her son, ate from the same pot. The old woman complained that there was no milk or meat, or even fish, to be had. As there was no man in the house, there was no one to go fishing.

The girl from next door turned up again during supper. She opened the door, saw Sasha, closed the door and hid herself on the porch.

"What are you hiding from, you little snake?" the old woman shouted. The girl remained quiet on the porch. "She's a bit touched," the old woman explained. "She's called Lukerya. Lukeshka!" she shouted again. "Come inside, then. The city folk have got something new to eat."

Sasha cut up the rest of the sausage he'd brought with him in his backpack and gave it to Kartsev.

Lukeshka came in and stood at the door.

"A dwarf of a girl," the old woman said, referring to Lukeshka's size. "She gets it from both sides, her father and mother both are little people. Where are your brothers?"

"The devil knows," Lukeshka replied, glancing at Sasha. "In the forest."

"Digging up stumps, doing some heavy work, or maybe a bit of drinking, just a glass or two, can't keep away from the stuff. Is your father with them?"

"Yes."

Lukeshka nodded at Kartsev. "Is he ill?"

"Yes, he is," the old woman answered. "He's been muttering away. Who to, I wonder? His soul is leaving his body. What are you standing there for? Come and sit down, come and talk, this one here's got a head on his shoulders," she said, gesturing toward Sasha.

But Lukeshka didn't sit down, she went on standing at the door, barefoot in her jacket and long skirt, chewing her resin and giving Sasha her laughing look. She emanated a scent of the river and new-mown hay. She was at that brief stage of a village girl's life when she had not yet been worn out with hard work, a household, and children, when she was still quick and strong and knew everything. She'd learned all about life on the crude village street and in the hut where the whole family slept together, her father and mother and her brothers and their wives. She was frank and naïvely brazen.

Sasha held out a piece of sausage to her. "Taste it."

Lukeshka made no move.

"Take it, devil-child, chew it up!" the old woman said.

Lukeshka took the sausage.

"Did they go out fishing the day before yesterday?" the old woman asked.

"Yes."

"Did they catch much?"

"Two bucketfuls."

"How old are you?" Sasha asked.

"What?" Lukeshka asked back.

"How old are you, when were you born?"

"How should I know? Sixteen, maybe. . . ."

"Some hope," the old woman interrupted her. "Our Vánka is fifteen and you're the same age as him, fifteen."

Lukeshka rubbed her shoulder up and down the doorjamb and said nothing.

"Lukeshka!" The shout came from the street.

"They're yelling for you," the old woman said.

"I know," Lukeshka replied, but stayed put.

"Lukeshka!"

"Hey, convict!" She swore and went out, slamming the door.

"She's a strange girl," the old woman said to Sasha. "Give her a choker and she'll go out with you."

"What's a choker?"

"Well, you'd call it a scarf."

"Interesting," Sasha said with a smile.

Kartsev moaned and wheezed during the night, and asked to be propped up, as he could no longer manage it by himself.

Sasha and Boris headed off for the hospital in the morning. There was a long line of people waiting for the doctor, stretching along the corridor and out onto the steps. Soloveichik went straight into the doctor's examining room, with Sasha following behind. The young doctor listened to Boris and, when he heard that it was about an exile, told him to bring a note from the NKVD district officer.

"A man's dying," Sasha said rudely. "What kind of note do you need?"

"Baranov knows what's required," the doctor replied.

It was a sleepy Baranov who came out into the yard to see them. He asked gruffly what was up, then irritably scratched a note that said: "To the district doctor. Administrative exile Kartsev is to be examined."

They returned to the hospital. Boris again barged straight into the doctor's domain without waiting in line and handed the note to the doctor, who said he'd come over after his regular patients had been seen to.

He came in the evening, examined Kartsev, diagnosed pneumonia and emphysema in one lung, and general malnutrition. Kartsev needed an oxygen tent, but there wasn't one; he needed hospitalization, but the hospital only had ten beds and there were already twenty patients. The doctor wrote out a prescription and told them to give him hot milk. Sasha could see from the grim, closed look on the doctor's face that he already regarded Kartsev as a dead man.

In the morning Kartsev was slightly better and he asked them to get Baranov.

"What do you want him for?" Sasha asked in surprise.

"Go and get him," Kartsev gasped and coughed. "They've got oxygen, they've got everything, just go, go and tell him to come."

They went. Boris suggested they get Volodya Kvachadze: "He knows how to talk to them."

Volodya listened to them calmly, even sympathetically. Was he trying to make up for his behavior on the Chuna, when he'd left Kartsev to sleep overnight in the cold barn? Hardly ... It was probably something else: there was an excuse to make a fuss — a big one, accusing the authorities of refusing an exile medical help.

"Kartsev asked us to get Baranov."

"He *what?*" Volodya turned to Sasha with a terrible look on his face. *"He asked for Baranov to come?"* His voice trembled, and as always when he was excited his Georgian accent became very pronounced.

"You can hardly expect him to go to Baranov, in his state."

"He asked you to get Baranov to go and see him?" Volodya repeated, looking at Sasha with hatred in his eyes. "And you said you'd do it?"

Sasha was annoyed by his attitude.

"What are you staring at, you've seen me before!"

"Calm down, Volodya, it's not Sasha's fault," Boris said.

Volodya fell silent and then said darkly, "Kartsev's an informer."

Sasha was staggered. "How can you say that? He was in special political prison, in isolation, for three years, he was on a hunger strike, he slit his wrists."

"Yes, he was inside, he went on a hunger strike, he slit his wrists!" Volodya shouted, pacing around the room. "Anyone can be thrown in jail, all kinds of people have been, and they starve like everybody else. . . . Why did they take him to Moscow?"

"They gave him exile," Boris remarked.

"And so what!" Volodya yelled again. "They need people like him in exile. 'You've come around now, admitted your errors? Well, sorry, but it's not enough, you've got to *prove* it with some real action! We need *reporters.*'"

"If that were true," Sasha objected, "Baranov wouldn't send him off to Chadobets, he'd keep him here in Boguchany."

"Baranov doesn't know a damn thing! That packet we gave him only contained our certificates. The *real* information will come later, by special messenger. Kartsev wants to explain to him that he's his man, that he has to be cured, he has to be saved. Everyone else from Verkhneuralsk was scattered all around to different camps and prisons, but he was sent to Moscow! What for? A visit to the Bolshoi ballet?"

"Anyone who doesn't agree with you is either a swine or an informer," Sasha said. "We're going for Baranov."

"Oh, well," Volodya said menacingly, "if you want to do that sort of work, go right ahead!"

"You can't frighten us! We haven't seen people like that."

"What *have* you seen?" Volodya shouted. "You haven't seen a thing. Mama's boy! You haven't felled trees when it's forty degrees below zero. You haven't seen people croaking in the snow, coughing up blood. You feel sorry for Kartsev! But what about all those who've been sent to their deaths by the likes of Kartsev — are you sorry for them?"

"Most of all, I'm sorry for you," Sasha said.

When they got to Baranov's house, Boris stopped.

"Let's think this over carefully, Sasha. You may not agree with Volodya, but you must admit there was some logic in what he said. What does Kartsev want Baranov for? To get into the hospital? We can ask that for him ourselves. So, what's he up to? You're just starting here, Sasha, but I'm already part of the landscape. There's nothing worse than this sort of suspicion, it spreads like wildfire. And for the rest of your life you can never prove it one way or the other. I'm willing to go to the hospital and to look after Kartsev, I'll do anything, I'll even empty his bedpan. But I can't fix up a meeting for him with Baranov."

"I'll go alone," Sasha said.

Boris thought for a moment, then made a suggestion. "Let's do it this way. We'll ask Baranov to get him into the hospital, but we won't mention the fact that Kartsev asked to see him. Then, when he's in the hospital, if he still wants to see Baranov he can make the request through the doctor."

"I've already given you the doctor, what more do you want?" Baranov asked with annoyance.

"He has to go into the hospital."

"But you've already been told, there are no beds."

"The man's dying."

"He's not going to die."

"If he does, we'll report to Moscow that you refused to get him into the hospital."

"You're starting off badly here, Pankratov," Baranov pronounced ominously.

Three hours later the hospital cart arrived at the hut and Sasha and Boris carried Kartsev out. The day was coming to an end, and a gentle breeze was blowing from the river. Kartsev lay with his eyes closed, breathing evenly and more peacefully.

That evening, Lukeshka was again sitting on top of the wind-break, wearing leather moccasins, her head and shoulders covered by a warm shawl.

She moved over, indicating that she wanted Sasha to sit next to her.

He sat down.

"Well, tell me something, Lusha. You are called Lusha, aren't you?"

"Lukeshka's my nickname."

"We say Lusha, but I'll call you Lushenka."

She covered her mouth with the shawl.

"Do you like Lushenka?"

She took the shawl from her mouth and her eyes were laughing.
"Do you work, or are you still at school?"

"I finished school."

"How many years?"

"Only three."

"Can you read and write?"

"I learned, but I've forgotten."

"Do you work?"

"I'm a cook. Where're you going to live?"

"In Kezhma."

"Oh," she sighed, disappointed. "It's a long way. A lot of exiles live here with us."

"Have you been to Kezhma?"

"No, I've never been farther than the forest."

"You're not afraid of the bears?"

"Yes, I am. The other day we were in the forest gathering berries and this bear came jumping out, roaring he was, fit to blow the forest down. We yelled and ran for the boat. It was too bad about the fruit, but it was heavy, it was weighing us down, so we threw it away. He didn't run straight, but pigeon-toed. We grabbed the oars, but he was already in the water. We just managed to start rowing, and he was still roaring, and we were scared to death.... Then we reached the other side.... Our whole trip had been for nothing. Now we don't go over there; we're too scared...."

She spoke in an animated way, yet she was shy and kept covering her mouth with the corner of her shawl.

"Will you come with me to Kezhma?" Sasha asked.

She stopped laughing and looked at him. "If you take me, I'll come."

"And what will we do there?"

"We'll get along. How long have you got to live in Kezhma?"

"Three years."

"So, we'll live together for three years and then you'll leave."

"What about you?"

"What about me? I'll stay here. It's the same with everyone — they live here awhile and then go away. Maybe you'll go native, become an Angarian?"

"No, I don't think so."

"We're going to the Sergunkin islands tomorrow. Come with us."

"What for?"

"We'll sleep together," she announced with naïve immodesty.

"Lukeshka!" a voice called from the neighboring yard.

"Will you come?"

"I have to think about it."

"Oh, you, you think too much." She laughed and ran off.

There were shavings in the coffin and Sasha wanted to clear them out, but Boris said, "You mustn't throw them out, don't you know that?"

Sasha didn't know; it was the first time he'd buried a man.

The undertaker and the driver went down into the cellar where the mortuary was. The doctor came out onto the steps, gave Sasha the same solemn look he'd given Kartsev, and said, "The death certificate has gone to the district officer."

Neither Sasha nor Boris replied. What did they want with a death certificate, who would they send it to?

The doctor didn't leave, but stood there looking at them. He was about their age.

The undertaker and the driver brought out the body and laid it in the coffin.

They nailed the lid down and the cart moved out of the yard. The driver, a short peasant, walked alongside the cart, while Sasha and Boris followed. Passing through the long village street with its gray-black log huts, they turned into a similar gray-black street, left the village behind them, and climbed a slope to the wooden, boarded-up church. The cemetery lay behind it.

They picked up shovels and began to dig. The earth was soft only on the surface. Farther down it was hard, frozen with layers of ice.

So, this was life's terminus for Kartsev, their chance fellow traveler, who had once worked at the Hammer and Sickle factory, a Komsomol activist, a prisoner in the Verkhneuralsk political isolation block, an exile. Was Volodya right? If so, what had made Kartsev do it? The wish to atone for his guilt, to demonstrate the sincerity of his recantation? Maybe they'd promised him his freedom? Or was it nothing more than weakness?

The answers were buried with Kartsev in far-off Siberia on the edge of the world.

But even if it was true, that wasn't the Kartsev Sasha had known. He had known only a sick and suffering human being.

The driver threw down his shovel.

"That should do it; the bears won't get down that far."

They took the coffin off the cart, slipped ropes under it, and, carefully negotiating the mound of earth, lowered it into the grave. Then they removed the ropes and filled the hole. It was all over. The driver jumped up onto his cart, picked up the reins, and trotted off back to the village. Sasha and Boris remained at the graveside.

"We should at least leave a marker with his name on it," Boris said.

But they couldn't find a piece of wood and they had no pencil.

From where they stood they could see the Angara amid the cliffs and forest, its waters rolling along from one unknown territory to another. On the horizon, the river became the same color as the sky, blending with it, as if God had not created the earth to separate water from water.

Sasha was pierced with a feeling of bitterness and joy. Standing in that desolate cemetery, full of anguish and despair, he suddenly had a clear sensation of the insignificance of his own misfortunes and sufferings. This vast eternity strengthened his faith in something higher than the values he had lived for so far. Those who send people into exile were mistaken in thinking that they could break a human being that way. You could kill a man, but you could never break him.

11

"**R**ead this!"
While Yagoda was reading what was his own last report, Stalin took a look at him: the coarse, narrow face the color of pale brick, the small mustache under his nose, just like Hitler's, the morose, cautious look. He was no beauty!

Stalin had picked him back in 1929. Menzhinsky had been seriously ill and had virtually stopped working, but it was not until the Seventeenth Congress that he was replaced on the Central Committee by Yagoda, his deputy. It would have been possible to release Comrade Menzhinsky from his duties as chairman of OGPU and appoint Yagoda in his place, but that would have been misunderstood, for Menzhinsky was generally considered to be Felix Dzerzhinsky's heir. A month later, Menzhinsky died. Immediately, the Politburo's long-prepared decision to create a commissariat of internal affairs could be carried out. It was to embrace the work of the chief board of state security, the militia, the border and internal security guards, the correction-labor camps and colonies, as well as the fire services and civil registration offices. Yagoda had been appointed people's commissar of internal affairs.

Yagoda's nomination had aroused no opposition in the Politburo. He was an old Party member, a career Chekist, not a political figure, not a member of the Politburo, but a "neutral" figure who would not upset the balance of the Party leadership.

Sverdlov, whose niece Yagoda had married, had not had a very high opinion of his relation. He'd started him off on the journal *Village Poor* and then sent him to a rank-and-file job in the Cheka.

But Sverdlov hadn't had much idea about people: he'd mistakenly boasted that he could replace the entire staff of the Central Committee from his notebook. He had even regarded Stalin as too much of an "individualist," and told him so to his face, way back when they were in exile in Turukhansk together. Not that Stalin had been offended. All in all, Sverdlov had been a decent sort, but he had had no personality. Lenin had put him in charge of the executive committee, which was a purely representative, figurehead job. When Sverdlov died, Lenin replaced him with Kalinin, the "all-Russian village elder," the little peasant from Tver who said "Russia is a peasant country."

The late Dzerzhinsky hadn't much liked Yagoda, either, and had given him second-rank jobs as a sort of office manager. For all his qualities, Comrade Dzerzhinsky had been an aristocrat by birth.

Naturally, Menzhinsky had also been an aristocrat, and a polyglot to boot, with fourteen languages, no less — what on earth did a Bolshevik want with fourteen languages! — and was therefore closer to Dzerzhinsky than Yagoda, who was a simple pharmacist from Novgorod. And for all his qualities, it had to be said, Comrade Dzerzhinsky was not entirely free of posturing, a characteristic that people hadn't liked in Trotsky, though he far outdid Dzerzhinsky in this kind of behavior. So it was natural that Yagoda, the undereducated "clerk," would not have greatly impressed the "Iron Felix."

The GPU, however, had no need of angels, nor of good looks, for that matter. The art of leadership lay in the ability to put the right man in the right job, and then — and this was the main thing — to remove him when he was no longer needed. For the moment, Yagoda was in the right job: he understood the real meaning of what was said to him.

The suspicion that Yagoda might have worked for the tsarist secret police — the Okhrana — was perhaps not entirely without foundation. But such cases were complicated and involved, and it was impossible to prove such suspicions. Circumstantial evidence was always shaky and unreliable, and direct evidence was practically nonexistent, as the Okhrana had destroyed nearly all their archives in the first hours of the Revolution. How many names of previous informers had we got hold of? Even what we did get was of little use as evidence, as the Okhrana knew how to cover its traces and leave false leads. And in any case, for a man who had dealings with the tsarist police and had had to maneuver to save himself for the Party, situations that might today, many years later, look distinctly dubious were unavoidable.

It was virtually impossible to prove either way whether a man was connected with the Okhrana or not, even if there was some evidence. Some such evidence in Yagoda's case had indeed been produced. It was circumstantial and unconvincing, and yet enough to accuse him of having been a police informer, *should there be a wish to do so*. Stalin told the person who had produced the evidence that the Party was not convinced and he had forbidden him ever to raise the issue again. But Stalin had retained the evidence himself, and Yagoda knew it. And Stalin had given orders that the man who had produced the evidence was not to be touched, and Yagoda knew that, too. Yagoda would be loyal out of fear, which was better than his being loyal out of conviction. Convictions change, but fear lasts forever.

Yagoda laid the letter on the desk without a word — Stalin had yet to ask him anything. Nor did he look at Stalin: to look at Comrade Stalin was to ask a silent question, invite conversation, and Stalin did not like that. Stalin knew without prompting when it was time for *him* to speak, and what to say. Of course, it was Yagoda's own report that Stalin had shown him, but as yet there was no knowing why.

Almost imperceptibly Stalin nodded toward the chair by which Yagoda was standing. The invitation to sit down meant it was going to be a long conversation, and as Yagoda was already aware, it was going to be a serious conversation, in the sense that he would have to work out its real meaning from Stalin's many hints and conundrums.

Pacing the room, Stalin said: "What does your report tell us? It tells us that Comrade Zaporozhets is not coping with his responsibilities. If it had been a simple matter to liquidate the Zinovievite opposition in Leningrad, we could have given the task to Comrade Medved and his crew. But Comrade Medved is a Kirov man, and Comrade Kirov is unfortunately unaware of the scale of the

Zinovievite danger to the Party and to himself personally. He is not evaluating the situation in Leningrad correctly."

Slowly and silently he paced back and forth on the carpet.

"What is special about this situation?" he went on. "It is special in Leningrad not merely because many Zinovievites still remain in the city Party organization. The main thing is that many of them still remain in the *leadership* of that organization, and in Comrade Kirov's own entourage. One wonders what happened to all those tens of thousands of people who voted for Zinoviev before the Fourteenth Party Congress. Where are they? They're still there, in Leningrad, in the same places and the same jobs. Comrade Kirov assures us that now they are all in favor of the Party line, now they are for the Central Committee. . . . But is that so? Oh, yes, they are for Comrade Kirov, but is that the same as their being for the Central Committee? How could they *not* be for Comrade Kirov, since he was the one who protected them and kept them safe and sound in Leningrad? Naturally they are for Comrade Kirov, of course they are devoted to Comrade Kirov. But perhaps Comrade Kirov is mistaking devotion to him for devotion to the Party? Is Comrade Kirov equating himself with the Party? Isn't he a little *ahead* of himself? Is it surprising that honest Communists in Leningrad are not happy with the situation in their Party organization? It is not at all surprising! Their dissatisfaction is wholly justified, especially among young Communists who grew up after the Zinoviev period, as you rightly say in your report. They protest against the situation, especially as their own growth and progress is being blocked by the old Zinovievite establishment, who naturally advance their own people and fail to make way for others, for outsiders. Outsiders as far as *they* are concerned, that is, but people who are in fact honest and sincere supporters of the Central Committee."

Stalin fell silent and maintained his slow, steady pacing of the room. Then he continued.

"What does Comrade Zaporozhets's task amount to? It amounts to changing the circumstances in Leningrad, changing the Leningrad organization's attitude to the Zinovievites, revealing the scale of the danger from Trotskyites and Zinovievites. So what has

Comrade Zaporozhets done? Nothing. He complains that Kirov and Medved *won't allow him* to do it, *won't allow him.* Such complaints are not worthy of a real Chekist. He complains that the apparatus is not subordinate to him, but to Medved. The fool! Let him either form his own apparatus or acknowledge his own impotence."

Stalin suddenly stopped in front of Yagoda.

"We've got to get rid of the supporters of Zinoviev and Kamenev once and for all. Comrade Kirov has surrounded himself with them and they are grateful for all his patronage." He returned to his pacing. "Undoubtedly, it would not be in the Zinovievites' interests, in the present circumstances, if Comrade Kirov were removed, as he is protecting them. But if the situation became more strained in a struggle for power, they would not need Kirov anymore. The threat of war could even make the situation more strained. For a war would only be useful to the enemies of the Central Committee, a war could open up the path to a change of leadership. At the moment, Zinoviev and Kamenev are trying to use Comrade Kirov as a weapon against the Central Committee, but the time will come when he will be of no further use to them and they'll remove him, causing a crisis in the country. Kirov is harboring a viper in his breast against Stalin, but who can say it will not bite Comrade Kirov himself?"

He picked up the report and tossed it to Yagoda.

"What the Party needs is action, not scraps of paper. You may go."

Had Yagoda understood him? Yes, he had understood everything. In fact, it would be best if Kirov would agree to transfer to Moscow. He was, after all, a Central Committee secretary, so let him work in the secretariat. We could keep an eye on him there. True, he'd also be closer to Ordzhonikidze, but we'd soon see how strong their tender friendship was when Kirov, as a Central Committee secretary, was running all industry, including heavy industry, which included Sergo Ordzhonikidze and his crew. Sergo was not all that bright, he'd always played second fiddle to Kirov, but he wouldn't want to be *directly* under Kirov's command. Still, healthy distrust was the best basis for working together.

Stalin went out to Poskrebyshev's office and told him to summon Comrade Yezhov.

Yezhov had appeared in the Central Committee apparatus in 1927. He was a short man, practically a dwarf. Stalin liked short people, being only five foot three himself.

Stalin couldn't remember — a rare situation — who had recommended Yezhov. Had it been Mekhlis? Poskrebyshev? Tovstukha? It was one of them. Before then, Yezhov had worked for the Party in Kazakhstan.

He had proved himself at the secretariat. He remembered who had worked where, when, and on what, and he kept hundreds of names in his head. A born professional. In 1930, Stalin had made him director of the Central Committee's personnel department, and it had been a good move. In ten minutes, Yezhov could produce an exhaustive report on any person on the establishment list, the *nomenklatura,* including even any member of the Politburo. Yezhov's index cards covered everyone. The tubby little man acknowledged no authorities, whether in terms of length of service in the Party, social origin, or past services — they were of no consequence to him. He regarded all such considerations as outdated and even harmful, since they gave those who harbored them an illusory right to be treated differently. When he reported on a member of the Politburo, his violet-colored eyes became expressionless. For him, members of the Politburo were no different from any other members of the establishment. Alone among the members of the secretariat, Yezhov had no personal ties. He was a hitherto unknown Party worker from distant Kazakhstan, and that was precisely why he detested the Party professionals, with their long-established connections, and pitilessly he broke up their "rings," removing their most important links, as he carried out Stalin's policy of uncoupling relationships in the organization. Of course, Yezhov was only a single unit; he had to fight to defend himself and his position against the mighty "rings." Blind hatred is a poor quality in politics; it tends to interfere with rational decision making. But even poor qualities have their uses. Yezhov was not a man of tender feelings — he was rough and ready and therefore useful to the cause. He didn't stand and ponder, he acted. He was free of all moral restraint or ethical convention. Outwardly modest, he was nevertheless vain. Like all small people he wanted to rule over others and to decide their fate, but he wanted to do it in secret, in the privacy of his own office, at his desk, with his dossiers and his almighty index cards. He was already virtually in charge of the security organization, the NKVD, and Yagoda hated him — this produced the desired balance. Stalin had advanced him into the Central Committee at the Seventeenth Congress, one of the few changes he had managed to accomplish on that occasion. Now it was time to get him into the secretariat where he could watch over not only the organs of the NKVD, but the courts and the prosecution service, and the balance would be complete. With Yezhov and Yagoda as two partners who hated each other, he didn't have to worry about that particular area.

Stalin nodded to a chair.

Yezhov sat down and opened up his notepad in front of him.

"There's a suggestion," Stalin said, "that we alter the structure of the Central Committee and supplement its machinery with new sections."

When Comrade Stalin said "there was a suggestion," it meant that it was Comrade Stalin's directive.

"What has given rise to this suggestion?" Stalin posed the question as if to himself.

And he answered it himself.

"I believe it has arisen from sound considerations."

Yezhov stared at his notepad, his fountain pen poised at the ready.

"We forgave Comrade Ryazanov for his action on that occasion," Stalin said. "We forgave him because he was provoked into doing it by Pyatakov. However, the action in itself was appalling. To arrest a commission from the center! There's not a single provincial Party secretary who would have dared do that. Yet, here was the manager of a factory who did it, and he did not even consult the local town Party committee secretary. It was a serious signal."

Stalin paused. Yezhov made notes, without raising his head.

"What does this signal tell us?" Stalin once more asked himself.

Came the reply: "The signal tells us that the leading figures in industry are out of control. The industrial machine is changing from a Soviet machine into a technocratic machine. A grave danger!"

At this point, Stalin paused, to signify that a *broad generalization* was about to be made and that it should be broadcast to the widest public. Yezhov concentrated.

"The technocratic machine is striving for economic supremacy, and it is one of the fundamental truths of Marxism that economic supremacy is political supremacy. We cannot allow the economic, and hence the political, supremacy of the technocracy, as it would mean the end of the dictatorship of the proletariat."

Having waited for Yezhov to write it all down, Stalin said: "Unfortunately, Comrade Ordzhonikidze does not recognize this danger."

Yezhov stopped writing. Whatever concerned members of the Politburo must be committed to memory, not written down.

"As a matter of fact, Comrade Ordzhonikidze is making the same error as many of our leaders who mistake the personal loyalty of their own staffs for loyalty to the Party and state. The technocratic machine is actually loyal to Comrade Ordzhonikidze, as well they should be. Comrade Ordzhonikidze does everything in his power to defend his staff, he protects them, he removes them from the Party's control, encourages their autonomous tendencies, protests against the arrest of any engineer-wrecker. Of course, under these circumstances the technocratic staffs are loyal to him. But they are loyal only for the time being, only while they are gathering strength. And once they have gathered that strength, they will do without Comrade Ordzhonikidze! Ryazanov arrested and threw out a commission appointed by Pyatakov. Yet Pyatakov is Comrade Ordzhonikidze's deputy! How can we be sure that tomorrow Comrade Ryazanov will not throw out a commission appointed by Comrade Ordzhonikidze himself? In treating a commission from Moscow like that, Comrade Ryazanov was performing a political act. Why did he not clear this political act with the political leadership in the person of the town Party committee secretary, Comrade Lominadze? Is Comrade Lominadze not a sufficient authority for Comrade Ryazanov? So it appears. But whatever Comrade Lominadze may or may not be, he is still the head of the Party organization, and nobody is allowed to bypass the Party organization."

At the point where Stalin stopped talking about Ordzhonikidze and starting talking about Ryazanov, Yezhov began writing again.

"Comrade Ryazanov," Stalin went on, "disregards both Moscow and the local Party leadership. What does this signify? This signifies that the technocratic machine feels itself to be beyond control and beyond reproach. Why is this?"

Stalin paused again, denoting that another *generalization* was on its way. Yezhov bent low over his notepad.

"The economic machine," Stalin went on, "feels itself beyond control because there is no Party mechanism to match it. What role can the Party cell of the Commissariat of Heavy Industry play, if a member of the Politburo is the head of the commissariat? What role can Party cells play in the central directorates, the trusts, the plants, and the factories, if the chairmen of the central directorates and the factory managers are members of the provincial Party committees, or even of the Central Committee, while the secretaries of those cells are at best members of the district Party committee? At that level, the role of the Party organizations is virtually reduced to zero. The case of Ryazanov prompts us to deal with a task of major importance: control of the economic machine must be carried out at the *equivalent* Party level. The Party machine must control *all* the country's administrations, including the economic, and above all the industrial machine, which has at its disposal the most independent, most educated, and most arrogant personnel."

Stalin's yellow eyes glinted maliciously at the word *arrogant,* and after a pause he went on.

"Any inclination to create a technocracy in our country must be torn up by the roots, smashed to smithereens. It is proposed therefore that to the existing Central Committee sections three new ones be added: an industrial one, an agricultural one, and one for transport. In this way, the three basic branches of the economy will be in direct contact with the Central Committee of the Party. In this way, the Party will be better able to help the decisive sectors of the national economy. The heads of these new sections should be executives of the same caliber as people's commissars, if not higher — men of weight and authority. Prepare a draft decree on the reorganization of the Party organs and show it to me. Select candidates for the posts of managers for the new sections and show me them, too. Each section will be under the care of a Central Committee member, possibly even a member of the Politburo. The industrial section, which is the most important, should definitely be under the care of a Politburo member. Perhaps Comrade Kirov. After all, he has a technical education. By the way, bring me his complete personal dossier."

Stalin got up.

Yezhov also rose hurriedly, closing his notepad and slipping his fountain pen into his breast pocket.

Stalin said: "To punish Ryazanov at this moment would be to justify Pyatakov's provocation. But the principle of democratic centralism must not be violated, even if the center is at fault. The provincial Party secretary should deal with this matter now. He should demand an explanation, carry out an investigation, and send the results here to us. The incident must be properly recorded."

12

It was still spring and Sharok was about to graduate from the institute when Malkova telephoned and ordered him to come next morning to the personnel department of the Commissariat of Justice.

So, a decision had been reached. The factory would be perfect, but if it was the court or the prosecution service it would at least mean Moscow; otherwise they wouldn't have summoned him to the commissariat. Everyone else at his institute had received their appointments and they were going to be stuck way out on the periphery.

He arrived at Malkova's office the next day at the appointed hour. She stood up when he came in and in a curt, businesslike way, said, "Let's go!"

She took him to a small, half-empty room with bare walls, a rickety office desk covered with green, ink-stained paper, and three chairs. A naked bulb hung by a wire from the ceiling. The room had an abandoned look, as if its function were long forgotten.

A short man was standing by a grimy window that had not been washed in a long time. He turned around as they entered and Malkova let Sharok pass in front of her and then left the room, closing the door firmly behind her.

The two men looked at each other for a while. The other man had an immobile, childlike face to which the large horn-rimmed glasses he wore gave an artificial maturity. Yuri had always tried to steer clear of such cold fish, because he thought them weak-willed, but easily offended and vindictive. This particular one was called

Dyakov. He invited Yuri to take a seat, and sat down facing him.

"You're just about to complete your work at the institute, Comrade Sharok," Dyakov began. "Your posting is about to be decided and I thought we should get to know each other. Tell me about yourself."

Malkova had opened their first conversation with precisely the same words — personnel staff weren't exactly original. And he gave Dyakov the same answer he'd given Malkova: he was the son of a clothing-factory worker, he'd had practical training as a milling-machine operator, he'd done such-and-such social work at the institute, and there was a *complication* — his brother had been sentenced for robbery. He tried to speak in such a way as not to compromise himself, and at the same time to suggest that he was unsuitable for work in the court or the prosecution service. They'd do better to send him to work at the factory.

Unlike Malkova, Dyakov did not lecture him about his brother. He had evidently been informed on that score. He did, however, question him closely about his parents' origin, who his relatives were, where they lived, what the Sharok apartment was like, and finally what his plans were after he left the institute.

"I'd like to go back to the factory."

Dyakov nodded sympathetically. "My job is just to clarify your intentions, the authorities will decide the rest. I'll call you again."

Evidently they wanted to recruit him either for the commissariat or the prosecution service, but what his work was to be they had yet to make clear. It was very flattering to have been selected out of the entire graduating class, but it upset his plans. And although a job in either the commissariat or the prosecution service would mean staying in Moscow, he had set his heart on a job at the factory.

A few days later Dyakov rang and asked him to return to the commissariat. Dyakov was waiting for him in the office where they issued passes. They took the elevator to the fourth floor, to the same room as before.

A burly man in army uniform, with four bars on his tunic collar, was sitting at the window reading a newspaper. The crimson tabs indicated that he was in the OGPU troops. Yuri shrank inwardly: now he knew the sort of work he was wanted for.

"Comrade Berezin," Dyakov announced.

Berezin put down the paper. Yuri saw the bronzed Eskimo face and again experienced a wave of alarm.

Berezin waved him to a chair.

Dyakov remained standing and only sat down during the interview when finally signaled to do so by Berezin.

Silently Berezin studied Yuri, then he said slowly: "The Party organization is recommending you for work in the NKVD. I have looked at your personal file. Your brother is serving a sentence for a criminal act. Were you acquainted with the people he was involved with?"

"I saw them for the first time in court."

"Were you on friendly terms with your brother?"

"He's four years older than I am. He had his friends, and I had mine."

"Do you maintain contact with him?"

"He writes to my mother and father. They write to him. They tell him I want him to finish his time and return to an honest life of work. I don't know if my advice has any effect on him."

Yuri knew perfectly well that it was he, not his brother, Berezin was interested in. Just as he did not want to arouse their doubts as to his sincerity, he also had to ensure they didn't recruit him into the security organization. But the decision must come from them. Berezin would never believe him, he was of the same stuff as Budyagin, the same iron cohort.

"And who are your friends?" Berezin asked.

"I haven't any particularly close friends," Sharok began cautiously, realizing that this was the most important question he was being asked. But who was it Berezin wanted to hear about? Sasha Pankratov or Lena Budyagina? But neither of them had been his friend for a long time. "I haven't any close friends," he repeated. "I have acquaintances from the institute, and from my old school, and the house where I live."

"You were at school number seven?"

That was it: he had either Sasha or Lena in mind.

"Yes, number seven."

"On Krivoarbat Street?"

"Yes."

"It's a good school. So, which of your schoolfriends do you see?"

Berezin was leading up to Sasha Pankratov. Should he say anything? But why not? Everyone knew about it. And what could they blame him for? There hadn't been any real friendship between them — to the contrary, there had been hostility. But he shouldn't mention the hostility, because they might think he was casting aspersions on an arrested man. There hadn't been anything, neither friendship nor hostility. They lived in the same apartment house, they were the same age, which meant they had been in the same school together, and had then worked in the same factory, but it had all been so long ago. . . .

"Well," he said, thinking over every word carefully, "in fact, we hardly ever meet at all. We used to meet casually, just because we lived in the same apartment house. But now we've all gone in different directions. For instance, Maxim Kostin has just finished infantry school and been sent out to the Far East. Pankratov has been arrested for something, though quite honestly I couldn't say what. Nina Ivanova is a schoolteacher; we occasionally pass each other in the yard and say hello and good-bye. . . . And there's Vadim Marasevich — though he doesn't live in my block, he does live on the Arbat and we see each other now and again. He's a linguist. Who else is there? Lena Budyagina lives in the Fifth House, but we also hardly see each other."

"Is she the daughter of Ivan Grigoryevich?" Berezin asked.

"Yes."

"Do you have a fiancée, or a girlfriend?"

Coming so soon after the mention of Lena, this question suggested they knew a lot about him. But they had to be well informed. The purpose of these questions was not so much as to discover the details of his private life, as to test his honesty.

"I haven't any intention of getting married just yet." Yuri smiled.

"Do you like going to the theater and the movies, do you like dancing?"

They knew that he used to go to restaurants with Lena.

"I like dancing."

"With pretty girls?"

"Preferably with pretty girls."

Berezin was silent, then he asked: "You mentioned Pankratov. Is that Alexander Pavlovich Pankratov?"

"Yes, but we knew him as Sasha. He was the secretary of our Komsomol cell. But he's been arrested. . . ."

"What sort of person is he?"

Sharok shrugged his shoulders. "It was a long time ago. Eight years. He seemed a nice enough boy back then, an honest" — he smiled — "Komsomol leader. But as for what happened later on, I couldn't say."

There was nothing else he could have said. A negative response, even a restrained judgment on his part, would have provoked questions to which he neither had any answers nor wished to have any. In the old days, Pankratov had been a good boy, in the old days when he and Sasha had been fifteen and he had looked at everything with young and trusting eyes. And he still did, for that matter, so what did they want with someone so open and frank and with a convict for a brother, to boot?

Sharok had not the slightest idea that it was this positive "sincere" response about Sasha Pankratov that sealed his fate. Berezin transferred his opinion of Sasha to Sharok, and just as he had seen a good, honest young man in Sasha, so now he saw the same honest young man in Sharok. In time, Berezin would pay dearly for this error.

Meanwhile he said: "We will consider your candidacy. But first of all you have to decide whether you want to work for us or not. It's a high honor to work for the Cheka, it's the armed unit of the Party. But we don't compel people to join, and if you decline there will be no hard feelings." He turned to Dyakov. "Give Comrade Sharok your phone number."

"Very good." Dyakov got up.

"Nothing has been settled yet," Berezin said, "so keep this conversation to yourself."

"I understand," Sharok replied.

Why had they picked him? He was an *average* student, he never got the best grades. And his social work was average, he only did what he was told. Average people had their uses, too, evidently.

He tried to imagine what they had said about him. Berezin

would have had his doubts. Why was the brother a convict? Why did he go to restaurants? No doubt the convict brother also liked the easy life, which was why he'd robbed a jewelry store. Do we need someone like this working for us? Dyakov, on the other hand, would be in favor of him. It was he who had spotted his application and he would therefore have to defend his choice. Something like a flash of mutual understanding seemed to have passed between them. Yuri would be able to work well with him.

But as for Berezin . . .

"Do you go to the racetrack with your father?" Berezin had asked.

"No, I don't."

This had been the most unpleasant of all the questions. They knew everything there was to know about him, they knew everything about everybody. And he had been afraid of Budyagin! Budyagin wasn't the one to be afraid of, it was Berezin. Budyagin was well known, Berezin was not, yet it was Berezin who had the most power. Possessing the power of secrets, people like Berezin stood behind the backs of those whose authority was on public view.

And Dyakov had power, too, even though he stood up every time Berezin spoke to him. Yuri recalled their introductory meeting, the way Dyakov had sat down with such authority. No, he hadn't asked for references from the institute, he had no need of them. Dyakov had already made his choice, and it was Sharok. Sharok had been created for this job, he was right for it, not open-hearted Maxim Kostin, or that spineless intellectual Vadim Marasevich, or that overconfident Sasha Pankratov. Nobody would be able to wriggle out from Sharok's grasp, or manage to justify themselves. He would not believe in anyone's sincerity — it was impossible to believe sincerely in *this whole business,* and anyone who claimed they did was lying.

So, that was it. He'd made the right decision. One must trust fate. He would agree and let them make up their minds. If they wanted him, they'd take him; if they didn't, they wouldn't. He'd be safe there, nobody would be able to touch him. He'd be one of those who could reach everyone else.

Yuri phoned Dyakov and told him he wished to accept.

"Come around this evening," Dyakov said.

*   *   *

With a pass in his hand, Yuri went down long corridors, studying the numbers on office doors. Was he really going to be working here?

Dyakov received him in a tiny office, but it was his own — here he was his own boss. He was in military uniform with three bars on the collar of his tunic. Strangely enough, the uniform suited him: it made his puny appearance quite imposing.

"You've made the right decision."

He used the familiar form of address and spoke in a welcoming way, as if Yuri already belonged. He took a file out of the desk drawer.

"This is your dossier. We have to complete it."

Yuri felt that Dyakov liked him.

"Listen Sharok," Dyakov said, "last time you mentioned Pankratov. What sort of person is he?"

"Well," Yuri said with a shrug, "as I already said, he was the Komsomol secretary in school, and he gave the impression of being an honest person at that time. I would say his weaknesses included a tendency to see himself as cleverer than others, more knowledgeable and better informed."

"Maybe he was better informed?"

"Maybe," Yuri agreed. Yuri saw exactly what was going on and he now knew what to say next. "His uncle, Ryazanov, is a construction chief. There were quite a few children of important workers in our school. Pankratov used to visit their homes. I would put it this way: he liked giving orders, and he wanted to be in charge."

"You've put your finger on it," Dyakov pronounced gravely. "He went just a bit too far. In addition to himself, he got some fine, honest young people into trouble."

"I heard he published a wall newspaper or something?"

"Yes, and he was involved in something else. Tell me, which important officials did he used to visit?"

Dyakov was obviously interested in Budyagin, but didn't name him, as he was too important. Yuri wouldn't mention him, either: information of *that* kind wouldn't come from him. He'd already mentioned Lena in his conversation with Berezin, and that was enough.

"There were people from the Fifth House in the class, and he visited them."

Dyakov gave Sharok a sideways look.

"Complete this questionnaire and write an account of yourself." He added cheerfully, "I think you and I are going to work well together."

Very quickly Yuri found himself comfortable in his new situation. He was right for this establishment and he even brought a touch of color to it with his youth, his affable smile, and open Russian face, and the somewhat Scandinavian correctness he had acquired on growing up, which distinguished him from these Latvians, Jews, Poles, and middle-aged Russian workers. Tall and lithe, he was quick-witted, businesslike, and reserved, qualities prized in him by both Dyakov and Berezin.

Berezin's patronage ensured that Yuri would move up fast, but it also made him uneasy, because he feared Dyakov. Berezin was high up in the organization and he didn't see Yuri for weeks on end. Yuri only came to mind when he was there, before his eyes. Dyakov, on the other hand, was with him all the time, and he might at any moment exploit Yuri's lack of experience to break him. Berezin was one of a kind, whereas the Dyakovs of that world were many. True, Yuri felt a closer affinity for Dyakov's machinations than he did for Berezin's straightforward style. Berezin believed, Yuri didn't believe, and Dyakov only pretended to believe.

With Dyakov he had to be on the alert; the man was a schemer, and Sharok had sensed it at once. Dyakov handed over to him a number of people he had been *working* with, and among them was Vika Marasevich.

Well, well, well, what a surprise! That meant that Vika ... Yuri wondered whether Dyakov had handed her over to him by mere chance, or whether he knew something about their relationship.

Just in case, Sharok said: "I know this Vika Marasevich, we were at school together. Her brother was in my class, and she was either a class above us or below, I've already forgotten."

Dyakov gave no hint as to whether he was aware of this, and he explained dispassionately: "The little lady has got in with foreigners. Take a look at her dossier and you'll see. But the point is, her father is Professor Marasevich and Glinsky visits him, that's the connection you have to work on with her. You'll meet her on Maroseika Street. Tuesday's her day, at eleven. She's never late, always there on the dot."

As expected, Vika turned up precisely at eleven. When Yuri opened the door and she saw him, she stepped back toward the elevator. She knew he was working for the NKVD, but she had never imagined he would be *running* her.

"Come in, come in, Vika darling, don't be shy." He smiled broadly. "It's been ages."

Tall and handsome in his uniform, he led her into the room and courteously placed a chair for her. Everything about him was shiny, gleaming, and new: his leather belt, the tabs on his tunic collar, his boots. He personified strength, authority, and success, and he spoke with her in a friendly, even cheerful way, as if there was nothing special about what she was doing for them.

But at their next meeting, she came wearing a low-necked summer dress, tight across the hips, and she casually adjusted a sleeve to bare a round, white shoulder. Yuri cast an indifferent glance over the naked flesh and, looking straight into her eyes, said: "You and I were in the same school but nobody's interested in the fact that when we were kids we may have secretly kissed during recess. There's nothing between us. Understand?"

She pulled up the sleeve to cover her shoulder and muttered in confusion, "Yes, yes, of course."

Dyakov had recruited Vika to penetrate Professor Marasevich's household in connection with the Lominadze case.

Glinsky and Marasevich were either related or from the same town. Glinsky was also a confederate of Lominadze. When Glinsky visited Marasevich's home, he met foreigners there. Why couldn't he have established a secret link through them with Lominadze's allies in foreign Communist parties?

This scenario would make it possible to create a *version,* and to add substance to Cher's shaky evidence by reinforcing it with the names of people not directly linked to the Comintern. But indirect connections always gave a case substance and credibility. Any fact, even Vika's trivial information, became important once it was linked to the *version,* if Glinsky's name appeared alongside those that Cher would *undoubtedly* recall, as he had those of Lominadze's messengers. And, at the same time, Glinsky's wife was the director of the institute where there had been a Trotskyite underground headed by her deputy, Krivoruchko.

Sharok had known Glinsky's son Jan in school. He'd heard Glinsky give a talk, reminiscing about Lenin, and had seen Jan's mother, a woman of some authority who later became director of the institute where Sasha Pankratov had studied, and incidentally was the person who had expelled Sasha. The silly woman hadn't realized that Sasha's case would one day form part of her husband's case, and consequently also her own.

This was what Sharok was now working on.

As he encountered these names from the old days, here in his new world, the past became linked with the present. For the first time Sharok felt a real sense of revenge against those who had humiliated him in the past, those who had slighted him. Sasha Pankratov had already got his — not from Sharok, but he'd got his, just the same. And the rest of them would get theirs, too.

13

The apartment where Yuri had met Vika belonged to Dyakov, although Dyakov actually lived elsewhere with his wife, Rebecca Samoilovna, a fat, lopsided, unbelievably ugly woman. She was, however, politically literate and taught political economy, and it was thanks to her that Dyakov had acquired a political education. Though as far as Sharok could judge, he'd read only one book — Stalin's *Questions of Leninism.*

Sharok did not like Rebecca. In fact, he didn't like Jews in general. No one in his apartment house or at school had ever made any distinction as to who was a Jew — only he, and his father and mother.

The Sharoks' anti-Semitism was deep-dyed, it was the anti-Semitism of their old neighborhood, Okhotny Row, where many of the storekeepers had been Black Hundreds.* They still remembered the Jews from way back, when the father and grandfather had been tailors on Moscow River Street, and in the nearby side streets of the Zaryad, by the town houses on Glebov Street, the Jews had lived and attended their nearby synagogue. The cocky young shop-assistants used to make fun of the tailors and hat-makers and furriers. Now, all of a sudden from second-class citizens, they had been promoted to the top and were the bosses. It was bad enough that ignorant peasants, Ivan-bumpkins, had been given power, but it was insufferable that that power was shared with the Moishes!

---

* *Translator's note:* An unofficial body that organized anti-Jewish pogroms in the period before World War I.

Old Sharok turned his protest against the new regime into hatred for the Jews. It was dangerous to protest against the regime itself.

Yuri thought Dyakov must have married Rebecca because he was so unattractive himself. He said nothing about Jews to Dyakov, in fact he never spoke about Jews. Even at home, when his father aired his views on the subject, Yuri merely grinned.

His family was now becoming a serious problem for him. He quickly straightened out his mother, forbidding her to gossip with the neighbors. Not that she had time anymore to sit around yakking: every morning she went to the special retail store to buy whatever they were dishing out on that particular day. And she no longer stopped in the yard outside the building. Why should she let people know what she had in her shopping bags? Things were more difficult with his father. The old man continued to moonlight at home. Not a great deal of it, no more than two or three suits a month, but it was this extra income, kept hidden from the tax inspector, that enabled him to go to the track and bet on the pari-mutuel. That could compromise Yuri and ruin his career.

The old man wouldn't give up his private income for anyone. It provided him with a form of independence from the accursed regime. At the factory he was nothing, a simple worker, but here he was his own boss. The most elegant women in Moscow were jostling to see him, and he was turning them away. They tried to ingratiate themselves and never haggled with him about his prices. He liked his pretty clients, their legs encased in fishnet stockings and their flirtatiousness, even if they only did it to get into his good graces. He preferred his clients to be young and beautiful and would even work for a pretty Jewish woman from time to time — some of them had such black eyes, it made your head swim! A girl had to be young, fresh, and juicy; he liked them full-bodied, big bosomed, and he never worked for old women, or even middle-aged women: they had no waists, and they lacked that certain look.

His father was the only man Yuri respected and to whom he felt attached. He valued his common sense. And he knew his father cared only for him. His father had been merciless toward his brother, Vladimir, but he had never laid a finger on Yuri. Father and son were both handsome, they even looked alike. They loved life, and they stood up to Yuri's mother, who was the scandalmonger of the family, and to his brother, the criminal. The old man gave no indication of what he thought about his son's new situation. In the same way, he had neither approved nor disapproved when Yuri had joined the Komsomol and the Party, and he had neither approved nor disapproved of the affair with Lena and its breakup. This was not because of indifference but because of his trust. Everyone was working for the new system, everyone was a state employee. It was no longer a question of whom you worked for, but how well you worked, everyone had to manage as best he could. Personally he protected his independence and refused to give up his trade. Even to mention it would be to inflict an insult his father would not forgive.

Should they split up? Could he bring himself to deprive both himself and the old folks of the rare possession of an apartment in Moscow? Could he fall out forever with his father?

He simply didn't know what to do. But nor did he dare to hide his domestic complications from his new employers. It would be better if they heard about them from him, rather than from an outsider.

He explained to Dyakov.

"We've lived in the apartment since before the war. They're all friends and acquaintances. This one needs a jacket turned, that one an overcoat shortened or a patch sewn on. And my father's not above taking a drink, you know."

"Your father works in a factory," Dyakov replied. "It's hardly a crime to sew on a patch or two in his own time, and it's not a crime to have a drink of vodka."

Dyakov was not concerned with what people thought or said. He and Sharok were deciding questions of life and death, they were at the cutting edge of the struggle with the enemy, they had special responsibilities and therefore a special morality. Not only their work, but their private lives were secret. Any excessive curiosity about their private lives was open to interpretation.

Yuri now wore the uniform of an NKVD functionary. He went out to work after dinner and arrived home in the small hours, rarely meeting anyone in the yard, and when he did, he pretended not to have noticed them.

Clients who lived in their block stopped coming to his father. There had never been many of them and now the old man turned them away. Yuri saw this as a tactful gesture of understanding. His father even became so discreet as to start seeing two of his best clients in their own homes. And then other clients started coming to see him there, which made him even more inaccessible, and therefore even more famous.

With their domestic life sorted out, the Sharok family acquired a sense of assurance that had been lacking, even to some extent removing the fear they had always felt. But there remained another side of his private life — women.

Yuri had always been wary of the cost of keeping a woman. Women at his new job began to flirt with him, but people didn't have affairs within the *collective*. He made no new ties, and he did not renew his old ones.

He was intrigued by Varya Ivanova. She had always had something and now she had turned into a real beauty! But she was a little bitch. He had met her in the apartment building's yard and given her a friendly smile and she had responded with a look full of hatred. She was part of Sasha's gang, she and that hysterical sister of hers, Nina. Yuri had never forgotten the New Year's party. Sasha had insulted him, but it was Nina who had started it, she was the one who had made a mountain out of a molehill. Sasha was finished. He'd been got rid of. The others could also be got rid of. Not that he would do such a thing! They were all from the same *backyard!* Dyakov would call this lower-middle-class pseudodecency. But his home was here, his father and mother were here, his brother would come back here. He couldn't surround them with enemies.

Only the thought of one woman troubled Yuri. Lena. He could not forget her face, so full of love and suffering. Apart from his father, she was the only person to whom he felt an attachment. She was someone whose loyalty he could trust. She had been willing to make sacrifices for him and she had proved it. That terrible night, and then the hospital, yet she had not given him away by a single word or sigh. She loved him. He remembered the smell of the hot mustard, and it aroused him even now. He was tormented by the thought that she loved someone else, or was living with someone else, or might marry someone else. He had practically killed her, but he was the only one who had a right to her. He would get her back and make her forget everything. He would make her submit to him again.

He hoped they would run into each other by chance, but there was little possibility of that. He knew where she worked, but it would be awkward to try to see her there. So, as he had done before, he phoned her at home. He put the receiver down, because her father answered.

The next day he called her at work.

She was not surprised, or a least she gave that impression. There was the familiar slow, deep voice. How are you? Fine. Can we meet? Well, I suppose so. But she would be going straight from work to their dacha. Maybe they should call everyone else up and all get together?

Yuri was amazed. "Who are you thinking of?"

She laughed. "Yes, in fact there's nobody around. I was thinking of Nina, but she's gone off to some seminar or other. What about Vadim, why don't you call him?"

"I'll try," Yuri replied, though he had no intention of doing so. "Where and when?"

"Sunday, I would think."

She didn't sound very sure, but she always spoke like that. She pronounced her word endings clearly and she lingered over the emphasis, which made her replies sound uncertain.

She gave him the number of the bus that left from Theater Square, the number of the line, which was how they labeled streets out at Silver Wood, the number of the dacha, and she explained how to get to it from the depot where the bus turned around to go back to Moscow.

Not a word of reproach, no injured tone, no joy or anger, no embarrassment. A certain offended tactfulness. The superiority of the aristocrat. But it suited him, all the same.

The thought of seeing her parents again embarrassed him, but probably they didn't know anything. Ivan Grigoryevich didn't like him, but so what, he never had. Maybe he wouldn't even see him. He would go swimming with Lena in the Moscow River, and he wouldn't stay for dinner. He only wanted to see her and reestablish their former relationship. And it was even possible that Lena would be alone.

Her parents might have gone on leave, taking Vladlen with them. Perhaps that was why she had asked him to bring Vadim: perhaps she was afraid of being alone with him.

The thought that he would be seeing her in two days brought the past back to him. He remembered sitting in Ivan Grigoryevich's study. Lena had been changing in her bedroom and he had been waiting for her, trembling with excitement. He was even more excited now.

❧ 14 ❧

His new work, his position, and his secret power had given Sharok self-confidence, yet when he got to Silver Wood he felt timid. The streets, or "lines" as they were called, were identified by nothing more than numbers. There were straight rows of fence, overhung with lilac and jasmine, identical garden gates made of the same fencing, and garden paths leading to the dachas hidden among trees and shrubs. There were neither barriers nor guards, such as you would find in a private park or forbidden zone. It was as if the very fact that these were government dachas prohibited anyone coming in and protected the people living there.

There was nobody on the streets, and behind the fences and scented shrubbery no one was to be seen. Automobiles would come in the morning to pick the dachas' owners up, then bring them back in the evening. The chauffeurs were well trained and took care of everything; they were partly bodyguards. There was yet another security system, although God knew where it was concealed. They had to do their work unnoticed; they were not to get in the way of the people they were protecting. Their charges were to feel free and unfettered, as it would be more comfortable that way. Nor should their children develop a feeling of fear. When you are being protected day and night, a sense of fear can undoubtedly arise.

The gate to the Budyagin dacha was not locked. Yuri walked along the path edged with flowers and found himself before a two-story dacha painted pale blue. There was no sign of life. The breakfast things had not been cleared from a table on the large verandah. The number of dishes and the number of chairs around the table suggested that Lena was not alone.

He hesitated in front of the verandah, unsure how to make his presence known. A maid poked her head out of a window and gave him a welcoming look of inquiry.

"I'm visiting Lena," he said.

"Then you must go round to the back, please." She indicated the way.

Yuri walked around the house and came to another verandah, a tiny one, overgrown by a wild vine. He heard a man's voice and at once recognized it as Vadim's.

He hadn't called him, so why was he here? An odd coincidence. Maybe he was a regular visitor? Had he been specially invited to spoil their tête-à-tête?

On the other hand, if the rest of them were at the house, Vadim's presence would be an advantage. With him there, Yuri would feel more sure of himself, he would appear the older schoolfriend. By inviting that blockhead, Lena had spared them both any awkwardness.

He went up the wooden steps and found Lena and Vadim sitting in wicker armchairs. There was a small table and a narrow wicker couch on which Yuri sat down. The verandah was off a small room.

If Vika had blabbed anything to Vadim, he would reveal it now in confusion and embarrassment. He showed nothing. Vadim was the same as ever, occupying center stage, prancing, fat and grandiose, like an elephant, talking as usual on subjects only he knew anything about.

Lena was listening to him intently. She hadn't changed at all. She still smiled her shy smile under her lowered brows. She still wore her black hair in a bun at the back, and her lips were as bright red as ever and slightly pouting. She looked at ease and natural, but Yuri knew instantly that she still loved him and it filled him with pride and joy.

Although, as before, he found he disliked being in a house that belonged to dignitaries. He was still afraid in some way, which was strange, as it was they who ought to be afraid of him. He had never fathomed the secret power of these intellectuals over him. Why should he feel a need to serve them? But being unable to understand was the same thing as being afraid.

Vadim was talking about a Soviet delegation to the Venice Film Festival. They had taken four new films: Mikhail Romm's *Boule de Suif* with Galina Sergeyeva, Alexandrov's *Moscow Laughs* with Leonid Utyosov, Poselsky's *Chelyuskin,* filmed by Troyanovsky, who had sailed on the *Chelyuskin,* and Ptushko's *The New Gulliver.*

Vadim made it clear he'd had a hand in their selection, and he talked about them, predicting their success, especially so for *Boule de Suif.* Apart from *Chelyuskin,* none of the films had yet been seen in Soviet movie theaters, so once again he was the one who was well informed, and everyone else knew nothing.

According to Vadim, a lot of films were ruined by formalistic idiosyncrasy and snobbish affectation. But *Boule de Suif* and *Moscow Laughs* gave grounds for optimism. Soviet filmmakers would soon be making films for the people.

"Maupassant's *Boule de Suif* for the people?" Yuri was dubious.

"Yes, absolutely!" Vadim cried. "Think about it! It's not just the story of a prostitute. The film is antimilitarist, anti-Fascist. It's important for the people, and they can understand it."

Yuri bit his tongue. He'd always thought of *La Boule de Suif,* like the rest of Maupassant, as erotic literature; he'd overlooked the fact that the girl was had by a Prussian officer.

"The Battleship Potemkin is also quite complicated, but the people went to see it," Lena said.

Yuri noticed that Lena was coming to his aid.

"Yes," Vadim agreed, "but look where Eisenstein's formalism ended up! *Ten Days That Shook the World* is utterly incomprehensible to the audience, a great theme vulgarized. And the same with Dziga Vertov! Have you seen his *Symphony of the Donbass?* Utter chaos, a parody of reality! And now Vertov's working on a film about Lenin" — he clenched his fat fingers into a fist — "imagine letting Dziga loose on such material! They may be great masters but it's time they defined themselves, time to say whose side they're on."

Yuri recalled Vadim going into ecstasies over Henri de Renier and other frivolous Frenchmen, and even giving him entertaining books about French pimps.

It probably wasn't worth arguing with him, but the temptation to get even over the Maupassant proved too much for him.

"Your taste has changed, Vadim," Yuri said.

"For the better, for the better, my friend," Vadim retorted challengingly. "We're all going through a process of evolution; the question is: In what direction?"

"What do you mean?" Yuri frowned. Vadim's aggressiveness had surprised him. It had nothing to do with Vika; this was Vadim feeling his own strength.

"I meant what I said," Vadim replied peevishly. "Man is developing, his direction is important. Everyone is leaping hurdles, but the important thing is: Which way to jump? *Which way?* In school, my literary taste was still vacillating. What matters is the point I have reached now. In school, you were in no hurry to join the Komsomol, now you're a member of the Party. I call that normal development."

Yuri knew he must not provoke an argument, he must be amiable, he must be amenable. He could only gain in Lena's eyes.

"Fine! Maybe even Eisenstein will end up a socialist realist!" he said.

He mentioned Eisenstein only because he couldn't quite remember the name of the other director and he didn't want to make a mistake. It was some wonderful name and equally wonderful surname. You could break your leg over so many Rabinoviches!

Lena gave him a look of gratitude.

"Perhaps the stagnation Vadim's talking about has to do with going over to talkies?"

Vadim objected at once. "I didn't say there was stagnation, and as for the future of talkies, I take a cautious view. Whatever you may think, the cinema is the great silence. Sound might turn cinema into theater on screen. Can you imagine Charlie Chaplin talking? I can't."

Lena had seen lots of talkies in London. They had become popular there and they would in the Soviet Union, too, but she didn't argue with Vadim. She just smiled as she remembered the way the audience had laughed at the American accents of actors during the demonstration of an American sound film.

"What do you think of *Counterplan,* and *Gold Mountains?*" Yuri asked, acknowledging Vadim's superiority.

Vadim smiled.

"Are they really talkies? They're more like film-strip with the sound of Shostakovich's music added. The music is good in its own right, and it's even better that Shostakovich uses folk melodies. That's important in the process of becoming a composer."

In showing how well informed he was, Vadim wanted Yuri to see that he could defend himself on all fronts. Yuri realized this and understood that Vadim was motivated by fear of him, Yuri. This explained his unusual aggressiveness. Yuri couldn't repress a smile, so he smiled at Lena and she smiled back, grateful to him for his patience.

"Shall we go for a swim before lunch or after?" Lena asked.

"You'll have to manage without me," Vadim announced, glancing at his watch. "I have to pop in on the Smidoviches, but I'll come back for lunch, if that's all right with you."

Lena went in to change, closing the door behind her, while Vadim and Yuri remained on the verandah. Lena's room looked out onto the verandah through a window hung with a light curtain that fluttered in the breeze and opened to reveal Lena with her arms raised, as she was pulling her dress off over her head. Yuri stood in front of the window to block it and held the curtain closed.

"How're things, Vadim?"

Vadim was looking through books on the table.

"Much the same as before. You never call or come over."

"Too much work."

Vadim picked up a book and showed it to Yuri. "Read it?"

"What is it?"

"Panaev's memoirs."

"I can't remember. I think I once had the memoirs of Panaeva, if I'm not mistaken."

"That was his wife. Loosely speaking. In fact, she was Nekrasov's legal wife. Her memoirs are not without interest. But this is Panaev himself" — he leafed through the book — "and there are some very interesting lines in it."

A pleasant male voice came from the neighboring dacha, singing *"Why do I love you, bright starlit night . . ."*

Vadim tore himself from the book and listened. "Music by

Tchaikovsky, words by Jacob Polonsky." Then he went back to the book.

Lena came out. She was wearing a red Gypsy-style shift with straps that revealed her shoulders and bare back.

She was a striking girl, voluptuous and big, just as Yuri liked.

Lena was embarrassed at showing so much flesh, and she smiled. "I put on my bathing suit, so I won't have to change there. Shall we go?"

"Wait, just one second!" At last Vadim found the place he had been looking for. "Listen to this. Panaev is quoting Belinsky, where Belinsky says: 'We need a Peter the Great, a new despot of genius, one who would deal with us mercilessly and implacably in the name of human principles. We must go through terror. Before, we needed Peter the Great's stick to give us at least a semblance of humanity; now what we need is to go through terror in order to make us human beings in the full and noble meaning of the word. Our brethren, the Slavs, cannot be awakened to consciousness quickly. It is a well-known fact that when the lightning does not strike, the peasant does not cross himself, he has no lord, however you interpret it, whereas the holy mother La Guillotine is a good thing.'"

Vadim put down the book.

"Well, what do you say to that?"

Yuri said nothing. He did not know how to react to such an obvious hint. The words were astounding. He could usually respond to Vadim, but this was so obvious. . . .

Again, Lena saved him. "I've read that passage. It isn't Belinsky, it's Panaev himself who says it. He attributes the words to Belinsky."

"He's citing Belinsky accurately," Vadim persisted. "The same words appear in other memoirs about Belinsky, in Kavelin's, for instance. The point is, Belinsky was a great man who realized that Russia needed firm leadership. But he was a man of his time, the early nineteenth century; he didn't know, he couldn't know that there was going to be a dictatorship of the proletariat."

Yuri secretly marveled at Vadim's political resourcefulness.

"And why do I love you, peaceful night . . ." It was the same voice from next door.

"He sings well," Yuri said. "Who is he?"

"Our neighbor," Lena replied. "He's a member of the Central Committee. Nikolai Ivanovich Yezhov."

Vadim turned his head to indicate that he had not heard the name before, he who knew everyone's name.

"I don't know who he is," Yuri said, "but he sings well."

"He's a very nice man," Lena remarked.

When they were alone together she said, "I hardly recognize Vadim. I'm afraid of him, I swear. He's become so dogmatic, so impatient and suspicious. Defending the Soviet régime like that! Who from? *Us?*"

Lena had always kept her opinions to herself and even now she was trying not to seem exceptional. But despite herself, she belonged among those who were running the state, and not simply serving it — like Vadim and his father. Now Yuri also belonged among those who ran the state. He came from the working class, he was a man of the people, the sort of man they were turning into leaders now. That was why he'd been recruited into security. There were high-level Chekists living in their apartment house on Granovsky Street and also here in Silver Wood. There were wonderful people among them. Her father had also been a member of the political board of the Cheka. Vadim's behavior was unnatural, it rang false and it grated when he said *"We* can," or *"We* can't," or *"We've* got," or *"Our* state." Nina Ivanova or even Sasha Pankratov could speak that way, they came from that world, they had the right. But Vadim did not. He could only serve, nothing more.

Just as she was thinking of Sasha, Yuri started speaking about him, and the coincidence made her shudder.

"Vadim changed the day they arrested Sasha," he said. "I saw it at once. Sasha's arrest frightened him. So now out of fright he shouts louder than everyone else."

"Yes," she agreed sadly. "Since Sasha's arrest we've all changed."

Yuri realized, as he had in his conversation with Berezin, that so much depended on what he would say about Sasha.

"It's a shame about Sasha. I was wrong. He had insulted me at that New Year's party and I wasn't seeing things objectively."

"What actually happened?" Lena looked at him as though she expected him to trust her.

Thinking over his words, he replied: "Sasha was used to leading. But at the institute, there were other people in the lead. Sasha attached himself to a group who wanted to replace them, a group of deviationists who were trying to overthrow the Party leadership of the institute. Sasha became implicated. Three years of exile, that's the best that could be done for him; the rest either got prison or camp, and long sentences."

It sounded as if he had helped Sasha.

"I was posted to work with the NKVD after finishing at the institute. I am a lawyer, after all," he continued. "My joining coincided with Sasha's case. To be honest, I didn't know till the last minute what they wanted with me."

"Really?" Lena was surprised. "But you trained at different institutes, and as for school, well, we were all friends at school."

His smile was full of meaning.

"Lena! Just because they weren't interested in *all* of Sasha's friends, it didn't mean they weren't interested in *any* of them. Don't forget that I live in the same house as Sasha, on the same staircase, and for two years we both worked at the same factory. Vadim had good reason to be scared. When they arrested Sasha, I had to make sure I didn't meet anybody, including you. I didn't want to complicate things for your father. He'd intervened in Sasha's case, about which he knew very little. Luckily, everything was disentangled. Sasha got off relatively lightly, his friends were freed of suspicion. Only Vadim is still nervous."

Lena was walking at his side, her head slightly bowed. Did she believe him? She had no reason not to. She knew what wonderful people worked in security, but she also knew what wonderful people they prosecuted. She could see that the others might have been called as witnesses and she not — it was all something of a lottery. And as Yuri said, there were enough complications and he hadn't wanted to make further ones for her father, and quite rightly. Stalin didn't like her father and the slightest excuse could lead to much unpleasantness. Anyone else in Yuri's position would probably have acted differently, they would have said something, tried to explain.

But Yuri was Yuri. The important thing was the principle that guided him.

There were only a few people at the bathing place. Some children were splashing noisily near the bank, a group of tanned teenagers in bathing suits were playing cards on the sand.

Lena took off her shift and stood there in a bathing suit that clung to her body, molding her breasts and hips. She gave him a shy smile, but did not turn away as he took off his underpants and slipped on his trunks.

"Let's go farther down, it's deeper," she said.

She swam with her arms bent at the elbow, and her head turning to right and left. Yuri had never seen this style of swimming before. He was amazed at how well she swam. This was a new side of her, but he still harbored the fear that things could not be straightened out between them all that easily.

Later, as they lay stretched out on the sand with their bare backs to the sun, she rested her head on her hands and looked at him sideways, and again he had the feeling that she still loved him.

And so she did. Perhaps it was because no other love had come along to take his place. Perhaps it was because she had a sensitive nature and Yuri had been the first and only man in her life. The suffering he had brought her had only strengthened her feelings. After all, he had suffered, too.

"When are we going to meet?" he asked.

She answered simply: "Whenever you want."

He'd be able to take her to his room again. His father would frown and his mother would wring her hands, but never mind, they'd get over it. But he was restrained by a primitive male cautiousness. They would rekindle their affair, fine, but this time he wasn't going to get in too deep. He wouldn't get away as easily the second time.

Where else could they meet? Where could he take her? There was only one place, and that was Dyakov's apartment. He virtually lived at his wife's place on the other side of the river. It wasn't the ideal place to meet, and if Lena ever found out . . . But she wouldn't. The bed was old and grubby and he didn't even know if it had any linen on it. That didn't matter. He could bring sheets with him from home in his briefcase.

"Well, at the moment," he said, "there are repairs going on at home. We're all camping out in one room at a time, dragging our things from room to room. But I've got this friend, I knew him at the institute, he's on leave right now and he's given me the keys to his apartment. We could spend some time there."

"We could," she agreed.

❧ 15 ❧

oe went into ecstasies when Varya told her she had danced with Lyova at the Metropole. His name was Sinyavsky and he was a construction draftsman, a nice, sweet boy who was always helping her at work. And the way he dressed! He went to only the best tailors. And the way he danced! As good as Vagan Khristoforovich. The plump, pretty girl with Lyova — she was also in drafting. Her name was Rina.

Zoe looked into Varya's eyes with envy. She had always dreamed of getting to know Lyova but had never managed it. That's what being beautiful meant. Everything just dropped into your lap.

"Oh, you're so lucky!" she sighed, sincerely.

Varya didn't especially like Lyova; he was not very manly. But he danced beautifully and, most of all, he was his own man, like the rest of his friends. They weren't like Vika and Vitaly, they didn't whore after foreigners. The only one of their friends who'd made an impression on her had been the architect Igor Vladimirovich. But he was already thirty, and he made her feel awkward. You had to be serious with him. But she could never fall in love with such an old man and she didn't want to string him along. He deserved respect, he had noble feelings and it would be shameful to hurt him. Varya had her own code of decency; she knew what was done and what was not done.

She hoped Lyova would include her in his group and she was waiting for his invitation. It took a little while, but two weeks after they had met at the Metropole it came.

An excited Zoe came bursting in to announce that the whole

group would be at the Hermitage Gardens the next day and that they were both expected.

And then Vika phoned at just the same moment to invite her the next evening to the Kanatik restaurant with Igor Vladimirovich.

"I can't," Varya replied. "I'm going to the Hermitage."

"With who?"

"Lyova and his friends. I'm going to be working with them."

"Does that oblige you to go out with them as well? Phone them and say you can't come. I'm telling you, Igor Vladimirovich is going to be there."

"I can't. I promised and I can't lie to them."

"But I gave my promise, too." Vika was becoming exasperated. "And not to some unimportant little shit like Lyova, but to Igor Vladimirovich. I'm not thinking of myself. He likes you. And he's not married."

"I'm sorry," Varya replied. "Let's make it another time, please. Call me. See you."

And she hung up.

As at the Metropole, the group in the Hermitage Gardens was in constant flux, with new people joining them for a while, then disappearing and coming back later. It was all perfectly natural. No one needed to stick with the group the whole time. They didn't actually go anywhere, but stood around at the main entrance to see and be seen by everyone.

It was a male company. Lyova, two boys from the design studio called Big Volya and Little Volya, a handsome young man with the strange name of Ika, then Willie Long, the son of a high Comintern official, a burly type with the face of a thug, and finally Miron, assistant to the great dance instructor Vagan Khristoforovich, a good-natured, curly-haired boy with the soul of a businessman. The only female among them was the eternal Rina, chubby and freckled as if she had a rash all over her body. Big Volya said she'd been kissed by the sun. Rina had been born to be cheerful and wherever she went she radiated joy, blazing like a nasturtium with her red hair.

Other girls joined the group haphazardly. Today it was Varya's turn. But nobody paid any special attention to her as a new arrival. They didn't baby each other in the group, they were all equals, just boys and girls, ordinary draftsmen, like Zoe. They would help Varya get a job in Shchusev's architectural studio, where they were designing the Moscow Hotel. Wages there were just as good as at the organizations that were designing the big projects for heavy industry.

Lyova was smiling sweetly, his crooked tooth bared, a boy with the face of an angel, and Rina was beaming like the sun itself, as they chatted idly, assessing the girls as they came. Their remarks were in fun and not at all in bad taste and the girls didn't mind, anyway.

Lyova's group seemed to own the place, even though they had no money, had got in without tickets, and would be going on to eat somewhere else. Miron, the curly-haired, kind-hearted business-man, said something obscure about someone called Kostya and then wandered off. Nobody minded; they'd all be leaving sooner or later.

Varya felt at ease among these people. She saw how much the boys liked her, both the silent Ika and Lyova, but she wasn't sure they'd take her with them to the restaurant, especially with Zoe tagging along. Zoe had stayed close to the group and was behaving in a noisy and excited way, and the others clearly wanted to dump her.

Just inside the entrance, a man with a little beard was sitting at a small table in front of a pile of envelopes and some pencils and a sign: "GRAPHOLOGIST — D. M. ZUYEV-INSAROV. *Your character analyzed from your handwriting. Fifty kopeks.*"

"I've always wanted to know my character," Zoe announced suddenly. "What about anyone else?"

Rina raised her eyebrows in puzzlement.

Willie Long sighed and threw up his hands in mock distress. "What a terrible pity there are no swings for us to play on."

Varya saw what a gaffe her friend had made. The group thought such things were childish and cheap.

Zoe went over to the table and called back: "Varya, come here!"

If she refused, she stood a chance of being asked to the restaurant, but if she did join Zoe, she'd probably be dumped with her.

Even so, she went to the graphologist's table. She leafed through his book of comments. Maxim Gorky had signed, and Lunacharsky, and some well-known actors: *"To Zuyev-Insarov from the unmasked Yaron."*

Zoe wrote on an envelope and handed it to the graphologist. She nodded at Varya. "Go on, write!"

"No, I don't want to," Varya declined. All she had was eight kopeks for the tram. Anyway, who could possibly read your character, especially from something scribbled on an envelope? It was just so much rubbish!

But Zoe had already given the graphologist a ruble. "For the two of us."

Varya wrote on the envelope and went back to the others, who paid no attention to the fact that she had returned. She could come and go like anyone else, it was their way.

Miron came back, said something incomprehensible and vanished again.

While Zoe was busy talking with one of the two Volyas, Rina said softly to Varya, "We're going to the Savoy, but not with Zoe."

"What am I supposed to do with her?"

Rina shrugged, as if to say, *That's your business, we'll take you, but not her, get rid of her any way you like.* Beaming brightly, she turned away as if she'd said nothing.

Then they started leaving, not all at once, but one at a time, very skillfully and unnoticed, like conjurors. And now, open your eyes and nobody's there!

Zoe and Varya found themselves on their own.

"They've gone!" Zoe whispered, and burst into tears.

"Were you expecting them to give you a ride in an automobile," Varya said mockingly, "or in a carriage with rubber tires, maybe?"

"What swines they are," Zoe muttered miserably. "And the biggest swine is that Rina, just freckles and red hair."

They walked along the path and mixed with the crowd. The audiences were strolling during the intermissions at the theater and the music hall where Tsfasman's band was playing. They had just completed their second boring circle when they saw Ika back where they'd been hanging around all evening.

"Girls," he shouted, "I've been looking for you! Let's go, come on!"

"Where to?" Varya asked.

"To the Savoy. We waited at the tram stop, but you'd vanished. The others have all gone on ahead; they sent me back to find you."

"Nobody said anything to us," Zoe protested.

"I don't know about that." Ika wasn't about to explain. "You must have misunderstood. Let's get going!"

⚜ 16 ⚜

The others were already sitting at a large oval table and the arrival of Varya and Zoe aroused little reaction: you've come, so sit down. Varya was still not sure whether Ika had come back for them on his own initiative or been sent.

They were talking about someone called Alevtina who'd been murdered out of jealousy by her husband who came from Bukhara. Rina had been at the trial.

"He was saved by the defense counsel, Braude," she related. "He was too much, the judges were fascinated: 'The revolving doors at the National are drawing our young girls into a vicious circle of restaurant life.'" She rotated her hand like revolving doors.

"He murdered a woman and only got two years?" Zoe was mortified.

"And that, no doubt, was on account of his cultural backwardness."

Lyova smiled angelically and showed his crooked tooth. "So, if we don't use the revolving doors, we won't be led astray?"

"People pass the time in restaurants and cafés all over the world," Willie Long said.

Little Volya covered his face and, rocking back and forth like a Muslim, murmured, "Poor Alevtina, sad Alevtina, why did the wild Bukharan have to cut her throat, cut her throat he did, like a chicken, just like a little chicken."

"Chicken broiled, chicken boiled," Big Volya chanted. "A chicken also has its rights."

"But if they removed the revolving doors and replaced them with

ordinary doors, would that mean there'd be no vicious circle?"
Lyova asked again.

Miron reappeared, sat down at the table, and announced, "He's
just finishing his game, he'll be here any minute."

"He's coming!" said Willie, who was facing the door.

A man in his late twenties was approaching their table. He was
thickset, broad-shouldered, and had a small mustache. His black
shoes had been polished to a high gloss and he looked better in his
superb suit, which he wore somewhat carelessly, than the immac-
ulate Lyova did in his. He crossed the restaurant with a light,
assured, and yet careful gait, nodding to acquaintances and smiling
in response to greetings. This was Kostya, the famous billiard player
about whom Miron had dropped a hint at the Hermitage Gardens.

The group greeted him. He surveyed the table with a slow gaze
that was at once strange, crazy, and distrustful, as if he were
wondering who all these people were, even though he knew them
perfectly well. He paused only when his eyes reached Varya and
Zoe.

He sat down next to Varya. "I see you haven't ordered anything,"
he said.

"Rina was telling us about the Alevtina case. She was at the trial,"
Lyova replied evasively.

Ika came straight to the point crudely. "We were waiting for you,
our 'patron.' "

Kostya looked attentively at Ika and said, "Pity about Alevtina,
she was a good girl. I warned her not to get mixed up with the
Bukharan, but she wouldn't listen."

He spoke slowly and precisely, stretching his lips and also,
slightly, his words, as they do in the south of Russia. He had dark
brown eyes, but his hair was a warm, bright golden color.

He turned to Varya. "You girls must be starving."

"I don't want to eat," Zoe said affectedly.

"But I do," Rina declared. "I'm starving. Let's eat now."

"Maybe we should have some snacks," Ika said.

He seemed to be the only one who wasn't dependent on Kostya.
A waiter came over.

"Bring us some cigarettes in the meantime," Kostya ordered.
"Hercegovina Flor?"

"Yes."

He said and did everything very slowly and deliberately. They were all desperate for something to eat, and he knew it, but he wouldn't hurry.

He opened the cigarette package with his fingernail and threw it on the table — here, help yourselves. But he asked only Varya if she smoked.

She sensed that he was expecting her to say she didn't, and evidently he was hoping she didn't smoke.

But she took a cigarette.

"I would have guessed you didn't."

"What a disappointment for you." She laughed, like a hard little flirt.

Kostya looked away from her slowly and, drawing out his words, asked, "So, what are we going to eat, and what are we going to drink?"

Lyova began reading out the menu, but Kostya interrupted him.

"Salad and meat in aspic," he said, surveying the numbers sitting around the table, "and two bottles of vodka and one of Muscat. Red or white?"

"Red's better," Rina said.

He turned to Varya. "And what do *you* say?"

"It's all the same to me."

"So, it's two bottles of vodka and one of red Muscat. And we'll have baked carp for the main course."

"Wow!" Willie Long exclaimed.

"Kostya, you don't have to throw your money around," Miron said.

"I want to treat you all," Kostya replied.

"Is it your birthday?" Varya asked jokingly.

"Yes. It is my birthday. In a manner of speaking."

He was the sort of person who went straight to the point. He wouldn't flirt with her by complimenting the slant of her eyes. But she could handle him if she needed to. For the moment, there was no need, as he was only showing off.

A man with the ugly face of an old gangster appeared, bent down, and whispered something in Kostya's ear.

"No," Kostya replied. "That's all for today."

The man disappeared.

Suddenly, without warning and unnoticed by the others, Kostya picked up Varya's purse from her lap, slipped a wad of money into it, and murmured under his breath, "This is so I don't gamble anymore today."

Varya was confused. If he wanted to gamble, he only had to take money out of his pocket, and if he didn't, he could leave it there. It was an obvious, showy ploy: he was making her an accomplice. Gangsters probably gave their money to their molls to look after the same way. But it would be awkward to give the money back to him in front of everyone, and she couldn't manage it as surreptitiously as he had. The money stayed in her purse, but she was not happy about it.

The waiter brought the drinks and the food. Kostya followed his movements like a host who wants his guests properly attended to. When they were at the Metropole or the Hermitage Gardens, the group was always shifting, as people came and went, and there was always disorder and vacillation. At the Savoy, they behaved themselves. And Varya realized that this was not the same casually formed group she had earlier thought. This group was centered around Kostya, it was his group. Only Miron permitted himself to depart from time to time on his business errands, and Ika, to show his independence, sat for a while at a neighboring table.

The chef, wearing a white apron and tall white hat, came out carrying a fish tank, in the bottom of which a live fish lay wriggling in a net.

"What's the name of this fish?" Kostya asked Varya, holding up his finger to stop anyone else answering for her.

"Well, since you ordered carp, I imagine that's what it is," she replied.

"Yes, but what sort of carp — ordinary or mirror?"

"I don't know."

"It's a mirror carp," he explained. "It has a tall, pointed dorsal fin and large scales. The ordinary carp has a wide fin and small scales. Right?"

"Right. Thanks very much. Now I can get into the Fish Institute."

Kostya nodded to the chef, who took the fish away.

"Are you an angler?" Varya asked him.

"Not an angler, a fisherman. I'm from Kerch, my father's a fisherman and my grandfather, too. I started going out to sea when I was a little boy."

"Since when has carp been a sea fish?" Ika asked, returning to the table.

"I didn't catch carp in the sea." Kostya tightened his lips. "I fished sea roach. Do you know the difference between sea roach and Caspian roach? You don't? Look, the band's here, go and dance and I'll tell you later."

Varya danced with Lyova, Ika, and Willie. Kostya didn't dance because he didn't know how. For some reason, even this did not seem like a shortcoming to Varya. If anything, it made him superior to the rest. He sat alone at the table, and only raised his head to look at her and smile. She felt sorry for him. They were having a good time at his expense but they left him on his own, they cared more about dancing than about their friend.

When they all started to get up for the next dance, Kostya held her back by the hand. "Sit with me."

She stayed with him.

"Are you studying to work?"

"I've finished school and I'm starting a job."

"Where?"

"In a design studio. We learned technical drawing at school."

"What about going to the university?"

"I don't want to yet."

"Why not?"

"There's no money in it. Does that satisfy you? This is a pointless conversation. Are you a designer, too?"

"A designer?" He grinned. "No, I've got a different speciality."

"Billiards?"

He heard the sarcasm in her voice and gave her a hard look; anger flashed in his eyes, but he stifled it. Slowly drawing out his words, he said: "Billiards is not a profession. As a highly educated man once said, 'Billiards is an art.'"

"Oh, I thought billiards was a game!" she said in mock surprise. She felt like teasing him, because he seemed a bit too full of himself.

"My speciality is electromedical equipment," he said seriously.

"Ultraviolet, sunray, quartz lamps, artificial sunlight, dentists' drills. Do you like the dentist's drill?"

"I hate it."

"So do I. I repair them."

He evidently thought he'd said enough about himself, for he asked, "Have you known Rina long?" — clearly trying to find out how she came to be part of the group.

"No, we only met today for the first time. She works with Zoe, and Zoe and I live in the same apartment house."

"In the same apartment house?" He seemed surprised. "Where would that be?"

"In the Arbat."

Again he showed surprise. "In the Arbat? With your mother and father?"

"I don't have a mother and father. They died a long time ago. I live with my sister."

He looked at her disbelievingly. Girls in restaurants always tried to seem out of the ordinary — to have had some particular success or some particular misfortune. Every one of them tried to invent a special fate for herself. Being an orphan at seventeen would pass as a *fate*.

But the girl sitting in front of him was no restaurant girl.

"All my family are still living," Kostya said. "My father and mother, four brothers, three sisters, grandfather, grandmother — we're a big family."

"Are they all in Kerch?"

"No, they moved," he replied evasively. "I've got nobody in Moscow. Nobody and nothing. Not even a place of my own."

"So, where do you live?"

"I rent a room out in Sokolniki."

Varya was amazed. "With so many friends, surely they could find you somewhere in the center of town?"

The idea occurred to her that she could fix him up at Sofya Alexandrovna's. The present lodger was moving out soon. She ought not to say anything to Kostya before talking to Sofya Alexandrovna, of course, but the desire to make up for his ungrateful friends was too much for her.

"I can't promise anything, but I'll ask a woman in the house. She's got a spare room, maybe she'll let you have it."

Again he looked disbelieving. But he saw that she was serious.

"It would be marvelous," he said. "It would be simply marvelous. Does she have a phone?"

"I must talk to her first."

He laughed. "No, I don't mean I want to telephone her, I mean does she have a phone, because I need one for my work."

"There's a phone."

She oughtn't to have said anything about the room. Maybe nothing would come of it.

"How did you manage to turn yourself from a fisherman into an electrical specialist?"

"Fisherman . . . I lived by the sea, so I was a fisherman."

"I've never seen the sea."

He was amazed. "Never seen the sea?"

"Only in the movies."

Now he looked straight at her. "But would you like to?"

"And how!"

The music stopped and everyone returned to the table.

Kostya leaned back in his chair and raised his glass. "I propose we drink to our new friends, Varya and Zoe."

"Hurrah!" Little Volya gave a mock cheer.

It was not the best time or place for toasts to be made: they'd already been eating and drinking, the table was in disorder, people were constantly coming over for a chat.

A young man with glasses and the face of a professor appeared next to Kostya. Varya noticed that he was holding a ten-ruble note in his hand.

"Odds or evens?" he asked.

"I'm not playing," Kostya replied.

Then he changed his mind.

"Wait! Varya, make a wish to yourself, any wish at all. Have you wished?"

"Yes." (She hadn't wished.)

"Now: you say, odds or evens."

"Evens."

"Evens?" the young man repeated.

"Evens," Kostya confirmed.

The young man laid the note on the table. Kostya grinned, picked up the note, and said to Varya, "I've won the money and you've got your wish. What did you wish?"

She said the first thing that came into her head: "That I'd get the job."

"You'll get it without wishing for it." He was disappointed.

"What is that game?"

Kostya smoothed the note out on the tablecloth and pointed to its serial number, 341672.

"There are six digits; you said evens, four, six, two, that makes twelve. He's left with the odd numbers, three, one, seven, which only makes eleven. Your total is higher, so you win, you get the ten rubles. If his total had been higher, we would have had to give him ten rubles. Got it?"

Varya laughed. "It's hardly higher mathematics."

"It's a good game, because as soon as he opens his fist, you can see if you've won or lost." His joy was like that of a child.

"And what do you call this highly complicated game?"

" 'Railroad.' Not *chemin de fer,* just plain 'Railroad.' "

"Railroad *à la* Savoy," she said.

Kostya laughed. "Did you hear that, Lyova, did you hear? 'Railroad *à la* Savoy.' "

"Do you mean 'Savoy' or 'Savoie'?" Ika gave a knowing smile, as if nobody — particularly Kostya — knew the difference between Savoy and Savoie.

"I mean the Savoy restaurant," Varya retorted, angry that Ika should be making fun of Kostya.

"Yes, obviously, the restaurant," Kostya agreed. He had spotted that there was a difference, though what or where Savoie was, he hadn't the remotest idea. He was sitting right on the edge of his chair with his arm along the back of Varya's, though he was not touching her.

He was trying to win her with his directness. He was pushy and persistent, but under control. Varya recognized all his moves, but she did not want to hurt him; after all, just like the rest of them, she was having a terrific time at his expense. And beyond that, there was something about him she found attractive. He was not only expansive, he was also kind and sincere.

The band started up again, everyone got up to dance, and again he held Varya back.

"Have you really never seen the sea?"

"No, I already told you."

He looked right into her eyes. "The train to Sevastopol, then by bus along the south coast to Yalta. We'll leave tomorrow, while we've still got some money." He nodded at her purse. "The train leaves during the day; bring only essentials, bathing suits, a coat, or we can buy what we need when we get there."

She looked at him in amazement. How could he propose such a thing? Had she given him any cause to think she was that kind of girl? What?

"Haven't you got anyone else to take on your *annual* holiday?" She put all the derision and irony she could into her words.

He threw back his head proudly and said slowly, "I don't have an *annual* holiday, I take off whenever I want to. I'm not dependent on anyone."

She now saw what attracted her to him. It was his independence, and now he was offering her a chance to share it. She knew what she would be agreeing to, but she wasn't worried about *that* — she had always known that *that* would happen sooner or later. Something else alarmed her. He was a gambler, he'd won some money, and now he wanted to have a spree with a *new* girl.

And he added, "We can buy the rest when we get back." So, there was going to be more to it than just a jaunt to the seaside.

Varya thought for a moment and then said, "How can I possibly go with you? I hardly know you."

"So, you'll get to know me."

"You're being pretty familiar already; it's not as if we've exchanged vows of friendship."

He reached for a bottle. "Let's drink to our friendship now," he suggested.

She pushed his hand away and said, realizing how banal she sounded but unable to find other words, "What do you take me for?"

"I take you for what you are — a delightful, good girl," he said with sincerity and laying his hand on hers.

Varya did not take her hand away. He didn't press her palm or stroke her fingers, but simply and softly laid his hand on hers, and she liked it. And she saw that he liked it, too.

Calmly and condescendingly he was surveying the noisy hall, an independent, powerful man, with money of his own, and with the only girl he would trust in the place, the only one he would pay any attention to. Even if there weren't any heroes left in the world, this was one man who wouldn't stand at attention and devour the authorities with his eyes, or drag his own suitcase along the platform under guard. . . .

Suddenly, without looking at her, he said thoughtfully, "Maybe with you along I could become a real person."

She frowned. He turned away.

"Okay," she said. "I'll come."

17

asha donned the harness and was surprised at how easily the laden boat moved against the current. With the towrope slung across a high beam at the prow, the boat pulled away and followed a course parallel to the bank.

They had had to row across the river. Sasha and Boris fitted the oars into the oarlocks and rowed with all their might against the strong current. Even at its deepest, the water was so clean that bright pebbles on the bottom were clearly visible, though the river changed color with the seasons, becoming steely gray, deep blue, or blue-green.

"We're going at a fair lick," Nil joked. "Ah, you young folks!"

Nil Lavrentyevich was a bustling little peasant with an expressive, if blandly featured, face. He had panned for gold on the Lena River, fought with the partisans against Kolchak and the Whites in the Civil War, and now he was a collective farmer, a kolkhoznik. He talked about his days with the partisans in vague terms, no doubt enlivening his account from stories he'd heard from others, but he told the truth about his gold-mining experiences. It was the custom among the people of the Angara that the young men went off to prospect for gold. If they came back with a gold ring on their finger, it meant they'd struck it lucky and would get married. It had been like this for Nil Lavrentyevich: he'd done his prospecting, come home, got married, and now he had his own homestead with six cows. By local standards, even ten cows didn't make him a landed farmer, a kulak, especially as he didn't hire poor peasants as laborers, or own a separator, or trade with the Tunguses. In the autumn he went into the forest where he would trap six or seven hundred skins during the winter. He had done well, but now the squirrels had moved north. The sables had been wiping them out, and anyway the collective farm was demanding more work from him. In the old days, you'd scythe a bit at haymaking and leave the rest of the work to your wife. Now there were no differences, the peasant and his woman were the same thing, just kolkhozniks.

They listened to Nil airing his views as they traveled along the bank, past overhanging cliffs, fallen rocks, and fords where the cliffs came right down into the water. During the day, the hot sun was high overhead. Only toward evening did it sink behind the forest, and then the bank would become striped with beams of the lilac light of the taiga.

An occasional, isolated fishing boat would appear; or a wooden float would be glimpsed at the opposite bank. They were trawling here. A raft would be seen floating in the distance with a solitary horse standing on it, and then there would be nobody, neither beast nor bird in sight. The noise of the small streams was like that of the taiga in a strong wind, as the water rushed between boulders and falls, seething in whirlpools and sending up spray into the sunlight. They all had to pull on the rope when the boat was going through these fast streams, while Nil stood at the tiller. Even his silent, sickly wife, wrapped in a large shawl, would put on the harness and pull.

Boris, his shoulder chafed and his shins bruised by rocks along the bank, said gloomily: "Volodya Kvachadze wouldn't have pulled any boat — he'd have made them pull *him.*"

Sasha replied, "As long as we're in harness, we don't have an escort."

The local exiles were waiting for them when they arrived at Goltyavino, a village on the bank of the river. One of them was a little, gray-haired old lady who had been a Socialist Revolutionary, another had been an Anarchist, a small gray-haired old man with a jovial face, and there was a startlingly beautiful girl named Freda. The old lady was Marya Fedorovna and the old man, Anatoly Georgyevich.

The mail had not been delivered for two months and Nil handed each of them a packet of letters, newspapers, and magazines, and there was a parcel for Freda, as well.

"Three days we've waited for you, from morning till dusk," Anatoly Georgyevich announced brightly.

"It was held up at the sorting office, Natoly Yegorych," Nil explained "We'll go on to Dvorets — there's a post office there now."

This news prompted a lively discussion. If the village of Dvorets was going to become a postal sector, then the winter post for the Taishet tract would come through much faster. On the other hand, the creation of a new postal sector might mean administrative changes. Maybe a new regional center was going to be established in Dvorets. And a new authority would mean a new broom, and a new broom that was closer at hand.

Marya Fedorovna hurried them along. "Collect your things, we have to arrange somewhere for you to spend the night."

"Thank you, but Nil has already offered us a place," Sasha replied.

"At Efrosinya Andryanovna's?"

"Yes," Nil confirmed, dragging the postbag out of the boat.

"Fine," she replied. "We'll spend the evening together. Freda will call for you. Is that all right, Freda?"

Freda was reading one of her letters.

"Freda, wake up!"

"Yes, yes." The girl put the letter back into its envelope and raised her huge blue eyes to look at Marya Fedorovna. Her long black hair fell onto an old blouse, which hugged her small waist.

"You can collect them," Marya Fedorovna repeated, "and we'll spend the evening at Anatoly Georgyevich's."

"Yes, yes." Anatoly Georgyevich was leafing through a journal.

"Comrades, you'll have plenty of time for reading later," Marya Fedorovna commanded. "Let's get going!"

Boris picked up Freda's parcel.

"You have your own things to carry," she said.

"I'll say!"

Boris swung the parcel up onto his shoulder with a spirited gesture and picked up his own suitcase. His fatigue had vanished.

"Leave the suitcase for the time being; you can come back for it," Marya Fedorovna advised.

Sasha helped Nil unload the boat. Boris came back and they

carried everything into a hut that was standing nearby on the bank.

While their hostess was cleaning a fish and cooking the supper, Sasha and Boris went outside.

"Well?" Boris looked at Sasha questioningly.

Sasha pretended not to understand the question.

"They're very nice, charming, welcoming people."

"Come on!" Boris retorted impatiently. "These are not like the lot at Chuna, Volodya's friends. These are real intellectuals, they don't care what you believe. What matters to them is that you're an exile, the same as them. Real people! Anyway, what do you think about Freda?"

"She's a beautiful girl."

"That's not the word for it! She's a Shulamith, an Esther! The Song of Songs! Something we had to preserve through thousands of years, through persecution, wanderings, pogroms."

"I didn't realize you were such a nationalist," Sasha said, laughing.

"If it was a Russian girl, it wouldn't be nationalism, but because it's a Jewish girl, it's nationalism. What I'm talking about is the type, the biology. My wife also came from a Jewish family, but I wouldn't give Freda's little finger for her. What bearing! What dignity! What a *woman!* What a wife and mother, what a housekeeper she'd make!"

"There speaks the Jewish male," Sasha said.

"Yes, and what of it?"

"You've got a sentence to serve, she's got a sentence to serve. You're in the Kezhma district, she's in the Boguchansk district."

"Nonsense! If we get married they'll put us together."

Sasha marveled at Boris's fantasy, but all he said was, "Maybe she's already married."

"That'd be too bad."

There was fish, sour cream, and blueberry jam. Nil and his wife spat their fishbones right out onto the table, but Sasha was already used to it.

Their hostess was a plump, bright woman. She complained about their son, who didn't want to work in the collective farm, and the "decruiters" who were trying to lure him to go and work on a building site.

"They won't leave you alone, that lot," Nil said of the recruitment people. "Know everything, they do, they pop up everywhere and they can really talk,"

The son, a real little Gypsy, sat watching Sasha and Boris with curiosity and listening in silence to his mother's complaints. The host, who also looked like a Gypsy, sat on a bench and smoked. Boris was watching the door, waiting for Freda. The hostess was still going on about her son.

"I found matches on him, he's got holes in his pockets where he hides cigarettes, lights them in his pocket, he does. What does he lack for here? We don't make him do a lot of work, we do it all ourselves. Yet as soon as he gets up in the morning, he's out of the house. It's what the bosses want, you mustn't complain."

The boy was silent, looking sideways at Sasha and Boris. His father was silent, too. At heart he was also a wanderer. And the mother didn't stop grumbling. Her boy would go away and get into bad company and end up in prison.

Freda entered, greeted everyone, and sat down without inter-rupting the conversation. She was wearing boots and an old coat, and tied around her hair and neck was a scarf, which she kept on while she waited for them to finish their supper.

Boris got up and looked at Sasha impatiently, urging him to get a move on.

There was a shrine with icons in one corner, and a corner table in another, with a mirror, a sewing basket, and a clean, embroidered towel laid out next to it. There were mineral specimens along the windowsills, boxes containing seeds and plants in jars.

"Anatoly Georgyevich is our resident agronomist, geologist, mineralogist, paleontologist, and I don't know what else," Marya Fedorovna said, laughing. "He's hoping they'll reward him for what he's doing. And so they will — with labor camp or the political isolator."

"The region ought to think it's of value," Anatoly Georgyevich replied. "There's nowhere else with the treasures that are here on the Angara. Coal, metals, oil, wood, furs, inexhaustible water power."

He turned the pebbles in his delicate fingers, and showed them pieces of lava lined with fine silver veins, pleased to have the attention of his unexpected visitors; there might not be any more for another year, if ever.

"I was exiled to the Angara even before the February Revolution of nineteen seventeen," he went on. "And now here I am again. But in those days, my articles on the region used to be published. Now I wouldn't even dare think of it. Still, I hope my notes might one day be useful."

"The exploration of mineral resources is very important for the development of a second metallurgical base in the east," Boris said, with a glance at Freda. "After the Kuznets Basin, industrialization is going to come here. It's just a question of time."

He spoke with gravity, like a senior official inspiring the local enthusiasts. Poor Boris! He was trying to look like a man of quality in Freda's eyes, but his qualities lay elsewhere.

Marya Fedorovna nodded mockingly.

"That's all you want, industrialization, the Five-Year Plan. They've taken away your freedom, that's what you ought to be thinking about. You talk about what will happen in the region fifty years from now, what sort of Siberia there's going to be. But try to imagine what sort of human beings there'll be when they've had the right to be good and kindhearted taken away from them for fifty years."

"But it's no good denying obvious facts," Anatoly Georgyevich said. "An industrial revolution is going on in Russia." The fluffy little old man was nothing like Sasha's idea of an Anarchist.

"What are you sitting here for!" Marya Fedorovna exclaimed. "Recant! You'll get straight into the Academy of Sciences!"

"No," Anatoly Georgyevich objected. "There must be those who differ. If there was no unorthodox thought, there would be no thought at all. But one must work, man cannot be idle." He pointed to his plants. "There, I'm growing tomatoes and melons."

"Those tomatoes will get you out of here and sent to a labor camp before anyone else," Marya Fedorovna remarked. "You're fussing about your tomatoes, but the kolkhozniks can't even grow grain for bread. They haven't even solved that problem in Russia, and they think it can be done out here on the Angara, where they've never grown it before." She sighed. "Things were more bearable in the old days: the exiles worked for the peasants or they lived on what was sent from home, and nobody took any notice of them. Now there are collective farms, there are authorities, government agents arrive. If you suggest a change, they accuse you of agitation. Whenever something goes wrong on the collective farm, they have to accuse someone and the scapegoat is the exile, the counterrevolutionary, he's a bad influence on the local population. If the potatoes don't grow, it's because of his influence; if no fish are caught or if the cows don't calve or give milk, it's because of his influence. For instance, they took Freda for a Baptist. One of them actually told her to stop her Baptist agitation! Isn't that what he said, Freda?"

"Yes." Freda smiled.

"One thing they have achieved," Marya Fedorovna said sarcastically, "and that is, the peasant won't fight. What has he got to fight for? He used to be afraid that the landlord would return and take his land back. Now the land has been taken away from him anyhow, so what is there for him to fight for?"

"It's a debatable question," Sasha said. "For the people, for the nation as a whole, there are values that he would fight for."

"But would you go and fight?" Marya Fedorovna asked.

"Certainly."

"What would you be fighting for?"

"For Russia, for Soviet power."

"But it's Soviet power that has exiled you to Siberia."

"That's unfortunately true," Sasha agreed. "But that's not the fault of Soviet power, it's the fault of people who abuse that power."

"How old are you?" Anatoly Georgyevich asked.

"Twenty-two."

"You're young." The old man smiled. "You've your whole life in front of you."

"What has he got in front of him?" Marya Fedorovna asked gloomily. "How long is your sentence?"

"Three years. How long have you got?"

"I haven't got any term," she replied coolly.

"How's that?"

"This is how: I began in nineteen twenty-two with exile, the Solovki Islands, the political isolation camp, then another exile, again either Solovki or the isolator. Now they say they're using us counterrevolutionaries to master the north. That's what you've got in front of you. Once you get into this orbit, you never get out of it. Do you imagine Freda would have got into this if they'd have let her go to Palestine?"

"You want to go to Palestine?" Sasha was amazed.

"Yes."

"What will you do there?"

"Work," she replied. "I'll work on the land." There was a slight burr in her voice.

"Do you know how to dig?"

"A little."

Sasha blushed. The question had sounded malevolent: "Do you know how to dig?" After all, she was working the land here, that was how she lived.

Trying to smooth over his tactlessness he asked her gently, "Are things so bad for you in Russia?"

"I don't want to be called a kike," she replied. She spoke calmly, but with a note of inflexible persistence. Nothing would work out here for Boris, Sasha thought. He wasn't likely to adopt her commitment.

Marya Fedorovna and Anatoly Georgyevich, the debris of a short period before the Revolution when people with different ideas were accepted as inevitable, were now regarded as unnatural. The Baulins and Stolpers and Dyakovs were convinced of their right to sentence old, powerless people who dared to think differently from them.

"I have a favor to ask you," Marya Fedorovna said. "When you're in Kezhma, find Anna Petrovna Samsonova and give her this for me."

She handed Sasha an envelope.

Ought he to take it? What was in it? Why didn't she send it by post?

The hesitation that flickered in his face did not escape her notice. She opened the envelope, which contained money. "There are twenty rubles. Please give it to her and tell her I'm still alive."

Sasha blushed again. "Fine, I'll give it to her."

They continued upriver, through fast streams, rowing from one bank to the other. It was hot, but Nil's wife, sitting at the tiller, remained wrapped in her shawl, and Nil himself did not take off his canvas raincoat.

They heard a distant noise.

"The Mura rapids," Nil explained with a worried look.

They were scraping underwater rocks more frequently. The current was getting faster and the noise rose to an unbroken and finally frenzied roar. The river ahead was shrouded in a huge white cloud, there were jutting bare rocks with great foaming waves breaking on them, and the noise was like the roar of hundreds of artillery guns. In a wild din, the river Mura came rushing in through a rocky gap in the left bank. Where it fell into the Angara there towered a vast granite-pointed crag.

They dragged the boat up onto the bank, unloaded it, and carried the things above the rapids, then came back and dragged the boat itself, using the towrope.

Boris no longer got tired; on the contrary, he was in a hurry to get to Kezhma where he intended to establish himself and get Freda transferred. He wasn't in any doubt that they'd get married.

"No, she has no fiancé or husband. Her mother lives somewhere near Chernigov. How can she be alone? We'll live in Kezhma, I won't let her go out to work, she'll look after the house, we'll have a child — they have children here, too, you know — and when our sentences are up, we'll leave. Can't you just see her in Moscow, in the theater, wearing an evening gown! It's worth a trip to the Angara to find a really good wife. Exile's only for a few years, but a wife is for life."

"She wants to go to Palestine," Sasha said.

"Nonsense. That'll pass. She hasn't yet experienced herself as a woman. When there's a family, a house, and children, she'll forget all about Palestine."

Sasha recalled the determination on Freda's beautiful face and he marveled again at Boris's blindness.

"She even says she believes in God," Boris went on. "You don't imagine she's being serious, do you? Show me one modern Jew who seriously believes in Jehovah. Religion for the Jews is no more than a form of national self-protection, a means for preventing assimilation. But assimilation is inevitable. My grandfather was a *tsaddik* and I don't even know Hebrew. What sort of a Jew am I, you might ask?"

"Boris, you've only seen her for one evening," Sasha said.

"You can find out about someone in five minutes. I saw you at the commandant's office and straightaway I knew we'd get on. And I wasn't mistaken. I've seen all kinds and colors of women, and when I find a real one, I don't need any other. Whereas a man who has been a milksop before marriage will grab the first piece of skirt that passes by, abandon his wife and kids and ruin his family."

Whatever lay beneath these words, whether it was loneliness, or sympathy for a girl who had ended up like himself in a remote region, Boris was certainly in love. This ladies' man and playboy was suddenly in love. When he spoke of Freda, his face became suffused with tenderness.

They passed by the village of Chadobets where Kartsev was supposed to have settled, and several other villages, staying the night with friends or relations of Nil's.

Sasha and Boris would go to bed soon after supper, while Nil would sit up late with their hosts. People would come and go, and Sasha would hear the door opening and closing and long snatches of peasant conversation in his sleep.

They would get up early, woken by the smell of frying fish, the clang of stove doors and saucepans being moved about.

"How did you sleep, did the bugs bite you?" the hostess would ask.

"Fine, thanks."

They would not linger over breakfast, as they were eager to be on their way. There would already be voices outside.

"They're rushing off to work," the hostess would say.

"Many thanks." Nil would get up and belch, and make a rough sign of the cross over his mouth.

Back in the boat, after such a night, Nil would air his views.

"Look at the collective farms we've got hereabouts. The earth is poor, taiga earth, frozen, it's not Russia, you can't export grain from here, there's hardly enough to feed yourself and your kids. What can we give the state? We can't give anyone anything, except some squirrel. They used to raise cattle on the Lena, now you can't even get milk. We used to hire the exiles, the politicals. They would dig up tree stumps; now we don't bother anymore. And nobody collects the pine nuts anymore."

They passed a Kalinin squat, a village built in 1930 by special settlers, kulaks banished from Russia.

"They brought them here at the very end of January," Nil related. "They just let them loose in the forest. They dug pits in the snow to put their children in, and the women lay on top of the children to keep them from freezing to death, crying fit to burst. Some of the peasants, the braver ones, went to the nearby village of Koda, five miles away, thinking they could at least find shelter for their kids. But the Koda people were scared. One of their families, the Rukosuevs, had kulaks of their own who'd been dragged off. The most hard-bitten ones had been taken away, so they were afraid. So, the peasants went back into the forest and started to make dugouts — just try making a dugout in the frozen ground, and with snow. Some died, some survived. In the spring they dug up stumps, plowed, and sowed. They were hardworking people, like workhorses, they were, and capable. They're still here, they plant tomatoes. Natoly Yegorych, the exiled politician, he planted tomatoes first. The people here used to laugh at him, but all they could do was scratch the earth. We've always been a wild lot, an ignorant people, but now the kulaks have proved it can be done. See how valuable they are to the state!"

The last sentence was pronounced with gravity and significance, as if to emphasize that he understood the interests of the state, both in the need to get rid of the kulaks and in the value of growing tomatoes.

But he could not hide his sympathy for the special settlers. He had children of his own. He had also been shocked by what had happened to them. He didn't know what lay ahead, and whether he would not suffer the same fate as the peasants from the Ukraine and the Kuban, *thrown out* of their native villages and driven only God knew where and for what. Sasha took a look inside the new huts, which were unlike the usual ones. They were typical Russian huts, with steps built out onto the street and earthen windbreaks built up around the walls — a little piece of Russia, cast out from its native place, abandoned in the snows of the taiga, but recreated and preserved there by Russian people.

Sasha would have liked to see these people, to see how they were now, but they were away at work. The village was quiet, peaceful, serene, and the riverbank was the same as it was at all the other villages along the Angara. There were boats and frames and nets.

They lived like everyone else. Those who had survived, that is. A group of children could be glimpsed in the distance on the hillside. They were the ones who had survived, had not frozen to death in the snow. Or maybe nobody had survived and they were new ones who had been born there.

Once again they took to the mighty river, now peaceful, the blue cliffs and limitless taiga, the sun in the bright blue sky, all of it created so lavishly and abundantly for the benefit of people. The quiet stretch of river, the little, nameless shallows. On the right bank was the village of Koda where all the Rukosuevs lived and where the special settlers had gone for help and not received any. Koda was also quiet and peaceful and showing no sign of life.

❧ 18 ❧

"Okay, I'll come." That had been easy to say yesterday, when they were sitting in the restaurant with music playing and pretty girls dancing with elegant men. That was her new, independent life. Kostya and his proposal to go to the Crimea had been part of that life, and Varya might have gone straight from the restaurant anywhere in the world with him. Next day, sitting in the dismal room in the shared apartment, everything seemed different, unreal, unrealizable. Yesterday seemed like a game or the idle chatter of a restaurant conversation. Vika's friends chatted like that about going abroad. Kostya's friends talked about going to the Crimea or the Caucasus.

What sort of person was this Kostya? A billiards player and a gambler. Look at the primitive ploys he used to try to seduce her: putting money in her purse, ordering the most expensive things on the menu and the best wines. He'd thrown money around. He'd shown off. He must have given dozens of girls this treatment. He must have asked dozens of them to go with him to the Crimea. She wasn't going to be taken in! She wasn't such an idiot as to get herself tangled up with a gambler! How would it look if he dropped her after the Crimea, or — worse — if he left her there? It would be all right if he gave her a return ticket to Moscow, but suppose he didn't, suppose he left her to make her own way back as best she could? Cable Nina, he might say, let your sister get you out of this mess. It'd be enough to give Nina a heart attack: you met someone in a restaurant yesterday, and today you go off with him to the Crimea! Anyway, why must it be today? What was the hurry?

She would speak to Sofya Alexandrovna about the room, as she had promised, and if Sofya Alexandrovna agreed, she would get to know Kostya better and possibly something would develop between them in time.

Kostya had brought her home from the restaurant in a taxi with Zoe, and as they said good-bye, he'd said, "Don't go out tomorrow, wait for my phone call. I'll call before noon."

It was already eleven o'clock and the sensible thing would be to go out, either to Sofya Alexandrovna or to Zoe at work. And then if he phoned in the evening, she'd say, "I waited all morning for you to call, and you didn't." Would he actually phone? Probably he'd already forgotten what he'd babbled about. How could he suddenly up and go to the Crimea, just like that? How could he stop work? How could he get tickets? It was hard enough to get a reservation if you were traveling on a warrant, but someone who came in cold off the street could wait at the station for weeks on end. She could also sit patiently at home. She'd promised to wait for his call, so she'd wait. It would be interesting to see whether he would or wouldn't telephone. How would he wriggle out of it?

At twelve-thirty Kostya called and said he had the tickets. The train would be leaving at four, he'd pick her up at three. He asked what floor she was on and the number of the apartment.

As soon as Varya heard his soft, masterful voice she was thrown into confusion. As he had the day before, he spoke slowly and precisely, with a slight drawl. At once, his face came back to her, and the strange, crazy, untrusting look he had fixed on her. She saw his broad build, his swagger, and at the same time his naïveté: he'd been surprised to hear that she lived on the Arbat, and was disappointed that she hadn't wished for the same thing he did. She also remembered how she had resented his friends, who were willing to eat and drink at his expense and then left him on his own. He'd said, "Maybe with you along I could become a real person." And at once he had frowned and looked ashamed of having made such an admission.

How could she possibly deceive him by breaking her word? She may only have made an idle promise, but it was a promise just the same. She simply couldn't bring herself to say "No."

"You don't have to come for me," she replied. "I'll be waiting for you on Nikolsky Street outside the second house from the corner."

"Fine, but don't be late or we'll miss the train."

Varya decided to get to Nikolsky Street by way of the connecting yard, to avoid a chance meeting with Nina at their entrance.

She had no need of a suitcase. Everything she was taking she was wearing, apart from another dress, a wrap, panties and a slip, a pair of stockings, a toothbrush, soap, and a comb, all of which she had crammed into a satchel.

It was just as well she hadn't taken a suitcase, as the passageway was closed. She remembered that all the passageways to the neighboring houses on the Arbat had been locked recently. Stalin had taken to traveling to his dacha along the Arbat and it had become a classified street. Varya had to go to Nikolsky Street by the normal route. Luckily, she met nobody, and even if she had, what would it matter? She was only walking along the street carrying her old school satchel.

She left a note for Nina: *"Gone to the Crimea with friends. Back in two weeks. Don't get bored. Varya."*

As she turned the corner of Nikolsky Street, she saw a taxi and, standing next to it, Kostya, in the same suit he had been wearing the previous evening at the Savoy.

They traveled in a sleeping-car. It was the first time Varya had seen one. When she and Nina had gone to their aunt in Kozlov (or Michurinsk, as it is now called), they had traveled in an ordinary car with reserved seats, just like all their friends. She knew there were cars with individual, closed compartments for four passengers, but a compartment for just *two* people, and with its own washbasin — that was something she'd never heard of. And here she was, actually traveling in just such a car and just such a compartment, all fitted out in velvet and brass, even with brass doorknobs. The corridor was carpeted, there were velvet curtains over the windows and a lamp with a beautiful shade on the table. A polite steward in uniform, who was particularly obliging to Kostya, served them tea in enormous glasses.

Varya realized that their car was for important, maybe even famous, people. There was a military man in the next compartment with four bars on his tabs, the highest rank. In the compartment beyond there was a beautiful middle-aged woman, most probably an actress, with her husband. Varya thought she might even have seen her in a film. And in other compartments there were probably commissars or deputy commissars, in their service jackets, boots, and breeches — the standard dress for high officials. But even the guard, and the wine-and-snacks steward, and the one who came around to take reservations for the restaurant car, and then the waiter and the barman in the restaurant car — they all treated Kostya with a special deference. There was something in his face and his bearing that instantly made these people single him out from the other passengers.

At first, Kostya's coarse familiarity jarred on her. He used the familiar form of address straightaway with all the service staff, but none of them took offense. They laughed at his jokes and were apparently only too happy to carry out his orders. For his part, Kostya accepted the efforts of the waiters with a benevolent smile, as was fitting for a man at the peak of success, who knew that his success acted like a magnet for others. But he was cheerful and friendly in his demeanor.

Kostya had no rank or official titles, nor had he any need of them. Independent, charming, and prepared to take risks, he always managed to get what nobody else could. Who, in the month of June at the height of the holiday season, could possibly have got hold of railway tickets for the Crimea on the very day the train departed, and in the sleeping car reserved for the most important people, at that? Only Kostya could, even though Varya reckoned he must have paid two or even three times more than the normal price. He gave tips to all and sundry, and he shared his good fortune with others.

He behaved with Varya as if they'd known each other a hundred years and there was nothing surprising in their traveling together in a compartment. He asked her nothing about herself, as if he already knew all about her. And, as if she knew everything there was to know about him, he told her nothing about himself. He talked about the places they were passing through as if it were the first time for him, as well. He did not make a pass. Not once did he try to embrace or kiss her. He was, as it were, starting from scratch with her. Only when they were standing in the corridor and looking out of the window did he lay his hand on her shoulder. It was a perfectly natural gesture and a natural position for him to adopt — they were a young couple admiring the view, the young husband with his hand on his young wife's shoulder. The rest of the passengers in the car indeed regarded them as newlyweds, smiling at them and, as it seemed to Varya, even admiring them, especially so in her case. She saw that Kostya was pleased and flattered by the admiration his "wife" was getting.

Only the thought of the night ahead tormented her. Naturally enough, Kostya was sure that, having agreed to go with him, she was also agreeing to do *it*. Men in general seemed to think that, if they've asked a girl to the theater or the movies or to go dancing with them, they were entitled to *it*, and they became offended and angry when they weren't allowed to have *it*. And here he was, taking her to the Crimea where they'd be sleeping in the same hotel room and he'd be buying her meals. No, this little arrangement did not suit her one bit, and she decided not to go along with it. She hadn't committed herself to that — the question hadn't come up. She was going to the Crimea for his sake — he had asked her and she had agreed, but that was all she had agreed to. If he liked the idea of wandering around the Crimea with a pretty young girl on his arm, then that was fine, she'd give him that pleasure. But no more.

It was growing dark outside. Kostya glanced at her and smiled. "Everything all right?" he asked.

"Yes, everything's fine." Varya answered him on the right note. But as the evening grew closer, she was becoming more and more nervous.

It would be different if she were in love with him or infatuated. But she wasn't, and she wasn't sure she ever would. Like everyone else, she was overwhelmed by Kostya's openhandedness and swagger, but she was used to more reserve than he had. In a word, Kostya was not properly brought up; he came from another world. Even though she had learned about life in the apartment-house yard, she was properly brought up. Her friends were also properly brought up. Lyova, Ika, Rina, and Big and Little Volya — they were all educated young people. Yet Kostya, the dominant member of the group, was not. The only reason they were all attracted to him was that he had the one thing none of them had — money — and he surrounded himself with these young people because they had something he lacked — education.

Of course, he was a man from the provinces, a man of the people, a character, an original. But that wasn't what appealed to Varya.

She was attracted by his independence. But she could be independent, too: she had only to work, even if she became his wife. Whether or not she wanted to become his wife, she didn't know. Obviously, they never had spoken of marriage. Was she going to become his mistress, then? But lovers *loved* each other. So, she would end up being a kept woman, and she had no intention of becoming that. Whatever she tried to tell herself, she knew that her arguments were shaky. Whatever was meant to happen would happen. She would have to put her foot down. She would have to end this farce.

❦ 19 ❦

They parted from the boatman and his silent wife in the village of Dvorets. Nil ran to the post office and came back with the inspector. Unloading his bags from the boat, he bustled about and argued, paying no attention to Sasha and Boris. His job had been to bring the two exiles to this place. He'd done it and that was that.

"Maybe we ought to go and call on the commandant?" Boris suggested.

"What for?" Sasha asked.

"To be sent on to Kezhma."

"We'll get there without his help. We've got our instructions."

"There could be difficulties if we don't report, if we don't show ourselves," Boris said with a frown. "It's not worth aggravating them over nothing."

Sasha did not want to go to the commandant's office. Another interview would only mean another humiliation. Boris was obsessed by his desire to start agitating immediately for some sort of position. He could think of nothing but Freda. Having heard that Dvorets might become a district center, he wanted to make contacts there, strike up acquaintanceships, in order to facilitate Freda's transfer to his place or his to hers. He was dreaming.

"Let's decide tomorrow," Sasha said.

"Okay," Boris agreed. "You stay with the things while I go find us somewhere to spend the night."

The sun had gone behind the clouds and a slender willow on the bank swayed in the chill breeze — the *khius* — that was coming off the river. Sasha threw his coat over his shoulders. He felt low. Why hadn't he wanted to see the commandant? Kvachazde would have gone and would have made demands. Boris had wanted to go, to try putting his affairs in some sort of order, as was his right. Yet Sasha hadn't wanted to go, and wouldn't. A week of traveling on the open river without a guard had given him a sense of freedom. Must it now come to an end? The idea seemed particularly wild and unnatural, here on the edge of the earth. No, he wouldn't go. Maybe he was deluding himself, but so be it!

Boris returned and announced triumphantly: "I'm about to introduce you to a little piece of the old empire — his majesty's chef! He cooked for Prince Yusupov and Rasputin. An amazing specimen."

He brought Sasha to a hut. A corpulent, red-nosed old man in a khaki quilted jacket and padded breeches tucked into tooled boots was sitting on a bench. His puffy, smooth-shaven face was as sleek as moss and his brush-cut gray hair gave him the appearance of a city man.

"Meet Anton Semyonovich!" Boris said excitedly. "Cook and chauffeur at the court of His Imperial Majesty."

"A life-chef, in other words," Sasha remarked, eyeing the old man with interest. The man was also watching Sasha attentively from under half-closed eyelids.

"Moscow is calling Anton Semyonovich back," Boris went on. "He's going to cook for ambassadors and envoys. *Cotolettes de volailles, sauce Provençal* . . . I used to know some chefs in Moscow. Nothing in your league, of course, but still they managed to survive. Do you know Ivan Kuzmych at the Grand Hotel?"

"Not as I recall," Anton Semyonovich replied blandly. He could hardly be expected to remember every Ivan Kuzmych, even if they all remembered him.

"A very decent cook, when there's anything to cook with, of course, is Maître Albert Karlovich," Boris continued.

"I know him," Anton Semyonovich replied shortly.

"He's well qualified and impressive." Boris was encouraged by the fact they had an acquaintance in common.

"It depends what he was impressive with," Anton Semyonovich said peevishly. "The first course, or the second or third . . ."

"That's precisely my point," Boris responded. "If there was anything to cook with. And for whom. If it was *boeuf Stroganov*, it was a dream...."

"And you really have to know how to prepare a *boeuf Stroganov*." Anton Semyonovich glanced at their hostess who was busily making their supper.

"When will you be leaving?" Boris asked.

"When they let me."

"Your release is being handled now, you say?"

"I work at the commandant's office. They also want to eat, so they're holding me back."

The hostess finished cleaning a fish and tossed it into a frying pan.

Nodding toward the stove, Boris said, "I can imagine what you'd do with that."

Anton Semyonovich maintained a majestic silence.

"You'll have to cook us a meal. When we get back to Moscow," Boris said with a laugh.

"I would right now, if I had the wherewithal," said Anton Semyonovich. He stared at Boris and his voice was badgering.

When Boris had given him some money he got up with an effort and went out.

"He's an alcoholic," Sasha said.

"No," Boris protested. "He just misses people."

Anton Semyonovich came back with a bottle of vodka.

"This is the most important thing. For the heart, I mean," he said.

He drank almost without eating, and became drunk at once. His neck turned purple, his face became angry. He was one of those capricious people who drink at someone else's expense and then insult him. Boris took no notice, but went on listing all the cooks and headwaiters he knew in Moscow.

"Why are you here?" Sasha asked.

Anton Semyonovich raised his bleary eyes, ready to curse these casual fellow drinkers, these idiots from Moscow whom he heartily despised because they allowed themselves so easily to be made fools of.

But it was not the delicate gaze of an idiot from Moscow that met his stare, it was the mocking, all-knowing look of the Moscow street, which was ready to give anyone an argument.

Lowering his eyes and breathing heavily, Anton Semyonovich spoke reluctantly.

"I was working in a district canteen. I wrote in the menu 'Lazy Soup.' Straight off the prosecutor asks me, 'Why "Lazy"?' They said I was mocking the shock-workers. I showed him a cookery book published in nineteen thirty which gives 'Lazy Soup.' All right? 'No, you're lying! Also, the book was written by a counter-revolutionary.' "

This was the most senseless story Sasha had yet encountered.

"Thank God it's all over," Boris said sympathetically. "Now they've let you go and you'll be heading home."

" 'Home'?" Anton Semyonovich looked at Boris with real hatred. "And where would *your* 'home' be? Some lousy kike *shtetl*?"

There! This was an object lesson for Boris: Don't fall for every dubious character you run into.

"Well, you can fuck off right now!" Sasha said. "Screw your mother through seven coffins!"

"Right!" Boris got up and bolted the door.

"What's the matter, boys?" Anton Semyonovich muttered in alarm. "I was only joking."

"It's your last joke, you piece of shit," Sasha retorted.

Boris threw himself onto Anton Semyonovich and pushed his head down onto the table.

"Let me go, boys," Anton Semyonovich whined, rolling his bleary eyes.

"Don't finish him off, Boris, leave something for me," Sasha said.

He found the ugly puffy face and bulging eyes repugnant. The scum! To think he could scoff at them! What a viper, what vomit! Some fellow exile, some colleague!

It was a revolting scene, but having reached the level of the gutter, it was the only way to deal with such scum.

"Apologize, you snake!"

"I apologize," Anton Semyonovich croaked.

"Now get the hell out!"

Boris booted him out of the door, threw him down the steps into the street, and then sat down on the bench exhausted.

"So much for His Majesty's life-cook," Sasha said with a laugh.

"And Freda has to live among such people," Boris said.

Next day they found the boat that was to take them on the next leg of their journey. It's owner, a member of a cooperative, agreed to take them if they would share the towing with him and the boatman. Kezhma was forty-five miles away, and if nothing went wrong they could make it in two days. They were in luck.

They carried their things down to the riverbank, where they found a large, heavily laden boat waiting. They were going to have to pull it. The owner was busy alongside. He was a fat-faced, jolly lad in a canvas cape and leggings, and high, thigh-length boots.

"Will we be leaving soon?" Boris asked.

"Once the paperwork is in order, we'll push off," the man replied.

"Listen, Sasha," Boris said, taking his friend aside. "We really should go and see the commandant. We'll tell him we've found a boat and loaded up and just came in to make ourselves known. Otherwise things could be hard for us in Kezhma. That bastard of an emperor's cook will have told them that we're here."

"You can do what you like, but I'm not going," Sasha replied in an offhand way. "And don't tell him I'm here. I've been given instructions to go to Kezhma, and that's where I'm going."

"Just as you like." Boris shrugged. "I'm going to see him all the same."

Boris was being driven by a demon. He was obsessed by the notion of marrying Freda and that was all he could think about. He did not want to miss any opportunity. Half an hour passed, then an hour, and he was still not back. The boat-owner had completed the documentation and had returned, but there was no sign of Boris.

"Better go find your mate," he said. "We've no time to lose; we'll have to leave without him."

Sasha didn't know what to do. He couldn't leave Boris behind, but he did not want to go to the commandant's office. Now it was late and they were bound to ask him why he hadn't reported at once.

"Let's wait a bit longer," he said.

At last Boris arrived and without a word took his suitcase out of the boat.

"What happened?" Sasha asked, knowing full well.

"They've sent me to Rozhkovo," Boris replied. His face was a blank.

Rozhkovo was a tiny village they'd passed the day before when they were with Nil.

"How can they do that without permission from the regional administrator?"

"They've got the right to fix a place of residence on their own authority."

"The hell with them! Come on, let's get going."

"They've taken my permit." Boris's voice was trembling.

"Calm down," Sasha said. "Go to Rozhkovo, then write to Kezhma or Kansk and ask for a transfer. There won't be any work for you in Rozhkovo. And I'll talk to the authorities when I get to Kezhma."

Boris waved an arm. "It's all over. I've been a fool!"

Sasha was sorry for Boris and sad to be parting from such a good friend, such a cheerful companion. They embraced and kissed each other. There were tears in Boris's eyes.

Sasha boarded the boat. The boatman pushed off and jumped in over the gunwale. They had to row for a while, as boats and nets were in the way of their towing the boat. Sasha gazed at the dejected figure of Boris. He was watching them leave. Then he picked up his suitcase and began to climb the hillside.

❧ 20 ❧

lone on the deserted river, Sasha was traveling to his future. All the others had reached their destinations, for better or worse; only he still had no idea what lay in store for him at his appointed place of exile. He would never see Volodya again, or Ivashkin, or the exiles they'd met in the various villages. He couldn't be certain he'd ever see Boris again, even though they'd be living in the same region. He felt sad at parting from the people with whom he'd covered the first few hundred miles of the journey.

The boatman was sitting at the tiller. He was a taciturn man of about forty with the severe face of an NCO. Sasha and the owner took turns towing the boat, and when they went through fast shallows they pulled it together.

The cooperative worker's name was Fedya. He was a sociable sort, a demobilized Red Army man, now working as a sales assistant in Mozgova, a village next to Kezhma, and he gave himself the grandiose title of manager of the village store. He had registered for some sort of course in Krasnoyarsk and would be starting his studies in the winter. With comic gravity, Fedya discussed the role of village sales assistant as the expression of state policy in the countryside. He was the new type of village activist, quick on the uptake, accepting everything on trust with cheerful willingness and without doubts and argument. He was also a songwriter and accordionist. The fact that Sasha was an exile was of no consequence to him. That was how things were organized — there were exiles, there always had been since the dawn of time, and they were people, like anyone else. But if Fedya were working on the commandant's staff right now and they told him to shoot Sasha, he would do it. Because that was how things were.

He asked Sasha about Moscow, what street he lived on, whether it was a good street, what other streets there were like, what his parents did, whether he'd been inside the Kremlin, if he had seen Comrade Stalin and the other leaders, and what the prices were in the shops. Everything amazed and delighted him. Moscow was the pinnacle of his dreams. He also admired Sasha, a genuine Muscovite! He treated Sasha to his Lux cigarettes, which were intended for the regional authorities.

Occasionally he sang "Forgotten and Abandoned," an exile's song that had become very popular on the Angara. He sang well: *"Nobody will come to see my grave. Only the nightingale will sing over it in the early spring. It will sing and whistle and fly away, and my lonely grave will be lonely again."*

Fedya had never gone prospecting for gold. It was no longer the custom. But before his army service, he'd served on Professor Kulik's expedition searching for the Tungus meteorite, but they hadn't found it because it was probably buried deep in the earth. Its crater had formed a lake, which then had turned into a swamp and was swarming with mosquitoes. There was no escaping them, so everyone got out. Fedya had also got out, especially as he was drafted. They started recruiting for the army here in 1926, the same year they opened the school. There had been no school previously, and he was the only boy in the village who could read and write, having been taught by his father. His father worked at a trading post and did business with the Tunguses.

"The people here are an uneducated, wild lot," Fedya said of the Tunguses in a good-natured way. "But they'll never cheat you. They call Russians Petrushka, Ivashka, Pavlushka, Kornilka.... They mangle the language. They love tobacco, they drink and smoke, men and women both, and the girls, and they all dress the same, man or woman, makes no difference. You can tell the difference because a man's got one pigtail and a woman's got two. They like beads, and they hang them on their fur coats and *kamasins*.

Kamus was the Tungus word for the skin from the foreleg of a deer or elk, and they made boots from it which they called *kamasins*.

Sasha was surprised by its similarity to the red Indian word *moccasin*. It proved to him that the Tunguses and the American Indians were related.

He would have liked to come here with an expedition to study the local dialects or with geologists to locate the untold wealth that was to be found in those parts. Instead, he had been exiled to a remote village without the right to leave it. Three years of his life would be wasted in idleness, of no use to himself or anyone else.

Why had it happened? Had it been his own fault? If he had talked about Krivoruchko, he'd be free now. But he hadn't talked, he had said that what was moral was what was in the interests of the proletariat.

But the proletariat were human beings and so proletarian morality was human morality. And it was immoral to save your own skin at the cost of another's.

Sasha spent the last night of his journey in the village of Zaimko, which was on an island with the unlikely name of Turgenev. The island was a dozen miles long, with the village of Aleshkino at its lower tip and Zaimko at its upper end.

The hut Sasha was brought to was extensive, and the yard was laid with boards. The woman of the house was a portly, imposing old lady who must once have been a beauty. Her husband was a bent old man with a ruddy complexion. Her sons — the elder was about forty, the younger thirty — had jet-black hair, hook noses, and thick eyebrows — typical Caucasians — and they both had wives and children.

"Father Vasily will be here shortly. You'll eat with him," the woman said.

The priest arrived. He had a light brown beard and the sort of kindly face seen in icons. He was wearing boots and a raincoat, which he removed, putting on a cassock. The woman served dried fish, eggs, and milk. As he ate, Father Vasily asked Sasha where he had come from and where he was going, where he was born and what his parents did. He said he was an exile, too. He did not ask why Sasha had been exiled, and said nothing about himself.

After supper they went into a small room containing Father Vasily's bed and a little table. It had a cloying, churchlike smell.

"Take off your clothes. We'll soak your feet and you'll feel better," Father Vasily suggested, bringing a kettle of hot water and a bowl. He gave Sasha soap and a towel. Sasha dipped his feet into the water and felt a momentary sense of weakness and a delicious feeling of release from fatigue.

Father Vasily leaned against the doorpost and watched Sasha with a benevolent look on his face. Now, when Sasha looked at him again, he seemed quite young, whereas at first he had thought him old. It was the beard and the cassock and the fact that he was a priest. In Sasha's mind priests were always old. In his mind, priests belonged to the prerevolutionary era.

"We could heat up the bath hut for you," Father Vasily said. "But it's on the bank and you'd catch cold coming back, and you have a journey in front of you."

"It's wonderful like this, thank you," Sasha replied.

"They use the bath hut here," Father Vasily went on. "In Moscow I imagine you had a bathroom?"

"Yes, that's right, a bathroom."

"Where I come from, they also use the hut," Father Vasily said, "or they just climb right on top of the stove and wash themselves there. The people here are much cleaner."

"Where are you from?" Sasha asked.

"The Korablin district of Ryazan province. Heard of it?"

"I've heard of Ryazan province, but not the district of Korablin."

"We come from southern parts, you and I," Father Vasily said with a smile. "You won't see an apple here, or a pear, and you're going to miss them. Red whortleberries, blueberries of different kinds, that's about it, plus cloudberries and small, forest blackcurrants. But no real fruit."

"I'll just have to manage without fruit," said Sasha, enjoying the warm water, which he swished with his fingers.

"Use soap on them, soap. Here, let me soap them for you." Father Vasily picked up the soap and the loofah.

"No, no, you don't have to," Sasha exclaimed.

But Father Vasily had already dipped the loofah into the hot water, rubbed soap onto it, and begun washing Sasha's feet.

"No, no, really!" Sasha protested, trying to get his feet out of the water, but afraid at the same time of splashing the floor.

"That's all right," Father Vasily said soothingly, as he scrubbed Sasha's feet. "It's difficult for you, but it's easy for me."

"No, really, thank you very much!" Sasha finally managed to get the loofah away from him.

"All right, you do it," said Father Vasily, wiping his hands on the towel.

"What do you do here?" Sasha asked him.

"I work. I help the households. They feed me and I'm grateful. The people here are good; they respond. If you are good to them, they repay you. But they will probably remove the exiles from here."

"Why?"

"Because of the kolkhoz. There's no private agriculture here, there's nowhere to earn a living, and they won't employ exiles in the kolkhoz. There are the special resettlers in some collective farms, but they won't take exiles there, either."

"Our hosts have strange sons, they look like Cherkesses," Sasha said.

Father Vasily smiled. "The good woman sinned in her youth. There was an exiled Caucasian lodging with them, they say. And she sinned."

"It seems to have happened more than once," Sasha observed. "There are two sons."

"Nine years he lived with them," Father Vasily explained readily. "Then he left. The children remained. Her husband regards them as his own, and they look on him as their father. Exiles have been sent here since time immemorial, the people have mixed with them. They live well and they've looked after me well. They don't have any particular religion, there never has been a real religion in these parts. It may be Siberia, but it still has to have a conscience of its own."

"Do you conduct services?" Sasha asked.

"The church has been closed down. But one talks and gives comfort."

Sasha dried his feet and pulled on his socks.

"Lie down and have a sleep; you need a rest," Father Vasily said.

"I'll empty the bowl out, then I'll lie down," Sasha replied.

"I'll take it," Father Vasily said, picking up the bowl. "You don't know where."

He returned with a cloth, wiped the floor, and took away the kettle.

Then he came back again and turned down the bedclothes.

"Lie down," he said.

"But what about you?"

"I'll find somewhere, I'm at home here. You lie down," he replied.

"Not for anything! I'll sleep on the floor."

"The floor's cold, you'll get a chill. I like to sleep on the stove," Father Vasily said.

"So do I," Sasha replied.

"Our hosts have already settled down for the night, so you'd disturb them," Father Vasily said. "I can lie down quietly, nobody will hear me."

He persuaded Sasha gently, but his was the gentleness of a man who would not be deflected from his duty. His duty was to give away whatever he had, and all he had, apart from a bowl of hot water, was a narrow iron bed.

Sasha lay down and felt the chill of the sheets. He had not slept between sheets for a long time, nor covered himself with a warm blanket. He stretched out, turned to the wall, and went to sleep.

He had learned to sleep lightly in prison and he was awakened in the morning by a rustling sound. It was Father Vasily getting up from the floor where he'd slept on a fur rug, covered by a fur coat.

"You said you'd sleep on the stove," Sasha said, sitting up.

"I tried to slip myself in on the stove," Father Vasily said cheerfully, "but it was fully occupied. I managed here perfectly and I've slept very well."

"You shouldn't give your bed up to everyone who passes through. There are lots of them and only one of you."

" 'Lots'?" Father Vasily objected. He was standing in front of a small pocket mirror that hung on the wall, combing his hair before tying it into a knot on the back of his neck. "There's been nobody for the past three months. They don't ship people off every day, and anyway the people are billeted in different houses. Maybe one or two people a year come to our house. I sleep in this bed every night, it's all the same to me, but you need rest wherever you can get it. Sleep, you've still got time."

He went out. Sasha turned over and went back to sleep.

He was woken again by Father Vasily who came to get his muddy boots and put on his cassock.

"Now you should get up and wash and we'll have breakfast."

For breakfast they were again given eggs, hot pies, and brick tea. Everyone had already gone off to work and only the woman of the house was left busying herself at the stove.

"How old are you?" Father Vasily asked Sasha.

"Twenty-two," Sasha told him. "How old are you?"

"Me?" The other man smiled. "I'm twenty-seven."

"How long did you get?"

Father Vasily smiled again. "Not long, just three years. I've already done two, there's only one left. I long for my native parts, but it will be sad to leave here, just the same. I've got used to this place."

"And you should stay here," the woman said. "Where will you go? They won't let you serve God in Russia."

Father Vasily turned to Sasha. "It will be tedious for you at first, then you'll become accustomed. Don't let your spirits fall, don't become bitter at heart, and remember good always follows bad. I remember reading Alexander Dumas, where he writes that misfortunes are like the beads of a rosary, strung on the thread of our life. The wise man will calmly say each bead. He was a secular writer who wrote adventure novels, but how well and how wisely he put it."

There was a knocking at the window. It was time for Sasha to go.

"How much do I owe you?" he asked the woman.

"You don't owe me anything," she said, waving her hand.

Father Vasily took him by the elbow. "Don't offend her."

He accompanied Sasha outside and helped him with his suitcase. The boatman untied the towrope, pushed the boat off, and sat down at the tiller. Fedya hung the harness across his shoulder and moved forward, gradually taking up the slack in the towrope and watching the boat behind him to see where the boatman was steering it. Once he was sure it was properly on course, he said: "As soon as we reach the end of the island, we'll cross to the mainland."

Sasha held out his hand to Father Vasily.

"Good-bye, and thank you for everything."

Fedya called cheerfully, "We're off!"

"May God protect you," Father Vasily said.

Part III

asha's place of exile had been determined as the village of Mozgova, eight miles farther up the Angara from Kezhma. He found a good room in a large, substantial house owned by a widow with two grown sons. The man she lived with was not an Angaran, but an ex-soldier who had settled here; her sons had opposed her remarriage, having no wish to share their property with a stepfather. Now the household had been incorporated into the kolkhoz, but when the old soldier got drunk, he would remember the long-standing offense and go on a rampage in the village, red-faced, and threaten to kill the two boys. They would catch him and lock him in a storeroom until he had slept it off.

The younger son, Vasily, was a fine-looking man with chiseled features. He'd no doubt slept with all the girls in the village, as the morals there were rather loose. He would get home first thing in the morning, if at all. Sasha hardly saw him, and when he did, Vasily would smile silently. Although he was not talkative, he was friendly.

The elder son, Timofei, was not interested in girls — he didn't "go out on the town" in the evenings, and he slept only at home. Without asking, he would come into Sasha's room and look at all his things, asking what this was for, and that? He looked distrustful and said little. His lack of manners jarred, but Sasha patiently answered all his questions. This was the real people, the *narod!* Great, mighty, but ignorant and uneducated. Like most Russian intellectuals, Sasha always felt guilty in their presence.

On one occasion Sasha went with Timofei to an island to help with the haymaking. He didn't know how to use a scythe, but he was determined to try. Sasha rowed while Timofei steered the boat. There were two scythes in the bottom of the boat, a whetstone for sharpening, and masks against the insects — a coarse, horsehair one for Timofei, and a silken net for Sasha, bought on Soloveichik's advice in Kansk.

Seeing Sasha's mask, Timofei said: "You city people have everything, and us peasants have nothing, we haven't been anywhere, but here you are, a burden on our backs." In his primitive way, Timofei was expounding the theory of surplus value: the peasants created material wealth and people like Sasha produced nothing.

This was in Sasha's mind as he rowed with all his strength to keep the boat from being carried below the island by the strong current.

"They exile you to sit on our backs," Timofei went on. "You live by our blood and sweat."

Sasha did not reply. What could he say? If Timofei would only think about it. . . . But he didn't want to think about it. He had an exile sitting there in front of him, a man without rights; it was a chance to taunt.

"Scared now, are you? Scared?" Timofei mocked. "I'll give you one with the scythe, chuck you in the river, and you'll vanish without trace. And nothing'll happen to me; I'll tell them anything I want on the mainland. You're a counter, a troksist, who's going to care about you? Yeah!"

Sasha rowed to the shore, jumped into the water, and pulled the boat in. Timofei remained sitting at the helm, grinning, and only when Sasha had pulled the boat right out of the water and dropped the painter did he climb out onto the bank.

"Why didn't you drown me?" Sasha asked.

"If you annoy me, I'll really drown you," Timofei said threateningly.

"You should have drowned me," Sasha said.

"How come?"

"Because I'm going to kill you right now," Sasha said.

Timofei took a step back. "Come on, stop fooling around!"

They were on a deserted island on the edge of the world. Somewhere on it there were reapers at work. The mosquitoes and flies were swarming and humming in the air and there was no other sound to be heard on the river. There was no world, no humanity, only the two of them, and at last Abel was going to repay Cain for his crimes.

Without taking his eyes off Sasha, Timofei slowly backed away, then he turned and leaped toward the boat and the scythes. Sasha caught up with him and hit him in the back with his fist. Timofei fell into the water, got up and turned, and Sasha punched him in the face. Timofei fell again and, spitting out water, crawled to the bank.

He wouldn't kill Timofei; he wasn't going to suffer because of this piece of shit. Timofei didn't get up, but lay on the bank looking up at Sasha in terror. What a revolting sight!

It was going to be a long three years!

Sasha went to the boat and threw out the scythes and the whetstone and Timofei's mask, then he took the oars and rowed back to the village.

At supper, Sasha announced that he would be moving to another house.

"Don't you like it here?" the old soldier asked. "You taught Timoshka a lesson, and a good one, too. He's nothing but threats, he's mean and nasty, never forgives anything. But you're really tough — you gave it to him! Go with Vaska, he's got all the girls, he can spare one for you."

"The teacher's been giving him the eye," Vasily said, laughing.

Timofei said nothing, and averted his eyes.

It was a good house, but living under the threat of possible vengeance was repellent, and also risky, given his situation. The next morning, Sasha transferred his belongings to another lodging.

This hut had a parlor as well as a kitchen, and that was the room they gave Sasha. His new landlords, an old man and woman, were poorer than the previous ones, but they fed him tolerably. They worked occasionally at the kolkhoz, but were home most of the time. They didn't quarrel; the old woman called her husband "my twisted one." He was small and slightly lopsided. It was quiet in the house. The old woman poked around in the oven and the old man chopped wood in the yard, or pottered about doing odd jobs. The room smelled of freshly washed floors, the time-blackened walls were hung with portraits of Lenin and Kalinin, and alongside them were photographs of the royal family in an open carriage, cut out of the magazine *Niva*.

Sometimes the old man would be gone all day and when he returned and was asked what he'd done at the kolkhoz, he would reply: "Whatever they tell me to do, I do it."

Kolkhoz was a relative term in those parts. Collectivization had been started later than in other provinces, and after Stalin's "dizzy with success" speech — and his brief retreat from collectivization — the kolkhozes had disintegrated totally. They had only begun to be reassembled a year and a half or two years after the others. What was there to be collectivized, after all? The short growing season barely produced enough grain to feed a family. And to market their grain, they would have to take it either four hundred miles by the sleigh road or down the Angara, through the rapids and the fast shallows, which was impossible.

As for cattle, each household had had about ten cows, so there were two thousand in the village, plus about a thousand horses. The cows had all been put into one herd and driven into the yards of the resettled kulaks, where more than half the stock had perished in the harsh winters. The remaining cows were returned to their original yards, not as private property, but as kolkhoz livestock. They hadn't raised their herds only to watch them die before their eyes. Who was going to milk them? Were they supposed to deliver the milk to Kezhma for the authorities? The only thing that remained was hunting. Before collectivization, they used to trade their squirrel pelts at the fur agency cooperative. But now they had to give them to the collective farm, which kept half their value. It was from here in Mozgova that the main path to the Tunguses lay, to the Vanarava. So the hunters hid their skins, then took them to the Tunguses where the trading posts paid full value.

Then the administrative center woke up — fur production had dropped. A loss of hard currency! A commission was sent. They hemmed and hawed and finally decided that the hunters were being distracted by agriculture — that was the trouble. Grain production wasn't profitable, it brought no good to the state, it was harmful, a dead loss, so the region was declared nonagricultural: it was to specialize in fur; and grain would be imported from agricultural provinces, just as it was for the Evenki tribe, who were hunters.

Now the kolkhozniks sold furs to the Tunguses in order to get grain, because they weren't allowed to grow their own, and none was being imported — it had somehow been forgotten. They explained to the authorities that the squirrels had migrated north, and it now took three weeks to reach them. Therefore they had to winter in new places, but the Tunguses destroyed their winter shelters, and it had all but come to shooting it out with them. In actual fact, they'd never had such good relations with the Tunguses, not only because of the grain they traded, but more for the vodka. The Evenki could get everything they needed at the trading posts. And they drank together.

These remote Siberian villages, which had once supplied the state with up to one hundred thousand squirrel pelts a year and had been self-sufficient, driving their herds into Irkutsk, feeding themselves with their own bread, milk, and fish, had now ceased hunting and sowing grain, reduced their herds to a tenth of their previous size, and, like the other Angara villages, they were now a burden on the Altai peasants, who barely had enough to eat themselves.

And yet the Angara did not suffer from the famine of the early 1930s. It was saved by the great distances, by its remoteness from the authorities, and its ancient, natural economy. It was fed by the river. All kinds of fish came here to spawn. You could scoop fish out of it with your hat. The forest fed them with berries and mushrooms. The cattle in their yards, though they belonged to the collective, also fed them. The collective farm had been established for three years. There were domestic fowl, pigs and piglets, and sheep kept for their wool, but they had not been pooled. Most important, there were no planned contributions, no state procurements, apart from furs, and even there the plan was reduced from year to year, while it was debated whether the region would be declared either nonagricultural or non-fur-trapping. The region was finally declared a dairy-trading region, and they were ordered to deliver fresh milk daily to the regional authorities, which the Kezhma kolkhoz was already failing to supply adequately. Mosgova delivered the milk regularly and without difficulty. There were two hundred cows left out of the two thousand — they just loaded ten churns of milk onto a cart and sent it off.

The village Sasha found himself in was not completely impoverished. They valued money. He paid twenty rubles for room and board, and sometimes he brought home a can of sour cream. He repaired the communal milk separator.

It was a Swedish model from the turn of the century, a so-called Laval Alpha-C, with plates that were very difficult to dismantle and clean. Sasha had first worked on a separator three years before at the institute during production practice. A combine team had been sent to a village and one of the dispossessed kulaks still had a separator, but nobody knew how to use it. A mechanic from the harvesting team had taken it apart, cleaned it, and put it back together. Sasha decided out of sheer curiosity to do the same thing here, and now it was usable again. But the machine was old: the thread on the main spindle was nearly worn out and the nut barely held. But there was nothing in the village with which to cut a new thread.

"Give it to the farm manager," Sasha said. "Let him take it to Kezhma where they can cut a new thread; otherwise it'll fall apart one of these days." But either the kolkhozniks did not tell the manager, or the manager didn't understand the problem.

The separator served as a social club for the married women. To gather around it meant an hour or so when they could get out of the house and chat while they waited their turn. It gave a brief respite. The women here did everything: the fields, the kitchen garden, the river, the cattle, the home. The true Anagaran male was a hunter, a nomad who hated work and especially hated domesticity. Soloveichik had been right: at twenty the women were workhorses, at thirty they were broken nags. Their best time was between thirteen and sixteen, before marriage. And although the young girls did equal work both in the kolkhoz and the home with the grown-up women, in the evenings they went "on the town." The girls walked in front, in two rows, singing, and behind them, also in two rows, came the boys, with an accordion player. They paraded to the edge of the village, then came back, turned around again, and kept this up until it began to get dark, when they would pair off and find a barn or hayloft. If a husband reproached his wife, it was most likely because she was a virgin, and that meant she'd been no good to anyone in her youth.

Much to his surprise, Sasha found that the incident with Timofei had raised his prestige among the villagers: an exile hadn't been afraid to beat up a local boy. Exiles, even in the time of the tsar, had not been forgiven for stealing or drunkenness, and a fight would be settled by the entire village; the guilty man would never be found. True, many had been ordinary criminals — the "politicals" hadn't got into fights. But this one, as the cooperative worker Fedya told it, was from Moscow itself, and he wasn't afraid of anyone. He had methods of his own. Fedya, telling the tale, used unfamiliar words to give greater weight to his own knowledge.

It was thanks to Fedya that Sasha ended up in Mozgova.

Unlike the sleepy NKVD officer in Boguchansk, the chief in Kezhma, Alferov, was an active, desperately emaciated type who looked at Sasha inquiringly and snapped: "How did you get here?"

"On the cooperative boat from Mozgova."

"Has it left yet?" he asked.

"No," Sasha replied.

"Go back on it to Mozgova," Alferov decided, apparently figuring Sasha would be less trouble there, and the boat was ready to leave.

Sasha was satisfied. He would be eight miles from Kezhma and things were all right for him, he was already known there.

One evening Fedya asked Sasha to come out onto the street. Sitting on a log in a side lane were Lariska, a divorcée, an unattractive, pimply woman who squinted, and Marusya, Fedya's sister, a square-built, good-natured girl with a broad, flat face.

Fedya sat down on the log next to Lariska and said to Sasha: "Sit with my sister."

Marusya looked at Sasha encouragingly, as if to say, *Come and sit by me, put your arm round my shoulders, you can see how broad and soft they are, and my bosom, too, it's warm, you can warm yourself.*

Nevertheless, Sasha sat down a little way off. Lukeshka in Boguchansk had been lively and adolescent, she had played with him in a naïvely immodest way. She had reminded him somewhat of Katya. But he had no idea what to say to this fat lump, and she no doubt had no need to say anything. She'd just fall down with him in a hayloft. . . .

The sound of songs and an accordion came from the street. The schoolteacher was passing. She was known as Zida. Her name was Nurzida Gazizovna and she was a Tatar, about twenty-five or -six. They also called her Zina, Zinka, but her pupils called her Zinaida Yegorovna. She walked unhurriedly past the side street where Sasha was sitting with his new friends, and she looked at them.

Smiling pleasantly, Marusya said to Sasha: "She's after you."

"Why me?"

"You looked at her. Want me to introduce you?"

Sasha liked her frank benevolence: If you don't want me, find someone else, or I'll find one for you. It was simple, and there was no offense.

"No need," he said.

"What don't you like about her?"

"She's skinny," Fedya answered for him.

"But she wears city clothes — dresses and silk pants," Lariska added.

"She's nothing but skin and bone under her silk pants," Fedya protested. He got up and stretched. "Come on, Lariska, the pies will get cold."

"I wrapped them in wax paper; they'll be hot."

In the yard Lariska said: "You go up to the hayloft, I'll bring the pies."

They climbed up to the hayloft by a wooden staircase. It smelled of last year's hay. There was a bright moon, and Marusya's round face shone white. Sasha sensed her expectant look and heard her heavy breathing. Fedya felt around under a mattress and a bottle appeared shining in his hand. There was a clink of glasses.

Sasha retained a hazy memory of that night. Lariska and Marusya drank little, but to show that he could keep up with Fedya, he drank half a glass of raw spirits, which burned his throat, then he drank water, and ate some dried fish. Then, to bolster his courage, he began boasting of how they drank in Moscow. He really got going and didn't give a damn; he broke loose from his self-control and from his bitterness. He asked for more vodka, but Fedya held the bottle upside down to show there was no more.

Then he threw up, not in the hayloft, but outside on the ground, which smelled of dung. Fedya and Marusya bent their white faces down to his, thrust a ladle against his teeth, and then poured water over his head and neck. He got up and tried to walk, but again was sick, convulsed by long painful spasms. The stars were shining in the sky, dogs were barking somewhere. They tried to drag him along, but he wouldn't go. Instead he crawled into his room through the window. He didn't want to disturb his hosts or disgrace himself.

He heard them getting ready to go off to work the next morning and he pretended to be asleep, and then in fact he went back to sleep, and when he awoke the house was empty. He got up and went down into the cellar where he was pleasantly engulfed by the damp, earthy chill. He found a wooden-lidded pot of sour cream and took it up to the kitchen. From under a cloth he took a loaf of white bread, still warm and soft, dipped it in the sour cream, and ate it. He felt better and slept until the evening, going outside only just before supper. His hosts said nothing, but Sasha was sure they knew.

He had completely recovered by the next day, but his mood was foul. He did not want to go out and perhaps run across Fedya, Marusya, and Lariska, because he was embarrassed at the thought of the mocking looks they would give him. He couldn't understand his behavior the night before. He had drunk too much many times, but he'd never boasted and bragged like that before. Still, he had to go to the cooperative, because he had run out of cigarettes. Fedya welcomed him with a smile. How's the head? Okay? Good! He sold him the cigarettes and matches, and suggested he buy a guitar and a beginner's primer. Three instruments had been sent, but nobody knew how to play them. Sasha didn't buy one, something he would later regret, as he could have learned to play.

He met Marusya in the street. She was bringing water from the river on a yoke. She smiled at him as if nothing had happened.

The village was utterly indifferent to his carouse; he had worried for nothing. Getting drunk was not an event. Moreover, Fedya had forbidden the girls to say anything, since he'd helped himself to the vodka from the cooperative.

The only person to mention it to Sasha was Vsevolod Sergeyevich, an exile from Moscow. He was a lean, sinewy man of about thirty, though he looked older. He was bald, and had a fleshy nose and a thin, sardonic mouth, but his laugh was good-natured.

He didn't say why he had been exiled: that wasn't done here. En route, companions told each other, but here they only mentioned the article they had been sentenced under. Most of them were under Article 58, Clause 10.

Vsevolod Sergeyevich had begun his exile in Kezhma and then landed up in Mozgova. He'd had an affair with a girl who worked in the district·financial office at Kezhma and such behavior by an exile was prohibited. He could have been sent farther away, another seventy-five miles at least, as the distances there were enormous, but he was allowed to continue working in Kezhma, though that meant a sixteen-mile hike every day. In the spring, however, they fired him, as another bookkeeper had been sent from the regional center. Now Vsevolod Sergeyevich earned his keep in Mozgova. He did some carpentry, mowed and gathered hay, dug vegetable gardens, went fishing with a drag-net, and astounded the natives with his short underpants. They'd never seen such things before, as they swam in their longjohns. He helped the kolkhoz accountant, a boy who had been trained in Kansk.

But his whole life revolved around women. He talked about them openly and cynically. Seeing Sasha frown, he said without offense, "What's left for us in this life? What do you intend to do? The only pleasure here is the women, there's nothing else. Value the crumbs the commandant leaves for us. You're a man, that means you're still a human being."

These notions grated on Sasha, but he became friends with Vsevolod Sergeyevich nevertheless. There was a touch of Moscow of the twenties about him, the Moscow of Sasha's childhood, in the words and phrases he used, his jokes, and the Gypsy songs he sang in his pleasant baritone voice. *"My love's delight lives in a chamber high, where no one can ascend . . ."* He carried himself with the lack of constraint characteristic of that period, and, as Sasha would realize later, the humanity of it, too. There was nothing in him of the Muscovite of the 1930s. Obviously he'd been away a long time.

When he heard that Sasha had had too much to drink, he didn't comment except to say with a frown: "Those aren't any friends for you. You should make friends with the teacher. She's charming and intelligent. I can't imagine how she ended up on the Angara."

"It surprises me, too," Sasha confessed. "Hiding herself away in a hole like this."

"Probably the result of a romantic disaster," Vsevolod Sergeyevich said. "But a woman approaching thirty, on her own, and an oriental to boot — that's quite a delicacy!"

"She doesn't look like a Tatar," Sasha observed.

"The Siberian Tatars are completely russified," Vsevolod Sergeyevich explained. "The Tatars of Tobolsk and Tomsk and Kuznetsk, they're just Russians, just Siberians. As for being Muslim, what Muslims are there now, anyway? And you won't find a Russian Orthodox, either. But they have preserved their national character, their mentality and outlook, especially the women. The women are the men's slaves, faithful, devoted, yet somehow arrogant. This one has the look of a Tatar princess. Frankly, I haven't got anywhere with her, and I've no idea why. You're a different matter, though. You've come just in time, Sasha! Nothing lasts, and all that's left for us are the women. Devote yourself to her, enjoy yourself. Believe me, women like her are a rarity these days. She'd be a catch even in Moscow."

"It might make difficulties for her," Sasha said.

"I doubt it. They can't get another teacher for this place. And as far as we know there's no informer here, and nobody is out to get her. Obviously, you don't have to put up posters announcing it. At the worst, you'd be sent to Savino or Frolovo, but the lady's worth it."

Compared with the stocky, broad-shouldered village girls, with their bare feet and long, billowing skirts, Zida seemed alien and defenseless. Small and thin, in her short little dress, she looked like an adolescent. She was the lonely outsider who'd come as the schoolteacher to a tiny village deep in the taiga, where study was regarded as a waste of time and school a burden.

She came into the store when Sasha was there, not by accident. She had a direct, calm, and slightly distant look in her gray eyes. Her smile was sweet and good-natured. She spoke to Sasha as to an acquaintance — in the village everyone knew everyone else. But there was something else in her look.

Fedya was complaining: for the second year now they hadn't sent any soap or brick tea or kerosene. At least they'd sent some calico, but not the colors the villagers wanted to buy. Zida listened attentively to Fedya's troubles and responded just enough to show that when there was nothing one could do, at least one understood.

Sasha leafed through some booklets on flax and cotton that had been sent. Neither flax nor cotton was grown there.

"We have some books at the school — perhaps you'd like to borrow some?" Zida said.

"Yes, that'd be fine!"

"Come to the boats this evening and I'll bring some."

She said it simply and naturally, but she chose the precise moment when Fedya was going into the storeroom at the back.

They met on the riverbank by the boats, which smelled of rotten wood, fish, and tar. She was wearing a coat buttoned all the way up, but her head was uncovered. Her evenly shaped face, with its etched features, looked very young in the moonlight, like a young girl's, but her eyes were those of an experienced, grown woman.

"I don't know what books you like. Come to my place and have a look."

Sasha pulled her toward him and kissed her soft lips. She closed her eyes and he could feel her heart pounding. She pulled back and gave him a quick glance and, gently releasing herself from his embrace, whispered: "Wait!"

Straightening her shawl, she took his hand and led him along the bank, then by a path past the little blackened bathhouses and up the hill.

"Wait here until I light the lamp, then come in."

Sasha leaned against the wall of a bathhouse. A light came on in a window. He leaped over the wicket fence and crossed the yard. The door was open.

He left before dawn, returning to his own place by the same path they had taken past the bathhouses, then along the bank, and he reentered the village from the other end.

They had not arranged their next meeting. The day lay ahead of them and they would find an opportunity. But it did not turn out that way; they did not see each other before Zida had to leave for Kezhma.

Late that evening Sasha went out onto the street. The village was asleep, but there was a light in Zida's window. Again, he jumped over the fence, and turned the handle of the door, which opened with a little squeak.

"Why don't you lock your door?"

"What if you came?"

Zida spoke pure Russian, with no trace of an accent, but in all other respects she was, as Vsevolod Sergeyevich had correctly observed, an oriental woman — obedient and passionate, aroused by Sasha's first touch . . . "What are you doing to me . . . ?" And combined with this there was an oriental reserve, even mystery. Of herself she said little, and with reluctance. Once she suddenly mentioned her husband and quickly corrected herself — ex-husband. At her parents' home in Tomsk was her daughter, Rosa, who was already six years old. Zida had completed her teachers' training in Tomsk, had taught for five years, and then had come here. "It was all so boring there." But why she had chosen to come to the depths of the taiga she did not say: "It turned out that way." She silently agreed with Sasha that their relationship must remain secret. Sasha wanted to save her from difficulties, though she knew perfectly well that it would be impossible to keep such a thing secret in the village. But she did not protest, she made no demands, there were no tears or quarrels or expressions of tempestuous joy or confessions of love. Only once when he awoke in the night did he see that she was not asleep but was leaning on her elbow and watching him.

He stroked her cheek.

"Why aren't you asleep?"

"I'm thinking."

"What are you thinking about?"

She laughed.

"I was wondering where such handsome men are born."

2

One day they came running for Sasha — the separator had broken down again. He'd told them countless times to take it to the machine and tractor station, but they still hadn't done so.

He went nevertheless. The women were standing by the separator, gossiping. The chairman of the kolkhoz, Ivan Parfenovich, was there, too. He was a tough, thickset peasant, and though Sasha didn't know him, he did know that he was severe and apt to use his fists to teach his kolkhozniks. He was talking to Zida. She cast a glance at Sasha.

"Hello," Sasha said cheerfully. "What's happened?"

He could see for himself what had happened: the separator had fallen apart. It was only to be expected.

"Is that your work?" asked Ivan Parfenovich.

"Why mine?" Sasha replied. "It's Swedish work. This separator was made by Swedes."

"The Swedes, the Swedes," Ivan Parfenovich muttered morosely. "You broke it, you fix it."

"I didn't break it. Nobody broke it. This machine's a hundred years old. The thread on the spindle's worn out. I've told them over and over again that it had to be taken to the machine station to have a new thread cut."

"Who did you tell?"

Sasha indicated the women. "I've told everyone — they've all heard me say it."

"You shouldn't have told them, you should have told me, for Christ's sake!"

"I'm not on your staff, as far as I know. I'm not under any obligation to you for anything."

"You snake, you wrecker!" Ivan Parfenovich exploded. "First you break the machine and now you want to blame it on the women!"

"Don't talk to me like that!" Sasha snapped back.

"What! I'm not supposed to talk to you? Damned troksist! Who do you think you're talking to?" Ivan Parfenovich shook his fists.

"I'm talking to an idiot, understand?" Sasha said, and laughed right in the man's face. "Just remember that: an idiot."

He turned and stalked off. Ivan Parfenovich said something to his back, but Sasha didn't hear what it was.

That evening a cart drew up outside Sasha's house and a peasant he didn't recognize jumped down, came in, and handed a note to him. It said:

To Administrative Exile Pankratov, A.P.:

On receipt of this you are to appear at once before the NKVD officer for the Kezhma district, Comrade Alferov, in the village of Kezhma.

It was signed by Alferov, quite a sophisticated signature, without flourishes.

Alferov impressed Sasha as an intelligent man, and it seemed strange that he was no more than a district officer. Not that his rank was apparent, as he wore civilian clothes, just as he had the last time Sasha had seen him.

His office was the front half of the hut where he also lived. He received Sasha in the domestic part of the house, in the large bedroom. A third doorway led to the kitchen, through which a cold draft was blowing in from the yard.

"Sit down, Pankratov." Alferov pointed to a chair next to a table. He sat on the other side of it. He looked friendly and animated. Sasha had the impression he was hung over. "So, how are you settling down in your new place?"

"I've settled in."

"Have you got decent lodgings, decent landlords?"

"Yes, everything's fine."

"Good, that's very good."

Alferov stood up and removed the glass from the lamp hanging above the table, lit the wick, adjusted the flame, and replaced the glass. The corners of the parlor went dim; the table was illuminated and on it Sasha saw there was a sheet of paper and at once guessed that it was a complaint against him.

"So," Alferov said, sitting down squarely on his chair. "So, everything's fine, everything's all right . . . good, good. But this" — he indicated the paper — "this, Pankratov, is not so good. They're complaining about you: premeditated sabotage, that's what it says — by means of sabotage you damaged the village's only separator. What have you got to say for yourself?"

"I did not damage the separator," Sasha replied. "I cleaned it three times, and to do that I had to dismantle it, which is quite complicated. When I dismantled it the first time, I noticed that the thread on the end of the spindle was wearing out and that the retaining nut wouldn't hold much longer, and that the machine ought to be taken to the machine station to have a new thread cut. Any mechanic or metalworker would confirm this. I told them this and I repeated it the second and third time when I fixed it. It is not my fault. The blame belongs to the people who didn't take it to the machine station in time. I couldn't take it myself, as I don't have the right to leave the village."

Alferov listened to him attentively, shifting his position in his chair and looking at Sasha from time to time in a peculiar way. His lunchtime drink had evidently inclined him to conversation. He had plenty of time.

"Right," he said. "So, the first time you dismantled the machine you noticed the thread was worn. Have I got that right?"

"That's right, and immediately I said —"

"Wait a moment. You say that any mechanic or metalworker would confirm that the machine is no use with the thread in that state?"

"Certainly, they'd confirm —"

"Yes, yes, Pankratov. A mechanic would confirm that at this moment — I repeat, at this moment — the thread is gone. But no mechanic could confirm that the thread had gone a month ago, when you first fixed the machine. And suppose I asked this mechanic, 'Could Citizen Pankratov, when tightening that nut, have overtightened it and stripped the thread?' What would he say? He'd say, 'Yes, that's possible, and he might have put the nut on askew, tightened it, and destroyed the thread.' Doesn't that make sense?"

"No, it doesn't," Sasha replied.

"Really?" Alferov expressed surprise. "And I thought myself good at logic. How am I being illogical, Pankratov?"

"When I took the separator apart the first time, I said right then and there that it ought to be taken to the machine station to have a new thread cut."

"To whom did you say this?"

"To everyone who was there."

"And who was there?"

"The women, the women kolkhoz workers, about twenty of them."

Alferov grinned at him.

"Pankratov, you're a clever, educated man! You told them, but what, in your view, were they supposed to do about it?"

"They ought to have reported it to the kolkhoz manager."

"Pankratov! These are uneducated peasant women who've never even heard such words as thread, nut, spindle. They can't even pronounce them! They wouldn't dare say anything to the manager — he'd only tell them to mind their own business. In any case, they don't want the machine taken away — it would be taken away and never brought back. Somehow it kept working. You were the one who ought to have told the manager, but you didn't, and as a result the machine is out of action. Well, what about that for logic?"

"Not very good."

"No? Why?"

"I don't work for the kolkhoz. I didn't take any money for cleaning the separator, I just wanted to help the people. There's only one question: Did I or did I not damage the machine? And since, when I dismantled it the first time, I said in public, in front of witnesses, that it couldn't be repaired, that shows I didn't damage it. And the fact that I said so can be confirmed by everyone."

Alferov looked at him with a smile and then said, suddenly becoming quiet and even a bit sad: "But will they confirm it?"

"Why shouldn't they?" Sasha replied uncertainly. Suddenly he was aware of the shakiness of his situation.

"Ah, Pankratov, Pankratov," Alferov said, still speaking quietly and with sadness, "you are so naïve. Where did you live in Moscow?"

"In the Arbat."

"So, we're neighbors," Alferov continued pensively, though he didn't say where he had lived in Moscow. "Yes, Pankratov, you are naïve. Imagine summoning those peasant women to court. First of all, can you provide their names, family names and first names? I doubt it. Second, they're all scared to death of the court and would do anything to get out of appearing. Supposing nevertheless you managed to drag two or three of them into court, there's only one thing they'd keep droning: 'We know nothing, we heard nothing, we saw nothing.' So, on one side of the scales there's you, an exiled counterrevolutionary, and on the other side there's the chairman of the kolkhoz, the power, the authority, the keeper of their fate. For whom will they testify? Come down from the clouds, Pankratov, and try to evaluate your position realistically. You won't have a single witness. Whereas the chairman of the kolkhoz will have the entire village as his witnesses. And the prosecutor will have all the grounds he needs to accuse you of causing premeditated damage to agricultural machinery, that is to say, sabotage. I take it you read the newspapers?"

"I haven't received any mail yet."

"But you read them in Moscow. Didn't you notice? There's sabotage everywhere, sabotage of tractors, combines, threshing machines, binders — sabotage everywhere. Is it really true? Are they really breaking everything on purpose? Who's causing the damage? The kolkhozniks? Why should they? It turns out there's no other answer for it: for hundreds of years our peasants have known only one piece of machinery, and that was the ax. Now we've put them to work on tractors and combine harvesters; we've given them trucks to drive, and they break them because they don't understand them, because they are not trained, because they are ignorant in the technological and every other sense. So what can we do? Wait until the countryside becomes technically literate and overcomes its ancient backwardness? Wait until the peasants change the character it has taken them centuries to form? And meanwhile should we let them break the machinery and let them learn on it that way? We cannot condemn our machinery to demolition and destruction; it has cost us too much blood to get it. Nor can we wait — the capitalist countries will strangle us. We've only got one method, it's a difficult one, but it's the only one, and that's *fear*. Fear embodied in the single word *wrecker*. You damaged a tractor, it means you're a wrecker, you get ten years. For a mowing machine or binder it's also ten years. So now the peasant begins to think, he scratches his head, he starts to take care of his tractor, he gives a bottle to someone who may know just a fraction about machinery — show me, help me, save me. A few days ago I was strolling along the riverbank and I noticed a kid sitting in his motorboat and he's crying: 'I pulled the string, something broke, the motor won't start, I'll get five years for it.' It was a very simple, primitive motor. I opened the lid and saw that a small lever had come loose, so I tightened it up and the motor started. But that boy would have been sentenced for damaging the motor, for sabotaging the plan for fish supply or something like that. That's how they do things in the courts. And there's no other way: we're saving the machinery, saving our industry, saving our country and its future. Why don't they do this in the West? I'll tell you why. We manufactured our first tractor in nineteen thirty, but in the West they made their first one in *eighteen* thirty, a full hundred years before us. They've got generations of experience; there the tractor is private property and the owner looks after it. Here, property belongs to the state, so it has to be looked after by state methods. If we give an uneducated peasant lad five or even ten years as a wrecker, what should we give you, an exiled counterrevolutionary and virtually an engineer? Any judge would convict you without hesitation, with a clear conscience — better still, he'd use you to clear his own conscience by telling himself that he was only obeying orders when he convicted those wretched peasants whereas at least he could convict you for doing something. You don't understand the situation you're in, Pankratov! You think that because you're in exile you're free. You're mistaken! And I'll tell you something else: the people in camps are better off! Yes, I know, it's tough there, they have to fell trees in the cold and there's hunger, they're behind barbed wire, yes, but there you're surrounded by prisoners like yourself, you're no different from each other. Here there are no sentries and watch-towers, you've got the forest all around you, you've got the river and the healthy air, but here you're an alien, here you're the enemy, and you've got no rights. We're obliged to put you inside on the first denunciation. Your landlady could come and say you were rude about Comrade Stalin. That would mean you were preparing a terroristic act."

He smiled at Sasha.

"So there it is, Pankratov, that's how things stand. You'll get ten years minimum. Do you understand?"

"Yes, I understand."

He understood it all right. If they could exile Soloveichik for a harmless joke, and Ivashkin for a misprint in a newspaper, and a cook for putting "Lazy Soup" on the menu, and if a pair of stolen soles could get you ten years according to the law of the seventh of August, and if he himself had been exiled for a few stupid rhymes, then for the separator — agricultural machinery — they would really give it to him.

"Right," Alferov said. "Now let's deal with the second point. 'Discrediting the kolkhoz leadership.' In the presence of kolkhoz-niks you called the chairman an idiot. Did you?"

"Yes. But he'd sworn at me, called me a snake, a saboteur, a Trotskyite, a counterrevolutionary, and God knows what else."

"That's very bad, of course," Alferov agreed. "But put yourself and him in front of the court, Pankratov. Your guilt in damaging the separator has already been established. And now the chairman of the kolkhoz, a man who suffers for the good of the collective, calls you a wrecker. He was right, and even if it stuck in their throats, the judges would understand him. As for the swearing, they'd take no notice — you don't get convicted for swearing here. But you, on the other hand, not only damaged the separator, you also called him an idiot in public. He is, after all, the chairman of the kolkhoz, his power depends on his authority, and you under-mined that authority. He'll have to leave his job now. You'll get ten years for that, and then the kolkhozniks will know what it means to insult the kolkhoz chairman. They'll respect him, they'll obey his orders. That's the way things stand, Pankratov. Do you understand?"

"I already said that I understand."

"I would like to hear just what it is you've understood."

"I understand that I have no rights, that they can do what they like with me, they can convict me of sabotage, of undermining authority, they can insult me and spit in my face. But bear in mind that I will answer every insult with an insult and every spit in the face with a spit in the face back."

Alferov looked at him with interest.

"And if you want to know," Sasha continued, "I regard your argument about sabotage as immoral. I admit that mistakes are being made, many mistakes, I've seen it for myself. But the idea that sabotage is state and Party policy, that I cannot believe. To admit such a possibility would mean losing my faith, and despite everything that's happened to me, I still believe in the Party."

Alferov continued to watch him with interest. "Anything else?"

"I've said it all."

"Well now," Alferov said earnestly, "as for the theory of sabotage, we'll discuss that further if the opportunity arises, of course. You believe in the Party, and that's very good. I joined the Party before the Revolution, I'm an old Bolshevik, Pankratov, and I daresay I can interpret Party policy no worse than you. But that is not the issue at present. The issue is you, and what I am to do with you. You look on me as your warder, your oppressor. Undoubtedly, I have to effect surveillance on you; it's part of my job. But I also have to answer for you, for your behavior and, incidentally, for your safety. You met the district officer in Boguchansk, Baranov? You saw what an idiot he is? If he'd been in my place, you'd have been stuck in jail long ago awaiting sentence. But, as you may have realized, I am not Baranov. I discuss the problem with you. Why do I do that? Out of boredom? Partly, I wouldn't deny it. But only partly. The main reason is that I have to make a decision. If I don't make it, others will, and with worse consequences for you. At any rate, I have to move you out of Mozgova for a start. Leaving you there would make it look as if you were right and the kolkhoz manager was wrong, and that would mean exposing you to the possibility of a new conflict. The chairman would set you up with something a bit more definite than the separator. What do you say about that?"

To have to move to yet another place, to begin all over again when he'd just met Zida and become attached to her, and also Vsevolod Sergeyevich, with whom he'd made friends. A new address — first there was Kansk, then Boguchany, then Kezhma, then Mozgova, and now something else. What would his mother think? The worst, naturally.... On the other hand, Alferov was right, he couldn't stay in Mozgova. Ivan Parfenovich was capable of anything. But why didn't Alferov make up his own mind? Why was he asking him?

"You've convinced me that I'll get at least ten years," Sasha said. "What difference does it make where I wait for the sentence? Mozgova would be best, as it's not likely to take very long."

Alferov shook his head. "Who can say how long it'll take. While I'm making inquiries in Kansk, and while they're making up their minds, it could take a long time, and then the road closes in September, so the reply won't get through till winter, when the sleigh road opens."

What was he up to? What was he thinking? He didn't have to make any inquiries. He could send Sasha to Kansk tomorrow with an accusation of sabotage; it was within his power to do so. What was he trying to get out of him?

"Do as you like. In any case, you'll do whatever you think is necessary," Sasha said.

Alferov got up, went to the sideboard, poured himself a glass of some darkish liquid, drank it, and then turned to Sasha.

"Would you like a glass? It's an excellent fruit liqueur."

"No, thank you."

"Don't you drink?"

"Not in a situation like this, I don't."

"Quite right, too. It would go to your head and you might say something wrong or sign something you oughtn't."

Alferov drank another glass and tossed a couple of berries into his mouth.

"An excellent fruit liqueur," he repeated. "My landlady infuses it from some forest berries and vows that it's very healthy, especially for men. For a young man like you, it doesn't matter, but when you get to my age, you have to take notice."

He returned to the table.

"So, what shall we do, Pankratov?"

"Send me to Kansk and get it over with. The exiles have a saying: The sooner you're inside, the sooner you'll get out."

Alferov did not react to the joke.

"Pankratov, I know you didn't break the separator, and I don't want your ten years on my conscience. In any case, there's no need for me to rush, as the complaint is now on file and can be activated any time."

He smiled again. Then he got up and walked across the room to close the kitchen door. He sat down and in a serious and authoritative tone, said: "Go back to Mozgova. But bear in mind that the chairman won't forgive you. Watch your behavior, get rid of your illusions, and don't get into fights with anyone."

Sasha detected a humane note in his voice, yet he couldn't bring himself to give in, to yield.

"Maybe I shouldn't go out at all?"

"If it's dangerous, don't."

"And what am I supposed to live on?"

"Doesn't your family send you money?" Alferov asked.

"Yes, but my mother earns a pittance, she works in a laundry, and my father hasn't lived with us for years."

"It's bad, but there's nothing I can do to help you. The exiles somehow take care of themselves. In general, exile here is an anachronism, a hangover from the pre-kolkhoz times when exiles could work for individual farmers. Apparently the exile system is going to be ended here soon anyway, they'll be moved into the towns. By the way, what's your specialization?"

"When I was arrested I was in my last year at the Transport Institute."

"You ought to be working for the machine and tractor station," Alferov said thoughtfully.

"I'm not familiar with agricultural engineering."

Alferov burst out laughing. "You're not familiar with agricultural engineering, yet you repaired the separator. And you accuse me of faulty logic! I say that out of vanity, as a former philosopher.

Anyway, how much engineering is involved? You can tell a pinion from a bolt, what more is there to it? The manager of the local machine station is a metalworker, and the chief mechanic is a tractor driver. If you know cars, you know tractors. I didn't know what your training was when you arrived, otherwise I'd have left you in Kezhma. You see how your fate hangs on such trivialities. Had I thought of asking then, you'd be living now in the regional center and working at the machine station. Well, we'll return to that another time. We have to wrap this thing up," he said, pointing at Ivan Parfenovich's complaint, "Go back to Mozgova, but, I repeat, be careful, or as we say nowadays, be on your guard."

They went out onto the dark street.

"Your cart's gone," Alferov said. "They probably decided they weren't going to have to take you back."

"It doesn't matter, I'll make it."

"Eight miles through the taiga, at night? Aren't you afraid?"

"No, the bear sleeps at night."

"Stay overnight, if you like," Alferov suggested. "My landlady's sister lives in the next hut, and she can put you up."

"No thanks, it's all right."

3

When they returned from the Crimea, Varya and Kostya moved into Sofya Alexandrovna's. Her lodger had moved by then and the room was vacant.

Sofya Alexandrovna took Varya's "marriage" stoically: so what, someone else had turned her back on Sasha. All his friends had forgotten about him, nobody called, nobody was interested, neither Vadim nor Lena Budyagina — never mind Yuri Sharok, who didn't even greet her. Nina Ivanova used to come by at the beginning, but she didn't anymore, she was boycotting Sofya Alexandrovna for giving a roof to Varya and Kostya. Sofya Alexandrovna was frankly pleased that Nina wasn't coming around. At first, Nina used to say that Sasha's arrest had been an absurd accident, but then new nuances began to creep into her conversation: there was the difficult internal and international situation, the sharpening of the class struggle, the activities of anti-Party groupings, and as never before particular precision and clarity of one's position was required, whereas unfortunately Sasha sometimes put his own understanding of events above the point of view of the collective. In a word, she hinted that Sasha's arrest had some foundation.

Until now Varya was the only one who had not abandoned Sofya Alexandrovna, which meant she had not abandoned Sasha. There hadn't been a romance between them, and yet Varya had stood in the prison lines with her, helped her make up parcels, protected her from rude customers at the laundry, and just by her presence brought some color into Sofya Alexandrovna's lonely life. And she had done all this not just out of compassion, but behind it, unseen, stood Sasha, her interest in him and her sympathy for his plight.

But there was nothing one could do; life must go on. Sofya Alexandrovna felt like a mother toward Varya and only wished her well. True, Varya was somewhat young to be jumping into a settled relationship. Would she be happy? Kostya was a generous boy, he liked to do things in a lavish way. He brought her all kinds of treats from the restaurants, and once he brought her an enormous cake. She had had no idea what to do with it — it was so big and might spoil. She had cut it up into slices and taken them around to her sisters. He made her gifts of all kinds of little things, like a box of ladies' handkerchiefs, stockings, and he'd even given her an umbrella. And although she declined his gifts every time, it was impossible to withstand his generosity.

Yet he made her feel uneasy. He didn't work anywhere — how was that possible in these times? Varya said he had invented some kind of substance for sealing electric light bulbs, he'd taken out a patent, and he was paying taxes. It all sounded rather odd, as if they had gone back to the time of NEP — the New Economic Policy of the 1920s. For her, the very word *nepman* smacked of the nouveaux riches, conspicuous luxuries, money-grubbing. And now, out of that long-gone age, there suddenly appeared this man who didn't work anywhere, who carried on incomprehensible conversations on the telephone, who dressed provocatively well, just as the young nepmen had dressed in their day. She was sorry that Varya, a girl from a working-class family, had become involved in that alien environment. Kostya spent every evening in a restaurant and Varya, if not every evening, then every Saturday and Sunday without fail. Varya admitted to Sofya Alexandrovna that Kostya played billiards and that it was in fact his main source of income. The electric bulbs and the sealing substance were covers, only serving to make it look as though he had a legal source of income. In fact, he was a gambler, a restaurant billiards player, and that was why he came home in the small hours. She had given him a street-door key and warned Varya to take the chain off the inner door so that he could get in. It was a breach in the age-old rules of the house — the door was supposed to be chained at night — but there was nothing else to be done; if the chain was kept on, Kostya would have to ring the bell.

Once Varya forgot to take off the chain. Kostya turned up at four in the morning and woke everyone up with the doorbell. Mikhail Yurevich said nothing, but their neighbor Galya screamed, "They're out at all hours and won't let you sleep!"

Galya had her eye on Sasha's room. She was living with her husband and child in a room about twelve feet square, while Sofya Alexandrovna was renting out a spare room she didn't need. She was profiteering from living space. Galya worsened their relationship in order to provoke a scandal and thereby bring this illegal situation to official notice and get the room for herself. Sofya Alexandrovna was worried. Naturally, her husband's claim on the room had been registered at the Moscow Soviet, and whose business was it if Varya was living in the room? Varya was registered as a resident in the same apartment house and she could hardly be expected to sleep with her young man in the same room as her sister! Sofya Alexandrovna was letting them stay temporarily in her spare room and it was no concern of anyone's! But what about Kostya? Varya said his residence permit was for the Moscow suburb of Sokolniki. But was that true? She could hardly ask to see his identity papers. If Galya called the militia and it turned out that Kostya did not have a residence permit for Moscow, what would happen then? And although she did not want to offend Galya, Sofya Alexandrovna decided to have a talk with her.

Varya was not feeling well. Kostya brought her dinner from the restaurant. He would not let her cook, in general, because he didn't want her to smell of the kitchen or to roughen her hands. He brought in elaborate dishes, and not only for her but also for Sofya Alexandrovna.

Varya usually heated up the meal, but on this occasion Sofya Alexandrovna offered to do it.

She laid the veal chops in the hot frying pan and the communal kitchen was permeated with their delicious aroma.

Galya observed with a smirk, "Goodness, how those smells make your mouth water!"

Pretending not to notice the irony, Sofya Alexandrovna said, "Varya's ill; Kostya brought it from the restaurant."

"They're good, these bourgeois dinners," Galya went on, still smirking. "And we have to make do with one piece of cod. Their dinner must have cost a good eight rubles, if not ten. . . ."

"I don't know what it cost," Sofya Alexandrovna answered calmly, and turned back to the stove.

"Where do people get that sort of money?" Galya would not be stopped. "He works at night, a night watchman is he? Surely night watchmen get less than janitors?"

"Stop it, Galya, please," Sofya Alexandrovna said. "You're a good, kind woman. Why are you saying these things?"

"They're riding on the backs of the good and kind people nowadays," Galya expostulated angrily. "The good and kind people do the plowing and carry the water. The good people stand in lines for half a day and can't trade their coupons for anything. They hang on to the steps of the tramcars and have to be careful not to fall under the wheels, while the not-so-good people ride in taxis and eat in restaurants."

Sofya Alexandrovna said nothing and took the dinner into her room. But Varya noticed her mood.

"Why are you upset, Sofya Alexandrovna?"

"It was Galya just now in the kitchen: 'bourgeois dinners,' 'they go out to restaurants, come in at all hours' . . ."

"What business is it of hers?"

"I suppose she's envious. . . ."

"Too bad!" Varya said.

"Maybe she just wants to get Sasha's room."

"But you've got it reserved."

"She thinks that if she can prove that I'm making money off the room, she'll get it away from me."

"Are you afraid of Galya?"

"I'm not afraid of her, but any kind of scandal these days . . ."

"She's a pig!" Varya swore. "I'll give her what for, I'll shut her up!"

"Don't do it, Varya, she can make trouble."

"I'd like to know what trouble she can cause me!"

"Not you, but Konstantin Fedorovich."

"And what is Kostya — a thief, a crook?"

"What are you talking about, Varya? But you must admit that

his position is ambiguous. He doesn't work anywhere, he's not employed anywhere . . ."

"Yes he is employed, in a cooperative workshop. And as for his billiards playing, he does it in a state billiards hall. It's not prohibited."

"Varya, I have nothing against him. But Galya might use the fact that he's not registered here."

"I'm also not registered with you."

"No, but you are registered in this apartment house."

"And he's registered in another one. What's the difference?"

"Are you sure he has a Moscow permit?"

"But of course!"

Sofya Alexandrovna sensed uncertainty in Varya's categorical response. But she could not bring herself to ask Varya if she'd seen the permit with her own eyes. She only said: "And your relationship also is not properly registered."

Varya laughed. "In this country, common-law marriage is equivalent to official marriage. We run a common household, we sleep in the same bed, so we're husband and wife."

"Varya, what are you saying?" Sofya Alexandrovna frowned.

"Well, what of it? I went to the court recently to find out about maintenance. The judge asked me straight out: 'Do you keep a common household budget, do you sleep in the same bed?' "

Sofya Alexandrovna frowned again.

"Sofya Alexandrovna, tell me honestly: Is it awkward for you having us here?" Varya said seriously. "Are you afraid?"

Sofya Alexandrovna answered her just as seriously: "Until you get yourselves settled properly, in your own place, you can stay here. But you must see that there are no scenes, no noise late at night. Do you agree?"

"Yes, and I'll think about what you've said."

"Also, Varya, there's a gun in your room, actually two."

"They're hunting rifles, Sofya Alexandrovna. Kostya hunts."

"It makes no difference. You must understand: the Arbat is now a classified street, and I can't allow guns in my house, given my position." Her voice had become firm and insistent. "They're very strict about such things now. Konstantin Fedorovich would be responsible if it was his apartment, but here, in my apartment, I'm responsible."

She was silent briefly and then added, "I must keep this room for Sasha, it's his room. I must protect it from every threat, even the most insignificant."

"Okay," Varya said. "There won't be guns here anymore."

Varya had never seen Kostya's residence permit with her own eyes. When they were in the Crimea, he used his identity card, together with hers, at the hotel, and filled out the registration form with his address as Moscow. He simply wrote what was on his identity card. That was all the receptionist needed to know.

But Varya had never seen Kostya's identity card either. Suppose she'd made a mistake? Suppose he hadn't written Moscow, but some other town? It didn't matter to her, but they mustn't deceive Sofya Alexandrovna.

That evening she said to Kostya, "Sofya Alexandrovna is worried about your permit."

"But I've told her where I'm registered — doesn't she believe me?"

"Yes, she does, but the neighbor, Galya, is making trouble. She wants to grab this room for herself, so she's claiming that Sofya Alexandrovna is making money out of her spare room. If your residence permit is not for Moscow, things will be hard for her."

"Should I show her my identity card?"

"That would be the best."

"But when? She's asleep when I get in, and when I wake up she's already out."

"Leave it with me and I'll show her."

He cast a sidelong look at her. "I can't leave my identity card — I need it. Wake me up early in the morning and I'll show it to her myself."

"Also, she doesn't want any guns in the house."

"But they're hunting rifles, it's not prohibited."

"It makes no difference. Galya could report them."

"Tell her I've got a permit for them."

"The permit may be for one rifle, but you've got more than one."

"They're hunting rifles, it's perfectly legal. And tell Sofya Alexandrovna to calm down," he muttered irritably.

"There's only one law here and that's Sofya Alexandrovna's," Varya said. "Either we do as she asks, or we'll have to clear out."

"Do it your way," he grumbled.

In the morning, he got up yawning and stretching, unused to rising early. He took his papers from his jacket pocket, knocked on Sofya Alexandrovna's door, went in, and then returned shortly after.

"Everything's okay."

Then he went back to bed.

Kostya had not shown Varya his identity card. She took note of this but did not dwell on it. In the short time she'd lived with him, she'd become accustomed to the idea that Kostya was a man with a complicated background and a complicated situation. It was no good asking him about anything he did not wish to talk about, because he never would. His parents were russified Greeks who had been fishermen on the Azov Sea. They'd been deported from Mariupol as kulaks. Kostya had been a sailor in the merchant navy at the time and had been abroad, which was the only reason he did not share their fate. He confessed to Varya that on returning home and hearing what had happened, he was sorry he hadn't stayed in Piraeus or Istanbul. He could be enjoying himself there right now. The merchant navy was not the place for him anymore: crews that went overseas were now being thoroughly checked, and they'd discover that his parents had been kulaks, and he'd be deported himself. He'd left for Moscow where it would be easier to lose himself. He'd worked as an electrical fitter, changed his job, invented the seal for the light bulbs, and joined the cooperative. But billiards was his real vocation. He had been spotted by Beilis, the top billiards player in Moscow. Beilis took him to the best billiards halls, where they hustled freeloaders, moneyed provincials visiting Moscow on government funds. Kostya was merciless with them. He would con them by losing the first game and then fleece them down to their last kopek.

Lyova once said that if Kostya lived in America, he'd be a millionaire. Ika had joked that it wasn't only shoeshine boys who became millionaires in America, it was also the Mafiosi. Varya had flared up and told Ika to hold his tongue. But she hadn't told Kostya about the conversation. He would never have forgiven Ika for the shoeshine boys.

By her common-law marriage to Kostya, Varya had bypassed all the rungs of the ladder. She was higher than Vika Marasevich, Nina Sheremetyeva, or Noemi. They were all kept by their lovers, whereas when she went to a restaurant it was with her husband. They all knew it and were now ingratiating themselves. Varya had no need to envy the foreign clothes that the girls sold and resold to each other. Kostya took her to the best Moscow dressmakers, the best shoemakers and furriers. Her coat was tailored by Lavrov, her dresses were made by Nadezhda Lamanova, Alexandra Lyamina, Barbara Danilova, and even Yefimova. Lubenets made her brassieres, Koshke on the Arbat made her girdles, Tamara Amirova her hats, Barkovsky, Gutmanovich, and Dushkin her shoes. Kostya went only to the best. His suits were made by Zhurkevich, the finest tailor in Moscow.

On the surface, everything seemed bright, festive, attractive. But Varya sensed that her relationship with Kostya would not last long. She didn't know why herself. There had been much in her previous life that she had not accepted, but everything had been clear and understandable. Now nothing was clear; she didn't know where she was going or where she was drifting. Kostya was more than ten years older than she, but he hadn't read anything, not even *The Three Musketeers*. He knew only four lines from all of Pushkin: "Alone, loaded down with calculations, armed only with a blunt cue, he played two-ball billiards from early morning." But he was clever — he quoted Pushkin not in order to pretend familiarity with Pushkin, but to show that billiards was something he and Pushkin shared.

Did she love him? It was hard to say. *It* had taken place in the hotel in Yalta. She had not resisted, perhaps out of a desire to experience the unknown, something they'd talked about as girls, perhaps out of a wish to become a woman in the full sense of the word.

But even after *it* had happened, there was no feeling of real intimacy; there was still a distance between them. Could it be simply because of the age difference? When they were at the beach he swam beautifully, yet she sometimes felt uncomfortable. He was thickset and broad-shouldered, but, as his bathing suit made all the more plain, he had short legs, and his arms, legs, and back were covered with hair — he was hairy all over and he had an eagle tattooed across his chest. On the beach, Kostya looked much older. Back in the hotel, he would lock their door, embrace her, and kiss her neck, her breasts, but she was ashamed of the daylight and afraid that when they went downstairs afterward to the restaurant, people would be able to tell that they had just been doing *it*. When they went to bed, she would turn out the light because she felt embarrassed undressing in front of him. She was too shy to caress him, or to embrace and kiss him. Nor did she very much want to.

Her new life brought her neither upheaval nor rapture. What had earlier seemed unattainable had suddenly become accessible and normal, as if this was how she had always lived. The festive feeling of an evening at the restaurant still appealed as it had before. She still liked beautiful clothes, but she was bored by the long fitting sessions, irritated by unobliging dressmakers and interminable waiting at Paul the hairdresser's, even though she saw the whole of Moscow's beau monde there.

Paul's salon was on the Arbat, next to the Prague restaurant. Kostya had supplied the salon with hair dryers, and Varya, like Paul's other regular clients, entered by way of his apartment. For some reason, Paul, whose real name was Pavel Mikhailovich Kondratyev, and his wife and manicurist, Vera Nikolaevna, singled Varya out. The fashion of permanent waving had just come in, but Pavel Mikhailovich refused to do it for Varya.

"How could I possibly deform such beauty as this?"

The ladies who were waiting to have their hair permed heard this and of course were offended. Varya didn't give a damn. She had her own circle of friends, Kostya's old friends. As before, they sat at the same table in the restaurant and she would dance only with them. Kostya would occasionally come out of the adjoining billiards room for a brief break, drink a glass of vodka, have a snack, embrace Varya tenderly as if to remind the others that this beautiful girl was his wife and that they were eating and drinking at his expense. Varya suspected that Lyova was buying his clothes at Kostya's expense, for such tailoring was beyond his means. But she could not reproach Lyova. He did not play billiards, he hardly drank, he was polite, gentle, and attentive, and he was a simple draftsman, a working man. Kostya needed people like Lyova around him, educated young people from good Moscow families, just as he needed a wife who was upright and decent. It gave him a place in society and heightened his reputation, at least in his own eyes. Although he read nothing himself, he knew what others were reading, he knew who was in fashion and who was well known. Not wanting to appear ignorant, he used to advantage his good memory for names and his lively mind.

Once at a restaurant, Ika asked, as if posing a quiz question, "A promising film director, two of his films begin with the letter O: what's his name?"

Kostya managed to intercept Ika's glance, turned around, and said at once, "Barnet."

Kostya didn't like movies, which he found pretentious. He preferred revues, operetta, ballets, and he hadn't seen Barnet's films, but he was the one to answer Ika's question first — and he gave a friendly nod to Barnet. "We've hunted together," he said casually.

"Yes, yes, I remember," Ika said mockingly. "You've told us the story of how you and he killed a wolf."

"That was with Kachalov," Kostya said, gritting his teeth, "and it wasn't a wolf, it was a family of wolves. We came across a lair and shot the wolf, then we shot the she-wolf and then we took the three cubs. You've presumably seen a wolf? If not, you ought to go to the zoo and have a look at one, though I don't advise you to try to stroke it — it might take your hand off."

He drank a glass of vodka, bent down to Varya, and said quietly: "And you criticize me for having guns, Varya." He cast his gaze around the salon. "They'd give anything to go hunting with me. Tomorrow we'll go to the Actors' Club and you'll see how they all fawn over me."

"But I thought they only let artists in."

He was genuinely surprised. "Varya! You don't believe me! We'll go there tomorrow."

Next day he got home early in order to help Varya decide what to wear. First she tried on a blue silk suit with a pleated flounce on the skirt and pleated collar, then she tried on a gray satin

Cossack-style coat embroidered in gold and worn with a straight slit-skirt, then a brown low-necked dress. She was constantly surprised that Kostya, who was so brusque in everything concerning his business affairs, could spend so long admiring her clothes and going into childlike raptures as he watched her dress.

"It's terrific, Varya, very chic!"

Varya trusted Kostya's taste. But suppose all those famous people were just condescending to Kostya? What, after all, was he? He was a billiards player and a hunter. And she, as his wife, wouldn't she look as stupidly overdressed as perhaps he did?

Her fears were groundless.

There were famous and not-so-famous people at the club, but they all tried to give an impression of knowing everyone to underline their importance. There were two billiards tables, but Kostya hardly played. The well-known expert Zakhar Ivanovich was there, giving advice to others, but if he played himself it was only for pennies, for he did not want to offend his famous friends. He relaxed from his business affairs at the Actors' Club on Staro-Pimenov, where he became jolly and good-natured, and Varya liked it when they visited him there.

The club was situated in the semibasement of an old ducal mansion and was furnished with comfortable antique furniture. It had small open alcoves along its walls for up to eight or ten people. Kostya sometimes brought Lyova and Rina to the club, and they would take a separate table for four. The alcoves were for large parties. Kostya pointed out Ilyinsky and Ktorov, and Varya recognized them from the film *The Trial about Three Million.* She also recognized Smirnov-Sokolsky, who often appeared in the revue at the Hermitage. He was sitting half-turned toward a bald man with a mustache, who was speaking with his hand over his mouth; either he was asking for something or he was saying something he didn't want others to hear. The bald man said little, but narrowed his bloated, cunning eyes that gave him the look of a satisfied cat.

"That's Demyan Bedny," Kostya said.

Varya liked the place. No vodka or wine was served, only mineral water and fruit juices. A notice warned: "MINERAL WATER IS NOT SERVED IN CARAFES." Also the food was delicious, the restaurant was run by the best cook in Moscow, Jacob Danilovich Rozental, or the Beard, as he was known.

As a sign of the establishment's sense of style, there was a notice on the wall which said:

REMEMBER ONE TRUTH ONLY,
WHEN COMING TO THE CLUB, BRING A WIFE,
AND DON'T BE LIKE THE BOURGEOIS,
BRING YOUR OWN NOT SOMEONE ELSE'S.

Rina said the first two lines were by the writer Tretyakov and the last two by Mayakovsky, just before his death.

Rina knew as many people as did Kostya. A companionable girl, she was on good terms with everyone, but she also knew how to keep people at arm's-length. Varya knew virtually nothing about her. She lived on the Ostrozhenka, next to the Monastery of the Conception, in a little wooden house. She never asked anyone in, joking that the house might collapse at any minute. Sometimes she arrived alone. They never managed to see with whom she came or with whom she left. People began to congregate at the club around eleven o'clock, when the theaters let out, and they usually left around two or three in the morning. Taxis would be waiting in the side streets.

"Would you like a ride home?" Kostya asked Rina.

She raised her eyebrows coquettishly. "I'm being taken. . . ."

Kostya helped Varya into the taxi and she leaned back comfortably in the seat. They went by Staro-Pimenov to Malaya Dmitrov Street, then along the boulevards. The city seemed strange and unfamiliar, empty and dark. The silently sleeping world seemed to conceal something uneasy. Varya was quiet as she mulled over her impressions of the evening.

Often, at the club, they would go upstairs to the auditorium to watch actors' parties. The actors themselves wrote parodies, one-act plays, sketches, and sometimes the writers gave them material. It was all done with brilliance. Gypsies sang, Ruslanova sang. It was the sort of thing you'd never see in an ordinary theater. Once Sergei Obraztsov came onto the stage carrying a puppet that had gray eyebrows and beard. The audience broke into applause and started looking around at Felix Kon, the head of the Arts Committee and chairman of the club's management. The puppet's likeness to him was astounding. In Kon's voice, Obraztsov announced that he was going to read a lecture on "The Soviet Lullaby." Pointing an admonitory finger at the audience, Kon's favorite gesture, the puppet said, "The Soviet lullaby is not like bourgeois song, it must be used to *waken* the infant." Just like that, without a murmur. And he could get away with it. It seemed to Varya that in general these people took quite a lot of license.

But Kostya said that they couldn't go to the club more than once a week: "There's no money to be made there, as you can see." He stuck firmly to this rule, breaking it only once, for Varya's benefit, when they put on *The Trial of Writers Who Don't Write Roles for Women*. Natalya Stas played the judge, the accused were Kataev, Olesha, and Yanovsky, and Meyerhold played the prosecutor.

Varya and Kostya sat in the seventh row alongside Alexei Tolstoy and the artists Deni and Moor. Varya caught a glimpse of Vika Marasevich, whom she had never seen there before. Vika's brother, Vadim, now an established literary and theater critic, was a regular, hobnobbing with the famous. He was moving up and down the aisle nearsightedly squinting as he searched for seats. Following him, evidently as his guests, were Yuri Sharok and Lena Budyagina. Lena spotted Varya and smiled at her sweetly, but when Yuri looked at Varya she turned away, for she couldn't bear the sight of him.

She at once recalled the New Year's party and the fight between Sasha and Yuri. Now Sasha was in Siberian exile, while Yuri and Vadim, Lena Budyagina and Vika Marasevich were enjoying themselves in this lovely club.

Lost in her thoughts, Varya did not hear what Natalya Stas was saying. She focused her attention back on the play just as they were calling on the "accused." Kataev was the first to rise. His voice sounded unpleasant, nasal, as if he had a cold. The audience thought his performance mediocre and gave him lukewarm applause, and Yanovsky got a similar response. But every one of Olesha's remarks was received with a burst of laughter. Meyerhold, tall and hook-nosed, swooped on Olesha like a hawk. Olesha, small, with hair flying all over the place, parried the blows with lightning

ripostes. Sitting in front of them was Yaron, who, as he turned to
Alexei Tolstoy and remarked on Olesha's performance, gave Varya
a lingering look. Then, when the trial was over, he got up, turned
to face Varya, and, standing awkwardly, blocked the aisle and
declared: "He glanced back at the beauty and turned to stone, like
Lot's wife." It was funny and Varya laughed.

"Are you an actress?" Yaron asked. "How is it I don't know
you?"

"I'm not an actress, that's why you don't know me," she replied
coolly. She didn't want Yaron to take her laughter as an encouragement.

Her attitude to all these famous people was complex. She was far
from sharing Kostya's and Rina's ecstasy: they were simply actors,
and they could get away with saying certain things. She preferred
to see actors on the stage, where she could applaud them with all
her heart — she could recognize talent. But why should she become
friends with them? What for? Kostya liked her attitude, it
delighted him, but he would not let her go either to the club or any
other public place without him, except to the movies with Zoe or
Rina.

⚜ 4 ⚜

After spotting Yuri Sharok in the Actors' Club, Vika Marasevich decided not to go there again. Why should she see him more than she had to? The meetings on the Maroseika were quite enough. She brought him routine information: on such-and-such date, in such-and-such restaurant, sitting at the same table were so-and-so and so-and-so, and they talked about this and that. Sharok insisted that she reproduce word for word everything each person said, even though the conversations may have been so empty that she could not remember them at all.

She began bringing him the news: "Noemi is still with her Japanese. But there's an Italian who wants to marry her and take her back to Italy with him. . . . Two new Germans have appeared on the scene, they are with girls from the Metropole, Susanna and Katya. The girls don't say who the Germans are. . . . Nelli Vladimirova, the beauty, has divorced her Gypsy Polyakov and got married to a rich French merchant called Georges — they have a large apartment, carpets, antique furniture, porcelain, appliances. . . ."

Vika tried to turn her meetings with Yuri into gossip sessions about the high life. Such gossip ought to impress the son of a tailor. But she soon discovered that he was not interested. Perhaps he didn't expect much from her, but as long as she was mixing with foreigners, she might as well provide some information. . . .

No, he was expecting something from her, but what was it? She caught his every word and reaction each time she uttered a name. And she finally guessed. Yuzik Liberman! That's who he was interested in! A tall, nimble young man, he was generally thought to be a high-level informer. He told anti-Soviet jokes openly, allowed himself risky stories and witticisms, and was not interested in foreigners, but, probably through his mother, had wide-ranging personal connections among the highest state officials. Yuri Sharok was interested in Liberman precisely because of those connections with high officials, for he was collecting material on them himself. What they said was unimportant. Yuzik Liberman might be the only one babbling, but he was babbling for the whole table: everyone was laughing, everyone was reacting, so in effect everyone was babbling.

As soon as Vika realized this, she began getting friendlier with Yuzik, and he gladly took up with her. Then she began writing detailed reports of where they'd been, when, and whom she'd seen and what she'd heard. This was what Sharok wanted to hear, this was exactly what he required. No doubt what Vika reported was nothing new compared to what Yuzik was reporting himself, but it was in this capacity that she was useful to Sharok.

She was not so stupid as to let Sharok know that she had guessed Liberman was his target. She had no higher ambitions in this enterprise and she preferred to look foolish and mindless in Sharok's eyes, so that he would not demand anything more serious of her.

In her cunning game with Sharok, she kept her main interest from him: the group of leading architects to whom her old friend Ivan Vladimirovich, himself an architect, had introduced her.

She had long given up her dream of marrying a glorious pilot, one of the newly created heroes of the Soviet Union. Where would she find one of them? They and even their provincial little wives were practically all Party committee members or in the leadership, as far up as Stalin himself. Even if she did carry it off, those heroes had no future, they were being sent as pilots to Chukotka. And the foreign connection was just as ephemeral. Erik? He was nice enough, but nothing special, just an ordinary foreigner. He took a daily bath and shaved and changed his underwear, he smelled nice. But what more was there to him? He hadn't popped the question, and without his daddy's and his mummy's say-so, he wouldn't. The honor of the company was at stake! At best, his father, his noble father, wouldn't arrive for another year, and she was already pushing twenty-four.

Vika needed a man with a powerful future. There was such a man, he was an architect, one of the architects of the Palace of Soviets, a major construction project and Stalin's brainchild. He was not yet old, forty-three, very young-looking, tall, and slim; he'd lived abroad for many years — he was a European! That would be some match! Not a pilot in flying-boots, but a world-famous architect, and she his wife, the daughter of a famous professor, an intellectual woman, and a Muscovite born and bred. No Sharok or Dyakov would dare to make demands on such an alliance; they'd soon get their fingers burned.

If they did dare, her husband would say to Stalin, "I understand, Josef Vissarionovich. If I'm not trusted I can be monitored by means of others. But it is immoral to have my wife watching me."

Then Dyakov and Sharok would evaporate from their little jobs, and it'd be a long way away, too.

True, the architect already had a wife. She was from Odessa and had lived with him in Italy where she'd acquired her polish and got herself in shape. She was a skinny brunette with a big nose, she smoked long thin cigarettes and squinted because she was short-sighted. She wouldn't wear spectacles. She never went anywhere with her husband. For twenty years they had been bored with each other. He spent all day at his studio and sometimes even the night. He often slept at Architects' House in the suburb of Sukhanovo, and was frequently abroad.

It would not be difficult to get rid of this woman from Odessa. At any rate the link had been forged: he had been attracted to Vika, and they now spent ecstatic hours in bed together. She was young, beautiful, experienced, capable, and he was a man of strong passions. They did not let a day pass without seeing each other, or at least speaking on the telephone.

But they kept their affair a secret. Everyone knew Igor Vladimirovich was an old friend of hers, an old flame. People knew that she went with him to Architects' House in the lawyer Plevako's former mansion on Novinsky Boulevard, and girls didn't normally go there. As a meeting place it wasn't fashionable; though it had a restaurant, it was only a third-class one. Architectural exhibitions were presented there, but who was interested in that?

It was all the easier for Vika to hide the affair. She would appear at Architects' House only with Igor Vladimirovich and then her architect would join them there.... The architect didn't think all this conspiratorial activity was necessary, but he valued the show of delicacy on Vika's part. He also appreciated her attention to his work. She went with Igor Vladimirovich to debates on projects in which the architect took part, and she listened attentively to the arguments and objections.

There would be middle-aged female architects at these debates, and they didn't bother Vika. What *did* bother her were the made-up little draftswomen from the design studios, but Igor Vladimirovich reassured her that for a leading architect, especially the Chief Architect, *her* architect, women assistants were unacceptable in any case.

"The first law of physical resistance in materials," Igor Vladimirovich would joke, "is that every connection limits freedom by one degree. And an architect must have absolute freedom in his own studio."

Vika played her role to perfection. Igor Vladimirovich believed that she was in love with his friend. For the architect it was a difficult period of struggle between architectural trends, schools, ideas, and traditions. Trained in Italy, having traveled to many countries and being familiar with contemporary Western architecture, he headed the school that based itself on the classical heritage but also took into account contemporary buildings, especially high-rise. He had been attacked for this, but Vika thought he was a genius. She thought his buildings, his designs, and ideas were brilliant innovations, and she said so to all his friends and enemies. He was a genius! Not a genius who would be appreciated five hundred years from now but an existing and recognized one. Everything he touched was the work of genius!

She had chosen her role well and she played it in a masterly fashion. She never contradicted the architect, never argued with him or behaved capriciously, and she was never offended. One had to behave oneself on a high level with a great man.

If he was unable to keep a date with her, he would always

telephone and ask in a concerned way: "What will you do with yourself?"

She would reassure him: "Don't worry, my dear, I'll rest, read for a while, I'll go to the movies with one of my girlfriends. Call me tomorrow morning without fail."

Of course, she did none of these things. She had her own affairs to attend to: dressmakers and shoemakers to see, and Yuzik Liberman and Sharok: she had to follow that routine strictly, there could be no misstep there. Nor could there be any as far as the architect was concerned, either. He must see her as a faithful, devoted friend. She was the daughter of a professor, descended from Cossack chieftains, after all! It was hardly her fault that she had been born among all these boors. She was an aristocrat, Goddammit!

Only once did she lose control.

The incident took place at the Museum of Fine Arts, where an exhibition of competing designs for the Palace of Soviets project was crowded from morning till night. The long line of viewers reached right out into Bolkhonka Street. The architects, including those from abroad, stood next to their projects, most of them accompanied by their wives, and answered questions and gave explanations. Vika was there every day and would meet her architect. She had many friends and acquaintances in that world and it was possible that someone might guess at her relationship with him, so she behaved decorously.

It was noisy and lively, and the crowds were constant. Only one person failed to come to the museum at all — the architect's wife.

"Don't criticize her," he said. "She's seen enough of my projects over the last twenty years, and she's bored to death with them."

"But this is your biggest project, this is the design of your life!" Vika protested.

"When my design has won and they start handing out the prizes, then she'll turn up," he joked.

"Oh, yes! Then she'll turn up and stand next to you and share your triumph!"

He looked at her intently. He saw that she wanted to be the one next to him, sharing his triumph.

Vika felt the pettiness of her remark and took his hand.

"I'm not claiming anything. It's just that I can't bear such indifference to you and your work. To stand next to you only when you're having a triumph, it's like ..." She twisted her face scornfully. "I'm sorry, but I suddenly felt terribly hurt for you."

She was awoken the next morning by the architect, who telephoned to say that there was to be a closed viewing that day and that she should not come. He would call later.

A closed session meant that Stalin and other members of the government would be visiting the exhibition.

Vika waited by the telephone all day. The architect phoned only toward the evening.

"I'm on my way," he said.

He arrived with a bottle of champagne. It was his moment of victory, their victory. Stalin had liked his project.

They left in the morning for two weeks at Sukhanovo.

⚘ 5 ⚘

S talin was sitting with his face to the sun in a wicker armchair on the verandah of his dacha in Sochi. He loved the house in Sochi. It was his own creation. And he loved the summer in the south, even though his doctors recommended the south only in the autumn. But what did doctors know, anyway? Even in his childhood he had loved this time of the year, and had loved to clamber over the ruins of Goris-Tsikhe, the ancient fortress on the mountain, built by the Byzantine emperors. It was there that he had fallen and maimed his arm. Sochi reminded him of Gori, even though Gori had no seashore, nor such vegetation. On the table in front of him was a pile of books by Solovyov and Klyuchevsky — both long-dead scholars — and Pokrovsky, the contemporary Soviet historian. There were also papers on the subject of "a plan for a textbook on the history of the U.S.S.R." Zhdanov was in charge of this project.

That had been *his* choice. That year he had commandeered Zhdanov from his post in Gorky and made him a Central Committee secretary. He had not done this because Zhdanov was running the region so successfully, including the building of the Gorky auto factory. Other regional Party secretaries were doing just as well. Nor was it because Zhdanov, at thirty-eight, was so young; other secretaries were the same age: Khrushchev, Vareikis, and Eikhe were forty, Khataevich was forty-one, and Kabakov was only forty-three. Zhdanov was an intellectual, he understood literature and art, but he was not the know-it-all type like Lunacharsky. He didn't flaunt his erudition, didn't show off with foreign words or claim to be a theoretician, like Bukharin, but he was an intellectual. There should be an intellectual in the leadership, and Zhdanov fitted the part. And he now appeared to be managing his first major task, the creation of the Writers' Union, very well. Its forthcoming congress would be a turning point in the Party's relations with the intelligentsia. The writers, as the main force of the intelligentsia, had always claimed the spiritual leadership of the people. Consequently the people could be tamed only if their intelligentsia was either destroyed or subdued. The best thing would be to destroy one part of it and subdue the other.

Lenin had relied on the intelligentsia in the struggle for power. And that had been the right thing to do. The intelligentsia was the time-honored standard bearer of heterodoxy, and independent thought was a useful weapon in the struggle for power. But once power had been won, one must no longer rely on the intelligentsia. The weapon now was not independent thought, but like-mindedness. RAPP, the association of proletarian writers, and other groups, had divided the intelligentsia and hence encouraged it to think in diverse ways. What was needed now was an organization that would unify, that would ensure people thought the same way, and that was to be the Writers' Union.

Maxim Gorky would be a good figurehead. He was in effect a left Social Democrat with strong leanings toward petit bourgeois liberalism. Lenin had been very careful with him, and rightly so. Gorky had a name, and he had connections with leading writers in the West. There was much he did not accept about what was happening in the Soviet Union, but life as an émigré had shown him that he had no future abroad. The true writer must live and die in his own motherland. Victor Hugo had been able to wait abroad for the fall of Napoleon the Third only because his works were being published in France. Russian émigré writers, however, were not being published in the Soviet Union, nor would they be. Arkadi Averchenko's trick would not be repeated. As for Bunin, what had he achieved? The Nobel Prize at the age of sixty-three — what good was that to him? Who read Bunin? He'd die in obscurity in his beloved Paris, where they would all die, and there'd be nobody left in Russian literature. Gorky wanted to survive, he wanted monuments to him built in his native land. One could understand that. And he would get his monuments. And his works would be published in collected editions. And he'd get his foreign royalties in hard currency. He was hard currency himself right now. He was even respected by Western writers, as well as by our own writers — even the former "Serapion Brothers," Fedin and Tikhonov, real writers, men of talent and experience who above all were serving the cause of socialism. But RAPP was edging them out of literature by pushing the "proletarian" versifiers into first place. What could be achieved with these rhymsters? What literary monuments would they leave to Stalin's epoch? Demyan Bedny? The only thing he'd leave would be his library, which was said to be a good one. Mayakovsky was capable and his poems were useful. But that was more like politics.

Once upon a time, even Stalin had flirted with writing poetry. As a seminarian he had sent his poem "Morning" to Ilya Chavcha-vadze, the editor of *Iberia*. He'd signed it Soselo, as writing poetry under one's own name was forbidden at the seminary. Chavcha-vadze had published five or six of his verses, reminiscences of Gori, of his father, of the road to Ateni, and of his father's friends meeting around the table. He had not written any more — his destiny did not lie in poetry. Were his poems any good? He'd never looked at them again. But he remembered that Ilya Chavchavadze had praised his "Morning":

> *The rose unfolds its bud,*
> *And tenderly embraces the violet,*
> *High in the clouds*
> *The lark breaks into a trill.*

Yet twenty years later, in 1916, the same poem, still under the pseudonym Soselo, had appeared in Jacob Gogebashvili's textbook for primary schools. If it could be chosen for a textbook, it must have had some value. Nevertheless, he had not been born to be a poet; a poet cannot be a fighter, for poetry softens the soul. Journalism — that was suited to struggle, and his pen had served the Revolution well. He had written a lot, and under all sorts of pseudonyms: David, Nameradze, Chizhikov, Ivanovich, Besoshvili, Kato, Koba. He had adopted Koba as his Party nickname, liking the sound of it. Koba was the noble hero of the novel *The Patricide* by Kazbegi. But when this pesudonym became known to the police, he could no longer use it, so he went back to using a whole range of others: K. Stefin, K. Stalin, K. Solin, until finally in 1913, he had settled on J. Stalin. And that was the name by which the whole world would come to know him.

He had given up writing poetry and had not become a writer, but he loved to read and did so widely. He could no longer recall the books that had entertained him as a youth, as they had melded with the things he'd read later, in prison and his various exiles. The profession of revolutionary left plenty of time for reading, indeed it made reading necessary.

The education at the seminary had been similar to that of a classical high school. They had studied Latin, Greek, biblical Hebrew, French, English, and German. But he had never managed to cope with foreign languages, and he'd not tried again while in exile, because he'd felt it was a waste of time. Yet he learned Russian well. The teaching at the seminary had been in Russian and he'd studied there for five years. He still had his Georgian accent and made no effort to lose it. Accent wasn't important. He'd known Russians who didn't know where to put a comma or where the stress fell on a word.

He didn't read second-rank, second-rate writers. What good were they? He'd read the classics — that was what a Russian revolutionary required: Gogol, Saltykov-Shchedrin, Chekhov, Gorky — they were the ones you could use in the struggle, they could be used in discussion, and if you wanted to take part you had better know them! He did not like, nor did he read, the peasant writers, like Zlatovratsky, Levitov, Karonin, nor even Nekrasov, Nikitin, and Surikov. They pitied the peasant, but the peasant pitied no one, as *he* knew only too well.

Tolstoy had been a great artist, but he had not understood the regime. He had idealized man, he had preached and exhorted, and hence he had debased his art. "The mirror of the Russian Revolution" — what wouldn't he say to please the liberal intellectuals! Dostoevsky was no philosopher. Like Tolstoy, he had no idea of the mechanism of social and state structure. But, unlike Tolstoy, Dostoevsky did not idealize man; he had understood man's insignificance and man's essential meanness all too well, and he had preached the doctrine of suffering. The doctrine had a powerful effect on people, but Dostoevsky was boring, he wrote badly and without artistry.

The greatest of all Russian writers was Pushkin. Pushkin understood and had a feel for everything, and he could do everything. How much his penetrating image of Peter the Great was worth! "He raised Russia on its hindlegs with his iron curb"! And in *Boris Godunov,* the peak of his creativity: "Our silly people are gullible; they're happy to marvel at miracles and novelties; but the boyars will remember Godunov as their equal.... If you're cunning and firm." Well said! "Silly and gullible": yes, that was the essence of the people. "Cunning and firmness": the essence of *his* regime. "They would remember him as their equal": the essence of *his* enemies. He'd been struck by *Boris Godunov* in his youth, and by the image of Otrepyev the pretender in particular: "the unfrocked monk, the fugitive novice, and only twenty years old.... Small of stature, broad of chest, one arm shorter than the other, his hair light brown." Stalin had perhaps read Pushkin in the seminary, as he was included in the curriculum, but he'd read *Boris Godunov* again at the physics observatory, where he'd worked as a statistician after being expelled from the seminary. They were now saying that he'd been expelled from the seminary for spreading Marxist propaganda, and he himself had filled in a questionnaire: "Thrown out of Tiflis Theological Seminary for propagating Marxism." But he'd been expelled for something else: nonpayment of fees, even though his mother sent him money every month, which she got from Igna-tashvili. He hadn't wanted to complete his theological studies; he had had no wish to become a priest. He was by then involved in a Marxist circle. But the version that claimed he had been expelled for his Marxism was the *desired* version, as it enhanced the image of the leader, and therefore served the cause of the Revolution.

He had reread *Boris Godunov* in the observatory. "Unfrocked ... fugitive novice ... only twenty years old.... Small of stature, broad

of chest, one arm shorter than the other, his hair light brown...."
Stalin was twenty at the time, a year from finishing, and he had
abandoned his religious career. He was also small, also broad-
chested, his hair was light brown, and one arm was disabled. He
was no longer a boy, or a sterile dreamer. Of course he did not draw
a comparison between himself and Otrepyev, nor was he even
attracted to that failure. But the physical similarity struck him. He
was also struck by Pushkin's insight into Otrepyev's defeat: he had
indiscreetly given away his great secret to an unstable Polish
woman. Starry-eyed and conscientious, he had been tormented by
the methods every politician had to resort to: "In fair Moscow I'll
show my enemies the cherished path." He was a romantic adventurer, but no politician. He had everything — the will, the vanity,
the dash, the ability to risk, the urge to victory — and an utter
inability to consolidate it. Such was the fate of unsuccessful
politicians: to hold on to power was harder than to seize it.
Otrepyev had not held on to it. This would not have happened if,
after his enthronement in Moscow, Dmitry Otrepyev had done
one-tenth of what the tsar, whose son he claimed to be, had done.

At any rate, that was what Stalin thought now, even though he
could not remember what his thoughts were then. All he remembered clearly was being impressed by their physical similarity. He
had been struck by the fate of the fugitive novice who had been
raised to the pinnacle of secular power. With time, this image had
faded in his mind, pushed out by other historical figures who had
captured his imagination. Yet still, somewhere in the recesses of his
mind, that image persisted.

Perhaps it floated unrecognized into his mind when he met Sofya
Leonardovna Petrovskaya, a Polish aristocrat in Baku? She had
liked him, the proletarian underground revolutionary, the *carbo-
naro* in fringed breeches, unshaven, sullen, taciturn, willful, and
strong. He visited her once when she was out, and when he came
the next time she told him, laughing: "The girl next door said:
'Sofya Leonardovna, a frightening-looking man came to see you.' "

He had grinned then, and had been pleased with the character-
ization: he wanted to be feared.

Sofya had been gentle and sensitive. She had cared for him and

had in fact been the greatest love in his life. She was a Socialist
Revolutionary, but she never argued with him, the Social Democrat.
She did not possess the inflexibility of most women Party function-
aries. She did not try to foist her ideas on him — on the contrary,
she avoided political argument, for she saw that any disagreement
annoyed him. She was the only woman who did not irritate him.
Their relationship ended, however, when she died of tuberculosis.

Of course, he was not Otrepyev and she was not Marina Mniszek.
Yet he now felt that somehow his first impulses had been stirred
precisely by the images that had lain dormant in his unconscious:
the Polish aristocrat and the obscure, unfinished priest, the underground revolutionary with his as yet unclear, but far-reaching plans.

In September at the Shikhovo cemetery, they had buried Khanlar
Safaraliev, an oil worker killed by thugs belonging to a gang of
Black Hundreds. It was the occasion of a great demonstration.
Factory whistles blew as he marched in the column, along with
Shaumyan, Enukidze, Azizbekov, Ordzhonikidze, Dzhaparidze,
and Fioletov. He had made a speech and Sofya had been there. Half
a year later they had buried her in the same cemetery, but then there
was no demonstration and the factory whistles didn't blow. Her
neighbors and her Polish acquaintances had walked in the cortège.
They had lowered the coffin into the grave, thrown earth on top of
it, and gone away. He had stayed behind, as he hadn't wanted to go
back with people he did not know and to whom he had nothing to
say. He stayed and sat on the fresh mound.

The rocky cape of Shikhovo thrust far out into the sea and rose
high above the Bibi-Eibat, which bristled with countless oil wells.
No workers were to be seen, but the rocker-arms moved up and
down, pumping oil. The spring had only just begun, yet the heat
from the sun was already strong. He sat alone on the mountain, on
the rocky headland of Shikhovo at the edge of the Caspian Sea, and
he looked at the bay and the innumerable oil wells. He had buried
Sofya, the only woman he cared for, yet his grief was not
all-consuming. He'd been in prison, in Batum and Kutaisi, he'd
been in exile in eastern Siberia, and he'd escaped from exile. Many
of his comrades had already left the field. Ketskhoveli had died in
prison, Tsulukidze had died. Everyone was passing away and
everyone would pass, as human life was only an instant in this

process. There was only *today,* which was also but an instant. For the revolutionary, however, it was a moment of real life. Only the revolutionary and only the sovereign understood the smallness and insignificance of human life, but only the sovereign had the right to spare himself. One's own life was worth nothing in the struggle for power. Once you had power, then life itself was the victor's reward. Now *he* was the victor, he could preserve life because he could preserve power.

All revolutionaries put their lives at risk, and he had risked his, but he had always been careful. On arriving in Baku, he'd entered the town on foot along the shore, by the oil wells. And when he tired, he sat down on the path and, just as now, lifted his face to the sun, or looked down the road to the oil wells, and the sea.

What is it that drives a revolutionary along his thorny path? Is it an idea? Lots of people have ideas, but they don't become revolutionaries. Love of mankind? Love of mankind was for ditherers, Baptists, and Tolstoyans. No. An idea was no more than a rationale for a revolutionary. Universal happiness, equality and brotherhood, the new society, socialism, communism — they were no more than slogans for raising up the masses for the struggle. To be a revolutionary was a matter of character, of making a protest against one's own oppression. It was the assertion of one's own personality. Five times he'd been arrested and exiled. He'd escaped from exile, he'd hidden, he'd starved, gone without sleep — what was it all for? Was it for the peasants who knew nothing except their own dung, and who didn't want to know? Was it for the sake of the "proletariat"? — those blinkered workhorses, dirty, ignorant, and dim-witted? In Baku he frequently spent the night in one of the workers' barracks, built by the Rothschilds on Bailov. He'd seen plenty of the "working class." He was already a prominent Party activist in Baku, he was the Bolshevik leader there. All the various efforts to dispute this fact had been unsuccessful. He'd managed to nip them in the bud.

Stalin got up from his armchair. A bee was buzzing about his head, close to his ear. He waved it away and it flew off and settled on the table. It crawled toward the ashtray and he swatted it with the volume of Klyuchevsky.

"Meanness!" he said in Georgian. "Meanness!" He sat down again in his armchair and turned his thoughts back to those times, and to the mean little book Enukidze had written.

Enukidze had suddenly decided to write about the underground press that had operated in Baku under the code name "Nina."

The press came under Lenin's direction, the correspondence went via his wife, Krupskaya, and the press itself was managed by Krasin, Enukidze, and Ketskhoveli. Nobody else, according to Enukidze, knew about it, and that meant that he, Stalin, hadn't known about it either, that they had never informed him about it.

One could understand Krasin, the suave electrical engineer who worked at Rothschilds and Mantashevs: Lenin had ordered him to maintain the strictest secrecy. Stalin wasn't angry with Krasin, who had died long ago, anyway. Ketskhoveli was dead, too. And the fate of the Revolution had not been determined by that one little press. That was the way things were then.

But things were different now. Stalin wasn't looking for laurels for his work in Baku or Tiflis or the Transcaucasus. He needed a real history of the Party, one that would serve the interests and authority of his leadership.

If he hadn't known of the existence of an underground press, right there under his nose in Baku, how could it now be claimed that he had been running the Party there? If he had been in charge, then he could not but have known about the press. To deny this would be to deny his role as Lenin's first lieutenant. Did Comrade Abel Enukidze really not understand that? He could not but understand. Why then had he published a book declaring that Comrade Stalin had had no connection with "Nina"? Why did Comrade Enukidze have to do this? What had suddenly drawn him to writing history? And this was the man to whom he had entrusted the security of the Kremlin, entrusted his life! Why were there only old Party members in the commandant's office of the Kremlin? Was that really the principle they applied in selecting security guards? If security officials regarded their work as political, then they were unreliable, as political views were changeable. Even personal sympathy was unreliable, for it was only one step from sympathy to antipathy. A guard must be devoted to his master like a wolfhound. That was the only kind of real guard. He knows only one thing: for the least negligence, for the least oversight he will lose his life, together with all his goods and privileges. That was the kind of guard they ought to be selecting for him. Instead, Comrade Enukidze had chosen Peterson as commandant of the Kremlin, the man who had once been in charge of Trotsky's train, a Trotsky man. Were they plotting a palace coup? Enukidze was one of them, that was plain from his little book. He had revealed himself through it!

That mean-minded provocation of a booklet had to be pulverized into dust. Abel would naturally make disclaimers, lamenting and repenting, and a repentant man is one who is finished politically. Whether he continues to exist physically is of no interest to anyone but his relatives and his dear ones. And even relatives and dear ones get over it.

Who should be given the job of writing a reply? It would be best if it were one of the old Baku group, but who was left of them?

Ordzhonikidze had spent time in Baku, where he had worked in the Shamsi Asadullayev oil fields in the district of Balakhnin as a medical assistant in a small house on the outskirts, a place called Ramanov. Stalin remembered that little house well. It had two rooms. Sergo had lived in one and the other had served as the receiving room. It had been an excellent cover, because anyone might be coming to call on the medical assistant. Sergo worked there for about a year, making flying visits to Baku. He was a real witness, and a good one, too; but he would try to avoid it on the grounds of being too busy. He was a friend of Enukidze's and not likely to want to give evidence against him.

What about Vyshinsky? He was a thoroughgoing scoundrel. All his life he'd been a Menshevik. That was understandable: among the Mensheviks you didn't have to do anything, other than engage in rhetoric. In 1908, the unofficial trial of the Baku union organizers who collaborated with the secret police had been arranged in the People's House in Balakhany. And who had spoken in their defense? Vyshinsky! In one night he spoke five times, so enamored was he of his own oratorical artistry. He was a demagogue and a phrasemonger. In the summer of 1917 he had been head of the

Arbat militia in Moscow and had posted notices announcing the search for and arrest of Lenin. And like a fool he had signed it "A. Vyshinsky." Then, after the October Revolution, he had an audience with Stalin and wept and recanted. But he never mentioned that they had shared parcels in Bailov prison, where they had once been together in the same cell. He had known that he would never be forgiven for such a reminiscence. Keeping quiet about those wretched little parcels was the price he was going to have to pay for his life. In 1920 Stalin had helped him join the Party, in 1925 to become rector of Moscow University, in 1931 chief prosecutor of the Russian Federation. And now Vyshinsky was deputy chief prosecutor of the U.S.S.R. But he was useless as a witness of the Baku period, because he was despised by the Party.

That left Kirov. He hadn't been in Baku before the Revolution, but for five years after he was boss of Azerbaijan and had access to all the archives. He had made a thorough study of the Baku Party organization, and he was well educated and meticulous. He ought to be the one to answer Enukidze's pamphlet. He had the authority to repudiate a version of history that was useless to the Party and, in addition, to support the one that reinforced the authority of the Party leadership. He extolled Comrade Stalin in words, but words were not enough. That was why he had summoned Kirov to Sochi. Let him do some work here, let him show what sort of person he'd become. The three of them would make good company. All three of them liked music. Stalin simply loved to listen to it. Zhdanov could play the piano and Kirov was a music-lover. He went to the opera, and didn't sit in the official box, but in the stalls, just to show what a good democrat he was. Kirov had always wanted to be seen as an intellectual. In his youth he had taken part in amateur theatricals, even though he was only studying at a technical school. Somewhere, either at Sergo's or maybe at Kirov's place itself, he'd seen a photograph of Kirov as a young man. Kirov's wife, Maria Lvovna Markus, had shown it to him. There was the lad in a uniform tunic with buttons, a uniform cap with a badge and on the badge the hammer and adjustable wrench intertwined, the emblem of the technical school. But to those who didn't know, it looked for all the world like a high-school or even university uniform.

But Kirov hadn't wanted to come to Sochi! He had tried to excuse himself because of illness — the doctors were recommending that he go to the spa at Mineralnye Vody for a cure. What's the matter with you? Heartburn. Who doesn't get heartburn? Can you call that an illness? Come here and we'll cure you, we'll do some work together.

"What do I know about history?"

"And what do *I* know about history? So we'll work on it together, you and me."

Let him stay for a while, let him be visible for a while. In fact, they had never been together. Before the Revolution they'd never met, and during the Civil War they only met two or three times. A closer link had been formed when Kirov was in charge of the Azerbaijan Party organization and had come to Moscow for congresses and Central Committee meetings, on business. He had made a pleasant impression. Ordzhonikidze had spoken well of him. He hadn't been abroad, he was not an émigré, but a professional Party worker, and an implacable enemy of Trotsky, Zinoviev, Kamenev, and Bukharin, although he maintained friendly personal relations with Bukharin. Stalin had advanced him. He had been a candidate, or nonvoting member, of the Central Committee at the Tenth Congress, and at the Twelfth Congress he was a full member. In 1930 he entered the Politburo. It had been Stalin who had sent him to Leningrad and entrusted him with the job of crushing that eternal stronghold of dissidence, arrogance, and opposition. Kirov had not fulfilled these hopes. He had not smashed the city; on the contrary, he had become its leader and won himself cheap popularity, as he was now trying to win popularity throughout the Soviet Union. He posed as moderate, good, and kind, in contrast to Comrade Stalin. He had spoken at the Politburo against the execution of Ryutin, and then against those of Smirnov, Talmachev, and Eismont. And he'd carried other Politburo members with him. Even Molotov and Voroshilov had wavered. Only Lazar Kaganovich had been unequivocally in favor of shooting them all.

Magnanimity toward a conquered enemy was dangerous: an enemy will never believe in your magnanimity; he will always regard it as a political maneuver and will attack at the first opportunity. Only a naïve person would reason differently. Kirov was a dangerous idealist. He was demanding material benefits for the working class, not realizing that when a man has material security he is not willing to make sacrifices, he cannot be appropriately enthusiastic, and he turns into a philistine, a petit bourgeois. The people's greatest energy could be evoked only through suffering. Suffering could be used for destruction or for creation. Human suffering leads to God: the people had been nourished by that basic postulate of Christianity for centuries, and it had become part of their flesh and blood, and we must use it. The earthly paradise of socialism was more appealing than a mythical heaven in the sky, even though to achieve it one also had to suffer. Of course the people must be convinced that their hardships were only temporary, that they served the attainment of the great goal, that the supreme authority understood the people's needs and cared for them and protected them from the bureaucrats, however high up. The supreme power was ALL-KNOWING, ALL-WISE, ALL-POWERFUL.

What was it he'd been thinking about the day before in this connection? Feeding the population? Abolishing ration cards? That had already been decided, and the cards would be abolished beginning the first of January. So what was it he'd been thinking about? Ah, yes! The conversation he'd had with the gardener, the Estonian, Arvo Ivanovich. Arvo Ivanovich had been transferred from the Voroshilov sanatorium to the government dacha because he was a local man and reported to be absolutely trustworthy. He was married to a Russian, had spent all his life in Sochi, and was said to be the best gardener there. Stalin had never met Estonians in the Caucasus, although he knew that at the beginning of the century several hundred had come from the Baltic provinces and settled in the area of Sukhumi, and also that three or four Estonian villages had sprung up on the Black Sea coast. The Estonians lived the same way as the local inhabitants: horticulture and cattle-breeding, though their cattle were a tougher breed than the local ones. But he hadn't known that Estonians had settled in Sochi. Arvo Ivanovich looked about fifty. He was a stocky man with high cheekbones, light brown hair, and pale eyes. Like all Estonians, he wore a waistcoat and jacket, but he tucked his wide trousers into his soft boots in the manner of the Caucasus. He spoke Russian with an accent, sometimes comically mispronouncing words. He had been cutting flowers the day before and Stalin, who loved flowers, had been watching him at work. Arvo Ivanovich had muttered something glumly and Stalin had asked him what the matter was. Arvo Ivanovich said his wife had been given short weight in the shop and been short-changed in the bargain. It must be reported to the town Party secretary: the guilty must be severely punished.

Russian merchants had always been crooks and they still were. Now they were afraid of robbing the state, so they robbed the population instead. The people could see what was going on but could do nothing about it. So Stalin would have to do something on their behalf. He didn't go to the shops, but he knew perfectly well his people's needs and the offenses they suffered. Stalin went from the verandah into the room. There behind a large secretarial desk sat Tovstukha, whom Stalin had brought to Sochi. Historians were doing research here, so they needed an intellectual like Tovstukha, the deputy director of the Marx-Engels-Lenin Institute. He knew history and understood what kind of history the Party needed right now. Tovstukha also understood current issues, for he had worked for many years as Stalin's secretary. Not only that, he suffered from tuberculosis, so it was good for him to warm himself in the sunshine. He was so thin and stooped, always coughing as he glowered under his brows. The doctors reported that he hadn't long to live. A pity, as he was a loyal man.

"Prepare a draft decree for the Central Committee," Stalin said. "On the struggle against giving short weight to the customer — no, the consumer. And against short-changing ... Better say this: on infringing retail prices in trade. Facts must be collected to show how this contravenes the Party's concern for the consumer in general. For these facts, Mikoyan, the commissar for trade and the chairman of the Union of Consumers' Societies, and Shvernik, the chairman of the Central Council of Trade Unions, should be admonished. They must also see that no one cheats or demeans the workers. It must be a harsh decree. The Central Executive Committee should decree ten years for short weight and short change!"

"It will take time to assemble the facts," Tovstukha said.

"In that case, write simply: facts have come into the Central Committee ... No: the Central Committee has at its disposal facts ... Write that."

Stalin went back to the verandah, sat down in his armchair, turned his face to the sun, and began thinking about Kirov again. They were calling him the heir. But he, Stalin, was only seven years older than Kirov. How could one talk of his inheriting? Who could say who would die first: the Caucasian people were long-lived. So, it was not inheritance *after* death they had in mind, but inheritance before death. They just couldn't wait. He didn't need a Convention of the sort that had sent Robespierre to the guillotine. Robespierre's fatal error had been to preserve the Convention. Napoleon had dispersed it and had been right to do so, for he was a great man, whereas Robespierre, despite all his harshness, was nothing more than a windbag lawyer.

Once, during one of Kirov's visits to Moscow, they had all gathered at Ordzhonikidze's. Stalin had been there, and Sergo, Kirov, Voroshilov, and Mikoyan. Kaganovich had also been there, although Sergo had not invited him, since he couldn't stand him. But Stalin had said: "Come on, Lazar, Sergo's invited us for supper." He couldn't imagine why, but Kirov had spent a good deal of the evening talking about how much he loved mathematics, physics, chemistry; that he had won an award when he completed technical school and had then started to prepare for the Tomsk Institute of Technology, wanting to become an engineer. Incidentally, hadn't it been there that he'd met Ivan Budyagin? Budyagin had also taken those same courses. Their friendship no doubt stretched back to that period.

As a man with a technical education, however minimal, and with such a love of things technical, Kirov was the right man to run industry. And, if he wanted, let him break industry into sections: machine-building, chemicals, construction, and so on. These conglomerates must be continually broken up, these networks of connected individuals must be shuffled and reshuffled. That was the sort of industry Comrade Kirov could run as a member of the Politburo and as a secretary of the Central Committee. There was nothing shameful about it: it was no disgrace to run the driving force in a country's economy — industry — particularly during a period of industrialization. And if it should turn out that Comrade Kirov did not agree and did not want to come to Moscow, it would mean that he wanted to remain independent and autonomous, that he wanted to continue his own particular line.

6

Sasha had not felt so depressed either in Butyrki prison or during the journey out. In Butyrki he had hoped that the charges would be reexamined and that he'd be released. During the trek there had been a goal: namely, to reach his place of exile, settle down, and wait patiently for his term to end. Hope had preserved his humanity, the goal had kept him alive. Now he had neither hope nor goal. He had simply wanted to help the people use their separator and now he was being accused of sabotage. Alferov had demonstrated it all to him with iron logic. Alferov, too, could smash him at any moment, if he chose to release Ivan Parfenovich's statement. Could one really live like this? What good were textbooks on French and politics and economics and philosophy that were on their way from Moscow? To whom was he going to expound them, with whom was he going to speak French? With the bears in the taiga? And even if Alferov left him alone, how and on what was he going to live in this place? He could learn to sew soles onto felt boots. That would be his fate. He'd forget everything he ever knew. The ideals he had grown up with had been taken over by the Baulins, the Lozgachevs, and the Dyakovs of this world, who flouted them and trampled on the people who were still loyal to them. He used to believe that you had to have strong hands and an inflexible will, otherwise you'd perish. Now he understood: you'd perish in any event, because your will would inevitably clash with a more inflexible one and your hands would wrestle with those that were even stronger because they held authority. In order to survive you had to submit to an alien will and an alien force. You had to protect yourself, adapt, live like a hare, afraid to poke your nose beyond the bush. Only at this price could one preserve oneself physically. Was such a life worth living?

Sasha was sitting in his room and trying to read. Outside in the yard, the old man tapped away with his ax, making something. The uniform, monotonous tapping only accentuated Sasha's sense of ennui. The old man left the yard, but Sasha could not read and he threw down the book. He simply would not be able to endure this life, he simply could not. He lay down on his bed and fell asleep, but even in his dreams the feeling of calamity would not leave him and he awoke in alarm with his heart pounding.

What did Alferov want from him? His benevolence had not been accidental. He wanted him to remain there for a reason. Logically, he ought to have formulated a case against Sasha in order to justify his own existence. Yet he had let him go back to Mozgova and hinted at a possible transfer to Kezhma and work at the machine station — and he had asked for nothing in return. Was he trying to win Sasha over or, on the contrary, to demoralize him? Perhaps he wanted to reduce Sasha to nothingness, to keep him in ignorance, under stress, in a state of permanent terror, knowing that there was a complaint against him and that he had to wait until he was summoned, and that he was not going to have a peaceful life. It was all so depressing.

The old woman called to him through the door: "Are you going to eat?"

"I've got a toothache, so I'm not going to eat," he replied.

He did not leave the house for two days. He sat in the yard and helped the old man. He knew Zida was waiting for him, but he did not want to see her, because she had witnessed his disgrace; she would try to console him, and this would only underscore his humiliation. In any case, he was indifferent to everything and everyone. He must end it all! He would never escape this vicious circle. But how would his mother take it? She wouldn't survive it, she couldn't withstand such a blow. He must go on, just so that his mother knew he was alive and would not lose hope.

Vsevolod Sergeyevich came to see him on the third day.

"What's the matter with you? You don't show up anymore. Are you sick?"

"I'm fine."

"Alferov get to you?"

"He proved to me that I'm a saboteur trying to overthrow kolkhoz authority. He proved it logically and convincingly."

Vsevolod Sergeyevich burst out laughing. "That's not surprising. He's a trained philosopher. Don't be fooled by his position. He's a real somebody. He's got three, maybe even four bars on his shoulder, more than his bosses in Kansk. That's why he doesn't wear a uniform. He's even been abroad, yet he ended up here. I'm afraid he may be, so to speak, one of our future colleagues or associates. Or he may of course land on his feet. It all depends on higher circumstances about which you and I know nothing. At any rate, he showed you his power, that he can grind you into dust simply on the statement of the kolkhoz chairman. You broke the separator and called the kolkhoz chairman an idiot. Was that what he accused you of?"

"Yes."

"Well, I want to reassure you. The very same day, they took the separator to Kezhma where they did exactly what you said they should. Then they brought it back and now it works perfectly. You can go and see for yourself."

"I haven't the slightest desire."

"And quite right, too. My advice to you, Sasha, is not to touch it again. Anyway, I think they'll drop the sabotage accusation. Don't worry."

"I'm not worried. I'm disgusted."

"I understand. And if you will let me be frank with you, I'll say one more thing. May I?"

"Of course."

"You, Sasha, are without doubt a human being. A real human being! A Soviet human being! I'm not paying you a compliment, I'm stating a fact. And it's good to be a real, high-principled, Soviet human being. But you want to be one in your present special circumstances, you want to behave the way a Soviet human being behaves. But that's not possible, Sasha: these people do not see you as a Soviet man, but as an *anti*-Soviet man. And that is the only way they see you and what you do here. You are walking along the street and you see that the separator isn't working, and since you understand about separators, you immediately go over and fix it. But the chairman of the kolkhoz and the district officer — I don't mean Alferov, but a run-of-the-mill district officer — they see it differently: why did he bother with the separator, which is none of his business? Obviously in order to break it. The enemy wrecks and plays dirty tricks whenever he can — I hope you know who spoke those words?"

"I know," Sasha replied.

"You don't want to be a social outcast, but you must take your position into account. You called the kolkhoz chairman an idiot, and that was your biggest mistake. If you'd cursed him to hell, nothing would have come of it. But the word *idiot* is insulting and humiliating, it smacks of superiority, it makes you clever and him a fool. Didn't Alferov suggest you move to another village?"

"Yes, he did."

"And? Did you refuse? On account of Nurzida Gazizovna?"

"I neither accepted nor refused. I told him to decide for himself. I don't want to be under any obligation to him; I don't want to be in his debt."

Vsevolod Sergeyevich thought for a while then said: "Well, maybe you've made the right decision. Though it would be more peaceful for you somewhere else. Here you've already had a fight with your landlord's son, then the incident with the chairman. Your reputation is not so great. But let's hope it will pass. You're suffering from nerves right now, Sasha. Your nerves are strained, under tension, like a spring: you had the arrest, prison, the transport, the trek, then Mozgova, the room, and then these troubles. And the way things happened, the spring snapped at the next turn of the screw. We've all been through it. The main thing is, it shouldn't become a habit. But you're tough, you've got a will of your own — learn from all of this. There's only one conclusion to be drawn: Don't fight with them and behave discreetly with the schoolteacher, because they'll be watching you from now on. Their fangs are bared, and they could get you for that as well."

He leaned over Sasha's bed and slapped him on the shoulder.

"Come on, that's enough! Get up! Let's go and have a game of Preference."

"I play badly."

"So what? Cards are our solace. The criminals play blackjack and we play Preference. Have a shave — you're all overgrown — get dressed, and we'll go. It's high time you met the local intelligentsia."

Sasha didn't want to go, but Vsevolod Sergeyevich insisted and Sasha realized that he should see how other people managed their lives in this place.

Mikhail Mikhailovich Maslov was about forty-five and had a gloomy, tormented face. He'd arrived from Solovki Islands a year before. It was plain from his bearing that he was an ex-officer.

"And we were sure you weren't coming," he said sourly to Vsevolod Sergeyevich when he arrived with Sasha.

"You've still got plenty of time to beat us," Vsevolod Sergeyevich replied with good humor.

During the game, Mikhail Mikhailovich didn't give the others any time to think. He pressed the game forward and criticized everyone's bad moves, except Sasha's. Sasha was from a different, hostile world, and he ignored him. For his part, Sasha found Mikhail Mikhailovich unsympathetic. He didn't like short-tempered, carping people. They reminded him of his father. It was a matter of character, not environment.

The fourth player was Peter Kuzmych, a former merchant from the town of Old Oskol in the province of Voronezh. He'd begun his term in Narym and was ending it here on the Angara. He was about sixty, stockily built, with broad shoulders, a barrel chest, and a short black beard streaked with gray. His breeches were tucked into his boots and he wore an old, worn-out jacket shiny at the elbows and lapels. Unlike the rest, he talked willingly about his misadventures.

"When they banned trading, I stopped doing business," he said. "And when they allowed it again, I sold everything the peasant needed. Scythes and sickles, pitchforks, all kinds of hardware and ironmongery, all the stuff I'd dealt with since childhood. There was a cooperative in the village, but the peasants all came to me, I had everything in stock in good time. I knew what the peasant needed. Well, then you know how things changed: there was the tax inspector, then another one, then there was the tax, then a new assessment, then self-assessment. In prison they demanded gold from me. Where was I supposed to find gold? My gold was in ironware: iron bars, graded iron, band iron, roofing iron. The only gold I'd ever seen was in ten- and five-ruble tsarist coins."

Peter Kuzmych spoke without bitterness. "Even the interrogator demanded gold. I was a trader, all right, I was dispossessed and disenfranchised. But what's it got to do with my children? Did they choose their father and mother? And of course they also wanted to live, they wanted to go with the rest of them into the Pioneers and the Komsomol, but everywhere they were chased away. Alyoshka, the youngest, a brainy boy, went off to Moscow, got himself a job in a factory. He writes to a newspaper: 'I, so-and-so, have broken with my father and have no connection with him.' It hurts. I raised him, I nurtured him, I fed him, and all of a sudden: 'I renounce you.' But what else could he do? Nothing. And anyway he believes commerce is harmful, alien, he says, one should live by labor.... Labor — just you try moving barrels of drying oil or plowshares around the shop, or kegs of nails, you know what my work's like.... All right! Alyoshka got himself into an institute. He decided to become an agronomist, drawn to the soil, he was. He lives in Moscow, in a hostel, but his mother doesn't sleep at night because her boy's starving. I sent him thirty rubles, he sent it back — it's ideological, he says. All right, so long as it's ideological, sit and starve! But it broke his mother's heart and she gave some neighbors food to take to him — a piece of pork fat and some homemade pies. The neighbors arrive at the hostel. Alyoshka's not there, so they leave the parcel on his stool — everyone had a stool by their bed — and there were four sharing the room. Alyoshka arrives, sees the parcel. Who's it from? People from your hometown brought it, they explain. No, he replies, the parcel is from my parents, I'm sending it back. But the others say, Why send it back, let's eat some kulak fat — they're young, healthy, and starving. They wolfed down the fat and the pies. And then one of them, one of the same people who'd eaten the pies, writes to the Party cell to say that Alyoshka's getting food from his parents and so he'd lied when he said he'd broken off relations with them. Alyoshka was expelled from the Komsomol and from the institute and went back to work at the factory. He had renounced his own folks, but the people he was trying to join had renounced him. . . ."

"That's the hundredth time we've heard it," Mikhail Mikhailovich interrupted. "Look at your cards."

"Why shouldn't I tell the young man?" Peter Kuzmych objected mildly. "Maybe he finds it interesting. Are your parents alive?"

"Yes, they are," Sasha replied.

"Have they been left alone?"

"Why should anyone bother them?"

"If they want to, they'll find a reason. It's easy for them: their son's in exile, so let them pine away in Siberia as well."

"You took pity on your boy the wrong way," Mikhail Mikhailovich muttered reproachfully. "You sent him a package and ruined his life. He wouldn't have died without your food — other students get by. And he was right to renounce you. Our lot is finished. 'The Revolution is the locomotive of history,' and we've fallen under its wheels. Better get used to the idea!"

"So a son is not a son and a father is not a father."

"Precisely," Mikhail Mikhailovich continued with irritation. " 'Honor thy father and thy mother' comes from God, and nobody needs God. Their religion is equality, and that's how it's going to be everywhere. They're going to make world revolution and everyone will be equal."

"That's enough about world revolution from you," Vsevolod Sergeyevich said, butting into the conversation. "The Bolsheviks themselves have given it up. The state, that's the religion for the Russian man, he even honors God in his sovereign. And he obeys. And he doesn't want freedom of any kind. Freedom would take the form of a universal bloodbath, whereas the people want order. I don't want Stepan Razin or Emelyan Pugachev. I prefer Lenin or even Stalin."

"That's why we're all here."

"Yes. And if we had Razin or Pugachev you'd be hanging from an aspen." Vsevolod Sergeyevich went on: "The Bolsheviks have saved Russia. They preserved it as a great power. If we had so-called freedom, Russia would fall apart. The new autocrat is strengthening Russia, all praise and honor and whatever else God grants him!"

"The state is supposed to protect its citizens, whereas your state fights against them," Mikhail Mikhailovich said. "It fights with me, with you, with Peter Kuzmych, it fights with the peasant on whom it depends, it even fights" — he nodded at Sasha — "with its own. I'm also a Russian and I'm all for Russia, but not for one like this."

"It's the only one there's going to be." Vsevolod Sergeyevich laughed.

The visit to Mikhail Mikhailovich did nothing to divert Sasha from his brooding, nor did it lift the weight and desperation from his shoulders.

He was all too familiar with such discussions, for and against a change of direction, and he found them tedious. Only Peter Kuzmych's story had had a human touch. Had it really been impossible to end the New Economic Policy without such excesses? And to ruin a boy's life just because his friends persuaded him to eat some of his mother's pies? It was all so impossible, so tedious. . . .

To this tedium was added his concern about his mother: up to this time he had not received a single letter from her.

On Wednesdays the exiles gathered on the bank of the Angara to wait for the mailboat. It was the main event in their monotonous lives. The peasant women would be rinsing their laundry, the young children would be swimming and would crawl trembling with cold out of the water, while the exiles strolled up and down the bank gazing into the misty distance of the river. Finally a tiny dot would be spotted downriver, the excitement would rise — was it the mailboat or not? The postman in his canvas raincoat with the hood down on his back would throw out a sack bearing a label marked "Mozgova," then he would hand out the letters and collect any for posting.

Sasha also went down to the river and waited for the mail with the rest of them, but the only letter he got was from Boris Soloveichik: "To Napoleon in exile" was the address on the envelope. Poor Boris, still making jokes, still full of optimism. He had petitioned for his transfer to Freda or Freda's transfer to him.

But Sasha received nothing from his mother in Moscow. He had sent a cable to her from Kansk in May and mailed his first letter at the same time. Allowing a week for a reply to get to Kansk and supposing a letter had arrived in Kansk when the mail for Boguchany had already left, it would wait in Kansk for another week. Then it would wait in Boguchany to be readdressed to Kezhma. In all, three weeks, and he'd already been here for over a month.

Vsevolod Sergeyevich tried to reassure him. "The first letter always takes forever. You have your way of counting and the post office have theirs. Letters from Moscow can take three weeks or three months, though nobody has a clue why. They could be tossed into the wrong bag, the cart could have broken down, the mail could have been left with a village soviet and half of it was lost. And if the postman drops the bag into the Angara, you'll be waiting the rest of your life. Then there's our dear Comrade Alferov, who's dying of boredom, so he gets a lot of pleasure reading our letters, and if something especially interests him, perhaps because of its literary merit, he could hang onto it for a month or so, or even keep it for good. Your reckoning of the time is wrong. They might have garbled your cable and your first letter to your dear mother may never have got there for any number of reasons, so she only got your second letter and you'll have to wait for an answer another month or six weeks. You have to be patient, my friend."

Vsevolod Sergeyevich was right, but seeing the others getting letters and newspapers and parcels, while he didn't, made Sasha edgy. He had sent two or three letters to his mother with every post. He'd written that he'd settled down well, that he had fine quarters, that the people here were fine, that she should not send him anything, as he had everything he needed.

Downcast, he walked home from the river along the village street. People greeted him as if nothing had happened, as if he hadn't been accused of sabotage or been summoned to Kezhma. Then he realized that as far as the village was concerned, nothing *had* happened. Nobody was concerned with him. Just as he'd been sent here, so he'd be sent away. They'd seen hundreds like him. They were used to the dead, the murdered, and the finished. They wouldn't even give shelter to the children of the special settlers.

Even the kolkhoz chairman, Ivan Parfenovich, paid no attention to Sasha and looked at him with indifference. He'd made his report to the proper authority; it was up to them to deal with it, he had enough worries of his own.

He ran into Zida several times. She looked at him inquiringly and he greeted her with a nod, but he didn't stop. He saw the light in her window in the evenings, but he didn't visit her. He felt sorry for her, but he could do nothing. He couldn't deal with her now. He couldn't deal with anyone or anything.

He saw Fedya only when he went to the store for whatever he needed. Fedya was as friendly as before, and once asked him to fix his bicycle for him.

"No way!" Sasha told him. "From now on I fix nothing. Repair it yourself!"

"Because of the separator?" Fedya asked.

"What do you think?"

"It might still turn out all right," Fedya said, without much conviction.

Sasha shuddered. The village did not regard the incident as closed. *It might still turn out all right.* And maybe it wouldn't turn out all right. They knew that if you got stuck with the label of saboteur, you didn't just walk away from it.

"I think it will turn out all right," Fedya went on with greater assurance, having reflected on it. "The separator works — they took it to the machine station and they said the thread had gone, just as you said. And he's not a bad man."

"Who's not a bad man?"

"Ivan Parfenovich, the kolkhoz chairman. He's not a bad man. You have to realize he's the boss. The squirrels have gone, there are fewer cows, they don't send grain, the peasants are recruited for the construction sites — try managing everything with just peasant women. And for the sake of that separator the women will tear your throat out because they have to have it. So, he had his say and you should have let it be, but you had to stand on your honor."

"Okay," Sasha interrupted him. "Just give me some cigarettes and matches, and fill this can with kerosene. I'm going!"

"Sasha, come on, be a man! The chain's come off my bicycle and

I can't put it back on. We'll have a drink later, and I've got some smoked grayling. What have I done wrong? I even told Ivan Parfenovich: Drop it, Ivan Parfenovich, I said, he's a city boy from Moscow, he just wanted to help and he told the women what to do, but they're such lumps! It'll all be all right, Sasha."

"Okay," Sasha said. "Show me the bike."

Fedya led him through to the yard and brought his bicycle out of the hut. As he checked it over, testing the bearings, the gears and chain, and the nuts, Sasha remembered the bicycle he'd had in his childhood. It had been an old lady's bike, assembled from various models. He could ride well in those days. He could stand on the saddle, ride with his back to the handlebars, leap off backward, letting the bike come out from under him. Max Kostin used to run around the yard and along the street after him and Sasha would let him ride it, and sometimes they rode together, with Max sitting on the saddle and Sasha pumping the pedals. Because it was a lady's bike, it had no crossbar.

The bicycle reminded him also of the dacha on the Klyazma. A lot of the boys and girls had bikes, not improvised ones like his, but Dukes and Enfields. They cost a lot, but their parents there weren't exactly poor — they were "experts," doctors, lawyers. The children used to ride down to the Klyazma to swim or more often to the Ucha, since it was wider. The path wound alongside the railway, then down a ravine, then back up to the railway, where the gravel flew out from under their wheels and the wind blew in their faces.

Toward evening the vacationers would gather on the station platform and wander up and down as they waited for the train from Moscow to arrive. Well-groomed women in light summer dresses with low necklines met their husbands, solid men in raw-silk suits and carrying heavy briefcases.

When Sasha appeared on the platform, wheeling his bike, black-haired, stripped to the waist, broad-shouldered and bronzed a deep, even tan, the women looked at him, smiled, and asked: "Whose chocolate boy is that?" It gave him a pleasant, sweet thrill. Only the word *boy* upset him.

In the evenings they played hide-and-seek in a clearing in the woods. One girl — he couldn't remember her name, but she was tall, slim, and long-legged — hid with him and pressed herself against him, as if in terror. Sasha could feel her hot body and wanted to pull her closer, but he hadn't the nerve. He said rudely: "Don't fidget, haven't you got enough room?"

Physical desire had arisen in him early, but he had suppressed it as unworthy of a real man. That was how he had thought at thirteen. The boys in the yard talked about girls cynically, boasting and bragging, and Sasha found their talk offensive. He wouldn't play kissing games, which he thought cheap and common — a man ought to have other, higher interests. He was a proud boy and didn't want to appear weak or cowardly. In the schoolyard he was thought strong and daring, but nobody knew what it cost him, what he had to overcome in himself.

The leggy girl latched onto Yasha Rashkovsky. Sasha could remember his name to this day. He was a tall boy who came from a famous ballet family in Moscow. He also studied at the Bolshoi. A year or two older than Sasha, the proud possessor of a Duke racing bike, he stood out among the cycling group. He once suggested that they go for a swim in the Klyazma, not the Ucha, because he'd found a good place for diving.

They arrived at the Klyazma, got off their bikes, and undressed, the boys wearing their bathing trunks and the girls their bathing suits. It was indeed a good place to dive. The bank was steep and overhung the water. But it was also very high, some twenty-five feet, and the girls were even too scared to stand at the edge. They would lie on their stomachs and peer down into the water over the edge. The boys wouldn't dive from so high a spot, either. Only Yasha would risk it. He jumped feet first into the water, surfaced, and then swam in long strokes back to the bank and climbed back up to the top by a steep path. The girls ogled him in ecstasy, including the leggy one. Yasha Rashkovsy was a well brought up boy and he didn't brag about his dive or put on airs or egg on anyone else to dive. He just lay on the ground sunning his back.

Sasha had dived off bridges and boats, but he'd never gone off a diving board or a bank this high. But since Yasha had done it, why shouldn't he? He had to jump, he had to overcome his fear. He was a good swimmer and he could dive well. The main thing was to stand straight, stretch out fully, and not to hit the water with your belly or back, but to enter it smoothly. It was not a spirit of competition that made him do it, but the need to overcome his own timidity. If he didn't do it now, he'd only be angry at himself. Sooner or later he'd come back and do it anyway, so why not now?

He got up and stretched. *I must just do it.*

He ran to the edge of the bank and plunged. He went in deep, and quickly stroked to reach the surface, where he turned onto his back and caught his breath. Above him, on the bank, Yasha was looking at him, and so was the leggy girl. . . .

These memories of his childhood tormented him now: Why had he cultivated such willpower, why had he toughened his character?

Someone was calling him and he recognized Zida's voice. He turned to see her standing at the steps.

"I've come to see Fedya's mother. I've brought her some medicine."

Sasha knew that Zida brought medicine from Kezhma and did what she could to help the villagers with cures. He also knew that her pupils missed lessons or gave up school altogether, and that in the school itself there were not enough textbooks or exercise-books, or even pencils. Zida tried to get what she could in Kezhma, and if she couldn't get anything, she managed with what there was. She went to the parents and tried to persuade them to send their children back to school. Sometimes she succeeded, sometimes not. She was a fine person, of course, staunch and uncomplaining, but why did she do it, why was she voluntarily wasting away in the backwoods?

"Why don't you come to me?" she said quietly.

"I'm in a rotten mood."

"Come and see me, Sasha, I miss you."

"They'll know and it could be dangerous for you. Do you think they don't realize who you're lighting your lamp for at night?"

"I won't light it. Come as soon as it's dark. I'll fry some fresh fish and bake some pies."

Her nearness, her voice, and the familiar scent of her cheap perfume excited him.

"I'm going to be drinking with Fedya; shall I come drunk?"

"Come, however you are."

"Don't think about that stupid business, don't torment yourself," Zida said. "Alferov went to the machine station and told them to fix the separator and they did it the same day. He doesn't want to make a case over it."

"How do you know about that?"

"The manager of the machine station told me himself. I'm friendly with his wife."

Sasha knew that she had invented this story to reassure him. Maybe Alferov had gone to the depot, since he was interested in the separator, but it was she, he was sure, who had asked the manager to repair it quickly. He said to her: "When this saga's over, they'll come up with a new one. They'll find something."

"It was no more than an accident, what happened to you. There's never been anything like it before."

"Listen," Sasha said suddenly. "Couldn't your manager friend ask to have me work at the depot? They must need people."

She propped herself up on her elbow and looked at him. Her face was next to his, and in the moonlight coming through the small window she looked unnaturally white.

"You want to move to Kezhma?"

"My darling," he said, "I have to do *something,* I have to make some sort of living."

She sank back on the pillow and said nothing. She didn't want him to move to Kezhma, she was afraid of losing him. Didn't the silly girl realize she was going to lose him anyway? Even if he managed to complete his term, even if he were free, he would not have the right to ask anyone to share his future. His sentence would always hang over him, he would always be in the sights of the Dyakovs. Could he take on the responsibility of another life, another's fate, could he condemn Zida to a life of hardship and wandering? He would have to lose himself, dissolve, hide himself without trace. He was a marked man. He would have to remain

alone. He didn't know if he would be able to look out for himself, but he was sure he wouldn't be able to look out for two of
them.

"I was joking," he said. "You don't have to ask for me. They
wouldn't give me a job there anyway. And besides, in Kezhma I'm
likely to get involved in another ruckus. They'd all be down on me
there."

Zida reached out in the dark and stroked his head.

"Cheer up, you're still young, your whole life is still in front of
you. How much longer have you got? Two years."

"Two years and four months." He was more precise.

"They'll soon pass, Sasha. You'll be free and you'll leave."

"Where will I go? They won't let me go back to Moscow, so it'll
mean wandering again, and with Article Fifty-eight still around my
neck."

"Maybe you ought to go somewhere like our place, in Tomsk
province. . . ."

He sensed she was leaving something unsaid.

"And what good would that do?"

"You're not known there," she replied, and again he felt she was
holding something back.

"Well, my name will be perfectly plain from my identity papers
and the sentence will be entered there, too. This is how it's done: on
the form there's a column that says, 'What documents serve as the
basis for the passport?' they write: 'Point II of government decree
of such-and-such date,' and that's the decree about the passport
system and its restrictions. So it doesn't matter whether I go to
Tomsk or Omsk, I carry the sentence. Do you understand?"

"Yes, I understand, but it is possible to lose one's passport."

He laughed. "If it was that easy, everyone who had served a
sentence would have got rid of his passport long ago and his
sentence with it. I don't think anyone has yet managed to do that.
When they issue a new passport, they make all the necessary
inquiries and it all comes out."

"I've got friends there, they can do anything," she said.

"I have no intention of living illegally on a forged passport."

"It would all be legal — you'd just have to change your
name."

"Really? That's very interesting!"

She sat up again and leaned close to him.

"If we both leave here when your time's up and we get married there, then under the law you can take my name and they'll issue you with a new passport, and in the column you mentioned they'll write: 'Issued on certificate of marriage.' You won't be a Pankratov anymore. That's not such a bad thing, is it?"

"And I'd become a Muslim." He laughed. "But won't they make me get circumcised?"

"I'm being serious. There are people there I can rely on."

"Have you just made all this up?"

"I've lived all my life in Siberia and I know how things are done. I'm not trying to force myself on you, I'm just thinking how to get you out of your predicament. Later on, if you want, we can get a divorce and you can still keep my name, but with a clean passport. You'll make me a *talak.*"

"What's a *talak?*"

"Tatar for divorce. When a husband wants to get rid of his wife, he pronounces the word *talak* three times."

Poor Zida. She thought there might be some happiness ahead for her. But there would be none, neither for her nor for him. She was offering him a kind of stowaway life, with a false name and a false passport. And if sometime, somewhere, he was to run into someone he knew, he would have to explain that he was no longer Pankratov, because, you see, he'd *got married.* And if Dyakov and his ilk were to catch up with him, they'd crow with joy and triumph: *So, you were trying to hide behind your wife, were you? No, my friend, you can't hide from us. And it's no accident that you're living on a false passport. No honest Soviet citizen needs a false passport, no honest Soviet citizen changes his name.*

But he didn't want to say this to Zida, because he didn't want to hurt her.

"Look, Zida," he said. "When you go for a job you have to fill out an application. You have to put down your life history: where you were born, where you went to school, who your parents are, and who their parents are. There's no way I could conceal Pankratov. They'd ask a few questions and it would all come out."

She was persistent. "We'll go to some remote district, you'll work as a driver or a mechanic, they don't use application forms for jobs like that, they don't make inquiries."

"That's enough," Sasha said. "This conversation is senseless. I was born with this name and I'll die with it. There'll be no changing it."

7

The tax inspector accused Kostya of concealing earnings and imposed a huge assessment. Nonpayment would result in a prison sentence. Meanwhile, an inventory was taken of his property at his address in Sokolniki, even though he insisted it did not belong to him but to his wife, Klavdya Lukyanovna. That was how Varya found out he was not divorced.

If he had told her right at the beginning that he hadn't formalized his divorce, she would have thought nothing of it. But he had concealed it. That was why he hadn't shown her his passport. It was humiliating. It was the first sign of Kostya's other life, about which she knew nothing.

"Varya," he pleaded, "there was nothing else I could do. I only registered my marriage with Klavdya to get a permit to live in Moscow, and it cost me a lot of money. I didn't tell you about it because I was afraid you wouldn't understand. Thousands of people do it all the time, otherwise nobody would be able to register in Moscow. In order to free myself from Klavdya I had to register myself somewhere. But where? At whose address? Who would register me? Sofya Alexandrovna? Who would let her? At Nina's? Nina wouldn't allow it; she refuses to acknowledge my existence."

"What's the solution?" Varya asked. "Does Klavdya Lukyanovna remain your legal wife and me your common-law wife?"

Mustering his dignity, he replied: "I'm installing a complicated electrical system in a research institute that's part of the Academy of Sciences. They're building housing for their staff and they've promised me a room."

As always, he sounded so plausible: an institute, the Academy of

Sciences, complicated technology ... But it didn't seem very likely to Varya.

"If they want to give you a room, they'll have to put you on the staff."

Kostya tightened his mouth and, speaking slowly, said: "Okay, I didn't want to tell you, but now I have to. What did you think, that I get jobs because of my beautiful eyes? No, Varya! I turn over half my pay to the people who get me the jobs. And to make sure they get their half, they hold me to a contract, a tough contract. I give them their half. But I pay the tax on the whole amount, so what does that leave me? Not a bean! Zero! But you and I have to live on something. So I didn't report on my return a couple of minor jobs I'd done at hospitals, and that's what the taxman pounced on. Believe me, I'd have quit doing this ages ago, but I've hung on because of the institute. I've been hoping for this room. And thank God you and I didn't register, otherwise they'd have come here to seize my property."

"What about Klavdya?"

"What about Klavdya?"

"Have they listed her property for this?"

"Don't worry on her account. She won't mind. She's been in worse scrapes than this. Don't worry about anyone or anything, everything's going to be all right, it'll all be fine. If I didn't tell you everything, it was only for your sake. Your peace of mind is the most important thing to me."

He could talk for hours when he wanted to convince someone of something. He found thousands of words and hundreds of arguments.

Did Varya believe him? She wanted to, otherwise how could she go on living with him? But she realized bitterly that nobody was really independent, neither she nor Kostya, and maybe he had even less independence than others. Lyova was dependent on his job, but however minor, it was legal, and he was dependent on his salary, but however piddling, it was legitimate. Kostya was dependent on a hundred circumstances beyond his control and danger dogged him at every step. Today he was rich; tomorrow he could be poorer than everyone else. Today he was riding high, but tomorrow he might be cast into the gutter.

Varya didn't know how Kostya managed to wriggle out of the whole mess, but evidently he did. For nearly two weeks he was hardly at home. He didn't go to the restaurants or billiards halls. Two weeks of feverish activity, of which she knew nothing, and finally he told her he'd paid off the entire obligation. However, he was finished for good with the workshop. What his future plans were she did not know: he did not tell her and she did not ask.

All he told her was that he'd taken a job in another workshop on Herzen Street, where they repaired typewriters. He knew about typewriters. He gave her the workshop phone number but said it might be difficult to reach him there, because he left the shop at ten in the morning for the various institutions whose machines he was to repair and sometimes, if he got the orders the day before, he went straight to his clients in the morning. Varya guessed, and in due course found out for sure, that Kostya was only employed on paper; other craftsmen were doing his work and getting his wages. But the job provided Kostya with an official position: he was an employee in a typewriter-repair shop. His sole employment, however, and his sole source of income, was billiards, nothing but billiards.

It was then that Varya decided that she'd had enough. It was time to get a job.

Lyova and Rina had promised to help her. They were employed in the design bureau for the Moscow Hotel where Zoe also worked. Varya could get herself a job without anyone's help, in fact — draftsmen were so very much in demand that there were job notices posted everywhere — but she preferred to work with people she knew. Lyova and Rina said that the Moscow Hotel, which was the biggest and most important structure in the capital, came under the direct control of the Moscow City Soviet, and as a result wages were higher there and the canteen excellent. The new building was being connected to the Grand Hotel, and together they would make one of the largest hotels in Europe. The best architects, artists, engineers, and technologists worked together on the project. In particular Lyova and Rina praised their boss, whom they called Igor, with the accent on the *or,* as if he were French. He was a talented young architect, one of the designers of the project, an attentive, kind, and responsive man. And if Varya did well, Igor could promote her as he had Lyova, who already had reached the grade of technician. Rina had similar prospects. The office was located on the fifth floor of the Grand Hotel in Okhotny Row, only seven stops from the apartment house on the Arbat, and there were two trams that went past it, the 14 and the 17. Zoe, who worked in a different section of the office, made a special point of that.

Varya turned up at the Grand Hotel on the appointed day.

The warehouses on Okhotny Row, the little church, and other buildings between the Grand Hotel and the Manège had been demolished and the site was surrounded by fencing. Varya entered the hotel from Voskresensky Square. A uniformed doorman looked her over but did not ask where she was going. Neither did the elevator operator who took her to the fifth floor.

She came out of the elevator and turned left, as Lyova had instructed her, and walked down a long corridor. She scanned the numbers on the doors, which were as they had been when that floor was part of the hotel. When she came to 526, she opened the door.

It was exactly like the room she and Kostya had had in the Hotel Orianda in Yalta, with a high ceiling and tall, narrow windows. Except that instead of hotel furniture, the rooms only contained three plain desks with sloping supports. They served as drawing boards.

Lyova was working by the window and looked up as she entered. He gave a welcoming smile, exposing his crooked tooth, and laid down his drawing pen.

"You've come! Good girl!"

"Where's Rina?"

"She popped out. She'll be back in a minute. Did you bring your diploma with you?"

He glanced over Varya's certificate.

"It's fine. Let's go."

He opened the door to the next office.

"May we, Igor Vladimirovich?"

He went in without waiting for an answer, taking Varya with him. As soon as Varya heard the name she grasped the situation. How could she not have guessed sooner? This was the man Vika had introduced her to at the National. Had she realized it sooner, she would not have come. But it was too late. Igor Vladimirovich recognized her at once. He raised his eyebrows in surprise, got up, and came around the desk, smiling in an inquisitive, though welcoming way. At the same time he looked slightly embarrassed.

"Igor Vladimirovich," Lyova said. "This is the girl I've been telling you about, Madame Ivanova. She has her diploma with her. Varya, show your diploma."

Varya took her certificate out of her bag again and laid it on the desk.

"Please sit down," Igor Vladimirovich said, as he sat down himself.

"Shall I leave?" Lyova asked.

"Yes, yes, thank you. . . ."

Lyova went out of the room.

Igor Vladimirovich looked over Varya's certificate.

"Have you worked anywhere?"

"No."

"No, of course not, you only left school three months ago." He smiled. "What an unexpected event! Lyova has been telling me about you and recommending you highly, but I had no idea who it was."

"And I didn't expect to see you, either," she said.

The first embarrassment had passed, but she now felt a certain sadness. She had met him only once, three or four months ago, yet it felt as though it had been an eternity. The walk in the Alexander Park, the conversation about Bové, the escape from the park guard, and her torn stocking — how far away it all was!

"You've changed a bit," Igor Vladimirovich said. "Or rather, you've grown up somewhat."

"I got married," she explained. She thought this statement would make their relationship perfectly plain.

"I had heard." He smiled again.

From Vika, she thought.

"Well now," he said briskly, "let's get down to business. You have no work experience, so you'll have to start as a copier."

"Yes, I know."

"Do you like drawing?"

"Yes, I love it."

"Good. There are two possibilities. Either you can work in the general drawing office, or in my own group with Lyova and Rina. What would suit you best?"

Varya did not want to work in the general office, where she only knew Zoe; she would prefer it here with Lyova and Rina, but that would mean working alongside Igor Vladimirovich, and under his supervision. Of course, he was nothing to her: they'd sat together in the National for an hour or two, whizzed around the Alexander Park and chatted. . . . She was a married woman now, but he still liked her, she could see that from his embarrassment, and working with him might be awkward.

So she replied, "I don't know, I don't mind either way."

"Start here with us," he suggested. "It's easier to start among friends. And when you've familiarized yourself with the place and had a look around, you can decide. Okay?"

She nodded her head to show her agreement.

He pushed a piece of paper and a pen toward her and dictated a statement about starting the job. He read it through, clipped it to Varya's school certificate, got up, opened the door to the next office, and ushered her out before him. Rina was now there as well as Lyova and she gave Varya an encouraging wink.

"Lyova," Igor Vladimirovich said, "I'll be back shortly. Show Varya around meanwhile."

He left and Rina burst out laughing.

"Do you see what an honor he's doing you? He's gone to register you himself."

"He's afraid the personnel staff will terrify her," Lyova joked. "Everything will be all right. Rina's being promoted to technician grade, so you'll be doing her job under my supreme authority."

But Rina had seen her with Igor Vladimirovich at the National. Wouldn't she make some remark?

"He offered me the general drawing office," she said, preempting anything Rina might say.

"That's odd," Lyova said. "We'd already agreed you'd work here with us. I even promised Kostya."

"What did you promise Kostya? That you'd keep an eye on me?"

"Varya! Come on! I just promised I'd help you over the first hurdles. . . . Right! Here's your desk, your board and T-square — you'll pick up your drawing instruments from supplies."

"Until you get a set of your own, that is," Rina added.

"That'll be later, when she's earned lots of money," Lyova observed sensibly. "You can work perfectly well with government issue."

He opened a cupboard to show her where the drawings and supplies were kept, while Rina kept up a running commentary. It was a good-humored and pleasant welcome.

They were chatting away when Igor Vladimirovich returned.

"Getting to know everything?"

"Yes, I am."

"Varya, come into my office for a moment."

She went back to his office, where he sat down and invited her to do so as well.

"Your application has been accepted. You can start work tomorrow morning. Here's your diploma, and here's something else. . . ."

Together with her school certificate he handed her an enormous, four-page questionnaire, and gave her a grin.

"You can fill this in at home and bring it with you tomorrow, when we'll hand it in to the personnel section. Since this is your first job, you won't have seen anything like this before. It's the stupidest thing you can imagine, but it's a formality we can't avoid. Are your parents alive?"

"No."

"Oh, I see. Well, just put the dates of their death and don't put in any other details about them. There is one other thing. . . . Please don't misunderstand me, it is needed for strictly official purposes, but are you and your husband registered as married?"

"No."

"I ask because there are a lot of questions on the form about spouses, their parents and grandparents, and it is very hard to fill it all in. A lot of it probably neither you nor your husband will know, and you'd have to write off somewhere to find out. But if you're not registered and have no children, you need not mention the relationship and then you can omit all the other tiresome questions."

Varya said nothing. She did not immediately understand what he was getting at. Probably he was being direct and she ought not assume there was any ambiguity. Yet she felt somewhat insulted. Vika must have said: "She's got herself involved with a gambler, he's not exactly a craftsman, not exactly a freelance — all in all, he's a shady fellow." And now Igor Vladimirovich was afraid this might complicate her application for the job. Well, to hell with it. She could find a job somewhere else, where they didn't make you fill out such complicated forms.

Igor Vladimirovich apparently knew exactly what she was thinking and said, "Do as you see fit. We'll give you the job in any case. I only wanted to make it easier for you to complete this unpleasant, troublesome, and tedious task."

"I'll see," she replied with restraint.

"I advise you to write out your answers on a separate piece of paper first, and check them thoroughly, then enter them on the form, because you can't cross anything out or make corrections — otherwise it has to be filled out all over again."

"All right, that's what I'll do."

"Excellent! We'll look forward to seeing you tomorrow, then. We start at nine and finish at four. I hope you'll like it here."

Varya walked home past the university, then along Vozdvi-zhenka and the Arbat.

The slightly unpleasant aftertaste left by the conversation about the form could not diminish the sheer joy she felt at having joined the real world. Lyova and Rina were wonderful. The restaurants and the Hermitage Gardens were only of secondary importance to them. The main thing in their lives was their work on this vast project in the center of Moscow. The drawing boards and T-squares, the rulers and curves, the pens and the smell of ink and finely sharpened pencils, all of this reminded her of school and drawing lessons, which she had never skipped. It augured a new and interesting life for her.

As for Igor Vladimirovich, she need not have felt awkward, she had not done anything wrong. On the contrary, she had refused to go with him and Vika to the Kanatik. Even then, he had seemed like someone from real life, not from Vika's world, and she hadn't wanted to lead him on. He had also seemed old to her, then. In fact, he was probably not that much older than Kostya.

He had advised her not to mention a husband: he didn't want her to run into problems with the questionnaire. A famous architect like him, yet he was afraid. But she wasn't afraid of anyone. Whatever kind of person Kostya was, she had no intention of hiding him. What business was it of theirs who her husband was and who his parents were? His parents weren't applying for the job, she was. Let them check up on her.

At home, she sat down at the table, opened the questionnaire and looked through it.

It turned out to be not four, but eight pages long. The questions were at first puzzling, then they made her indignant, then furious, and finally utterly confused.

As Igor Vladimirovich had suggested, she wrote all her answers first on a piece of scratch paper.

1. Surname, first name, patronymic. If changed, indicate former name. That was easy: Ivanova Varvara Sergeyevna. She hadn't changed her name.

2. Date and place of birth. Easy. Fifth of April, 1917, Moscow.

3. Nationality and citizenship (indicate if you have held another citizenship). Also easy: Russian, citizen of the U.S.S.R.

4. Class or social origin before the Revolution (peasant, lower middle class, merchant, gentry, honorary citizen, clergy, military, etc.). Her parents had been teachers. What social class was that? She'd have to ask Nina. But what was it like for those unfortunates whose parents had been clergy — "priest's child" — or military — "officer's son"?

5. Education. That was simple: completed secondary school with construction-drawing specialization.

6. What foreign languages do you possess? Answer: Some ability in German.

7. Party membership and length of service. Non-Party.

8. Date of joining Komsomol. Did not join.

9. If you have been in either the Communist Party or the Komsomol previously, indicate when and reason for leaving. Have you been in other parties? She wrote: I have not been a member of either the Communist Party or the Komsomol or any other party.

10. Have you ever been penalized during your membership of either the Party or the Komsomol (where, when, from whom, what were they, what were they for, have they been lifted, if so, by whom)? Answer: As

I have not been in the Party, I have incurred no penalties, and since none have been imposed, none have been lifted.

11. Have you wavered in carrying out the Party line, have you participated in any opposition or anti-Party grouping (where, when, which)? Here she would say: As I have not been a member of the Party, I have not carried out its line anywhere, and therefore have not wavered and have not participated in any opposition or anti-Party groupings.

12. Have you or any of your relatives been subject to court prosecution or investigation, arrest, and punishment under the court and administrative procedures, been deprived of voting rights, or are at present before the court and under investigation or serving a sentence?

She had nobody in prison, before the court, or under investigation. She had no other relatives, apart from an aunt in Kozlov. Maybe the aunt in Kozlov had someone in prison or deprived of their voting rights? She would of course write "No," but she had the feeling she was hiding something and that in the mysterious personnel section they would dig up some arrested relative of whose existence she was completely unaware. Surely Sofya Alexandrovna hadn't had to fill in such a form when she went for her job. Had she had to write about Sasha?

13. Have you been abroad, to which countries, what were you doing? I have not been abroad.

14. Have you or your wife (husband) now or in the past any relatives abroad (who, where)? Do you (or did you in the past) maintain contact with them? Indicate any relative with foreign citizenship.

In school there had been children of former nobility from the side streets of the Arbat with relatives abroad, just as many of Pushkin's and Tolstoy's descendants were living abroad. It would be interesting to see how those poor devils answered this question. After all, you had to say where, but everyone was afraid to write and receive letters from abroad.

15. Were you or any of your relatives prisoners of war or interned during either the Imperialist or Civil War? Now they want to go back to the Great War!

Questions 16, 17, 18, 19, 20, and 21 concerned service in the Red Army, the partisans, and the revolutionary underground, and wounds or shell-shock. She put "None" to all of them.

22. *Which of your relatives (as listed in paragraph 27) have been in other parties, worked before the Revolution in the police, gendarmes, prosecution service or court, the prison authority or the border guards or exile escort service?*

Now, let's see who they include in paragraph 27? *Wife, husband, children, mother, father, brothers, sisters. A husband should list both his own and his wife's relatives, a wife should list her own and her husband's relatives.* Good God! She not only had to list all her own relatives, but also Kostya's, and to say whether any of them had worked in the border guards or exile escort service before the Revolution. Did Kostya even know? Why must a person answer for her spouse's relatives?

23. *Family situation (married, single, widowed): list the members of your family, giving their ages. If married, divorced, or widowed, give the surname, first name, and patronymic of your first wife (husband).* Well, what difference does a wife who died twenty years ago make to a design bureau? What possible significance could it have for planning a hotel?

24. *Present address.* Fine.

25. *All previous home addresses since birth.* That was easy for her: she had never lived anywhere except in the house on the Arbat. But suppose a middle-aged person was filling it in, how many addresses did they have to remember? Especially since birth! If their parents had died, how were they supposed to find out where they had lived in childhood?

Question 26 was the one Igor Vladimirovich had warned her about. *Information about your close relatives (give details on your wife [husband], children, mother, father, brothers, sisters). Surname, first name, and patronymic, how related, date and place of birth, nationality, Party membership, name and address of place of employment and position held, residential address. The same information on relatives of spouse.* That meant she would have to give all this information not only on Nina and her dead mother and father, but also on all of Kostya's relatives, and he had five brothers and sisters, all scattered throughout the Soviet Union, and his father and mother had been dispossessed at that.

Now she understood: Igor Vladimirovich's warning had been with the best intentions. But she wasn't going to go along with that sort of appeasement, she wasn't going to accommodate herself. She wasn't that sort of person!

Right, what next?

Physical features: height, color of hair and eyes, other distinguishing marks.

The pigs! The only thing they haven't asked for is my finger-prints, like they do in prison! *Fingerprints weren't enough for them!* No, this was just too much! To hell with it! She wouldn't answer such a demeaning questionnaire. She'd find a job where they didn't make you fill out such forms, in one of the ordinary run-of-the-mill offices where they also needed draftsmen and copiers. If worse came to worst, she wouldn't get a job at all, but would prepare for higher education and apply the following year to the Institute of Architecture. And if she didn't get a grant, she'd tell Kostya not to buy her any more expensive clothes; she would use the money for education. The fur wrap he'd given her recently was probably the equivalent of two or three years' expenses. If she sold her clothes, she'd have enough for several years. Not only that, she'd be a student, she'd be studying, they wouldn't check up on her this way. And when she became a qualified architect, they wouldn't dare impose such a stupid form on her.

Varya closed the questionnaire and threw it on the table. She'd show it to Kostya tomorrow and he could have a good laugh.

She changed into her housecoat and hung her dress in the closet. But as she was closing the door, she suddenly realized something was missing. The fur wrap that Kostya had given her only recently was not there. It must have cost a fortune, it contained at least six or seven silver-fox skins. She had only worn it once, when they had gone to Staro-Pimenov Street.

She pulled dresses out of the closet, coats and jackets; she rummaged through everything, but there was no fur wrap. Nothing else had been touched, only the wrap. She thought at once of the neighbor, Galya. Or her son, Petka, a fifteen-year-old hooligan.

Sofya Alexandrovna had already come home from work. Varya knocked on her door, went in, and closed it firmly behind her.

"Sofya Alexandrovna, my silver-fox wrap's gone."

"What do you mean, gone?" Sofya Alexandrovna was puzzled.

"It was hanging in the closet this morning, and now it's not there."

"Have you looked properly?"

"I took everything out of the closet. It's been stolen!"

"Stolen! Who would steal it?"

"I don't know. Maybe Galya, or Petka."

"But they haven't got a key to your room.... I've been living with them for so many years. Such a thing has never happened before."

"Petka was only a little boy before. Now he's growing up and has started stealing, it isn't strange at all."

"We must call the militia," Sofya Alexandrovna said.

Varya did not want to call the militia without talking to Kostya. She did not know why, but she felt she ought to speak to him first.

"We must wait for Kostya."

"What are you talking about, Varya? Konstantin Fedorovich won't be home until late. We must tell the militia at once. Otherwise they'll ask why we didn't call them right away."

"How will they know when I opened the closet? I'll go to them tomorrow and say that I just opened my closet and discovered the loss."

"It'll be harder for them to look for it tomorrow," Sofya Alexandrovna insisted. "You have to search when the trail is still warm, not when it's gone cold. I can understand that it's all very unpleasant, but it's the only way. That wrap is worth a fortune. And if it was Petka who stole it, it's all the more reason not to let him get away with it, otherwise he'll rob us again. What would life be like here then?"

"I'll find Kostya right away and see what he says," Varya said.

She changed, threw on a raincoat, and left the house.

What had stopped her from calling the militia? Why was she being so cautious and why was she running to Kostya now? Was it because of the tax inspector? He had, after all, made an inventory of Kostya's property. The militia might ask her where she got such an expensive wrap and she would have to say Kostya had given it to her, and that meant ... What precisely did that mean? She didn't know. All she knew for sure was that she must not go to the militia without Kostya's say-so. After all, she didn't even know where the wrap had come from. He'd brought it home, opened it up, and said: "Try this on!"

It had fit her perfectly.

"It's a present from me," he'd said.

"Thank you," she'd said. "How much did it cost?"

"What difference does it make? It cost. It wasn't cheap."

The wrap was new, probably bought from someone, or made by some underground furrier, or maybe from the foreign goods store. At any rate, it couldn't have been stolen, otherwise Kostya would not have let her wear it to the Actors' Club. Still, he never told her where he got it. He always appeared to be skating on thin ice.

She found him in the Metropole billiards hall. She hated billiards halls, they were no place for women. There were only men there: some sober, some drunk or half-drunk, some looking at her with curiosity, others mockingly as though she were a tiresome wife who'd come to drag her man home. The place was full of smoke, stuffy. The faces looked haggard and white.

Kostya did not see Varya. He saw nothing but the balls and the pockets and his own cue. He followed his opponent's shot, made a note on the slate, and turned back at once to the table, tense, concentrated, and focused on the game.

Varya had no idea who had won. Kostya said something to the scorekeeper, who immediately racked up the balls for a new game. Kostya was chalking his cue and gazing around the billiards room with a hard, guarded stare when he caught sight of Varya standing at the entrance. He showed no surprise, as if he had been expecting her. He merely frowned more fiercely and went over to her carrying his cue.

"Let's go outside," he said.

They went into a small lobby outside the billiards room. It had two small sofas and an armchair. Varya guessed it was where they went to smoke. She felt suddenly calmer: she saw from his expression that there was no need to call the militia.

"What is it?" he asked, without looking at her.

"The wrap's gone."

"What wrap?"

"The silver fox."

He was silent for several seconds, and turned his head to one side as if he did not understand what she was saying. She felt that here was a man she knew absolutely nothing about.

Finally he said: "I'll buy you another one, a better one. I lost, I couldn't lay my hands on any money, so I used the wrap to pay up — otherwise they would have murdered me. Go home, I'll be there myself soon."

Varya went home.

"Well?" Sofya Alexandrovna asked.

"Konstantin Fedorovich took the wrap to a furrier to have something done to it. It's a good thing we didn't call the militia." Varya went into her room, took off her raincoat, kicked off her shoes, and sat down on the bed to think.

He'd gambled away the wrap. And she still didn't know where he'd got it. Maybe he'd won it from another player who, like him, was gambling with his wife's property.

She didn't give a damn about the wrap itself. But today it was her wrap, and tomorrow it could be her coat and then her shoes the day after. A drunk drinks his wife's things away, a gambler gambles with them. Vika, Noemi, or Nina Sheremetyeva might be whores, but they didn't run the risk of seeing their clothes on someone else's back. Today he was gambling away her clothes, maybe tomorrow he'd gamble with her. What a fool she'd been! She'd deluded herself about his imaginary independence. Now she knew the price he paid for that independence. And now she too was dependent on the roll of the balls on a billiards table.

Such a fate did not appeal to her, she could not remain dependent on him, she didn't want gifts that he was going to gamble away, that was no good to her. She wouldn't be able to finish her education with his help. She could count only on herself. Damn that form! Nothing but forms, everywhere the same degrading procedure. But it would be better to go through with it where she had some friends, rather than among strangers she did not know. Igor Vladimirovich was right — she would not mention Kostya. What she revealed about herself was enough. Anyway, why say anything about Kostya? She saw everything clearly now. She had always felt the casual and temporary nature of this relationship.

It was easy to write about herself. She had the same answer for all the difficult questions: no. As for her dead father and mother, she'd ask Nina, who knew everything.

True, Nina was avoiding her because of Kostya. She didn't visit or phone, and when they passed each other in the building she didn't stop but just gave an indifferent nod of the head. As if it was any business of hers! But she would tell Varya about their mother and father; they were, after all, her parents too.

She telephoned and Nina was there.

"It's Varya. I'm coming over. I've got something to discuss."

"Okay, if you want to talk about something," Nina replied casually.

She shouldn't have phoned — it sounded as if she was asking permission. She should have just gone.

Had Varya simply made a bad marriage, Nina would have shared her sister's fate, come to her rescue, and consoled her. But what had taken place was not simply a failure, it was the betrayal of everything decent and irreproachable their parents had inculcated in them.

Once, meeting Nina in the yard, Yuri Sharok had said to her: "Your Varya's mixed up with a thief." Nina did not like Sharok. But Lena Budyagina was back with him and because of Lena Nina did not want to start a quarrel. Nevertheless, she did not need Yuri's warnings.

"So, why is a thief at large?"

"He'll be inside soon enough," Sharok had promised.

Whether or not Yuri was speaking the truth, Varya's so-called husband was obviously a very dubious character. He was from another world, a world of restaurants, gamblers, speculators, and crooks, a world that Nina found utterly repugnant. She and Varya were now on opposite sides of the barricades. And it was not coincidence that Sofya Alexandrovna was giving her shelter; she was also on the other side of the barricades, unable to forgive the Soviet regime for Sasha's exile. But even if that had been a mistake, the Soviet regime as such was not at fault, there wasn't a government in the world that did not make mistakes. And when a fierce class struggle was going on, and the Party was forced to liquidate the remnants of hostile parties and factions and oppositions, occasional mistakes were likely to be made.

And anyway, what sort of mistake had they made over Sasha?

According to Lena Budyagina, who reported what Yuri Sharok had told her in strict confidence, there had been an anti-Soviet organization at Sasha's institute. Sasha had defended them and he'd been arrested together with them. He'd only been given three years, because they realized he was not the ringleader. But he had to bear some of the responsibility, especially as, according to Sharok, he had been defiant and uncooperative during the investigation. He had not acknowledged his mistakes, and he had relied on the help of his powerful uncle, Ryazanov. But neither Ryazanov's intervention, nor that of Ivan Grigoryevich Budyagin, had helped.

Sofya Alexandrovna ought to accept the situation; she was a grown woman, she should understand. But she was full of hatred. She wanted everybody else to suffer, and by taking in Varya with her profiteering, she was throwing down a challenge not only to Nina but to all of Sasha's friends.

Anyway, Varya had chosen her life while still at school. She had gone out with lots of boys, used lipstick, spent all her money on clothes. Even then Nina had been unable to control her, and she certainly couldn't now. It had to happen. Now, whatever was wrong, Varya would have to get out of it herself. She'd better not be counting on registering her little man at Nina's. The living area there was just enough for two, and Nina wasn't going to give up one single square inch for a thief, a speculator, and gambler. They could live how and where they liked. Varya was obviously coming around to moan about her accommodations.

But instead Varya had something quite different on her mind. She needed information for a job-application form. Varya getting a job? She hadn't expected that. It was strange. Maybe she wasn't enjoying her new life-style?

"Where are you going to work, if it's not a secret?"

"There's no secret. At the design bureau for the Moscow Hotel."

Nina understood it all: the good life wasn't so wonderful and the husband wasn't doing so well, either. She wouldn't ask Varya anything, she'd let her talk if she felt like it.

"What do you need?"

Varya held out the form and pointed to item 27: *Information on your close relatives.*

"Write it on a piece of paper and I'll put it on the form later," Varya said. She sat down and looked around the room. The only thing new was a photograph on the wall of Maxim Kostin, wearing his military tunic with the tabs on his collar. There was his good, kind, open face. So, Nina was writing to Max. She ought to marry him, they suited each other so well. Eventually, as the wife of a commander, she'd become a mother and that would suit her, too.

Everything else in the room was as it had been before. On the bookshelf, next to the children's encyclopedia, was the photo of their mother and father when they were young; there was the table with its worn-out oilcloth; the battered house slippers under Nina's bed, and on her own bed, a bright scarf across the pillow, and next to it the bronze athlete holding a lamp in his outstretched muscular hand. Varya had not even taken her bed-linen to Sofya Alexandrovna's, nor her phonograph. And although she had quickly discovered that there were a lot of things she needed, she had preferred to buy new things. She had come back to the apartment only once, to pick up her school certificate. Nina had not been in then, and thank God she hadn't.

But now, as she sat and looked around the room and saw all the familiar things and was aware of the familiar smells, she felt like a schoolgirl again. It made her sad and she realized clearly that despite all of Nina's tediousness, this was the only place she could be at peace, here in her own home. She had no other home, or soon would have none.

Nina handed her the list of facts.

Varya checked them against the form and found Nina had answered all the questions.

"Yes, good, thank you. Well, fine then. Good-bye."

"Keep well."

Had she behaved decently to her sister? Nina wondered. What else was she supposed to do? Jump up and down for joy just because Varya got a job? Everyone worked, it was a basic thing. Varya wasn't making anyone happy. She could have gone on to higher education but wanted to be a copier. Well, everyone must choose her own path. We talk about women's dignity, and forget all about it as soon as a man comes along.

Varya — all right, Varya was just a child who'd grown up in the yard and the street. But Lena Budyagina, my God! Lena was an older woman, and look at the family she'd been raised in! Nina now knew that Yuri had given Lena an illegal abortion, and that she'd practically died, and the swine hadn't even visited her once when she was in the hospital. Six months later he turns up and Lena's going out with him again. Couldn't she see what he was? They weren't all genuine Chekists in the NKVD, there were plenty of opportunists, too, and Yuri was one of them. Lena must realize that. And now there was this new story — another "tragedy": Yuri, it turned out, was having an affair with another woman as well. And instead of kicking the creep out of her life, Lena was suffering and tormenting herself again. Nina despised women's dependence on men. She saw it in her own sister, and just because Varya was now getting a job, it didn't mean her fundamental nature had changed. So, it wasn't yet time to celebrate. Lena had told Nina in a moment of desperation that Yuri was being unfaithful. She gave no details: "He's being unfaithful" was all she would say.

The details, or more accurately the detail, consisted of the fact that Yuri was sleeping with Vika Marasevich. Lena and Vika had come face to face at the Maroseika, on Starosad Street, on a staircase landing. Lena had stepped out of the elevator just at the moment that Vika was closing the door to the apartment that Lena was about to enter. They had looked at each other in confusion for a few seconds, then Vika had said, "Hello!" Lena had muttered something in reply. Vika had got into the elevator and closed the door.

Lena's first impulse had been to run away and she scurried down the stairs. She stopped at the floor below to catch her breath and to listen. The elevator door slammed shut and she knew Vika had left. Let her go a bit farther. Lena slowly went down to the next floor. My God! So what had happened at the New Year's party had not been a casual incident, but had been going on between them for a long time. The others had all seen it, but she had been blind. Nina had got into a row with Yuri and Sasha had said to her, right out in front of Yuri: "Couldn't you find yourself a bigger piece of shit?" Yuri had had no mercy and even now she felt sick at the thought of the abortion. They told her in the hospital that it was a miracle she had survived, but he had behaved like a coward, he'd hidden and hadn't come to see her once. And now he was waiting for her in the same bed that Vika had just got out of. No doubt she was not the only one to use that bed. He hadn't even been ashamed to make a date with her on the same day, practically at the same time, as he had with Vika.

It was then that she realized she was an hour early: Yuri had asked her to come at five. She'd forgotten and come at their usual time. He needed an hour to rest! The bastard, the sex maniac! Soon he'll suggest they both go to bed with him at the same time. It was all finished, as far as she was concerned. She wanted no explanations. She had no wish to hear his lying justifications.

Yuri called her that evening and asked in a whimsical voice why she hadn't come that day.

"I was held up at work."

"Will you manage Tuesday?"

"No."

"When, then?"

"I don't know. If I can, I'll phone you. But don't call me anymore. Good-bye, Yuri."

What was the matter with her? Sharok couldn't understand. Everything had seemed to be going well. They weren't meeting very often, because of his work, but they went to the theater and the movies, the Actors' Club, exhibitions.... What was she so upset about? It was strange.

Sharok discovered the cause of her discontent all too soon.

After bumping into Lena, Vika panicked for an instant. She realized that Lena had come for a rather different purpose than her own, because Vadim had told her that the relationship between Yuri and Lena had been revived. And he was seeing Lena there at the secret apartment! He'd given Vika away! Lena would obviously demand an explanation and Sharok would have to admit that the room was used for other than intimate purposes. Secret informers should never be exposed, but he would have to explain why Vika happened to be there.

Vika was at once reassured by this thought. She realized what luck it was: now Yuri would have to let her go, and he couldn't wriggle out of it. He had been particularly nasty that day and he was going to pay for that little conversation.

"Yuri," Vika had said, "I'm married."

"Yes?" he replied breezily. "I'd be interested to know to whom."

She gave the name of her architect. Sharok knew the name but showed no particular surprise.

"Congratulations! He's a famous man."

"Stalin liked his design."

"I saw it at the exhibition," Sharok said guardedly, as if he was afraid to discuss a design that had been approved by Stalin himself.

"You and I have got to part, Yuri."

He looked as if he had not understood. "In what sense?"

"I'm a married woman now, and you know whose wife I am. I've changed my style of life. I don't go to restaurants anymore and I don't see my old circle of friends."

"You'll be meeting new people."

"No, my husband leads a very quiet life. He's in his studio from nine in the morning till eleven at night, and I sit at home and wait for him. Alone. But that isn't the point. The point is, I can't — I haven't the right to hide anything from him."

"So, don't," Sharok said calmly.

"You mean tell him about our meetings?"

"Tell him, if you think you must."

"But I signed an agreement that I wouldn't tell anyone."

"In the interests of family harmony, I authorize you to divulge our little secret," Sharok said with a smirk.

"He'll leave me at once."

Sharok shrugged his shoulders. "What for? For doing your duty?"

She looked him straight in the eyes. He knew perfectly well that she could never tell a soul. He wasn't going to let her out of his clutches; he wanted her to inform on her own husband, and she hadn't the slightest doubt that he'd make her do it. Still, she said: "All right, I'll tell him everything."

He grimaced. "Yes, yes, you tell him, and we'll add some information. We'll throw in all your foreign friends. And then you can tell him how it is with them, with foreigners. It must be nicer sleeping with them, isn't it?"

"Yuri, what are you saying?"

He smashed his fist down on the table and roared: "I know what I'm saying! You sleep with them, you whore, you wander from one hotel bedroom to the next. You've tied yourself hand and foot to foreign spies. You're up to your eyes in shit. Yes, you tell your nice new husband what you like about them, let him hear it from you!"

"Yuri, how can you? I only met those people around the table in restaurants."

"That's a lie. You slept with them. The last time it was with the Swede. We know about him, and we know about all the others before him, right down to the last one. What is it with you, aren't there enough Russians? What's wrong with Russians? Answer me!"

The bastard could at least have been polite. She had slept with him, too, after all, and he was a Russian. But she said nothing. She was stunned at how well informed he was.

Looking at her with hatred in his eyes, he went on: "Oh, but they were all Papa's friends, all famous people ... Professor Kramer, Rossolini" — there was disgust in his voice — " 'talented violinists,' ah, yes, Fritz and Hans and Michel ... all part of the family. Tomcats! And all these tomcats are active members of the Nazi Party, they're all Fascists and spies! And those Japanese you had a good time with, spies every last one of them, and big ones, too. One of them holds the rank of colonel. Don't you know why they come here, why they love us so much? You've got yourself mixed up with them and now you come running and want to be let off the hook, otherwise you'll tell your husband everything. No, my dear, you won't tell him anything, because we're going to do it for you, and then we'll see if he still wants you!"

She had sat silent, feeling powerless and doomed.

But now, as she walked along the Maroseika, she felt differently. He had miscalculated, the little tailor's boy! It was his fault that she had been exposed. Her argument about her husband had not convinced him, but he'd have to reckon with other arguments now. Just you wait, Yuri, just you wait.

She telephoned him at home on Sunday.

"Yuri, it's Vika. Hello. I need to talk to you urgently."

"What's happened?"

"Not on the phone. I'll come to your place and we can meet outside in the street and go for a walk."

She was afraid to go to the Maroseika, afraid of being alone with Sharok, which was fine with him since he couldn't go there anyway — it wasn't his day. He realized that Vika was going to try her delaying tactics about her husband again, so he saw no special reason for haste. But there was something alarming about her insistence.

"What's the rush? We'll meet at our usual time and talk then."

"This won't wait," Vika persisted. "And it's not in your interest to delay."

"You can wait."

"All right," she said coldly. "I have warned you. You'll only have yourself to blame later."

"What is this, a threat?"

"Look at it anyway you like. I'm asking you for the last time: Will you come out onto the Arbat right now?"

"All right, we'll meet in an hour at Sobachy Square, I have to go that way, in any case."

"Let's sit." Vika pointed to an empty bench in the square.

"No," Yuri said. "Let's walk down this street; I have to get to Vorovsky Boulevard."

They went down Trubnikov Street.

"So, what's up?"

"What's up?" she repeated with a smirk. "What's up is that you ought not to turn the apartment where we meet into a love-nest."

He knew at once that she must have run into Lena there.

Playing for time, he said: "What are you talking about?"

"I met Lena Budyagina on the landing. We even exchanged greetings — we're old schoolfriends, after all. Obviously, she guessed why I was coming to you — she knows what work you're in. That means I've been exposed, I'm of no further use to you as an informer. Let's part as friends, Yuri."

He walked in silence, pondering the situation. Now he understood: Lena had come too early, she'd mixed up the times, the silly fool. She'd bumped into Vika, taken offense, and that was why she didn't want to see him anymore, damn her! Nothing but trouble, that woman! But Vika's little trick wouldn't work. The idiot was trying to blackmail him.

Vika suddenly took his arm, smiled, and looked tenderly into his eyes. "Don't be angry, Yuri! You've had a setback, but you're clever, you'll cover it up and nobody need ever know about it. It's much worse for me: now I won't be able to show my face anywhere. Everyone will avoid me and I'll just have to stay at home."

He didn't remove his arm from hers. She was a smart little bitch, say what you like. Very cool and merciless. In fact, she was just the sort of female he needed, not that wet hen, Lena. He could go far with Vika. Lena might be the daughter of Budyagin, but the prison cells of the Butyrki would be getting him soon enough, whereas Vika came from a neutral professor's family. . . .

But it was a bit late for such thoughts. "Didn't it occur to you that Lena thought you were my mistress?" he asked.

Vika stopped. She was no longer smiling but looked at him with her gray merciless eyes.

"Don't take me for a fool. I gave in to Dyakov because I lost my head and signed the piece of paper he pushed in front of me. But you're not Dyakov. We've known each other since childhood, you're my brother's friend, you visit our house, and, on top of everything else, you've slept with me. You could have been decent to me, but you weren't. And now I'm not going to be decent to you, just remember that. I've written a letter to Yagoda telling him that you've set up a brothel in Starosad Street and that you exposed me to one of your lovers, the daughter of a deputy commissar and my friend since childhood. The letter is written and ready to be sent. If you arrest me now and take me away, the letter will be sent. Keep that in mind."

"Arrest you, take you away?" Sharok was scornful. "Who needs you?"

And he walked ahead. She walked alongside him, but she did not take his arm.

"If I'm not needed, so much the better. Let's part. Otherwise, I'll take it to the bitter end, I won't stop, I won't retreat, I promise you."

"Oh dear, how terrifying!"

Ignoring this, she went on: "I dealt honestly with you. I met repulsive people for you, like that Liberman. But you gave me away because of one of your amorous adventures. Let's see how your bosses like that."

"Don't try to threaten me." He grimaced. "It won't help you, it'll just make things worse."

"And don't you threaten me — I'm not afraid of anything. I'm married and I'm making a new life for myself and I'm going to defend it. I may go under, but so will your career. They'll never forgive you for this. But if you act sensibly, all this will remain just between ourselves. You can trust me."

Now it was he who stopped.

"Look, Lena did see you and she made a scene about it. I confessed to her that you and I have a romance going — after all, there was one, wasn't there? I gave her my word I wouldn't see you again. And you can rest assured that Lena won't tell a soul about it. So from that point of view, you're not under any danger. As for your letter, it won't work. Lena is, in practical terms, my wife. You bumped into her, she made a wrong assumption — such things happen. We just take a statement of nondivulgence from her and the matter's closed. All you'll achieve with your letter is that they'll transfer you to someone else, and I'm not sure it would be better for you."

Vika listened to him intently and looked straight at him with her big, gray, shameless eyes. Then in a firm, decisive, and malicious voice, she said: "Well, everyone has to go his own way. Keep well."

But he held her back.

"Wait, there is another thing to be considered. Last time you asked to be released from cooperating, I was obliged to report this request to my chief, the same day on which I sent in my report. I don't know what the result will be. You'll have to be patient."

"How long must I wait?" she asked, aware that he had thought this up on the spur of the moment, and that he hadn't sent in any report, though perhaps he would, which meant he was afraid of her.

"You'll get a reply at our next meeting."

To have to wait ten days! And to have to hang around in that apartment again.

"All right," she said. "I'll wait ten days."

ika would not yield. Having become the wife of the
architect, she imagined she held all the cards. The real
power was of course on the other side, but Vika was brazen,
decisive, and capable of anything. And it had to be admitted,
he had dealt her an ace.

Sharok thought it sensible to tell Dyakov: "Marasevich has
declared herself married to her architect and she wants to appear
like a good little girl to him."

"Is she being a nuisance?"

"She's stopped seeing the Liberman crowd, she doesn't meet her
old friends or go to restaurants. She just sits at home. And she has
made no new acquaintances, as yet. Perhaps we should leave her
alone for a while, give her time to settle into her new life, become
part of a new circle, make new friends. The architect has a lot of
people around him, and some of them are very interesting."

"That sounds sensible," Dyakov agreed. "Let her run for a while.
Now we have this, Sharok. . . ." Dyakov sorted through some
papers on his desk, an activity that meant he was collecting his
thoughts, preparing what to say.

"Ah, yes," he went on. "This conversation is confidential," he said
with a telling look at Sharok. "Comrade Zaporozhets has arrived
from Leningrad and wants to take three or four reliable people from
the central organization back with him. It would of course mean
greater responsibilities and higher pay. Among the candidates your
name has been mentioned. How do you feel about it?"

Sharok shrugged. "How should I feel? I'll go where I'm sent. I
hope I would still be able to retain my Moscow apartment?"

"Yes, of course, your parents live there, anyway. You'll spend a couple of years working on the periphery, though the second capital is hardly the periphery. You'd come back here to a higher position. Think about it. It's an offer you can accept or turn down, it's not an order. A lot of people would like to work with Zaporozhets. He's a good, cheerful type who takes care of his crew. This is just a preliminary chat. He will want to talk to you himself, and anyway he may choose someone else. But think about it. In my opinion it's a real opportunity for you."

The proposal was unexpected but interesting. Nobody ever spent their entire career in Moscow — it wasn't done. One had to spend some time working on the periphery and then return to Moscow with practical experience. Leningrad was the best possible choice: it wasn't some provincial hole and it was only an overnight journey from Moscow. Also, Zaporozhets would no doubt soon be taking over from the old man, Medved, and that could mean that Sharok would move up with him. But he ought to have some base of support here. Dyakov wasn't a source of support, he was only a minor functionary. What about Berezin? He was powerful enough, but he didn't get on with Yagoda and was likely to be transferred to the Far East. As for going to the Far East — no thanks, Leningrad would do very nicely.

Sharok found the proposal an attractive one in general. It would provide a natural break with Lena. And with his brother, too. His brother's term was about to end and he'd be coming home. He could look after himself. Sharok wasn't his nursemaid.

Sharok was in a good mood when he next met Vika at the Maroseika.

"Well, my love, you can celebrate. We're letting go of you entirely. And not because of Lena. I reported that you had run into my wife and that matter has now been taken care of. We're stopping our meetings because my bosses found my argument persuasive: If you're sitting at home like a good little wife, what can we get out of you? Enjoy your honeymoon!"

"Thank you," Vika replied cautiously. "But ... what about my original agreement?"

"Your agreement? It's in the archives. Do you want it back?"

"Yes."

"Well, you don't want much, do you! Who do you think is going to remove a document from the file? It's been numbered and sent to the archives. The mice are reading it."

Vika realized that as long as they had that document, they had her by the throat. But at least for the time being she was free; as for later on, one would see.

"Thanks, Yuri," she said, getting up. "I hope we never meet again under such circumstances." She waved her arm around the room. "Nor for the same purpose."

"Never," he promised, smiling.

It was a sincere reply. He would never deal with Vika Marasevich again. If the need should arise, as it surely would, someone else would run her.

He was already preparing himself mentally for the departure to Leningrad. He had never been there. Many of his schoolfriends had visited it during the holidays. It was regarded as terribly fashionable to vacation in Leningrad. They had relatives and friends there, but he had nobody. He envied the Arbat intellectual families this, as he envied them much else. Now he was going to Leningrad, too, and not for a cozy stay with relatives, but to do important work. He would stay in a hotel first, and then he'd be given an apartment.

That day Sharok had taken some papers into Berezin's office for his signature.

After signing, Berezin had said: "A new class for the NKVD staff school is about to be chosen. Would you like to study?"

Sharok was taken aback. The staff school was also very tempting; it prepared personnel for the higher ranks. But what about Leningrad?

"I don't know," he said uncertainly. "The point is, Comrade Zaporozhets wants me to go to Leningrad with him."

Berezin looked hard at him, then lowering his head to hide his gaze, he said: "That's another matter. The question of the staff school doesn't arise, then."

His face was impenetrable.

Sharok left the room and Berezin locked the door after him. From the same bunch of keys he found the one to his safe, which stood in a corner of his office. He opened the safe, stood a chair next to it, and began piling up files that he was removing from the safe, looking at them one by one.

He finally found what he was looking for and set it aside, putting all the other files back in the same order he had found them. He inserted a sheet of paper to mark the place of the file he had removed.

He studied the file closely, stopped at one page, and lit a cigarette. The information Sharok had inadvertently given him confirmed his belief that some sort of action was being prepared in Leningrad.

His suspicion had first been aroused by the dispatch of Alferov to eastern Siberia. Kirov had requested that Alferov be assigned to him, but instead of sending Alferov to Leningrad, he'd been sent to the Angara as district officer, the reason given that while he was in Siberia checks could be run on certain of his earlier activities in China. He hadn't even been allowed to come back to Moscow. He'd been ordered to remain in Kansk and then dispatched from there to the district office.

In place of Alferov, Ivan Zaporozhets went to Leningrad. Tall and broad-shouldered, he was "a fine figure of a man," a wit and a joker who loved good wines and women and who sang well. He lived in Palikh and complained that there was no bathroom and that his wife nagged him about it. He had a beautiful wife — Rosa Proskurovskaya. . . .

Berezin bent over his desk and read again through Zaporozhets's dossier. Although he was a former Left Socialist Revolutionary, he'd remained in the Cheka's central organization. He had of course been protected by Yagoda. They were always together. Among the operations he'd been involved in, the most important one in the file was when he had been dispatched to the Anarchist Makhno's headquarters. He had the luck of a daredevil. And now he was preparing a new adventure. Berezin's man in Zaporozhets's crew had given him a copy of an intercepted letter from a certain Nikolaev. It was a strange letter and it put one on one's guard. Berezin read it again.

Leonid Nikolaev had joined the Party in 1920 when he was still fighting at the front, aged sixteen. He came from a worker's family and had himself been a worker. Until 1934 he'd worked in the Leningrad branch of the Workers' and Peasants' Inspectorate as a price inspector. According to him, he was removed from that job through the machinations of Trotskyites who were entrenched in the regional Party committee. However, the secretary of the factory Party cell, who was also a Trotskyite, assigned him to the transport sector to organize Party mobilization. He was willing to work anywhere the Party sent him, but it wasn't the Party but the Trotskyites who wanted him out of Leningrad. He had refused to go. For that he had been expelled from the Party and since March he had been unemployed. He'd sent twenty letters to Comrade Kirov asking for a review of his case and an investigation into the domination of the Leningrad organization by Trotskyites. Not one of his letters had produced a response. Either Comrade Kirov did not think his letters required a reply, or they were not getting to him. The blame for this lay with the Trotskyite entourage, which Comrade Kirov trusted blindly. Nikolaev had spent fourteen of his thirty years in the Party. He could not imagine his future existence without the Party, he was at the limit of his patience and was ready to do anything. . . .

Ready to do anything . . . What did that mean?

Suicide? Anyone who'd been in the Party for fourteen years would know he'd never frighten anyone with that. A terrorist act? Such things were not put into letters, and one didn't issue warnings about them. You could be shot for such a threat. But he had written it, he had issued a threat. Was he psychologically unbalanced?

But to whom were his threats directed? And, most important now: Zaporozhets was working with this man. What did he want him for?

What was Zaporozhets's purpose in taking new people to Leningrad? Whom were they supposed to replace? For what reason? Why such secrecy? Even he, Berezin, who was a member of the board, had only learned about it by accident.

Stalin was not pleased with the situation in Leningrad — that was widely known. He was demanding that Kirov suppress the so-called participants in the Zinovievite opposition; he wanted to unleash terror in Leningrad. But why? As the detonator for terror throughout the country? Kirov was refusing and evidently it was Zaporozhets's task to provoke an incident that would make it possible to overcome Kirov's resistance. But whatever Zaporozhets managed to pull off, the investigation of it would take place in Leningrad. Kirov would never let it be held anywhere else; he would never yield over such a matter; he'd take it to the Politburo.

That meant Zaporozhets had to do something that would stun everyone, something that even Kirov would have to yield to.

What could it be? Sabotage, an explosion, a railway disaster? Kirov wouldn't be deceived by that! The murder of one of his lieutenants? Chudov, Kodatsky, Pozern? Was that Nikolaev's role? It would certainly make a big noise, but there was no way Kirov could be kept out of the investigation.

What else was there?

Berezin clearly recalled Stalin's words to him in 1918 at Tsaritsyn. Stalin had demanded the execution by firing squad of a number of military specialists, former tsarist army officers. Berezin, who was then in charge of a special unit, proved that the charges were without foundation and suggested that the executions might provoke complications and problems.

Stalin had replied instructively: "Death solves all problems. No man, no problem."

And Stalin had turned out to be right. A cable arrived rescinding the executions, but the people had already been shot. It didn't cause any problems.

That was the man's philosophy. Was he applying it now? Yes, undoubtedly! Berezin could not come right out and say so — one unguarded word from him and he'd be liquidated. But he could sound a warning.

That evening he called on Budyagin. They lived in different parts of the Fifth House of Soviets, and while they did not know each other well and met only rarely, they were sympathetic to each other: they both belonged to the iron phalanx of old Bolsheviks who had traveled along the same path of life and both were devoid of vain ambitions.

Berezin did not express his suspicions to Budyagin. It was enough that Berezin had come to Budyagin's apartment for the first time in his life, ostensibly to borrow a book on the economy of the Far East that he could have obtained from any library. Budyagin took full account of the point, made almost imperceptibly by

Berezin, that Ivan Zaporozhets was selecting a group of people to take to Leningrad and that this was a closely guarded secret.

After he'd seen Berezin out, Budyagin went into the kitchen to make himself some strong tea. He was sorry that his wife was away, as he would have liked to discuss Berezin's information, information that was very worrying.

Next morning, Budyagin went past his own office to Semushkin's. He nodded toward Ordzhonikidze's door.

"Is he in?"

"He is," Semushkin replied.

Budyagin did not mention Berezin's name when he told Ordzhonikidze about the appointment of new people to Zaporozhets in Leningrad. The source of information in such cases was not revealed.

Ordzhonikidze became pensive. If the new appointments were simply the result of the usual bureaucratic intrigue in the NKVD apparatus, then Medved ought to inform Kirov about it. However, interested parties were using Budyagin to inform him, Ordzhonikidze, a Politburo member and personal friend of Kirov. In other words, this information was not of an internal, administrative nature, it was political.

"What do you think about it?" Ordzhonikidze asked.

"Something's being cooked up in Leningrad. The object is to compromise Kirov."

"How?"

"It's difficult to say. They want to force him to carry out arrests, they want to make it impossible for him not to. And if he still refuses, he'll be removed from Leningrad."

"I think you're right," Ordzhonikidze agreed.

The thought would never have occurred to him. It took a career Chekist like Berezin to spot it at once.

ꙮ 10 ꙮ

He had a toothache. The tooth had been loose for a long time, but it had been kept in place by the plate he wore. When he had removed the plate the night before, however, Stalin had felt a twinge of pain. He put the plate back and the tooth was firm again. But when he touched it with his tongue, it felt loose. The gum seemed to be aching, too.

Stalin went to bed without removing the plate and had a peaceful night. He removed it gingerly next morning, touched the tooth with his tongue and then with his fingers. It wiggled and he wanted to pull it out, he wanted to push it out of his mouth with his tongue. Stalin ordered his dentist to be brought from Moscow. That evening, he was informed that Dr. Lipman and his technician had arrived by plane and were installed in dacha number three.

"Tell him to come as soon as he's settled in," Stalin instructed.

Half an hour later the dentist appeared. He was a handsome, good-natured Jew less than forty years old. He had treated Stalin before and Stalin had been pleased with him. He had even said something like "You've got a gentler touch than Shapiro."

Shapiro had been Lipman's predecessor. He was also a good dentist, but Stalin didn't like to be asked a lot of questions, to be felt all over, have medicine prescribed, and then never have anything explained. They never told you what was wrong with you or what their prescriptions were supposed to do. They had a terribly self-important manner and turned their profession into an enigmatic mystery. These qualities had been especially unpleasant in the small, quiet Shapiro.

Lipman, on the other hand, explained what he was doing, he told Stalin how his teeth were, how to hold the plate, and when he first removed one of Stalin's teeth, he didn't just throw it away in the basin, as Shapiro had done. He showed it to Stalin, pointing out what had happened to the root and why it had been necessary to pull it. He was an unhurried, affable man. Stalin said of him jokingly: "He charms the teeth right out of your mouth!"

He could see that Lipman was afraid of him, but there was nothing special about that: everyone was afraid of him. But if a dentist is so scared that his hand shakes, he might do something wrong. And so he gave a friendly welcome to Lipman. As usual, he asked: "How are you and how are things at home? Everything all right?"

He knew absolutely nothing about Lipman's family or his household.

"Fine, thank you, Josef Vissarionovich."

Lipman opened a suitcase that was almost as big as a traveling trunk, and took out his instruments and a headrest, which he attached to an armchair. Stalin was pleased to see that he installed the headrest first, whereas Shapiro had done it only when Stalin was already in the chair, and Stalin never liked people to fuss about behind his back.

Having attached the headrest and made sure it was firm, Lipman asked Stalin to sit down. Lipman tied a napkin around his neck and with a gentle touch of the hand lowered his head onto the headrest.

"Is that comfortable?"

"Yes."

"What is the trouble?"

"There's a loose tooth, especially when I take out the plate."

"We'll look at it right away." He gave Stalin a glass of water. "Rinse, please. . . . Yes, good. . . . Now put your head back, please. . . . Yes, that's good. . . ."

Cautiously, Lipman removed the plate and touched the tooth. His touch was gentle and his hands smelt of something pleasant. Then from among his instruments he selected an inspection mirror and examined the teeth again.

"The tooth will have to come out, there's nothing else to do. It'll only go on giving you trouble. The plate won't hold it, it's completely gone."

"How long will this take?"

"Well, the gum should heal in a couple of days and we can make the new plate in a day. I think it will take five days in all, no more."

"And I'll be walking around without any teeth for five days?" Stalin frowned.

"Why without any teeth?" Lipman smiled. "You'll only be without the upper molars. We could of course adapt this plate temporarily" — he turned the old plate over in his hands — "and that way you'll only be without one tooth. The problem is that if there is any distortion, you could damage a healthy tooth, by putting too much pressure on it. Why take the risk? Can't you wait for just a few days?"

"All right," Stalin agreed. "When do you want to take it out?"

"Anytime it's convenient. What about right now?"

"Or tomorrow morning?" Stalin asked.

"Tomorrow morning will be fine."

"I've got guests arriving today. It's awkward to greet one's guests with no teeth, don't you think?"

"If your guests want to eat," Lipman laughed, "the main thing is that they should have their own teeth."

Stalin got up and Lipman hurriedly removed the napkin from around his neck.

"Enjoy yourself," Stalin said. "Tomorrow morning after breakfast they'll call for you."

Kirov arrived during the day. Stalin told Zhdanov to show him the work they were doing on the history textbook and to invite him to supper that evening.

The three of them dined together. As the host Stalin sat at the head of the table.

"I'm glad you came, Sergei Mironovich. Andrei Alexandrovich, here" — he nodded at Zhdanov — "doesn't drink and doesn't eat, but sits at the table like Jesus Christ and is trying to starve me to death. But I agree with Chekhov: all these illnesses have been dreamed up by doctors. One must of course eat a little of everything in moderation. Here they use very good herbs, like coriander and tarragon. And the fruit is good, and dry wine, Georgian wine, good wine. Eat and drink, it's all good for you. Whatever's on the table, you can see for yourself — you're from the Caucasus. Or maybe since you've been in Leningrad you've forgotten cheese-bread and lobio beans and stewed cold turkey."

"I haven't forgotten," Kirov said with a laugh as he helped himself from each dish. "I remember it all and I love it all."

"I don't know what sort of cooking is in fashion at the moment in Leningrad," Stalin said thoughtfully. "The gentry used to like French cooking and the people ate German cooking, sausage and salami. What about now?"

"Now it's proletarian cooking that's in fashion," Kirov said. "Cabbage soup, borscht, chops, and macaroni. Whatever we issue on coupons, the people eat."

"Yes, the coupons," Stalin mused. "We're going to abolish the coupons."

Kirov said nothing. The abolition of coupons from the first of January had already been decided on.

"A good harvest is expected this year," Stalin continued. "There should be enough grain. The word from Kazakhstan is that the harvest there is unprecedented, they haven't seen one like it for decades. They expect to get more than one thousand pounds per acre. I'm afraid your friend Mirzoyan won't be able to handle such a large harvest."

"Mirzoyan's an energetic man, he won't let us down."

As if he hadn't heard Kirov's reply, Stalin continued thoughtfully: "A rich harvest is of course a good thing, but it's dangerous as well: it takes people by surprise, it brings with it a mood of complacency, well-being, security. A rich harvest is good when it has been gathered and delivered, not plundered or frittered away."

Kirov knew that Stalin never said anything without a reason. He had not begun the conversation about Kazakhstan by chance. Normally Stalin did not talk business at the table, but this was an exception. He would start by talking about something remote, making some banal remarks as a way of introducing some of his most unexpected decisions. And again he was talking about agriculture. A month before, at the June meeting of the Central

Committee, Kirov had been criticized for not fulfilling the grain and meat quotas, even though they had supposedly been reduced. In fact, they had not been reduced, but merely adjusted for the various sectors. Some had been raised, others reduced. Stalin did not understand such things, because he did not understand agriculture. Nor had there been any delay in handling the harvest: June was the decisive month for deliveries in the Leningrad region. But Kirov had not protested against the decree criticizing him: the Party was preparing to abolish the ration-card system, so it was necessary to concentrate every effort on securing grain for the country, and everyone had to be stretched. If anyone was to be criticized, then of course it would be best to make an example of the leading Party organization. It was the usual thing, and Kirov did not see anything personal behind it, although a better example could have been made of the Moscow organization, as it was in the capital. But the Moscow organization was headed by Kaganovich, and Stalin didn't want to offend *him*. It was typical of him to insult one while rewarding another and to play them off against each other. Stepan Shaumyan once said of Stalin: "Koba has the mind and morals of a snake." But Kirov was above that: when Party matters were being decided, there was no room for personal feelings. Moreover Kirov detested Kaganovich as a murderer, bootlicker, and coward. At any rate, Kirov had understood the Central Committee decree on the delays in Leningrad. What he did not understand was the conversation about the harvest in Kazakhstan. And the idea of his helping to write the history textbook must be a fiction — he was no historian! Stalin was no historian either, though he thought he was. So why had he brought him here?

"Right," Stalin said suddenly. "Why are we talking about harvests and Kazakhstan and Mirzoyan? There's only one thing we want to talk about, and that's the question of history." He turned to Zhdanov. "Have you put Sergei Mironovich in the picture?"

"Yes, preliminarily," Zhdanov replied.

"We have to take the writing of history into our own hands," Stalin said sternly. "Otherwise it'll fall into the wrong hands, the hands of the bourgeois historians. Not that our historians are much better. And I don't mean Pokrovsky — he's a bourgeois historian anyway."

"Pokrovsky undoubtedly made mistakes," Kirov protested. "But Lenin assessed his work in a different way...."

Stalin fixed Kirov with a searching look.

"And how did Lenin assess him?"

"You must be aware of his letter to Pokrovsky about *Russian History in a Brief Outline?*"

"And what did he write to Pokrovsky?"

He knew perfectly well what Lenin had written, but he thought he could catch Kirov out in an error.

"I don't remember the text word for word. One could have a look at it, it's been published many times. But Lenin congratulated him on the book and said it ought to be translated into other languages."

"Yes," Stalin agreed, "Lenin did pay him those compliments. But at the same time, he suggested that a chronological table be added to the book to avoid superficiality. And that was the essence of Lenin's assessment of the book."

"I'm not a historian," Kirov said. "But I don't agree. The general assessment was clear, precise, and positive. The suggestion that a chronological table be added was a detail, it did not detract from his generally positive assessment. Pokrovsky wrote his book in nineteen twenty and in effect it was the first attempt to throw light on Russian history from the Marxist-Leninist point of view. And he wrote it as a book for the masses on Lenin's orders. For all its shortcomings, the work has considerable merits — we have all learned from it. No doubt historical science has moved on and a new textbook is needed, but to criticize Pokrovsky's work, as some historians are doing, is not right, and to persecute him, as he has been persecuted in recent years, is intolerable. Pokrovsky was without any doubt an honest man —"

"See?" Stalin grinned. "And you say you're no good at history. You'll show us all up! And you're quite right, we do need a new history textbook. That's why I asked you to come here. You didn't want to come, but as it turns out you're really needed. The issue now is not Pokrovsky. I'm talking about certain members of the Party, certain *old* members of the Party. Comrade Krupskaya, for instance, is also writing history. Have you seen her memoirs of Lenin?"

"Yes, I've read them." Kirov nodded his head.

"And Pospelov's article in *Pravda* about the memoirs?"

"Yes, I've read that, too."

"It's a good article, it's to the point." Stalin turned and took a file off a table, leafed through it, and found the cutting from *Pravda* and looked over the passages he'd marked in red pencil. "Yes, here . . . Pospelov writes: 'Krupskaya uncritically exaggerates Plekhanov's role in the history of our Party, and she depicts Lenin as Plekhanov's respectful pupil.' He's right. And why is he right? Because Krupskaya is looking at these figures from the distant past, whereas Pospelov is looking at them with today's eyes. And from our experience of today, despite the respect we may have for Plekhanov as the 'Father of Russian Marxism,' despite our high regard for his activity, we cannot *now* put these two figures on the same level."

Kirov again listened carefully to Stalin. He remembered Pospelov's article well. The point of it was not of course Plekhanov. The offending words were in Krupskaya's following remark: "After October, people began to come to the fore who had not had a chance to show themselves earlier because of the circumstances of the old underground. . . . Among these was Comrade Stalin." Kirov knew perfectly well how furious those words would have made Stalin and he knew a reply would not be long in coming. And that's how it had turned out. The answer was Pospelov's long article in *Pravda* in which he criticized various aspects of the memoirs in order to be able to make the following point: "Even during the underground period the *leading* role of such authoritative organizers — Party leaders — as Stalin and Sverdlov, was entirely obvious to the grassroots Bolshevik activists who were working not abroad but right inside Russia." That of course was not true. But Stalin would not countenance the slightest attempt to alter the claim that, even before the Revolution, he was the second man in the Party, that Lenin ran the Party from abroad while Stalin ran it inside Russia. This version did not correspond with the truth, but it did rally the Party around the new leadership. And Kirov accepted this version. But it was one thing to accept it for the sake of political expediency, and quite another to accept it as history.

Stalin grinned.

"Everyone's been writing memoirs. Even Abel Enukidze's doing it."

From the same file which he'd put back on the table, Stalin retrieved Enukidze's pamphlet and showed it to Kirov.

"Have you read this?"

Kirov had read Enukidze's piece and knew exactly what Stalin did not like about it. For a moment he felt like saying he hadn't read it just to avoid the conversation. But then Stalin would suggest he read it, so ultimately he wouldn't be able to avoid discussing it.

"Yes . . . I glanced through it . . . I came across it. . . ."

Stalin seized on his evasiveness. " 'Came across it,' 'glanced through it.' According to this, only three people knew about the existence of the illegal press known as 'Nina': Krasin, Enukidze, and Ketskhoveli. How does Abel Enukidze know that?"

"He was one of the people who ran the press," Kirov replied.

"Precisely, he was *one* of them. But there were also Krasin and Ketskhoveli. And Ketskhoveli did not conceal its existence from me. But neither Krasin nor Ketskhoveli are alive. Only Abel Enukidze's still alive, but that doesn't give him the right to depict the history of the press any way he likes, instead of the way it actually was."

"Apparently Enukidze didn't know that you were aware of what was going on," Kirov said. "He no doubt believed that Lenin's directive had been carried out to the letter."

"What directive?" Stalin pricked up his ears.

"The one that said that nobody apart from Krasin, Enukidze, Ketskhoveli, and the typesetters was to know about the press."

"How do you know about this directive?"

"It's common knowledge."

"What do you mean 'common knowledge'? The fact is, Enukidze dreamed it up and everyone believes it. The press was indeed under the control of the overseas center, but why should it follow that I didn't know anything about it? Yes, Lenin ran the press personally, but that doesn't mean, as Enukidze writes, that nobody, apart from them, knew anything about it. And if Comrade Enukidze really thought that, why didn't he check first with the people who were in Baku at the time? And why has he published this just at this moment? Why does he emphasize that point particularly? Why was it necessary? It was necessary in order to repudiate the idea of the leadership succession, to prove that the present leadership of the Central Committee is not the direct successor to Lenin, that before the Revolution Lenin did not rely on the current leadership, but on other people. More than that, he trusted those other people, whereas he did not trust the present leadership. What game is Comrade Enukidze playing?"

"I don't think that is what Comrade Enukidze was trying to do," Kirov protested. "I think he simply wrote about what he knew. He undoubtedly did not know that Ketskhoveli had kept you informed. I'm sure of it."

"I see no grounds for such conviction," Stalin replied coldly. "I see no grounds for such assurance. Comrade Enukidze didn't join the Party yesterday, Comrade Enukidze is a member of the Central Committee, he cannot *not* think through the political consequences of his actions. Comrade Enukidze cannot be unaware of whose interests his pamphlet serves. If an ordinary historian had written it, one could have ignored it. Historians often make mistakes — they are the prisoners of bare historical facts and as a rule they are poor dialecticians and make even worse politicians. But this pamphlet was not written by an ordinary historian, it was written by one of the leaders of the Party and state. Why did he write it? Why was he drawn to write his memoirs? It's a bit early for that. Comrade Enukidze is still a young man. We're practically the same age, and I certainly don't regard myself as an old man who's ready to start writing his memoirs. These are not memoirs, this is a political act. It is an act aimed at distorting the history of our Party, an act aimed at discrediting the present Party leadership. *That* was what Comrade Enukidze set out to achieve."

"I think you're overreacting," Kirov said with a frown. "Granted, it's simply not Comrade Enukidze's business to write such pamphlets. He's neither a historian nor a writer. But I doubt that he w nts to discredit the present leadership. He's an honest, sincere m n and he loves you."

Stalin stared at Kirov from under his brows. His eyes were yellow, like a tiger's. Becoming angrier all the time, which caused his accent to grow heavier, he said: "Honesty, sincerity, love — they aren't political categories. In politics there's only one thing: political calculation."

The conversation had become painful. It had been difficult in general to talk to Stalin lately, especially when he was irritated.

"Comrade Enukidze could be corrected," Kirov said in a conciliatory way. "His incompetence in questions of history could be pointed out to him."

"Yes," Stalin was quick to respond. "If some historian had written it, another historian could correct him. But this was written by a Central Committee member, one of the most prominent leaders of the country. He can be corrected only on that level." He stared at Kirov. "You ran the Baku Party organization for five years. A statement from you would carry the most weight."

Kirov was astounded. Such a thing had never happened before. He, a member of the Politburo, must testify publicly that Stalin had run the press known as "Nina," of whose existence he had in fact been unaware — Enukidze was right about that. Why was such a demand being made of him? Was it to test his loyalty? It had been tested enough, but if it was to be tested again, then it should not be on this issue.

"I've never done any history," Kirov said. "And I'm not knowledgeable on this particular issue. And, anyway, during the period in question, I wasn't even in Baku."

"Ah, well," Stalin said calmly, "nobody can blame you. I hope there are comrades in the Party who are capable of replying to Abel Enukidze." He turned to Zhdanov. "The Central Committee of the Party shouldn't deal with this question. It's not a question for the whole Party, but only for one of its organizations. Let the Transcaucasian organization deal with its own history. Summon Comrade Beria and inform him of the Central Committee's point of view. He's the secretary of the Transcaucasian regional committee, it comes within his scope."

ext morning after breakfast Stalin ordered them to call the
dentist.

Lipman appeared with his suitcase. He laid out his
instruments, set up a bowl, sat Stalin in the armchair, and
tied the napkin around his neck.

"How did you sleep?" Stalin asked.

"Wonderfully," Lipman replied, as he prepared the syringe. "It
couldn't have been better — so quiet and peaceful here. . . ." With
a gentle touch of the hand he eased Stalin's head back onto the
headrest, and asked him to open his mouth. "I don't know how it
affects others, but the sound of the surf always has a good effect on
me."

Stalin felt a small jab in the gum, but thought that perhaps he
had only imagined it. Lipman's face showed nothing. He was
looking into Stalin's mouth and smiling. Then he sat back, rested
his hands on his knees, and, still smiling, said: "We'll just wait a
minute, while the anaesthetic takes effect. You can close your
mouth, you can talk, and you can walk about, but it's better if you
sit."

The gum became numb and then heavy, as if it was filling up
with something. Stalin had had teeth out under local anaesthetic
before, but he couldn't remember how long it took for the drug to
take effect.

"Do we have long to wait?" he asked.

"Ten minutes, I think. Open your mouth again and I'll have a
look."

He examined Stalin's mouth again, passing a metallic instrument along the gums. "It'll soon be frozen, just be patient."

He looked at Stalin. Calm and benevolent, he had given the injection well, without causing any pain. Comrade Stalin ought to be pleased with him.

Stalin did indeed appreciate people who knew their jobs and were good at them. This surgeon would probably live to be a hundred: he was happy in his job, happy in his life and his position. He worked in the Kremlin, treating members of the Politburo. He was well looked after and was no doubt envied; there were always people who envied you. But he evidently paid no attention to them. He was a man without ambition, like the overwhelming majority of people in the world. Once upon a time, as a very young man, he, Stalin, had begun struggling for the people. He did not know then the other, real motives for his struggle. But now he was ruling these people, and they believed in him as if he were a god. But you can only believe in gods blindly, without thinking. They called him Father. People only respect a father who has a heavy, strict, but strong and reliable hand. And this man was dedicated to him only because he had this close physical contact. Such people were also necessary in his entourage; not just his henchmen and wolfhounds and his ambitious assistants, but also simple, modest people who loved him and were loyal to him.

Lipman, sitting next to him, looked at his watch and smiled at Stalin. Now and again he asked him to open his mouth and he would insert an instrument and after one such examination he showed Stalin the tooth he had just pulled out with pliers.

"When did you manage that? I didn't feel a thing."

"Well, it was anaesthetized. And the tooth was nearly out, it could have been taken out by hand, as we say."

"Why didn't you?"

"Then you would have felt it."

Stalin spat out a long stream of bloody saliva into the bowl, rinsed his mouth, and spat again.

"You shouldn't eat anything for two hours," Lipman said, giving him a clean napkin. Stalin wiped his lips. "And nothing hot at all today."

He picked up the dental plate from the table and examined it.

"This is a good plate, it's well made with good materials — a blend of gold, platinum, and palladium. You won't need it anymore, we'll make you a new one. But you know, Josef Vissarionovich, it might be best to make a more simple one."

"What do you mean, simple?"

"Well, here the teeth are held by a metal plate, whereas we could make it entirely in plastic."

"Why is that necessary?"

"The point is, Josef Vissarionovich, that the metal plate is fixed to the teeth by these two little hooks — what we call clasps. As long as the plate itself is light, it doesn't put pressure on the teeth. But you've already got seven false teeth on this plate and it's heavy, too heavy. And now we're going to put another tooth on it and it will become even heavier, the load will increase. A plastic plate can cling to the palate and can carry any number of false teeth."

"You want to give me false teeth like an old man?"

"Why like an old man? Old men have no teeth whereas you have your own teeth. And you will have for a long time yet, please God."

Some years earlier, when Stalin had had some molars removed and it was suggested that he have a plate, he'd been terribly upset: he wouldn't do it! An old man with false teeth! He'd seen old men take out their false teeth at night and put them in a glass of water. That's what Solts, who was not that old, had done when they were sharing a safe house in Petersburg. Solts's false teeth were in fact the first ones he'd seen. When Solts spoke, and he was always excited when he spoke, his false teeth slipped and he'd have to hold them up with his tongue, which made him lisp and pronounce his words badly — it was not a pretty sight.

But the dentists had explained to Stalin that what they had in mind was not a full denture, but a gold plate to hold false molars, so he'd have something to chew his food with. They'd made the plate and he'd got used to it. It didn't get in the way and he did not feel toothless. Later, when two more teeth were taken out, they suggested making him a thin plate of the sort Lipman was now suggesting, and for the same reasons. But he had refused and they'd made the gold plate that Lipman was now holding in his hand, and despite all the warnings, it had served him well.

Now Lipman was suggesting an old man's denture. Lipman was

a dull-witted man, seeing him only as a patient and forgetting that millions of people gazed at this "patient." He couldn't stand up in front of them with a loose denture and lisp and talk as if he had a mouthful of porridge.

"Make me a gold one," Stalin said.

Lipman did not dare to object further. "Yes, of course. If the wound hurts, take one of these tablets and call me if necessary. And let me see how the healing is progressing tomorrow."

"They'll come for you at the same time."

Lipman left. Stalin went over to the mirror and opened his mouth. He bared his teeth. It made an unappealing picture: only five teeth left in his upper jaw, five yellow, smoke-stained teeth. Never mind, Zhdanov would just have to stand him for a few days with five teeth. And Kirov, too.

The thought of Kirov made him frown. Kirov didn't want to join in the struggle, he didn't want to reinforce the leadership of the Party.

That day he saw nobody, but allowed the anaesthetic to wear off and the wound to heal. Following Lipman's orders, he ate nothing for two hours and for lunch he had cold beet soup and some lukewarm meatballs. They served him the right thing, as he had nothing to chew with. The wound did not hurt, nor did the gum, and he had no need of painkillers.

Lipman came in the morning, examined his mouth, and pronounced that he was satisfied.

"It's all going well. We'll start the new plate in two days."

"How do you relax?" Stalin asked. "Aren't you bored?"

"But, Josef Vissarionovich, how can one be bored with the sea and the beach right here, and I found writing paper and sharp pencils on my desk, so I sat down and wrote."

"What are you writing about?"

"A specialist piece on prosthetic appliances."

"I wish you luck."

Stalin ate both lunch and dinner alone: he had no desire to be seen without teeth. But he had to work. Zhdanov and Kirov came to see him during the evening. They sat on the verandah and read the newspapers.

"So, Hitler is to be the Führer of the German people for the rest of his life, and chancellor of the empire," Stalin commented.

"You'll see, he'll pronounce himself emperor," Kirov said with a laugh.

"He wouldn't be so stupid," Zhdanov remarked.

"Yes," Stalin agreed. "It wouldn't make any sense. There have been a lot of emperors, but only one lifetime Führer. And he hasn't got any children, he can't create a dynasty." His eyes slid down a newspaper column. "I see Zinoviev has burst into print again; every day he writes something. Open any newspaper and you're bound to see something by Zinoviev or Kamenev or Radek. Scribble, scribble, scribble . . ."

"They've nothing else to do, so they write," Zhdanov said.

"But what is interesting," Stalin went on, "is that every article extols Comrade Stalin. He's this, he's that, he's great, he's a genius and wise and practically higher than Marx, Engels, and Lenin. Why all this praise? How can Zinoviev praise Comrade Stalin sincerely? He cannot! He hates Comrade Stalin. So, he's lying, he's writing what he does not think. Why is he lying? After all, he knows perfectly well that nobody, least of all Comrade Stalin, believes him. Is he afraid? Who is he afraid of? After all, nobody's bothering him."

"He wants to prove that he is harmless, disarmed, that he had no ambitions," Kirov said.

"Let's allow that," Stalin agreed. "It's dubious, but let us allow it. But he is belittling himself. And nobody ever forgets their own debasement. One can forget all sorts of things — insults, hurts, injustices — but nobody can ever forget his own belittlement, it's simply human nature. The animals hunt each other, they fight and kill and eat each other, but they don't debase themselves. Only human beings do that. And no man can ever forget being belittled and he can never forgive the one before whom he has debased himself. On the contrary, he will always hate him. And the more Zinoviev praises Stalin, the more he debases himself before Stalin, the more he will hate Stalin. Radek is also parading himself, also praising, but Radek is a windbag, he's not a serious person. Yesterday he was praising Trotsky, today he's praising Stalin, tomorrow, if he has to, he'll praise Hitler. Give him a mustard sandwich and he'll drool and lick his lips and even say thank you. But Zinoviev and Kamenev, no, they have other ambitions. All their lives they aimed at becoming leaders and they still do, especially as their regiments have increased with the addition of Bukharin and Rykov and their company."

Kirov shrugged his shoulders. "Zinoviev and Bukharin? What's the connection?"

"Sergei Mironovich," Zhdanov said mildly, "Bukharin secretly ran to Kamenev and tried to form an alliance with him."

Kirov liked Zhdanov, but there were matters that members of the Politburo discussed only among themselves, and Zhdanov was not a member of the Politburo. Stalin had begun this conversation in front of Zhdanov purposely to show that he saw no difference between Zhdanov and Kirov.

"But you see, Comrade Zhdanov," Stalin objected dryly, "that took place eight years ago, at a time when the Party leadership had not been stabilized and when Zinoviev and Kamenev were still aiming at gaining power. They know perfectly by now that they have no chance and they are reconciled to their position, and to their defeat, if only because they have publicly repented and been compromised for so many years and, I think, now can count on nothing."

Zhdanov wanted to reply but Stalin stopped him with a gesture.

"They're politicians, and therefore they always want power. And the more they are humiliated the more they hope to get revenge. They can never forgive anyone for their humiliation, you and me most of all. Zinoviev regarded Leningrad as his patrimony. On the eve of the Fourteenth Congress the Leningrad organization voted for Zinoviev against the Party. And now for eight years Comrade Kirov has led the Leningrad organization and it follows him. The Leningrad organization no longer acknowledges Zinoviev, it only acknowledges Comrade Kirov. Will Zinoviev forgive you for that? No, he will not, and he will take his revenge at the first opportunity."

"I find that incomprehensible." Kirov shrugged. "I can't imagine and I can't see or even guess how they might get at me."

"Ways can always be found," Stalin replied. "For such work, ways can always be found. And especially in Leningrad where there are still plenty of old Zinovievites, people you refuse to discard because you believe in their so-called recantations and self-disarmament."

Stalin stared at Kirov and became aware of the other man's pockmarks. They spoiled his face. It became unpleasant to look at him. You might think: So what, so he has a few pockmarks? But it was unpleasant. Kirov's pockmarks reminded him of his own.

"Comrade Stalin," Kirov said firmly, "the Leningrad organization voted for Zinoviev in nineteen twenty-five. But the leadership had been pressing them day and night to do so — virtually ordering them to. These were ordinary Party members. Not to obey would have been a breach of discipline. This, unfortunately, is the cost of democratic centralism: any Party organization might temporarily follow its leadership down the wrong path. The ordinary members of the Party are not to blame, and we should not punish them for it. But in nineteen twenty-six they voted for us, for the Central Committee."

"The 'ordinary members of the Party,'" Stalin said, smirking, "are bad members of the Party if the district secretary can raise them against the Party, against its Central Committee. The Leningrad Communists are not as simple as you make them out. Even now, they still regard their city as the cradle of the Revolution and themselves as the vanguard of the Russian working class. And there are still those in Leningrad who not only voted as Party discipline dictated, but whose repentance is no different from that of Zinoviev and Kamenev: they're biding their time, they know that it could come during the slightest confusion in the Party, in the country, or in the state. It would be enough to get rid of me, of you, and two or three other members of the Politburo to create such a moment of confusion, and they would exploit it at once — they are experienced politicians. And you and I would get no mercy from them. If they were to manage a takeover and grasp power, they'd slaughter us down to the third generation. And you trust them, you deal with them like a liberal. You think they'll thank you? Not a bit of it! You like to walk the streets or sit in the balcony at the theater. You're careless, extremely careless. Don't you understand? Must the Politburo issue a special decree about your safety?"

"I don't want any special decrees," Kirov said hastily. "I have enough bodyguards and they're reliable."

"That's what you think," Stalin objected. "The Politburo might take a different view. There is an agreed procedure for the protection of Politburo members, and you're the only one who is breaking it."

"I've been in Leningrad eight years and nothing's happened," Kirov said. "Not even a hint of anything."

"Yesterday there was nothing and today there was nothing, but it could happen tomorrow," Stalin protested. "Nothing is eternal, nothing lasts forever. Hitler's coming to power changes the situation fundamentally. The opposition forces in our country find comfort in Germany's militaristic aspirations. The Germans may be aimed first and foremost against the West, but the West is trying to divert them against us. Such a turn of events could create a crisis here. Who would be able to exploit it? The opposition forces. What opposition forces are there in our country? Monarchists? Constitutional Democrats? Socialist Revolutionaries? Mensheviks? No, none of them, they've all been swept away; they are not capable of revival. The people have bound themselves forever to the Soviet system. Therefore the only danger is within the Soviet system itself, that is, within the Party. Who are they? The Trotskyites, Zinovievites, Bukharinites. Are they themselves aware of this? Of course they are. And meanwhile they are maneuvering. Their main task is to protect themselves and their supporters. Are they few in number? Only a few thousand people? But how many of us Bolsheviks were there in nineteen seventeen? Also only a few thousand. But we exploited the situation correctly and we won. What reason have we to suppose that people like Zinoviev, Kamenev, and Bukharin wouldn't be able to exploit the appropriate situation, with not a few thousand but tens of thousands of hidden supporters? Don't you think all the former Mensheviks are supporting Zinoviev? Or that Bukharin does not have the support of all the rich peasants whose lands we collectivized and the

Kadets? They would see Zinoviev and Bukharin as a springboard, only as transitory figures, but they would see them as the only acceptable ones in the crisis: the people know them and the Party knows them. Nobody will remember the fact that they recanted and admitted their errors. Look at the mistakes Zinoviev and Kamenev made in nineteen seventeen, and yet it was all forgiven and forgotten. For fifteen years Trotsky fought against Lenin, but when he came over to the Bolsheviks, it was all forgiven and forgotten. The people are not interested in a politician's past, but in what he is now, at the present time. Zinoviev, Kamenev, and Bukharin understand this perfectly; it's basic strategy. The main thing for them is to protect themselves and bide their time. In this they are more cunning than Trotsky. Trotsky was a poor politician: he was impetuous, and so were his supporters. But we knew them all, and we had them under surveillance. Zinoviev and Bukharin are more cunning. They capitulated in time, they did not expose their supporters. Their supporters are in hiding and ready to come out at any moment. There are vast numbers of them. They include all the people in the Party who feel aggrieved, as well as all the people in the country who feel badly treated. It's a large and dangerous potential force. And yet it's *we* who are protecting them, we who nourish them, and yet we are afraid of offending them."

"Are you talking about Leningrad?" Kirov asked.

"Yes," Stalin replied harshly. "I am talking about Leningrad, Leningrad as an undestroyed bastion of opposition, and I am thinking of Comrade Kirov as a man who does not want to destroy that bastion."

"It isn't like that," Kirov replied calmly. "The history of the Party teaches us otherwise. There always were differences within the Party over strategy and tactics, there always were arguments and discussions. But when the Party made a decision, the argument ended, no more opposition existed, and none of the former oppositionists were cut off from the Party. On the contrary, Lenin taught us to take a solicitous and comradely attitude toward those who have been wrong on this or that issue. I can say with confidence that there are no Trotskyites, Zinovievites, or Bukharinites in the Leningrad organization. Undoubtedly, we come up against occasional anti-Party and anti-Soviet moods, but in the main they stem from the bourgeois classes and are in no way connected with the former opposition. As for the Leningrad worker-Communists who voted for Zinoviev in nineteen twenty-five, they broke with him long ago, they've forgotten all about him. And I cannot and will not punish them eight years after they voted for their Party leadership — in accordance with Party discipline. If you find my policy mistaken, you can always recall me from Leningrad. But as long as I'm there that's the policy I intend to pursue."

The tension that had been rising perceptibly in Stalin suddenly subsided and he spoke blandly, almost with indifference:

"The Party can't have a separate policy in each city. It has a unified policy for the whole country and every district Party secretary has to submit to that policy. We will discuss how to deal with the former Zinovievites at the Politburo. But until we do discuss it, I want you to be careful and take my warnings seriously: the Zinovievites are becoming active. I have a wider range of information than you. You're too trusting, Sergei Mironovich. Be careful that your trusting nature doesn't blind you."

"In what sense?"

"You've only seen Zinoviev and Kamenev on the platform at congresses, whereas I've spent years with them: I even shared a cell with Kamenev. They're liars, cheats, and hypocrites. And the people who support them are also liars, cheats, and hypocrites. Don't trust them, they are capable of anything. And they hate you. By the way, that is one of the reasons it was thought you ought to move to Moscow. If someone else were to take your place and to cope with Leningrad as well as you do, they'd realize that success isn't just a question of Comrade Kirov, but of the Party. The Leningrad Communists wouldn't be following Comrade Kirov, they'd be following the Party. And they wouldn't have a grudge against your successor. You are a secretary of the Central Committee, after all, it's high time you moved to Moscow. See through the abolition of ration cards in Leningrad, let the Leningraders remember you for that, let that be, so to speak, your act of farewell, and then come to Moscow."

Suppressing his mounting fury, Kirov lowered his gaze. The hint that he hungered for popularity was crude like all of Stalin's hints. It was quite clear: Stalin wanted him out of Leningrad, he wanted him at his side in Moscow where he could keep him under full control. He would give him only second-rank jobs to do and keep the top jobs for such bootlickers as Molotov, Kaganovich, and Voroshilov.

"Comrade Stalin," Kirov said, "I request that you do not recall me from Leningrad before the reconstruction of the city has been completed. I began it and I would like to finish it."

Kirov said this in a tone that suggested that he would brook no argument.

Stalin understood and asked calmly: "But when will the reconstruction be finished?"

"I hope by the end of this Five-Year Plan."

"Oh, well," Stalin joked, "we'll just have to try and finish the plan in four years and get you to Moscow sooner."

12

Varya arrived at work promptly at nine. She laid the drawing that was to be copied on her board, covered it with a pale blue linen sheet, and pinned them both down with thumbtacks. She then wiped a thin film of machine oil over the surface, as Lyova had shown her, in order to make the tracing linen transparent, allowing the drawing to come through clearly and preventing the ink from running. The drawing had been done by Lyova who, having been made a technician, had graduated to "pencil work," as his new position was defined. He was a very nice boy without a technical education and he was terribly proud of his new title as design technician. Igor Vladimirovich made the sketch, Lyova the technical drawing, and Varya the copy. The linen was sent down to photostating, where they produced the blueprint, which was the working drawing issued to the construction site. The hotel was going up right next door. It was easy to work from Lyova's drawings as he had what was called "high graphics" — precise, quality representation. When Lyova handed over his drawing to Varya, he explained its features: the windows, doors, vestibule and lobbies, the banquet hall in the restaurant. Igor Vladimirovich would then elaborate. He would emerge from his office and stand next to Varya, leaning over the drawing: this line means this, and this line means that. He taught them in a friendly and informal way.

"And don't be afraid to ask if there's something you don't understand," he would say.

Lyova and Rina told Varya that Igor Vladimirovich had explained the plans to them in exactly the same way when they had started as copiers, because he didn't want their work to become mechanical. He wanted them to understand it. Ordinary bosses would come over, look at your work, and say: "Hmm, that's not it, my dear. Let's take it off and start again." That was not Igor Vladimirovich's style. He was as much a teacher as he was a boss, and he was treating Varya just like everyone else. He did not appear to single her out, but Varya knew that this was not the case, and in order not to encourage him, she would tend to go to Lyova or Rina for help.

She settled down in the job very quickly, feeling no anxiety or fear or uncertainty. She knew all the drafting instruments from school, and was expert at stretching the linen and making sure the ink did not drip onto the drawing. Lyova and Rina were full of admiration for her ability, if ink did spill, to remove it with a razor blade without leaving a mark. And to their amazement she could draw a free-hand curve with a fine pen.

They all went off in a noisy crowd at twelve o'clock to have their lunch in a special canteen on the corner of Tverskaya and Belinsky streets. Lunch consisted of salad, cabbage soup or broth, kasha with a piece of meat or a meatball, and watery stewed fruit. It only cost forty kopeks and they didn't take a coupon from your food card. You could also buy from the canteen and take a couple of salami, cheese, or herring sandwiches with you, also without using your ration coupons. There were forty people working at the bureau, half of them pretty young girls, some of whom Varya had seen at the Hermitage Gardens, the National, or the Metropole. Some got to the canteen early in order to keep a place in the line and they all joked and seemed cheerful and friendly. And their bosses — the architects, engineers, and technicians — seemed equally friendly and informal.

They would walk back in twos and threes as and when they finished their lunch.

Zoe pointed out the hotel construction, which had a high fence around it. They were laying the foundations and installing all the other underground systems. Rolling her eyes, Zoe said: "Last year they tore down Okhotny Row, and all those little shops and warehouses where they used to sell the meat and fish were full of rats. And just imagine, all the rats ran into the Grand Hotel, scrambled right up to all the floors and got into the rooms, and they

were really fat and huge, the size of cats. It was awful! We died of
fright, the girls all jumped up on their desks. Special crews had to
come and exterminate them and the hotel even had to be closed for
a time."

Zoe hadn't changed at all. She was still the excitable, pesky,
talkative girl she had always been. Nobody at the office had made
friends with her or showed any interest in her. Varya also found it
hard to be friendly, but she didn't want to snub her old friend, so
she patiently listened to her interminable chatter.

"The hotel project belongs to Igor Vladimirovich and another
architect," Zoe explained. "They both won first prize in the
competition and Academician Shchusev was appointed co-designer.
Not only that, Shchusev was made overall manager. Of course, they
didn't like that, but Shchusev doesn't even have an office here, he's
on Bryusov Street — you know, in the same house as Kachalov and
the other famous actors. You know?"

"I don't know, and how do *you* know? Have you visited
Kachalov at home?" Varya asked sarcastically.

"I haven't visited him, but I know where his house is because I've
delivered drawings to Shchusev there."

Varya saw Shchusev when he came to the bureau, which was
nearly every day. He was a pleasant old man, about sixty. Once he
came into their room. Lyova was at work on a perspective drawing
of the hotel for some high-level authority. The job was urgent and
he had been working on it day and night.

Shchusev looked over the drawing and nodded in approval. "It's
very good, but the windows ought to be narrower."

Then he left.

Lyova collapsed on his stool in despair.

"What's the problem?" Rina asked.

"The space between the windows is brickwork. If I narrow the
windows, I'll have to redraw each brick. It means another night's
work."

"I'll help you, if you like," Rina offered.

Igor Vladimirovich, who had overheard them, interrupted:
"Don't touch it. When he comes tomorrow, tell him you've done
it."

Next day Shchusev duly turned up.

"Have you done it?"

"Yes."

"There, you see? A completely different effect!"

They laughed about that for a long time. Shchusev in fact provided a lot of amusement. He was designing the columns supporting a box structure, which was going to be the restaurant. In the bureau they jokingly but affectionately called this box "the Trunk." They were all enthusiastic about the project and were irritated by alterations. They rejoiced at successes and were, all in all, a friendly little team.

Igor Vladimirovich never criticized Shchusev, nor would he allow them to do so in his presence. He never argued with Shchusev's instructions, but he did everything his own way, as he had with the windows. Varya liked this — it was Shchusev, after all! Had Igor Vladimirovich spoken ironically about him, he would only have demeaned himself. Igor Vladimirovich had style! When he looked over his subordinates' sketches and outlines, he would make a few strokes with charcoal — they called it his "flavoring" — and these were his instructions, which they would carry out unquestioningly. He was correct, reserved, elegant. Many of the girls were in love with him, but he was irreproachable.

Once the four of them were returning from lunch: Varya and Igor Vladimirovich were walking along together and Rina and Lyova were slightly ahead. Looking at the windows of the National, he said: "Aren't you reminded of anything?"

Varya passed the National twice a day on her way to the canteen and back, and it had not reminded her of anything. She had been there once with Vika, back in the spring, but her memory of that visit had long been replaced by her impressions of the other restaurants she'd visited with Kostya.

"I remember," she replied calmly. "We met there when I was with Vika Marasevich."

"And do you remember the Alexander Park? The entrance that was blocked by a bench, the guard's whistle? Our running away? Your torn stocking?"

Apparently they were memories he cherished. She also found

them poignant: it had been another time, another life, she'd had other hopes. She caught a note of expectation in his voice. But why? After all she had a husband! But maybe not for much longer. Still ...

"Yes," she replied casually, "I remember. ..."

Of course she liked Igor Vladimirovich, but only as a person, a colleague. Even then, at the National, she had realized he was not like Vika and her friends. And now she had seen him at work, among extraordinary people. Shchusev came, and the well-known artist Lanseré, who had decorated the halls of Kazan Station and who was now going to decorate the ceiling in the hotel's main restaurant. Then there was an American consultant on refrigerators and other modern kitchen technology, and there were architects and engineers who came to finalize details on the project. Lyova would tell her who they were after they'd gone, and they were all famous people, every one of them.

Varya did not want to leave work at night. She didn't want to go home and she no longer wanted to share the life Kostya lived. She did not love him, she merely pitied him. He had said: "With you beside me, I could become a real person." They were empty words. He hadn't become a "real person" and he never would.

After the business of the fur wrap, he acted as if nothing had happened: such was the life of a gambler — today you're in the money, tomorrow you have to tighten your belt. So what, you had to be patient and overcome temporary failures. Varya said nothing but he knew she did not accept his arguments. He saw how she had become distant and enclosed, yet he still tried to involve her in his way of life. One day he brought home a gold bracelet for her and put it on her arm, saying casually: "Wear it."

She took it off and put it on the table. "I'm not going to wear it."
"Why not?"
"I've never worn gold and I don't intend to start now."

He was enraged, but managed to restrain himself. "You don't have to wear it, but it's yours anyway." He put the bracelet in its box, wrapped the box carefully in paper, and put it in the table drawer which he locked. He joked: "A lady is supposed to have a casket for her jewels. But since you haven't got one yet, it can stay here."

She said nothing. She was sure the bracelet would disappear as suddenly as it had appeared.

The same day, he put some money in the table drawer. Varya did not touch it and didn't even know how much was there.

"Why don't you take any money?" he asked one day.

"What for? You don't eat at home and I eat at work."

"You still have to pay for your meals," he said.

"My wages are enough for that."

Soon the money disappeared, and with it the gold bracelet. She didn't need the money or the bracelet, but she would tell him about their disappearance so that there would be no misunderstandings.

"Varya," he had replied tenderly, "forgive me this time, too. I'll win it back, I'll win it back, don't be upset."

"I'm not upset and you don't have to return anything. I don't need the money or the bracelet. They went and I thought I should let you know, even though I was sure you had taken them."

He raised his voice. "If you knew I'd taken them, why bother to tell me?"

"Don't you like hearing such things? Don't bring any more expensive things or money here anymore. Keep them somewhere else."

"What do you mean by that?"

"This isn't a pawnshop or a savings bank. Your things would be safer there, but here, if anything happened to them, Sofya Alexandrovna and I have to answer for it."

"You just don't want to understand how I have to live my life, do you!"

"No, I don't! I don't understand your way of life and I cannot accept it."

"You talk to me as if I was a stranger."

She turned and looked him straight in the eye. "Yes, we are strangers, and it would be best if we parted."

"Ah, so that's how it is, is it!" His mouth twisted and he spoke deliberately. "As long as I'm winning I'm all right, but as soon as I start losing I'm not wanted anymore."

"You know perfectly well it's not like that. I didn't ask to go to the Crimea with you, and I didn't ask you for the silver fox and gold bracelet. It's simply that I realize we have nothing in common and we can't live together."

He spoke scornfully through clenched teeth: "You're having an affair with the architect."

"Idiot!" she flung at him contemptuously. But she wondered if someone had been gossiping. But who? Rina or Lyova?

"Oh, yes, of course, I'm an idiot." He dragged out his words, repressing his rage. "You don't like restaurants, do you? But where did I meet you, if it wasn't in a restaurant?"

"You mean you picked me up in a restaurant, so I'm a restaurant whore?"

He kept himself under control.

"All I'm saying is, we met in a restaurant and you shouldn't distort the facts."

"I don't have to distort anything, and we don't have anything to discuss. We have to split up. And right now! We have to get out of this room today!"

He raised his eyebrows in surprise and mockery. "Today? Interesting ... And where will we go?"

"*I'm* going home. And you've got an apartment where you're registered."

He grimaced again, this time in a grin.

"I've already explained to you, that registration is just a formality. I can't live there and I'm not going anywhere. I like it here."

He smiled broadly, victoriously, knowing what this did to Varya, and he triumphed in her distress. And she was indeed distressed. She could not leave him here. Sofya Alexandrovna did not like him, but she'd be afraid to go to the militia to get him out. She was afraid of anything that might cause her to lose her room. My God, how irresponsible it had been of her to drag Sofya Alexandrovna into such a mess!

"Sofya Alexandrovna gave the room to me."

He interrupted her: "To us, not to you, to us. And anyway I pay for it."

"I'll give you back the money."

"Now, you listen to me carefully," he said forcefully. "When we met, back in the Savoy, you told me about this room, you promised to speak to the landlady. In other words, it was for me that you took it. And now I'm supposed to get lost. Where am I supposed to go? Onto the street? Well, I'm not going to live on the street, I'm going to live here. You can live wherever you like."

Varya hung her head. He was pitiless, unscrupulous; he didn't care about anyone but himself. And she had called him her husband. Worst of all, she had to put up with him because she had no right to leave him alone with Sofya Alexandrovna.

Kostya was enjoying her humiliation and her helplessness.

"If you don't want to live with me, that's up to you. We're not registered, we can go our separate ways. I'm not forcing myself on you." A note of pride came back into his voice. "I never force myself on anyone, Sofya Alexandrovna included. I'll leave here, I'll give up the room. But not until I find another one in the center of town, with a telephone and all the conveniences. It'll take me two or three months. I'll stay here alone, or we can stay here together, it's all the same to me. We don't get in each other's way. Those are my terms: two or three months. If a room comes up sooner, I'll move out sooner." He grinned again. "And since you're so very desperately concerned, you can help me find another place."

"I can't help you find another room, but I agree to wait two months," she said.

He broke in: "Two or three months, I said."

"All right, two or three months. But you promise me that in two or three months we'll be out of this room."

He gave her one of his typical, big charming smiles.

"So, we've agreed. Why quarrel and get on each other's nerves? Let's make peace! Hurrah! What do you say we change and go out somewhere?"

"I'm not going anywhere with you anymore. I'm only staying on here for the sake of Sofya Alexandrovna, for her peace of mind. As for the rest, forget it! I shall sleep on this sofa."

"On this sofa?" He laughed. "Will you have enough room?"

"Don't worry, I'll have enough room."

"It's your life."

✶   ✶   ✶

How could she have deceived herself so badly? She had not seen or guessed what lay behind his showy generosity and independence. How could she have yielded to such cheap words as "with you beside me I could become a real person," when in fact he already regarded himself as one? She had been the most beautiful girl in her class, the most capable. She had been head and shoulders above all the others, yet not one of them had got themselves into a mess like this. No billiards player would have flattered his way into the heart of any of those girls.

She had to straighten herself out, she had to understand what she felt about herself.

Varya reread Zuyev-Insarov's analysis of her handwriting. She'd kept it in the same envelope in which it had been mailed to her. The stamp on the envelope bore three profiles: one of a worker in a cloth cap, another of a Red Army soldier in a pointed *budyonovka* helmet, and the third of a bearded peasant in a peaked cap.

> You are an exceptionally talented person. You have a critical mind and a strong will, but you have an impulsive character. You show independence in behavior and you make decisions without the advice or help of others. You are intelligent and capable of handling scientific questions independently. You lean toward creativity in science, a trait that possibly is as yet unrevealed because of your lack of purpose. You are sincere and capable of great sacrifice, but you can change your opinions radically after an argument. You are touchy and quick to take offense, and you are not easily dissuaded from a course once decided upon. You have a hot temper and are capable of making caustic remarks. You are bold and not always cautious in your relationships. You do things on a grand scale and are unable to deny yourself pleasure. You like people who are self-confident and you do not suffer spineless people gladly. You are impeccably honest in money matters, often to your own detriment. You are unforgiving, but not vengeful. You crush enemies with scorn. You have a heightened sensitivity. You hide profound feelings and you suffer alone. Your character is divided and changeable, the joy of life

being replaced by melancholy. In intimate relations you do not tolerate familiarity and monotony. Out of pride, you are capable of breaking off a relationship over a trifling cause.

Zuyev-Insarov, graphologist

She didn't know about her talents and capabilities — he no doubt paid the same compliments to everyone. On the other hand, he hadn't written that to Zoe. But the character sketch did explain a lot about her marriage. She did like people who had self-confidence, she did decide everything for herself and hated being contradicted, she wasn't cautious and didn't like denying herself pleasure. All that fitted. It was a very positive portrait and for that reason she had never shown it to anyone. The most accurate point in it was that she hid her deepest feelings and suffered alone. She was suffering alone now.

She hardly saw Kostya these days. As usual, he came home late, when she was already asleep on the sofa, and he was still asleep when she went out to work in the morning. He didn't bother her, but behaved in a friendly manner as though he was tolerating her female whims. Money appeared again in the table drawer and one day she noticed fur boots in the closet. Kostya waited patiently. Her days off would have been difficult, but she did not take any. As in all other institutions, the bureau worked seven days a week, with a sliding schedule for days off. There was a lot of work and the management was delighted when any of the staff worked straight through. Any free day not taken was added to one's vacation. She took extra work home in an effort to earn more and be independent of Kostya, and she hardly even went to the movies with Zoe.

Varya spent her free evenings down the hall in Mikhail Yurevich's room, packed as it was with cupboards, shelves, and cases full of books, albums, and files. His narrow bed stood in one alcove formed by bookshelves. In another alcove was his writing table covered with jars, tubes of glue and paint, glasses full of paintbrushes, pens, pencils, scissors, razor blades, and other tools with which he worked. Next to the table was an old armchair with a high back and a sagging seat. Varya sat on it with her legs tucked up under her.

The paints and glue gave the place a cozy smell, and Mikhail Yurevich had the comfortable appearance of an old-fashioned bachelor in a pince-nez. He worked somewhere and left early in the morning, arriving home every day promptly at six, and if he were delayed, he would turn up with a newly acquired book, or an engraving or maybe a reproduction. This was his whole life. He glued in pages and re-bound the books himself, and he kept a complicated catalogue that enabled him to find whatever he was looking for on his innumerable shelves. When Varya took down a book, he would watch with a jealous, suspicious look to see how she held it, how she turned the pages, and whether she put it back in exactly the place she'd got it from.

Mikhail Yurevich bought his books with the pittance he earned, denying himself everything; summer and winter he wore the same suit with worn-out elbows and lapels.

"Of all of man's inventions," he said, gluing a half-decayed page to a thin, transparent sheet of paper, "the book is the greatest, and of all the people on earth, the writer is the most amazing phenomenon. We only know Nicholas I and Count Benckendorff because they had the honor of living at the same time as Alexander Sergeyevich Pushkin. What would we know of the history of mankind if there were no Bible? Or about France if there had been no Balzac, Stendhal, or Maupassant? The word is the only thing that lives forever."

"What about the pyramids and the cathedrals?" Varya protested. "The monuments of architecture and the great painters of the Renaissance?"

"In order to enjoy the works of Michelangelo and Raphael you have to go to Rome or Florence or Dresden, you have to visit the Louvre or the Hermitage. But I don't have to go anywhere for Dante or Goethe, I always have them with me," he said, surveying his shelves.

"This library is your fortress, you take refuge here," Varya said, smiling, and she told him she had bought a book by Pilnyak.

"They say he's a good writer," Mikhail Yurevich said guardedly. "There are quite a few interesting writers at the moment: Zoshchenko, Babel, Tynyanov. But at my age, Varya dear, people prefer to stick to their old friends. With an author I know, I feel as if I'm with a well-tried friend, and when I reread him I return to my youth or my childhood. I can journey through my whole life."

Sometimes, either from under the bed or from behind a shelf, he would drag out baskets covered with sacking. Varya would open them and bring out bundles of journals: *The World of Art, The Scales, Apollo, The Golden Fleece,* all printed on fine paper and illustrated with drawings and illuminations by leading artists.

"None of this will ever come back," he mused sadly. "The flowering of Symbolism, the heyday of Russian art ... Benois, Somov, Dobuzhinsky, Bakst ..."

"I like the Peredvizhniks, the Wandering Artists," Varya said. "They were great artists. Look how long their art has lasted, but who knows about the *World of Art* people anymore?"

Mikhail Yurevich peered at her over the top of his pince-nez.

"They're not recognized now, they are not being shown, but they had undoubted qualities: a high order of graphic art, elegant ornamentation, precision."

She shouldn't have said that nobody knew the *World of Art* people anymore. He was hurt.

"Mikhail Yurevich, I could sit here for hours, but aren't you tired of me?"

"Not at all, Varya, not at all! I'm delighted when you come."

He mentioned Sasha often.

"Sasha has an artistic nature. He is open-hearted, contemplative, very observant, and his comments on the books he has read show that he has subtle taste. But the times stimulated the active sides of his nature and he did not take the path his own character intended for him. But he used my library extensively, he read a lot."

"What books did he like?"

"He knew the Russian classics very well, especially Pushkin. He could recite pages of Pushkin by heart. He knew Tolstoy, Gogol, Chekhov, Saltykov-Shchedrin. He didn't like Dostoevsky."

"I don't either," Varya said. "He tears you apart."

"Maybe you'll come to like him. ... Yes, about Sasha: he loved the French writers, especially Balzac and Stendhal. After all he can read French."

"Really?" Varya was surprised. "We did German in our school."

"Sasha finished school five years before you, I imagine, and in those days they studied both French and German. Later there was only German. I've got quite a good collection of French books and Sasha read them in the original. It was a pity he didn't enter the language faculty, but he thought the country needed engineers. As a matter of fact, the situation he is now in might well change his life: suffering sharpens one's mental observation and develops artistic talent. In any case, he's not likely to be able to return to public work after exile."

"Maybe they'll review his case, maybe they'll exonerate him. After all, he didn't do anything."

Mikhail Yurevich shook his head doubtfully. "Free him? I've never come across such a thing. It'll be good enough if they let him go when he's finished his sentence."

"What do you mean?" she asked in amazement.

"I don't know for sure, but it's a possibility that they won't ever free him. I know of such cases where they add a further term for political exiles. You know Travkina who lives in our block?"

"I've seen her, and I know her daughter," Varya replied.

"It's the younger daughter you know. The elder one's been in exile since, I believe, nineteen twenty-two. First she was on Solovki, then Narym. But she is a Socialist Revolutionary and she won't renounce her views, so maybe that's why. It might well be different for Sasha." He looked at Varya sideways over his pince-nez. "We mustn't say any of this to Sofya Alexandrovna. Let's hope everything will go as it should for Sasha."

"Of course I won't say anything, it would kill her. She lives for only one thing, and that is to see Sasha again. That's all."

"That's right. We'll wait for him, too. Sasha will come back and he'll develop the talent given to him by nature. He's too honest for politics, too trusting. You need different qualities for politics. When he was expelled from the institute, I advised him to go away — to his father or to his uncle. It would have saved him, they would have forgotten about him. But he wouldn't listen to me. He believed in justice. That shows how trusting he was."

Sasha not be freed? Varya was shocked. It had never occurred to her that she might never see him again. She was living in his room, surrounded by his things, next door to his mother. She assumed it was temporary and accidental that he was not there. Would he never come back? It was absurd! It was dishonest, unfair, and illegal!

What would happen to Sofya Alexandrovna? She was counting the days to his return. The biggest events in her life were his letters. She read them to Varya. They were laconic, witty, full of tenderness for his mother and his effort to cheer her up and console her. He never complained, never asked for anything. He wrote often, but his letters arrived irregularly. He numbered them and sometimes the later ones arrived before the earlier ones. Sofya Alexandrovna worried that perhaps there was something important in the letters that hadn't arrived. Varya tried to reassure her by pointing out the difficulties of the mail from Siberia. And she would be proved right when the letters finally did arrive.

Varya helped Sofya Alexandrovna prepare a package of winter clothes that Sasha would have to receive before the roads became impassable in the autumn. He had his overcoat and his hat with earflaps: he'd been wearing them when he was sent into exile. Sofya Alexandrovna mailed him felt boots, two sets of woolen underwear, woolen socks, a scarf, and a sweater. Varya put it all in a plywood box, wrapped it up with sacking that she sewed closed and addressed with an indelible pencil. When she came to pick it up to send off, it reminded her of the times she had gone with Sofya Alexandrovna to search for Sasha. It reminded her of the suffering and torment of the people waiting in the long lines at the prisons.

She recalled the episode in the Arbat Cellar, when Sasha had condemned the prostitute and then stood up for her as a woman. That was Sasha. And at the New Year's party, he'd given that bastard Yuri Sharok what he deserved. He wouldn't allow him to insult Nina, and when everyone else had sat silent, he hadn't. He was only in Siberia because he had refused to behave like a scoundrel. Several people had put out that newspaper, but he was the only one who had taken the blame. And when he had walked so obediently between those escorts? What else could he have done? He was alone and unarmed and there were three of them with rifles. He had seemed pitiful to her then. How stupid of her! The cross that it was Sasha's lot to bear had not humbled him, but had raised him even higher. Now she understood this.

Sasha's textbooks and pencils, his pens and various nuts and bolts, probably from his bicycle, were in the table drawer. His exercise weights were under the table, and his books were on the shelves, though perhaps they also belonged to his father and mother. It was the sort of library that builds up in a family over the decades. But Varya found Sasha's own books: Jules Verne, Fenimore Cooper, his childhood books; the six-volume edition of Pushkin published by Devrien in 1912; Gogol in one volume, Lermontov, Tolstoy's *War and Peace, Till Eulenspiegel,* the *Kalevala,* the *Song of Hiawatha, Blood and Sand* by Blasco Ibañez, *Kira Kiralina* by Panait Istrati, books by Ilf and Petrov, Zoshchenko, Babel, Sholokhov, and the ten-volume *Short Soviet Encyclopedia.*

She remembered how she had pressed against him when they were dancing in the Arbat Cellar, and again at the New Year's party, and it excited her to think of it now. Of course, she liked him. Maybe she had even been in love with him and hadn't realized it because she thought of him as a grown-up. Yes, she had realized it, that was why she had asked him to go skating with her. She had wanted to skate with him and hold him by the arm. . . .

Sasha sent her greetings in all his letters. Always at the end: "Say hello to Varya." Perhaps it was simply politeness or for the sake of her relations with Sofya Alexandrovna. But he sent greetings only to her, not to any of the others — he didn't even write "Greetings to all the family and friends." Varya felt there must be some significance in this, something unspoken but understood between them. She asked Sofya Alexandrovna to send him her best wishes in return.

"Write him a few words yourself," Sofya Alexandrovna suggested one day.

But Varya was not yet ready for that. It would be shameful to write empty phrases, and stupid to write "come home soon," as if it depended on him. She could not bring herself to write meaningfully to him, to let him know that she was thinking of him, missing him.

She said, "What can I write to him about? The bureau? As if that would interest him!"

𝕭

ikhail Mikhailovich Maslov's wife, Olga Stepanovna, came to visit him. From Kalinin to Krasnoyarsk by train, then up the Yenisei by steamer, then by such boats as she could find up the Angara through shallows and rapids. And all for the sake of three days with her husband.

She was a pleasant woman with unhurried movements and a welcoming look. They had not seen each other for seven years. They had two children. Where and when and in what circumstances had they married? He was a former officer, she was an accountant.

Looking at her, Sasha suddenly saw Mikhail Mikhailovich as young and handsome, and Olga Stepanovna next to him, young and full of joy and hopes, both tall and their faces lit up with happiness. And just as clearly, down to the smallest detail, he could see their real life, compressed into seven frightful years.

Olga Stepanovna arrived in the morning with the mailboat and in the evening Mikhail Mikhailovich invited everyone to come for a game of Preference. This amazed Sasha. He would have thought that Mikhail Mikhailovich and Olga Stepanovna would have wanted to spend their three days alone together. Of course, any new person arriving, especially one who was free, was an event, but even so.... They hadn't seen each other for so many years, and they wouldn't see each other for many more, and he wants to play Preference.

Sasha was even more astounded by the irritable way Mikhail Mikhailovich spoke to his wife. It wasn't his usual peevishness, but a deliberate, emphatic rudeness and his cold eyes became increasingly furious.

She did not play, but sat next to her husband, watching his cards and saying nothing, though it was clear she knew the game. And only once did she say, after Mikhail Mikhailovich had played badly, "You shouldn't have played the trump card."

Mikhail Mikhailovich twitched.

"I don't need your prompting, thank you very much! I do know how to play this game."

"I'm not prompting, the game was over," she replied, smiling sweetly, forgiving her husband. She expected the others to excuse his behavior, which had been distorted by life in exile.

Everyone felt uneasy. Peter Kuzmych wheezed, Vsevolod Sergeyevich tried to change the subject, and only Sasha, who was boiling with rage, could not contain himself and got up and said he was throwing in his cards.

Vsevolod Sergeyevich went out with him. Once they were on the road, Sasha said: "Maslov's a swine! For his sake that woman made a grueling journey; she's loyal to him and yet look at the way he treats her!"

"Yes, she's self-sacrificing all right," Vsevolod Sergeyevich agreed. And he added with his ambiguous smile, "But whether or not she's faithful to him we cannot know."

"Some people have a one-track mind. . . ."

"Meaning me?" Vsevolod Sergeyevich grinned.

"Meaning you."

"You don't know me very well," Vsevolod Sergeyevich protested. "I think very highly of Olga Stepanovna's devotion in coming here. But just think of her life there, in Kalinin. Young, beautiful, alone . . ."

"That's a rotten thing to say."

"You're a romantic, Sasha," Vsevolod Sergeyevich said mildly. "And I like you for it, as it happens. There's something of the unselfishness of an earlier generation in your naïveté. Olga Stepanovna undoubtedly is a woman willing to make sacrifices, the highest female type. But don't forget she's the mother of two children, she has to work, and our employers don't take pity on counterrevolutionaries or their wives and children. Now you just think about it, dear boy! Especially as children have to eat, and not once, mark you, but three times a day. You still don't know real life, my boy, you've still got your head in the clouds."

"There are some things one should not say, whatever the circumstances," Sasha said. "You have no grounds for implying that Olga Stepanovna has done anything wrong."

"I'm not saying she has, I'm only suggesting the possibility."

"You've no grounds for that, either. All we know is that she has not abandoned Maslov, she hasn't renounced him or gone off with someone else. She's trekked all this way to see him, and he's behaving like a boor."

"Yes," Vsevolod Sergeyevich agreed, "he is behaving like someone with no manners. I'm trying to understand precisely why."

"What's to understand?" Sasha scowled. "He's a boor and that's it. You talk as if our status as exiles compels a woman to become immoral. But kindly tell me what circumstances compel Maslov to behave like a lout? Don't blame it all on the Soviet regime — that has nothing to do with this. Maslov is taking advantage of his wife's weakness; she's weaker than he is, as is any sensitive person confronted by a boor and a lout."

"You amaze me, Sasha," Vsevolod Sergeyevich said. "You've got some ideas that are quite uncharacteristic of your generation. I wonder if that isn't why you've landed in this place? Were you always like this, or did you get this way being here?"

"I'm no different in any way from my generation," Sasha objected. "It's just that you don't know us. Lenin also didn't deny the eternal truths; he himself grew up on them. What he said about a particular class morality was prompted by the needs of the moment: the Revolution was a war, and a harsh war at that. But in essence our ideas are both human and humane. What for Lenin was temporary and prompted by harsh necessity, Stalin elevated into something permanent, eternal. He raised it into dogma."

"You didn't say anything about Stalin and I didn't hear you," Vsevolod Sergeyevich said with a laugh. "As for Maslov, I'm afraid you're oversimplifying. Life is complicated and it can't be made to fit into some kind of pattern, especially the life of someone like Maslov. For all your nobility, Sasha, you've got one weak spot: you're trying to make a new vessel out of the broken fragments of your faith. But it won't work, because the fragments will fit together only in their original shape. Either you must return to your faith, or you must renounce it forever."

They said good-bye outside Vsevolod Sergeyevich's house.

Sasha saw the light in Zida's window. She was waiting for him. He went down to the river, the route he normally took. But he didn't feel like being with her. Love brings joy, it relieves life's boredom. But if there is no life, no love will relieve it.

All right, he'd sit for a while on the riverbank and maybe go to her later. He often sat here in a boat, gazing at the river and the silver path reflected by the moon on the water.

What Zida was offering him was no way out. She was satisfied with very little, which was her virtue, but why was she living in this outback? What sort of person was she to hide herself away, concealing herself from someone or something and wanting him to hide himself in a remote corner, too, like a cockroach. No, he had no intention of living a cockroach's life. They wouldn't make a cockroach out of him!

He heard footsteps. Could it be Zida?

The moon was barely breaking through the low-lying clouds. Sasha could just make out the figures of people walking along the bank and only when they were already quite close to him did he recognize Maslov and Olga Stepanovna. They did not see him as they stopped by some nets which were strung over supports.

"Olga, I beg you, hear me out. . . ."

Sasha didn't know what to do. He didn't get up at once but stayed there, thinking the Maslovs would walk on. But they had stopped and it would be awkward to reveal himself now, and the fact that he could hear their conversation.

"Try to understand me, I beg you," Mikhail Mikhailovich went on. "Otherwise I cannot do anything. Leave me, erase me from your life, renounce me for the sake of the children, and for your own. Get remarried and change your name and the children's name, free yourself. Why should you be destroyed along with me? I can't sleep at night, thinking of you and the children, worrying that they'll fire you, that they'll exile you, too. You can end these torments for me.

I haven't got much longer and I'd like to die in peace, knowing that you and the children are out of danger."

"Oh, my God, how can you say such things?"

"I can say anything, I no longer have a life. Why did you come? How will you explain it to them back there? I'm going to give you a written agreement to divorce — you can say you came here to get it. You don't need one to get a divorce from a man under sentence, but you can say you didn't know that and you thought you had to have it, so you came."

"I don't torture you. It's you who are torturing me," she said. "Let's go. I'm cold."

The letters from home finally arrived, and, as Vsevolod Sergeyevich had predicted, they came in a bundle. Sasha's mother had written every day and addressed them all to Boguchany. He opened them according to their dates and read them in that order.

His mother wrote practically nothing about herself: "Everything's fine with me, I'm working and that's fine, too." She said nothing about his father, which meant that he had abandoned her altogether, and nothing about Mark, which presumably meant he hadn't been in Moscow. She said nothing about Nina or any of his other friends, which meant they didn't come to see her. She mentioned her sisters, who were all fine. Her letters were composed mostly of questions: "How are you? Have you settled down? What do you eat? What do you need? — don't be afraid to ask, we'll get everything for you, we'll send you everything." Obviously she had only him in her thoughts. She was yearning for his return and she was suffering. But she was holding on, she hadn't broken down, she was living for his sake, and he must therefore live for hers. As long as he was alive, she would be alive. Nor was she alone: in every letter she mentioned Varya. "I came to see you with Varya" meant that they had searched the prisons for him together. "When Varya and I stood in the lines" — Sasha knew what lines she meant.

All his comrades had abandoned him. And only Varya, little Varya, had stuck by his mother. Sasha recalled her delicate, translucent face, her oriental eyes and her hair hanging in a neat fringe over her high forehead. He remembered her bare knees on which she had written crib notes in school. And he remembered that look with which pretty teenaged girls embarrass boys. She was petite, gracious, and elegant. He recalled her standing in the apartment building entrance with the other teenagers, in a dark coat with her collar casually turned up. He recalled her delight in the Arbat Cellar, and dancing with her. . . . *"Wherever I wandered in the flowering spring, I had a wonderful dream that you were with me . . ."* And how she had pressed against him, using her simple means of seduction . . .

Only Varya had stood by his mother in her most difficult days. She was just the sort of stable and fearless person his mother needed. How had she developed such strength? He was filled with tender feelings for this brave girl. And he had lectured her, seeing her through Nina's eyes. How narrow his point of view had been in those days!

An old woman named Travkina lived in their block with her younger daughter. The elder one, who was either an SR or a Menshevik, was on Solovki. Nobody would have anything to do with the Travkins. The old woman would cross the yard, thin and straight, wearing a black coat and black old-fashioned hat. The younger daughter also walked across the yard in silence. There was something pitifully ingratiating in her bright eyes, but the looks she got in return were only those of indifference or malicious pleasure.

Sasha too had regarded her with hostility: they were a family of enemies.

And now his mother was crossing the yard getting just such looks: the mother of an enemy. But she was not alone, she had Varya to share her misfortunes with, Varya to ease her suffering.

The mail arrived every week. Sasha took home letters and sometimes a package wrapped in white canvas, dotted with brown wax blobs. Sometimes there were rolled bundles tightly bound in wrapping paper, striped yellow from dried glue. The bundles had been addressed of course by Varya in her neat, draftsman's hand, and she had carefully written: "Kansk Region, Kezhma District, Mozgovaya Village." The same address appeared on the letters. Sasha had written to say it was "not Mozgovaya, but Mozgova," but she continued to write Mozgovaya, which she evidently thought was more correct.

Prolonging the pleasure, Sasha would look through the letters, leaf through the newspapers, reading the more interesting parts. Then he would set them aside and open the package. There would be cakes, sweets, cocoa, dried or crystallized fruit — all of it costly. He had told his mother not to send him food, but she did anyway.

When he had looked over everything and knew what pleasure lay in store, he would start to enjoy the celebration he'd been waiting for all week. Again, but this time slowly and attentively, he would reread the letters. His mother wrote to him every day, sometimes taking several days over the same letter, and she always included the date and gave the letter a number. Not all of them arrived. In every letter there were greetings from Varya, but that was all: she never wrote to him herself. Why? He, too, only sent her greetings in return, though he did once add a postscript to one of his letters to his mother: "Dearest Varya, thank you for everything." Maybe she would write to him after that.

After the letters, he started in on the newspapers, drawing out the pleasure for two days, and if there were also magazines he could make them last the whole week. The newspapers had already been read — they didn't have that fresh smell of newsprint that they did in Moscow, first thing in the morning at the kiosk on the corner of the Arbat and Plotnikov Street. Sometimes there would be a day's issue missing, but Sasha would not let it upset him, he mustn't blame his mother, she was doing everything she could for him. Whatever irritation he felt came from the intolerance he'd been brought up with. His mother's vagueness now reminded him of his home and his childhood, and they were far more precious to him than a missing newspaper.

They'd got rid of the trams from the Arbat and had asphalted the road. He found it hard to imagine the Arbat without trams. A Metro station had been built in Arbat Square. That was something he'd like to see with his own eyes. It was already the second year of the Five-Year Plan and the cars and tractors were coming off the conveyor belts, blast furnaces were making iron, the open-hearth furnaces were producing steel, the people were models of zealous labor. But alongside this there were countless trials, reinforcing the organs of repression. The punishment for attempting to escape abroad was now execution, with ten years' imprisonment for an escapee's family, who were held responsible even though they had not committed the crime. All this in order to consolidate the power of one man. And that man was the symbol of the new life, the symbol of everything the people believed in and were struggling and suffering for. Did that mean that everything done in his name was just?

A letter arrived from his father: "Forgive me for not writing sooner, but I couldn't get your address" — it was a typical crack at his mother's muddle-headedness; she couldn't even provide their son's proper address. He couldn't believe that she didn't know where Sasha was and viewed it as an attempt to prevent him from contacting his own son — one of the innumerable reproaches Sasha had heard him make for as long as he could remember.

His father wrote that while he understood the misfortune that had befallen Sasha, Sasha was young, he had his whole life in front of him, everything would turn out all right, he mustn't let it get him down. Whatever the relations within the family — and they were not his fault — he was not only a father, he was also a loyal friend, and Sasha must know that.

Sasha put the letter away. He was seized by the distress he always felt when he had anything to do with his father. His father had never been interested in Sasha; he was concerned with only one person's life, and that was his own. And if he "understood" the misfortune that had befallen Sasha, it must be because it had introduced a degree of inconvenience into his own life. His usual order had been disrupted, and *order* was the essence of his life, it was his philosophy.

When Sasha was a child, his father would come into his room, switch on the light, waking the boy up, and turn him onto his right side, as it was harmful to sleep on the left side and Sasha had to be taught to sleep properly. He would sort through Sasha's books on his desk and put them in neat piles: everything had to be in its proper place. And everything had to be made ready in the evening, because one would be hurrying to work in the morning and it was essential that one learned it in childhood. Sasha wanted to go to sleep, in hopes that his father would leave the room, but he did not say anything — it would have been useless anyway, for his father did not hear very well. Pavel Nikolaevich would ask Sasha to repeat what he'd said and then he'd become irritated, convinced that Sasha was talking quietly on purpose.

Order, order, order! He observed order himself and he expected everyone else to do the same. Whether it was at home or at work, he was the indignant, irritable, aggressive pedant. "The struggle against production losses" was the main theme of his work. The token of successful production — he was a food technician — was cleanliness. And cleanliness was also the token of both physical and moral good health, key to orderliness and longevity. A slovenly person could not be an orderly person! Order, cleanliness, hygiene! Fruit should always be washed, like vegetables, in several changes of water, and should then be peeled, even though the peel contained valuable nutrients. He peeled apples slowly in the thinnest of layers, and he ate slowly, too, concentrating and masticating his food thoroughly, eating everything down to the last crumb, and making little Sasha eat all his food. Nothing was to be wasted, nothing to be left on the plate.

His father's clothes and shoes lasted for decades. Every night he put his shoes out on the windowsill to air them, and before that he cleaned them in the hallway. It was a narrow hallway and, with his shoes, his brushes, his tins of polish, and a newspaper spread out on the floor, he used to get in everyone's way. But he already knew this and was always ready with a rebuff if anyone complained. Nobody liked to offend him, and nobody would have anything to do with him. He, on the other hand, would be filled with his loud indignation if someone so much as left the light on in the lavatory or hadn't turned off the tap completely in the bathroom. Everyone would stay quietly in their rooms until finally someone would lose patience and run out into the corridor and demand to know whom he was talking about, and then a slanging match would ensue, with mutual recriminations and accusations.

His militant pedantry, which was absurd and unbearable at home, was the other side of his attitude toward work. He was a good worker, a highly qualified specialist who loved his job, possessed an amazing capacity for work, but he didn't get on with management or his fellow workers, whom he regarded as a bunch of idlers, loafers, and scoundrels. He was interested in nothing but his job, which consisted of making proposals for economizing on resources. And he could talk of nothing else. Sasha was sorry for him and tried to make contact but failed. Conversation with his father was unendurable. When he told Sasha about all his problems at work, he expected the boy to share his hatred for his enemies. Sasha's brain would burst with countless names he didn't know. He would ask, "Who is that?" and his father would get angry and say, "I told you about him last year, but of course you're not interested in your father's affairs!"

He gave Sasha his written proposals to correct for style, although Sasha did not know the terminology of the food industry. Instead of explaining it, his father would grumble: "It's not so hard to remember such elementary things." Sasha tried to avoid reading his father's work, as it only provoked arguments and pushed them even farther apart.

Everyone who lived in the communal apartment had his own way of coming in. Galya slammed the door and rushed down the corridor. Mikhail Mikhailovich came in quietly, delicately, almost without being detected. Sasha's father would rattle the key irritably in the lock. Something was always bound to annoy him: the inner door had not been properly closed and the warmth was going out onto the stairs, or the doormat wasn't where it was supposed to be. Was it in someone's way? Some people!

He would come into the room each evening with a gloomy face, and without a greeting — they'd seen each other in the morning, hadn't they? He would look around the room with a scowl, searching for disorder but not finding any, as Sasha's mother would have put everything away carefully. Silently he would take off his coat and hang it in the closet on a coathanger, then take off one jacket and put on another. Then he would go off to the bathroom to wash his hands and they would hear his discontented grumbles issuing from there. Finally he would sit down at the table and follow his wife's every move with a scowl on his face, inspecting his plate, his fork, and his spoon carefully and wiping them fastidiously with his napkin, and then in silence and concentration he would eat his food. It was the only time when he was not making comments, as nothing could distract him from the intake of food. If he'd emptied his plate before his wife, he would ask sullenly: "Is there a second helping? Ah, there *is*, thanks very much!"

And yet Pavel Nikolaevich was his father. Whether he was a good one or a bad one, he was still his father, he was a part of his life, a part of his childhood and of everything Sasha now remembered with yearning and tenderness. He did not regard his father as harsh; it was his egoism that was harsh. There was only his work, his health, his convenience. He was punished with loneliness for this, but he did not understand it, putting it down to other people's malice, which only made him lonelier. Sasha pitied him especially now, when he himself had learned what loneliness was.

August came to an end and the brief autumn and the yellowing of the taiga began. The days were warm and windless, the nights cold, even icy; the ground dried out and became hard and, in places, to Sasha's surprise, red for some reason. Along the shallow Mozgova River the ground was slightly frozen and crunched underfoot in the dips and hollows of the footpath. Hares ran along the bank in the evening. The bellowing of the elk in rut echoed from the taiga. And in only one week the taiga shed its foliage and became dead and bare. Great wedge-shaped flocks of geese honked above the lakes as they set off on their migration south. The sun appeared briefly and the nights began to lengthen.

Then the Angara became filled with thin autumn ice and no more mail would come until the winter, when there would be a sleigh road. His only link had been cut with the outside world, with his home, his mother and with Varya, whose presence Sasha felt in every letter, though she still had not once written to him. Without letters or newspapers, and without sweet Varya's writing on the newspaper bundles, life became even more tedious. Zida gave him things to read from the Kezhma library, usually old stuff he'd already read, but occasionally something new turned up. For instance, Makarenko's *The Educational Poem,* Bruno Yasensky's *A Man Changes His Skin,* Gladkov's *Energy.* Zida brought him the books by cart, when there was one, but often she carried them herself on foot. Sasha would get angry: why lug them herself? She would laugh and say someone had helped her, and in any case what did two or three books weigh?

He would come for the books during the day, but not because he had given up being cautious. They still kept their relationship secret, but they became open about their friendship. He behaved like a friend, visiting during the day, sometimes with Vsevolod Sergeyevich, and he would sit with her during the evening. But when he stayed overnight, he would leave at dawn, as he had before, going along the riverbank and arriving at his house from the opposite end of the village.

Zida felt his distance, his cooling off, and one day said, "Don't think that I want to marry you. You've probably got someone in Moscow anyway. It's just the tedium and boredom. And I'm glad to have some joy in my life."

He stroked her cheek tenderly and did not protest. It was just as well that she understood. As for his already having someone in Moscow, she was right about that, too. Varya. He couldn't get her out of his mind.

Sasha could not imagine surviving until the winter without mail. And yet the others had managed, whether it was winter or summer; they got used to it, so why shouldn't he? The same fate was shared by everyone. Why could he not share the burden, like the rest? Why couldn't he be patient, as they were?

He didn't want to resign himself, he could not be patient. The notions of resignation and patience had always been alien to him, signs of weakness. According to his earlier ideas, strength was possessed by people who were quite different, people with whom he compared himself, people he numbered himself among. Here everything was the other way around: the people he had looked down on had turned out to be stronger than he precisely because they had the capacity for suffering and patience. He had been strong when he was among the strong, but he had been torn from his usual environment, deprived of the medium in which he had existed, and at once it emerged that he had nothing to fall back on: on his own he was nothing. The people here, on the other hand, relied on themselves alone, on their own resources, however pitiful, yet they were sufficient to bear all their misfortunes without complaint, and to live in hope.

Sasha came to these pitiless conclusions about himself. And yet he could still not overcome the feeling of desperation, a further proof of his pathetically weak will. He thought of nothing but his despair. The village news, the muddle in the school department, inattentive pupils — what did he care? It was all uninteresting, alien, boring. . . .

Early in the morning he would take his landlord's old shotgun and Eskimo dog Zhuchok, and go into the forest after grouse. He would return at midday and then two or three hours before sunset he would go out again. He went not because that was regarded as a good time to hunt, but to tire himself out by walking. He wanted somehow to free himself of his damnable thoughts. The shotgun was old, but the shot was a good size — number six — the most appropriate. And Zhuchok with his wolf coloring was a good dog: he had a pointed muzzle, slanting eyes that glowed red in the dark, sharp upright ears, a powerful well-muscled neck, and a bushy tail curled over onto his back. The dog was alert and would quickly put up the grouse, which would fly up into a tree and stay close to the trunk, becoming almost invisible, especially if it was a spruce overgrown with lichen. Zhuchok would bark at it to draw the bird's attention, while Sasha would fire from twelve paces. The grouse would fall to the ground and the dog would rush to retrieve it, bringing it to Sasha in its mouth. Sasha would bring five or six grouse to Zida from each shoot. She cooked them in sour cream and they were delicious. Sasha ate them with pleasure, especially if he had also managed to get a little liquor from Fedya in return for some of his birds.

One day Fedya said to Sasha: "You're catching a lot of grouse, but you go too far into the forest. You want to watch out the bear doesn't get you."

Sasha shrugged his shoulders. "I haven't come across bear for some reason. They've probably forgotten we're here."

"He'll be there when he remembers," Fedya answered enigmatically. But Sasha thought nothing of it: the locals liked to make jokes at the expense of the exiles, and they didn't think much of them as hunters.

The next day Sasha went into the forest again. The dog was not in the yard or on the street, and it was used to going out with him early in the morning and would normally be jumping up and down waiting for him. Sasha whistled, but there was no bark in reply. Maybe the landlady had taken him to the farm or the landlord gone to Kezhma with him. Sasha decided to go alone. The hunt wouldn't be as successful, but he had a good eye himself and would be able to make out where the frightened grouse had flown.

He went by the usual path to the familiar clearing where grouse abounded. The dried-up yellow leaves rustled under his feet and thin twigs cracked. A grouse took wing and settled on a tree. Sasha thought he heard another bird taking off nearby but he did not look around, afraid to lose sight of the bird in the tree, which he could see plainly. It seemed to be looking back at him with curiosity, and he raised the shotgun and took aim. He fired and at once, close by, a second shot rang out and a bullet flew past him. Sasha ran behind a tree for cover — this wasn't buckshot, this was a bullet, and what he had taken for the sound of another grouse had been the footsteps of a man.

As these thoughts rushed through his mind, he pressed himself against the tree, holding his breath and listening to the forest.... All was quiet. Sasha would have liked to fire in the direction the bullet had come from, but he had only loaded one barrel, and, having fired, was now disarmed. He laid the gun on the ground and began to load the second barrel with one of the six shells in his pocket. But as soon as he began to move, a second shot rang out and a bullet struck the tree. He quickly rammed the shell home, cocked the gun, and waited silently in anticipation. He heard a rustling noise, the crackle of branches, and finally the stamping of feet. The man who'd shot at him was running away. It was quiet again.

Sasha waited a little longer, listening intently, not yet ready to leave his cover. Then, bending low, he went in the direction opposite from that in which the other man had run. He did not use the path but went through the trees, pushing through the over-hanging branches, and came out onto the Angara. He did not go down along the bank, but returned to the village along the edge of the forest.

Who had shot at him? A casual vagrant who wanted his gun? Hardly. The man already had a gun of his own. It was someone from the village. Timofei, that's who it was! Fedya hadn't been joking when he'd warned him: this was the bear he'd been talking about. Timofei had obviously been boasting that he was going to pay Sasha back, and in this place they got their revenge with a bullet or the lead slugs they used to hunt bear. Fedya could have warned him that Timofei was out to get him, but he had chosen not to. He hadn't wanted to get involved; he was afraid that if Sasha heard about Timofei's threat, he'd go to the authorities and make him, Fedya, a witness. Nobody would say anything if Timofei killed Sasha. What was Sasha to them? He was here today and gone tomorrow, whereas this was home to Timofei and his family. Fedya would have said nothing. And nobody would have taken any notice. They'd have written him off as a dead man. Why carry out an investigation here, on the edge of the world?

It was only when he got back to his room and had collapsed on his bed that he realized he'd been standing at the very edge of an abyss. The life that had seemed interminable could be cut off at any second — by a bullet, an overturned boat, another exhausting trek, a casual illness. And nobody would come to his aid. His death would affect nobody, nobody needed him, nobody would defend him, there was nobody to complain to! Alferov? He'd want to know why Sasha particularly suspected Timofei. Ah, I see, you once gave him a beating? You shouldn't quarrel with the local population, they are also human, they have their dignity, and their own morality that you have to take into account. And a few things: Do you have the right to go so far away from your place of settlement? Do you have permission to use firearms? Since a complaint would not result in any investigation, Sasha would become all the more defenseless and his enemies would regard themselves as beyond any punishment.

Making it public would achieve nothing. He had to look after himself. But how? Not go into the forest? Timofei could lie in wait for him on the bank of the Angara or simply kill him there, at home, with a shot through the window. How could he live with the fear of a bullet in his back? On top of everything else, this! How absurd! It was his own fault! Why did he have to get to know Timofei? Why had he gone haymaking with him? He ought to have kept himself at a distance, whereas he had relaxed, he'd behaved as if they were equals, and Timofei had thought that Sasha was seeking his protection and so he decided to taunt him. He hadn't liked losing and resolved to take his revenge. Sasha shouldn't have been arrogant, but he shouldn't play up to people — people vary.

In the evening Sasha went to Fedya's store and, waiting until the customers had left, said, "You were right. There are bears in our forest."

Fedya rolled his eyes. "So, now you see...." He knew without asking what kind of bear Sasha meant.

Sasha left the store and slowed his pace as he passed Timofei's house. Should he go in and see the bastard? No, he must keep a grip on himself, he mustn't do anything hasty.

He told only Vsevolod Sergeyevich about the incident and warned him that Zida knew nothing about it.

Vsevolod Sergeyevich frowned. "It's more serious than you think."

"I know it's serious. I also know that if he'd killed me, he would have got away with it."

"You must be careful," Vsevolod Sergeyevich advised. "You shouldn't go into the forest alone. If you like, I'll come with you."

"Well, we'll see," Sasha said evasively.

At home he asked where Zhuchok had been that morning. It turned out they didn't know — no one had gone anywhere with the dog. "I thought he was with you," the landlady said.

It was obviously Timofei at work; the bastard had somehow managed to tie up Zhuchok somewhere.

Zhuchok meanwhile was lying on the threshold and moving his eyes from the landlady to Sasha, seemingly aware that they were talking about him. Sasha stroked his muzzle. "We'll go out and get a bear tomorrow, boy. You be ready."

Sasha found a bar of lead in the landlord's storeroom from which he cut some slugs. He loaded one barrel with birdshot and the other with lead. Now let Timofei try something.

But Sasha did not have the chance to go back into the forest.
Early in the morning, while he was still in bed, a peasant from
the village soviet arrived with a note:

On receipt of this notice, Administrative Exile Pankratov, A.S.
is required to appear before the Kezhma District NKVD
officer-in-charge, Alferov, V.G., in the village of Kezhma.

It was signed with Alferov's now familiar signature.

14

Lyova told Varya it was time for her to join the union. It was a pure formality, but it was necessary. Varya put in her application.

It turned out to be no pure formality. Membership was decided at a general meeting, where they asked the same kind of questions she had answered in her job application. Varya was again angered by the question "Are you married?" She wanted to reply, "Yes, I am married," but because she had put something different on the application form, they would only start asking questions and humiliate her even more. She said, "No, I am not married." She saw the look of amazement on Zoe's and some of the other girls' faces, but nobody cross-examined her. They asked her questions about politics: Who was the chairman of this state committee, who was the chairman of that board? What was the difference between building the socialist society and building the foundations of the socialist society? What precisely have we already built? Varya was amazed that people she knew well, whom she saw every day and with whom she had the friendliest relations, suddenly became suspicious, ready to find her out in a lie, just as if they were carrying out some important state affair, though God only knew what. Even Rina and Lyova — even Igor Vladimirovich — had a look of concentration. It was so stupid. They were going to enroll her in the union anyway — she'd already been approved from her job application; everything was in order. It was simply a ritual being acted out, with the appearance of a debate and the appearance of a task they had all become accustomed to.

The questions ended. Igor Vladimirovich got up and said that

Ivanova worked in his studio, that she carried out her work conscientiously and was entirely suitable to become a member of the union. Varya was surprised to hear him using such official language.

The vote was unanimously in favor, and with that the business came to an end.

As soon as they got up, everyone's face changed, the formal expressions giving way to normal friendliness: they had done their civic duty, they congratulated Varya and hurried home.

Igor Vladimirovich suggested they go down to the second-floor restaurant to celebrate Varya's acceptance into the union. Rina said she wasn't dressed for the Grand Hotel and proposed the Kanatik instead — it was less fancy and the service was faster. Lyova supported her — Igor Vladimirovich would be paying and it would be embarrassing to run up a big bill.

Varya didn't want to go anywhere. She could understand Rina's and Lyova's behavior at the meeting — they were only minor employees who were afraid of losing their jobs. But Igor Vladimirovich? Couldn't he have been different from the others? What could he have to be afraid of, a famous architect like him? Yet he had used exactly the same words, even though he knew how banal they were and how ridiculous the whole procedure had been. It suddenly occurred to her that Sasha Pankratov, even if he thought such an assembly was important, would have remained himself. Probably he would have got up and said it was pointless to ask all those questions, since they'd already been answered in the questionnaire, so why waste time? That's what he would have said, because he had character. But Igor Vladimirovich didn't! And so she didn't want to go anywhere, but as the celebration was in her honor, it was difficult to refuse.

The Kanatik was on the corner of Theater Square and Rozhdestvensky Street opposite the monument to the printing pioneer Ivan Fedorov. It was in a cellar. Varya had never been there before: it had no billiards hall, so Kostya never went there. She remembered that Vika had once asked her to go, as it happened, with Igor Vladimirovich, but she had refused because she had preferred Lyova's company. But here she was with Igor Vladimirovich after all.

There was nobody she knew in the restaurant. Rina said everyone came there on Fridays for the roast capon. By "everyone" she meant the restaurant habitués.

"Still, there are quite a few people here," Igor Vladimirovich observed, looking around the low-vaulted room.

"It's in the center of town, so a lot of people come in after work," Lyova explained.

"When the working day finishes for office workers, it's just beginning for the tarts," Rina added, not at all inhibited by Igor Vladimirovich's presence. He wasn't the boss here, just one of the party.

People were coming and going all the time. Three girls came in and sat down not far from their table. Varya noticed them only because she could not miss the sudden look of alarm exchanged between Rina and Lyova.

These were "restaurant girls" whose working day, as Rina had just observed, began only now. For them it was the best time of the day, when they could sit for a while without any men, before "business" began. They could have a bite on their own money, talk about their own concerns, leave the waiter a tip, and feel like ordinary women.

One of the girls was sitting with her back to them. Her neighbor bent over and said something to her and she turned toward Varya's table, nodding casually to Rina and Lyova. They nodded back with radiant smiles. But she wasn't looking at them, she was looking at Varya. She smirked, turned back to her friends, and said something, and they all laughed. She was a skinny blonde with close-set eyes, around twenty-five, with a pale, badly made-up face. She was decently dressed, not fashionably or provocatively.

Varya again caught an anxious glance passing between Lyova and Rina and she felt awkward herself: the girl was looking at her too doggedly, too mockingly, too derisively.

"Who's the madame?" she asked.

"I don't know, we've met somewhere, I can't remember where," Rina answered with a casualness that was plainly artificial. And the girl obviously knew Lyova, too, they'd met somewhere, and not just casually.

Igor Vladimirovich also felt the awkwardness of the moment and looked at his watch, making it plain that he hadn't time to stay much longer. He raised his glass.

"Congratulations, Varya, you're now a fully paid-up worker. I wish you luck."

Everyone was drinking.

The girls at the other table burst out laughing at something the blonde had said.

Igor Vladimirovich looked at his watch again.

"Are you in a hurry?" Rina was also keen to leave.

"I'm afraid it's time ..."

"Yes, of course," Lyova chimed in.

The blonde turned around.

"Lyovushka!" she exclaimed.

Lyova went over to her table and bent down to say something to her. He smiled sweetly and stroked the blonde's shoulder tenderly. Then he returned to his friends. And again loud laughter exploded from the next table at one of the blonde's remarks.

Back at their own table, Lyova talked in the same sweet way about Skomorovsky's dance band, which had just begun a tour in Moscow. Rina was listening to him chattering away, but Varya could see that she was worried.

The blonde got up and came over to their table with a cigarette in her hand. First she glanced at Varya and then at Igor Vladimirovich.

"Anyone got a light?"

Her movements expressed deliberately restrained familiarity and a hidden but perceptible challenge. Igor Vladimirovich handed her a box of matches. She struck one and lit her cigarette. Suddenly she turned to Varya: "How are things with you and Kostya?"

"Klavdya, Klavdya ..." Lyova touched the girl's elbow.

"What's the matter? I'm interested. She's his new wife and I'm his old one. I was number two hundred, she's number two hundred and one. So, how are things? Has he given you your reward yet?"

Varya did not understand the question at first and thought perhaps the girl was hinting at pregnancy.

"Klavdya, stop right now!" Rina snapped sternly.

"All right, you!" the blonde retorted crudely. "Shut your mouth! She thinks she's his wife and he's her husband," the blonde raged on. "He's got a cartload and a half of wives like that. And every one of them's got the clap. Right, Rina? You got it, too, didn't you? And now you're finding teenagers for him. A bunch of whores, the lot of you!"

The meaning of what the blonde had said sank in, and Varya, speaking very calmly and precisely, said: "Madame prostitute, why don't you just fuck off."

They were all stunned and froze as they waited for the storm to break.

Igor Vladimirovich shouted in a shrill and unexpectedly high voice, "Leave this table at once! Go away! Unless you want to spend the night at the militia? I can easily arrange it for you!"

"Oh, oh, I'm terrified!" The blonde laughed hysterically.

Her friends leaped up from their seats and tried to drag her back to their table, but she tore herself away and shouted: "I spoke to her like a civilized woman, but she had to call me names, the slut! She hasn't even left school yet, and she's already turning tricks!"

Igor Vladimirovich summoned the waiter and paid the bill.

They finally got out of the restaurant.

"I go this way," Lyova said, as he lived on Sretenka Street. "Just forget it, she's crazy. See you!"

Varya, Rina, and Igor Vladimirovich went down to Theater Square.

"What a repulsive person! Such slander! What other lies would she have dreamed up!" Rina was indignant.

"One shouldn't go to such places," Igor Vladimirovich remarked.

"You can run into psychopaths like that anywhere," Rina replied.

"You mustn't be upset," he said to Varya. "Don't pay any attention, it was nothing."

"I'm not upset," Varya replied, frowning.

When she got home, it was ten. She had worked late and it was time to go to bed. If she had been able to take time off, she would not have gone to work the next day, after what had happened in the Kanatik. Rina and Lyova weren't the problem, they were Kostya's friends, though apparently Rina had been something more than just a friend — she was on his "list." Such were the morals of Kostya's world. Igor Vladimirovich could not have expected to hear about her married life like that. On the other hand, she had been surprised by his behavior at the union meeting and by his shrill voice in the restaurant. If they were attacked by hooligans on the street, he would undoubtedly shout for help in the same shrill voice. A sheep and a coward to boot! Sasha would have defended her differently. Now she felt that she and Igor Vladimirovich were even, they were quits. She had felt ashamed of herself when the whore spoke to her as if she were one of them. The blonde had been Kostya's whore in the past and now she'd taken her place. Varya had never before felt so humiliated. How would she be able to go to work the next day, how would she be able to look people in the eye?

What could she do? God, where could she go to hide from all this? She could turn her back on it and go home to Nina, but she could not let poor Sofya Alexandrovna down, she didn't have the right to do that. Kostya had ruined her life utterly. But to bring a crook into the house and then run away — she'd never forgive herself. Should she start a fight with him? She would achieve nothing by it except a din in the apartment and even more trouble for Sofya Alexandrovna.

There was a knock at the door.

"Come in."

It was Sofya Alexandrovna.

"Good evening, Varya."

"Good evening, Sofya Alexandrovna. Please sit down. How are you?"

Sofya Alexandrovna sat down and looked at Varya intently. "Something's upsetting you," she said.

"I'm just tired. I had to go to a meeting. I've been accepted into the union."

"It's only a formality, but you have to go through it," Sofya Alexandrovna remarked.

Again she looked at Varya.

"Varya dear, why I'm here . . . Konstantin Fedorovich brought some man here today, and he didn't even lock the door behind him, and they were in here taking the guns to pieces and clicking the bolts. . . . Varya, we did have an agreement. How could this happen?"

Varya opened the closet and saw the two hunting rifles leaning against the wall, behind the clothes.

She sank onto the bed and let her hands fall helplessly. "I have behaved very badly toward you, Sofya Alexandrovna. I had no right to bring him into your home."

"But you are his wife after all."

"Wife? What sort of wife am I to him, and what sort of husband is he to me? I cannot imagine how I let this happen. I have no life with him, I hardly see him, and we haven't been man and wife for a long time."

Sofya Alexandrovna remained silent.

"But I can't do anything, I'm in a trap," Varya said in desperation.

"In a trap?" Sofya Alexandrovna sounded surprised. "I don't understand. What sort of trap? You're relationship isn't registered, you're a free person, you earn your own living."

"Yes, that's true, but I can't just walk away from here."

"Why not?"

"Because then he won't leave. He said as much: 'You can leave, but I like it here.' Oh, yes, he promised to look for another place for himself, but he's lying, he won't look for anything. And I can't leave him here, you and he don't get on. He even brings the guns back while I'm still here. Can you imagine what he'd do if I weren't here at all? He wouldn't even let you into the room."

Sofya Alexandrovna smiled and stroked Varya's head. Varya suddenly realized that her smile was exactly like Sasha's. And they both had the same eyes.

"Varya, Varya, my dear," Sofya Alexandrovna said tenderly. "You're worrying about me. You've got such a good heart. But you mustn't concern yourself. If you really want to leave him —"

"I left him ages ago!"

"Dear girl, one always has tiffs. Young people take everything too much to heart and they part and then they come together again. . . ."

"Tiffs . . ." Varya's voice was trembling. "He gambles with my things. You remember the wrap? I didn't tell you the truth about that. He lost it playing billiards. He'll gamble *me* away when he has to. All his deals are shady. The lamps and the electrical equipment — he's a speculator. His property has all been listed and I was afraid they'd come here, but thank God they didn't. His women insult me. I can't bear to look at him, and you call that having a *tiff*. . . ." She burst into tears.

Sofya Alexandrovna stroked her head again. "There, there, my dear, calm down, there's no need to despair, it's not a catastrophe, believe me. But why didn't you tell me about all this before?"

"I was ashamed," said Varya, swallowing her tears.

"What nonsense, you silly girl. I'm an old woman with experience, after all. The two of us could easily have found a way out a long time ago. Tell me, do you want to go back home or do you want to stay here with me?"

"Naturally, I'd like to stay here with you. But it's quite impossible, Sofya Alexandrovna. If I stay, he won't leave, and if he leaves and I'm here, he'll keep phoning and causing trouble. He'll ruin your life. It's important for me to get him out of your life."

"Don't worry." Sofya Alexandrovna was quite composed. "I'll get rid of him myself. If you've made up your mind . . ."

"Sofya Alexandrovna!"

"All right, all right . . . So, collect your things together right now and go back to Nina. I'll do the rest."

Varya was amazed at how firm and composed Sofya Alexandrovna was. Just like Sasha. Good God, she really didn't know her at all. Until then she had seen her as a mother broken with grief, and that image had overshadowed Sofya Alexandrovna's true character.

"I'm not taking anything that he bought me," Varya said.

"That's up to you, but get your things quickly — he could come in at any minute."

Kostya never came home this early. But Varya knew that Lyova or Rina would probably tell him about the incident in the Kanatik, so he might come home at any time. As she was packing her suitcase, she said: "I can't take everything at once, and I must take my drawing board and T-square. Could I leave a few things in your room and collect them later?"

"Need you ask!"

Varya put on her coat. She had her suitcase in one hand and the drawing board and T-square in the other.

"Go by the back stairs in case you meet him coming in."

"I don't care. I'm only worried about you."

"I've already told you not to worry about me," Sofya Alexandrovna said assertively. "But go by the back door anyway. You don't want to have a fight on the stairs."

"All right."

Varya kissed her. "Thank you for everything and please forgive me."

"My dear child, what is there to forgive? I should be thanking you for not having abandoned me. When everything's settled down, come back here. It'll make me happy."

Varya opened the door of the apartment. The room was not locked and Nina was sitting at the table correcting exercise-books.

Nina saw Varya's suitcase, her drawing board, and T-square.

"No more domestic bliss?"

Varya put the suitcase down and laid the drawing board on her bed.

"It's finished."

15

Varya was nervous, fearing that Kostya would arrive home early and start telephoning her. But he didn't call, which meant that, as usual, he had come in late.

Then, the next day at work, two hours before the end of the day, Igor Vladimirovich called Lyova into his office to take a phone call. It was unusual for him to get a call on that phone.

Lyova came out a few minutes later and told Varya she was wanted on the telephone.

"Is it Kostya?"

"Yes."

"How does he know the number?" she asked.

Lyova shrugged his shoulders in reply.

"We're not supposed to make personal calls on Igor Vladimirovich's private phone. There's the office phone, and Kostya knows the number."

Lyova shrugged again. "He says it's urgent and you must come immediately. I asked Igor Vladimirovich if it was all right and he said it was."

"Go back and tell him to call me on the other number."

"Go yourself, I'm not a messenger."

"Not a messenger? And I suppose it wasn't you who told him about what happened in the Kanatik!"

It was a wild guess, but Varya had hit the mark.

Lyova went back into the office, then returned and said sullenly: "He'll be waiting for you at five o'clock today by the gate of the Culture and Recreation Park."

"Does he want to go on the swings?" she asked sarcastically.

"I'm only telling you what he said."

"Have you quarreled?" Rina asked, without lifting her eyes from her drawing board.

"What business is it of yours?" Varya snapped.

"I only asked. . . ."

"Well, don't!"

The first thing Varya did on getting home was to telephone Sofya Alexandrovna. She was worried about her.

"How is everything, Sofya Alexandrovna?"

"Everything's fine."

"Has he left?"

"Yes."

"And has he taken his things?"

"Yes."

"How did you manage it?"

"I managed. . . . Come over and I'll tell you."

She did not want to talk on the telephone, quite rightly. Varya couldn't wait to hear how Sofya Alexandrovna had managed to get Kostya out, but first she had to talk to Nina. They had to come to terms on how they were going to live together.

Varya unpacked her suitcase and hung her clothes in the closet where they used to be. She looked through the drawers in her desk and found everything as it had been, untouched and in exactly the same place, as if Nina had known she'd be back. She was her sister and it was after all the family home. She attached her drawing board to the table and began to work.

She was still working when Nina came home. Varya smiled at her and asked if she would like something to eat, indicating the sandwiches she'd brought from the office. Nina was also conciliatory. She looked at Varya's work and asked her what she was drawing and listened with interest to what she said. As for their household budget, Nina said that since they both ate at work there was no problem. Varya protested: there was the rent, the telephone, the gas and electricity, breakfast and supper. She would pay half of all these expenses. They agreed that they would keep track of all their expenses and then divide the total equally at the end of the month.

Then they sat and drank tea with Varya's sandwiches, and talked. Varya told Nina about the building of the hotel and about the people she worked with, and Nina was pleased to see how immersed she was in her work. But Varya said not a word about Kostya. And Nina did not ask. Varya would tell her in her own good time.

It was around ten o'clock when the telephone in the corridor rang. Nina went to answer it.

"It's for you, Varya."

Nina looked at her anxiously, and Varya sensed it was Kostya. And it was.

"Did Lyova give you my message?"

"Yes."

"Why didn't you come?"

"I don't play on swings anymore; I've grown up."

"We have to talk."

"I'm listening," she said.

"This is not for the phone. We have to meet."

"We've got nothing to talk about and no need to meet."

"It's very important. For me, for you — and for Sofya Alexandrovna."

He was lying, of course. Trying to blackmail her. She was gripped with fear, just the same.

"All right. Come to the Grand Hotel at four tomorrow. We'll talk then."

"No, we have to talk right now, this minute. You can't imagine how important it is. Tomorrow will be too late. Come outside on the Arbat in a few minutes."

"All right," she said. "I'll come now."

She went back into the room and threw on her raincoat.

"I'll be right back."

"Was it him?" Nina asked.

"Yes."

"Do you want me to come with you?"

"Why?"

"Anything could happen. . . ."

Varya laughed. "Don't worry about a thing."

*   *   *

Kostya was pacing up and down outside. He was wearing a coat with the collar turned up and a cap pulled down over his eyes, looking like a cross between a detective and a Hollywood gangster. She had never seen him in this role before. It was an idiotic costume.

They walked along the Arbat.

"Who was it who answered the phone?" he asked.

"My sister."

"Does she know you've come out to see me?"

"Of course."

They turned into Plotnikov Street, then Krivoarbat, and then they walked as far as the vacant lot opposite the school, where they sat down on a bench. It was dark by then. The dim streetlights were on and there were lights shining in the windows of the houses. Only a few people were about.

"You shouldn't go out without your husband," Kostya began. "That's how you can have a nasty experience. If I'd been there nobody would have bothered you. But you went without me and that's what happened."

"Before you came along," she replied, "before I had a husband, so to speak, nobody ever pestered me and nobody ever insulted me. But this *person* insulted me precisely because I was your wife and she regarded me as just another whore."

"She's a psychopath, she's ill," Kostya protested.

"What's she got?"

"I've told you, she's psychologically ill. Psychopaths are capable of saying anything."

"I haven't got time, Kostya," she interrupted him. "My sister's waiting. I'm not interested either in your psychopath or in what happened at the Kanatik. It's over between us."

He said nothing, then he suddenly smiled and tried to take her hand.

"Wait, Varya, don't get worked up. I can understand that you're angry, but after all it wasn't so bad when we were together. You did exactly what you wanted. You wanted to work, so you got a job. If you want to get a degree, I'll help you. I feel you're like a stone wall behind me, holding me up."

She took her hand away. "Don't fool yourself, Kostya. It's all over."

He said spitefully: "No, it's not! You promised to wait until I'd found another place to live. But I'm out on the street now, I've nowhere to spend the night."

"That's not true. You yourself said you couldn't care less where I lived, whether with my sister or at Sofya Alexandrovna's. I left the things you bought me. You can pick them up and gamble with them, or give them to your whores. That'll make us even."

"No," he snarled, "we're not even at all, far from it. What did you tell Sofya Alexandrovna about me?"

"Me? Nothing."

"You're lying!"

"I'm not lying. I only told her about the fur wrap because I had to, otherwise she would have called the militia and that wouldn't have been very nice for you, I imagine. Anyway, there was no need to tell her anything, she could see it all for herself. You promised you wouldn't bring guns into the house, but yesterday you did. I was fed up with it all, so I left. What you do is your own affair."

"I know what to do, don't you worry," he muttered sullenly. "I'll settle the score with that old bag, she'll get what's coming to her, she'll be spitting blood. . . ."

"Who are you talking about?" Varya was puzzled.

"I'm talking about that old vulture, your Sofya Alexandrovna, that's who. I'll remind her of a thing or two. 'There's no law now, nothing but anarchy.' She'll pay for that. And the things she's said about Comrade Stalin . . . Because they sent her son into exile, she reviles our government. . . ."

This was the last thing Varya had expected. "Kostya, what are you talking about? Come to your senses!"

"I can give as good as I get. You think you can throw me out just by giving me back the clothes I bought you? Well, you can't!"

"What a pig you are!" she cried, choking with anger. "You're nothing but an informer, that's what you are. But just you try. You can't do anything to Sofya Alexandrovna, just remember that. If you say one word about her, I'll swear that it was you who said all that — you, not her, do you understand? I'm the only witness and they'll believe me, not you. I'll say you're slandering her for revenge, because she wouldn't let you keep guns in her home and that you were keeping them on a classified street. If you raise one finger to hurt Sofya Alexandrovna, I'll smash you to smithereens. And nobody will help you. All the Rinas and Lyovas will be only too glad to sell you down the river."

She couldn't speak. Her anger and spite and indignation stuck in her throat.

"Speak, come on, speak," his voice was a whisper. "It's the last chance you've got — before I shoot you!"

She felt calm as soon as he said this. His hand was in his pocket, where he kept a Smith and Wesson revolver. He had shown it to her once, saying it belonged to some famous friend and that he was going to repair it. He had been lying, as usual. But she was not afraid of him; she knew he was too much of a coward to shoot. Nor would he report Sofya Alexandrovna; he was too scared to do that, too. She, on the other hand, felt reckless and totally unafraid. Let him do his worst!

"Oh, yes?" she said with a smirk. "You're going to shoot me, are you? I suppose that's why you asked me if my sister knew who I was going to meet. She knows I came to meet you, she knows, so shoot me and it'll be the firing squad for you, they'll make sure of that. Coward!" Her voice rose to a scream. "Shoot, you coward, shoot!"

Curtains were drawn back and people peered out into the darkness.

Varya went on screaming: "Go on, then, why don't you shoot, you coward, you piece of shit!"

A man's voice rang out loudly: "Hey, what's going on down there?"

Passersby in the nearby side street stopped.

"Stop your yelling, you psychopath," he snapped. "You won't get away from me, you'll see."

He turned and walked quickly away down a side street.

"I was just going to come and find you," Nina said when Varya got back home. "What happened, or is it a secret?"

Varya laughed. "Nothing much, he only threatened to shoot me."

"I don't believe it!" Nina expostulated. "Has he forgotten where he lives?"

"He's just a fool, a nobody."

* * *

Immediately after work the next day, Varya went to see Sofya Alexandrovna.

She found her sitting at the table writing a letter, apparently to Sasha.

"Well, tell me what happened, Sofya Alexandrovna."

Sofya Alexandrovna put down her pen and took off her spectacles. "I asked him to leave. He resisted at first, but then he went."

"No, tell me the details, please."

"I told him I had forbidden him to bring guns into the house and that he had done it just the same. I said I had given you a good dressing-down. You'd gone back to your sister's and I wanted him to leave, too, especially as the neighbors were complaining that because of him the apartment door was never chained. He started swearing and making threats and uttering all sorts of rubbish about my making money out of the room —"

"The pig!"

"I told him I would be chaining the door that day and that nobody would open it for him, and if he tried breaking in we'd call the militia and tell them that he was selling guns, that he was engaged in very peculiar business. I told him that all the neighbors were against him and that both the house manager and the militia have asked about him. He started to threaten me again, so I said: 'My son was arrested and he's in exile, so I know how to reach the prosecutor, and the detectives and the lawyers, so you can't scare me. You'd better think about your own skin. If you are not out by tomorrow morning, you'll only have yourself to blame, because I won't stop at anything.' And with that I went back to my room. He'd taken his things and gone by morning."

"His things? What about the things he gave me?"

"He left them."

"That gives him an excuse to come back. . . ."

"Perhaps he's hoping to make it up with you?"

"He'll have a long wait."

"One thing I didn't expect," Sofya Alexandrovna said, "was that he left his keys. I was sure we'd have to have new locks put in."

"He was thinking ahead." Varya laughed. "If there was a

break-in at the apartment, he'd be the first person they would suspect. That's why he gave the keys back to you."

"Possibly," Sofya Alexandrovna agreed.

"As for the things he left, don't worry, I'll take them to my own place, and if he comes around or telephones about them, you can tell him I've taken them and he should ask me about them."

"Yes, that's right, they're your things, you must take them."

"Yes, maybe," Varya said vaguely, having made up her mind definitely to give Kostya his things back via Lyova next day.

She embraced Sofya Alexandrovna tenderly.

"I feel so guilty, you've been through so much on my account."

"Nonsense, my dear, just put that out of your head. And you mustn't be afraid of him. People like that are only strong when they're up against weak people and only brave if you're timid."

"I know," Varya said, smiling ruefully. "Last night he called me out onto the street and threatened to kill me."

"Really?"

"Yes. I just laughed at him and left."

"Good girl, that's the way!"

Varya felt good about it herself. She sensed her own strength and independence. Yes, her independence at last! She was no longer subject to someone else's will. Now she could leave all this filth behind her. Maybe she had got herself into this mess and had made a terrible mistake, but you only learn by your mistakes. All over the world people were struggling for a crust of bread and a place in the sun. Everywhere they were adapting to circumstances. It was important to remain a human being and not let anyone trample on your dignity. She had achieved this and could be proud of herself.

"Are you writing to Sasha?"

"Yes, my dear. I must mail it tomorrow. I'm afraid it won't get to him before the roads close. In October and November, there's no transport of any kind, not until the Angara freezes. I want to make sure he gets a letter with the last delivery."

Varya pictured Sasha standing alone on the bank of the far distant river in Siberia and she also wanted to write to him, at least a couple of words to bring him some comfort. After what she had just been through, and having stood up to things as she had, she now felt better, and somehow it was easier to write to Sasha — the best man in the world.

"Could I write something to him too?"

"But of course, my dear Varya," Sofya Alexandrovna replied with delight. "It'll make him so happy. After all, nobody writes to him, except me."

Varya took a sheet of writing paper, thought for a moment, dipped her pen into the inkwell, and then wrote:

Greetings, Sasha!

I'm at your mother's now and we're both writing to you. Everything's fine here. Your mother is well, and I'm working on the Moscow Project . . .

She reflected and then added: *"How I'd love to know what you're doing right now. . . ."*

⚜ 16 ⚜

Sochi was becoming a burden to Kirov. His work on the textbook was no more than a formality: he read what had been written and he approved what had already been approved by Stalin. He realized that Stalin wanted to reshape history not only in order to extol himself but also to justify the harshness of his past, present, and future actions. And Kirov could not object. It would be pointless to try to argue on the theoretical level, first because he was not a historian, but also because Stalin had at his disposal a host of historians and ideologues who could prove anything they were told to. Kirov did not want to get into that kind of debate, nor did he feel he should write an article on Stalin's role in the Caucasus.

For five years Kirov had headed the Party organization in Azerbaijan and he had a thorough knowledge of its history. He knew that Stalin's role in Baku had been that of a rank-and-file professional revolutionary. The idea that he had done something special had only recently been invented, like a lot of other things, for that matter. Kirov himself had contributed to this process, but it had concerned general questions of history. For instance, confirming that Stalin was Lenin's heir. This was necessary for Party purposes, and Kirov had accepted it, believing that some departure from the truth was permissible. But everything had now been accomplished. Stalin was the leader, the battle had been won. Why did he now need to be credited as the head of an underground press called "Nina"? Did he want Kirov to settle his score with Enukidze for him? Kirov would have nothing to do with it.

He knew every street in Baku, every house and factory and oil well. In those days, he had not associated any of it with Stalin. Now the whole of Baku was being turned into one big memorial to the living Stalin. Streets, districts, oil installations, institutes, and schools all bore his name. A museum had even been opened in Bailov prison, though nobody knew which cell Stalin had occupied. They were afraid to ask him in case he thought the question revealed the triviality of the fact itself. He might suspect the Baku comrades were not convinced that such a monument was really necessary. So they had decided everything for themselves. They selected a cell in which it was easy to make a new door from the outside, so that tourists could look into it without entering the jail itself. The museum had been established and the tourists were being shown it, though Stalin knew it was a pure fiction. As a matter of fact, Kirov had noted that Stalin on numerous occasions erased the borderline between reality and myth where the past was concerned. Kirov had even talked to Ordzhonikidze about it.

For Kirov, however, the line remained and he had no intention of creating new myths. Stalin's demand that he stay in Sochi was an annoying waste of time. Food rationing was about to be abolished and his place was in Leningrad. In four months the citizens of the U.S.S.R. would be able to buy as much bread as they liked. This was proof that the collective farm system worked, even though it had been created at the cost of countless losses and sacrifices and suffering. The new measure must not be allowed to go wrong. It must be carefully prepared for, especially in those districts with no grain of their own, such as Leningrad. And instead, here he was wasting time in Sochi.

Kirov read the comments on the textbook synopsis on the beach. He didn't so much read as glance through them, and then put them down with a stone on top to prevent their being blown away.

Fenced off by a double thickness of wire fence, the beach was deserted. Behind the wire to the right and left, the beach was a prohibited zone. There was a sentry in a box at the entrance with a telephone, and another one who marched up and down on the paved path beyond the fence. The beach itself was only used by guests, as Stalin never went into the water or strolled on the beach. The domestic and other staff and the security guards at the dacha bathed somewhere else.

The only person Kirov met there was the dentist from Moscow. The man was respectful and affable, and was not at all ingratiating. He had a soft voice and swam superbly without showing off. It was plain to see that he was enjoying everything about the place — the sea, the sun, and the sandy beach — and Kirov liked to see people enjoying themselves. Of course, people had enjoyed themselves a thousand years ago, and they would go on doing so as long as there was life on the planet. Yet somehow he could never separate the pleasure he observed in Soviet people from the state he represented, with its structure that he had affirmed and would continue to affirm, and with the new society he was building. The smile he saw and the laughter he heard was his and the Party's reward, justifying the hard and at times harsh decisions they had to make. As a Marxist, Kirov thought on the grand scale, but he was always aware of the individual behind the thousands and millions. For him, an audience was never featureless. When he got up on a stage, he always tried to achieve a rapport with each person in the hall. Perhaps that was the secret of his success as a speaker.

He was never patronizing in person, either, but would willingly enter into conversation with anyone. He even found the dentist interesting. They talked about everyday things, like the temperature of the water, the sulfur springs that welled up from the seabed, the effect of Matsesta waters on the human organism. Kirov was glad that Lipman didn't talk like an expert, but rather as if he were having an ordinary conversation. Even when he was talking about teeth, his special subject, it was on the simplest level, such as whether it was best to clean one's teeth with a big or a small toothbrush. But Lipman did not once say whom he was treating here. The name of Stalin did not pass his lips.

"Matsesta performs miracles," Lipman said. "One of our neighbors in the apartment was a complete invalid, he couldn't walk at all, but he had a spell at Matsesta and now he's running around like an eighteen-year-old."

"Have you got a good apartment?"

"Well . . . we have a fine room in a shared apartment, about fifteen feet square, on Second Meshchansky Street, not far from the center of town, with our own telephone in the room. The neighbors don't like that very much and want the phone moved into the corridor. I wouldn't mind — I can't see why other people shouldn't use it — but the Kremlin Medical Service won't allow it. They put it in, so they could call me to see patients at any time."

Kirov knew that Kremlin doctors weren't telephoned about their important patients: they were simply picked up and taken. And they were never told the name of the patient they were being taken to. Ordzhonikidze had joked about it: "Imagine, they bring my doctor to me, and they don't even tell him my name. But the doctor knows it anyway: if Ivanov comes to get him, then he's coming to see me. If it's Petrov, then Kuibyshev is the patient. Those are the sort of games we're playing now."

The wind was beginning to blow and whitecaps appeared on the sea. "There are a lot of jellyfish near the shore, which means there's going to be a gale," Kirov said. This was the sort of casual remark they made to each other as they lay on the sand, or took a swim or toweled themselves. The dentist tactfully said very little, as he had noticed Kirov's papers and did not want to distract him from them.

Kirov read the various commentaries without making any effort to understand them. The direction this revision of history was taking was obvious, so the details were of no importance. He thought about Stalin. In recent years he had taken to thinking about him a lot. In Leningrad these thoughts were pushed into the background by work, but here he had no work. Here there was only Stalin to think about. Kirov was meeting him every day and thinking about him incessantly.

He had supported Stalin all these years. He had upheld his line, fought with his enemies, supported his authority. And he had done so sincerely and with conviction, even though he found many of Stalin's personal characteristics unpleasant. One had to know how to separate the personal qualities from the political. He didn't have much faith in Stalin's promise to take Lenin's criticism of him seriously and improve himself. Kirov was convinced of something else, namely that the dark side of Stalin's character had been made worse by the struggle for power inside the Party. Once it was over, there had been no further need for extreme measures. At that point the negative aspects of Stalin's personality ought to have given way to the positive ones, those characteristics that the leader of a great country must have if he wants to earn the grateful memory of future generations. And certainly Stalin wanted that, so anger ought to give way to magnanimity and suspiciousness to trust.

Kirov's hopes, however, had not been realized. To the contrary, as Stalin's position strengthened, the more intolerant he had become, the more capricious and malicious, the more he manipulated intrigues, poisoning relations between the other Party leaders, and the more he made the security organs into his chief weapon of government. Under Kirov in Leningrad, the NKVD chief, Philip Medved, was subordinate to the regional Party committee. But secretaries of other regional committees were beginning to mutter that the security police were becoming independent of the local Party leadership and were taking their orders only from the center. They were getting into every nook and cranny of the state. Their main weapon was gathering information, and they were even forcing Communists to keep an eye on each other. A concerned Maria had told him several times that even he was being watched. Well, Maria was his wife, she was entitled to be worried. But her sister, Sofya, a level-headed, seasoned Party member since 1911, had confirmed it. Kirov did not share their alarm. Nothing of the sort would be allowed to happen in Leningrad, where his chief of personal security, Borisov, changed the deployment of his teams too often, no doubt the reason why the women thought he was being followed.

Moscow was a different matter. There, they watched his every step, just as they watched all the other members of the Politburo: seeing who was meeting whom, who was visiting whose house. It was disgusting and there had never been anything like it before in the Party. But that was how things were now, and there was nothing anybody could do about it. Stalin's suspiciousness was getting worse. He didn't trust anyone. It was impossible to be frank with him, as he could turn your sincerity against you at any moment. All this was creating an atmosphere of insecurity, alarm, and even helplessness. Yet nevertheless it was impossible to come out against Stalin. That was the tragedy of it all. His line was correct, but his methods were unacceptable. He had turned Russia into a mighty industrial power. To come out against Stalin would mean to come out against the country and the Party. Nobody would support such a move. And if they would, who should replace him?

A lot of people would like to see him, Kirov, in the post of general secretary, but he didn't want it, he wasn't up to it. He wasn't a theoretician, he was one of the practical organizers of the Revolution. His brightest memory of his revolutionary youth was probably the duplicating machine he had made with his own hands, which the students used for printing their leaflets. He had been extremely proud of his duplicator as his first material contribution to the cause. The Party leadership had often praised him and they were always pleased with the weighty and handsome results of his labor and that of the people he led. It was enough for him that he was a Communist, a Party member, and that the Party put such trust in him.

But Stalin no longer took account of the Party leadership which had come into being after the death of Lenin, even though it had defended Lenin's inheritance against Trotsky and Zinoviev. It no longer called itself collective, nor was it: the Party had only one leader now, and that was Stalin. But its core had remained. Lenin had also been the leader of the Party and the state, yet he had taken account of the core which surrounded him. And that was despite the differences that had then existed between them. Stalin was bypassing the Politburo. Now, people like Zhdanov, Malenkov, Beria, Yezhov, Mekhlis, Poskrebyshev, Skiryatov, and Vyshinsky carried more weight than the members of the Politburo. Kirov understood perfectly what Stalin's aim was in demanding that he get rid of the former Zinovievites: he wanted to create an atmosphere of terror, at a time when there were no grounds for it. Stalin, however, wanted to rule by means of fear, and fear alone: it was essential in order to consolidate his one-man rule. And where that would lead, who could say?

Kirov recognized with bitterness that the Party had made a grave error in not taking Lenin's advice and removing Stalin as general secretary. They should have done it. Trotsky still would not have got the upper hand, for he was regarded as an outsider by the Party. Nor would Zinoviev and Kamenev have become the leaders, for the Party did not trust them. The Party today would have been led by its true Bolshevik core, the present Politburo, plus Bukharin and Rykov, and even Stalin, but as an equal member. Well, it was impossible to correct that error. Stalin was now immovable.

It was also impossible to convince him of anything. He only gave the appearance of agreeing with you for the sake of maneuvering. He calculated his political moves on the long term. There was some ulterior political goal behind his apparently innocent suggestions that Kirov write an article against Enukidze and move to Moscow. Lenin had written that Stalin was capricious. But he was also patient and persistent, and he always carried his intentions through to the end.

Stalin knew the secret of power. People could understand his simplified seminary logic and dogmatism and they were impressed by it. He had managed to inspire the people with a belief in his omniscience and omnipotence. The people liked his majestic grandeur, and they also liked the fact that, after so many years of chaos, civil war, and conflict inside the Party, order had been restored. They identified this order with Stalin. It had already become impossible to overthrow the deity, this idol. Kirov was overwhelmed by the realization of his own helplessness.

When Kirov had first moved to Leningrad in 1926, he had known how difficult his job would be. The Communists there had voted for Zinoviev. Then, using all the organizational and propaganda means at its disposal, the Central Committee had succeeded in persuading them to vote against the Zinovievite opposition, in favor of the resolutions passed by the Fourteenth Congress and the Central Committee's policies. It was the first time in the Party's history that tens of thousands of Communists had renounced the views they had held the day before and voted for those they had just condemned. And Kirov had been responsible for bringing about the change. It had been a bitter victory, and since then he had devoted all his efforts to restoring the Leningrad Communists' dignity and erasing the psychological trauma that had been inflicted on them.

Of course, he was in favor of iron discipline in the Party, but the Party did not need an organization that was nothing more than a dumb and obedient voting mass, and Kirov had no desire to head such an organization. The revolutionary city must remain the cradle of the October Revolution and its workers the vanguard of the Russian working class. Leningrad must remain a city of advanced European science, art, and culture. That was why Kirov had opposed the transfer of the Academy of Sciences to Moscow. The Politburo had not supported him. They had been guided by the simple notion that, since science served socialist construction, it must be close to the center that directed this construction, alongside the commissariats and other agencies. Kirov had disagreed. But they hadn't supported him. They'd laughed and said that he wouldn't even hand over his aged academicians. And Stalin had laughed, too. But Stalin had known that Kirov was against anything that hurt the pride of the Leningraders.

In any event, Kirov's policies had yielded results. Over a number of years, he had tactfully and persistently persuaded the Leningrad Communists that their vote on the eve of the Fourteenth Congress was regarded as an isolated episode with no further consequences, that their distrust of Stalin was groundless, and that Stalin's policy was the correct one. Convincing them of all this had been no easy matter. They had a high degree of political awareness. It was during those years that the collectivization had taken place, accompanied by the violent dispossession of the kulaks and Stalin's unconvincing maneuvers, exemplified by his "Dizzy with success" speech. During the same years the country had experienced famine and the severe rationing of food and goods. Kirov had done everything he could to make sure the population of Leningrad was fed, frequently coming into conflict with the commissariats in Moscow on this score.

But Leningrad had done its duty by the Party, sending tens of thousands of Communists into the countryside to work on the machine and tractor stations and the state farms, as well as on transport and the main sites of the Five-Year Plan. They had been the best of the city's workers. In demanding and accepting these sacrifices, the Party had, as it were, restored its former role to Red Petrograd. And the dissident vote on the eve of the Fourteenth Congress and the local lack of trust associated with it were entirely forgotten, and for good.

And now that the wound had healed, Stalin had decided to open it again. After eight years, he was going to remind the Leningraders of the old episode, to punish them and take revenge, for behind Stalin's order "to liquidate those still hiding and not disarmed" lay his intention to smash the backbone of the Leningrad Party organization. Kirov would not allow it to happen. And the

Politburo would support him. Stalin would not succeed in turning the Central Committee and his Politburo into obedient executives of his will. And this would provide a guarantee that Stalin would never manage to rise above the Party.

Stalin had done much for the reconstruction of the country, and like all great historical figures he had stamped the mark of his personality on the epoch. Lenin would have carried out the task with more acceptable methods. But Lenin wasn't there. Stalin was there instead. Lenin had always worn shoes. Stalin wore boots. There was no question, however, that Russia was becoming one of the most powerful industrial countries in the world, with advanced science, mighty technology, and high culture. It was not a country that should be ruled by terror. Science, culture, and technology demand the free exchange of ideas. Coercion would become an obstacle on the path of the country's development. Marxism taught that the objective laws of history were higher and more powerful than the individual personality. The logic of the historical process was implacable, and Stalin would have to submit to that logic. History must be allowed to take its course.

The main thing, Kirov thought, as he got up, bored with lying on the sand too long, the main thing was to protect the core of the Party organizations. As long as the Bolshevik hard core was alive and strong, the Party was indestructible.

"You're slightly sunburned," Lipman said to Kirov. "You should put your shirt on, or ..."

He didn't finish what he was about to say as the telephone rang in the sentry box and both men turned toward it. The sentry came over and told Lipman he was required in the first dacha.

"You'll have to put some lotion on to prevent it from hurting," he said to Kirov, as he dressed hurriedly.

17

Lipman examined Stalin's mouth and pronounced that it was healing well and that he would be able to start preparing the new plate in two days.

"Tomorrow, maybe?" Stalin asked.

"We could," Lipman said, smiling, "but it would be better to wait until the day after tomorrow."

"If you think so," Stalin said with a frown. "How's the work going?"

"The work only begins after we've made a mold."

"I meant your book," Stalin explained irritably.

"I'm sorry, I didn't realize.... Thank you, I'm working on it."

Stalin got up.

"Good-bye."

It was not the dentist who had irritated Stalin, but Kirov. They had had no more confrontations, and Kirov was always on time to discuss the commentaries on the plan for the textbook, agreeing to everything without a word. But he was behaving like someone forced to do something both uninteresting and unnecessary. Their meetings had become tiresome. Stalin could have sent Kirov away, but he wanted to avoid an open rift with him. He must be patient. It was getting on his nerves, but he knew how important it was to maintain an appearance of calm, composure, and imperturbability. He had the capacity to contain himself when he was alone, otherwise he would not have been able to do so when he was with others. And if he did lose his temper, it was not with the object of his irritation. On this occasion, it was the dentist who served the purpose.

Lipman appeared at the appointed hour and began to make the wax mold. Stalin did not like this procedure and felt, when the dentist took the wax out of his mouth, that he was taking his remaining teeth with it. Nor did he like the feeling of the wax fragments that were left in his mouth.

"Everything seems to be fine," Lipman said finally. "It's quite a good mold, but I just wonder whether we shouldn't make a simple plate, after all, Josef Vissarionovich?"

Stalin struck the arm of his chair with his fist. "I've told you in plain Russian that I want a gold one!"

"Yes, yes, of course," Lipman muttered hastily. "We'll do as you say. It'll be ready tomorrow morning."

Stalin watched silently as Lipman gathered up his things with trembling hands. The blockhead was scared! What a population!

Lipman suddenly stopped clearing up and asked timidly: "Josef Vissarionovich, I have to match the color for the tooth. Would you mind sitting down again for a moment, please?"

Stalin put his head back on the headrest and opened his mouth. Lipman tried several different samples. His expression was worried, even frightened, and he seemed to be taking a long time. Stalin was bored sitting there with his mouth open for so long.

"Are you going to be done with this soon?"

"Right away," Lipman said, as he tried one model after another. He eventually came to a decision and said: "You can get up now, Josef Vissarionovich. I'll try to have everything done by tomorrow morning." He had a worried look on his face as he closed his case.

The next morning Stalin ordered them to bring the dentist.

"He hasn't finished yet, Comrade Stalin," Tovstukha reported. "He said it won't be ready until tomorrow."

Stalin's face darkened. "Bring him here."

Lipman appeared a few minutes later, out of breath.

"You promised the plate today. Why don't you keep your word?" Stalin said.

"It hasn't been possible, Josef Vissarionovich."

"What's holding it up?" Stalin glowered at the dentist with a look that would scare anyone.

Lipman spread his hands helplessly.

"Tell me the truth," Stalin said.

"Well," Lipman began timidly. "Not one of the false teeth that I brought with me matches yours properly."

"Why didn't you bring the right ones?"

"I brought everything we had, including the same ones that were used for you before."

"So?"

"People's teeth change color, especially if they smoke. The teeth I brought with me come very close to yours, very close indeed, but there is nonetheless a slight difference in shade."

"Is it very noticeable?" Stalin asked.

"No, not very, but a specialist would spot it."

"What do I care what specialists think?"

"I didn't want it said that I'd done bad work for you," Lipman replied.

Stalin smirked. "So, because of your professional vanity, I have to walk around without any teeth. How much longer is this going to go on?"

"I've requested that Moscow be telephoned and asked to send me more teeth. I gave the catalogue numbers."

Stalin stared intently at Lipman. "But you just said you'd brought everything you had in Moscow."

"They'll get them . . ."

"Where from?"

Lipman mumbled without raising his eyes: "Berlin."

"Berlin?"

"I bought them from a German catalogue."

"Why didn't you tell me that right away?"

Lipman said nothing.

"Were you forbidden to tell me?" Stalin smirked again.

Lipman said nothing.

"Was it Tovstukha?"

Lipman gave a barely perceptible nod of the head.

"Bear this in mind," Stalin said reprovingly. "You *may* tell

Comrade Stalin everything, you *must* tell Comrade Stalin everything, and you must *not* hide anything from Comrade Stalin. And
another thing: *it is impossible* to hide anything at all from Comrade
Stalin. *Sooner or later he will find out the truth."*

The delay over the plate was of course tiresome, but it would
turn out all right in the end. It was the fact that they had forced the
dentist to lie that was annoying. Nobody in his entourage had the
right to utter a single untrue word. A small lie always brings a
bigger one in its wake. If the people around him were lying to him
about trivialities, then they were unreliable. Everyone, from the
members of the Politburo right down to the cooks in the kitchen,
must know that they should speak the truth to Comrade Stalin, the
whole truth and nothing but the truth.

He let the dentist go and called Tovstukha.

"Why did you make the dentist deceive me?"

"What happened was this," Tovstukha said. "The dentist told
me yesterday that he hadn't got teeth of the right shade and that
they could be obtained only in Berlin. I immediately phoned
Litvinov and gave him all the information from the catalogue.
Litvinov phoned Khinchuk —"

"Is Khinchuk still in Berlin?"

"Yes, Surits is only leaving for Berlin today."

"Right. And, so?"

"Litvinov informed me that everything had been bought and was
being delivered to Moscow today. I'm expecting the shipment to be
here by this evening, and the dentist has said they'll do the work
overnight."

"They should sleep at night. If they work all night they'll only
make a mess of it. But my question was, why did you make the
dentist deceive me?"

The reply was unexpected. "I was afraid you'd forbid the
purchase of the materials from Berlin."

Tovstukha was afraid of Stalin's modesty: it was a subtle way of
flattering him. On the other hand he might really have thought that
and decided to take the responsibility himself, at his own risk. He
was a tested and loyal man. Nevertheless, he shouldn't have tried to
save himself with a lie.

"You did all this yesterday without my knowledge," Stalin said. "You have presented me with an accomplished fact, and whether or not I am pleased with it, it's too late to change anything now. But why did you make the dentist tell a lie?"

"I was afraid he'd tell you everything and you'd forbid it."

Stalin paced back and forth on the verandah and then stopped with the sudden thought that it wouldn't be a bad idea if he were to take a little bromide again. He'd started sleeping badly after Enukidze's nasty little article had appeared. Kirov had disappointed him, avoiding the responsibility of writing a reproof to Enukidze. Kirov's presence in Sochi wasn't good for Stalin's nervous system. But he must distinguish between important and minor matters. He mustn't lose control over trivialities. Ordering the teeth from Berlin was a minor matter. Tovstukha had spoken sincerely, even convincingly. But the lying had to be nipped in the bud once and for all.

Stalin's face darkened again. He stuck his face right next to Tovstukha's and stared at him. Tovstukha reddened and stepped back a pace.

"I don't want to be surrounded by liars and deceivers. I must be able to trust the people around me *absolutely!* They must not lie even on trivial matters, they must not so much as think of it."

Tovstukha felt that Stalin had said the last words in a slightly more conciliatory tone.

"Forgive me, I acted without thinking."

But Tovstukha had misjudged and Stalin measured him again with a threatening look.

"I will punish the smallest lie severely. And I will be especially severe with those who force the service staff to lie. I hope you understand?"

"Yes, Comrade Stalin. It won't happen again."

The next day after lunch Tovstukha reported that the dentist had everything ready.

"Let him come," Stalin ordered.

Lipman appeared, smiling apologetically. He greeted Stalin and opened his case.

Pacing up and down the room and watching the dentist's movements, Stalin said: "Have you thought over the conversation we had yesterday?"

"Yes, of course, Josef Vissarionovich."

"I talked about it with Comrade Tovstukha and it turns out he made you lie."

Lipman put his hand on his heart. "Comrade Stalin, we didn't want to tell you a *lie!* Comrade Tovstukha asked me not to *bother* you, he didn't want to *distress* you with such a minor complication. God forbid that he'd tell me to lie to you!"

" 'Bother,' 'distress' — that's talk for children. We're both grown men."

Stalin sat down in the armchair and put his head back on the headrest. Lipman immersed the new plate in a glass of water, then shook the water off and carefully put it in place with a gentle movement. It was made of gold.

There then followed the usual procedure with pencil and blue paper: clamp your teeth together, now unclamp them. This did not take long, as the plate was an excellent fit.

"It all seems fine," Stalin said.

As Lipman was leaving, he asked Stalin not to remove the plate until the next morning and to call him if it became uncomfortable.

There proved to be no need for this and Stalin was very pleased. When Lipman appeared two days later, Stalin said to him: "It's a very comfortable plate. It doesn't press anywhere or trouble me at all. It already feels as if I've been wearing it for a long time."

Lipman nevertheless asked him to sit down. He removed the plate, examined the gum, and then replaced the plate.

"Yes," he affirmed. "It's turned out well."

"There you are," Stalin said. "And you didn't want to make it out of gold."

Lipman was silent, then, after some hesitation, said: "Comrade Stalin, since you are pleased with my work, I would like to ask you for a small favor."

"Yes?" Stalin frowned. He didn't like people to make direct requests. There was a proper procedure for such things; he had staff who knew how to prepare questions and who knew which requests should be forwarded and which should not. It was indiscreet to ask him for something in person.

Lipman's request was unexpected.

He took a package out of his case and unwrapped it to reveal a plastic plate.

"I would ask you, Comrade Stalin, to wear this plate for just one day. See which of the two is more comfortable and decide for yourself."

Stalin raised his eyebrows in amazement. He had said plainly enough that he preferred gold, he'd even hit the arm of his chair with his fist, and the dentist's heart had sunk to his boots. Yet here he was, still insisting on getting his way. Well, God knows, maybe he ought to give it a try.

"All right," he agreed reluctantly.

Lipman changed the plates. The fitting, as before, took no time. Everything seemed fine.

"Please call me tomorrow and tell me which one you prefer," Lipman said. "We'll leave whichever one is more comfortable."

The next day before lunch, Stalin called Lipman in.

"By way of self-criticism, I have to admit that you were right. This plate is much lighter and more comfortable. But it might break, so you'd better make me a spare."

Lipman gave a big smile of delight. "I'll make ten, if you like!"

"Have you had lunch?"

"Yes, of course."

"Well, never mind, have another bite with me."

He took Lipman into the neighboring room where there were wines and snacks on the table. "I don't have any vodka or brandy. I don't drink it and I don't advise anyone else to. Now, wine — that's quite a different matter. Which ones do you like?"

"I'm not very knowledgeable about wines," Lipman said with embarrassment.

"That's bad. One should know about wines. I never drink coffee. I drink tea, though rarely. But I do like wine. Two or three glasses of wine make you feel better, and it doesn't cloud the mind," Stalin said.

He poured some wine into two small glasses, almost the size of liqueur glasses.

"Let's hope the plate you've made me lasts a long time. Have something to eat."

Lipman took a pâté sandwich.

"Would you like to relax a little longer in Sochi?" Stalin asked.

"It's wonderful here, but I must get back to my work in Moscow. That's if you don't need me here any longer, of course."

"I'll tell your boss I kept you here. You can relax and swim and write your book."

"My patients are expecting me back in Moscow. I've already begun treatment on some of them — I've removed bridgework and taken out teeth and they're sitting there with their mouths open waiting for me to come back. How can I leave them like that?"

"You're right," Stalin agreed. "When do you want to fly back?"

"As soon as possible. Tomorrow would be good."

Stalin opened the door to the office and called Tovstukha. "Arrange for the dentist to fly back to Moscow tomorrow and see that he has everything he needs" — he nodded toward the bottles — "some of that wine, for instance."

He disappeared briefly and then returned carrying a large colander full of grapes, which he handed to Lipman.

"Will you be able to take these home with you? If you can't, someone will help you." He turned to Tovstukha. "Arrange for someone to meet him in Moscow and take him home. Good-bye, doctor! Keep well!"

After the dentist had left, Stalin asked for Zhdanov and Kirov to be called.

Zhdanov reported on the commentaries on the next chapter of the textbook. Stalin listened, pacing the room. Kirov was sitting at the magazine table and sketching on a piece of paper, which irritated Stalin, though he had the same habit of doodling while listening. In his case, it helped to concentrate the mind, whereas in Kirov's it was a means of distraction, demonstrating his lack of interest in what was going on and that he was having nothing to do with it.

Stalin gave no sign of his irritation, however. On the contrary, when Zhdanov had finished he said: "They seem like sound judgments to me. I think we should adopt them."

"I have no objections," Kirov said, without raising his eyes from the sketch.

Stalin picked up a summary of grain procurements and held it out to Kirov. "Look at this!"

Kazakhstan had been underlined in red, showing that the average figure for the amount of grain collected was seventy percent of the planned total.

"Mirzoyan is falling behind," said Stalin. "It seems our fears were justified."

"It's not that bad," Kirov replied. "Seventy percent ... But of course the situation will have to be improved."

"This *average* figure conceals major delays in particular areas," Stalin objected, reaching for another sheet of paper from the table. "For instance, in eastern Kazakhstan they only achieved thirty-eight percent of the plan. And this is against a background of an excellent harvest. But, just as we thought, the local authorities were caught unawares by this excellent harvest and became complacent. Reports from Kazakhstan indicate poor use of machinery, an antipathy to mechanization specialists, the squandering and stealing of state property, penetration of the land agency organizations by outside, criminal elements and crooks carrying Party cards in their pockets. This situation has got to be corrected urgently, or it will be too late. If Kazakhstan fails in its procurements, it could seriously affect the country's bread supplies, and just at the moment when we are about to abolish bread rationing. I think we ought to send someone to help Comrade Mirzoyan."

"Won't he be offended?" Kirov queried. "It'll look as if we don't have faith in his abilities. Maybe we should write to him, suggesting that he tighten up his Party people, and offering him extra workers and transport?"

"Why should he be offended?" Stalin wondered. "One should never be offended by the Party. If we all got offended by the Party, what would be left of it? Of course, we must be tactful. We won't send an instructor, but a Central Committee secretary. Listen, Sergei Mironovich, maybe you yourself ought to go and see him.

You're on friendly terms and he would take it as an honor if a member of the Politburo were to go there."

This was a turn of events Kirov had not been expecting. To go to Kazakhstan would mean tearing himself away from Leningrad for at least a month. On the other hand, Stalin could just as easily keep him here in Sochi for all of September. But Stalin did not want that: their relations had become strained and Stalin no doubt thought it best that he leave. Perhaps Stalin was using Kazakhstan as an excuse to send him away. Simply to return to Leningrad would indicate that the work they had intended to do together hadn't gone well. Now there was a specious excuse: Kazakhstan needed help urgently and there was a whole host of good reasons why Kirov was the best man to send, not least his personal friendship with Mirzoyan. In these circumstances, his sudden departure from Sochi would not arouse false rumors. One thing made him suspicious, however, and that was that Stalin had mentioned Kazakhstan the very first day he had arrived in Sochi. Why? Had he foreseen that they wouldn't work well together? Had he been preparing for Kirov's departure well ahead of time? It was possible, as Stalin was farsighted. In any event, the suggestion gave Kirov the opportunity to leave sooner than otherwise. Of course, another excuse could have been found. It would have been simpler to let him go for the cure at Minvody, for which no excuse was needed, since it was what his doctors had ordered. He had already refused to write about Enukidze or to return to Moscow, and a third refusal would make relations between them impossible.

"Well, if it's necessary," Kirov said, "I'll go."

"It is necessary, as you well know. And anyway" — Stalin nodded at the notes on the history project — "you don't seem terribly taken with this work. Am I right?"

"Yes, you're right," Kirov confirmed. "I'm no historian...."

"Well, there you are! In Kazakhstan you'll be working on a current problem. It won't occupy you for more than a month and it'll get Kazakhstan out of a mess and ensure that we have enough bread. What are Kazakhstan's difficulties? First of all, it's on the periphery, a long way from the center. Second, the population is very mixed, and is virtually new to agriculture. A lot of the former kulaks have resettled there. Some of them are good, diligent workers." He turned to Zhdanov. "Please check, if you can, Andrei Alexandrovich: I have already requested a decree restoring the rights of former kulaks who have done well in their new locations over the last three or five years, especially the youth. Anyway, among these people there are some hardworking ones, but there are also many who are embittered and are doing us harm. On the other hand, we have not yet inculcated into our own people, our own rank-and-file workers and run-of-the-mill toilers, the basic ethics of labor: which is to do your work to the best of your ability. We haven't developed in them a sense of pride in the quality of their work or in their professions, or any personal pride in their own reputation as workers. For example, I just had a dentist here from Moscow. He suggested his own way of doing things, which I rejected. He started insisting and I had to raise my voice, but he persisted. But what was interesting was that he made both what I wanted and what he had suggested and asked me to try both, first mine, then his. I did. His was better, and I admitted this to him. In other words, he had been right to insist on his own solution. Why had he done this? He could just as easily have done what I wanted and gone in peace. But, no, he had stood his ground, and had not been afraid to do so. His virtue got the better of him. In other words, he is a real worker with a high order of professional pride, of the kind we have to inculcate into our people. And when they have absorbed this feeling, the need for coercive measures will disappear. In the meantime, we talk a lot about devotion to the cause, we make vows and accept responsibilities. But there is only one responsibility, and that is to one's conscience in what one does, one's pride in the job, like the Georgian wine-growers, for instance, or that dentist."

"The dentist was a very nice man." Kirov smiled.

Stalin came to a halt.

"Has he treated you, too?"

"No, I saw him on the beach. He swims well."

Stalin continued to pace in silence, then said: "So, it turns out you weren't bored after all, and I was afraid that our poor Sergei Mironovich was bored stiff by these commentaries."

Kirov caught the familiar note of envy and suspicion in Stalin's voice.

"The beach was deserted. There was nobody swimming, apart from the dentist and myself. I saw him twice. He made a good impression on me."

"Yes, he was talkative," Stalin added with indifference. This kind of indifference on Stalin's part was also something Kirov was very familiar with.

Stalin went on pacing the room in silence and then stopped in front of Kirov and said: "Can you fly to Alma-Ata tomorrow?"

"Certainly."

"That's fine, then."

That evening, as he was signing papers, Stalin said to Tovstukha: "Replace the dentist Lipman with someone else."

After a moment, he added: "He should be released from the Kremlin hospital, but he should not be touched."

❧ 18 ❧

As before, Alferov was wearing civilian clothes and again received Sasha in his parlor, pulling up a chair for him at the dining table. The table was a simple one made out of planks, but the chairs, which were from town, had upholstered seats.

"Sit down, Pankratov. Would you like some tea?"

Such a welcome boded no good.

"Thank you, I've already had breakfast," Sasha replied.

"A glass of tea won't hurt you just after a journey. How did you get here?"

"I walked."

"All the more reason ..."

Alferov opened the door to the kitchen. "Anfisa Stepanovna, prepare the samovar." He came back to the table and looked at Sasha with a friendly expression on his face. "Well, now, Pankratov, is the separator working?"

"I don't know, I'm not interested."

"Nonsense. Anyway, it is working. And you can thank me. I asked the machine and tractor station to deal with it immediately and they repaired it the same day."

So, Zida had told him the truth.

Alferov gave him a sidelong look.

"As I'm sure you realize, I did not do it for altruistic reasons. I did it because, since it was one of *our* charges who had broken it, it was *our* responsibility to fix it."

"One of your 'charges' didn't break it."

"That's not what they think in the village. At any rate, it's fixed and the incident has been closed. Or to be more precise, silenced. The accusation against you is here with me." He pointed to his desk drawer. "I have no intention of blackmailing you with it. Of course, the chairman of the kolkhoz could bring it up again, but we'll return to that question another time. Ah, here's the tea!"

A portly, impressive-looking middle-aged woman, wearing a long skirt and short blouse, brought in the samovar, then she brought in a plate of fish baked in eggs, some fish pies, and a dish of whortleberries and blueberries.

"I'll make the tea myself," Alferov said, filling the pot. "It's a great art, you know. I learned it in China."

He stood the pot on the crown of the samovar and covered it with a folded tea towel.

"Have a bite while the tea is brewing," he said, indicating the food.

"Thank you, I'll have some tea, but I won't eat. I've already had breakfast," Sasha replied.

"Well, just look and if you feel like it, eat something. The appetite grows with eating. How are you managing in Mozgova? Are you bored?"

"There's not much fun there."

"It's not the good life, to be sure," Alferov agreed. "But you've got some quite interesting people there. The philosopher Vsevolod Sergeyevich Zhilinsky, for instance. He used to be a pupil of Berdyaev. He could have gone abroad at one time, but he refused out of his love for Russia, as he put it. He might still be able to go, though it's late. If one loves Russia, one ought to work for her, not against her. Don't you agree?"

Sasha shrugged. "In principle I agree, but I don't know what he did against Russia."

"Zhilinsky and all the rest will tell you they've landed here for no reason at all. But you can take my word for it, nobody is sent here for no reason."

Sasha smirked, and it was not lost on Alferov.

"You're thinking of yourself, but you're quite a different matter. Your exile has to do with our internal Party affairs. It is, as Pushkin said, 'An ancient fraternal quarrel.' You got into a particular situation and you did not behave very cautiously. Do you think I wanted to get stuck in this hole? You've met the district officer in Boguchany. Someone like him can get by just fine here. I'm somewhat different, I hope you'll agree. But I wasn't on top of my situation and ended up here. Well, so what? I'm a Communist and I'm doing my duty. Yes, about Zhilinsky. He's a clever man, very well read, but be on your guard with him."

"I have very little to do with him. We're only on nodding terms."

"You have to associate with him willy-nilly," Alferov objected. "You can't take a vow of silence for three years, so inevitably you'll associate with him. There's also Mikhail Mikhailovich Maslov, a former colonel on the general staff."

"That's someone I haven't the slightest interest in," Sasha said, beginning to see where Alferov was heading.

"Yes, of course, he's of a different generation and different mentality entirely. The people you came out here with were at least nearer to you in age. Kvachadze, for instance. Do you correspond with him?"

"No, I don't even know where he is."

"Why have you abandoned all your old friends?" Alferov asked with surprise. "On the other hand, I can understand. Kvachadze is a Trotskyite, and a dyed in the wool one, too. But there was also Soloveichik. . . ."

"We've corresponded a little."

Of course, he needn't have said it. He could have asked why he had been summoned. For an interrogation? If so, then he ought to get on with it in the proper way — this kind of chat didn't suit Sasha. Sasha didn't say this, however. Alferov hadn't harmed him, and if he just wanted to talk to another human being, Sasha could accept that.

"Was it some time ago when you received his last letter?"

"Don't you know?" Sasha replied. "I thought you were up to date on all my correspondence."

"Yes, sometimes we have to look through the exiles' letters, that is part of our duties," Alferov affirmed. "But I do it on an irregular and selective basis."

"My envelopes are always open."

"What would be the point of resealing them?" Alferov laughed. "You'd be able to tell they'd been opened, anyway. But, as I said, I do it selectively and I might have missed Soloveichik's last letter."

"Has something happened to him?" Sasha asked.

"Nothing in particular. He wants to be transferred to Goltyavino. He says his fiancée is there. Is it true?"

"Yes," Sasha asserted. "His fiancée is there. I met her when we were passing through Goltyavino."

"I accept that he has a fiancée in Goltyavino, but that doesn't give him the right to leave his appointed place of settlement of his own accord. He went to Goltyavino without permission. I might have shut my eyes to it — young people, true love, and all that. But Goltyavino comes under the jurisdiction of the Dvorets commandant's office, and they are not prepared to shut their eyes to it."

"I didn't know anything about it," Sasha said. "But I can understand it. If anyone has ended up here by accident it's Soloveichik. He's anything but political. He's easygoing and makes friends quickly, but the restrictions here are very hard for him to bear. Of course, it's strange that he did this, but then love knows no frontiers."

"Your lyrical sentiments, Pankratov, are what is called in official language *escape!* And for that they don't just punish the escapee, but all those who helped him. There are other exiles in Rozhkovo. He has involved them all in it."

"So, if someone escapes from Mozgova, am I responsible?"

"Yes. Think about it: one runs away and everyone else is responsible. So the innocent have to protect themselves from the egoists who only think about themselves. You have to tell the authorities about any escape that is being planned, that's the system. And you have to help in this. You say you're an honest Soviet citizen, so help us!"

"So, *that's* what you're trying to turn me into!"

"Alexander Pavlovich! Don't say that — we have the severest punishments for provocation. We're not asking you to report on moods or on conversations you've heard. We want to prevent escapes, we want to save the unthinking people who run away and the trusting people who help them. We're going to transfer you to Kezhma as an itinerant mechanic for the machine and tractor station. You'll be able to move freely around the district and you'll meet other exiles, among them some who are planning to escape.

And you will persuade them not to. At least, you can tell us so that we can prevent it happening. You'll earn a living, you'll be living in the district rather than a village, and you'll be saving people from committing foolhardy acts."

"You're wasting your time," Sasha said. "I'm not going to do what you're proposing. I regard it as immoral."

"Do you also regard my work as immoral?" Alferov asked.

"You've got a job and you are doing your duty. I'm an exile and I'm also going to do my duty."

"What would that be?"

"To complete my term."

Alferov was silent, then he smiled and said: "Alexander Pavlovich, you put me in a very difficult position."

"I don't understand."

"You said, 'Love knows no frontiers.' Let's suppose you're right. But your wife is the teacher. Can we entrust the education of the new generation to the wife of a man who is politically disloyal?"

"I haven't got a wife. Where did you get that from? The teacher? I go to her occasionally for books — and that's all."

"Alexander Pavlovich, we're both grown men and we understand each other. Not that I expected a different reply. But the teacher is for all intents and purposes your wife. If you are sensible, we could bring you both here to Kezhma, since we need a teacher here."

"I haven't got a wife," Sasha repeated, scowling. "You could just as easily call any woman in Mozgova my wife. If you touch the teacher, you'll be committing the greatest injustice."

"Nobody's going to touch her. But we are obliged to shield her from alien influences. That's what we'd say if we moved you to another place."

"You're in charge." Sasha sighed with relief. To hell with them! They could move him to another village, as long as they left Zida alone.

Alferov got up and paced around the room.

"Tell me, Pankratov, what do you propose to do in life?"

"After exile, I'll go home and try to get my case reviewed."

"You won't be going back to Moscow; it'll be out of bounds for you."

"There are other places besides Moscow."

"Get your case reviewed?" Alferov continued. "That's not very likely. Your conviction will hang over you."

"They sometimes lift a conviction."

"Yes, sometimes," Alferov agreed. "But they do that as a reward for services to the state. And I don't see any particular desire in you to do anything special in that regard. After all, you feel aggrieved."

"I'm not aggrieved. But I can't forget the way my mother struggled in the corridor when they took me away, and I can't forget the way the interrogator handled my case."

"All right." Alferov sat down opposite him. "Let's get down to business. Soloveichik has escaped."

He watched for Sasha's reaction. Sasha looked back at him, stunned. "That's impossible. Soloveichik isn't that stupid, he knows there's nowhere to hide."

"Yet he has escaped. Did he write anything to you?"

Sasha grimaced. "Escaping is stupid enough, writing about it is even more stupid."

"Undoubtedly," Alferov agreed. "But you're his only friend here, his only comrade."

"Are you accusing me of being an accomplice to his escape?"

"Pankratov," Alferov said reprovingly, "I'm more concerned about you than you think. Nobody is accusing you of this. But Soloveichik must have thought out his escape route very well. There are two obvious routes. One is down the Angara to the Yenisei, and the other is through the taiga to Kansk. He won't get far by either route, as he'll be held in the first village. To avoid all the settlements he'd need a large supply of food, which he does not have. But there is a third possibility, and that's *up* the Angara to Irkutsk. It's a longer route, but it passes through Mozgova, where you live, and there are two more settlements farther up where there are people with the same ideas as his fiancée. He may well have chosen this route, and it is possible that he will show up at your place."

"How can he show up at my place? With the entire village watching?"

"I don't know. Maybe he won't show up, but maybe he will. In which case you will have to think carefully about what to do."

"Should I detain him?" Sasha laughed. "And what happens if I can't handle him?"

"You don't have to detain him, we'll do that. The best thing would be to persuade him to go back. In that case, the charge of escape would be dropped, and it would simply be voluntary absence, which could be dealt with by administrative means. I'm telling you honestly, Pankratov, I don't want there to be an escape. I don't need any extraordinary incidents."

Sasha felt that Alferov was being sincere. But he did not believe that Boris had escaped. Maybe he'd been hunting in the taiga and got lost.

"So, there you are, Pankratov. The simplest thing is for you to persuade him to go back. And if he won't, then tell the village soviet or the kolkhoz authorities. They'll know what to do."

He added after a pause: "Take this business seriously, Pankratov. Harboring an escapee or giving him aid can have very serious consequences for you. You have been warned!"

Boris on the run! Sasha simply could not believe it. He could believe that Boris would hang or drown himself: his life had been ruined. Hadn't he himself been close to suicide? But escape? The practical, rational Boris would have known perfectly well how absurd such an attempt would be. The best chance to escape had been when they were in Kansk: he could have stowed away on a train and gone. But as long as he remained here he could still hope to live with Freda. Once he'd gone, that hope would be gone, too, forever. Also they'd drag Freda into it, and Boris wouldn't want to put her on the spot.

So what was the trap Alferov had set for him? Your comrade has escaped from exile and you can get out of answering for it if you hide behind our broad back! You're living with the teacher and she could suffer because of it, so, again, let us shelter you behind our broad back! You can't make a living in Mozgova, so who's going to feed you for three years? Well, I'll give you a job and you needn't be a burden to your family. And don't forget, the separator's still hanging over your head — the paper's right here in my desk drawer. It was all so primitive.

At the same time, Sasha had sensed an exceptional quality in Alferov, something different. He was no Dyakov; he was a bird of a quite different feather. He'd been in China. You wouldn't send Dyakov to China. On the other hand, Dyakov was in Moscow, working in the central organization, and Alferov was here in the sticks. It was evidently a punishment. The suspicious look he had in his eyes was a sign of his own insecure situation. And he didn't have Dyakov's crude methods of applying pressure. Maybe he wasn't trying very hard?

Sasha told Vsevolod Sergeyevich that he'd been summoned because of Zida. He said nothing about the escape, which he did not believe had taken place, anyway.

Vsevolod Sergeyevich reacted calmly.

"At the last resort, you can go to Savino or Frolovo — a small price to pay for two months of happiness. And nothing will happen to Nurzida Gazizovna. She's worth more here than Alferov. They can find another district officer, but not another teacher."

Sasha told Zida about Boris, thinking that, like him, she would not believe it. But she did.

"They run away from the anguish and tedium. Even the most rational ones. It's normal."

Strangely enough, the conversation with Alferov had a calming effect on Sasha. It put an end to his torture. Alferov had confirmed what he himself had thought: he would never see Moscow again and there was no hope of having his case reviewed. He'd been written off. Well, that meant he would have to start thinking differently. He finally accepted his fate and felt that he was now capable of mastering himself. He had no more illusions. His case was not special, he was just one of an enormous number. He now had to find the resources within himself to survive.

One day he met Timofei on the street. The other man looked at him warily and wanted to go past, but Sasha blocked his path.

"Are you a bad shot, Timofei, or have you got a rotten gun?"

"What do you mean?" Timofei mumbled, stepping back onto the grass as he had the last time, when he'd been afraid Sasha was about to hit him.

"Don't be afraid," Sasha laughed. "I'm not going to touch you here — but if I come across you again in the forest, I'll shoot you like a dog. You've got birdshot, but I've got slugs and the barrel of my gun is rifled, so watch out! And if I don't get you, someone else will. We have our own code of punishment. Just remember that, you scum!"

He walked off. That was the only way to deal with such people; that was how they'd dealt with the boys who had murdered the exiles on the Kansk road, as everyone on the Angara knew. And Timofei knew it, too. The coward would keep his nose clean from now on! When Sasha went into the forest now it was with his barrels loaded, and more than one lump of lead in his pocket. He did not go without Zhuchok, he did not stand still on open ground, and he went by a different path each time.

The second or third day after the conversation with Timofei, Sasha was in the forest when Zhuchok suddenly stopped and sniffed and then dashed off into a thicket. The bark was not a call to Sasha to come and see something. The dog was barking angrily, deep in its throat, at a man or maybe a bear. Sasha hid behind a tree and loaded both barrels with lead slugs.

The barking went on with mounting rage, now getting farther away, now closer. The dog was obviously running away and then returning to the charge. It couldn't be Timofei, as the dog knew everyone in the village, so either it was someone Zhuchok didn't know, or it was a bear.

It seemed to Sasha that there was a man behind a tree, he sensed a stirring, maybe a movement of air or the crackle of a twig. . . . Zhuchok sprang out into the clearing and threw himself at the stranger, who chased him off with a long stick.

Sasha recognized him at once. It was Soloveichik, in buttoned breeches and a padded coat, a fur hat with earflaps, and marsh boots. He now had a small beard and he looked thin.

Sasha called to the dog and went over to Soloveichik.

They embraced.

"Let's go back into the forest," Sasha said.

They went into a thicket and sat down under a tree where it was relatively dry. Boris took off his backpack, put it alongside him, laid his head back against the tree, and closed his eyes.

"That's a nasty dog you've got."

"He found a stranger. Do you want something to eat?"

"Not at the moment. I've just eaten." He nodded at his bag. "Had you heard about me?"

"Alferov called me in and asked about you."

Boris lay with half-closed eyes.

"Why did you do it?" Sasha asked.

Boris began to cough, hacking long and painfully. "I asked them to transfer me to Freda, or her to me. They refused. I went to see her. They arrested me on the road. I escaped. I can't go back to Rozhkovo, they'd put me in prison and sentence me for the escape. So, I came in this direction. They'll look for me lower down or on the Kansk road. This way, I might manage to get to Bratsk."

"Alferov said you might come this way."

"He said that to you?"

"Yes."

Boris was silent.

"It's a month's trek to Bratsk. Winter will start any day now. You'll freeze to death in the forest," Sasha said.

"I've no choice," Boris replied, exhausted. "If I get there, I get there, and if I don't, I don't."

"But what about Freda?"

"Nothing will happen to her. She doesn't know anything about it. I never saw her after we got here. Did I write to her? I wrote to a lot of people."

"It's not quite that simple," Sasha objected. "You said she was your fiancée, so she's someone very close to you. They're bound to bring her in."

"They called you in, too, but what could you tell them? She's got nothing to tell them, either."

"Listen, maybe it would be best for you to show up in Kezhma and present yourself to Alferov. You can say you've come to ask him to transfer you to Freda or Freda to you. It will look quite different then: you wouldn't have gone outside the district, you'd have turned up in Kezhma."

"It sounds shaky." Boris frowned. "I came to Kezhma, but they arrested me not on the road to Kezhma, but farther down the river. No, I can't go to Alferov, he'll only send me on to Kansk."

"There's no road to Kansk," Sasha said. "And there won't be one for at least another month. And there's no jail in Kezhma, so where will they keep you? It's easier for Alferov to accept your version: you came to plead for yourself and Freda. He himself said: 'I don't want any extraordinary incidents.' The fact that they arrested you lower down doesn't matter. Tell him there were no boats in Rozhkovo, and that you were hoping to hire one at maybe Koda or Pashino."

"Alferov must already have announced my escape," Boris objected. "After all, if he called you in it means he has taken measures."

"But it's the only chance you've got," Sasha insisted. "You'll never get to Bratsk. You'll be picked up in the first village and you can count on a sentence for escaping."

"I'm not going to go into the villages."

"What will you eat?"

"You'll give me some grub — some fat and sugar, some dry bread, whatever you can get hold of. . . ."

"Of course I will. But how long will that last you? How much can you possibly carry? You'll find nothing to eat in the forest, it's already winter. You haven't got a gun. You'll turn yourself in at the first village, just out of hunger. Think about it — your life is at stake. If you present yourself to Alferov, you can save yourself. And you have the chance of getting out of the mess you're in. If you go on, either you'll die in the forest or they'll catch you and you won't have a chance in hell."

Half-lying with closed eyes, Boris seemed not to be listening to Sasha. Perhaps he had dozed off.

"Will you spend the night at my place?" Sasha asked.

Without opening his eyes, Boris shook his head in refusal. "They'd get me. And then you'd be in it, too."

"Don't worry about me," Sasha said.

Boris opened his eyes and said with sudden energy: "If they see me here, Alferov will follow this trail. I've got to cover forty-five miles to where I can get help. I'm not going to put you on the spot. You won't even be able to say you didn't know I was a fugitive, since Alferov had already told you. We must agree that you haven't seen me and I haven't seen you. Whatever happens, whether in a year, or two years, or ten years — I haven't seen you and you haven't seen me."

"Well, I still think you're making a mistake," Sasha said. "You could be in Kezhma in a couple of hours. Alferov will give you a bit of a rough time, but that'll be the end of it. I can't guarantee it, but I think that that's what would happen. And I repeat, it's the only chance you've got."

"I've made up my mind," Boris said firmly. "Can you get me some fat, dry bread, and sugar?"

"I can get the fat and I'll try for some sugar. The bread has to be dried, but if you can wait, there'll be dry bread, too."

"I can't wait. Bring the bread as it is."

"Boris!" Sasha said. "I beg you to think! I can't understand what you're counting on. Even if you get to Bratsk — which you won't, but even if you do — what then?"

"There are people in Bratsk who'll help me get to Irkutsk, where I'll get the train for Moscow."

"And then what?"

"I shall seek the truth."

He seemed to have gone crazy. What truth was he going to seek? Perhaps he was leaving something unsaid? Perhaps there really were people on the route he could trust? Freda's friends? If he had forty-five miles to go, that could be either Frolovo, or Savino, or Usoltsevo. But they were all on islands. How was he going to get across the Angara? The river hadn't yet frozen and would not for a while, so the current was still strong. But Boris was clearly counting on something. Obviously even here in exile he could have made contacts and created opportunities that Sasha didn't know about. The state had always seemed to Sasha so all-powerful, all-knowing, and all-pervasive. In fact, it wasn't so. You could avoid the state. Zida had offered him *other* ways. And Soloveichik no doubt also had his own ways. It was simply that Sasha didn't know what they were.

"How long do you need to get back to the village?" Boris asked.

It was a hint to Sasha to move. He got up.

"I'll be back in three hours."

"I'll wait for you."

Boris huddled against the tree and closed his eyes.

* * *

Everything that had happened before — his arrest, prison, exile — was nothing compared to what was happening now. Then, he had been completely innocent. Now he was breaking the law for the first time. Having been warned, he was helping a fugitive. Boris of course would never give him away, but still the charge of "complicity in an escape" would hang over him. And the penalty would be doubly painful: Boris's escape was an absurdity — either he'd perish on the way or they'd catch him.

He had to help his friend nevertheless. The main thing was to make sure that nobody in the village suspected anything. Should he ask his landlords for fat and sugar? Who was it for? Too obvious a clue. Zida was the only person he could ask for help. If she didn't have anything, she could go to her neighbors. She was always buying food from them, so they wouldn't suspect anything. A piece of fat, some bread or flat cakes, a couple of dozen hard-boiled eggs, she'd have sugar, he had the sweets his mother had sent from Moscow, some salt . . .

He'd say to Zida: Please get this for me. I need it. Don't ask why and forget that I asked you.

Zida didn't ask him anything. She went to her neighbors and came back with fat, dried meat, and flat cakes. She boiled the eggs and got the sugar and sweets. She wrapped it all up and put it in a canvas bag of the sort the local hunters took with them into the forest.

The fact that she used just such a bag made it plain that she knew what was going on.

Sasha turned in the doorway as he was leaving, and said: "I haven't taken anything from you."

Whatever happened, however it all turned out, Zida was to have no part in it.

She nodded her head. "All right."

Hearing Sasha, Boris opened his eyes and propped himself up. He shook his head as if to clear it, then put the food into his backpack. He did not take the salt.

"I have some already."

He got up. Sasha helped him on with the backpack.

"Well, my friend, it's good-bye!" Boris said.

Hampered by the backpack, he awkwardly embraced Sasha and they kissed each other.

"I'll be in this place tomorrow from the morning on," Sasha said. "If you change your mind and come back, I'll be here."

"I won't change my mind," Boris replied. "Will you be all right? Did you take precautions when you got this stuff?"

"Don't worry about it."

❧ **19** ❧

Ordzhonikidze was still upset about the incident with the Pyatakov commission, when Ryazanov had practically thrown them out of the plant. And he was still smarting from the dressing-down he'd got from Stalin, thanks to Ryazanov. Stalin had supported Ryazanov, even though there was not a single document to authorize the housing or the other communal and recreational facilities he had started building. It was all based on words alone, and words were easily forgotten. Ryazanov was in an exposed position.

For that reason Ryazanov had readily accepted an invitation from the journal *Bolshevik* to write an article on the plant and the problems facing the country's ferrous metal industry. *Bolshevik* was the Party's chief journal and the article was bound to help the plant, as suppliers and subcontractors would see it as a directive. And, what was more important, the article would give Ryazanov an opportunity to give public notice of the additional building he had initiated, and hence legalize it.

Mark Alexandrovich wrote the article in the course of two evenings. He argued that the Americans had developed the project in great haste and that many adjustments had been necessary as a result. He listed the chief ones. At the same time, he urged that Soviet metallurgists be made acquainted with the best models of American industrial practice and showed in detail the areas in which Soviet methods were lagging.

The main task facing the ferrous industry in the East was to retain and consolidate a technically qualified and stable work force.

For this reason, it was essential to build living accommodations, as well as communal and recreational facilities on a large scale. He listed the works that had already been carried out (and which had prompted the sending of the Pyatakov commission), and those that had already received the approval of the Party Central Committee (meaning Stalin's approval), and he indicated that this work would continue.

He concluded with sharp criticism of faulty suppliers. The article appeared in the middle of November and at the end of the month Mark Alexandrovich went to Moscow to attend a plenary session of the Central Committee.

The meeting discussed only one issue: the abolition of ration cards for bread and other foodstuffs from the first of January, 1935.

All the speakers voiced their concern: the system had been in existence since 1928 and had guaranteed a fixed level of supply, however inadequate. Now the sale of food was to be free and the market would be revived, but people had forgotten how to manage it.

Stalin did not speak, but sat silent on the platform.

During an interval on the second day of the session, a smiling Ordzhonikidze, accompanied by Kirov, approached Ryazanov in the foyer.

"Sergei Mironovich wants to meet you," Ordzhonikidze said. "He liked your article."

Kirov shook hands with Mark Alexandrovich. "Yes, it was a sensible, intelligent article. What you say about the new regions applies to the old ones, too, you know. The problem of maintaining a stable work force of qualified people has become a major priority everywhere. I agree that we ought to learn from the Americans — there's no disgrace in that, even if they are capitalists. As for your criticism of certain Leningrad enterprises, I promise to deal with the situation."

"Thank you, that would be our highest reward," Mark Alexandrovich replied.

Ordzhonikidze said with good humor: "He's a real diplomat. His article officially legalizes the illegal costs he has incurred."

"Oh, come, Grigory Konstantinovich," Ryazanov protested. "All I did was to make known what had been done and been approved."

Ordzhonikidze had no chance to reply. Stalin had stopped next to them. They had not even noticed from which direction he had come.

"What's the argument about?" he asked.

"We were talking about Ryazanov's article," Ordzhonikidze replied.

"What article is that?" Stalin asked, glancing coldly first at Ordzhonikidze and then at Ryazanov, but passing over Kirov.

"It's in the most recent issue of *Bolshevik*," Kirov said.

"I haven't read it," Stalin said, without looking at Kirov. He walked away.

Mark Alexandrovich watched him go and as he looked at the narrow back and slightly rounded shoulders in the khaki-colored, almost brown tunic, his heart filled with pride. Only a moment ago he had been standing next to *Stalin,* with Kirov and Ordzhonikidze, and everyone at the meeting had seen them talking together. Stalin hadn't seen his article in *Bolshevik,* but that was only to be expected, as he would have been busy getting ready for this meeting. It was enough that Kirov had read it and praised it. And Ordzhonikidze's friendly demeanor showed that he was no longer angry with him. His actions had been legitimated, and the article had served its purpose. Everything was all right, and his fears had been groundless. In a period of great accomplishments, whatever is true and valuable will inevitably triumph because Stalin's wise thoughts and mighty hand are guiding everything. There Stalin was, walking through the foyer packed with people, and nobody seemed to be making way for him, nobody stepped to one side, and yet the way before him was open. He was walking calmly, unhurriedly, lightly in his soft boots, and nobody seemed even to look at him or cast a glance in his direction, and yet they all knew he was there. He disappeared behind a door leading to a room set aside for the presidium. It was only then that Ryazanov realized that Ordzhonikidze was leaning against the wall and with trembling hands was taking a nitroglycerine tablet from a pillbox and placing it under his tongue.

"What's the matter?" Kirov asked in alarm.

Ordzhonikidze caught his breath. "Nothing."

Mark Alexandrovich took his arm.

Gently Ordzhonikidze removed his hand.

"Grigory Konstantinovich, let's go to the first-aid post, it's right here."

"No, it's all right, it's passed."

"No," Kirov said resolutely. "You're going home. Come on, I'm going to take you."

Stalin's unfriendliness came as no surprise to Kirov. Their relations had deteriorated in Sochi, from where Stalin had virtually sent him packing to Kazakhstan. Kirov had been there from the sixth to the twenty-ninth of September, and when he had returned to Leningrad, his NKVD chief, Medved, had reported that, without his agreement, his own deputy, Ivan Zaporozhets, had brought people from the central organization in Moscow and had put them into key positions in the secret political section. He was demonstrating in general that he was autonomous and subordinate only to Moscow. The situation was intolerable. The NKVD could not have two chiefs, one of them answering to the local Party secretary and the other to Moscow. Medved therefore demanded the immediate recall of Zaporozhets, as well as the people he had appointed without the agreement of the local organs.

The problem was a tricky one. These appointments had undoubtedly been approved. Probably they had been made on Stalin's instructions to "root out the remains of the opposition" and to spite Kirov: you won't do it yourself, so we'll do it for you. That explained why Zaporozhets was proclaiming his autonomy in every way possible. To demand his recall would mean direct conflict with Stalin, and on the delicate question of *personnel,* in which Stalin would not tolerate anyone's interference.

Yet to allow the existence in Leningrad of a body that was not subordinate to the local Party committee would mean losing all authority in due course.

Kirov gathered the bureau members of the Party committee in his office, and only the bureau members. There were no secretaries or technical experts, and no minutes were taken. He asked Medved to repeat what he had told him and he asked the bureau members for their opinions. Unanimously, they demanded that Zaporozhets and his people be recalled immediately.

Kirov picked up the phone and asked for Moscow.

"I'll report at once," Poskrebyshev said.

They waited a long time. It was quiet in Kirov's office. Everyone was silent, knowing that Stalin never answered the phone by chance.

Finally he picked it up.

"Yes?"

"Comrade Stalin," Kirov began, "Zaporozhets is operating on his own here, and does not answer to NKVD chief Medved. The bureau of the Party committee requests that Zaporozhets be recalled from Leningrad."

Stalin was silent, then he said: "What is he actually doing on his own authority?"

"The last thing he did," Kirov said, "was to bring in five of Yagoda's people, and without Medved's knowledge he put them into important positions in the NKVD's secret political section. . . ."

"Well, there you are," Stalin replied. "They are internal transfers within the NKVD organization."

"But am I the secretary of the local Party committee, or not?" Kirov said angrily, and he struck the table with the edge of his palm.

"Why all these childish questions?" Stalin protested. "The NKVD is a new commissariat, and as in any new commissariat, there are bound to be personnel changes. It's practically impossible to clear each appointment with all the local organizations."

"The bureau, and I personally, insist on the recall of Zaporozhets," Kirov declared.

"I've explained it to you as best I could, I can't do more than that," Stalin said coldly, and he put down the phone.

They all sat in silence for a moment, and then Kirov turned to Medved. "Well, Philip, you're the boss of your organization. The bureau only acknowledges you. You must cut off any of Zaporozhet's separate operations at the root. And we'll support you."

Kirov returned to the plenary session after taking Sergo to his apartment. The bell had rung, the break was over, and the participants had all filed back into the hall. Mark Alexandrovich waited for Kirov to return.

"Excuse me, Sergei Mironovich, but how is Grigory Konstantin-ovich?"

"He seems to be all right for the moment. He's gone to bed and Zinaida Gavrilovna is calling the doctor."

But Ordzhonikidze had forbidden his wife to call the doctor. He felt better and got up, though he decided not to return to the meeting. He was familiar with the draft decree and they would pass it without him.

He sat down in an armchair and pondered.

During the two-minute conversation in the foyer, he got a clear and precise understanding of Stalin's attitude to Kirov. He knew Stalin well, and he knew what it meant when Stalin spoke to someone without looking at him.

It was getting dark and they turned on the lights in the apartment. Zinaida Gavrilovna looked in: "How are you?"

"I'm fine, but please don't put my light on, I want to sit here alone for a while."

He sat and thought. After Budyagin's report on the strange appointments in the Leningrad NKVD, he had tried on several occasions to talk to Stalin about Kirov, with the intention of feeling out the situation, but Stalin had always changed the subject. Then he had suddenly raised it himself.

The Politburo had been discussing Kirov's report from Kazakhstan about the progress of the grain procurements, and, as if by the way and not connected with the question under discussion, Stalin had said: "I've suggested to Comrade Kirov, as a secretary of the Central Committee, that he move to Moscow, but he refused. How long can one stay in one town? Eight years! It's enough. Having Kirov in Leningrad is a luxury we can no longer afford. Kirov is a worker of national dimensions; the whole Party needs him."

He had said no more and gone on to the next item of business.

After the meeting, when everyone had gone, except Stalin, Molotov, Kaganovich, and Kuibyshev, Stalin had said to Ordzho-nikidze: "Talk to Kirov. After all, you're friends. He should transfer to Moscow. We need a Russian in the central leadership. You and I are Georgians, Kaganovich is a Jew, Rudzutak's a

Latvian, Mikoyan's an Armenian. What Russians are there? Molotov, Kuibyshev, Voroshilov, and Kalinin. That's not many."

When Kirov had returned from Kazakhstan, Ordzhonikidze went to see him in Leningrad and talked about Stalin's proposal. Kirov again refused. He told Ordzhonikidze about the friction with Stalin in Sochi and of the new conflict over Zaporozhets. He said calmly and with assurance: "We're not going to let Zaporozhets commit excesses here."

How naïve they had all been, himself, Budyagin, and Kirov. How naïve! As if Stalin had not known that Kirov wouldn't give in over Zaporozhets. "Rooting out the old pals" was a cover for something else, a camouflage. Zaporozhets wouldn't root out anything, they wouldn't let him.

What could be done? The only thing left was to gain time. Kirov must be kept in Moscow for at least a few days or a week. Ordzhonikidze knew he must think everything out carefully. He might consult some other friends; maybe they would be able to persuade Kirov to move to Moscow. The main thing was that if Kirov remained unexpectedly in Moscow, Stalin might smell a rat and might change his mind and recall Zaporozhets.

Kirov got back from the plenary session just before eleven o'clock and Ordzhonikidze opened the door to him himself.

"Feeling better?" Kirov asked breezily, as he entered the apartment. "How are you?"

Ordzhonikidze sat down again and caught his breath. "Not good, Seryozha, not good at all. Stay here with me for a few days."

Kirov, who was packing his briefcase, looked at him.

"What are you talking about? The day after tomorrow it's the first of December, I have to give my report to the Party activists. . . . About the plenary session —"

"What does that amount to? It's just a report," Ordzhonikidze said, breathing with difficulty. "Can't Chudov or Kodatsky give it for you? Stay here with me for a while, Seryozha. It may be the last time we'll see each other. . . ."

Kirov went over to him and took his hand, and looking into his eyes said: "You must stop thinking like that. Go to bed and call the doctor. Chest pains like that always makes one afraid of the worst. Pull yourself together. Where should I call for a car?"

"I'll call one for you."

Ordzhonikidze got out of the armchair and went into the next room, where he called the garage on the internal number and asked for his own driver, Barabashkin.

"Vasili Dmitryevich, bring round the car to take Kirov to the station." He added quietly, cupping the mouthpiece with his hand, "And make sure he's late for his train. Got it?"

Ordzhonikidze went back into the dining room, where Kirov had already got his things together and was standing, with his coat on, chatting to Zinaida Gavrilovna.

"I'd rather you stayed here with me for a couple of days," Ordzhonikidze muttered sadly. "Eh, Seryozha, won't you?"

"I can't. I've told you . . . December the first . . . the activists . . ."

There was a short blast from the car horn at the entrance downstairs.

Kirov embraced and kissed first Ordzhonikidze and then his wife.

"Don't listen to him," he admonished her as a friend. "Make him get treatment."

He picked up his briefcase and left hurriedly. It was eleven thirty.

They had gone no distance, when Barabashkin stopped the car, jumped out, and raised the hood.

"What's up?" Kirov asked.

"There's something wrong with the motor, Sergei Mironovich. I'll fix it in a jiffy."

"I can't wait."

Barabashkin's mistake had been to pull up near a tramstop. A tram was approaching and it was number four, which went to the railway station. Kirov managed to jump aboard. The guard at the station got him into the coach of the Red Arrow one minute before its departure for Leningrad.

⚜ 20 ⚜

It was still dark when Sasha left the house and reached the place where he had left Boris the day before. He whistled and called to the dog a few times to let Boris know he was there, but there was no response. He exhausted himself searching the forest all day until twilight, but he found no sign of Boris, which meant he had decided to go on. Over the next few days Sasha searched in large circles. The snow was already hanging on the spruce like fat white pillows and covering the ground and the fallen trees in powdery clumps. The marshes were frozen over. Sasha found it hard going. He stopped frequently and listened, but the forest was silent. Occasionally he heard the loud crack from a tree as it froze, or the clucking of a crossbill as it flew from one spruce to another, shaking the hoarfrost from the branches and dropping pine needles and cones onto the snow.

Once he raised a white hare, which ran off between the trees with its long ears lying flat against its back. He came across squirrels that must have been born that year, they were so inexperienced: they sat on branches out in the open and peeled cones, turning them over rapidly in their paws and looking Sasha up and down. He watched a fox trotting at a leisurely gait, pausing now and again to listen for the squeak of a mouse or vole under the snow; when it heard one it would make a dash and dig for it like a dog. Once he saw a wood-grouse feeding: stepping gingerly over the fresh snow, it was picking leaves from the twigs of a juniper tree as it went, or the shoots of a blueberry bush that was not yet entirely snow-covered, or the topmost sprouts of a young pine.

Every day for a week Sasha ventured out into the forest, but

Soloveichik did not show up, which meant he had either gone farther, or he'd vanished, frozen, become ill, fallen through the ice or got lost and died of starvation.

But they hadn't caught him. Had he been caught, everyone would have known. An escape was an event, but the capture of a fugitive was an even bigger occasion. News of it would have flown all around the Angara, and people would have been asking who had helped him, who had hidden him, who had given him food?

The exiles in Mozgova also discussed Soloveichik's escape. But since none of them, apart from Sasha, knew him, and Sasha did not expand on their acquaintanceship, the discussion was of a general nature. The consensus was that he had no hope and was doomed. Even if he managed to get out of Siberia, he would not survive, since it was impossible to live without legal status. Everyone agreed on that.

But they also knew that Soloveichik's escape would not end there. To leave it unanswered, so to speak, would only encourage additional escapes. If it was not possible to punish the fugitive, then those who remained must be punished. They would be taken from the places where they had made themselves a home and deprived of any means of earning a living. They must understand that they would answer for every escape and that they themselves must prevent any similar events in the future. And indeed, all the exiles from Boris's village of Rozhkovo were soon dispersed among other villages.

Two were sent to Mozgova — one named Kayurov and the other a woman who was said to have been a member of the Party since 1905. She had the unusual name of Zvyaguro and was called Lidya Grigoryevna. An old-fashioned, unattractive woman with buck teeth, she had with her a little boy of six called Tarasik.

Arriving by the sleigh road, she left the driver outside the hut where Sasha lived, came in and said: "Soloveichik told me about you. Do you have any idea where I might get a room?"

"I'll have to think," he replied. "Come through and sit down."

"I must let the driver go."

She went back outside. In the sleigh, wrapped in a shawl, sat Tarasik. Lidya Grigoryevna hauled him out and Sasha took out her things — two battered suitcases tied with string — and they all went back into the house. They heard the swish of the runners as the sleigh moved off.

Lidya Grigoryevna unwrapped Tarasik's shawl, removed another garment resembling a fur coat, took off his fur cap, and told him to sit on the bench. Tarasik sat, and gazed at Sasha.

Sasha opened the door to the kitchen and asked the landlady to come in. Both the landlady and landlord came into the parlor.

Indicating Lidya Grigoryevna, he said: "This is a friend of mine. Who would take her in?"

The old woman looked at the little boy.

"Your grandson, is he?"

"Yes," Lidya Grigoryevna said with a frown.

"It's hard to find a place when you have a child. Get up to all kinds of mischief, they do. . . ."

"He doesn't get into mischief," Lidya Grigoryevna said.

"Who can say?" the old woman muttered.

"But surely there have been other exiles here with children before?" Sasha asked.

The old woman did not answer, but went on looking at the boy.

"What's he called, then?"

"His name is Taras."

"The Bryukhanovs might let a room," the old man said.

"The daughter is touched in the head," the woman said, "but she's a quiet girl and wouldn't hurt him."

Lidya Grigoryevna frowned again.

"Who else is there, apart from the Bryukhanovs?"

The old woman ruminated. "What about the Syzykhs?" she asked the old man.

"He likes to pour it down his gullet, all right," the old man said with approval.

"No, no, I don't want that. Tarasik is afraid of drunks."

"You're too choosy," the old woman said disapprovingly, and then turned to Sasha. "Try the Verkhoturovs, next door to the teacher."

On their way there, Lidya Grigoryevna said: "It's not easy finding a place with the child, not that he's a nuisance to anyone. They're afraid that if I'm taken away, he'll be left on their hands. And it could be a year or two before the authorities would send him to a children's home, and there would be applications to be made and letters to write, and they can't write."

The Verkhoturovs wanted thirty rubles a month.

From the expression on Lidya Grigoryevna's face, Sasha could see she was going to turn it down at once. He took her by the elbow.

"Fine," he said. "They'll move in today."

Lidya Grigoryevna was not pleased. "You shouldn't have agreed on my behalf. I can't afford to pay that sort of money, and I have no intention of doing so."

"My agreement isn't binding on you, you can always change your mind. Stay at my place for a few hours, just to rest and have something to eat, and meanwhile I'll go and look for something else for you. If I find something cheaper, you can take a look at it and decide if you want it. And if I don't find anything, you can stay at the Verkhoturovs' for the time being, while we go on looking."

"The Verkhoturovs' place is impossible," she replied. "I've only got twenty-five rubles. How can they ask such prices? In Rozhkovo I paid fifteen rubles."

"It is more expensive here," he agreed. "Rozhkovo is off the beaten track, but Mozgova is next door to Kezhma, the district center, and living costs there are higher. I pay twenty rubles. They added another ten for the boy. I'll lend you some money, and you can pay me back."

"I won't take money from you," she protested. "My nephew in Yaroslavl sends me money, but the mail is going to be chaotic now, what with the move. I know only too well what happens to mail when it's readdressed, and I'll be lucky if I get anything before six months. I earned my living in Rozhkovo by sewing. My landlady had a machine. Will I find one here?"

"The place is full of fashionable women," Sasha said breezily. "They compete with the local intelligentsia. A large clientele awaits you. And we'll find you a machine."

"It won't make any difference, it'll be like Rozhkovo, where they paid me in eggs, sour cream, or fish. My nephew sends me twenty rubles a month, and that's all I can pay."

Sasha took Lidya Grigoryevna to his house and asked the old

woman to give her and Tarasik some tea, while he went off to talk to Zida. She knew everyone in the village and might have some practical advice.

The door to Zida's hut was open, but she was not there. There was wood smoldering in the stove, and there were textbooks and exercise-books on the table, which meant she had come home from school. She wouldn't allow her pupils to take their books home and made them do their work at school: they wouldn't do any schoolwork at home, the books would be used to cover the milk bowls and they'd tear up their exercise-books for cigarette papers.

He began automatically looking at the childish scribbles, when his attention was drawn to a thick, cloth-bound notebook. It was the proper kind he used to have in Moscow when he was at the institute. Equally automatically, he opened it.

Even without reading it, from the dates indicated — August, September, October, November — and the letter "S" for Sasha and "V.S." for Vsevolod Sergeyevich, and isolated phrases which he glimpsed, like "Yesterday he said," and "He's very brave and noble," Sasha realized that this was Zida's diary. His first impulse was to close it instantly — he would not sink to reading someone else's diary. Yet ... Had this been Moscow, his past life, he would never have read someone else's diary, but here, in his present situation ... After all, she was writing about *him!* What was she writing? Why commit it to paper? He had to know what was written there. Every word he said and every step he took could be misinterpreted. Trouble could come from any direction, even from the woman he loved. What did he really know about her? Why was she here? What was she doing in this hole?

He paced the room.

And what did she mean by "brave and noble"? Was it an allusion to his having supplied Soloveichik with food and not given the fugitive away? Just two words like that would be enough to get all the exiles in Mozgova kicked out. Because he had trusted her, others could suffer. Of course, she had not intended to harm anybody, but why write such things? Didn't she understand? And why leave the diary on the table? Was it accidental? Did she just forget to hide it away? Was it merely absent-mindedness?

He paced the room again, tore a piece of bark off a log, and threw it into the stove, where it flared and curled for a moment before dying.

Should he look at the diary? Should he read what she had written about him and find out once and for all just who she really was? If he did, he would be crossing the borderline between decency and dishonor. It was too late in any case: he had hesitated too long and he heard her coming across the yard and then scraping her boots in the porch. She came into the room and smiled at him.

"Have you been waiting long?"

By way of reply, he pointed to the diary. "What's that?"

She heard the anger in his voice and realized he had opened the notepad. She was flustered for a moment, but then looked at him with a clear, open gaze. "It's my diary."

"Why do you keep one?"

She was slow to reply.

"Are you offended by something I wrote?"

"I don't read other people's diaries. But ... Apparently you do write things about me?"

"Yes, I do."

He looked at her and said: "Why are you here, Zida?"

She lowered her head and said nothing.

"I'm asking you, what brought you here?"

"That is something I'll never tell you," she whispered.

"It's your own business, but I have to know what you've written about me."

She held out the notepad to him. "Read it for yourself."

"I'm not going to read your diary. But I will ask you to tear out any pages about me and burn them, right here in this stove. And don't write anything else about me. I explained my situation to you, I'm only sorry you don't seem to have understood."

She leafed through the diary pensively, turning down the corners of some of the pages and then she handed it to Sasha.

"That's what I've written about you."

"I've told you I'm not going to read it. Just tear out the pages and burn them."

He knew he was making a harsh demand, but there was nothing

else to do. Soloveichik's action had been paid for dearly by people who were already suffering enough. Sasha could not let anyone else suffer because of Zida's thoughtlessness.

Zida went to the stove and opened the iron door. She tore a page out of the diary, read it, crumpled it up, and threw it into the fire. She did the same with a second page, and a third and fourth.... Kneeling in front of the stove with her back to Sasha, she went on tearing out pages and throwing them into the fire, no longer reading what she had written. The last part of the diary was about Sasha, but perhaps she was by now indifferent, for she went on tearing out pages right to the end of the pad.

"It's hot," she said suddenly.

Only then did he realize that she hadn't had a chance to take off her outdoor clothes, that she was still in the fur coat, felt boots, and shawl she had been wearing when she came in.

Now he felt sorry for her and cursed himself. It was disgusting and awful! He couldn't wait for the torture that he had created to end.

Zida stood up and put the remains of the notepad on the table, smiling through her tears.

"That's all of it."

Sasha left her. It had been terrible, it had been appalling and loathsome, but there was nothing else he could have done. He was living by new laws. Perhaps Zida would understand and they'd remain friends.

He went to Fedya's store and asked him about a room. He added that the lodger had a child of six, that she could sew well, and that the landlady must have a sewing machine.

"What about sending her to Lariska?" Fedya suggested. "She's alone, and she's got a machine. She likes new dresses and she can't sew, so there's always a dressmaker in the house."

"She can't pay more than twenty rubles."

"Fifteen'll be enough for Lariska," Fedya said with a wave of the hand, "especially if she does her sewing for her. She might even be able to do some sewing for Marusya."

"But will Lariska agree?"

"She will if I say so."

The business concluded, Sasha took Lidya Grigoryevna's suitcases to Lariska's, where he inspected the sewing machine and oiled it. It was an ancient model, but a good one — a Singer.

"Good luck," he said. "If you need anything, call me."

He would have liked to know the details of Soloveichik's escape, but Lidya Grigoryevna said nothing about it and he felt it would be indiscreet to ask.

When he heard that Sasha had found a place for Lidya Grigoryevna at Lariska's, Vsevolod Sergeyevich said, with his usual grin: "An alliance of the old maid and the whore. But she had nowhere to go with the boy. By the way, do you know who Tarasik is?"

"She says he's her grandson, but there's no family resemblance."

"He's the son of some special settlers who died — kulaks, to be more precise."

Sasha was amazed. "She undertook to raise the child here? That's a brave thing to do."

Vsevolod Sergeyevich nodded. "Or it's an attempt to find meaning in life, to have something to cling to."

"Whatever her motive," Sasha said, "it's a noble and humane act. And personally it gives me hope: even here, people are still upholding the highest human values, and one of those values is compassion."

"It makes me think of the changes that have taken place in present reality," Vsevolod Sergeyevich said. "It's quite likely that in her day as a Party functionary Lidya Grigoryevna actually dispossessed Tarasik's kulak parents and sent them off to Siberia. And now here she is herself in Siberia, raising their son and bearing torments and deprivation because of it. Doesn't it reinforce the notion of redemption?"

"I don't know much Christian theology," Sasha replied. "But I think that what moved Lidya Grigoryevna was above religions and ideas, it was the capacity to sacrifice oneself for others. And the fact that it can take place even here, as I said, gives me hope: human feeling has not been killed in people and it never will be."

When Sasha had offered Lidya Grigoryevna money, he had all of thirty rubles to his name. He'd have a few rubles left for cigarettes and kerosene, he'd just make ends meet, but at least he would have helped her out. In any case, he didn't have to pay his landlords until the end of November, or December, at the latest, when the mail would start coming again by the sleigh road.

As he had expected, the mail came at the beginning of December. And, as he had hoped, there was plenty of it. There was money, a package of winter clothes, addressed in Varya's precise hand, a batch of letters from his mother, and a pile of newspapers to read. The postmarks were from August and September and occasionally November, which meant some of it had been sent before the roads had broken up and it had been mixed up with the mail that was sent later. There must still be more to come.

He could look forward to a week of pleasure, maybe even two. December was going to be delightful.

As usual, he read the letters first, putting them in order of their postmarks. His mother said nothing new, but then what news could she possibly have? She sent greetings from the aunts and Varya, and said nothing about his father, or Mark, or his friends. He opened each envelope with the secret hope of getting even two words from Varya. He had written to her, after all. But in letter after letter all he found was "Greetings from Varya." And her neat, expert handwriting on the parcels and newspaper rolls.

And then, when he had lost all hope, he opened the very last letter and saw another page:

Greetings, Sasha! I'm at your mother's now, and we're both writing to you. Everything's fine here. Your mother is well, and I'm working on the Moscow Project. How I'd love to know what you're doing right now.

Varya

He read the lines again. *"How I'd love to know what you're doing right now ..."* My God, how *he'd* love to know what *she* was doing. How he'd love to see her, hear her, touch her, stroke her face ... *"How I'd love ..."* He felt a sharp pang of love and attraction to this girl. He imagined her suddenly there with him....

His heart was pounding and he got up and paced the room to regain control of himself. He read the newspapers for August and

September, but every minute or so he picked up the letter and reread those lines: *"How I'd love to know ..."*

Dammit, there was still everything ahead of him! Varya was his, he now felt sure of it. There was Varya, there was his mother, there were the people around him, there were his thoughts and ideas, and everything that makes a man human.

The sun's rays were coming through the little square windows into the room. The hut was well heated, warm and cozy. Never mind, one could live! Life was bad for those who had no roof over their heads.

Someone had entered the porch and was stamping his feet and brushing the snow off his felt boots with the twig broom. The door opened and Vsevolod Sergeyevich came in.

"Come in!" Sasha was delighted to see him. "Take your things off."

Vsevolod Sergeyevich took off his fur coat and hat, unwrapped his scarf, and laid his gloves on the stove. Then he paced up and down the room, rubbing his hands. He nodded toward the table: "Going through your mail?"

"Yes, there's a lot of it. I imagine you got plenty, too?"

"So, what's new?" Vsevolod Sergeyevich said, answering the question with another.

"Nothing special ... letters from my mother, and friends. I'm happy to get them."

"Yes, yes, of course." Vsevolod Sergeyevich seemed not to have heard him.

"What's the matter?" Sasha asked. "You look worried."

"Things are bad, Sasha, very bad." He went on pacing the room, rubbing his hands continually.

The first thought that came into Sasha's mind was Soloveichik — surely they hadn't caught him?

"Why? What's happened?"

Vsevolod Sergeyevich stopped in front of him.

"Kirov was murdered in Leningrad on the first of December."

"Kirov?" Sasha repeated with a puzzled frown. "Who killed him?"

"I don't know the details. It's in a government statement: 'On December the first at sixteen thirty hours in the Smolny Institute in the city of Leningrad, Kirov died at the hands of an assassin dispatched by the enemies of the working class. The assailant has been apprehended. His identity is being established.' "

"Have you got the newspaper?" Sasha asked.

"No, I haven't got the newspaper, but that's the government's account. There was a second statement: the assassin was someone called Nikolaev. And third, cases of terrorism are now being dealt with inside ten days. The defendant has no say, in other words, there's no defense, or appeal, or pardon. They are shot as soon as sentence is pronounced. So, there you are, Sasha! 'The assassin was dispatched by enemies of the working class.' Not bad, eh?"

"What is so significant about those words? They aren't the main point."

"You think not?" Vsevolod Sergeyevich replied. " 'The assassin was dispatched by enemies of the working class,' yet 'the identity of the assailant has still to be established.' Does that make any sense? The man's identity was still unknown then, yet they knew who had sent him? It's incomprehensible, quite incomprehensible. Or it is completely comprehensible."

"They say Kirov was a good man, a good speaker, and the Party's favorite. Who would dare to raise their hand against him?"

Vsevolod Sergeyevich sat down on the bench and put his head back against the wall.

"Whoever did it, Sasha, I can tell you with utter certainty that there are dark days ahead."

1966–1983
Moscow